America the Beautiful

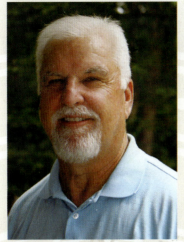

Jeff Jones, Publisher

This past May, Ed Tillett (WG General Manager) and I attended the grand opening of a municipal marina in Slidell, LA, on the north shore of Lake Pontchartrain. Officials from the U.S. EPA were on hand to recognize the City of Slidell with an Excellence in Site Reuse Award for developing the marina on a former Superfund site, turning an environmental problem into a community asset. Waterway Guide was there to cover the event and our hosts were Bill and Laura Borchert, who we had met on Waterway Guide's rally to Cuba in 2017. Bill is a City Councilman and largely responsible for the marina build-out and was the city's point person for the weekend festivities. While the main event included the marina opening, concerts and fireworks, it was Slidell's weekend salute to U.S. war veterans and the respect shown for those heroes and their families that resonated with me.

At the time I was monitoring the declining health of my uncle, William Henry Graham who was our family's all-American veteran hero. Having retired as a Command Sergeant Major from the U.S. Army in 1972, Bill Graham landed at Normandy, fought in the Battle of the Bulge and helped liberate France during World War II. A career military man, he also saw action in Korea and Vietnam. He earned numerous medals, including the French Legion of Honour. He passed away on May 23, 2018, at the age of 95, just 3 days after my return from Slidell. He was buried over Memorial Day weekend, a few days short of his 96th birthday. I attended his military funeral in Kentucky, where he was buried in uniform beside his wife and son. To say I was caught up in a moment of patriotism during those couple of weeks is an understatement.

Patriotism is a year-round event, and I can't help but be humbled daily by the military folks who make it possible for all of us to freely enjoy this great country, including the beautiful waterways we travel so frequently. Many who engage with us at Waterway Guide are active or former service members, and we salute you and your loved ones for your hard work and sacrifices. When you provide your keen observations, they are passed along to our readers through timely updates to our digital and print publications.

As Waterway Guide heads into its 72nd year, we thank all of you for your continued support of our advertisers and vendors, many of whom are veterans. They have greatly contributed to this industry and without them we could not have achieved our many improvements, including the online Waterway Explorer planning tool (waterwayguide.com) and other new digital offerings. With the help of our partners, the entire WG team will continue to deliver you safely and enjoyably to your destination for years to come.

Thanks to all of you who make this lifestyle possible.

Best,

Jeff Jones, Publisher

PUBLISHER'S LETTER

WATERWAY GUIDE OFFICES

Corporate/Production Office
16273 General Puller Hwy.
P.O. Box 1125
Deltaville, VA 23043
804-776-8999
804-776-6111 (fax)
www.waterwayguide.com

BOOK SALES

waterwayguide.com/shipstore
800-233-3355

FOUNDED IN 1947

Publisher	**JEFF JONES** jjones@waterwayguide.com
General Manager/ Editor-in-Chief	**ED TILLETT** etillett@waterwayguide.com
Managing Editor	**JANI PARKER** jparker@waterwayguide.com
Graphic Design/ Production Manager	**SCOTT MCCONNELL** scott@waterwayguide.com
Product Manager	**HEATHER SADEG** heather@waterwayguide.com
Marketing & Advertising Traffic Manager	**SANDY HICKEY** sandy@waterwayguide.com
Book Sales Manager	**LINDA JERNIGAN** linda@waterwayguide.com
Business Development & National Sales Manager	**GRAHAM JONES** graham@waterwayguide.com
Comptroller	**ARTHUR CROWTHER** acrowther@waterwayguide.com
Senior Advisor/ Skipper Bob Editor	**TED STEHLE** tstehle@waterwayguide.com
News Editor	**LISA SUHAY** lisa@waterwayguide.com
Web Master	**MIKE SCHWEFLER**
Office Assistant	**LEON HOLZMAN**

ADVERTISING SALES

National Sales & Northern, Chesapeake Bay, Atlantic ICW & Gulf Coast	**GRAHAM JONES** graham@waterwayguide.com
Bahamas	**BOB BOWER** bobby@waterwayguide.com
Florida East Coast & Great Lakes	**PETE HUNGERFORD** pete@waterwayguide.com

REGIONAL CRUISING EDITORS

BAHAMAS	BOB BOWER TOM & CINDY CASEY LUCY & MATT CLAIBORNE
NORTHERN, CHESAPEAKE BAY, ATLANTIC ICW & THE GULF COAST	MARK BAKER SCOTT RICHARD BERG MICHAEL CAMERATA TOM DOVE CAPT. GEORGE & PAT HOSPODAR DEB & DENNIS JANSMA CAPT. DENA HANKINS & JAMES LANE DUD & ELAINE LLOYD BOB SHERER (CONTRIBUTING EDITOR)
GREAT LAKES	CAPT. GEORGE & PATRICIA HOSPODAR CAPT. JOHN JOHNSTON MICHAEL O'REILLY & ANN PHILLIPS MARY & THERON RODRIGUEZ
CUBA	ADDISON CHAN NIGEL CALDER (CONTRIBUTING EDITOR)

@Waterway Guide

@WaterwayGuide

@waterway_guide

YOUR ISLAND IS CALLING

With more than 700 islands and cays, 2,200 miles of coastline, and 100,000 square miles of the world's clearest water, it won't be easy to see all of the breathtaking beauty in one boat trip. But that doesn't mean you shouldn't try.

THE ISLANDS OF THE
bahamas

Bahamas.com/boating

CUTWATER

THE WORLD'S FINEST SPORT CRUISERS

View all seven trailerable models at CutwaterBoats.com

C-242C • C-242SC • C-28 • C-30S • C-30CB • **C-302C** • C-302SC

Southern Coverage

Ch1
Ch2
Ch3
Ch 4
Ch 5
Ch 6
Ch 7
Ch 8
Ch 9
Ch 10
Ch 11
Ch 12
Ch 13
Ch 14
Ch 15
Ch 16
Ch 17

MISSISSIPPI
ALABAMA
GEORGIA
FLORIDA

GULF OF MEXICO

Gulfport
Mobile
Pensacola
Panama City
Apalachicola
Carrabelle
Tarpon Springs
Tampa
St. Petersburg
Sarasota
Ft. Myers
Sanibel I.
Flamingo
Key West
Dry Tortugas
Miami
Ft. Lauderdale
Palm Beach
Stuart
Vero Beach
Cocoa
New Smyrna Beach
Daytona Beach
Jacksonville
Fernandina Beach

St. Johns River
Ponce de Leon Inlet
St. Lucie Inlet
Lake Okeechobee
Okeechobee Waterway
Biscayne Bay
Channel Five

MILE 135 EHL
MILE 292 EHL
MILE 380 EHL
GIWW MILE 150
GIWW MILE 74
GIWW MILE 0
ICW MILE 897
ICW MILE 830
ICW MILE 740
ICW MILE 717
ICW MILE 986
ICW MILE 1085
ICW MILE 1240

N

Contents

2019 Southern Edition, Volume 72, No. 3

Cruising south on the ICW, mariners enter Florida at Mile 714. As you cross Cumberland Sound and the St. Marys River, the broad expanses of the marsh-bordered Georgia ICW give way to the narrower, more protected and more populated Florida route. Below St. Lucie Inlet, the coastline becomes truly tropical, with a profusion of palm trees and exotic flowers. The Florida ICW is well marked and easy to follow.

More than 300 miles of mostly navigable inland waterways carve through the Fort Lauderdale area, making it the "Venice of America." It is well known as a yachting center and boating amenities and services are readily available. Fort Lauderdale to Miami is known as "Florida's Gold Coast," and it glimmers with glamour and charm.

Extending in a sweeping southwesterly curve from Miami and the mainland, the Florida Keys offer the cruising boater an environment unlike other Waterway areas. In many ways, the Keys resemble the islands of the Bahamas. However, a main highway and a total of 18.94 miles of bridges tie them together.

TABLE OF CONTENTS

FLORIDA'S WEST COAST

Zoologically and geographically, Florida's lower west coast differs substantially from the east. The cruising, too, is entirely different. The sophistication, glamour and luxury so prevalent on the east coast comes in more measured doses here. The pace is slower, the atmosphere more relaxed and the amenities somewhat more limited and spaced farther apart, but the cruising is superb.

UPPER GULF COAST

Florida's Panhandle, stretching from Carrabelle or Apalachicola on the eastern end to Pensacola and Perdido Bay on the west, is sometimes called the Forgotten Coast. It can be reached in one of three ways: From the east, either directly across the Gulf of Mexico or by skirting the Big Bend area just offshore; or from the west, where the inland rivers of the Midwest merge into Mobile Bay.

INDEXES

Wifi Solutions for Cruising and Long Distance Boating

A mystery for many boaters on the water today is how we ever survived without internet connectivity, either on the boat or at the dock. As we know, more of us are able to spend more time on the water and away from the office while conducting business, transactions and updates to make our boating more safe and enjoyable.

One of the more progressive companies offering systems for your vessel is Wave WiFi. At the core of all Wave WiFi products is their Graphic User Interface (GUI). This is where users often get frustrated in setting up and managing their onboard systems, but Wave WiFi has solved that.

Wave WiFi's proprietary firmware allows you to see all available WiFi signals and determine their encryption status, signal strength (signal to noise ratio in real time) and frequency. You can choose the best access point available for your specific requirements including WEP, WPA and WPA2 encrypted as well as unlocked networks.

Their advanced signal processing technology optimizes internet speeds in both directions by combining superior receiver sensitivity with high transmitter output power to provide fast and reliable internet connections even when access points are at distances that could be miles away. Dual frequency 2.4/5Ghz solutions provide access to the most reliable and fastest connections available.

The key to Wave WiFi's continued success and growth has been finding solutions for mobile users of all types. They specialize in recreational boats and have products that run the gamut from small runabouts up to large superyachts.

Cruisers looking to connect to open hot spots get easier access and better connections. Onboard routing solutions deliver vessel-wide voerage even in propagation is limited on larger boats. 3G/4G/LTE cellular solutions provide internet access when WiFi is no available. The products are just as effective in maritime commercial applications including oil and gas, tug and barge, as well as a variety of fishing vessels.

We've confirmed that their systems are solid. As you continue to bring your boat, yacht or runabout into the 21st century, see what Wave WiFi has to offer. They are boaters who designed their systems for boaters and the marine environment. While many of us use our boats to get away from it all, onboard connectivity can keep us cruising longer while cellular and WiFi solutions allow us to travel farther.

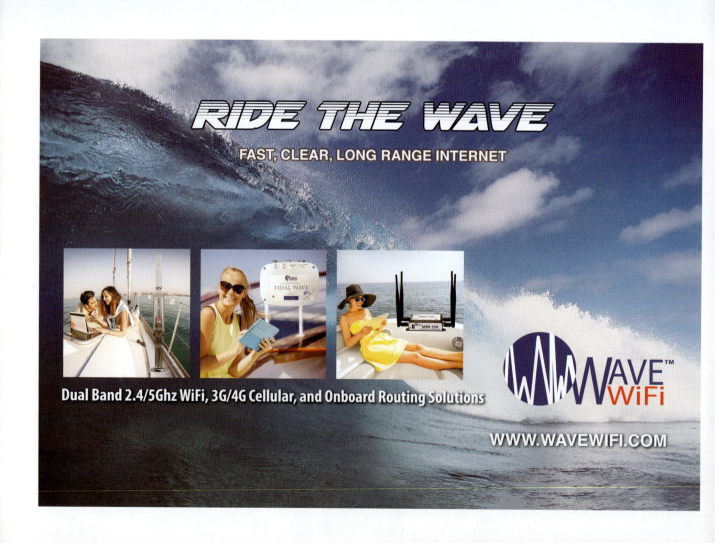

RIDE THE WAVE

FAST, CLEAR, LONG RANGE INTERNET

Dual Band 2.4/5Ghz WiFi, 3G/4G Cellular, and Onboard Routing Solutions

WAVE™ WiFi

WWW.WAVEWIFI.COM

How to Use This Guide

Marina listings and locator maps

Mile-by-mile navigation

Dockage/mooring and anchorage details

Detailed Goin' Ashore for select ports with locator map and key featuring attractions, shopping and dining

Includes Skipper's Handbook with bridge schedules, selected inlets, GPS waypoints, customs procedures and more!

The adventure of a lifetime
America's Great Loop

2+ Countries • 14+ States and Providences • 100+ Locks • 5,250+ Miles...
... all aboard your own boat!

America's Great Loop Cruisers' Association

AGLCA is a group of over 6,000 people who share a passion for the Great Loop. We provide information and inspiration that help our members move the Great Loop from their bucket list to reality. Whether you're brand new to the idea of the Great Loop, you're actively planning for it, or you're ready to drop the dock lines and head out now, AGLCA offers something for you!

Membership includes:
- Events
- Discounts
- Newsletters
- Podcasts
- Camaraderie
- Blogs
- Cost Calculators
- and so much more!

Visit our website:
www.GreatLoop.org

500 Oakbrook Lane,
Summerville, SC 29485
Tel: 877-GR8-LOOP

Cruising Editors

Waterway Guide's on-the-water Cruising Editors bring us firsthand information about the navigation, news and trends along the waterways we cover. In addition to contributing to the annual guide, they provide daily updates on the Waterway Explorer at waterwayguide.com. We are pleased to introduce you to our crew.

Bahamas

Matt and Lucy Claiborne met while studying together for their pilot's license and have been sharing adventures ever since. They lived aboard a 31-foot sailboat as newlyweds, then owned a 19-foot runabout while living in Key Largo, which they used for sunset cruises. They upgraded to a 21-foot cuddy cabin, which they used as a platform for diving in the Florida Keys and for week-long camping vacations exploring different parts of Florida's beautiful coasts. Fueled by the desire to be on the water full-time, they sold their house, purchased a 38-foot sailing catamaran (*Independence*) and moved aboard, along with their cocker spaniel, Captain Hastings. They are in the middle of a planned three-year cruise and have traveled to Florida, the ICW, the Chesapeake Bay and the Bahamas (twice). They both hold USCG 50-ton Master licenses and love every minute spent on the water.

Bob Bower worked at his family business in Nassau for 21 years, where edited the Bahamas Tourist News, and the promotion boards' Bahama Out Islands Travel Guide and Nassau/Paradise Island Tourist News. Born in Nassau and schooled in the UK, Bob lived in Australia for seven years, where he co-partnered a successful public relations firm in Sydney. For the past two years he served as executive director for the Association of Bahamas Marinas. He also writes for *Fodor's Travel Guides*. Bob loves to travel the Bahama Out Islands and his further journeys have taken him to the Caribbean, Spain, Malta, France, Belgium, Ireland, the UK, the US and Canada. Since 1987 Bob has resided in Nassau with his wife and three children and loves his faith, reading, chess, travel and photography.

Tom and Cindy Casey, originally from Martinez, CA, cruised a Navigator 4400 on the west coast of California from San Francisco to Mexico. Now full-time residents of Marathon, they enjoy fishing, free diving, scuba diving and spearfishing. As travel agents for the last 30 years, they have dove in more than 35 countries. They cruise the Bahamas extensively every spring in a 44-foot power cat, *Aquila*, with their dog, Captain Caper.

Northern, Chesapeake Bay, Atlantic ICW & the Gulf Coast

After being long-time sailors, **Bud & Elaine Lloyd** decided that in order to fulfill their dream of living aboard and cruising full time they needed a trawler. *Diamond Girl* was the choice, and after many years they still believe that their decision was good. From their homeport of Long Beach, CA, they cruised all over Southern California and parts of Mexico. Finally they decided that it was time to get serious about fulfilling their dream of cruising, so they put *Diamond Girl* on a ship and sent her to Ft. Lauderdale, FL. They have been cruising on the East Coast for a number of years now and have found the lifestyle even more rewarding than they ever imagined. After 30,000 miles on the ICW, many crossings of Lake Okeechobee and numerous summers spent on the Chesapeake Bay, they truly enjoy passing along information and sharing some of their favorite spots with the *Waterway Guide*. If you see *Diamond Girl*, knock on the boat and say "hi."

Capt. George and Patricia Hospodar have been boaters for over 40 years and have cruised more than 43,000 miles together aboard two sailboats and their 48-foot Symbol motor yacht, *Reflection*. Since 2008 they have traveled up and down the Atlantic ICW numerous times between their home on Barnegat Bay in Brick, NJ, and their "adopted" home at Banana Bay Marina in Marathon, FL, and have completed the America's Great Loop journey twice through the waterways of the U.S. and Canada. George, a retired business owner, has been a 100-ton licensed U.S. Coast Guard Captain for 26 years and is a Past Commodore of the Bristol Sailing Club in Bay Head, NJ, a Past Director of the New Jersey

Marine Trades Association and a Past President of the Chesapeake Marine Canvas Fabricators Association. He and Pat (a retired music teacher and choral director) are Platinum lifetime members of the America's Great Loop Cruisers' Association, as well as members of the Marine Trawler Owners Association and the Marathon Yacht Club. Together they have also authored two popular boating books: *Reflection on America's Great Loop* and *The Great Loop Experience from Concept to Completion*, and they are often featured speakers at boat shows, TrawlerFests and other nautical events.

Capt. Dena Hankins and James Lane left Seattle, WA, aboard a William Garden Seawolf ketch in 1999 and have been traveling ever since. They sailed the Puget Sound and the San Juan Islands, the Georgia Strait and the Strait of Juan de Fuca, the northern Pacific Ocean and the San Francisco Bay. There, they downsized to a Gulf 32 pilothouse sloop and jumped the trades to the Big Island of Hawai'i. They sailed throughout the archipelago for a year and sold that boat in Oahu in order to move to the Indian Subcontinent in 2008. In 2009, they chose the Chesapeake Bay as the restarting point for their circumnavigation, titled "Around the World in 80 Years." They settled aboard their new old boat, a 1961 Philip Rhodes Chesapeake sloop, and gunkholed from Norfolk, VA, to Winter Harbor, ME, and south to Cape Fear, NC. Dena is a multi-published novelist and short-story writer with a 50-ton Master License. James is an accomplished photographer and indefatigable traveler, storyteller and sailor. Together, they can face anything, even a head rebuild, and honestly say they're living the dream.

Debi and Dennis Jansma both have a long-lived love of the sea and boating. Dennis began sailing as a teenager on a Hobie Cat in Hingham MA, while Debi grew up helping in marinas managed by her parents along the Erie Canal. The two met in high school in Rumson NJ, and sailed together in the Navesink River. After they married, they became members in the Monmouth Boat Club, where Dennis enjoyed racing Flying Scots. In 2005, Debi and Dennis moved to the Miami area, seeking a longer sailing season, and joined the Coconut Grove Sailing Club. Both became very active on the CGSC Race Committee, and traded their Flying Scot for a 27-foot Stiletto catamaran to sail on Biscayne Bay. After their youngest left for college, wanderlust set in for real and they started planning to make the liveaboard life

reality. They spent three years having their dream boat built, a kit catamaran from Australia called a Fusion 40 (*XYZZY*). They have cruised both coasts of Florida, the East Coast north as far as Kittery, ME, and spent 5 months in the Bahamas during their second winter aboard. Both Debi and Dennis are SSCA members.

Scott Richard Berg is a lifelong boater and full-time cruiser with five decades of experience on a range of vessels from el Toro prams to a 135-foot Baltic Trader. He operated Chardonnay Boatworks, a full-service marine repair company, for many years from a series of cruising sailboats (all named *Chardonnay*). He is the immediate past president of the SSCA, an ABYC-Certified Master Technician and holds an Amateur Extra Class radio license. Scott is *Waterway Guide's* on-the-water Cruising Editor for the Potomac River.

Michael Camarata started his sailing/boating life in the early 1970s when he decided to buy a Sunfish-type sailboat with his future wife, Carol Zipke. A few years later they bought a larger sailing dinghy with TWO sails. This was to set a pattern of larger and more complicated sailing vessels that continued to the vessel they now own and live aboard, a 44-foot sailing catamaran, *Infinite Improbability*, which Michael says is their last upgrade. Michael and Carol's cruising area originally ranged from New York City to Nantucket and north of the Cape Cod Canal. Now, having sold all of their "dirt-based property" the couple roams from southern New England to the Florida Keys and the Bahamas. They live in Mystic, CT, in the summer and Marathon, FL, in the winter. They are both Past Commanders of the Waterbury (CT) Power Squadron, as well as Senior Navigators in the U.S. Power Squadron.

Mark Baker and his partner Ann have been avid "part-time liveaboards" since purchasing their 37-foot, shoal-draft, racer/cruiser 9 years ago. Since that time they have put over 2,000 nautical miles under the keel and have personally made all repairs and upgrades to their sailboat. Along with their canine companion Guimauve, they enjoy meeting new folks in the towns and cities along the way and also seeking out secluded spots to enjoy the natural world and to experience some good ol' gunkholing. Ann is a talented birdwatcher and Mark enjoys underwater photography and the study of geology. Both being former teachers, they are practitioners of life-long learning.

Tom Dove began sailing in 1955, created popular programs for Annapolis Sailing School in the 1960s (including the world's first flotilla cruises), and has cruised on a variety of sailboats in the U.S. and various other parts of the world. He has been writing about boating for books, national and regional magazines and television for the past 30 years. In 2017, he chose a more "age appropriate" vessel and now ambles happily along the Atlantic coast with his wife, Kathy, on *SNOWBIRD*, a renovated 1977 Grand Banks 32 trawler.

Long-time skipper **Bob Sherer** is a contributing editor at *Waterway Guide*. Bob (better known in cruising circles as "Bob 423") focuses on navigational alerts along the Atlantic ICW. Bob and his wife, Ann, just completed their eighth trip down the ICW from Poughkeepsie, NY, to Key West. Bob is best known for his activity on numerous cruising forums and the couple has a popular blog at fleetwing.blogspot.com. Bob and Ann spend 9 months of the year aboard *Fleetwing*, a Beneteau 423, with four-legged crew member, Hoolie, a Brittany.

Great Lakes

Michael O'Reilly and Ann Phillips came to sailing by first messing about with canoes and kayaks while living on the Canadian shore of Lake Superior. Sailing replaced the smaller boats, and over the last 15-plus years they have enjoyed many extended summer cruises. Most recently they completed a cruise through four of the five Great Lakes, and currently plan on exploring Lake Ontario, the St. Lawrence Seaway down to Newfoundland, and beyond. Mike is a long-time freelance journalist, writing mostly about the sciences. With the transition to this new watery life, Mike now spends most of his work time writing about traveling, destinations and cruising. Ann is an accomplished photographer. Together they are chronicling their life afloat.

Mary and Tharon Rodriguez enjoy cruising the Great Lakes in Michigan Summers and Florida Keys/Bahamas the remainder of the year. Their fleet includes *Fuzz*, an S2 7.3, located on the Great Lakes, and *Tipsy Gypsy*, 36-foot Hinterhoeller Nonsuch, located in Florida. They are both digital nomads working and cruising full-time and sharing their adventures through writing blog posts, taking pictures for Instagram, and uploading videos on YouTube. They are fun-loving, adventure-seeking, mid-westerners with a whole lot to offer our team. Learn more about them by visiting maryandtharon.com.

Captain John "JJ" Johnston is our expert on the Erie Canal and the New York State Canal System. He is originally from Pittsburgh, PA, but calls Fairport, NY, his home canal town. Capt. JJ retired from Kodak's motion picture division in 2007 and became a captain on *Sam Patch*, a popular Erie Canal tour boat. He also served as Executive Director of CANAL NY, a destination marketing organization, traveling on his 29-foot diesel inboard C Dory, *Penguin*, across the State of New York, promoting the waterway and learning about its history, operation and navigation. He's motored all 524 miles of the NY State Canal System, been up and down all 57 locks, overnighted in 42 canal communities and participated in more than 20 canal events.

Cuba

Addison Chan is the Cruising Editor for the Cuba edition of *Waterway Guide*. He and his wife, Pat, have cruised from the U.S. to Cuba and The Bahamas multiple times aboard their 42-foot sailboat, *Threepenny Opera*. Addison has a popular Facebook group called *Cuba, Land and Sea*, which is a clearinghouse of current information about cruising and traveling in Cuba. The Cuba cruising guide addresses questions posed there that encompass not only the boating aspects of Cuba but the other aspects of experiencing Cuba as well. Addison's world travel, seamanship, navigation skills and spirit for adventure all combined to offer what we consider to be the most experienced view of Cuba's culture, its people and insight for anyone taking their boat there.

Other Contributors

Waterway Guide gathers information and photos from a variety of sources, including boaters, marinas, communities and tourism divisions. We would like to thank everyone who contributed to this edition, with special thanks to:
Bill Hezlep
Rudy & Jill Sechez
Brad Whitmore (Cocoa Village)
Royce Hall ("Crossing to the Bahamas")
Elizabeth Kelch (ICW navigation alerts)

Sag Harbor Yacht Club

FUEL
GAS/DIESEL

OPEN SEASONALLY
APRIL - NOVEMBER

TRANSIENT DOCKAGE UP TO
200FT

ELECTRIC 30-200AMPS

ALL VISITING YACHTSMEN
WELCOME

COVERED PATIO AREA
WITH GAS GRILLS

SAG HARBOR YACHT CLUB IS LOCATED WALKING DISTANCE TO HISTORIC SAG HARBOR, NY. CLUB AFFILIATIONS NOT NECESSARY FOR TRANSIENT DOCKAGE.

Est. 1899

631.725.0567/VHF 09

WWW.SAGHARBORYC.ORG

Marinas   **Services**   **Anchorages**   **Bridges & Locks**   **Nav Alerts**   **Fuel**

Waterway Explorer provides
6 different icons that overlay
on the maps as modes
Modes

Info Pane with details

Plan your time on the water with Explorer

www.waterwayguide.com

ATLANTIC OCEAN

N

DAYTONA BEACH, FL (WX-2)

Fernandina Beach

Jacksonville Beach

St. Augustine

Palm Coast

Daytona Beach

Ponce de Leon Inlet

New Smyrna Beach

Cape Canaveral

Cocoa Beach

Cocoa

Melbourne

Titusville

FORT PIERCE, FL (WX-4)

ICW MILE 717

ICW MILE 740

Jacksonville

JACKSONVILLE, FL (WX-2)

ICW MILE 748

ICW MILE 776

PALATKA, FL (WX-4)

ICW MILE 802

ICW MILE 830

ICW MILE 846

ICW MILE 872

ICW MILE 897

ICW MILE 917

MELBOURNE, FL (WX-1)

MORRISTON, FL (WX-1)

TAMPA BAY, FL (WX-1)

GIWW MILE 150

GIWW MILE 136

Tampa

Bradenton

GEORGIA

FLORIDA

SALEM, FL (WX-4)

Steinhatchee

Suwanee

Cedar Key

Homosassa

Spring Hill

Tarpon Springs

Dunedin

Clearwater

St. Petersburg

LARGO, FL (WX-5)

TALLAHASSEE, FL (WX-2)

St. Marks

EAST POINT, FL (WX-6)

MILE 380 EHL

Carrabelle

Apalachicola

MILE 351 EHL

GULF OF MEXICO

Sebastian

Vero Beach

Fort Pierce

Stuart

St. Lucie Inlet

Jupiter

Palm Beach

Lake Worth

Del Ray

Pompano

Ft. Lauderdale

Hallandale

Miami

Key Biscayne

Biscayne Bay

Key Largo

Islamorada

ICW MILE 933

ICW MILE 952

ICW MILE 965

ICW MILE 986

OKEECHOBEE MILE 0

OKEECHOBEE MILE 40

ICW MILE 1005

ICW MILE 1027

ICW MILE

ICW MILE 1057

ICW MILE 1063

ICW MILE 1085

ICW MILE 1094

ICW MILE 1142

ICW MILE 1160

MIAMI, FL (WX-1)

WEST PALM BEACH, FL (WX-3)

PRINCETON, FL (WX-4)

Lake Okeechobee

OKEECHOBEE MILE 78

Okeechobee Waterway

BELLE GLADE, FL (WX-2)

TEA TABLE, FL (WX-5)

Channel Five

Marathon

ICW MILE 1192

Cape Sable

Flamingo

Fort Myers

Punta Gorda

GIWW MILE 90

GIWW MILE 74

GIWW MILE 58

OKEECHOBEE MILE 144

GIWW MILE 0

Cape Coral

Sanibel I.

San Carlos Bay

FORT MYERS, FL (WX-3)

Naples

Marco Island

Everglades City

KEY WEST, FL (WX-2)

NAPLES, FL (WX-7)

Anna Maria Island

Sarasota

Venice

Port Charlotte

Key West

ICW MILE 1240

Southern Planning Map

Grid is approximately 5 nautical miles. For Planning purposes only. Not to be used for navigation.

SKIPPER'S HANDBOOK

Rules of the Road

Anyone planning to cruise our waterways should make themselves familiar with the rules of the road. *Chapman Piloting: Seamanship and Small Boat Handling* and *The Annapolis Book of Seamanship* are both excellent on-the-water references with plentiful information on navigation rules. For those with a penchant for the exact regulatory language, the Coast Guard publication *Navigation Rules: International–Inland* covers both international and U.S. inland rules. (Boats over 39.4 feet are required to carry a copy of the U.S. Inland Rules at all times.) These rules are also available online at navcen.uscg.gov. Click on NavRules on the top menu bar.

The following is a list of common situations you will likely encounter on the waterways. Make yourself familiar with them, and if you ever have a question as to which of you has the right-of-way, let the other vessel go first. Sailors need to remember that a boat under sail with its engine running is considered a motorboat.

Passing or being passed:

■ If you intend to pass a slower vessel, try to hail them on your VHF radio to let them know you are coming.

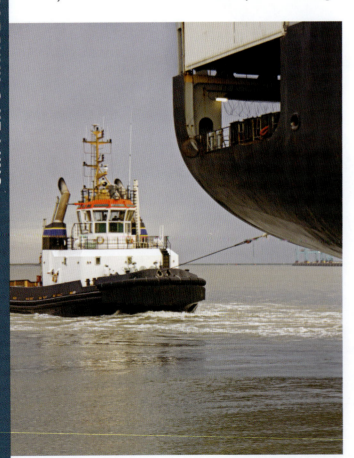

■ In close quarters, BOTH vessels should slow down. Slowing down normally allows the faster vessel to pass quickly without throwing a large wake onto the slower boat.

■ Slower boats being passed have the right-of-way and passing vessels must keep clear of these slower vessels.

■ As you pass a slower boat, take a look back to see how they were affected by your wake. Remember: YOU are responsible for your wake. It is the law to slow down, and it is common courtesy.

At opening bridges:

■ During an opening, boats traveling with the current go first and generally have the right-of-way.

■ Boats constrained by their draft, size or maneuverability (e.g., dredges, tugs and barges) also take priority.

■ Standard rules of the road apply while circling or waiting for a bridge opening.

Tugs, freighters, dredges and naval vessels:

■ These vessels are usually constrained by draft or their inability to easily maneuver. For this reason, you will almost always need to give them the right-of-way and keep out of their path.

■ You must keep at least 100 yards away from any Navy vessel. If you cannot safely navigate without coming closer than this, you must notify the ship of your intentions over VHF Channel 16.

■ Keep a close watch for freighters, tugs with tows and other large vessels while offshore or in crowded ports. They often come up very quickly, despite their large size.

■ It is always a good practice to radio larger vessels (VHF Channel 13 or 16) to notify them of your location and your intentions. The skippers of these boats are generally appreciative of efforts to communicate with them. This is especially true with dredge boats on all the waterways.

In a crossing situation:

■ When two vessels under power are crossing and a risk of collision exists, the vessel that has the other on her starboard side must keep clear and avoid crossing ahead of the other vessel.

■ When a vessel under sail and a vessel under power are crossing, the boat under power is usually burdened and must keep clear. The same exceptions apply as per head-on meetings.

■ On the Great Lakes and western rivers (e.g., the Mississippi River system), a power-driven vessel crossing a river shall keep clear of a power-driven vessel ascending or descending the river.

Power vessels meeting any other vessel:

■ When two vessels under power (either sailboats or powerboats) meet "head-to-head," both are obliged to alter course to starboard.

■ Generally, when a vessel under power meets a vessel under sail (i.e., not using any mechanical power), the powered vessel must alter course accordingly.

■ Exceptions are vessels not under command, vessels restricted in ability to maneuver, vessels engaged in commercial fishing or those under International Rules, such as a vessel constrained by draft.

Two sailboats meeting under sail:

■ When each has the wind on a different side, the boat with the wind on the port side must keep clear of the boat with the wind on the starboard side.

■ When both have the wind on the same side, the vessel closest to the wind (windward) will keep clear of the leeward boat.

■ A vessel with wind to port that sees a vessel to windward but cannot determine whether the windward vessel has wind to port or starboard will assume that windward vessel is on starboard tack and keep clear.

VHF Communications

Skippers traveling the U.S. inland waterways use their VHF radios almost every day to contact other vessels and bridgetenders, make reservations at marinas, arrange to pass other vessels safely and conduct other business. *Waterway Guide* has put together the following information to help remove any confusion as to what frequency should be dialed in to call bridges, marinas, commercial ships, or your friend anchored down the creek. Remember to use low power (1 watt) for your radio transmission whenever possible. If you are within a couple of miles of the responding station (bridge, marina or other craft) there is no need to broadcast at 25 watts and disturb the transmissions of others 25 miles away.

Channel Usage Tips

- VHF Channel 16 (156.8 MHz) is by far the most important frequency on the VHF-FM band. VHF Channel 16 is the international distress, safety and calling frequency.

- If you have a VHF radio on your boat, FCC regulations require that you to maintain a watch on either VHF Channel 09 or 16 whenever you are underway and the radio is not being used to communicate on another channel. Since the Coast Guard does not have the capability of announcing an urgent marine information broadcast or weather warning on VHF Channel 09, it recommends that boaters normally keep tuned to and use VHF Channel 16, but no conversations of any length should take place there; its primary function is for emergencies only.

- The Coast Guard's main working VHF Channel is 22A, and both emergency and non-emergency calls generally are switched to it in order to keep VHF Channel 16 clear. Calling the Coast Guard for a radio check on VHF Channel 16 is prohibited.

- Radio-equipped bridges in SC, GA and FL use VHF Channel 09, with a few exceptions.

- Recreational craft typically communicate on VHF Channels 68, 69, 71, 72 or 78A. Whenever possible, avoid calling on VHF Channel 16 altogether by prearranging initial contact directly on one of these channels. No transmissions should last longer than 3 minutes.

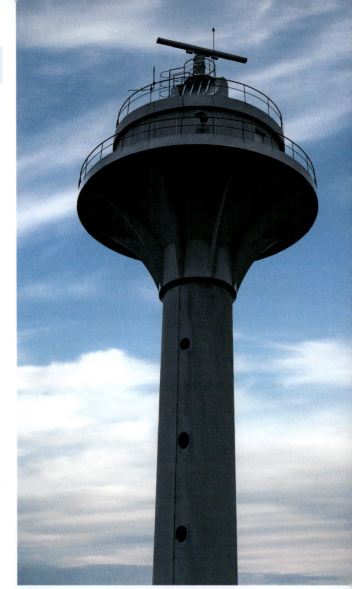

Coast Guard radio communication radar tower

- The Bridge-to-Bridge Radio Telephone Act requires many commercial vessels, including dredges and tugboats, to monitor VHF Channel 13. VHF Channel 13 is also the frequency used by bridges in several states.

Distress Calls

MAYDAY: The distress signal "MAYDAY" is used to indicate that a vessel is threatened by grave and imminent danger and requests immediate assistance.

PAN PAN: The urgency signal "PAN PAN" is used when the safety of the ship or person is in jeopardy.

SÉCURITÉ: The safety signal "SÉCURITÉ" is used for messages about the safety of navigation or important weather warnings.

VHF Channel 16 is the distress call frequency. The codeword "MAYDAY" is the international alert signal of a life-threatening situation at sea. After a MAYDAY message is broadcast, VHF Channel 16 must be kept free of all traffic, other than those directly involved in the rescue situation, until the rescue has been completed. If you hear a MAYDAY message and no one else is responding, it is your duty to step in to answer the call, relay it to the nearest rescue organization and get to the scene to help. Remember, a MAYDAY distress call can only be used when life is threatened. For example, if you have run on the rocks but no one is going to lose their life, that is NOT a MAYDAY situation.

Note: The Coast Guard has asked the FCC to eliminate provisions for using VHF Channel 09 as an alternative calling frequency to VHF Channel 16 when it eliminates watch-keeping on VHF Channel 16 by compulsory-equipped vessels.

VHF Channels

09	Used for radio checks and hailing other stations (boats, shoreside operations). Also used to communicate with drawbridges in Florida.
13	Used to contact and communicate with commercial vessels, military ships and drawbridges. Bridges in several states monitor VHF Channel 13.
16	*Emergency use only.* May be used to hail other vessels, but once contact is made, conversation should be immediately switched to a working (68, 69, 71, 72, 78A) VHF channel.
22	Used for U.S. Coast Guard safety, navigation and Sécurité communications.
68 **69** **71** **72** **78A**	Used primarily for recreational ship-to-ship and ship-to-shore communications.

How to Make a Distress Call

Hello All Ships. **MAYDAY! MAYDAY! MAYDAY!**

This is: Give your vessel name and call sign.

Our position is: Read it off the GPS, or give it as something like "two miles southwest of Royal Island." (Your rescuers must be able to find you!)

We are: Describe what's happening (e.g., on fire/hit a reef/sinking)

We have: Report how many people are on board

At this time we are: Say what you're doing about the crisis (e.g., standing by/abandoning ship)

For identification we are: Describe your boat: type, length, color, etc. (so your rescuers can more readily identify you)

We have: List safety equipment you have e.g., flares/smoke/ocean dye markers/EPIRB

We will keep watch on Channel 16 as long as we can.

Port Security

In the U.S., the U.S. Coast Guard and Customs and Border Patrol–both components of the Department of Homeland Security–handle port security. Local law enforcement agencies and the FBI also have a role in port security at the local and regional level. Each year, more than 11 million maritime containers arrive at our seaports. At land borders, another 11 million arrive by truck and 2.7 million by rail. Homeland Security is responsible for knowing what is inside those containers, whether it poses a risk to the American people and ensuring that all proper revenues are collected.

As an example, one in five food items is now imported. American consumers demand fresh limes and blueberries all year round and, as a result, during the winter months in the U.S., nearly 80 percent of the fresh fruits and vegetables on our tables come from other countries. With the ever-increasing amount of trade, the agricultural risks to the United States grow. The threat to crops and livestock is real.

In response to this threat and others, the U.S. Coast Guard has established "protection zones" around all

U.S. Navy vessels, tank vessels, and large-capacity cruise vessels, even when underway. U.S. Navy bases, U.S. Coast Guard bases and some shoreside facilities, such as nuclear power plants, are also in protection zones. Non-military vessels (this means YOU) are not allowed within 100 yards of these protection zones. To do so can rack up serious civil penalties and even imprisonment. These protection zones vary from port to port and from facility to facility, but ignorance of the protection zones is not a viable excuse. Having said that, law-abiding boaters sometimes find themselves unable to comply with the letter of the law without hitting a jetty, for example. In such cases, common sense and good communication should prevail.

America's Waterway Watch Program

Government officials view the recreational boating community as an ally. We can do our part (and perhaps stave off more stringent regulations and surveillance measures) by becoming familiar with the Coast Guard's

America's Waterway Watch program. Think of it as a neighborhood watch program for the waterways.

It is not the intent of America's Waterway Watch to spread paranoia or to encourage spying on one another, and it is not a surveillance program; instead, it is a simple deterrent to potential terrorist activity. The purpose of the program is to allow boaters and others who spend time along the water to help the authorities counter crime and terrorism. To report suspicious behavior, call the National Response Center at 877-249-2824 (877-24WATCH). For immediate danger to life or property, call 911, or call the Coast Guard on Marine VHF-FM Channel 16.

This section includes a list of ports and places that require a little forethought and vigilance on your part. Following the steps in the action plan below will help ensure a trouble-free journey and keep you and your crew out of the headlines.

Prepare:

◼ Before you leave, check the current charts for the area in which you will be traveling and identify any security areas. Security zones are highlighted and outlined in magenta with special notes regarding the specific regulations pertaining to that area.

◼ Check the latest *Local Notice to Mariners* (available online at navcen.uscg and posted at some marinas) and identify any potential security areas that may not be shown on the chart.

◼ Listen to VHF Channel 16 for any Sécurité alerts from the Coast Guard (departing cruise ships, U.S. Navy vessels, fuel tankers, etc.) for the area you will be cruising prior to your departure.

◼ Talk to other boaters in your anchorage or marina about the areas where you will be traveling. They may have tips and suggestions on any potential security zones or special areas they may have encountered on their way.

Stay Alert While Underway:

◼ Mind the outlined magenta security areas noted on your charts.

◼ Look for vessels with blue or red warning lights in port areas and, if approached, listen carefully and strictly obey all instructions given to you.

◼ Keep your VHF radio switched to VHF Channel 16 and keep your ears tuned for bulletins, updates and possible requests for communication.

◼ Avoid commercial port operation areas, especially those that involve military, cruise line or petroleum facilities. Observe and avoid other restricted areas near power plants, national monuments, etc.

◼ If you need to pass within 100 yards of a U.S. Navy vessel for safe passage, you must contact the U.S. Navy vessel or the Coast Guard escort vessel on VHF Channel 16 to let them know your intentions.

◼ If government security or the U.S. Coast Guard hails you, do exactly what they say, regardless of whether or not you feel their instructions have merit.

Additional Resources

Department of Homeland Security: dhs.gov

U.S. Customs and Border Protection: cbp.gov

Local Notice to Mariners: navcen.uscg.gov (then click on "LNMS" on the top menu bar)

Atlantic Intracoastal Waterway Association: atlintracoastal.org

America's Waterway Watch: americaswaterwaywatch.org

Florida Ports Council: flaports.org

Alabama State Port Authority: asdd.com

U.S. Coast Guard

The Coast Guard stands watch at all times to aid vessels of all sizes and the persons on board. The Coast Guard locations listed below cover the areas included in this edition of *Waterway Guide*. In some areas, you can quickly reach the Coast Guard by dialing *CG on a cellular phone. If you have a question of a non-emergency nature, the Coast Guard prefers that you telephone the nearest station. As always, if there is an emergency, initiate a "MAY DAY" call on VHF Channel 16. (Directions for initiating a "MAY DAY" call are provided in the following section.)

■ SEVENTH COAST GUARD DISTRICT

District Office: Brickell Plaza Federal Building, 909 SE 1st Ave., Miami, FL 33131
305-415-6860

FLORIDA (SECTOR JACKSONVILLE)

10426 Alta Dr., Jacksonville, FL 32233
904-714-7500 or -7558 (emergency)

FLORIDA (SECTOR MIAMI)

100 MacArthur Causeway, Miami Beach, FL 33139
305-535-4300 or -4472/-4520 (emergency)

FLORIDA (SECTOR KEY WEST)

100 Trumbo Rd., Key West, FL 33040
305-292-877 or -8727 (emergency)

GULF COAST (SECTOR ST. PETERSBURG)

600 8th Ave., SE, St. Petersburg, FL 33701
727-824-7534 or -7506 (emergency)

■ EIGHTH COAST GUARD DISTRICT

District Office: Hale Boggs Federal Building, 500 Poydras St., New Orleans, LA 70130
504-589-6225

GULF COAST (SECTOR MOBILE)

1500 15th St., Mobile, AL 36615
251-441-5720 or -6211 (emergency)

For more information: uscg.mil

Coast Guard Requirements

In addition to aiding boaters in distress, the Coast Guard also enforces maritime law and conducts safety inspections. While a Coast Guard boarding can be unnerving, if you are responsible and prepared, it will only take 15 to 30 minutes and will be a non-event. First, have your boat in order. This includes having your vessel documentation, registration and insurance documents on hand, as well as your passport. Organize this in a binder and keep it in the nav station so you don't have to fumble around looking for documents and paperwork. You will need to acknowledge the location of any weapons on board and show a permit (when required by state law).

As they begin to inspect your boat, the officers will focus on areas with the largest safety concerns, including the following.

Life Jackets: One Type I, II, II, or V per person plus one Type IV throwable device is required. PFDs must be U.S. Coast Guard-approved, wearable by the intended user and readily accessible. The Type IV throwable device must be located such that it is immediately available.

Visual Distress Signals: All vessels 16 feet and over must be equipped with minimum of 3 day-use and 3 night-use or 3 day/night combination pyrotechnic devices. Non-pyrotechnic substitutes: orange flag (for day use) and electric S-O-S signal light (for night use). Flares must be up to date (e.g., not expired).

Sound Producing Devices: A whistle, horn, siren, etc. capable of a 4-second blast audible for 0.5 mile must be on board for use during periods of reduced visibility. Boats 65 feet and over must have a bell and one whistle or horn required to signal intentions.

Navigation Lights: All boats over 16 feet must have working navigational lights and an independent all-around anchor light. Sailboats under power are considered powerboats and must follow "power" rules.

Fire Extinguisher: U.S. Coast Guard-approved, marine-type fire extinguishers are required on any boat with enclosed fuel or engine spaces, enclosed living spaces, or permanent (not movable by one person) fuel tanks. They must be in good working condition and readily accessible. (Number of units required depends on vessel length.)

Ventilation: Boats built after August 1, 1980, with enclosed gasoline engines must have a powered ventilation system with one or more exhaust blowers.

Backfire Flame Arrester: All gasoline-powered inboard/outboard or inboard motor boats must be equipped with an approved backfire flame arrester.

Pollution Placard: It is illegal to discharge oil or oily waste into any navigable waters of the U.S. Boats over 26 feet must display a durable oily waste pollution placard of at least 5 by 8 inches in a prominent location.

MARPOL Trash Placard: It is illegal to dump plastic trash anywhere in the ocean or navigable waters of the U.S. Boats over 26 feet must display a durable trash placard at least 4 by 9 inches in a prominent location.

Navigation Rules: Boats 39.4 feet and over must have a copy of current Navigation Rules on board. You can download a copy at uscgboating org.

Marine Sanitation Devices: The discharge of treated sewage is allowed within 3 nm of shore except in designated "No Discharge Zone" areas. The Coast Guard will check that overboard discharge outlets can be sealed (and are sealed, if within 3 nm of shore).

These requirements are detailed in a **downloadable boater's guide** at uscgboating.org/images/420.PDF. State and local requirements are also considered. If there is a minor violation, they may give you a written warning explaining what needs to be fixed to be in compliance. If you are found with a small violation and correct it quickly, then this will merely be a chance to interact with those whose goal is to keep you as safe as possible on the water.

Customs Reporting Procedures: Arrival in the U.S.

Operators of small pleasure vessels, arriving in the U.S. from a foreign port are required to report their arrival to Customs and Border Patrol (CBP) immediately. The master of the vessel reports their arrival at the nearest Customs facility or other designated location. These reports are tracked in the Pleasure Boat Reporting System. An application to lawfully enter the U.S. must be made in person to a CBP officer at a U.S. port-of-entry when the port is open for inspection.

CBP has designated specific reporting locations within the Field Offices that are staffed during boating season for pleasure boats to report their arrival and be inspected by CBP. The master of the boat must report to CBP telephonically and be directed to the nearest Port of Entry to satisfy the face-to-face requirement, or report to the nearest designated reporting location, along with the boat's passengers for inspection.

You may be required to rent a car or take a cab to the nearest airport or federal office several miles away for the inspection. These offices are often closed on weekends. If your arrival is after working hours, you are required to stay on board and clear in the next morning. You must, however, clear in within 24 hours of your arrival. Everyone on board, regardless of nationality, has to report in person. U.S. nationals must take their passports or passport cards. All non-U.S. Nationals should take their passports with valid visas and a Green Card, if held. Take your boat papers, either U.S. documentation or state registration with state decal number. You should also present a list of firearms and ammunition on board.

Exceptions to Face-to-Face Reporting

Alternative Inspection Systems (AIS) satisfy the boat operator's legal requirement to report for face-to-face inspection, but boaters must still phone in their arrival. There are currently five exceptions to the face-to-face inspection at a designated reporting location: CBP ROAM (new in 2018), Small Vessel Reporting System (SVRS), NEXUS, Canadian Border Boat Landing Permit (I-68) and Outlying Area Reporting Stations (OARS). Participation in any of the programs does not preclude the requirement for physical report upon request by U.S. Customs and Border Protection.

NEW in 2018: CBP ROAM

This free mobile application provides pleasure boaters with a convenient and efficient way to report their U.S. entry from a personal device, as opposed to calling their local CBP number. Travelers can use their personal smart device to satisfy reporting requirements in select areas. All travelers, regardless of nationality or citizenship, are eligible to use the CBP ROAM app.

Currently, the CBP ROAM app can be used to report U.S. entry by pleasure boat in Florida, select locations in Minnesota, and in the Great Lakes and Saint Lawrence River area between Buffalo and Ogdensburg, NY. Additional locations are being added, and travelers should contact their local port of entry to confirm whether arrival submissions via the CBP ROAM app are accepted.

Travelers enrolled in the LBO Program, NEXUS and other Trusted Traveler Programs can save their traveler number in their profiles to save additional time when returning to the U.S. For more information on the CBP ROAM app, visit cbp.gov/travel/pleasure-boats-private-flyers/pleasure-boat-overview/roam.

Small Vessel Reporting System (SVRS)

This is a voluntary effort that allows eligible, frequent pleasure boat operators and passengers who are U.S. Citizens or Lawful Permanent Residents (LPRs) of the U.S. to register with CBP. SVRS offers facilitated customs and immigration clearance for recreational low-risk boaters at time of arrival. Enrollment in SVRS is voluntary and will allow CBP to expedite the arrival reporting process to boaters who have enrolled into the program. This program will satisfy the boat operator's legal requirement to report to a port-of-entry for face-to-face inspection but boaters must still phone in their arrival. Note that pleasure boaters currently enrolled in the LBO program (described below) are not required to re-apply for participation in SVRS.

Please note: At press time in 2018, SVRS was being discontinued (no date provided) and replaced with CBP ROAM. Your SVRS, Local Boater, or Registered Traveler numbers will remain in effect and can be utilized and saved within the app to expedite reporting.

For more information: cbp.gov/travel/pleasure-boats-private-flyers

NEXUS (entry from Canada)

This joint Canada-U.S. initiative offers facilitated customs and immigration clearance for recreational low-risk boaters entering either country through registration into the program. NEXUS is valid for 5 years and satisfies the boat operator's legal requirement to report to a port-of-entry for face-to-face inspection, but boaters must still phone in their arrival.

Canadian Border Boat Landing Permit (I-68)

Under this program, applicants for admission into the U.S. by small pleasure boats are inspected and issued an I-68 permit for the entire boating season. The I-68 permit allows boaters to enter the U.S. from Canada for recreational purposes with only the need to report to CBP by telephoning in their arrival.

Outlying Area Reporting System (OARS)

This is another northern border method for boaters to report entry into the U.S. from Canada. The OARS program uses videophones, typically located at public marinas, which boaters may use to report to CBP.

Local Boater Option (LBO) Program

Participants in this program may report their arrival to U.S. Customs and Border Protection (CBP) by calling one of the telephone numbers listed in the accompanying table. Unless directed by a CBP officer, a participant in this program does not have to report for an in-person inspection. The program is designed to provide participants an easy to use web-based tool to record and update their intended international travel on a private vessel by filing a float plan.

Please note: At press time in 2018, LBO was being discontinued (no date provided) and replaced with CBP ROAM.

VISA Waiver Program (Canadian Residents)

Permanent residents of Canada who are nationals of a designated Visa Waiver Program country may enter the U.S. by means of a pleasure boat along the northern border if in possession of a valid, unexpired, passport issued by his or her country of nationality, and an unexpired Non-immigrant Visa Waiver Arrival/Departure Form (I-94), or an unexpired passport, valid unexpired U.S. non-immigrant visa and I-94 Form. Entry may be made only as a visitor for pleasure.

Designated Ports of Entry		
Florida: East Coast & Keys *(Report to individual stations or call 800-432-1216 or 800-451-0393 after hours.)*		
Fernandina Beach	403 N. 3rd St., Fernandina Beach	904-261-6154
Jacksonville	2831 Talleyrand Ave., Jacksonville	904-360-5020
St. Augustine	394 Estrella Rd., St. Augustine	904-209-0099
Daytona Beach Intl. Airport	720 Coral Sea Ave., Daytona Beach	386-248-8043
Port Canaveral	200 George King Blvd., Cape Canaveral	321-783-2066
Melbourne	One Air Terminal Parkway, Melbourne	321-674-5796
Ft. Pierce/St. Lucie County Intl. Airport	2990 Curtis King Blvd., Ft. Pierce	772-461-1733
West Palm Beach	1 East 11th St., Riviera Beach	561-848-6922
Palm Beach Intl. Airport	Bldg. 1612, South Perimeter Rd., West Palm Beach	561-233-1083
Ft. Lauderdale Gen. Aviation	1050 Lee Wagner Blvd., Ft. Lauderdale	954-356-7946
Ft. Lauderdale Executive Airport	5575 NW 15 St., Ft. Lauderdale	954-356-7412
Port Everglades	1800 Eller Dr., Ste. 110, Fort Lauderdale	954-761-2000
Opa Locka Airport	4371 NW 150th St., Opa Locka	305-687-5475
Port of Miami	903 South America Way Terminal H, Miami	305-536-4758
Tamiami Executive Airport	14720 SW 128th St., Miami	305-969-7511
Key West	301 Simonton St., Ste. 20, Key West	305-296-5411

The Sojourner Permit

Florida has a unique form of short-term registration of a vessel called a Sojourner Permit. This is a temporary registration that is most applicable to those non-residents who leave their boats in a marina for the entire winter season.

The permit is required for any vessel owned by a non-Florida resident that is registered in another state or federally documented and that stays in Florida waters for more than 90 days or is used in Florida waters more than 183 days in a 12-month period. U.S. Coast Guard documented vessels from another state may also apply for a Sojourner Permit and will be granted an additional 1 year of use in Florida waters.

The intent is to ensure that boats used in Florida are registered in Florida, thus making them taxable under Florida's law regarding items purchased out of state but stored or used in Florida. However, under the Sojourner permit, your stay is deemed temporary and no tax is collected if you meet all of the following conditions:

- You are a legal resident of another state;
- You have owned the boat 6 months or longer;
- You have shown no intent to use the boat in Florida at or before the time of purchase; and
- The boat has been in use 6 months or longer within the taxing jurisdiction of another state.

Florida law requires that a vessel be registered in a U.S. jurisdiction at the time the boat enters Florida waters so as to be eligible for the initial 90-day grace period. Individual county tax offices issue the Sojourner Permit. State law is subject to local interpretation, depending on the tax district. Therefore, if you are going to keep a boat in Florida longer than the allotted 90 days, you will want to educate yourself in advance. Note that this is related to the USE tax and not the SALES tax on a vessel purchased in the State of Florida. Also, the Sojourner Permit applies only to Florida, and does not supersede, cancel or impair the home-state registration of the vessel.

A $50.00 non-resident commercial vessel fee is charged if the vessel is being used for commercial purposes. If the vessel is used exclusively for commercial shrimping and is registered in Mississippi, North Carolina or Texas, the fee is not applicable.

> The permit required is HSMV 87244, "Application to Register Non Titled Vessels," which is available at flhsmv.gov/resources/forms/all-forms. You will also need a copy of the current out-of-state registration.

State Registration & Fees

Remember that as you cross state lines in your vessel, boating laws will change. Mandatory education requirements to operate a boat, for example, vary from state to state. The bottom line in vessel registration and education is: Know before you go. Make sure you display a valid registration sticker from your home state and follow your host state's regulations. Some specifics are provided here, but this information is subject to change, so visit the individual websites listed below for additional information and updates.

Alabama
Registration Grace Period: 90 days
Boat Sales & Use Tax Rate: 2%
Boating Registration:
outdooralabama.com/boat-registration
State Tax Department: revenue.alabama.gov

Florida
Registration Grace Period: 90 days
Boat Sales & Use Tax Rate: 6%
Notes: Sales tax is capped at $18,000. Vessels brought into the state for repair exempt from registration requirement.
Boating Registration: flhsmv.gov
State Tax Department: floridarevenue.com

Mississippi
Registration Grace Period: 60 days
Boat Sales & Use Tax Rate: 7%
Boating Registration:
mdwfp.com/license/boating-registration
State Tax Department: dor.ms.gov

SKIPPER'S HANDBOOK

Florida Anchoring Restrictions

For over a decade, Florida legislators have grappled with the rules of anchoring. Following the completion of an 8-year pilot program conducted by the U.S. Fish & Wildlife Service that provided insight into the multitude of issues associated with vessels anchoring in the state's waterways, the Florida legislature approved House Bill 7043 that codified anchoring regulations in the state. The new regulations, which offer clear guidance and specific requirements for boaters, localities, public safety agencies and law enforcement, went into effect July 1, 2017.

It will be illegal for any vessel to be at anchored any time during the period between one-half hour after sunset and one-half hour before sunrise in the areas noted (with the exceptions listed below).

- The section of Middle River lying between Northeast 21st Court and the ICW in Broward County.

- Sunset Lake in Miami-Dade County.

- The sections of Biscayne Bay in Miami-Dade County lying between:
  Rivo Alto Island and Di Lido Island
  San Marino Island and San Marco Island
  San Marco Island and Biscayne Island

Exceptions

- If the vessel suffers a mechanical failure that poses an unreasonable risk of harm to the vessel or the persons onboard unless the vessel anchors. The vessel may anchor for three business days or until the vessel is repaired, whichever occurs first.

- If imminent or existing weather conditions in the vicinity of the vessel pose an unreasonable risk of harm to the vessel or the persons onboard unless the vessel anchors. The vessel may anchor until weather conditions no longer pose such risk. During a hurricane or tropical storm, weather conditions are deemed to no longer pose an unreasonable risk of harm when the hurricane or tropical storm warning affecting the area has expired.

- During special events, including public music performances, local government waterfront activities or fireworks displays. A vessel may anchor for the lesser of the duration of the special event or three days.

- Vessels engaged in recreational fishing if the persons onboard are actively tending hook and line fishing gear or nets.

The bill provides that citations will result in a mandatory court appearance and a $50 civil penalty. Those failing to show up for court may be found guilty of a misdemeanor of the second degree, with more severe penalties.

The Bottom Line

House Bill 7043 effectively prevents cities, towns, counties or other municipal entities from passing laws or ordinances preventing boaters from anchoring. HB 7043 now provides specific language related to where vessels may anchor in proximity to marinas, docks, boatyards, mooring fields, superyacht repair facilities and other vessels, as follows:

- Vessels are prohibited from anchoring or mooring within 150 feet of a marina, boat ramp, boatyard or other vessel launching or loading facility, and within 300 feet of a superyacht repair facility.

- Anchoring is prohibited within 100 feet of the marked boundary of a mooring field. A local municipality may establish a distance less than this (not more).

This new measure also provides clear guidance on the definition of derelict vessels, use of unpermitted moorings and proof of pump-out when anchored for 10 days or longer in permitted mooring fields or No-Discharge Zones.

Dinghy Restriction in Miami Beach

It is also important to note that the City of Miami Beach passed an amendment to an ordinance in 2015 making it unlawful to tie a dinghy to a canal wall to visit the city. The city is also strictly enforcing the 20-minute limit for the dinghy dock at the end of 17th St. These restrictions carry stiff civil fines.

Anchoring in the Keys

Bottom conditions in the Keys include, mud, rock, broken coral, sand and grass. Often the cover over ledge rock can be thin. Carry a couple types of anchors on board, as no anchor design excels in every situation, and cruisers should always carry a spare. Many anchor designs function well but testing shows modern, spade-type anchors give the best all-round performance. These anchors feature a chiseled point designed to improve penetration and a good surface area to weight ratio to hold in softer conditions. They also provide good hooking action. Once deployed, always use reverse engine power to set the anchor and test it's hold.

In many of these anchorages you will experience strong tidal flows and 180-degree swings. You should check position on changing tides; anchor alarms are of limited use. Boats with fin keels should be prepared for "anchorwinder" situations where the anchor line gets wrapped around the keel. This happens when strong winds oppose a strong current.

Some use a "fore and aft" anchor configuration to reduce swing or a Bahamian Moor configuration to increase holding force. Cruisers should be aware that any two anchor configuration is difficult to deploy and worse to retrieve. This guide is not a resource on anchoring technique but we advise that if you choose to deploy two anchors also deploy a float and a trip line on at least one to make retrieval simpler. Conditions can change and you may have to move in a hurry. Be prepared to release or cut one anchor free so you can make a quick getaway. Whatever configuration you choose, remember that current and tidal flow always win over wind for sailboats, where as wind will generally have a stronger influence on powerboats.

Mileage indicated here is in statute miles, and no effort has been made to tell you how far off the channel the anchorage is located. You should be able to find these spots easily on your chart. Each of these anchorages has been visited or observed by a Waterway Guide contributor. There are other places, though, where a prudent boater can anchor. Let us know how these anchorages are, or if you find other good ones. Visit us online at waterwayguide.com to submit information.

ICW ROUTE

Ragged Keys (Mile 1106). East of the ICW, 7-foot approach, 8 feet to shoal west of Keys. Holding fair to good in grassy mud. Limited protection from northeast through southeast.

Sands Key (Mile 1108). East of the ICW, 6.5-foot approach, 5 feet in area west of northern portion of the key. Holding fair to good in grassy mud. Protected from south to northeast.

Elliott Key (Mile 1109 to Mile 1114). East of the ICW, 5-foot approach, 5 feet to shoal anywhere along west side of the key. Holding fair to good depending on rocky to grassy mud bottom. Protection from northeast through southeast.

Caesar Creek (Mile 1115). East of the ICW, anchorage open to both routes. Four-foot approach from ICW; 12 feet in best area between Rubicon and Reid keys. Holding good; mud and some grass. Well protected.

Angelfish Creek (Mile 1120). East of the ICW, anchorage open to both routes. Five-foot approach from both ends. Anchorage in side creeks north of channel is 5 feet deep. Holding mixed: some rocky areas, some hard. Strong currents. Well protected.

Pumpkin Key (Mile 1122). East of the ICW, 9-foot approach, 7 feet to shoal anywhere in lee of key depending on winds. Holding fair to good in grassy mud with some rocks.

Steamboat Creek in Card Sound (Mile 1125). East of the ICW, 9-foot approach, 7 feet to shoal north and in mouth of creek off Jew Point. Holding good in grassy mud. Protection only from southwest to east.

Manatee Bay in Barnes Sound (Mile 1132). West of the ICW, 5-foot approach and 5 feet to shoal in area near marked channel leading into Manatee Creek. Holding good in hard bottom. Protection fair to good except in strong winds from north to northwest.

Sexton Cove (Mile 1135). East of the ICW, 7-foot approach, 6-foot depth to shoaling close in. Holding fair in grass and hard bottom with some rocks. Protection from northwest through southeast.

Stellrecht Point (Mile 1136). Southeast of the ICW, 7-foot approach, 6 feet to shoal just south of the point. Holding fair to good in grassy mud. Protected from north through southwest.

Tarpon Basin (Mile 1139). Southeast of the ICW, 7-foot approach, anchor in 5-6 feet south of shoal in center of the basin. Holding fair to good in grassy mud over rock. All-round protection.

Sunset Cove, Buttonwood Sound (Mile 1142). Southeast of the ICW, 5-foot approach, 4 feet or less close in, 5 feet near Pelican Key and near Upper Keys Sailing Club docks. Holding fair to good. Protection from east through south and to west. From the north, close in to the key.

Butternut Key (Mile 1146). Northwest of the ICW, 6-foot approach, 5 feet near eastern Butternut Key just north of marker "60." Holding fair in soft bottom. Protection only from northwest to north.

Tavernier Community Harbor (Mile 1150). South of the ICW, 5-foot approach, 5 feet outside basin, 4 feet inside. Holding poor to fair in dense, grassy bottom. Protection fair to good in all but strongest north winds.

Cowpens (Mile 1155). Southeast of the ICW, 5-foot approach and depth. Numerous spots to anchor in Cowpens anchorage area. Fair to good holding in soft bottom, some grass. Protection from east through west, depending on exact anchoring spot.

Upper Matecumbe Key (Mile 1160). South of the ICW, 6-foot approach and 5 feet in the anchorage off of the restaurant/bar. Protection from south and southeast. Holding fair in soft bottom.

Shell Key (Mile 1161). Southeast of the ICW, 7-foot approach from the west. Can drop anchor close to shore for good protection from east winds. Holding good in grass and sand.

Lignumvitae Key (Mile 1164). Southeast of the ICW, 7-foot approach to either side of key. DO NOT ANCHOR; use the heavy moorings provided. Protection is dependent on being in the lee of the key.

Long Key Bight (Mile 1170). On ocean side of Channel Five Bridge, 9-foot approach, shoaling to 5 feet at center. Anchor as far in as draft allows. Holding good, some grass. Protection good from all but east winds.

Rachel Key (Mile 1190). Southwest of the ICW, south of Rachel Bank, 7-foot approach, 5 feet in area southwest of Rachel Key and southeast of charted shoal. Holding fair to good in sand and grass. Anchoring in the bight southeast of Rachel Key is also possible. Protection fair to good depending on exact anchorage.

Boot Key Harbor (Mile 1195). East of the ICW, accessible through Knights Key Channel or Moser Channel, then east to Boot Key Channel. See details in anchorages for Hawk Channel route.

Bahia Honda Area (Mile 1205). Southwest of the ICW in charted cove, 7-foot approach, 7 feet to shoal inside 6-foot line. Holding fair in grassy mud. Protection from east through southwest only. You can, with care, anchor just outside the park basin in 8 feet if you can get under the 20-foot clearance at the bridge.

HAWK CHANNEL ROUTE

Caesar Creek (Mile 1118). Anchorage open to both routes. Seven-foot approach from Hawk Channel, 4 feet from ICW. Anchorage best between Rubicon and Reid keys. Twelve-foot depth, holding good. Well protected.

Angelfish Creek (Mile 1122). Anchorage open to both routes. Five-foot approach from both channels. Anchorage in side creeks north of channel. Five-foot depth, holding mixed, some hard and some rocky areas. Strong currents, well protected.

Largo Sound (Mile 1141). Five-foot approach, some 5-foot depths near the channel, but 3 feet is the norm. Holding fair, some grass, well protected.

Rodriguez Key (Mile 1145). Seven-foot approach, 7 feet or less close in. Anchor in lee as required for protection. Holding good. Note wrecks north of key and shoal to the west.

Rock Harbor (Mile 1144). Seven-foot approach, anchor as close in as draft will permit. Protection from north to northeast. Mandalay Restaurant (cash only) has a dinghy beach.

Tavernier Key (Mile 1150). Six-foot approach, less close in. Anchor in Tavernier Harbor area. Holding good. Some protection from northwest to north, southwest through south.

Whale Harbor (Mile 1158). Five-foot approach, 5 feet in anchorage. Anchor in lee relative of keys to north and to small key to southwest near marker "5A." Holding fair, some grass. Protection fair northwest through east. Note shoals.

Indian Key (Mile 1165). Seven-foot approach, 7 feet or less at anchorage close in. Anchor on southeast side of key in lee. Holding good in sand and sea grass. Protection fair from northwest through northeast.

Long Key Bight (Mile 1172). Nine-foot approach, shoaling to 5 feet in center. You can anchor as far in as draft allows. Holding good in some sea grass. Good protection from all but due east.

Boot Key Harbor (Mile 1193). Five-foot approach from Sister Creek, 7-foot approach from Boot Key Channel. Eleven feet to shoaling near head of harbor. Holding good. Good protection for 360 degrees except in severe east-northeast winds. Little room to anchor outside of mooring field. Alternative is to harbor outside, just west of Boot Key in 5 to 8 feet.

Bahia Honda Key (Mile 1207). Ten-foot approach, 9 feet or less close in between bridges. Holding fair to good. Fair to good protection. Strong tidal currents. Anchor checks on tide swings are advised.

Newfound Harbor (Mile 1215). Seven-foot approach. Most anchor in the cross-bar of the "H" etched by the deeper channels in 7 to 8 feet. Or in 9 feet or less close in toward highway bridge. Holding good. Fair to good protection in all but worst southerly winds. .

Niles Channel (Mile 1215). Seven-foot approach, depths of 7 to 21 feet in sand and grass. Holding fair to good in mud and grass. Fair to good protection in all but worst winds from the south.

Saddlebunch Harbor (Mile 1228). Six-foot approach through narrow channel between Saddlebunch Keys and Pelican Key. Anchor in 7 to 8 feet of water just inside. Holding fair. Strong currents. Buoy your anchor. Fair to good protection.

Key West (Chart 11447). Anchorages in the Key West area are limited. The best is the northernmost of the two small islands off Key West Bight., Wisteria Island, at Mile 1245. Anchorage is north or east, as south of the island the holding is poor. Seven-foot-depth approach, with 7 feet to shoal near shore. West of Fleming Key is another alternative. Note: The anchorage is adjacent and contiguous to the harbor and is exposed to the wash and wake of passing vessels. Holding is good in fairly hard bottom. Protection from east and south, with shoals providing wave reduction from the north. Or proceed around the north end of Fleming Key and anchor north of the mooring field and off of Sigsbee Park.

Anchoring Doesn't Have to be a Drag

by Rudy & Jill Sechez

As you seek anchorages along the coasts or in the various waterways, you will encounter a variety of sea beds. Add to that Mother Nature's quirky sense of humor, throwing at you a wide range of wind speeds, currents, and wave conditions… it's no wonder that anchoring is often looked upon as a challenge. However, it doesn't have to be, and here are a few suggestions to ease the challenge:

Sand, mud, and weeds are the types of sea bottoms cruisers will most likely encounter; and as there won't always be a choice, cruisers should outfit with anchors that will enable them to securely anchor in all three.

SuperMax, Spade, Delta, Bruce, Fortress and other general-purpose anchors, in addition to the Fisherman-style anchors, all work well in sand. However, anchors with a 45 degree fluke angle do not do well in sand; if they do set, once the wind picks up, they usually do not hold.

For "sand" anchors, unless the manufacturer suggests differently, for wind speeds from zero to around 25 knots, the anchor sizes listed in the manufacturer's sizing chart are adequate; gale force winds usually require an increase of at least one size, and storm force winds, two sizes.

Any anchor that works in sand will most likely work in mud, but the holding power of the anchor will be less in mud than in sand–as little as one sixth. Therefore, an anchor used in mud, regardless of whether it has a 45 degree fluke angle–the optimum angle for mud–will need to be bigger than that used in sand, at the very least one size bigger than that mentioned above.

In weeds, general-purpose anchors usually just hook into the weeds, instead of the seabed, often pulling out once the wind picks up. For an anchor to hold well in a weedy bottom, it must have the weight to crush down to the seabed, and have palms or flukes long enough to dig below the weeds, into the seabed. The one anchor that can do this reliably is the "fisherman-style" anchor. Having one of these anchors onboard, such as a Luke take-apart anchor, not only broadens your choices of anchorages, if sized appropriately–two pounds per foot of boat–it also makes for a great storm anchor.

A fourth type of bottom is the "solid bottom", either rock or coral. With little or no soil for the anchor to dig into deep enough, as you try to set the anchor, or as the wind rises, the anchor will just drag along the bottom, or maybe catch and release. In this type of bottom, unless the vessel is moored to a massive-enough weight, or to an augured-in anchor, as the wind speed rises, the wise captain will seek an anchorage with better holding.

It is Mother Nature that dictates the amount of rode that must be deployed, and as the wind rises, a scope of at least 10:1 may be needed. When calculating for scope, add together the depth of water, height of the freeboard, and any additional tide. But if the wind is expected to rise toward gale force levels, or higher, also include the: depth that the anchor buries, height of waves, and the height of any storm surge. Adequate scope is too important, so when high winds are expected, don't skimp; if there isn't enough room to let out enough rode, move the boat to where there is.

There are also times when more than one anchor may be required, but not just any little old anchor is suitable for this job. Additional anchors must also be sized appropriately, and be of a design that is compatible with the type of seabed. Multiple anchors are not an opportunity to use "ill-sized" or "ill-suited" anchors.

If your current ground tackle does not conform to the above recommendations, plan to upgrade it, and don't forget to follow the applicable "rules" concerning the display of day-shapes and anchor lights

Rudy and Jill Sechez are the authors of ANCHORING–A Ground Tackler's Apprentice. To read more, order a copy of this book through waterwayguide.com or call 800-233-3359. Rudy and Jill are Anchoring Consultants, providing one-on-one onboard sessions, consultations, and group seminars. They are also available to talk to groups and clubs; to arrange to have them speak to your organization, contact them at rudyandjill@yahoo.com.

Float Plan

BoatU.S.

1. Phone Numbers

Coast Guard:_____

Marine Police:_____

Local TowBoatU.S. Company:_____

2. Description of the Boat

Boat Name:_____ Hailing Port:_____

Type:_____ Model Year:_____

Make:_____ Length:_____ Beam:_____ Draft:_____

Color, Hull:_____ Cabin:_____ Deck:_____ Trim:_____ Dodger:_____

Other Colors:_____ # of Masts:_____

Distinguishing Features:_____

Registration No:_____ Sail No:_____

Engine(s) Type:_____ Horsepower:_____ Cruising Speed:_____

Fuel Capacity, Gallons:_____ Cruising Range:_____

Electronics/Safety Equipment Aboard

VHF Radio:_____ Cell Phone:_____ CB:_____ SSB:_____

Frequency Monitored:_____ Loran:_____ SatNav:_____

Depth Sounder:_____ Radar:_____ GPS:_____

Raft:_____ Dinghy:_____ EPIRB:_____ A/B/C/406M

(Indicate Type)

3. Trip Details

Owner/Skipper (Filing Report):_____

Phone:_____ Age:_____

Address:_____

Additional Persons Aboard, Total:_____

Name:_____ Age:_____

Address:_____ Phone:_____

Boating Experience:_____

Name:_____ Age:_____

Address:_____ Phone:_____

Boating Experience:_____

Name:_____ Age:_____

Address:_____ Phone:_____

Boating Experience:_____

Name:_____ Age:_____

Address:_____ Phone:_____

Boating Experience:_____

Name:_____ Age:_____

Address:_____ Phone:_____

Boating Experience:_____

Departure Date/Time:_____ Return No Later Than:_____

Depart From:_____

Marina (Home Port):_____ Phone:_____

Auto Parked At:_____

Model/color:_____ Lic. #_____

Destination Port: _____

_____ ETA:_____ No Later Than:_____

Phone:_____

Anticipated Stopover Ports:_____

_____ ETA:_____ No Later Than:_____

Phone:_____

_____ ETA:_____ No Later Than:_____

Phone:_____

_____ ETA:_____ No Later Than:_____

Phone:_____

_____ ETA:_____ No Later Than:_____

Phone:_____

_____ ETA:_____ No Later Than:_____

Phone:_____

Plan Filed With:_____

Name:_____ Phone:_____

Get in the habit of filing a Float Plan. It can assure quicker rescue in the event of a breakdown, stranding or weather delay. Fill out the permanent data in Sections 1 and 2. Then, make enough copies to last for the season. If you file a Float Plan with someone not at your home, such as a harbormaster or boating friend, be sure to notify them as soon as you return. Don't burden friends or authorities with unnecessary worry and responsibility if you are safe.

Check your *BoatU.S. Towing Guide*. Some listed companies will accept a verbal Float Plan via telephone or VHF.

Talking About the Weather

Every day on the water can't entail balmy breezes, abundant sunshine and consistently warm weather; however, staying out of bad weather is relatively easy if you plan ahead. The National Weather Service (NWS) provides mariners with continuous broadcasts of weather warnings, forecasts, radar reports and buoy reports over VHF-FM and Single Side Band (SSB) radio. Reception range for VHF radios is usually up to 40 miles from the antenna site, although Florida stations are frequently picked up in the near Bahamas. There are almost no areas on the U.S. coast where a good quality, fixed-mount VHF cannot pick up one or more coastal VHF broadcasts. Also, there is no substitute for simply looking at the sky, and either stay put or seek shelter if you don't like what you see.

SSB Offshore Weather

SSB reports are broadcast from station NMN in Chesapeake, VA and from station NMG in New Orleans, LA. The broadcasts are not continuous, so refer to the latest schedules and frequency lists (see sidebar) to catch them. SSB reports provide the best source of voice offshore weather information. Two major broadcasts alternate throughout the day. The High Seas Forecast provides information for mariners well offshore, including those crossing the North Atlantic Ocean. Coastal cruisers will be more interested in the Offshore Forecast, which includes information on waters more than 50 miles from shore. The forecast is divided into regions.

Weather Apps
Boating Weather (FREE)
Buoy Weather (FREE)
Marine Weather by AccuWeather (FREE)
NOAA SuperRes Radar HD ($3.99)
PredictWind (FREE)
Storm Radar with NOAA Weather (FREE)
Weather Underground (FREE)
Windfinder (FREE)
Windy (FREE)

Weather Online
Accuweather (accuweather.com)
Windfinder (windfinder.com)
Buoy Weather (buoyweather.com)
National Hurricane Center (nhc.noaa.gov)
National Weather Service (weather.gov)
NOAA Marine Forecasts (nws.noaa.gov/om/marine)
Passage Weather (passageweather.com)
Predict Wind (predictwind.com)
Sailflow (sailflow.com)
The Weather Channel (weather.com)
Weather Underground (wunderground.com/MAR)

SSB Weather Frequencies

UTC	Chesapeake, VA NMN Frequencies (kHz)	New Orleans, LA NMG Frequencies (kHz)
0330 (Offshore)	4426.0, 6501.0, 8764.0	4316.0, 8502.0, 12788.0
0515 (High Seas)	4426.0, 6501.0, 8764.0	4316.0, 8502.0, 12788.0
0930 (Offshore)	4426.0, 6501.0, 8764.0	4316.0, 8502.0, 12788.0
1115 (High Seas)	6501.0, 8764.0, 13089.0	4316.0, 8502.0, 12788.0
1530 (Offshore)	6501.0, 8764.0, 13089.0	4316.0, 8502.0, 12788.0
1715 (High Seas)	8764.0, 13089.0, 17314.0	4316.0, 8502.0, 12788.0
2130 (Offshore)	6501.0, 8764.0, 13089.0	4316.0, 8502.0, 12788.0
2315 (High Seas)	6501.0, 8764.0, 13089.0	4316.0, 8502.0, 12788.0

(UTC, or Coordinated Universal Time, is equivalent to Greenwich Mean Time)

VHF-FM/NOAA Weather Frequencies

WX1	162.550 MHz
WX2	162.400 MHz
WX3	162.475 MHz
WX4	162.425 MHz
WX5	162.450 MHz
WX6	162.500 MHz
WX7	162.525 MHz

Lightning Safety

Water and metal are excellent conductors of electricity, making boating in a thunderstorm a risky prospect. Several coastal Florida cities are among the most lightning-prone in the U.S., according to the World Meteorological Organization (WMO). Some of the cities that made the "Top 10" and average number of thunderstorms per year are: Fort Myers (88 days), Tampa (82.7 days), Tallahassee (82.5 days), West Palm Beach (76.8 days), Daytona Beach (73.4 days) and Miami (72.3 days). But Florida isn't alone in this dubious honor: Lake Charles, Louisiana, also made the top of the list (75.8 days), as did Mobile, Alabama (75.5 days). While the odds of a given boat being hit are small, the consequences are severe and deadly. Do not try and play the odds!

The best advice if you are out on the water and skies are threatening is get back to land and seek safe shelter, but that's not always practical for cruisers who live aboard or are not near land.

Reading the Skies

Thunderstorms occur when air masses of different temperatures meet over inland or coastal waters. An example of this would be when air with a high humidity that is warm near the ground rises and meets cooler air, which condenses and creates water droplets. This releases energy, which charges the atmosphere and creates lightning. This is why thunderstorms are a daily occurrence between March and October near southern waterways.

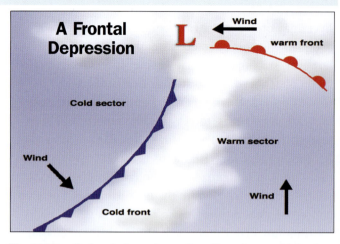

The trigger of change is a depression. Here, in a cold front, a counterclockwise flow of cold air comes in from the northwest. Warm air is sucked in from the south, which rises above the cold air, causing wind sheer and rain. The wind veers. A falling barometer is one of the warnings of a developing front.

A tell-tale sign of a thunderstorm is cumulonimbus clouds: those tall clouds with an anvil-shaped (flat) top. Thunderstorms can also precede even a minor cold front. Keep in mind that thunderstorms generally move in an easterly direction so if you see a storm to the south or southwest of you, start preparing!

Don't Wait Until It's Too Late

Almost all lightning will occur within 10 miles of its parent thunderstorm, but it can strike much farther than that. Also, the current from a single flash will easily travel for long distances. Because of this, if you see lightning or hear thunder, you CAN get struck!

The ability to see lightning will depend on the time of day, weather conditions and obstructions, but on a clear night it is possible to see a strike more than 10 miles away. Thunder can also be heard for about 10 miles, provided there is no background noise, such as traffic, wind or rain.

If you see lightning, you can determine the distance by timing how long it takes for you to hear the thunder. The old rule that every 5 seconds of time equals 1 mile of distance works well. So if it takes 20 seconds to hear thunder after you see lighting, then the storm is 4 miles away. This is the time to drop anchor and "hunker down."

Safety Tips

Lightning tends to strike the tallest object and boats on the open water fit this profile to a tee. The lightning will try to take the most direct path to the water, which is usually down the mast on a sailboat or the VHF antenna on a powerboat. However, both sailboats and powerboats with cabins–especially those with lightning protection systems properly installed–are relatively safe, provided you keep a few things in mind:

If You Are Struck

1. Check people first. Many individuals struck by lightning or exposed to excessive electrical current can be saved with prompt and proper cardiopulmonary resuscitation (CPR). Contrary to popular belief, there is no danger in touching persons after they have been struck by lightning.

2. Check the bilge as strikes can rupture through-hull fittings and punch holes in hulls. Props and rudders are natural exit points on power boats.

3. Check electronics and the compasses. Typically everything in the path of the lightning is destroyed on the way down to the water, including instruments, computers and stereos.

4. Consider a short haul to check the bottom thoroughly. Lightning strikes sometimes leave traces of damage that may only be seen when the boat is out of the water.

- Before the storm strikes, lower, remove or tie down all antennas, fishing rods and flag poles.

- Stay down below and in the center of the cabin. Avoid keel-stepped masts and chain plates (on sailboats) and large metal appliances, such as microwaves or TVs. Remove any metal jewelry.

- Disconnect the power and antenna leads to all electronics, including radios. Do not use the VHF radio unless absolutely necessary.

- If you are stuck on deck, stay away from metal railings, the wheel, the mast and stays (on sailboats) or other metal fittings. Do not stand between the mast and stays as lightning can "side-flash" from one to the other.

- Stay out of the water. Don't fish or dangle your feet overboard. Salt water conducts electricity, which means that it can easily travel through the water toward you.

- Don't think your rubber-soled deck shoes will save you; while rubber is an electric insulator, it's only effective to a certain point. The average lightning bolt carries about 30,000 amps of charge, has 100 million volts of electric potential and is about 50,000°F.

Don't Rush Back Out

Because electrical charges can linger in clouds after a thunderstorm has passed, experts agree that you should wait at least 30 minutes after a storm before resuming activities. And remember: If you can hear thunder, you can still be struck by lightning!

NOAA National Severe Storms Laboratory: nssl.noaa.gov

Hurricanes

While all coastal areas of the country are vulnerable to the effects of a hurricane (especially from June through November), the Gulf Coast, Southern and Mid-Atlantic states typically have been the hardest hit. But northern locales aren't immune; several destructive hurricanes have dealt a blow to areas in New England over the last 100 years, including Hurricane Sandy in 2012 and Matthew in 2016. While hurricanes can create vast swaths of devastation, ample preparation can help increase your boat's chances of surviving the storm.

According to the National Weather Service, a mature hurricane may be 10 miles high with a great spiral several hundred miles in diameter. Winds are often well above the 74 mph required to classify as hurricane strength, especially during gusts. Hurricane damage is produced by four elements: tidal surge, wind, wave action and rain.

- Tidal surge is an increase in ocean depth prior to the storm. This effect, amplified in coastal areas, may cause tidal heights in excess of 15 to 20 feet above normal. Additionally, hurricanes can produce a significant negative tidal effect as water rushes out of the waterways after a storm.

- Wind gusts can exceed reported sustained winds by 25 to 50 percent. So, for example, a storm with winds of 150 mph might have gusts of more than 200 mph, according to the National Weather Service.

- Wave action is usually the most damaging element of a hurricane for boaters. The wind speed, water depth and the amount of open water determine the amount of wave action created. Storm surges can transform narrow bodies of water into larger, deeper waters capable of generating extreme wave action.

- Rainfall varies but hurricanes can generate anywhere from 5 to 20 inches or more of rain.

If your boat is in a slip, you have three options: Leave it where it is (if it is in a safe place); move it to a refuge area; or haul it and put it on a trailer or cradle. Some marinas require mandatory evacuations during hurricane alerts. Check your lease agreement, and talk to your dockmaster before a hurricane if you are uncertain. Keep in mind that many municipalities close public mooring fields in advance of the storm. In some localities, boaters may be held liable for any damage that their boat inflicts to marina piers or property; check locally for details. Because

of this, rivers, canals, coves and other areas away from large stretches of open water are best selected as refuges.

Consult your insurance agent if you have questions about coverage. Many insurance agencies have restricted or canceled policies for boats that travel or are berthed in certain hurricane-prone areas. Review your policy and check your coverage, as many insurance companies will not cover boats in hurricane-prone areas during the June through November hurricane season. Riders for this type of coverage are notoriously expensive.

Natural Seasickness Remedies

Take slow, deep breaths. This helps with upset stomach and dizziness.

Focus on the horizon. Keep your body still and head facing forward and watch a stationary object. Taking the helm always helps.

Ginger can help. Eat ginger snaps, drink ginger tea or ginger ale or digest ginger in capsule form ahead of time.

Peppermint works too. Sucking on a peppermint candy, drinking peppermint tea or breathing in peppermint oil dabbed on a cloth can help with stomach issues.

Acupuncture wristbands apply pressure to specific points in your wrist and can reduce nausea.

Hurricane Categorization

CATEGORY	PRESSURE	WIND SPEED	SURGE
1	Above 980 mb (Above 28.91 in.)	64–82 knots (74–95 mph)	4–5 ft. (1–1.5 m)
Visibility much reduced. Maneuvering under engines just possible. Open anchorages untenable. Danger of poorly secured boats torn loose in protected anchorages.			
2	965–979 mb (28.50–28.91 in.)	83-95 knots (96–110 mph)	6-8 ft. (1.5-2.5 m)
Visibility close to zero. Boats in protected anchorages at risk, particularly from boats torn loose. Severe damage to unprotected boats and boats poorly secured and prepared.			
3	945–964 mb (27.91–28.50 in.)	96–113 knots (111–130 mph)	9-12 ft. (2.5-3.5 m)
Deck fittings at risk and may tear loose, anchor links can fail and unprotected lines will chafe through. Extensive severe damage.			
4	920–944 mb (27.17–27.91 in.)	114–135 knots (131–155 mph)	13-18 ft. (3.5-5.4 m)
Very severe damage and loss of life.			
5	Below 920 mb (Below 27.17 in.)	Above 135 knots (131–155 mph)	Above 18 ft. (Above 5.4 m)
Catastrophic conditions with catastrophic damage.			

Preparing Your Boat

- Have a hurricane plan made up ahead of time to maximize what you can get done in amount of time you will have to prepare (no more than 12 hours in some cases). You won't want to be deciding how to tie up the boat or where to anchor when a hurricane is barreling down on you. Make these decisions in advance!

- Buy hurricane gear in advance (even if there is no imminent storm). When word of a hurricane spreads, local ship stores run out of storm supplies (anchors and line, especially) very quickly.

- Strip everything that isn't bolted down off the deck of the boat (canvas, sails, antennas, bimini tops, dodgers, dinghies, dinghy motors, cushions, unneeded control lines on sailboats), as this will help reduce windage and damage to your boat. Remove electronics and valuables and move them ashore.

- Any potentially leaky ports or hatches should be taped up. Dorades (cowls) should be removed and sealed with deck caps.

- Make sure all systems on board are in tip-top shape in case you have to move quickly. Fuel and water tanks should be filled, bilge pumps should be in top operating condition and batteries should be fully charged.

You will need many lengths of line to secure the boat; make certain it is good stretchy nylon (not Dacron). It is not unusual to string 600 to 800 feet of dock line on a 40-foot-long boat in preparation for a hurricane. If you can, double up your lines (two for each cleat), as lines can and will break during the storm. Have fenders and fender boards out and make sure all of your lines are protected from chafe.

- If you are anchored out, use multiple large anchors; there is no such thing as an anchor that is too big. If you can, tie to trees with a good root system, such as mangroves or live oaks. Mangroves are particularly good because their canopy can have a cushioning effect. Be sure mooring lines include ample scope to compensate for tides 10 to 20 feet above normal.

- Lastly, do not stay aboard to weather out the storm. Many people have been seriously injured (or worse) trying to save their boats during a hurricane. Take photos of the condition in which you left your boat and take your insurance papers with you.

Returning Safely After the Storm

- Before hitting the road, make sure the roads back to your boat are open and safe for travel. Beware of dangling wires, weakened docks, bulkheads, bridges and other structures.

- Check your boat thoroughly before attempting to move it. If returning to your home slip, watch the waters for debris and obstructions. Navigate carefully as markers may be misplaced or missing.

- If your boat is sunk, arrange for engine repairs before floating it, but only if it is not impeding traffic. Otherwise, you will need to remove it immediately. Contact your insurance company right away to make a claim.

Northern Hemisphere Hurricane Evasion Tactics

Evasion Route

PREDICTED HURRICANE TRACK

Dangerous Semicircle

Navigable Semicircle

Evasion Route

NOAA Hurricane Resource Center:
hurricanes.noaa.gov

National Hurricane Center:
nhc.noaa.gov

BoatU.S. Hurricane Resource Page:
boatus.com/hurricanes

Reference Materials

NOAA Charts & Corrections

Print on Demand Paper Charts: Updated weekly and available from NOAA-certified agents. Orders shipped next business day. For a complete list, see: nauticalcharts.noaa.gov/staff/print_agents.html.

PDF Nautical Charts: Updated weekly. Available at charts.noaa.gov/PDFs/PDFs.shtml.

Raster Nautical Charts: Full-color digital images of NOAA paper charts. Compatible with most marine navigation software and available for free at charts.noaa.gov/InteractiveCatalog/nrnc.shtml.

Booklet Charts: Reduced in scale and divided into pages for convenience, but otherwise contains all the information of the full-scale nautical chart. Updated weekly. Available at nauticalcharts.noaa.gov/staff/BookletChart.html.

USCG *Local Notice to Mariners:* Provides timely marine safety information for the correction of all U.S. Government navigation charts and publications from a wide variety of sources, both foreign and domestic. Divided by district. Updated weekly and available as a PDF at navcen.uscg.gov. (Select LNMs tab at top of page.)

Navigation

- *NAVIGATION RULES, INTERNATIONAL—INLAND*, U.S. Dept. of Homeland Security. The U.S. Coast Guard requires all vessels over 12 meters [39 feet] carry this book of the national and international rules of the road. Can be downloaded as a PDF at navcen.uscg.gov.

- *U.S. Coast Pilot (1-5)*, NOAA. Includes piloting information for coasts, bays, creeks and harbors. Also includes tide tables and highlights restricted areas. Updated weekly and can be downloaded as a PDF at nauticalcharts.noaa.gov/nsd/cpdownload.htm.

- *A Boaters Guide to the Federal Requirements for Recreational Boats*, U.S. Coast Guard. Can be downloaded as a PDF at uscgboating.org.

NOAA Chart No 1. Symbols, Abbreviations and Terms, NOAA/DoD can be downloaded as a PDF at nauticalcharts.noaa.gov.

Maintenance

- *Boatowner's Mechanical & Electrical Manual* (4th Edition), Nigel Calder

- *Boatowner's Illustrated Electrical Handbook*, Charlie Wing

- *Boat Mechanical Systems Handbook*, David Gerr

Seamanship

- *The Annapolis Book of Seamanship* (4th Edition), John Rousmaniere

- *The Art of Seamanship*, Ralph Naranjo

- *Boater's Pocket Reference*, Thomas McEwen

- *Chapman Piloting & Seamanship* (68th Edition), Charles B. Husick

- *Eldridge Tide and Pilot Book* (annual), Robert E. and Linda White

- *Heavy Weather Sailing* (7th Edition), Peter Bruce

- *Nigel Calder's Cruising Handbook*, Nigel Calder

- *Offshore Cruising Encyclopedia*, Steve and Linda Dashew

- *World Cruising Essentials*, Jimmy Cornell

- *Anchoring: A Ground Tackler's Apprentice*, Rudy and Jill Sechez

First Aid & Medical

- *Advanced First Aid Afloat* (5th Edition), Dr. Peter F. Eastman

- *DAN Pocket Guide to First Aid for Scuba Diving*, Dan Orr & Bill Clendenden

- *First Aid at Sea*, Douglas Justin and Colin Berry

- *Marine Medicine: A Comprehensive Guide* (2nd Edition), Eric Weiss and Michael Jacobs

- *On-Board Medical Emergency Handbook: First Aid at Sea*, Spike Briggs and Campbell Mackenzie

Lionfish Management

Lionfish are an edible, venomous fish invading Florida and Bahamian waters. They can be found in the Atlantic, Caribbean and Gulf of Mexico and are voracious eaters of valuable game fish, crustaceans and, perhaps, even coral. Lionfish are usually found floating in a stationary position around coral heads, swaying beautifully with their mouths open and ready to feed. Game fish and crustaceans don't even seem to register that they are in danger; scientists think that they fool prey into thinking they are sea fans, seagrass or seaweed. Researchers have discovered that in just five weeks, lionfish can reduce the number of young native fish on a reef by as much as 80 percent. The ramifications for grouper, lobster, shrimp and similar fishery resources are grave.

In Florida, the Fish and Wildlife Conservation Commission (FWC) organizes lionfish derbies to rid Florida's waters of the non-native species. Teams collect lionfish by hook and line, spear, hand-held nets or any otherwise legal harvest gear. Prizes of up to $5,000 are awarded. FWC encourages dive shops and charter captains to implement lionfish excursions into their regularly-scheduled charters to meet diver demand and contribute to statewide removal efforts. Further, FWC educates and trains divers to confidently and safely harvest lionfish. See details at myfwc.com/fishing/saltwater/recreational/lionfish/events.

It is important to note that lionfish are venomous, not poisonous. Eating the cooked fish is a gastronome's delight, not a gourmet danger, and is another way to minimize their impact. Order lionfish when offered or cook your own. Reef Environmental Education Foundation (REEF) has published "The Lionfish Cookbook" (2nd edition), which is a unique blend of 45 recipes, background on the lionfish invasion and its impacts and a section on how to safely catch handle and prepare the fish. Lionfish range from bluegill size, all the way to 18 inches long.

A lionfish "sting" can be as painful as a stingray's or as mellow as a honeybee's. If you do get stung, remove the spine if it is stuck in your flesh and immerse the digit in the hottest water that you can possibly stand as soon as possible. The pain does not last as long as a stingray's (nor is there the possibility of an embedded sheath), but it is just as nasty in the immediate sense.

Onboard Waste & No-Discharge Zones

Up until the late 1980s, many boaters simply discharged their untreated sewage overboard into the water. After a revision to the Clean Water Act was passed in 1987, the discharge of untreated sewage into U.S. waters within the three-mile limit was prohibited. Shortly thereafter, pump-out stations became a regular feature at marinas and fuel docks throughout the U.S. waterways.

Simply stated, if you have a marine head installed on your vessel and are operating in coastal waters within the U.S. three-mile limit (basically all of the waters covered in the guide you are now holding), you need to have a holding tank, and you will obviously need to arrange to have that tank pumped out from time to time.

Government regulation aside, properly disposing of your waste is good environmental stewardship. While your overboard contribution to the waterways may seem small in the grand scheme of things, similar attitudes among fellow boaters can quickly produce unsavory conditions in anchorages and small creeks. The widespread availability of holding tank gear and shoreside pump-out facilities leaves few excuses for not doing the right thing.

No-Discharge Zones

- No-Discharge means exactly what the name suggests: No waste, even waste treated by an onboard Type I marine sanitation device (MSD), may be discharged overboard. All waste must be collected in a holding tank and pumped out at an appropriate facility.

- Keep in mind that there are some areas that forbid overboard discharge of any waste, including gray water from showers or sinks. Familiarize yourself with local regulations before entering new areas to ensure you don't get hit with a fine.

- No-Discharge Zones in Florida include Destin Harbor, the Florida Keys National Marine Sanctuary and the City of Key West.

The Law

- If you have a marine head onboard and are operating on coastal waters within the U.S. three-mile limit (basically all of the waters covered in this Guide), you need to have an approved holding tank or Type I MSD. In a No-Discharge area even a Type I MSD system must have a holding tank.

- All valves connected to your holding tank or marine head that lead to the outside (both Y-valves AND seacocks) must be wire-tied, padlocked or absent of the valve handle and in the closed position. Simply having them closed without the (non-releasable) wire ties will not save you from a fine if you are boarded.

- You may discharge waste overboard from a Type I MSD in all areas except those designated as No-Discharge Zones. A Type I MSD treats waste by reducing bacteria and visible solids to an acceptable level before discharge overboard.

- While small and inconvenient for most cruisers, "Port-A-Potties" meet all the requirements for a Type III MSD, as the holding tank is incorporated into the toilet itself.

Pump-Out Station and Holding Tank Basics

- Some marinas are equipped with pump-out facilities, normally located at the marina's fuel dock. Note that some marinas charge a fee for the service.

- Several municipalities and local governments have purchased and staffed pump-out boats that are equipped to visit boats on request, especially those at anchor. Radio the local harbormaster to see if this service is available in the area you are visiting. There is normally a small fee involved.

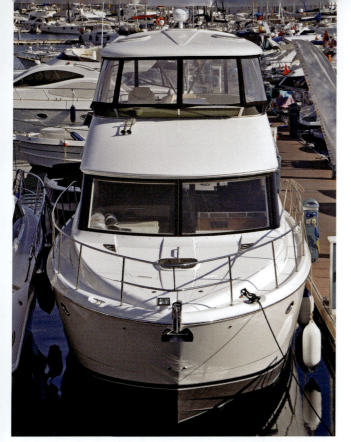

■ Type I MSD: Treats sewage before discharging it into the water using maceration. The treated discharge must not show any visible floating solids and must meet specified standards for bacteria content. Raritan's Electro Scan and Groco's Thermopure systems are examples of Type I MSDs. Not permitted in No-Discharge Zones.

■ Type II MSD: Type II MSDs provide a higher level of waste treatment than Type I units and are larger as a result. They employ biological treatment and disinfection. These units are usually found on larger vessels due to their higher power requirements. These may not be discharged in No-Discharge Zones.

■ Type III MSD: Regular holding tanks store sewage until the holding tank can either be pumped out to an onshore facility or at sea beyond the U.S. boundary waters (i.e., three miles offshore).

Additional Resources
BoatU.S. Guide to Overboard Discharge:
boatus.com/foundation/guide/environment_7.html

EPA Listing of No-Discharge Zones:
epa.gov/vessels-marinas-and-ports/no-discharge-zones-ndzs-state

■ You will want to keep an eye out on your holding tank level while you are cruising, especially if you are getting ready to enter an area where you many not have access to proper pump-out services for a few days. Plan a fuel stop or marina stay to top off the fuel and water tanks and empty the other tank before you set out into the wild.

Marine Sanitation Devices

Florida Statute 327.53 requires that vessels 26 feet or longer with an enclosed cabin and berth facilities must have one of the three types of MSDs described below on board when in state waters.

Distances: Fernandina Beach to Apalachicola, FL

Inside Route Distances - Fernandina Beach, Florida to Key West, Florida
(nautical and statute miles)

	Key West	Flamingo	Marathon	Matecumbe Harbor	Tavernier	Miami	Port Everglades	Fort Lauderdale	Port of Palm Beach	Jupiter	Fort Myers	Moore Haven	Clewiston	Port Mayaca	Stuart	Salerno	Fort Pierce	Vero Beach	Melbourne	Eau Gallie	Cocoa	Titusville	New Smyrna Beach	Daytona Beach	Marineland	St. Augustine	Jacksonville	Fernandina Beach	Norfolk, VA
Norfolk, VA	1061	1050	1045	1017	999	947	927	925	885	873	975	926	915	892	865	860	839	827	798	795	780	764	735	722	692	676	659	623	•
Fernandina Beach	458	427	422	394	378	324	304	303	262	251	353	303	292	269	242	237	216	204	175	172	157	141	113	99	69	53	36	•	717
Jacksonville	454	423	418	390	374	320	300	299	258	247	349	299	288	265	238	233	212	200	171	168	153	137	108	95	65	49	•	41	758
St. Augustine	405	374	369	341	324	271	251	249	209	197	299	250	239	216	189	184	163	151	122	119	104	88	59	46	16	•	56	60	778
Marineland	389	358	353	325	309	255	235	234	193	182	284	235	223	200	173	169	148	136	106	103	89	72	44	30	•	18	75	79	796
Daytona Beach	359	328	323	295	279	225	205	204	163	152	254	204	193	170	143	138	117	105	76	73	58	42	14	•	35	53	109	114	831
New Smyrna Beach	345	315	309	282	265	211	191	190	150	18	240	191	180	157	130	125	104	92	63	59	45	28	•	16	51	68	124	130	846
Titusville	317	286	281	253	237	183	163	162	121	110	212	163	151	128	101	97	76	64	34	31	17	•	32	48	83	101	158	162	879
Cocoa	301	270	264	237	220	166	146	145	105	93	195	146	135	112	85	80	59	47	18	14	•	20	52	67	102	120	176	181	898
Eau Gallie	286	255	250	223	206	152	132	131	90	79	181	132	120	97	70	66	45	33	3	•	16	36	68	84	119	137	193	198	915
Melbourne	283	252	247	219	203	149	129	128	87	76	178	128	117	94	67	62	41	29	•	14	21	39	72	87	122	140	197	201	918
Vero Beach	254	223	217	190	173	119	99	98	58	46	148	99	88	65	38	33	12	•	34	38	54	74	106	121	157	174	230	235	952
Fort Pierce	242	211	205	178	161	107	87	86	46	34	136	87	76	53	26	21	•	14	47	52	68	87	120	135	170	188	244	249	966
Salerno	224	193	188	161	144	90	70	69	28	17	119	70	58	35	8	•	24	38	71	76	92	112	144	159	194	212	268	273	990
Stuart	229	198	193	165	149	95	75	74	33	22	111	61	50	27	•	9	30	44	77	81	98	116	150	165	199	217	274	278	995
Port Mayaca	256	225	220	192	176	122	102	101	60	49	83	34	23	•	31	40	61	75	108	112	129	147	181	196	230	248	305	310	1026
Clewiston	279	248	243	215	199	145	125	124	83	72	61	11	•	26	58	67	87	101	135	138	155	174	207	222	257	275	331	336	1053
Moore Haven	290	259	254	227	210	156	136	135	94	83	49	•	13	40	70	81	100	114	148	152	168	188	220	235	270	288	344	349	1066
Fort Myers	339	309	303	276	259	205	185	184	144	132	•	56	70	96	128	137	157	170	205	208	224	244	276	292	327	344	402	406	1122
Jupiter	207	177	171	144	127	73	53	52	12	•	152	96	83	56	25	20	39	53	87	91	107	127	159	175	209	227	284	289	1005
Port of Palm Beach	196	165	160	132	116	62	42	41	•	14	166	108	96	69	38	32	53	67	100	104	121	139	173	188	222	241	297	302	1018
Fort Lauderdale	155	125	119	92	75	21	1	•	47	60	212	155	143	116	85	79	99	113	147	151	167	186	219	235	269	287	344	348	1064
Port Everglades	154	123	118	91	74	20	•	1	48	61	213	156	144	117	86	80	100	114	148	152	168	188	220	236	270	289	345	350	1067
Miami	134	104	98	71	54	•	23	24	71	84	236	180	167	141	109	104	123	137	171	175	191	211	243	259	293	312	368	373	1090
Tavernier	83	52	47	19	•	62	85	86	133	146	298	242	229	203	171	166	185	199	234	237	253	273	305	321	356	373	430	435	1150
Matecumbe Harbor	65	35	29	•	22	82	105	106	152	166	318	261	247	221	190	185	205	219	252	257	273	291	323	339	374	392	449	453	1170
Marathon	42	34	•	33	54	113	136	137	184	197	349	292	280	253	222	216	236	250	284	288	304	323	356	372	407	425	481	486	1203
Flamingo	73	•	39	40	60	120	142	144	190	204	356	296	285	259	228	222	243	257	290	293	311	329	362	377	412	430	486	491	1208
Key West	•	84	48	75	96	154	177	178	226	239	390	334	321	295	264	258	278	292	326	329	346	365	397	413	448	466	522	527	1244

Coastwise and Inside Route Distances – Key West, FL to Apalachicola, FL
(nautical miles)

	Apalachicola, FL	Carrabelle, FL	St. Marks, FL	Cedar Key, FL	Tarpon Springs, FL	Clearwater, FL	Tampa, FL	St. Petersburg, FL	Bradenton, FL	Sarasota, FL	Venice, FL	Port Boca Grande, FL	Fort Myers, FL	Naples, FL	Everglades, FL	Cape Sable, FL	Flamingo, FL	Matecumbe Harbor, FL	Marathon, FL	Key West, FL
Key West, FL	406	389	367	310	250	234	232	218	210	186	172	144	134	96	88	57	70	65	42	-
Marathon, FL	408	391	389	313	253	237	235	221	213	189	174	146	136	100	80	31	37	29	-	
Matecumbe Harbor, FL	411	394	392	316	255	240	237	224	215	191	177	149	139	103	81	32	35	-		
Flamingo, FL	396	379	377	301	240	225	222	209	200	176	162	134	124	88	66	17	-			
Cape Sable, FL	379	362	360	284	223	208	205	192	183	159	145	117	107	71	49	-				
Everglades, FL	350	334	332	255	195	179	177	163	155	131	116	88	79	38	-					
Naples, FL	316	299	297	221	160	145	143	129	120	96	82	54	44	-						
Fort Myers, FL	297	280	278	202	142	126	124	110	102	78	63	35	-							
Port Boca Grande, FL	262	245	244	167	107	91	89	75	67	43	28	-								
Venice, FL	234	218	216	139	79	63	61	47	39	15	-									
Sarasota, FL	221	204	202	125	65	49	42	33	25	-										
Bradenton, FL	209	193	191	114	54	38	36	22	-											
St. Petersburg, FL	202	186	184	107	47	31	18	-												
Tampa, FL	218	202	200	123	63	47	-													
Clearwater, FL	174	157	155	79	18	-														
Tarpon Springs, FL	164	147	145	68	-															
Cedar Key, FL	118	101	91	-																
St. Marks, FL	69	52	-																	
Carrabelle, FL	25	-																		
Apalachicola, FL	-																			

Routes used in table:
- Hawk Channel – between Marathon and Key West
- Northwest Channel (Key West) and outside to places between Cape Sable and San Carlos Bay, thence inside to Anclote Keys, thence outside to St. George Sound.

Distances from Everglades northward are inside via Big Marco River and Gordon Pass.

Distances on St. Johns River, Florida
(nautical and statute miles)

	Lake Harney	Sanford	Astor-Volusia	Georgetown	Leesburg	Moss Bluff Lock	Silver Springs	Welaka	Crescent City	Palatka	Doctors Lake Inlet	Jacksonville	Broward River (mouth)	Intracoastal Waterway	Mayport	St. Johns River (mouth)
St. Johns River (mouth)	161	143	109	95	162	145	136	86	89	68	32	20	12	4	2	•
Mayport	159	141	107	93	160	143	134	84	87	66	30	18	10	2	•	2
Intracoastal Waterway	157	139	105	91	158	141	132	82	85	64	28	16	8	•	2	5
Broward River (mouth)	149	131	97	83	150	133	124	74	77	56	20	8	•	9	12	14
Jacksonville	141	123	89	75	142	125	116	66	69	48	12	•	9	18	21	23
Doctors Lake Inlet	129	111	77	62	129	112	104	54	56	36	•	14	23	32	35	37
Palatka	93	75	41	26	94	76	68	18	20	•	41	55	64	74	76	78
Crescent City	101	83	49	35	102	85	76	26	•	23	64	79	89	98	100	102
Welaka	75	57	23	8	75	58	50	•	30	21	62	76	85	94	97	99
Silver Springs	123	105	71	56	31	14	•	58	87	78	120	134	143	152	154	157
Moss Bluff Lock	131	113	79	65	17	•	16	67	98	87	129	144	153	162	165	167
Leesburg	148	131	96	82	•	20	36	86	117	108	148	163	173	182	184	186
Georgetown	66	49	14	•	94	75	64	9	40	30	71	86	96	105	107	109
Astor-Volusia	52	34	•	16	110	91	82	26	56	47	89	102	112	121	123	125
Sanford	18	•	39	56	151	130	121	66	96	86	128	142	151	160	162	165
Lake Harney	•	21	60	76	170	151	142	86	116	107	148	162	171	181	183	185

GPS Waypoints

The following list provides selected waypoints for the waters covered in this book. The latitude/longitude readings are taken from government light lists and must be checked against the appropriate chart and light list for accuracy. Some waypoints listed here are lighthouses and should not be approached too closely as they may be on land, in shallow water or on top of a reef. Many buoys must be approached with caution, as they are often located near shallows or obstructions. The positions of every aid to navigation should be updated using the Coast Guard's *Local Notice to Mariners*, which is available online at: navcen.uscg.gov/lnm.

The U.S. Coast Guard will continue to provide Differential GPS (DGPS) correction signals for those who need accuracy of 10 meters or less, even though most GPS receivers now come with an internal capability for receiving differential signals.

Prudent mariners will not rely solely on these waypoints to navigate. Every available navigational tool should be used at all times to determine your vessel's position.

Florida East Coast

LOCATION	LATITUDE	LONGITUDE
St. Marys Entrance Lighted Buoy STM	N 30° 42.900'	W 081° 14.650'
St. Johns Lighted Buoy STJ	N 30° 23.583'	W 081° 19.133'
St. Augustine Lighted Whistle Buoy STA	N 29° 54.917'	W 081° 15.283'
Ponce de Leon Inlet Lighted Bell Buoy 2	N 29° 04.767'	W 080° 53.483'
Cape Canaveral App. Chnl. Lig. Buoy 8	N 28° 23.867'	W 080° 33.433'
Fort Pierce Inlet Lighted Buoy 2	N 27° 28.650'	W 080° 15.417'
St. Lucie Entrance Lighted Buoy 2	N 27° 10.017'	W 080° 08.383'
Lake Worth Inlet Lighted Buoy LW	N 26° 46.367'	W 080° 00.600'
Boca Raton Inlet North Jetty Light 2	N 26° 20.167'	W 080° 04.183'
Hillsboro Inlet Entrance Lighted Buoy HI	N 26° 15.133'	W 080° 04.467'
Port Everglades Lighted Buoy PE	N 26° 05.500'	W 080° 04.767'
Bakers Haulover Inlet Jetty Light	N 25° 53.933'	W 080° 07.183'
Miami Lighted Buoy M	N 25° 46.100'	W 080° 05.000'

Florida Keys

LOCATION	LATITUDE	LONGITUDE
Biscayne National Park N. Lig. Buoy N	N 25° 38.733'	W 080° 05.367'
Fowey Rocks Light	N 25° 35.433'	W 080° 05.800'
Triumph Reef Light 2TR	N 25° 28.267'	W 080° 06.917'
Pacific Reef Light	N 25° 22.267'	W 080° 08.517'
Carysfort Reef Light	N 25° 13.317'	W 080° 12.683'
Elbow Reef Light 6	N 25° 08.667'	W 080° 15.500'
Molasses Reef Light 10	N 25° 00.717'	W 080° 22.583'
Davis Reef Light 14	N 24° 55.550'	W 080° 30.167'
Alligator Reef Light	N 24° 51.100'	W 080° 37.133'
Tennessee Reef Light	N 24° 44.767'	W 080° 46.933'
Coffins Patch Light 20	N 24° 40.550'	W 080° 57.500'
Sombrero Key Light	N 24° 37.667'	W 081° 06.650'
Big Pine Shoal Light 22	N 24° 34.117'	W 081° 19.550'
Looe Key Light 24	N 24° 32.800'	W 081° 24.150'
American Shoal Light	N 24° 31.500'	W 081° 31.167'
Pelican Shoal Light 26	N 24° 30.367'	W 081° 35.983'
Stock Island Approach Channel Light 32	N 24° 28.483'	W 081° 44.533'
Key West Ent. Lighted Whistle Buoy KW	N 24° 27.683'	W 081° 48.033'
Key West NW Chan. Ent. Lig. Bell Buoy 1	N 24° 38.867'	W 081° 53.967'
Sand Key Light	N 24° 27.233'	W 081° 52.650'
Cosgrove Shoal Light	N 24° 27.467'	W 082° 11.100'
Twenty-Eight Foot Shoal Light	N 24° 25.800'	W 082° 25.533'
Halfmoon Shoal Light WR2	N 24° 33.500'	W 082° 28.433'
Rebecca Shoal Light	N 24° 34.733'	W 082° 35.117'

Location	Latitude	Longitude
Dry Tortugas Light	N 24° 38.000'	W 082° 55.233'
New Ground Rocks Light	N 24° 40.000'	W 082° 26.650'
Ellis Rock Light	N 24° 38.950'	W 082° 11.033'
Smith Shoal Light	N 24° 43.100'	W 082° 55.300'

Florida Bay and West Coast

LOCATION	LATITUDE	LONGITUDE
Bullfrog Banks Light BB	N 24° 50.733'	W 081° 20.567'
Arsenic Bank Light 1	N 24° 52.250'	W 080° 53.017
East Cape Light 2	N 25° 05.000'	W 081° 04.967'
Northwest Cape Light 4	N 25° 12.833'	W 081° 11.750'
Little Shark River Entrance Light 1	N 25° 19.350'	W 081° 09.233'
Broad Creek Light 6	N 25° 26.317'	W 081° 12.200'
Lostmans River Light 8	N 25° 32.567'	W 081° 14.983'
Pavilion Key Light 10	N 25° 40.917'	W 081° 21.400'
Cape Romano Shoals Light	N 25° 41.300'	W 081° 38.783'
Indian Key Pass Light 1	N 25° 47.983'	W 081° 28.067'
Coon Key Light	N 25° 52.900'	W 081° 37.933'
Capri Pass Light 2	N 25° 58.500'	W 081° 46.267'
Gordon Pass Shoal Light	N 26° 05.483'	W 081° 48.683'
San Carlos Bay Light SC	N 26° 25.133'	W 081° 57.550'
Sanibel Island Light	N 26° 27.183'	W 082° 00.850'
Charlotte Harbor Ent. Lig. Bell Buoy 2	N 26° 39.850'	W 082° 19.567'
Venice Inlet Light 1	N 27° 06.767'	W 082° 28.217'
Big Sarasota Pass Light 1	N 27° 15.567'	W 082° 33.767'
New Pass Entrance Light NP	N 27° 18.917'	W 082° 35.883'
Longboat Pass Approach Light LP	N 27° 25.850'	W 082° 41.850'
Southwest Channel Ent. Lig. Bell Buoy 1	N 27° 32.333'	W 082° 48.600'
Tampa Bay Lighted Buoy T	N 27° 35.317'	W 083° 00.717'
Pass-A-Grille Entrance Light PG	N 27° 40.583'	W 082° 46.017'
Johns Pass Light JP	N 27° 46.500'	W 082° 48.033'

Location	Latitude	Longitude
Clearwater Pass Channel Light 1	N 27° 58.267'	W 082° 50.850'
Anclote Anchorage South Ent. Light 1	N 28° 08.283'	W 082° 51.950'
Anclote River Entrance Light 1	N 28° 10.383'	W 082° 49.533'
Anclote Anchorage North Ent. Light 2	N 28° 15.050'	W 082° 52.900'
Homosassa Bay Entrance Light 2	N 28° 41.433'	W 082° 48.650'
Crystal River Lighted Buoy 2	N 28° 47.517'	W 082° 58.583'
Withlacoochee River Entrance Light 1	N 28° 58.133'	W 082° 49.717'
Cedar Keys Main Channel Light 1	N 29° 04.000'	W 083° 04.550'
Cedar Keys NW Channel App. Light 2	N 29° 08.483'	W 083° 07.850'
Suwannee River, Alligator Pass Light 2	N 29° 14.583'	W 083° 11.783'
Suwannee R., McGriff Pass Daybeacon 1	N 29° 18.583'	W 083° 12.017'
Steinhatchee River Light 1	N 29° 39.383'	W 083° 27.433'
St. Marks River Lighted Buoy SM	N 30° 04.300'	W 084° 10.800'
Carrabelle Channel Lighted Bell Buoy 2	N 29° 44.550'	W 084° 39.200'
St. George Island W Jetty Lig. Buoy 1	N 29° 36.167'	W 084° 57.217'
St. Joseph Bay Lig. & Ent. Rg. A Rear Lig.	N 29° 55.100'	W 085° 22.833'
St. Andrew Bay Ent. Lig. Whistle Buoy SA	N 30° 05.500'	W 085° 46.433'
Choctawhatchee Bay Ent. Lig. Whi. By CB	N 30° 22.250'	W 086° 30.900'
Pensacola Bay Ent. Lig. Gong Buoy 1	N 30° 16.267'	W 087° 17.550'

Alabama

LOCATION	LATITUDE	LONGITUDE
Perdido Pass Ent. Lig. Whistle Buoy PP	N 30° 15.517'	W 087° 33.400'
Mobile Entrance Lighted Horn Buoy M	N 30° 07.517'	W 088° 04.117'

Bridge Basics

Bridges have to be factored in when planning a trip. Depending on where you cruise, you may be dependent on bridge openings; a particular bridge's schedule can often decide where you tie up for the evening or when you wake up and get underway the next day. While many are high (over 65 feet), and some usually remain open (such as railroad bridges), others are restricted for different hours in specific months, closed during rush hours and/or open on the quarter-hour, half-hour or even at 20 minutes and 40 minutes past the hour. To add to the confusion, the restrictions are constantly changing. Just because a bridge opened on a certain schedule last season does not mean it is still on that same schedule. (See the Bridges & Locks section in this guide or waterwayguide.com for the most current schedules.) Changes are posted in the Coast Guard's *Local Notice to Mariners* reports, which can be found online at navcen.uscg.gov. It is also a good idea to check locally to verify bridge schedules before your transit.

Most bridges monitor VHF Channel 09, designated by the Federal Communications Commission as the "bridgetender channel." Bridges in NC and VA still answer on VHF Channel 13, as do the locks in the Okeechobee. In any waters, it is a good idea to monitor both the bridge channel and VHF Channel 16–one on your ship's radio and one on a handheld radio, if your main set doesn't have a dual-watch capability–to monitor oncoming commercial traffic and communications with the bridgetender.

When using VHF, always call bridges by name and identify your vessel by name and type (such as sailing vessel or trawler) and whether you are traveling north or south. If you are unable to raise the bridge using VHF radio, use a horn signal. (For further information, see the *Coast Pilot 4, Chapter Two: Title 33, Navigation Regulations, Part 117, Drawbridge Regulations.*) If the gates do not come down and the bridge does not open after repeated use of the radio and the horn, call the Coast Guard and ask them to call the bridgetender on the land telephone line, or you may be able to call the bridge directly. Phone numbers for many bridges are given in the following Bridges & Locks section, although some of the numbers are not for the actual bridgetender, but for a central office that manages that bridge. Some bridges are not required to open in high winds. If you encounter a bridge that won't open, it is prudent to drop the hook in a safe spot until the situation is resolved.

Swing Bridges:
Swing bridges have an opening section that pivots horizontally on a central hub, allowing boats to pass on one side or the other when it is open.

Lift Bridges:
Lift bridges normally have two towers on each end of the opening section that are equipped with cables that lift the road or railway vertically into the air.

Most bridges carry a tide board to register vertical clearance at the center of the span. (Note that in Florida waters the tide board figure–and the one noted on the chart–is generally for a point that is 5 feet toward the channel from the bridge fender.) In the case of arched bridges, center channel clearance is frequently higher than the tide gauge registers. So check your chart and the tide boards and, unless it specifically notes that vertical clearance is given "at center," you may be able to count on a little extra height at mid-channel, under the arch of the bridge. Some bridges may bear signs noting extra height at center in feet.

Because many bridges restrict their openings during morning and evening rush hours to minimize inconvenience to vehicular traffic, you may need to plan an early start or late stop to avoid getting stuck waiting for a bridge opening.

Pontoon Bridges:

A pontoon bridge consists of an opening section that must be floated out of the way with a cable to allow boats to pass. Do not proceed until the cables have had time to sink to the bottom.

Bascule Bridges:

This is the most common type of opening bridge you will encounter. The opening section of a bascule bridge has one or two leaves that tilt vertically on a hinge like doors being opened skyward.

Bridge Procedures:

- First, decide if it is necessary to have the drawbridge opened. You will need to know your boat's clearance height above the waterline before you start. Drawbridges have "clearance gauges" that show the closed vertical clearance with changing water levels, but a bascule bridge typically has 3 to 5 feet more clearance than what is indicated on the gauge at the center of its arch at mean low tide. Bridge clearances are also shown on NOAA charts.

- Contact the bridgetender well in advance (even if you can't see the bridge around the bend) by VHF radio or phone. Alternatively, the proper horn signal for a bridge opening is one prolonged blast (four to six seconds) and one short blast (approximately one second). Bridge operators sound this signal when ready to open the bridge, and then usually the danger signal–five short blasts–when they are closing the bridge. The operator of each vessel is required by law to signal the bridgetender for an opening, even if another vessel has already signaled. Tugs with tows and U.S. government vessels may go through bridges at any time, usually signaling with five short blasts. A restricted bridge may open in an emergency with the same signal. Keep in mind bridgetenders will not know your intentions unless you tell them.

- If two or more vessels are in sight of one another, the bridgetender may elect to delay opening the bridge until all boats can go through together.

- Approach at slow speed and be prepared to wait, as the bridge cannot open until the traffic gates are closed. Many ICW bridges, for example, are more than 40 years old and the aged machinery functions slowly.

- Once the bridge is open, proceed at no-wake speed. Keep a safe distance between you and other craft, as currents and turbulence around bridge supports can be tricky.

- There is technically no legal right-of-way (except on the Mississippi and some other inland rivers), but boats running with the current should always be given the right-of-way out of courtesy. As always, if you are not sure, let the other boat go first.

- When making the same opening as a commercial craft, it is a good idea to contact the vessel's captain (usually on VHF Channel 13), ascertain his intentions and state yours to avoid any misunderstanding in tight quarters.

- After passing through the bridge, maintain a no-wake speed until you are well clear and then resume normal speed.

Locks and Locking Through

Many rivers in North America are a series of pools created by dams. When the dams also include locks, navigation is possible beyond the dam. Locks are watertight chambers with gates at each end. They raise and lower boats from one water level to the next. Many cruisers find locking through a pleasant experience and part of the adventure of boating.

Lock Types

- Conventional lift locks are single chambers that raise and lower boats.

- Flight locks are a series of conventional lift locks.

- Hydraulic lift locks have water-filled chambers supported by rams or pistons that move in opposite directions. The movement of one chamber forces the movement of the other via a connected valve. The chamber in the upper position adds sufficient water to cause it to drop, forcing the lower chamber to rise. The chambers have hinged gates fore and aft that contain the water and allow boats to enter or leave.

- Marine railways convey boats over obstacles, usually a landmass, by containing boats in a gantry crane that moves over the land and deposits the boat on the other side of the obstruction.

River locks are usually conventional lift locks. The dam deepens water around shoals, and the lock allows vessels to bypass the dam. Conventional lift locks work by gravity alone. Water passively flows into or out of the lock. When the lock is filling, the valve at the upper end of the lock is opened, and water flows in. The downstream lock gate is closed, preventing the escape of the water. This is the time of greatest turbulence in the locks and the time of greatest vigilance for boaters. When the upper water level is reached, the upper lock gate opens to allow boats to exit or enter.

When the lock empties, both lock doors are closed, a valve on the lower end of the lock is opened, and water exits. This creates a surge of water outside the lock, but inside the lock, the water recedes like water in a tub. When the water level in the lock is the same as the lower river level, the lower lock gate opens and vessels leave.

Locking Protocol

1. Call ahead on the VHF (Channel 13 or sound three blasts) for permission to lock through. Indicate whether you are northbound (upbound) or southbound (downbound). Your presence and communication indicate to the locktender your desire to lock through.

2. Wait a safe distance from the lock, or find an anchorage nearby and within sight of the lock.

3. Prepare for locking by placing large fenders fore and aft and having lines ready. Fender boards are useful because they protect your fenders and provide a skid plate against the dirt and algae on the lock wall.

4. When approaching the lock, stay back to allow outbound vessels to clear the lock. Do not enter until signaled to do so. Signals vary. Look for a telephone/pull rope at the lock wall; listen for a whistle blast—one long and one short blast, or three

SKIPPER'S HANDBOOK

blasts; look for a "traffic" light–green, yellow or red. Follow directions given by the locktender. The order of priority is:

U.S. Military
Mail boats
Commercial passenger boats
Commercial tows
Commercial fishermen
Pleasure craft

5. When the locktender turns on the green light or calls for you to enter, enter in the order that boats arrived at the lock. The longest waiting boat goes first, unless directed by the locktender, who may call boats in according to size and the configuration of the lock. Do not jump the line; do not scoot in front of others; defer to faster boats so you do not have them behind you after you leave the lock.

6. When entering the lock, leave no wake, heed instruction, and respect other boaters. If they are having trouble and appear unsettled, stand by until they are secure. Listen to the directives of the locktenders. Some lock systems require all line handlers to wear personal flotation devices (PFDs). Crew members on the bow should wear PFDs.

7. You will be directed by the locktender to a place along the lock wall. You will find an inset mooring pin (floating bollard), vertical cable or a rope. If there is a floating bollard, secure the boat to the pin via a center cleat by wrapping the line around the pin then back to the boat cleat. If there is a vertical cable, wrap the line around the cable, and bring it back to the boat; the loop will ride up or down the cable. If there is a drop-down line, bring the line around a cleat, and hold it. DO NOT TIE LINES! If you are asked to provide a line, throw it to the locktender. After the locktender has secured it, take the bitter end and wrap, but do not tie, around a cleat. Attend the bow and the stern, and adjust the line(s) as the boat rises or falls in the lock chamber.

8. In crowded locks, move forward as far as you can to make room for others coming in behind you. Small boats may raft to bigger boats. Set adequate fenders for fending off another vessel.

9. Inside the lock chamber, turn off engines when secure. Exhaust fumes contained in the lock chamber are an irritant to people in small, open boats. Attend the lines at all times. Be prepared for turbulence when the lock fills. Never use hands or feet to fend a boat off a lock wall. Stay alert to other boats. Be prepared to quickly cut a line if needed.

10. When the lock reaches its determined depth/height, the locktender will loosen the line and drop it to you if you are using a line attached at the top of the lock. After receiving a whistle blast by the locktender, recover any lines used, and prepare to exit. Leave the lock in the same order as entering. Do not rush ahead of those in front of you.

Lock Fees

Unlike locks in other countries (including Canada), there is no fee for transiting locks managed by the Army Corps of Engineers.

Bridge & Lock Schedules

KEY:

| **Statute Miles from ICW Mile 0** |
| **Vertical Clearance** |

Drawbridge clearances are vertical, in feet, when closed and at Mean High Water in tidal areas. Bridge schedules are subject to schedule changes due to repairs, maintenance, events, etc. Check Waterway Explorer at waterwayguide.com for the latest shedules or call ahead.

FLORIDA BRIDGES MONITOR (VHF) CHANNEL 09

Florida's East Coast ICW

720.7 / 5' — Kingsley Creek Railroad Swing Bridge: Usually open.

720.8 / 65' — Kingsley Creek (FL A1A) Twin Bridges: Fixed

739.2 / 65' — Hecksher Dr. (Sisters Creek) Bridge: Fixed

St. Johns River

13.1 / 169' — Dames Point Bridge: Fixed

21.8 / 86' — Mathews Bridge: Fixed

22.8 / 135' — Hart-Commodore Point Bridge: Fixed (Also known as Isaiah D. Hart Bridge)

24.7 / 40' — Main Street Lift Bridge: Opens on signal except from 7:00 a.m. to 8:30 a.m. and from 4:30 p.m. to 6:00 p.m., Mon. through Sat. (except federal holidays), when the draw need not open.

24.8 / 75' — Acosta Bridge: Fixed

24.9 / 5' — FEC Railroad Bascule Bridge: Usually open, displaying flashing green lights to indicate that vessels may pass. When a train approaches, large signs on both the upstream and downstream sides of the bridge flash "Bridge Coming Down," the lights go to flashing red, and siren signals sound. After an 8-minute delay, the draw lowers and locks if there are no vessels under the draw. The draw remains down for a period of 8 min. or while the approach track circuit is occupied. After the train has cleared, the draw opens and the lights return to flashing green.

25.4 / 75' — Fuller-Warren Bridge: Fixed. Contractor will have floating equipment in the vicinity of the bridge to include barges, cranes, and other work vessels. Future waterway restrictions may be necessary for the replacement of the bridge fender system and girder erection. This work is anticipated to start September 2017 and will be completed by the Fall 2020.

35.1 / 65' — Buckman (I-295) Bridge: Fixed (Also known as Three-Mile Bridge)

51.4 / 45' — Shands Bridge: Fixed (Note: A new fixed 65-foot vertical clearance bridge has been in the planning stages for several years.)

79.8 / 65' — Palatka Memorial Bridge: Fixed

90.2 / 7' — Buffalo Bluff Railroad Bascule Bridge: Usually open.

122.2 / 20' — Astor Hwy. Bascule Bridge: Opens on signal. (Note: Open bascule overhangs channel above a height of 72 feet.)

138.2 / 15' — Whitehair (SR 44) Bascule Bridge: Opens on signal.

156.2 / 7' — Port of Sanford Railway Bascule Bridge: Usually open.

156.3 / 45' — U.S. 17/U.S. 92 Bridge: Fixed

156.6 / 45' — St Johns River Veterans Memorial Twin Bridges: Fixed

Florida's East Coast ICW (cont.)

742.1 / 65' — Wonderwood Drive Twin Bridges: Fixed. The vertical clearance will be reduced to 61 feet MHW over one-half of the navigational channel during installation of a containment system. Estimated completion date is January 2019.

744.7 / 65' — Atlantic Beach Twin Bridges: Fixed (Note: May be less than charted clearance.)

747.5 / 65' — McCormick (U.S. 90) Bridge: Fixed

749.5 / 65' — Butler Blvd. (Pablo Creek) Twin Bridges: Fixed

758.8 / 65' — Palm Valley (SR 210) Bridge: Fixed

775.8 / 65' — Usina (Vilano Beach) Bridge: Fixed (Note: May be less than charted clearance.)

777.9 / **18'** — **Bridge of Lions (SR A1A):** Opens on signal, except from 7:00 a.m. to 6:00 p.m., when the draw need only open on the hour and half-hour; however, the draw need not open at 8:00 a.m., 12 noon, and 5:00 p.m. Mon. through Fri. (except federal holidays). In addition, from 7:00 a.m. to 6:00 p.m. on Sat., Sun. and federal holidays, the draw opens only on the hour and half-hour. (Note: Additional 4 feet of vertical clearance at center of bridge.) 904-824-7372

780.3 / **65'** — **SR 312 Twin Bridges:** Fixed

788.6 / **25'** — **Crescent Beach (SR 206) Bascule Bridge:** Opens on signal.

803.0 / **65'** — **Hammock Dunes (Palm Coast Hwy.) Bridge:** Fixed

810.6 / **65'** — **Flagler Beach (Moody Blvd.) Bridge:** Fixed

816.0 / **15'** — **Bulow (L.B. Knox) Bascule Bridge:** Opens on signal.

824.9 / **65'** — **Ormond Beach (SR 40) Bridge:** Fixed

829.1 / **65'** — **Daytona Beach–Seabreeze Twin Bridges:** Fixed

829.7 / **22'** — **Main Street (Daytona Beach) Bascule Bridge:** Opens on signal.

830.1 / **65'** — **International Speedway Blvd. Bridge:** Fixed

830.6 / **21'** — **Veterans Memorial Bascule Bridge:** Opens on signal, except from 7:45 a.m. to 8:45 a.m. and 4:45 p.m. to 5:45 p.m. Mon. through Sat. (except federal holidays), when the draw opens only at 8:15 a.m. and 5:15 p.m. Contruction was underway at press time on 65-foot vertical clearance replacement bridge.

835.5 / **65'** — **Dunlawton Ave. (Port Orange) Bridge:** Fixed (Note: May be less than charted clearance during high tide.)

845.0 / **24'** — **George E. Musson (Coronado Beach) Bascule Bridge:** Opens on signal, except from 7:00 a.m. until 7:00 p.m. daily, when the draw opens only on the hour and half hour. (Note: Hydraulic bridge; slow in opening.)

846.5 / **65'** — **Harris Saxon (New Smyrna) Bridge:** Fixed

869.2 / **27'** — **Allenhurst (Haulover Canal) Bascule Bridge:** Opens on signal. 321-867-4859

876.6 / **7'** — **NASA (Jay-Jay) Railroad Bascule Bridge:** Usually open, displaying flashing green lights to indicate that vessels may pass. When a train approaches, the lights go to flashing red, and the draw lowers and locks if there are no vessels under the draw. The draw remains down for a period of 5 min. or while the approach track circuit is occupied. After the train has cleared, the draw opens and the lights return to flashing green.

878.9 / **65'** — **Max Brewer (Titusville) Bridge:** Fixed

885.0 / **27'** — **NASA Causeway Twin Bascule Bridges:** Open on signal, except from 6:30 a.m. to 8:00 a.m. and 3:30 p.m. to 5:00 p.m. Mon. through Fri. (except federal holidays), when the draws need not open. (Note: May be less than charted closed clearance.)

894.0 / **65'** — **Bennett Causeway (City Point) Twin Bridges:** Fixed

897.4 / **65'** — **Merritt Island (Cocoa) Twin Bridges:** Fixed

909.0 / **65'** — **Pineda Causeway (Palm Shores) Twin Bridges:** Fixed

914.4 / **65'** — **Eau Gallie Causeway (SR 518) Bridge:** Fixed

918.2 / **65'** — **Melbourne Causeway (SR 516) Twin Bridges:** Fixed

943.3 / **65'** — **Wabasso Bridge:** Fixed (Note: May be less than charted clearance.)

951.9 / **66'** — **Merrill P. Barber (Vero Beach) Bridge:** Fixed

953.2 / **65'** — **Alma Lee Loy (17th St.) Bridge:** Fixed

964.8 / **26'** — **North Fort Pierce (SR A1A) Bascule Bridge:** Opens on signal.

965.8 / **65'** — **Fort Pierce (SR A1A) Bridge:** Fixed

981.4 / **65'** — **Jensen Beach Causeway (SR 707A) Bridge:** Fixed

984.9 / **65'** — **Ernest Lyons (SR A1A) Bridge:** Fixed

SKIPPER'S HANDBOOK

Okeechobee Waterway (East to West)

3.4
65'
Evans Crary (SR A1A) Bridge: Fixed

7.3
65'
Roosevelt Blvd. (U.S. 1) Bridge: Fixed

7.4
7'
Florida East Coast Railroad Lift Bridge: Usually in the fully open position, displaying flashing green lights to indicate that vessels may pass. When a train approaches, the navigation lights go to flashing red and a horn sounds four blasts, pauses, and then repeats four blasts. After an 8-min. delay, the draw lowers and locks, if there are no vessels under the draw. The draw remains down for a period of 8 min. or while the approach track circuit is occupied. After the train has cleared, the draw opens and the lights return to flashing green. Note: Only 50 feet of charted horizontal clearance.

7.4
14'
Old Roosevelt (Dixie Hwy.) Bascule Bridge: Opens on signal. The draw opens on signal, except from 7:00 a.m. to 6:00 p.m., Mon. through Fri. (except federal holidays), when the draw need open only on the hour and half hour. However, the draw need not open between 7:30 a.m. and 9:00 a.m. and 4:00 p.m. and 5:30 except at 8:15 a.m. and 4:45 p.m. On Saturdays, Sundays, and federal holidays from 8:00 a.m. to 6:00 p.m. the draw need open only on the hour, 20 minutes after the hour, and 40 minutes after the hour. When the adjacent railway bridge is in the closed position at the time of a scheduled opening the draw need not open, but it must then open immediately upon opening of the railroad bridge to pass all accumulated vessels. 772-692-0321 (Note: This is a change from the 2018 published schedule.)

9.5
54'
Palm City (SR 714) Bridge: Fixed

10.9
55'
Indian St. (SW Martin Hwy.) Bridge: Fixed

14.0
56'
I-95 Twin Bridges: Fixed

14.6
55'
Florida Turnpike Twin Bridges: Fixed

15.1
St. Lucie Lock: Opens 7:00 a.m. to 5:00 p.m., on request. Normally make fast on south wall. 772-287-2665

17.1
56'
SR 76A Bridge: Fixed

28.1
55'
Indiantown (SR 710) Bridge: Fixed

28.2
7'
Seaboard (Indiantown) Railroad Swing Bridge: Opens on signal, except from 10:00 p.m. to 6:00 a.m., when the bridge opens on signal only if at least 3-hour notice is given. 772-597-3822

38.0
7'
Florida East Coast (Port Mayaca) Railroad Lift Bridge: Usually in the fully open position, displaying flashing green lights to indicate that vessels may pass. When a train approaches, it will stop and a crewmember will observe the waterway for approaching vessels, which will be allowed to pass. Upon manual signal, the bridge lights will go to flashing red, and the horn will sound four blasts, pause then repeat four blasts. The draw will lower and lock, if there are no vessels under the draw. After the train has cleared, the draw will open, and the lights will return to flashing green. (Note: Vertical clearance when open is 49 feet, setting the overhead clearance for the OCWW.) The bridge is not constantly tended.

38.8
55'
U.S. Hwys. 98 & 441 Bridge: Fixed

39.1
Port Mayaca Lock: Opens on signal, 7:00 a.m. to 5:00 p.m. Last lockage at 4:30 p.m. Normally make fast on south wall. 561-924-2858

60.7
11'
Torry Island (Belle Glade Dike) Swing Bridge: Opens on signal from 7:00 a.m. to 6:00 p.m., Mon. through Thurs., and from 7:00 a.m. to 7:00 p.m., Fri. through Sun. At all other times, the draw need not be opened for the passage of vessels. Manual operation. (May not open in winds in excess of 20 mph.) 561-996-3844

75.5
Clewiston Lock: Normally open. If the lock is closed due to high lake levels, an operator will be on site.

78.0
Moore Haven Lock: Opens on signal, 7:00 a.m. to 5:00 p.m. Last lockage at 4:30 p.m. Normally make fast on south wall. 863-946-0414

78.3
5'
Seaboard (Moore Haven) Railroad Swing Bridge: Opens on signal, except from 10:00 p.m. to 6:00 a.m., when the draw need not open. (Note: Normally open. Manual operation.)

78.4
55'
Moore Haven (U.S. 27) Twin Bridges: Fixed

93.5
Ortona Lock: Opens on signal, 7:00 a.m. to 5:00 p.m. Last lockage at 4:30 p.m. Normally make fast on south wall. 863-675-0616

103.0
28'
La Belle (SR 29) Bascule Bridge: Opens on signal, except from 7:00 a.m. to 9:00 a.m. and from 4:00 p.m. to 6:00 p.m., Mon. through Fri. (except federal holidays), when the bridge need not open. The bridge will open from 10:00 p.m. to 6:00 a.m. on signal only if at least 3-hour notice is given. 863-674-4663

108.2 / 9' — **Fort Denaud Swing Bridge:** Opens on signal, except from 10:00 p.m. to 6:00 a.m., when the bridge will open on signal only if at least 3-hour notice is given. 863-675-2055

116.0 / 23' — **Alva Bascule Bridge:** Opens on signal, except from 10:00 p.m. to 6:00 a.m., when the bridge will open on signal only if at least 3-hour notice is given. 239-278-2704

121.4 — **W.P. Franklin Lock:** Opens on signal from 7:00 a.m. to 5:00 p.m. Last lockage at 4:30 p.m. Normally make fast on south wall. 239-694-5451

126.3 / 27' — **Wilson Pigott (Olga) Bascule Bridge:** Opens on signal, except from 10:00 p.m. to 6:00 a.m., when the bridge will open on signal only if at least 3-hour notice is given.

128.9 / 55' — **I-75 Bridge:** Fixed

129.9 / 5' — **SCL Railroad Lift Bridge:** Usually open. (Note: Span overhangs channel when open, resulting in a vertical clearance of 55 feet.)

134.6 / 56' — **Edison Twin Bridges:** Fixed

135 / 55' — **Caloosahatchee Bridge:** Fixed

138.6 / 55' — **Veterans Memorial (Mid-Point) Bridge:** Fixed

142 / 55' — **Cape Coral Bridge:** Fixed

Florida's East Coast ICW (cont.)

995.9 / 21' — **Hobe Sound (SR 708) Bascule Bridge:** Opens on signal. 772-546-5234

1004.1 / 25' — **Jupiter Island (CR 707) Bascule Bridge:** Opens on signal. (Hail as "707 Bridge.")

1004.8 / 26' — **Jupiter (U.S. 1) Bascule Bridge:** Opens on signal.

1006.2 / 35' — **Indiantown (SR 706) Bascule Bridge:** Opens on hour and half-hour.

1009.3 / 35' — **Donald Ross Bascule Bridge:** Opens on the hour and half-hour.

1012.6 / 24' — **PGA Blvd. Bascule Bridge:** Opens on the hour and half-hour.

1013.7 / 25' — **Parker (U.S. 1) Bascule Bridge:** Opens on the quarter hour and three-quarter hour.

1017.2 / 65' — **Blue Heron Blvd. (SR A1A) Bridge:** Fixed (Note: Actual clearance may be as low as 60 feet. Check the tide boards.)

1020.8 / 21' — **Flagler Memorial (SR A1A) Bascule Bridge:** Opens on signal at 15 min. and 45 min. past the hour. (Note: This is a change from the 2018 published schedule.)

1022.6 / 21' — **Royal Park (SR 704) Bascule Bridge:** Opens on the hour and half-hour.

1024.7 / 14' — **Southern Blvd. (SR 700/80) Bascule Bridge:** Opens at 15 min. and 45 min. past the hour. (Note: Bridge under construction at press time. The new closed vertical clearance will be 21 feet. Be aware that you may have delays due to the construction. The project is planned to be completed in 2019. Check waterwayguide.com for updates.)

1028.8 / 35' — **Lake Worth-Lake Ave. (SR 802) Bascule Bridge:** Opens on signal.

1031.0 / 21' — **E. Ocean Ave. (Lantana) Bascule Bridge:** Opens on the hour and half-hour.

1035.0 / 21' — **E. Ocean Ave. (Boynton Beach) Bascule Bridge:** Opens on the hour and half-hour.

1035.8 / 25' — **E. Woolbright Rd. (SE 15th St.) Bascule Bridge:** Opens on signal.

1038.7 / 9' — **George Bush Blvd. Bascule Bridge:** Opens on signal. 561-276-5948

1039.6 / 12' — **Atlantic Ave. (SR 806) Bascule Bridge:** Opens on signal at 15 min. and 45 min. past the hour.

1041.0 / 30' — **Linton Blvd. Bascule Bridge:** Opens on the hour and half-hour. (Note: Actual vertical clearance may be as low as 27 feet. Call ahead to verify.) 561-278-1980

1044.9 / 25' — **Spanish River Blvd. Bascule Bridge:** Opens on the hour and half-hour.

1047.5 / 19' — **Palmetto Park Bascule Bridge:** Opens on the hour and half-hour.

23' — **Boca Raton Inlet Bascule Bridge (to ocean):** Opens on signal.

1048.2 / 9' — **Camino Real Bascule Bridge:** Opens on the hour, 20 min. past the hour and 40 min. past the hour.

1050.0 / 21' — **Hillsboro Blvd. (SR 810) Bascule Bridge:** Opens on the hour and half-hour.

SKIPPER'S HANDBOOK

13' **Hillsboro Inlet Bascule Bridge (to ocean):** Opens on signal, except from 7:00 a.m. to 6:00 p.m., the draw will open only on the hour, quarter hour, half-hour, and three-quarter hour.

1055.0 **15'** **Pompano Beach (NE 14th Street) Bascule Bridge:** Opens on the quarter hour and three-quarter hour.

1056.0 **15'** **Atlantic Blvd. (SR 814) Bascule Bridge:** Opens on the hour and half-hour.

1059.0 **15'** **Commercial Blvd. (SR 870) Bascule Bridge:** Opens on the hour and half-hour.

1060.5 **22'** **Oakland Park Blvd. Bascule Bridge:** Opens on signal at 15 min. and 45 min. past the hour.

1062.6 **25'** **East Sunrise Blvd. (SR 838) Bascule Bridge:** Opens on the hour and half-hour. On the first weekend in May, the draw need not open from 4:00 p.m. to 6:00 p.m. on Sat. and Sun. and, on the first Sat. in May, the draw need not open from 9:45 p.m. to 10:45 p.m.

1064.0 **24'** **East Las Olas Blvd. Bascule Bridge:** Opens on signal at 15 min. and 45 min. past the hour. On the first weekend in May, the draw need not open from 4:00 p.m. to 6:00 p.m. on Sat. and Sun. and, on the first Sat. in May, the draw need not open from 9:45 p.m. to 10:45 p.m.

New River (North & South Forks)

1.4 **16'** **SE 3rd Ave. Bascule Bridge:** The draw opens on signal, except from 7:30 a.m. to 9:00 a.m. and 4:30 p.m. to 6:00 p.m., Mon. through Fri. (except federal holidays), when the draw need not open.

2.3 **21'** **Andrews Ave. Bascule Bridge:** The draw opens on signal, except from 7:30 a.m. to 9:00 a.m. and 4:30 p.m. to 6:00 p.m., Mon. through Fri. (except federal holidays), when the draw need not open. The draw need not open for inbound vessels when the draw of the Florida East Coast Railroad Bridge is in the closed position for the passage of a train.

2.5 **4'** **Florida East Coast Railroad Lift Bridge:** Usually in the fully open position, displaying flashing green lights to indicate that vessels may pass. When a train approaches, the navigation lights go to flashing red and a horn sounds four blasts, pauses, and then repeats four blasts then the draw lowers and locks. After the train has cleared, the draw opens and the lights return to flashing green. The bridge shall not be closed more than 60 minutes combined for any 120-minute time period beginning at 12:01 a.m.

2.7 **20'** **William H. Marshall Memorial (7th Ave.) Bascule Bridge:** The draw opens on signal, except from 7:30 a.m. to 9:00 a.m. and 4:30 p.m. to 6:00 p.m., Mon. through Fri. (except federal holidays), when the draw need not open.

3.3 **3'** **11th Ave. Swing Bridge:** (Located on North Fork.) Opens on signal. (Note: This is a hand-operated swing bridge; expect delays.)

0.9 **21'** **Davie Blvd. Bascule Bridge:** (Located on South Fork.) The draw opens on signal, except from 7:30 a.m. to 9:00 a.m. and 4:30 p.m. to 6:00 p.m., Mon. through Fri. (except federal holidays), when the draw need not open.

2.0 **55'** **I-95 Twin Bridges:** (Located on South Fork.) Fixed

2.1 **2'** **SCL Railroad Bascule Bridge:** (Located on South Fork.) Usually open

4.4 **21'** **SR 84 Bascule Bridge:** (Located on South Fork.) Opens on signal if at least a 24 hour notice is given. No VHF; call 954-776-4300.

4.5 **40'** **I-595 Bridge:** Fixed

Florida's East Coast ICW (cont.)

1065.9 **55'** **SE 17th St. (Brooks Memorial) Bascule Bridge:** Opens on the hour and half-hour.

1069.4 **22'** **Dania Beach Blvd. (A1A) Bascule Bridge:** Opens on the hour and half-hour.

1070.5 **22'** **Sheridan St. Bascule Bridge:** Opens at 15 min. and 45 min. past the hour.

1072.2 **25'** **Hollywood Beach Blvd. (SR 820) Bascule Bridge:** Opens on hour and half-hour.

1074.0 **26'** **Hallandale Beach Blvd. (SR 858) Bascule Bridge:** Opens at 15 min. and 45 min. past the hour.

1076.3 **65'** **William Lehman Causeway (SR 856) Bridge:** Fixed

1078.0 **30'** **NE 163rd St. (Sunny Isles) Twin Bridges:** Opens on signal, except from 7:00 a.m. to 6:00 p.m. on Mon. through Fri. (except federal holidays), and from 10:00 a.m. to 6:00 p.m. on Sat., Sun., and federal holidays, when the draw need open only at 15 min. and 45 min. past the hour.

32' **Bakers Haulover Inlet Bridge (to ocean):** Fixed

1081.4 **16'** **Broad Causeway Bascule Bridge:** Opens on signal, except from 8:00 a.m. to 6:00 p.m., when the draw need open only s at 15 min. and 45 min. past the hour.

1084.6 **25'** **West 79th St. Bascule Bridge:** Opens on signal.

1087.2 **56'** **Julia Tuttle Causeway (I-195) Bridge:** Fixed (Note: Bridge is less than standard ICW vertical clearance.)

1088.6
12'
Venetian Causeway Bascule Bridge (West): Opens on signal, except from 7:00 a.m. to 7:00 p.m., Mon. through Fri. (except federal holidays), when the bridge need only open on the hour and half-hour.

1088.8
65'
MacArthur Causeway (SR A1A) Twin Bridges: Fixed

1089.3
65'
Dodge Island Hwy. Bridge: Fixed

1089.4
22'
Dodge Island Railroad Bascule Bridge: Usually open.

Miami River

23'
Brickell Ave. Bascule Bridge: Opens on signal, except from 7:30 a.m. to 7:00 p.m., Mon. through Fri. (except federal holidays), when the draw need only open on the hour and half-hour; however, from 7:35 a.m. to 8:59 a.m., 12:05 p.m. to 12:59 p.m. and 4:35 p.m. to 5:59 p.m., the draw need not open.

75'
Metro Train Bridge: Fixed

21'
Miami Ave. Bascule Bridge: Opens on signal, except from 7:30 a.m. to 7:00 p.m., Mon. through Fri. (except federal holidays), when the draw need only open on the hour and half-hour; however, from 7:35 a.m. to 8:59 a.m., 12:05 p.m. to 12:59 p.m. and 4:35 p.m. to 5:59 p.m., the draw need not open.

75'
SW 1st Ave. Bridge: Fixed

11'
SW 2nd Ave. Bascule Bridge: Opens on signal, except from 7:30 a.m. to 7:00 p.m., Mon. through Fri. (except federal holidays), when the draw need only open on the hour and half-hour; however, from 7:35 a.m. to 8:59 a.m., 12:05 p.m. to 12:59 p.m. and 4:35 p.m. to 5:59 p.m., the draw need not open.

75'
I-95 Twin Bridges: Fixed

18'
SW 1st. St. Bascule Bridge: Opens on signal, except from 7:30 a.m. to 7:00 p.m., Mon. through Fri. (except federal holidays), when the draw need only open on the hour and half-hour; however, from 7:35 a.m. to 8:59 a.m., 12:05 p.m. to 12:59 p.m. and 4:35 p.m. to 5:59 p.m., the draw need not open.

35'
W. Flagler St. Bascule Bridge: Opens on signal, except from 7:30 a.m. to 7:00 p.m., Mon. through Fri. (except federal holidays), when the draw need only open on the hour and half-hour; however, from 7:35 a.m. to 8:59 a.m., 12:05 p.m. to 12:59 p.m. and 4:35 p.m. to 5:59 p.m., the draw need not open.

12'
NW 5th St. Bascule Bridge: Opens on signal, except from 7:30 a.m. to 7:00 p.m., Mon. through Fri. (except federal holidays), when the draw need only open on the hour and half-hour; however, from 7:35 a.m. to 8:59 a.m., 12:05 p.m. to 12:59 p.m. and 4:35 p.m. to 5:59 p.m., the draw need not open.

22'
NW 12th Ave. Bascule Bridge: Opens on signal, except from 7:30 a.m. to 7:00 p.m., Mon. through Fri. (except federal holidays), when the draw need only open on the hour and half-hour; however, from 7:35 a.m. to 8:59 a.m., 12:05 p.m. to 12:59 p.m. and 4:35 p.m. to 5:59 p.m., the draw need not open.

75'
Dolphin Expressway Bridge: Fixed

17'
NW 17th Ave. Bascule Bridge: Opens on signal.

25'
NW 22nd Ave. Bascule Bridge: Opens on signal.

Florida Keys

1091.6
65'
William M. Powell (Rickenbacker) Causeway Bridge: Fixed

1126.9
65'
Card Sound Bridge: Fixed

1134.1
65'
Jewfish Creek (U.S. 1) Bridge: Fixed

1152.0
15'
Tavernier Creek Bridge: Fixed

1156.0
27'
Snake Creek Bascule Bridge: Opens on signal, except from 7:00 a.m. to 6:00 p.m., when the draw need open only on the hour.

1157.0
10'
Whale Harbor Channel Bridge: Fixed

1162.0
7'
Upper Matecumbe Key Bridge: Fixed

1162.1
10'
Teatable Key Channel Bridge: Fixed

1163.0
27'
Indian Key Channel Bridge: Fixed

1164.5
10'
Lignumvitae Channel Bridge: Fixed

1168.5
10'
Channel Two Bridge: Fixed

1170.0
65'
Channel Five Bridge: Fixed

1176.0 / **23'** — **Long Key Viaduct Bridge:** Fixed

1179.0 / **8'** — **Toms Harbor Cut Bridge:** Fixed

1180.0 / **7'** — **Toms Harbor Channel Bridge:** Fixed

1188.0 / **13'** — **Vaca Cut Bridge:** Fixed

1194.0 / **19'** — **Knight Key Channel Twin Bridges:** Fixed

1197.0 / **65'** — **Seven Mile (Moser Channel) Twin Bridges:** Fixed

1205.0 / **20'** — **Bahia Honda Twin Bridges:** Fixed

1209.0 / **11'** — **Spanish Harbor Channel Bridge:** Fixed

1215.0 / **15'** — **Little Torch Key (Pine Channel) Bridge:** Fixed

1215.0 / **40'** — **Niles Channel Bridge:** Fixed

Florida's Gulf ICW (GIWW)

34.3 / **22'** — **Boca Grande Swing Bridge:** Opens on signal, except from 7:00 a.m. to 6:00 p.m., Mon. through Fri., when the draw opens on the hour and half-hour. On Sat., Sun. and federal holidays the draw opens every 15 min. (Note: Vessels must request an opening.)

43.5 / **26'** — **Manasota Key (Tom Adams) Bascule Bridge:** Opens on signal. (Note: Actual clearance may be closer to 23 feet.)

49.9 / **26'** — **Manasota Bascule Bridge:** Opens on signal.

54.9 / **25'** — **Tamiami Trail (Circus) Twin Bridges:** Opens on signal.

56.6 / **30'** — **Venice Ave. Bascule Bridge:** Opens on signal, except from 7:00 a.m. to 4:30 p.m., Mon. through Fri. (except holidays), when the draw opens only at 10 min. after the hour, 30 min. after the hour and 50 min. after the hour. Between 4:35 p.m. and 5:35 p.m., the draw need not open.

56.9 / **30'** — **KMI (Hatchett Creek) Bascule Bridge:** Opens on signal, except from 7:00 a.m. to 4:20 p.m., Mon. through Fri. (except federal holidays), when the draw opens only on the hour, 20 min. after the hour and 40 min. after the hour. Between 4:25 p.m. and 5:25 p.m., the draw need not open. On Sat., Sun. and federal holidays from 7:30 a.m. to 6:00 p.m. the draw will open only on the hour and every 15 min. thereafter.

59.3 / **14'** — **Albee Road (Casey Key) Bascule Bridge:** Opens on signal.

63.0 / **9'** — **Blackburn Point Swing Bridge:** Opens on signal.

68.6 / **18'** — **Stickney Point (SR 72) Bascule Bridge:** Opens on signal, except from 6:00 a.m. to 7:00 p.m. daily, when the draw need open only on the hour and half hour thereafter. (Note: This is a change from the 2018 published schedule.)

71.6 / **25'** — **Siesta Drive Bascule Bridge:** Opens on signal, except from 6:00 a.m. to 7:00 p.m. daily, when the draw need open only on the hour and half hour thereafter. (Note: This is a change from the 2018 published schedule.)

73.6 / **65'** — **Ringling Causeway (SR 789) Bridge:** Fixed

23' — **New Pass Bascule Bridge (to Gulf):** The draw need only open on the hour, 20 min. past the hour, and 40 min. past the hour from 7:00 a.m. to 6:00 p.m. From 6:00 p.m. to 7:00 a.m., the bridge will open on signal only if at least 3-hour notice is given.

17' — **Longboat Pass (SR 789) Bascule Bridge (to Gulf):** Opens on signal.

87.4 / **22'** — **Cortez (SR 684) Bascule Bridge:** Opens on signal, except from 6:00 a.m. to 7:00 p.m. daily, when the draw need open only on the hour and half hour thereafter. (Note: This is a change from the 2018 published schedule.)

89.2 / **24'** — **Anna Maria Island (Manatee Ave. West) Bascule Bridge:** Opens on signal, except from 6:00 a.m. to 7:00 p.m. daily, when the draw need open only on the hour and half hour thereafter. (Note: This is a change from the 2018 published schedule.)

99.0 / **180'** — **Sunshine Skyway (Central Span) Bridge:** Fixed

110.5 / **65'** — **Sunshine Skyway (Meisner) Bridge:** Fixed

114.0 / **18'** — **Pinellas Bayway 'A' Span Bridge:** Fixed

114.0 / **65'** — **Pinellas Bayway 'C' Span Bridge:** Fixed

117.7 / **23'** — **Corey Causeway (SR 693) Bascule Bridge:** Opens on signal, except from 8:00 a.m. to 7:00 p.m., Mon. through Fri., and from 10:00 a.m. to 7:00 p.m., Sat., Sun. and federal holidays, when the draw need only open on the hour, 20 min. after the hour and 40 min. after the hour.

118.9
21'
Treasure Island Causeway Bascule Bridge: Opens on signal, except from 7:00 a.m. to 7:00 p.m., Mon. through Fri., when the draw will open on the hour, 20 min. after the hour and 40 min. after the hour and on the quarter hour and three-quarter hour on Sat., Sun. and federal holidays.

27'
Johns Pass Twin Bascule Bridges (to Gulf): Opens on signal. (Note: Located 1.25 miles SW of GIWW.)

122.8
25'
Welch Causeway (SR 699) Bascule Bridge: Opens on signal, except from 9:30 a.m. to 6:00 p.m. on Sat., Sun. and federal holidays, when the draw opens only on the hour, 20 min. after the hour and 40 min. after the hour.

126.0
20'
Park Blvd. (SR 248) Bascule Bridge: Opens on signal.

129.3
25'
Indian Rocks Beach (CR 694) Bascule Bridge: Opens on signal.

131.8
75'
Belleair Causeway Bridge: Fixed

74'
Clearwater Pass (SR 183) Bridge (to Gulf): Fixed

136.0
74'
Clearwater Memorial Causeway (SR 60) Bridge: Fixed

141.9
18'
Dunedin–Honeymoon Island Bascule Bridge: Opens on signal. (Note that charted clearance is 24 feet but actual clearance is 18.)

GIWW, East of Harvey Lock (EHL)

361.4
65'
Apalachicola-St. George Island Bridge: Fixed

351.4
65'
John Gorrie Memorial (U.S. 98/319) Bridge: Fixed

347.0
11'
Apalachicola Railroad Swing Bridge: Maintained in the fully open-to-navigation position and untended.

329.3
65'
White City (SR 71) Bridge: Fixed

75'
Port St. Joe (U.S. 98) Bridge (to Gulf): Fixed

315.4
65'
Overstreet (SR 386) Bridge: Fixed

295.4
50'
Dupont (U.S. 98) Bridge: Fixed

284.6
65'
Hathaway (U.S. 98) Bridge: Fixed

271.8
65'
West Bay Creek (SR 79) Bridge: Fixed

250.4
65'
Clyde B. Wells (Choctawhatchee Bay) Bridge: Fixed

234.2
64'
Mid-Bay Bridge: Fixed

49'
Destin Twin Bridges (to Gulf): Fixed

223.1
50'
Brooks Memorial Bridge: Fixed

206.7
50'
Navarre Beach Causeway (CR 399) Bridge: Fixed

189.1
65'
Pensacola Beach (SR 399) Twin Bridges: Fixed

171.8
73'
Gulf Beach (SR 292) Bridge: Fixed

54'
Perdido Pass Channel Bridge (to Gulf): Fixed

158.7
73'
Foley Beach Expressway Bridge: Fixed

154.9
73'
Gulf Shores Parkway (Portage Creek) Twin Bridges: Fixed

127.8
83'
Dauphin Island (SR 163) Causeway Bridge: Fixed

Ditch Bag Checklist

Rescue Items

- [ ] Functioning, registered EPIRB
- [ ] Handheld VHF radio (waterproof or in sealed pouch, with extra batteries)
- [ ] Sea anchor, drogue and line
- [ ] Manual inflation pump
- [ ] Selection of flares (parachute and handheld) and smoke signals
- [ ] Strobe light (may be present in inflatable PFD)
- [ ] Flashlight & batteries (headlamp is ideal)
- [ ] Whistle (may be present in inflatable PFD)
- [ ] Signal mirror
- [ ] Handheld GPS or compass (for position)
- [ ] Small pair of binoculars (to confirm a boat or plane spotting before using flares)

Survival Items

- [ ] Sponges and bailer (with handle)
- [ ] Patch kit for inflatable dinghy or life raft (or emergency clamps)
- [ ] Water (individually sealed or in collapsible containers)–at least 2 gallons per person
- [ ] Emergency food rations and can opener (if needed)
- [ ] Power Bars
- [ ] Prescription medications
- [ ] Seasickness medications/remedies
- [ ] First aid kit
- [ ] Multipurpose tool or sailor's knife
- [ ] Waterproof matches

Other Items

- [ ] Solar blanket
- [ ] Heavy-duty coated gloves
- [ ] Duct tape
- [ ] Sewing kit
- [ ] Simple fishing gear (line, jigs, hooks, etc.)
- [ ] Polypropylene line
- [ ] Waterproof sunscreen and zinc oxide
- [ ] Bug repellent
- [ ] Ziploc bags (gallon size)
- [ ] Paper and pen in Ziploc bag
- [ ] Spare prescription glasses and sunglasses (polarized to reduce glare)
- [ ] Laminated copies of passports or license
- [ ] Cash ($50 in small bills)
- [ ] Copy of the yacht's papers (including insurance)

Crossing to the Bahamas

For vessels crossing between the Florida east coast and Bahamas, the Gulf Stream is the principal navigational consideration. It is a wide, deep and warm river of fast moving water flowing north, where sea conditions are deeply influenced by the wind. Crossing this river requires careful planning while considering the characteristics of your vessel and crew and the expected wind and weather.

The Gulf Stream current generally begins a few miles out from the Florida coast, and extends for approximately 43 nm eastward. The current will gradually increase as you travel east, reaching a maximum of roughly 3.6 knots about 8 to 11 miles from the western wall. The current gradually subsides to little or no current at the eastern edge of the Stream. The average northerly speed over the 43 mile width is 2.5 knots while the average direction of flow is 1 degree True when north of Lake Worth Inlet, and about 2 degrees True south of the inlet.

The sea state in the Stream is largely a function of the prevailing ocean swell in the area combined with local wind generated waves. The National Weather Service marine forecast provides the Significant Wave Height expected for the Stream, that is, the average height of the highest one-third of the combined swells and wind waves. Be sure to check this when planning your departure. For a useful rule of thumb, south to southeast winds at 10 knots will develop 2-foot seas; 15 knots, 4- to 5-foot seas; 20 knots, 7-foot seas; and 25 knots, 9-foot seas.

For most cruising boats it is generally not advisable to cross the stream in winds higher than 15 knots. And it is never a great idea to cross in winds with any significant northerly component as winds against the current cause a very steep, choppy sea. Winds of 10 knots or less offer a relatively comfortable ride for the typical semi-displacement recreational boat 35 to 45 feet in length, provided there are no significant swells in addition to the wind waves.

In winter, the location of the Stream will sometimes be marked by mist rising from its warm waters, significantly warmer than the colder coastal water. In winter too, and whenever a northerly wind is blowing, the horizon looking toward the Stream will often look jagged or saw-toothed. Sailors observing from inshore say there are "elephants" out there–giant square topped waves are kicked up by the Gulf Stream's determination to win its way north against the wind. In bright sunlight the Gulf Stream is a deep cobalt blue in which if the sun is right, you may see light dancing in its depths. You will usually see blond colored patches of Sargasso weed drifting in its waters. Fish will often congregate near and under these patches. You can be sure you have entered the Stream when the water temperature noticeably increases over a short distance from the near shore ocean temperature. If you are navigating using GPS, you will likely see the effects of the current quickly as your course and speed over ground change significantly.

Magnetic Heading & Time-To-Cross

Direction (M) / Distance (nm)	From	To	Top Number = Heading to Steer (Magnetic) — Bottom Number = Time Between Waypoints (Hours) — Based on Boat Speed (Knots)								
			5 kn	6 kn	7 kn	8 kn	9 kn	10 kn	15 kn	20 kn	25 kn
312° 82.3 nm	West End	Fort Pierce	297° 14.5	299° 12.3	301° 10.6	302° 9.4	303° 8.4	304° 7.6	307° 5.2	308° 4.0	309° 3.2
302° 67.4 nm	West End	Saint Lucie	283° 12.4	286° 10.4	289° 9.0	290° 7.9	292° 7.1	293° 6.4	296° 4.3	297° 3.3	298° 2.6
282° 55.7 nm	West End	Lake Worth	259° 11.9	263° 9.7	266° 8.2	268° 7.1	269° 6.3	271° 5.6	274° 3.7	276° 2.8	277° 2.2
101° 55.7 nm	Lake Worth	West End	124° 12.3	120° 9.9	117° 8.4	115° 7.2	114° 6.4	113° 5.7	109° 3.8	107° 2.8	106° 2.2
65° 69.3 nm	Port Everglades	West End	83° 11.9	80° 10.1	78° 8.8	77° 7.8	75° 7.0	74° 6.3	71° 4.3	70° 3.3	69° 2.7
111° 69.0 nm	Lake Worth	Freeport	129° 15.6	126° 12.6	124° 10.6	122° 9.2	121° 8.1	120° 7.2	117° 4.7	115° 3.5	114° 2.8
78° 74.5 nm	Port Everglades	Freeport	95° 13.9	92° 11.7	90° 10.0	88° 8.8	87° 7.9	86° 7.1	84° 4.8	82° 3.6	81° 2.9
259° 74.5 nm	Freeport	Port Everglades	242° 17.6	245° 14.1	247° 11.8	248° 10.2	249° 8.9	250° 8.0	253° 5.2	254° 3.8	255° 3.1
291° 69.0 nm	Freeport	Lake Worth	273° 13.6	276° 11.3	278° 9.6	280° 8.4	281° 7.5	282° 6.8	285° 4.5	287° 3.4	288° 2.7
336° 74.6 nm	Bimini	Lake Worth	319° 10.7	322° 9.3	324° 8.2	325° 7.4	327° 6.7	328° 6.2	330° 4.4	332° 3.4	333° 2.7
306° 48.2 nm	Bimini	Port Everglades	279° 8.6	284° 7.2	287° 6.2	289° 5.5	291° 4.9	293° 4.4	297° 3.0	299° 2.3	301° 1.9
281° 43.8 nm	Bimini	Miami	251° 9.9	257° 7.9	260° 6.6	263° 5.7	265° 5.0	267° 4.5	272° 2.9	274° 2.2	275° 1.8
126° 48.2 nm	Port Everglades	Bimini	152° 14.3	147° 10.8	144° 8.7	142° 7.3	140° 6.3	138° 5.6	134° 3.5	132° 2.6	131° 2.0
101° 43.8 nm	Miami	Bimini	130° 10.2	125° 8.1	121° 6.7	119° 5.8	117° 5.1	115° 4.5	110° 3.0	108° 2.2	106° 1.8
07° 49.8 nm	Lake Worth	Memory Rock	113° 10.1	108° 8.3	105° 7.0	103° 6.1	101° 5.4	100° 4.9	96° 3.3	93° 2.5	92° 2.0
306° 70.2 nm	Memory Rock	Fort Pierce	288° 12.6	291° 10.6	293° 9.2	295° 8.1	296° 7.3	297° 6.6	300° 4.5	302° 3.4	303° 2.7
105° 61.7 nm	Fort Pierce	Matanilla Shoal	126° 13.8	122° 11.2	120° 9.4	118° 8.1	116° 7.2	115° 6.4	112° 4.2	110° 3.1	109° 2.5
286° 61.7 nm	Matantilla Shoal	Fort Pierce	265° 12.6	269° 10.4	271° 8.8	273° 7.7	274° 6.8	276° 6.1	279° 4.1	281° 3.1	282° 2.5

Corrected courses and estimated elapsed times at varying speeds under normal sea conditions

Departure/Destination Waypoints				
Location	Latitude N		Longitude W	
	degrees	minutes	degrees	minutes
Fort Pierce	27°	28.489	80°	16.216
Matanilla Shoal	27°	20.000	79°	07.500
St. Lucie	27°	10.020	80°	08.530
Memory Rock	26°	55.000	79°	07.000
Lake Worth	26°	46.345	80°	01.879
West End	26°	42.250	78°	59.786
Freeport	26°	30.000	78°	47.060
Port Everglades	26°	05.627	80°	05.416
Miami	25°	45.354	80°	06.888
Bimini	25°	42.630	79°	18.450

Planning to Cross

Crossing the Gulf Stream is like traversing a wide, moving walkway–your boat is being steadily pushed northward. The longer you spend in the Stream, the further north you will be unless you compensate for that movement. Your best strategy is to take advantage of that push, starting as far south, or upstream, of your destination as possible. To the extent that is not possible, careful planning and navigation can minimize the time it takes to cross.

NOAA weather broadcasts give daily information about the Gulf Stream, including its width, speed, distance offshore at different locations along the Florida coast, and its temperature. Many online sources also give daily, detailed maps of the Stream. But for planning, a reasonable rule of thumb is to assume the entire distance you have to run from a Florida departure to a point lying along the W 79° 15.000' line of longitude

will be subject to an average 2.5-knot, north-flowing current. For fast boats, this may have relatively little effect on your course and time to cross. But for slower boats, particularly under sail, the effect is profound and must be taken into account. There are essentially three ways to navigate this challenge:

■ In the days before GPS and chartplotters, boats would compute a heading based on the average current and then steer that constant heading. The disadvantage to this approach is that it is based solely on averages, while the actual current and wind will vary from day to day and during the crossing. But it usually works because it generally gets the boat close enough to your destination that it can be recognized.

■ The boat can be steered to stay pointed at the destination waypoint. This works, but is not the most efficient method and will take more time.

- For boats equipped with GPS, a chartplotter and preferably autopilot, steer to constantly keep the boat on the route from starting point to destination. The actual heading will vary constantly; adjusting to the actual current and wind drift as you move along the route. This is the most efficient way to navigate the crossing.

There are as many opinions on when to depart Florida and at what time to arrive at your Bahamian waypoint as there are vessels crossing the Gulf Stream. Night crossings are common, but they do present the additional challenge of traveling amidst the ever-growing number of freighters and cruise ships in very busy shipping lanes to and from Florida. Dawn departures provide easier travel in the shipping lanes and arrival in Bahamian waters with the sun behind you. And if you decide to continue across the banks, night passage will be in many ways easier there than in the Gulf Stream. You should consider your speed of travel, destination, and what conditions are expected when you arrive. A vessel departing for and planning to visit North Bimini will have a much different crossing schedule than one headed non-stop to Nassau. Regardless, pay attention to the weather and don't develop forward-only vision.

Be vigilant about frequent checks for other vessels to starboard, port and aft! Don't become another victim rundown by an inattentive skipper traveling on autopilot. And don't forget to file that float plan. (A number of free iOS and Android apps allow you to create a float plan and email it to participants or emergency contacts.)

The Constant Heading Table

If you choose the constant heading approach to your passage, the Magnetic Heading and Time-to-Cross table included with the satellite graphic provides for a given boat speed, the single heading to steer and the time to cross on that heading. This data will always be an approximation but is a good estimate for your constant heading, and also a good tool for planning passage time if you will be steering to stay on a route line. The tables are based on the WGS84 datum and 2019 magnetic variation from the National Centers for Environmental Data at NOAA. The results are accurate to within one degree. The current was assumed to be the average current in the Gulf Stream, 2.5 knots. They do not consider wind drift or leeway; compensating for these for your vessel will improve accuracy.

The from/to locations correspond to the waypoints identified in the Departure/Destination Waypoints table.

They can be used regardless of your destination, but you will have to adjust your total trip plan for additional distances to be run.

For example, assume you want to leave from Lake Worth inlet and go to West End. The fourth entry in the table shows the distance traveled between these waypoints is 55.7 nm at a bearing of 101 degrees magnetic. Also assume you plan to travel at 8 knots boat speed. The table shows that at 8 knots, you must steer on average 115 degrees magnetic to arrive near the destination waypoint. The time enroute will be approximately 7.2 hours between the two waypoints. So if you plan to leave your anchorage or slip early, arriving at the departure waypoint at 7:00 a.m., you should arrive at the destination waypoint at approximately 2:12 p.m. Of course you need to allow for the time required to get from there to your final overnight stop, wherever that may be. Remember that if you use GPS and remain on the route line between points, your heading will vary with the current and wind conditions, but you will average 115 degrees magnetic over that time. On the other hand, if you steer a constant 115 degrees magnetic, you will deviate from the route line, but should end up at or near the destination.

Listen to the Forecast

The Gulf Stream is a relatively constant, predictable force. The weather is not. Listen to the forecasts. Believe the bad ones, and don't trust the good ones. Go to the beach if you can and look out over the ocean. What is happening out there? As stated before, the most difficult and dangerous time for any vessel to cross the Gulf Stream is when the wind is from the north, including the northeast and the northwest. Whether you are running a 180-foot motor yacht or skippering an 18-foot sailboat, northerly conditions are definitely not the ones in which to cross. Remember that the Gulf Stream is flowing north at 2.5 knots. When the wind blows from the north, it is like rubbing a cat the wrong way; all the fur kicks up and the results are the "elephants" mentioned earlier. These are high, ugly waves as closely spaced as elephants holding each other's tails in a circus parade. In those conditions, the Gulf Stream is not where you want to be.

Weather is available on the VHF NOAA weather channels, from numerous online sources, and with many weather apps. Pay close attention, plan carefully, pick your weather window and enjoy a pleasant crossing to the wonderful Bahamas.

Inside vs. Outside Mileage

Heading north or south, many skippers mistakenly assume that they will shorten their trips by going out to sea and running down the coast. The distances shown here–both inside (red boxes) and outside (blue boxes)–demonstrate that this is not necessarily true.

Keep in mind that while outside distances from sea buoy to sea buoy are virtually the same as the ICW distances, the mileage in and out to the buoys adds to the total distance. These differences, which may seem insignificant at first, do add up.

Skippers should consider the safety factor, as well. Some of the outside stretches are easy while others can be more hazardous. Watch the weather carefully; it can be uncomfortable outside despite the inside passage being calm and unaffected.

Do, however, be prepared to run outside for a day if the ICW is obstructed locally by a malfunctioning bridge or severe shoaling. (The fixed Julia Tuttle Bridge at Mile 1087.2 sets the restricted vertical clearance at 56 feet. See the bridge tables for more information.)

Most importantly, prepare your boat early, plot the course in advance and only go if the forecast is good.

Outside Distance to Big Ship Inlets

St. Johns River to Port Canaveral Inlet: 150 nm

Port Canaveral Inlet to Fort Pierce Inlet: 65 nm

Fort Pierce Inlet to Lake Worth Inlet: 45 nm

Lake Worth Inlet to Port Everglades Inlet: 40 nm

Port Everglades Inlet to Government Cut: 20 nm

Fernandina Beach — ICW MILE 717
Jacksonville — ICW MILE 740 — St. Johns River
ICW MILE 776 — St. Augustine
Palm Coast
ICW MILE 830 — Daytona Beach
Ponce de Leon Inlet
ICW MILE 846 — New Smyrna Beach
150 nm
ATLANTIC OCEAN
ICW MILE 878 — Titusville
Cape Canaveral
Cocoa — ICW MILE 897
Cocoa Beach
65 nm
ICW MILE 917 — Melbourne
ICW MILE 935 — Sebastian
Vero Beach — ICW MILE 952
Fort Pierce — ICW MILE 965
ICW MILE 986 — Stuart
45 nm
St. Lucie Inlet
Lake Okeechobee
ICW MILE 1005 — Jupiter
Okeechobee Waterway
Palm Beach
Lake Worth — ICW MILE 1027
40 nm
Pompano
Ft. Lauderdale — ICW MILE 1063
Port Everglades Inlet
Hallandale
20 nm
ICW MILE 1085 — Miami
Government Cut
ICW MILE 1094 — Key Biscayne
Biscayne Bay
ICW MILE 1142
Cape Sable — Flamingo — Key Largo
Channel Five
ICW MILE 1240
Key West

FLORIDA
Tampa
Bradenton
Venice
Punta Gorda
Cape Coral
Ft. Myers
Sanibel I.
San Carlos Bay
Marco I.
Everglades City

For many boaters, the thought of leaving the safe confines of the Intracoastal Waterway (ICW) for the open seas is terrifying, and, for some of us, that is as it should be. While the open waters of the Atlantic can be serene, they can also turn nasty; therefore, it is no place for the unskilled or poorly prepared. Plan for every contingency while underway. If things start to go wrong, head for the next inlet and deal with the problems from dockside. There are no awards for being foolish when you are offshore.

Offshore Runs: Despite what you may have heard, it is not always shorter to run offshore. When you add the distances involved in leaving and returning to the ICW, you are often better off time-wise staying inside. Having said that, for those mariners who have the skills, a capable well-found vessel and the mettle to venture out into the deep blue off the coast, the beauty and challenge to be found offshore is reward enough.

Cautions and Warnings: If conditions are bad when you reach the sea buoy for an inlet, you may find yourself in an untenable position, being driven ashore by wind or waves and unable to find the inlet buoys. It might be far better to remain well offshore in rough conditions, possibly continuing to a better inlet, unless the inlet you are considering is a Class A inlet for big ships, or one of the more easily run inlets, such as Government Cut. Should you find yourself at an inlet

and needing direction, a call on VHF Channel 16 for local knowledge is likely to bring you a response. Sea Tow and TowBoatU.S. are two other knowledgeable sources. The Coast Guard may also be able to assist you.

Online Resources: Prior to your voyage, there are a number of online sources that can familiarize you with the inlets; the Waterway Guide website (waterwayguide.com) has both chart and satellite views of the inlets via the Waterway Explorer, plus cruising details from local boaters, both of which are quite useful. Obviously, this guide can give you helpful advice, particularly on what you will find inside the inlet. You will also need Coast Pilots, which can be downloaded free at nauticalcharts. noaa.gov. With inlets, it is also vital that you keep up with the *Local Notice to Mariners*, which are available online at navcen.uscg.gov/ and then click on the LNMs tab. The Tide Tables for the areas you are traveling through are also necessary and are provided in this guide and online at tidesandcurrents.noaa.gov.

Some inlets have recent U.S. Army Corps of Engineers surveys in Adobe PDF format, which can be found at saw.usace.army.mil/Missions/Navigation/ HydrographicSurveys/InletsCrossings.aspx. These particular charts, when available, provide waypoint information, although it takes some patience to familiarize yourself with the format. Of particular use are the centerline waypoints and controlling depths provided within the inlet. The exact locations of all aids to navigation in the inlet are also noted. However, be advised that the markers at some inlets are moved on a regular basis and the buoys should be honored.

Check carefully the date of the survey to determine its applicability for your passage. Inlets change rapidly and even recent surveys may be inaccurate.

Skills and Equipment: Before you begin an offshore passage, take an honest accounting of your vessel, your crew and yourself. Is each of you up to the task? Is the vessel properly outfitted? Do you have the necessary safety equipment, charts, long distance communications gear such as single sideband radio (SSB), an Emergency Position Indicating Radio Beacon (EPIRB) and life raft? Do you and your crew have adequate experience in boating and navigation to attempt an offshore coastal passage?

Always file a float plan with a reliable person. If all your good planning goes awry, this could well be your "ace in the hole" and someone will be able to locate you if you need assistance. A sample float plan is provided in this guide.

About the Weather: Mother Nature is capricious and the National Weather Service is not omniscient. Sometimes a day that begins with clear skies promised by the weatherman ends in tumult, with the captain swearing he will buy a motor home—in Idaho no less—if only he can get safely into port. Check the weather using as many sources as possible. If you have access to weather routing services, they are a good option, particularly for longer offshore passages. You are seeking a weather window with enough space on each side to get you safely out and back in, with room for unexpected contingencies. Plan your trip so that you enter in daylight, with the tide, particularly if your boat is slow or underpowered. Remember that wind against tide can create short, steep waves in an inlet that can quickly make even a ship channel impassable for slower boats.

A safe offshore passage is an accomplishment. You will always remember your first one; the serenity of a calm dark night passage, the thrill of the sun rising after an endless night and the quiet confidence you feel deep inside as you bring your boat to anchor or dockside after many miles outside. Knowing that you have a convenient inlet to duck into should conditions offshore deteriorate certainly adds confidence, as well as an additional margin of safety, to your plans.

Florida's East Coast Inlets

Big ship inlets are denoted with the following symbol:

Gulf Coast Inlets

The big ship channels on the Gulf Coast are Boca Grande Channel, Tampa Bay Entrance, St. Andrew Bay Entrance, St. Joseph Bay Entrance, Pensacola Bay Entrance and Mobile Bay Entrance. There are several smaller channels (labeled as "Passes") that are available for smaller vessels. See Waterway Explorer for details (waterwayguide.com).

Note: All inlets require some degree of caution. Weather, depths and tides are important factors for safe navigation. Be aware that in any inlet shifting bottom conditions can result in aids to navigation being incorrectly located or nonexistent. Charts provided here are not intended to be used for navigation.

St. Johns River Entrance

Sea Buoy: RW sea buoy "SJ" is located at N 30° 23.600'/W 81° 19.140'.

Overview: Big ship inlet frequented by freighters, U.S. Naval vessels and commercial fishermen, especially shrimpers, who you will see in the early morning hours. Wide, deep and trouble-free entrance. Naval Station Mayport is to the south of the entrance.

Navigation: Approach from the east. Ocean approach landmark is St. Johns Light, which stands 83 feet above the shore and 1 nm south of the St. Johns north jetty. Offshore waypoint is located nearly 3 nm from the jetties. Use waypoint N 30° 23.860'/ W 81° 22.000', which is located about halfway between flashing red buoy "4" and flashing red buoy "6" and over 0.25 nm from the jetties. Follow buoys in. Landmarks include a tower at Jacksonville Beach and a water tank (painted in a red and white checkerboard design) at the naval station.

Cautions and hazards: None, other than the large vessel traffic, which can be heavy at times. Slower boats are well advised to pick their tide coming in here, or settle down for a very long transit; the tide can run up to 3 to 4 knots.

ST JOHNS RIVER ENTRANCE

Mercator Projection

Depth: See interactive charts on Waterway Explorer at waterwayguide.com.

ICW connection: Mile 738 of the ICW is 5 nm from the jetties. If going south, be sure of your markers; there is an underwater jetty at the south entrance to the ICW channel. The current here can also quickly push you out of the channel. Caution is advised.

Nearest recommended inlet: It is approximately 30 nm to the St. Marys (Cumerberland Sound) Entrance.

Use Chart 11490

St. Augustine Inlet

Sea Buoy: RW sea buoy "STA" is east and north of N 29° 55.000'/W 81°15.230'.

Overview: Located north of Anastasia State Park.

Navigation: From the sea buoy, proceed slightly south of east towards the inlet, paying close attention to the markers. You will see a tall cross ahead on shore providing an approximate range to the inlet, which will help you to orient yourself. Once past Cape Francis on the south, bear to the middle and south side of the channel as you proceed. There is a large shoal at marker "2A." If headed north once inside the inlet, note that you keep red nun buoy "60" to port, as that is part of the ICW.

Cautions and hazards: There is some infrequent dredging activity in this inlet, but it should be regarded as a fair weather-only inlet with no protection until well inside the inlet. There are extensive shoals with breaking water to the north and south of the inlet extending well offshore. Proceed with caution at slow speed as the temporary markers–which are frequently moved by the USCG to mark deeper water–can be very difficult to see. The currents in this inlet are very powerful and dictate appropriate boat handling skills as well as advanced local knowledge.

Depth: See interactive charts on Waterway Explorer at waterwayguide.com.

ICW connection: Connects directly to the ICW at Mile 776. If going north, stay closest to the eastern side of the channel to avoid the marked shoal to port.

Nearby facilities: There are several marinas to both the north and south of the inlet, including in Salt Creek. St. Augustine provides a mooring field to the north and south of the Bridge of Lions and in Salt Creek to the south.

NORTHERN RIGHT WHALE CRITICAL HABITAT
(precautionary area: 50 CFR 226.203c, 224.103c; see note A)
It is illegal to approach any right whale anywhere closer than 500 yards.

Use Chart 11485

Ponce de Leon (New Smyrna) Inlet

Sea Buoy: Red buoy "2" is located at
N 29° 04.700'/W 80° 53.700'.

Overview: Used extensively by locals and sport fishermen and convenient point to enter or leave the ICW between Daytona and Cape Canaveral. Sometimes referred to as New Smyrna Inlet. This is a fair weather inlet only.

Navigation: Coming from the offshore waypoint, the jetty on the north side of the inlet provides protection from north and northeast swells. Hold close to the jetty until inside the inlet, as there is a shoal building north and east from green buoy "7." The USCG station is located on the south channel of the inlet and will respond to calls for inlet conditions, and the local TowBoat US is up to date on local conditions. Both can be hailed on VHF Channel 16.

Webcam: For a live view of the port, visit volusia.com/explore-a-city/ponce-inlet.

Cautions and hazards: Seemingly constant reclamation, dredging and seawall construction, yet shoaling has been reported in the approaches both north and south of the inlet coming from the ICW. Inlet markers are continually moved by the USCG to reflect deep water. Expect substantial traffic at all hours. This is a fair weather inlet only, particularly for weather out of the south and east, which creates large swells into the inlet. Local knowledge is strongly advised before using this inlet.

Depth: See interactive charts on Waterway Explorer at waterwayguide.com.

ICW connection: The inlet is 2.5 miles from ICW Mile 840 with one channel leading north, another south. The north channel is not as well marked as the south channel until well inside and shows charted depths of just 7 feet MLW.

Nearby facilities: There is one marina immediately to the north of the inlet in the north channel and several more in New Smyrna Beach. There are anchoring possibilities as well.

Use Chart 11485

Port Canaveral Inlet

Sea Buoy: Flashing red buoy "4" (2.5 sec) is located at N 28° 22.560'/W 80° 31.740'.

Overview: Well-marked, deep ship inlet protected from the north by the long and shallow Southeast Shoal off Cape Canaveral. The lock inside the inlet eliminates current, making this one of the easier to use inlets on the Florida coast.

Navigation: Southbound cruisers can make for N 28° 23.490'/W 80° 33.000' after rounding red buoy "4," while northbound craft could go in much closer, at N 28° 24.570'/W 80° 34.480'. The channel is well marked; simply run down the channel, turning due west at Middle Reach. Lock operating hours are 6:00 a.m. to 9:30 p.m., 365 days a year. (The observation area is open 6:00 a.m. to 9:00 p.m.) Lockage takes 20 to 30 minutes.

Webcam: For a live view of the port, visit portcanaveralwebcam.com.

Cautions and hazards: Coming from the north, the Southeast Shoal off Cape Canaveral keeps boaters several miles offshore. Stay east of W 80° 27.00' before turning in to the sea buoy after rounding red buoy "4" at N 28° 23.470'/W 80° 29.100' marking the southern edge of the shoal. Note that this cuts off the offshore waypoint. From the south, cruisers can approach from within 0.5 nm of the shore in depths greater than 20 feet MLW.

Depth: See interactive charts on Waterway Explorer at waterwayguide.com.

ICW connection: Inlet is 7.5 nm from ICW Mile 894 (across the Banana River and through the Barge Canal).

Nearby facilities: There are several marinas inside the inlet, as well as a U.S. Customs office for clearing in.

Cape Canaveral Lock

Use Chart 11478

Sebastian Inlet

Sea Buoy: No sea buoy. Steer to waypoint N 27° 51.675'/ W 80° 26.500', which will place you directly east of the inlet.

Overview: This is the only charted inlet between Cape Canaveral and Fort Pierce and is a local knowledge, fair-weather inlet used largely by smaller recreational fishing boats. Crossed by a fixed bridge (A1A) with 37-foot vertical clearance.

Navigation: If you must enter, do so only from the east using the waypoint; there is an unmarked shoal blocking any approach from the south. From the waypoint, proceed due east keeping to the center of the jetties. There are no buoys and only a light at the end of the north jetty. A 3,000-foot-long by 100-foot-wide and 9-foot-deep channel provides access to the ocean, but as with all ocean inlets, a cautious approach is warranted, as shoaling is ever present and continuous.

Webcam: For a live view of the inlet, visit sebastianinletcam.com.

Cautions and hazards: Swift cross currents and the resulting shifting channel make navigation difficult without up-to-date local information. The currents in this area can also affect travel on the ICW.

Depth: See interactive charts on Waterway Explorer at waterwayguide.com.

ICW connection: The inlet is 2 nm from ICW Mile 935 (across the Indian River) over an area of 5- to 6-foot depths following privately maintained aids.

Nearby facilities: There are a few small local marinas along the west shore of the Indian River on the ICW route.

Use Chart 11472

Fort Pierce Inlet

Sea Buoy: Red sea buoy "2" is located at N 27° 28.640'/ W 80° 15.410' (1.5 nm seaward of the channel).

Overview: This is a big ship inlet and one of the best and easiest inlets on Florida's east coast. Currents are strong; slower boats will want to have the tide favoring their passage. There is an inner channel and a turning basin.

Navigation: Above waypoint takes you 1.5 nm from the channel in deep water. Smaller craft can approach in over 20 feet MLW to green buoy "5" and red buoy "6" at

N 27° 28.160'/W 80° 16.900', which is just 0.2 nm from the jetties.

Webcam: For live view of the inlet, go to visitstlucie. com/fort-pierce-inlet-webcam.

Cautions and hazards: Watch for the many small fishing boats throughout the channel. Eastbound swells can create rough conditions within the inlet proper, preventing smaller boats from leaving.

Depth: See interactive charts on Waterway Explorer at waterwayguide.com.

ICW connection: Connects directly to the ICW at Mile 965.

Nearby facilities: There are marinas in the inlet itself and more to the north and south of the inlet, including repair facilities. There is an anchorage to the north of the inlet off the ICW and to the south on the backside of Causeway Island.

Use Chart 11475

St. Lucie Inlet ("The Crossroads")

Sea Buoy: Flashing red buoy "2" (4 sec) is located at N 27° 10.000'/W 80° 08.380'.

Overview: This marks the intersection of the Indian River, Saint Lucie, Okeechobee Waterway and ICW (hence "The Crossroads"). Used by sport fishermen, megayachts and offshore sailors.

Navigation: The entrance marker at N 27° 10.00'/ W 80° 08.380' can be used as an entrance waypoint. The jetties are visible directly west of this point.

Webcam: For a live view of the inlet, visit stlucieinlet. com.

Cautions and hazards: Conveniently located and frequently dredged but requires caution due to problematic shoaling. Jetty to the north and small breakwater to the south offer protection once inside, although protection from the south is marginal in east to southeast winds. The USCG has placed temporary markers denoting best water. Local knowledge should be obtained before using this inlet. The current can be strong.

Depth: See interactive charts on Waterway Explorer at waterwayguide.com.

ICW connection: ICW is approximately 1 nm away at Mile 988. Due to constant shoaling, several temporary buoys have been placed between the inlet and the ICW.

Nearby facilities: There are several marinas and areas to anchor inside Manatee Pocket, to the west of the ICW. There is also a mooring field in Stuart beyond the fixed Evans Crary Bridge (65-foot vertical clearance). Three nautical miles to the south is Peck Lake, with deep anchorage and easy access to the Atlantic beaches via the State Park.

COLREGS DEMARCATION LINE
80.727d (see note A)

ST LUCIE INLET

SOUTH POINT

Hole in the Wall

The Narrows

Long Island 80°10'

Long Point

Horseshoe Point

Cable Area

(see note B)

NOTE B
eacons are private
ns are approximate.

Rocky Point

Rocky Point Cove

(see note B)

Use Chart 11472

Jupiter Inlet

Sea Buoy: No sea buoy. Steer to waypoint N 26° 56.620'/ W 80° 03.790' (0.4 nm east of the inlet).

Overview: Fair weather inlet only. Prone to severe shoaling and cited by the USCG as "not navigable without local knowledge."

Navigation: If you must enter, proceed in a westerly direction from the waypoint to the markers on the jetties. Once inside the jetties, depths increase substantially.

Webcam: For a live view of the inlet, visit evsjupiter.com.

Cautions and hazards: Severe shoaling to both the north and south of the entrance. With any swell, mariners should divert to another inlet. The inlet is considered impassable in a northeast swell of any size.

Depth: See interactive charts on Waterway Explorer at waterwayguide.com.

ICW connection: Connects directly to the ICW at Mile 1005.

Nearby facilities: Marinas located to the north and south of the inlet, with provisioning nearby.

JUPITER INLET
CAUTION

Inlet entrance continually shoaling. Passage through the inlet is not recommended without local knowledge of all hazardous conditions affecting this area.

LOXAHATCHEE RIVER

The Intracoastal Waterway follows the Loxahatchee River through U.S. Route 1 bascule bridge, then makes a sharp turn southward just east of Florida Route A1A ALT bascule bridge.

CAUTION

Fixed and floating obstructions, some submerged, may exist within the magenta tinted bridge construction area. Mariners are advised to proceed with caution.

Lake Worth (Palm Beach) Inlet

Sea Buoy: RW sea buoy "LW" is located at N 26° 46.360'/W 80° 00.610' (1.1 nm east of the jetties).

Overview: Deep, easily navigable big ship inlet that is sometimes referred to as the Palm Beach Inlet. Vessels returning from the Bahamas can clear Customs and Immigration here.

Navigation: Straight shot from the sea buoy with no hazards of any sort. There is a long jetty to the south and a much shorter one to the north.

Webcam: For a live view of the inlet, visit pbcgov.com/webcams/lwi.

Cautions and hazards: Large commercial vessels frequently use this inlet. Further in, many small fishing boats can cause problems, particularly beside Peanut Island. Currents are strong but do not cause much difficulty in the inlet.

Depth: See interactive charts on Waterway Explorer at waterwayguide.com.

ICW connection: Connects directly to the ICW at Mile 1027.

Nearby facilities: Port caters to megayachts with numerous marinas and marine facilities. Several good anchorages also close by. No convenient dinghy dockage.

LAKE WORTH INLET

Boca Raton Inlet

Sea Buoy: No sea buoy. Steer to N 26° 20.15'/ W 80° 04.270' and pick up the quick flashing green buoy "1" on the south jetty and quick flashing red buoy "2" on the north jetty.

Overview: Narrow, dredged cut located 5 nm northward of Hillsboro Inlet Light. Boca Raton Inlet (A1A) Bascule Bridge (23-foot vertical clearance) crosses the inlet and opens on signal.

Navigation: Tall, pink Boca Raton Resort & Club is a landmark visible from many miles offshore. The inlet's entrance has short jetties marked by private lights. Be sure to request a bridge opening upon arrival in the inlet to avoid circling in the strong current. It is strongly recommended to head south of green buoy "1" (south jetty) and approach the inlet from the south.

Webcam: For a live view of the inlet, visit video-monitoring.com/beachcams/bocainlet.

Cautions and Hazards: There is heavy traffic in the area, especially on weekends. Local knowledge is required, as shoaling outside the inlet can limit access at low tide. Depths change frequently due to shoaling and shifting sandbars, and swift-moving currents cause swells where the outflow meets the ocean. The inlet channel and markers are not charted and transit is considered dangerous. Be aware that the current usually reverses in the ICW as it passes the Boca Raton Inlet.

Depth: See interactive charts on Waterway Explorer at waterwayguide.com.

ICW connection: Connects directly to the ICW at Mile 1048.

Nearby facilities: Marine facilities are available on the ICW and farther south off the Hillsboro River. A small anchorage is located just south of the Palmetto Park Bridge (Mile 1047.5) at the northeastern end of Lake Boca Raton.

Use Chart 11467

Hillsboro Inlet

Sea Buoy: RW sea buoy "HI" is located at N 26° 15.070'/W 80° 04.630' (approximately 0.4 nm from the inlet). A course to the northwest (paying close attention to the green day marks and lighted buoys) will bring you past the jetty.

Overview: Frequently used and offers reliable 7-foot MLW depths; nevertheless this inlet requires attentiveness when entering.

Navigation: Easily identified by 136-foot high Hillsboro Lighthouse. Hillsboro Inlet Bascule Bridge (13-foot closed vertical clearance) inside the inlet opens on signal, except from 7:00 a.m. to 6:00 p.m., the drawspans need only open only on the hour, quarter-hour, half-hour and three-quarter hour. Due to the very strong currents in this inlet, vessels should contact the bridge tender before entering the inlet.

Webcam: For a live view of the inlet, visit hillsborolighthouse.org/inlet-cam.

Cautions and Hazards: A southeast wind against a tide situation can kick up a short, vicious chop that can set an unwary boater onto the shoals to the south of the inlet. More than one vessel has been bounced onto the bottom here in the troughs. Currents to 6 knots have been reported. There is a 64-foot clearance power cable at the bridge.

Depth: See interactive charts on Waterway Explorer at waterwayguide.com.

ICW connection: Connects directly to the ICW at Mile 1053.

Nearby facilities: Marinas are to the north and south of the inlet, with provisioning nearby. No nearby anchorages.

Use Chart 11467

Port Everglades (Fort Lauderdale) Inlet

Sea buoy: RW sea buoy "PE" is located at N 26° 05.500'/W 80° 04.790'. From the sea buoy, head due west into the cut.

Overview: This big ship inlet, located 9 nm south of Hillsboro Inlet, is also known as Fort Lauderdale Inlet. Wide, deep, straight and completely free of hazards; accommodates naval vessels, container ships, freighters and cruise ships. Be aware that larger vessels will often be escorted and have an enforced security perimeter.

Navigation: At the turning basin, swing south into the ICW, or north to the ICW and the various marinas of Fort Lauderdale.

Webcam: For a live view of the inlet, visit portevergladeswebcam.com. Fort Lauderdale ICW can be seen at ftlauderdalewebcam.com.

Cautions and hazards: Frequent large ship traffic in and out of this inlet necessitate a careful watch, particularly at night and in poor weather. The cut can get bouncy with sportfishing boats running in and out at high speeds.

Depth: See interactive charts on Waterway Explorer at waterwayguide.com.

ICW connection: Connects directly to the ICW at Mile 1066.

Nearby facilities: Several marinas are located to the north of the inlet. Some transient dockage is located in Dania Cut to the south. Las Olas Bridge mooring field is north of the inlet, in the center of town. Anchorages are available nearby, although access to shore is difficult.

Use Chart 11470

Bakers Haulover (North Miami Beach) Inlet

Sea Buoy: No sea buoy. Steer to waypoint
N 25° 54.000'/W 80° 06.730'.

Overview: Popular and busy with local recreational
fishermen and tour boats.

Navigation: There are no markers, other than a light on
the south side of the inlet and once you have turned
north, deep water is close to the shore on your port side.
The inlet has a fixed bridge (A1A) with 32-foot
vertical clearance.

Cautions and hazards: Strictly a fair-weather inlet for
cruising vessels due to problems with continual ICW
shoaling. Cruisers would be wise to forgo this inlet in
favor of Miami's Government Cut (8 nm to the south) or
Port Everglades Inlet (11.5 nm to the north). Mariners
are advised to exercise extreme caution while transiting
the area.

Depth: See interactive charts on Waterway Explorer at
waterwayguide.com.

ICW connection: Proceed due east into the inlet,
turning south once inside to head for the ICW Mile
1080. Severe shoaling exists in the vicinity of Biscayne
Bay buoy "7B" on the ICW. The shoal protrudes into
the channel on the east side, which reduces the channel
width by approximately half of the charted width.
Biscayne Bay Buoy "7B" has been relocated by USCG to
mark the best water.

Nearby facilities: There is a marina just to the north of
the inlet.

NORTH
ATLANTIC OCEAN

Mg

Obstn
Fish Haven
(auth min 6 ft)

Spoil Area

R "4A"
Subm pile
Mkr

Fl G 4s 16ft
5M "5"

R "6"

10 FT
MAY 2004 - OCT 2009

Bkw

OCT 2009

Spoil Area

9 FT
OCT 2009

9 FT

9 FT OCT 2009

Piling

St M

R "6A"

Piles

G "7"

Subm piles

Obstn rep.

NW Bn

G C "7B"

G C "7C"

Sign

Subm pile

1080

Obstn
Fish Haven
(auth min 6 ft)

Ruins

Co Bakers Haulover

Inlet

25°54'

570

R "8"

INTRACOASTAL WATERWAY

Fl G 2.5s
16ft 5M "9"

Q 13ft PA Priv

Piles

FIXED BRIDGE
HOR CL 125 FT
VERT CL 32 FT
OVHD PWR CAB
AUTH CL 53 FT

COLREGS DEMARCATION LINE
80.727k (see note A)

G "11"

A1A

Piles

Use Chart 11467

Government Cut (Miami) Inlet

Sea Buoy: RW sea buoy "M" is located at N 25° 46.088'/W 80° 04.998'.

Overview: This big ship inlet is wide and deep and is free of hazards. Runs between Miami Beach (to the north) and Fisher Island (to the south).

Navigation: In settled conditions, use the waypoint N 25° 45.400'/W 80° 06.880', which brings you in to just over 0.5 nm from the jetties; otherwise, the sea buoy at N 25° 46.130'/W 80° 04.960' is the preferable waypoint. Follow a course of 253° M inside the channel, then 299° M from green buoy "7" through the jetties. Closures are announced on VHF Channel 16. During closures, Fisherman's Channel south of Dodge Island is the alternate inlet. It is similarly free of hazards, although when entering from the ICW heading south, leave buoys "53A" and "55" well to port before turning in to the channel due to shoaling extending into the channel.

Webcam: For a live view of the inlet, visit portmiamiwebcam.com.

Cautions and hazards: A car ferry runs between Dodge Island and Fisher Island with frequent crossings. Both channels are subject to strong currents.

Depth: See interactive charts on Waterway Explorer at waterwayguide.com.

ICW connection: Connects directly to the ICW at Mile 1089.

Nearby facilities: There are marinas and anchorages nearby as well as provisioning opportunities.

Cape Florida (Biscayne Bay) Inlet

Sea buoy: Use flashing (4 sec) 37-foot Biscayne Channel Light "6M" located at N 25º 38.742'/W 80º 05.373'.

Overview: This inlet is primarily used by cruisers heading to the islands. Located 6 nm south of Miami.

Navigation: Pass Biscayne Channel Light to port, then continue to entrance buoy green "1" and follow the marked channel.

Cautions and hazards: Local knowledge should be obtained before entering this inlet for the first time. It is a well-marked channel, but attention is required in some shallow areas (7 to 9 feet).

Depth: See interactive charts on Waterway Explorer at waterwayguide.com.

ICW connection: Connects to ICW (0.5 nm) at Mile 1094.

Nearby facilities: There are anchorages nearby at No Name Harbor and Hurricane Harbor. No Name Harbor is part of a State Park with a restaurant, making it busy on weekends. Coconut Grove is located across the Bay and to the west and offers facilities.

Use Chart 11465

Angelfish Creek

Sea Buoy: No sea buoy. Steer to waypoint N 25° 19.600'/W 80° 14.914'.

Overview: For vessels wanting to take advantage of the Gulf Stream for a transit to Bimini Island in the Bahamas, Angelfish Creek provides a more southerly approach than Miami. Be aware that the 1.8-nm-long inlet adds 14 nm to the Bahamas trip, making it 56 nm instead of 42 nm.

Navigation: Entering from Card Sound at flashing red buoy "14," the depths will increase quickly to 7 to 10 feet, then to over 13 feet until you approach the exit to the Atlantic. At red buoy "4" you will see three green daybeacons ahead. Favor the red side as you approach flashing red buoy "2" and proceed slowly through to the Atlantic while watching your depth. There is a cross current here; pay attention to your track so that you don't get pushed out of the channel.

Cautions and hazards: The channel is a fair weather proposition only, particularly from the Atlantic. The depth from the Atlantic side is approximately 4 feet at the beginning of the channel. Because of this, an ocean side approach is not recommended for cruising vessels. Vessels traveling offshore in inclement weather would be best advised to continue on to Government Cut in Miami (26 nm).

Depth: See interactive charts on Waterway Explorer at waterwayguide.com.

ICW connection: Inlet leads into Card Sound, with the ICW 1.4 nm away at Mile 1120.

Nearby facilities: Several anchorages are nearby.

Skipper's Notes

Florida's Upper East Coast

- FERNANDINA BEACH TO ST. JOHNS RIVER   ■ SIDE TRIP ON THE ST. JOHNS RIVER
- ST. JOHNS RIVER TO PONCE DE LEON INLET
- NEW SMYRNA BEACH TO VERO BEACH   ■ FORT PIERCE TO ST. LUCIE INLET   ■ OKEECHOBEE WATERWAY

GEORGIA

FLORIDA

St. Marys River

Fernandina Beach **ICW MILE 717**

Jacksonville
ICW MILE 740
St. Johns River

ICW MILE 776 St. Augustine

ICW MILE 830 Daytona Beach
Ponce de Leon Inlet

ATLANTIC OCEAN

ICW MILE 878 Titusville

Cape Canaveral

Cocoa **ICW MILE 897**

ICW MILE 917 Melbourne

Vero Beach **ICW MILE 952**

ICW MILE 986 Stuart
St. Lucie Inlet

Lake Okeechobee

Gulf of Mexico

Okeechobee Waterway

N

Ft. Myers

GIWW MILE 0

San Carlos Bay

FLORIDA'S UPPER EAST COAST

Visit Waterway Explorer at waterwayguide.com

Florida's Upper East Coast

Cruising south on the Intracoastal Waterway (ICW), boaters enter Florida at Mile 714 and Fernandina Beach. As you cross Cumberland Sound and the St. Marys River, the broad expanses of the marsh-bordered Georgia ICW gives way to the narrower, more protected, and more populated Florida route. In the 375 statute miles (326 nm) to Miami, navigational aids are plentiful, and marinas and urban centers proliferate as you travel south.

The Upper Florida ICW is well marked and easy to follow. Keep track of your position by checking off markers on the chart as you pass. Take a little extra care where inlet, river and ICW channels meet; a few moments' study of the chart ahead of time will prevent confusion in those areas where a buoy system changes direction. With a few exceptions, the ICW here is protected from strong winds and is usually free of rough water. Tidal range is more than 7 feet at Fernandina, and currents up to 4 knots may be encountered between Fernandina and Haulover Canal, especially at inlets. Tidal variances and currents decrease as you head south to Miami.

The ICW passes the birthplace of NASCAR (Ormond Beach); the Space Coast, where manned NASA flights have launched since 1972; artsy Melbourne and Eau Gallie; and "Velcro" (Vero) Beach, where cruisers wait out weather but never seem to want to leave.

We also take two side trips in this section–one on the St. Johns River and one on the Okeechobee Waterway.

The Bridge of Lions is a double-leaf bascule bridge that spans the Intracoastal Waterway in St. Augustine, Florida. It connects downtown St. Augustine to Anastasia Island across Matanzas Bay.

The St. Johns River is one of the few north-flowing rivers in the U.S. and travels 248 miles from the heart of central Florida to Mayport. This is the route to the City of Jacksonville and is well worth the effort.

The Okeechobee Waterway crosses Florida at the St. Lucie River and divides central and south Florida. It ends at Mile 0 on the Gulf ICW (GIWW) at San Carlos Bay, south of Cape Coral.

No Wake Zones

Idle-Speed/No-Wake Zones are set up to protect shorelines, wildlife, shore facilities and berthed boats from wake damage and help cut down on boating accidents. Idle speed means putting the engine in gear with no increase in throttle, while taking care to maintain control of the vessel. Other areas have Slow-Speed Zones where a minimum wake is required, while others may have a limit on wake height. Read the signs!

Manatee zones also have speed restrictions that are strictly enforced. Many are seasonal, and the posted signs may be difficult to read, so keep an eye out for them.

Crab Pot & Trap Markers

The terms "pot" and "trap" are somewhat interchangeable when referring to the enclosed traps (usually a framework of wire) used to catch crabs in shallow waters. These are identified by markers, which can range from colorful buoys to empty milk jugs (or anything else that floats). They are so ubiquitous that some creeks and rivers along the ICW are clogged with pots, making navigation tricky. Darker colored markers are especially difficult to see in the best of conditions. You do NOT want to get a line wrapped around your prop, so it is advisable to have a spotter on the foredeck when traversing fields of pots. Be advised that it is against the law to place crabpots with marker buoys inside navigational channels but they sometimes break loose and find their way there.

Docking & Anchoring

Much of Florida's eastern ICW is narrow and shoal-bordered, with scattered anchorages. As the population continues to increase, favorite anchorages become more crowded. Good anchorages are still available if you plan ahead. Using an anchor light is important and required by law, and in some places you will be ticketed for not having one on at night. Florida restrictions on anchoring are being changed on a regular basis. Before planning to anchor in an area, be sure to check to make sure you can.

The same space shortage applies to marina dockage, so you should reserve ahead or plan to arrive early at your chosen marina during the winter cruising season. Most dockmasters make every effort to find room for one more, and the friendliness of the boating community more than makes up for the crowded conditions.

See up-to-date navigation alerts, dockage and anchorage listings and bridge schedules on the Waterway Explorer at waterwayguide.com.

Fernandina Beach to St. Johns River

ICW Mile 716–Mile 740

VHF FL Bridges: Channel 09

CHARTS NOAA 11489, 11490, 11491

■ FERNANDINA BEACH AREA– ICW MILE 716 TO MILE 720

As you cross the St. Marys River and enter the State of Florida, you will notice a change in the characteristics of the ICW. Georgia's long, open sounds and wide rivers gradually transform into a series of creeks and rivers connected by narrow land cuts, and you will see much more development. The ICW crosses several navigable inlets that no doubt attracted the early explorers. The first settlers built strategic, profitable ports along these protected inside waters. Today's cruisers use improved and connected passages that link many of these original settlements.

Florida's northernmost city, Fernandina Beach, is on Amelia Island, east of the ICW. Although discovered in 1562 by the French explorer Jean Ribault and named *Isle de Mai*, it was the Spanish who ultimately settled the island in 1567. They renamed it *Santa Maria*, established a mission and built Fort San Fernando. In 1702, the British captured the island and gave it the name that finally stuck: Amelia, in honor of King George II's daughter.

Amelia Island has enjoyed a colorful history. In its earlier years, pirates and smugglers used it as their stronghold and rum runners continued the tradition during Prohibition. Eight different flags have flown over Amelia Island, among them the standard of the Conquistadors and the French Huguenots, the British Union Jack and the Stars and Bars of the Confederacy. The island is the only place in the U.S. to have been claimed by so many governments.

The very charming historic downtown district, next to the waterfront, has several restaurants, taverns and gift shops. The Convention and Visitors Bureau at 102 Centre St. can provide a helpful map or visit ameliaisland.com for maps and interactive guides to the area.

NAVIGATION: Use NOAA Chart 11489. This area was dredged in early 2018 and has changed very little except that the depths have improved somewhat. On the Amelia River at Mile 718 past the Fernandina Beach waterfront, swing wide between red daybeacons "14" and "16" and favor the north side between red daybeacons "16" and "18" due to 6-foot depths between the two. After passing daybeacon "18," stay to the western side until you pass daybeacon "1" and you will find deeper water. Red daybeacon "18" appears to be too far to the west but head toward it to give the shoal at the bend marked by flashing green "1" a wide berth, both above and below.

FERNANDINA HABOR MARINA

Fernandina Beach

After passing flashing green daybeacon "1," swing to the east side of the channel as indicated by the magenta line on the chart. The shoal moving out from the west side is about 6 feet or less at MLW, as noted by our Cruising Editor in summer 2018. In response to frequent groundings here, the Coast Guard has established a red daybeacon "2" near green daybeacon "3. Follow the buoys for a minimum of 9 feet at MLW. A helpful chart of the Fernandina south shallows with the new buoys in place is shown on the Waterway Explorer at waterwayguide.com.

The Amelia River breaks off to the west of the ICW at Mile 719.8. Just southwest of the Jackson Creek entrance to the Amelia River (near Mile 720), the ICW turns south and leaves the Amelia River for Kingsley Creek. Two bridges span the ICW at Mile 720.7—the **Kingsley Creek Railroad Swing Bridge** (5-foot closed vertical clearance, normally open) and the **Kingsley Creek Twin Bridges** (65-foot fixed high-level highway bridges carrying U.S. A1A).

Although the railroad bridge is usually open, trains hauling logs to the area's two paper mills can delay your journey. The bridge gives no warning when it is going to close, and it does not have a VHF radio. If you are in this area and you hear train whistles, be aware that the bridge could close as you approach it. After passing beneath the bridges, you could see either a wide expanse of water or mud flats on either side of the channel, depending on the state of the tide.

 Note that most charts are not up to date in the area of Kingsley Creek at Mile 720. Stay in the visual center for 20-foot MLW depths.

Dockage: At Mile 715.3 is the entrance to Egans Creek (east of the ICW), which leads to Tiger Point Marina, the first marina you will encounter as you enter Florida from the north. Tiger Point has a full-service repair yard as well as limited transient slips. Diesel fuel and gas can be found at Port Consolidated at Mile 716.5. It is usually best to dock alongside the fixed dock during higher tides. Many commercial vessels fuel up here, so there may be a wait, plus there is a 200 gallon minimum. Transient overnight dockage is not permitted here.

The Fernandina Harbor Marina is located at Mile 716.7. This marina was heavily damaged from Hurricane Matthew in 2016 and Hurricane Irma in 2017. At press time in summer 2018, rebuilding was planned but with no set operational date. Moorings are available on a first-come, first-served basis and the dinghy dock is open. The fuel dock is also gone but will be rebuilt; again, no projected date is available. They can accommodate approximately five 40-foot transient boats. You will need to call two weeks in advance for availability. Be sure to check the Waterway Explorer at waterwayguide.com for the latest information.

Oyster Bay Harbour Marina off Lanceford Creek no longer accepts transients unless you are a homeowner or the guest of a homeowner. Call ahead for current information.

Amelia Island Marina, in a cove just north of the bridges to the east past green daybeacon "13," is a full-service marina (including gas and diesel) with haul-out capabilities and personalized boat service. They also have a courtesy car and an on-site eatery (The Galley Bar and Grille, 904-261-7447). The narrow channel leading to the marina at Mile 721 should be traversed with a mid-tide or higher. This is a good choice in strong winds when other marinas may be too exposed, but the 30 transient slips fill quickly in bad weather, so call ahead.

Anchorage: The mooring area in Fernandina Harbor is marked with yellow buoys, but anchoring is still permitted outside the marked area in 7 feet at MLW. Anchored boats may use the dinghy dock and showers for a modest fee. If you choose to anchor, take care that your swinging circle does not extend into the channel or the mooring area. Also make sure that you have adequate scope on your anchor for the varying depths and sometimes fast-moving current. Although it is a relatively short dinghy ride to the marina dinghy dock, the anchorage and mooring areas are open to winds, wakes and considerable tidal current.

Caution is advised in this area; sunken boats have been present in the past and debris may still be on the bottom. Several sunken boats have been observed outside of the channel between red daybeacons "14" and "16."

Boats have been seen anchoring off of the Amelia River in Bells River and also in Lanceford Creek. Approach with caution as the chart contours show varied depths with snags and mud banks. The tidal range is greater than 7 feet, and tidal currents run up to 2 knots here. Although it is a relatively short dinghy ride to the marina dinghy dock, the anchorage and mooring areas are open to winds, wakes and considerable tidal current. Always display anchor lights, as commercial and other traffic can be heavy at all hours.

Note that the **high-level bridges** along this stretch are unofficially considered to be among the "lowest" of the 65-foot bridges on the ICW; expect no more than 64 feet at high tide. If in doubt, check the clearance boards and go through at half tide. With the wide tidal range (7 feet), currents can be unexpectedly strong.

The Amelia River breaks off to the west of the ICW at Mile 719.8 (Piney Island) with 6-to 7-foot MLW depths. Although it is preferred over Jackson Creek to the north, it is also quite narrow. Enter slowly with the depth sounder on. Be sure to lay out plenty of scope due to the swift currents but also be aware of your swing room.

■ TO FORT GEORGE RIVER

ICW Mile 721 to Mile 729

NAVIGATION: Use NOAA Chart 11489. South from the Kingsley Creek Railroad Swing Bridge (5-foot closed vertical clearance, normally open) and the Kingsley Creek Twin Bridges (65-foot fixed vertical clearance) to flashing red "14," shoaling reduces depths along the west side of the channel to 5- to 8-foot depths. In the ICW channel at green daybeacon "21" and flashing red "24" (just north of the entrance to Alligator Creek), the narrow channel makes a sharp sweep to the east.

⚠ Round the turns between green daybeacon "21" and green daybeacon "25," staying off the greens by 50 feet for 7.3 at MLW. If you go directly from green to green, you will run into shoaling.

Just past flashing red "28" (about Mile 724), you will pass Amelia City, a small waterside hamlet tucked into a bend on the east side of the river. You will see bulkheads, some private docks and a few houses. Inside the marsh, past the bulkhead area, are more houses.

The shallowest part of the south Amelia River is between red daybeacon "34" and red daybeacon "36." There is an 11-foot MLW passage closer to flashing green "37" but the channel is narrow and you can easily stray into 5 feet in the marked channel. To avoid doing so, split red daybeacon "32" and the docks. Pass 100 feet off flashing green "33" and aim at flashing green "37" until halfway, then turn to split red daybeacon "36" and flashing green "37," where you should have 11 feet at MLW. If you turn too soon, you will find 5 feet at MLW.

Next, round flashing green "37" 300 feet off and aim for red daybeacon "38" and pass that 300 feet off. Most charts shown a tongue of deep water starting by red daybeacon "38," which you should follow. When the tongue of deep water ends, aim for flashing green "41" and when close, split flashing green "41" and red daybeacon "42." Do not turn towards flashing green "45"

GOIN' ASHORE: **FERNANDINA BEACH, FL**

SERVICES

1	Library
2	Post Office
3	Visitor Information

ATTRACTIONS

4	Amelia Island Museum of History
5	Maritime Museum of Amelia Island
6	Marlin & Barrel Rum Distillery

SHOPPING

7	Amelia Island Paint & Hardware
8	Fantastic Fudge
9	Fernandina Food Mart
10	Tho Book Loft

DINING

11	29 South
12	Brett's Waterway Café
13	Marina Seafood Restaurant
14	Palace Saloon

MARINAS

15	Fernandina Harbor Marina

The downtown historic district, a 50-block section surrounding Centre Street, is an attractive and popular gingerbread seaport dating from the 1850s, when Florida's first cross-state railroad ran from Fernandina to Cedar Key. (The railroad tracks still run past the waterfront with occasional traffic.) The area is listed on the National Historic Register and is is a wonderful cruising stopover with many great restaurants, shops and supplies within an easy walk of the marina area and waterfront.

Attractions: With local attractions such as Fort Clinch State Park, Cumberland Island National Seashore, Amelia Island State Park and the island itself, Fernandina makes a pleasant stopover. A good place to start is at the Welcome Center, located in an old train depot at 102 Centre St. (904-277-0717). Your next stop should be the Amelia Island Museum of History at 233 S. 3rd St., which is located in an old jail. Here you can see exhibits on the island's 4,000 years of history and local preservation efforts. Docent-led tours of all types originate here, from home tours to pub tours to even ghost tours. Call ahead for hours at 904-261-7378.

The Maritime Museum of Amelia Island is located just off the waterfront (115 S 2nd St.) with maritime history, pirate lore and marine artifacts. Highlights includes

U.S. Navy memorabilia, a Soviet-era KGB diving suit, an artifact from an expedition to the *Titanic* and, of course, Spanish treasure. Open Tuesday through Saturday; call for hours (904-432-7086). The museum is co-located with the Marlin & Barrel Rum Distillery, which is also worth a look-see. Stop for a sampling and stay to hear about the distilling process and the owners' use of locally sustainable organics for distilling their unique liquors.

If you have transportation, be sure to visit Florida's oldest lighthouse, Amelia Island Lighthouse, built in 1838. To register for a tour of the lighthouse (for a small fee), call 904-310-3350. It is located on Egans Creek.

Shopping: Be sure to try Fantastic Fudge (218 Centre St., 904-277-4801). The Book Loft (214 Centre St., 904-261-8991) offers a large selection of new and used books. Amelia Island Paint, Hardware and Marine Supply (516 Ash St., 904-261-6604) has a good selection of hardware and boating staples. BuyGo Gourmet Groceries (22 S. 8th St., 904-310-9766) is a small store with a good selection of basic food products and personal items, as well as a fresh meat counter and gourmet coffees. Winn-Dixie and Publix are about 2 miles away.

The popular weekly farmers' market is not to be missed, with fresh local fruits and vegetables, baked goods, food carts, arts and crafts, and live music. You'll find it on the corner of Centre and 7th Streets every Saturday from 9:00 a.m. to 1:00 p.m. Visit fbfl.us for more information.

Dining: There are a surprising number of shops and restaurants in this small town. Do take the time to explore all of the side streets, you're sure to be rewarded with the perfect café to suit every taste. Not far from the waterfront you will find the Palace Saloon (117 Centre St., 844-441-2444), Florida's oldest tavern. Originally named the "Ship Captain's Bar," the Palace Saloon has been a bar since 1903. (Prior to that, it was a haberdashery.) The original bar was a true "gentleman's establishment" with complimentary towels for patron's to wipe the foam from their mustaches and solid brass spittoons for those who enjoyed a good chew with their beer. Check out the original carved mahogany bar, brass cash register, hand painted wall murals, tin ceiling and inlaid tile floors. The bar is open every day from 12:00 p.m. to 2:00 a.m. Be sure to try the Pirates Punch, made from their own secret recipe. See history, specials and more at thepalacesaloon.com.

Brett's Waterway Café is located at Fernandina Harbor Marina. You can't find a better view in town (1 S. Front St., 904-261-2660). A local favorite and the oldest restaurant in town is Marina Seafood Restaurant, located just across the street from the marina (101 Centre St., 904-261-5310). 29 South gets great reviews. Find them two blocks from the waterfront (29 S. 3rd St., 904-277-7919).

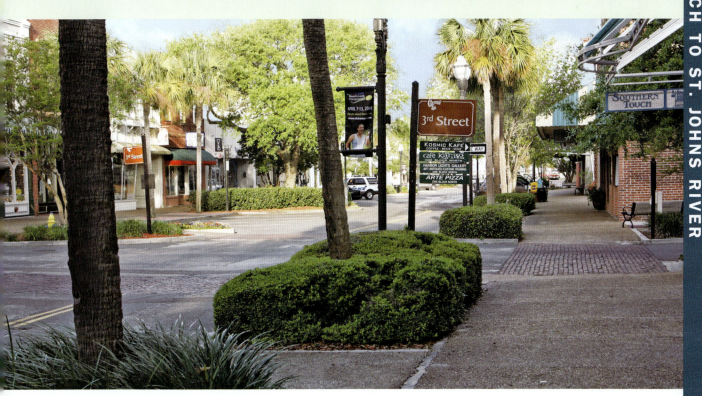

Amelia River, FL

FERNANDINA BEACH AREA		Largest Vessel Accommodated	VHF Channel Monitored	Transient Berths / Total Berths	Approach / Dockside Depth (reported)	Floating Docks	Gas / Diesel	Groceries, Ice, Marine Supplies, Snacks	Repairs: Hull, Engine, Propeller	Lift (tonnage), Crane, Rail	Min/Max Amps	Laundry, Pool, Showers, Courtesy Car	Pump-Out Station	Nearby: Grocery Store, Motel, Restaurant
				Dockage			**Supplies**		**Services**					
1. Tiger Point Marina ▢ ⓦⒾⒻⒾ 715.3	904-277-2720	55	16/11	4/50	7/8	F	–	M	HEP	L50	30/50	S	–	MR
2. Port Consolidated 716.5	904-753-4258	285	16	0/13	50/30	–	GD	–	–	–	–	–	–	GMR
3. Fernandina Harbor Marina ⓦⒾⒻⒾ WG 716.7	904-310-3300	50	16/68	5/	18/8	F	GD	–	–	–	30/50	LS	–	GMR
4. Oyster Bay Harbour Marina–PRIVATE ▢ ⓦⒾⒻⒾ	904-261-4773	65	–	0/76	15/6	F	–	I	–	–	30/50	PS	P	R
5. Amelia Island Marina ▢ ⓦⒾⒻⒾ WG 721	904-277-4615	110	16/72	call/147	5/6	F	GD	IMS	HEP	L50	30/50	LSC	P	GMR

▢ Internet Access ⓦⒾⒻⒾ Wireless Internet Access WG Waterway Guide Cruising Club Partner onSpot dockside WiFi facility
See WaterwayGuide.com for current rates, fuel prices, web site addresses, and other up-to-the-minute information. *(Information in the table is provided by the facilities.)*

until halfway there. There is a 5-foot MLW shoal coming from the port side, as shown on most charts.

> ⚠️ Because this is such a changeable area, remember to be on the alert for shoaling and the possibility that there may be additional aids in place when you make passage here. There were reports of dredging in the area at press time in summer 2018 and hopefully the passage will be clear by the fall. See the Waterway Explorer (waterwayguide.com) for new alerts and updates.

The current across Nassau Sound's ocean inlet, at the southern end of Amelia Island, may be very strong, so watch your set and drift; slow boats may have to crab across. The deepest water is closer to the inlet. The twin **A1A Bridge** (21-foot fixed vertical clearance) and **George Crady Bridge** (15-foot fixed vertical clearance) cross the Nassau Sound inlet. The charted red daybeacon at the entrance to the cut to the south is red daybeacon "46," which may not appear on older charts. The lower portion of Amelia Island is home to a large and lovely resort community, Amelia Island Plantation. No dockage is available on the premises.

Anchorage: As the chart clearly shows, the ICW channel hugs the Amelia Island shore just south of Amelia City. There is an anchorage just north of Mile 726 off the entrance to Alligator Creek. Enter by turning to the northeast between red daybeacon "36" and flashing green "37." Be careful here; the entrance is shallow, carrying only 6-foot depths at MLW, and then increasing to 8-foot depths at MLW off Alligator Creek. Tugboats have been observed taking a shortcut through this anchorage area at high tide. It is also possible to anchor at the mouth of Harrison Creek with 9 feet and excellent holding in mud.

Sawpit Creek and Gunnison Cut– ICW Mile 730 to Mile 734

NAVIGATION: Use Chart 11489. Between ICW Miles 730 and 735, shorelines close in somewhat as the channel runs through narrow land cuts and two natural creeks. The dredging of Sawpit Creek in the past corrected the persistent shoaling in the vicinity of flashing green "49" for a while, but it is back.

Favor the deep natural channel along the west (red) side of the ICW when rounding the bend marked by flashing green "49" and "49A." Sawpit Creek and Gunnison Cut lead to Sisters Creek and the St. Johns River crossing. In the summer of 2018, our Cruising Editor reported 3-foot MLW depths on the green side of the channel, so staying to the red side is highly recommended.

Anchorage: At Mile 731, you will find 7 to 15 feet with excellent holding in mud behind the island between the bridge over Nassau Sound's ocean inlet and the ICW. However, be aware that the entrance is charted as shallow and should not be used except at high tide. This offers good protection but expect a strong current.

Fort George Island–ICW Mile 735

At Mile 735 the ICW meets the Fort George River. One mile east of the ICW channel, Fort George Island makes an attractive side trip, with its Indian mounds, wildlife sanctuary and lush jungle growth.

NAVIGATION: Use NOAA Chart 11489.

> ⚠️ There is a 5-foot MLW shoal in the middle of the channel at Mile 735. Favor the red side for 8.6 at MLW, passing 150 feet off both green daybeacon "73" and flashing red "74."

FERNANDINA BEACH AREA, NOAA CHART 11489

Anchorage: Once inside the river, the water will deepen and you can enjoy a beautiful anchorage. Drop the hook in 6 to 15 feet at MLW with excellent holding in mud. Hug the southern shore for deeper water and be mindful of your swinging room and the state of the tide. This is exposed to the northwest. Anchor just past the plantation, which you can explore with your dinghy.

Sisters Creek–ICW Mile 736 to Mile 740

South of the ICW junction with the Fort George River, the ICW route runs a straightforward path through Sisters Creek to the St. Johns River. (The ICW picks up on the other side at Pablo Creek.) As you travel along some sections of Sisters Creek, you may see the superstructures of large ships headed up or down the St. Johns River. The suspension bridge at Dames Point, at the western end of Blount Island, can be used as a landmark when you are headed south.

NAVIGATION: Use NOAA Chart 11489. Favor the east bank just south of flashing red "82" on Sisters Creek as shoaling has created MLW depths of 6 to 8 feet along the west bank. The **Hecksher Dr. (Sisters Creek) Bridge** at Mile 739.2 has 65-foot fixed vertical clearance. Expect heavy currents when passing under the bridge and approaching the St. Johns River.

Stay alert for large ships traversing the St. Johns River. Shipping traffic may be heavy. Keep in mind that large oceangoing vessels have the right of way. The pilots and captains of large vessels in this area always announce their approach and intentions at the Sisters Creek and St. Johns River intersection via Sécurité warnings. Listen on VHF Channel 16. Smaller vessels in the area should stay clear of these large vessels.

At this point, the St. Johns River is narrow compared to some of its broad expanses south of Jacksonville. Crossing can present problems to lightly powered vessels, given the strong currents (2 to 3 knots on the ebb), obstructed visibility and continuous commercial traffic. Observe markers closely until you are safely into the ICW land cut (Pablo Creek) across the St. Johns River. This area has a clearly marked channel that should be very carefully followed. Be aware that the shipyard on the east side of the Sisters Creek entrance to the St. Johns River creates a blind spot for small boats heading into the river.

The land cut from this point southward through the Jacksonville Beach area is well marked, but at low tide the dredged channel is narrow. Follow the markers carefully to stay on the channel's centerline and be prepared to squeeze over for tugs with barges.

Dockage: The City of Jacksonville operates the Jim King Park and Boat Ramp at Sisters Creek Marina. The facility has floating concrete face docks on either side of the bridge, restrooms and pump-out service. Dockage is free for 72 hours. The current is strong here but manageable. There is also a large boat ramp area, which causes congestion, particularly on weekends. The marina is closed to transients during the Greater Jacksonville Kingfish Tournament in July.

There is additional free overnight dockage (no restrooms) that can handle larger cruising boats in the small creek just north and west of the launching area.

Anchorage: It is possible to anchor north of the Hecksher Dr. (Sisters Creek) Bridge at Mile 739. There is 8 to 11 feet at MLW with good holding in mud. It is exposed, however, to the north and wakes.

■ ST. JOHNS RIVER ENTRANCE

The St. Johns River entrance is one of the safest and easiest gateways from the Atlantic Ocean. Ocean freighters use it, as do military craft and fishing skiffs. Recreational boats make it a point of entry and departure for passages along the coast, coming into and leaving marinas at Mayport (2 miles upriver) and on the ICW (5 miles upriver). It is 150 nm from St. Johns Entrance to the next big ship inlet, Port Canaveral Inlet.

NAVIGATION: Use NOAA Charts 11489, 11490 and 11491. The ocean approach landmark is St. Johns Light, standing 83 feet above the shore, 1 mile south of the St. Johns River north jetty. The light shines from a square white tower and is easy to spot from the ocean. The St. Johns River red and white sea buoy, flashing Morse (A) "STJ," located 3 miles east of the jetties, guides boaters into the marked inlet channel.

Other landmarks include a tower at Jacksonville Beach and a water tank (painted in a red and white checkerboard design) at the Mayport Naval Air Station. Other water tanks line the beaches to the south. (See the Inlet section in the front of this guide for more information on the St. Johns River Entrance.)

Kingsleys Creek

AMELIA ISLAND MARINA

St. Johns River Entrance, FL

ST. JOHNS RIVER		Dockage					Supplies		Services					
		Largest Vessel Accommodated	VHF Channel Monitored	Transient Berths / Total Berths	Approach / Dockside Depth (reported)	Floating Docks	Gas / Diesel	Groceries, Ice, Marine Supplies, Snacks	Repairs: Hull, Engine, Propeller	Lift (tonnage), Crane, Rail	Laundry, Pool, Showers, Courtesy Car	Min/Max Amps	Pump-Out Station	Nearby: Grocery Store, Motel, Restaurant
1. Jim King Park and Boat Ramp at Sisters Creek Marina	904-630-0839	40	–	call/15	35/15	F	–	–	–	–	–	–	P	–
2. Fort George Island Marina (WiFi)	904-251-0050	70	16/68	5/13	40/25	F	GD	IM	–	L14	30/50	LS	–	R
3. St. Johns Boat Company (WiFi)	904-251-3707	200	16	call/5	41/26	–	–	M	HEP	L100,R300	15/100	–	–	R
4. Morningstar Marinas Mayport (WiFi)	904-246-8929	200	16/74	10/10	30/30	F	GD	IMS	–	L6	30/50	C	–	R

⌨ Internet Access 📶 Wireless Internet Access **WG** Waterway Guide Cruising Club Partner ☁ **onSpot** dockside WiFi facility
See WaterwayGuide.com for current rates, fuel prices, web site addresses, and other up-to-the-minute information. *(Information in the table is provided by the facilities.)*

ST. JOHNS RIVER, NOAA CHART 11491

Mayport

NAVIGATION: Use NOAA Chart 11489. Inside the jetties, the St. Johns River runs unobstructed and naturally deep past the Mayport Basin, which is usually occupied by enormous naval craft. The basin is off-limits to recreational craft, except in extreme emergencies.

Dockage: The town of Mayport, 3 miles inside the entrance jetties on the south side of the river, is an important commercial and sportfishing center that provides dockage for cruising boats. Mayport is a good place to lay over before you start your cruise up the St. Johns River, as supplies are readily available here. On the north side of the river is Fort George Island Marina with fuel and transient dockage for vessels up to 70 feet. St. Johns Boat Company is a full-service boatyard with a 100-ton lift and a 300-ton railway that can handle all manner of repairs but they have no transient slips.

On the south side of the river, Morningstar Marinas at Mayport provides fuel, transient dockage and excellent local seafood. A ferry runs across the St. Johns River to Fort George Island. You could spend hours watching the constant activity. A Coast Guard station is located at the south end of the Mayport waterfront, as well as a luxury residential and marina project (Fort George Harbour).

■ NEXT STOP

The splendid St. Johns River, which winds its way from Mayport to Sanford, is described in the following chapter. Cruisers continuing south on the ICW will find their course resuming in Chapter 3, "St. Johns River to Ponce de Leon Inlet."

ST. JOHNS BOAT COMPANY

St. Johns River Entrance

Side Trip on the St. Johns River

VHF FL Bridges: Channel 09

CHARTS NOAA 11487, 11491, 11492, 11495, 11498

Southbound on the ICW, the waterway crosses the St. Johns River just west of Mile Point, about 5 miles from the St. Johns Entrance and a little over 1 mile west of Mayport. At that point, the ICW leaves Sisters Creek and enters Pablo Creek at red nun "2" (Mile 740) for the run south. However, in this chapter we are going to make a turn to starboard and then travel south "up" the St. Johns River (green markers to starboard), which flows from the heart of central Florida northward for 248 miles to the Atlantic Ocean at Mayport.

If you are not in a hurry while heading south in the fall or going north in the spring, stop and take a cruise "up" the river. With Atlantic Ocean access and the St. Johns River and the ICW within easy reach, the Jacksonville area is a prime playground for boaters. The City of Jacksonville offers good restaurants, museums, a zoo, a National Football League team (the Jacksonville Jaguars) and plenty of full-service marinas. Sanford on Lake Monroe is a good place to spend the winter if you like daytime temperatures in the 60s and low 70s.

From the intersection of the St. Johns River and the ICW at ICW Mile 739.5, you are likely to meet several types of commercial vessels, from freighters, tankers and container ships to tugs towing large barges and even cruise ships. Upriver from Jacksonville, commercial traffic consists of the occasional tug and barge.

Residential areas with private piers line the shore south of Jacksonville to the Green Cove Springs area, but the trees have been carefully preserved, making it difficult to see some of the houses. The river is less developed and more scenic farther south; part of the river is a wildlife sanctuary and many skippers make this beautiful trip an annual cruise. Unfortunately, exploring the most beautiful part of the St. Johns River is limited to boats able to pass under the Shands Bridge (45-foot fixed vertical clearance), south of Green Cove Springs at Red Bay Point, 48 miles from the ICW.

The river boasts infinitely varied scenery. It is as broad in places as a great bay; it is sometimes placid, sometimes wild, with pockets of civilization scattered sparsely along its shores. In its narrow, winding sections, subtropical vegetation and heavy stands of trees grow right down to the water's edge. Its sloughs, creeks, oxbows and backwaters are often choked with water hyacinths but restraining fences and bulkheads help keep most of this floating vegetation out of the channel.

Hundreds of creeks and small rivers, deep or shoal, flow into the St. Johns River, and all have something to offer. A good outboard-powered dinghy will enhance

One reason for the popularity of the **St. Johns River** is its fishing. The river, its lakes and its tributaries comprise what is widely known as the "Bass Capital of the World" and evidence suggests that its reputation is well deserved. Florida requires fishing licenses for freshwater and saltwater. (Licenses are not required for those under 16 or over 65, or certified as totally and permanently disabled.)

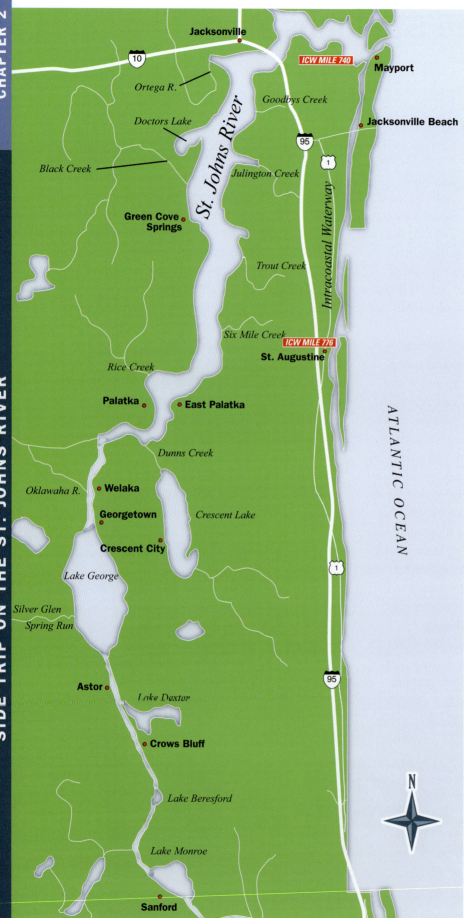

St. Johns River

Jacksonville

ICW MILE 740

Mayport

Ortega R.

Goodbys Creek

Doctors Lake

Jacksonville Beach

Black Creek

Julington Creek

Green Cove Springs

Trout Creek

Intracoastal Waterway

Six Mile Creek

ICW MILE 776

St. Augustine

Rice Creek

Palatka

East Palatka

Dunns Creek

Oklawaha R.

Welaka

Crescent Lake

Georgetown

Crescent City

Lake George

ATLANTIC OCEAN

Silver Glen Spring Run

Astor

Lake Dexter

Crows Bluff

Lake Beresford

Lake Monroe

N

Sanford

your pleasure in discovering the quiet and scenic anchorages along the St. Johns River's upper reaches. Here, too, is a proliferation of bird life: osprey, turkey vultures, pelicans, anhinga, terns, cranes, herons, egrets, bald eagles, cormorants, ducks and many songbirds are visible along the river. Alligators are common enough to warrant wariness in letting your pets roam.

From November through March, the great manatees (sea cows)–which are protected by law–live along stretches of the river. There are manatee zones along all banks of the St. Johns River in Duval and Clay counties, including Doctors Lake. Shoreside development includes state parks, fish camps (both primitive and luxurious) and a few proper marinas, some large and some small. None of humanity's intrusions detract from the overall scene, but rather all blend so well that they seem like natural outgrowths of river life.

The St. Johns River is a cruising ground with reliably mild winter weather, interesting towns, villages and secluded anchorages that should not be missed. The beauty is astounding and the cruising is wonderful.

Cruising Conditions

Between Mayport and Sanford, the St. Johns River is deep and easy to cruise with well-marked channels and shoals, but follow charts carefully and keep an eye on the depth sounder. If the chart looks doubtful, then go marker-to-marker. Overhead clearance is set by two fixed bridges. (The first is the Shands Bridge at Mile 47.9 at Red Bay Point, which carries a 45-foot vertical clearance.)

Several unmarked shoal spots extend toward the channel between Palatka (Mile 76) and the Buffalo Bluff Railroad Bridge at Mile 86.5 (7-foot closed vertical clearance, usually open) near Murphy Island. The Coast Guard reports that the overhead power cable just north of the Astor Highway Bridge at Mile 123 has less than the charted 50-foot clearance, but we do not have an exact figure.

Snags are seldom a problem in main channels of the St. Johns River, but approach side streams and sloughs carefully. Keep a sharp eye out for the ubiquitous crab trap markers, which vary from commercially produced floats to plastic bottles, and may drift into the channels. Some are painted black, some are heavily fouled with dark vegetation and some are even pulled under water by the current.

In the narrow snakelike reaches beyond Lake George, it is safest to stay in the center of the channel, although depths tend to hold close to the riverbanks.

Recreational craft use the river year-round. On weekends and holidays, especially when the weather is good, parts of the river carry heavy traffic. You will see everything from mid-sized cruisers and small runabouts to bass boats and personal watercraft, all in a great hurry to reach their destinations. No-Wake Zones abound, especially in the Astor/Blue Springs area, where the rules are strictly enforced to protect manatees. Maintain only steerageway here (even sailboats), particularly from November through mid-April, when the manatees are in residence. Marine patrol vessels often stand by to enforce regulations.

Dealing with River Currents

Skippers of sailboats with auxiliary power or low-powered motor cruisers should check their tidal current tables before starting upriver to Jacksonville from the ICW or Atlantic Ocean entrance. River currents meeting strong ocean tides can create tricky conditions. Currents are more important than tidal range, as the ebb in the river can run 2 to 3 knots, making for a slow passage for underpowered boats. Up-to-date tide tables (tidesandcurrents.noaa.gov) give corrections to the Shands Bridge (45-foot fixed vertical clearance) at Red Bay Point near Green Cove Springs. The average maximum flood given is 0.9 knots, and the average maximum ebb is 0.6 knots.

The next location is Tocoi, approximately 15 miles upriver, where the current is weak and variable. Current past Tocoi can be strongly influenced by the water level

in the upper (southern) part of the river, which varies with seasonal rainfall. Summer is wet, while winter is dry. It can be strong enough to make docking across the current difficult for the unwary.

River Tides & Depths

The spring range (full and new moon) at Mayport can exceed 5 feet and at Palatka, around 1.5 feet. Wind and rainfall affect depths dramatically in the upper reaches. Lake Monroe (Mile 164) may be 5 feet deeper after summer rains and storms than at the end of a dry winter in March. River currents respond to these changes.

Up-to-date tide information can be found at tidesandcurrents.noaa.gov.

If you plan to gunkhole, it would be advisable to carry a lead line or long boat pole to supplement your depth sounder. We find the crowd-sourced Navionics Sonar Charts useful along the St. Johns River, as fishermen have explored most of the creeks and uploaded their soundings.

■ TO JACKSONVILLE

The route to Jacksonville is a big-ship channel, well marked and simple to run. It generally follows the wide, natural course of the river. For the most part, deep water prevails alongside the marked channel, there are no intricate ranges and the next light or marker is always within sight. Even for slow sailboats, the trip is less than a day's travel and your efforts will be rewarded.

NAVIGATION: Use NOAA Chart 11491. (This chart covers the mouth of the St. Johns River on the Atlantic Ocean to the Ortega River just past downtown Jacksonville.) While currents gradually decrease upriver on the St. Johns River, the flow runs up to 3 knots at first and can be a major factor near the downtown Jacksonville bridges. Plan your trip for a fair current by calculating slack before flood and maximum flood at Mile Point (at flashing red buoy "22") on the St. Johns River to get an interval of time to arrive at the ICW crossing. Our mileage guide starts with Mile Zero at the mouth of Sisters Creek.

Coast Pilot (Volume 4) points out four critical traffic areas on the St. Johns: (1) the junction of the St. Johns River and the ICW; (2) Dames Point Turn; (3) Trout

St. Johns River Area, FL

WG

TROUT RIVER	Largest Vessel Accommodated	VHF Channel Monitored	Dockage — Transient Berths / Total Berths	Dockage — Approach / Dockside Depth (reported)	Floating Docks	Supplies — Gas / Diesel	Supplies — Groceries, Ice, Marine Supplies, Snacks	Services — Repairs: Hull, Engine, Propeller	Services — Lift (tonnage), Crane, Rail	Services — Min/Max Amps	Services — Laundry, Pool, Showers, Courtesy Car	Pump-Out Station	Nearby: Grocery Store, Motel, Restaurant
1. Seafarer's Marina 🖵 📶 904-765-8152	80	16	5/75	10/10	–	–	IMS	–	–	30/50	LS	P	GMR

🖵 Internet Access   📶 Wireless Internet Access   **WG** Waterway Guide Cruising Club Partner   onSpot dockside WiFi facility

See WaterwayGuide.com for current rates, fuel prices, web site addresses, and other up-to-the-minute information. *(Information in the table is provided by the facilities.)*

TROUT RIVER, NOAA CHART 11491

River Cut; and (4) Commodore Point. Commercial vessels must give a Sécurité call on VHF Channel 13 to avoid meeting one another at these points. Recreational boats do not need to do so (as you will have enough maneuvering room to stay out of the way), but monitor VHF Channel 13 so you will know whether you will be meeting a big ship or a tug with tow.

Dames Point–Fulton Cutoff

West of Sisters Creek and the ICW, the channel enters wide and straight Dames Point–Fulton Cutoff, dredged to eliminate a bend in the St. Johns River's natural course. The impressive high-level bridge at Mile 5.8 across the St. Johns River and Mill Cove is officially named the Napoleon Bonaparte Broward Bridge but is known by locals as the **Dames Point Bridge** (169-foot fixed vertical clearance above the main channel).

Mainly a complex of wharves, warehouses and a container terminal, Blount Island (created by dredge spoil) is on the north side of the Dames Point–Fulton

Cutoff channel. Although the loop behind the island is deep, three low bridges (with 5-, 8- and 10-foot fixed vertical clearances) prevent a complete circuit. Blount Island Marine Terminal Entrance Channel (Back River) pierces Blount Island from the Dames Point–Fulton Cutoff Channel; it is entirely commercial. Recreational craft should not attempt to anchor or fish in the channel.

Anchorage: You may anchor off Little Marsh Island east of Blount Island and across the Blount Island East Channel if necessary but be sure to stay clear of the channel. Watch for pot markers and do not interfere with the private docks along Little Marsh Island. There is no place to go ashore here, and it is very busy with commercial traffic.

A better anchorage is at Reed Island, across from Blount Island, in at least 10 feet at MLW with good holding in mud. It is open, however, to north and south wakes.

Broward and Trout Rivers

The unmarked Broward River requires local knowledge and is blocked off by a wharf extending 500 yards from shore, as well as the **Route 105 Bridge** (20-foot fixed vertical clearance) crossing the entrance. Many shallow-draft local boats use the Trout River just 2 miles to the south. (Note that the dinghy dock at the Jacksonville Zoo on the Trout River was destroyed by Hurricane Irma and there are no plans to resume waterfront access to the zoo.)

NAVIGATION: Use NOAA Chart 11491. Turn off the main St. Johns River channel between flashing red buoys "64" and "66" into the Trout River and then pick up red daybeacon "2" and green daybeacon "3," which mark the Trout River Channel. The **Main Street (U.S. 17) Bridge** (29-foot fixed vertical clearance) and the **CSX Railroad Swing Bridge** (usually open) cross the river a short distance upstream.

Dockage: Twin daybeacons red "2" and green "3" mark the entrance to Seafarer's Marina, which has some transient space and dockside and approach depths of 10 feet at MLW. Groceries and restaurants are nearby.

City of Jacksonville

NAVIGATION: Use NOAA Chart 11491. Along the St. Johns River from the ICW the posted speed limit in the channel is 25 mph between flashing red buoy "24" and flashing green buoy "25" near Mile 739.5 to the Hart-Commodore Point Bridge, just past flashing green buoy "79." Manatee zones are designated as Slow-Speed/Minimum-Speed Wake or Idle-Speed/No-Wake Zones from the channel to shore. A No-Wake Zone lies from the Hart-Commodore Bridge to the Fuller-Warren (I-95) Bridge. The St. Johns River is patrolled, and speed limits are enforced.

From the ICW crossing, the river generally winds in an east-west direction until it broadens at Hendricks Point in South Jacksonville and turns south. Most of the development is on the western shore, south of the Ortega River, ranging from summer cabins and elegant homes to large commercial complexes. The heavily industrialized riverfront (with the largest deep water harbor on the southern Atlantic coast) begins just off the Trout River near red buoy "64."

The St. Johns River runs wide and deep past the yards and wharves. About 12 miles past the high-rise Dames Point Bridge, the downtown bridges appear. At Mile 15.7 is the red **Matthews Bridge** (86-foot fixed vertical

Side Trip: Fort Caroline

About 1.7 miles west of the ICW, on the south side of the river (opposite flashing red buoy "34") at St. Johns Bluff, a national park features a recreation of French-built Fort Caroline. The French (who discovered the St. Johns River in May 1562 and called it Riviere de Mai) established North America's first Protestant settlement in 1564. They built Fort Caroline to secure their landholdings, but the Spanish, who had established St. Augustine, temporarily defeated them. Under Spanish rule it was called Fort San Mateo, but the French retook it two years later and restored its original name.

Fort Caroline is worth visiting, but the current is strong and the water, even close in, can carry 45-foot depths. It is best to rent a car in Jacksonville and drive to the fort. Do not attempt to anchor by Blount Island and then dinghy across to the fort. There is no place to land a dinghy, and the steep banks are home to rattlesnakes and water moccasins.

GOIN' ASHORE: **JACKSONVILLE, FL**

SERVICES	
1	Library
2	Visitor Information
ATTRACTIONS	
3	Jacksonville Landing
4	Museum of Contemporary Art
5	Museum of Science and History (MOSH)
6	Southbank Riverwalk
7	USS Adams Museum
SHOPPING/DINING	
3	Jacksonville Landing
MARINAS	
3	Jacksonville Landing
8	River City Brewing Co. & Marina

Following the Civil War, Jacksonville became a popular winter resort. Visitors arriving by steamboats and railroad enjoyed the mild winters, fine restaurants and hotels until Henry Flagler extended the railroad south to Palm Beach and then Miami in the 1890s.

In the early 1900s, Jacksonville promoted its mild climate, low labor cost and easy rail access to become the "Winter Film Capital of the World," with more than 30 studios. In the 1920s, local politicians forced the studios to go elsewhere, and Hollywood was born.

Jacksonville International Airport, 10 miles north of the city, has commercial air service to all major cities.

Attractions: Beyond the busy commercial area, the Jacksonville waterfront is delightful. Tranquil riverside parks and open space line the waterfront. The city's riverfront redevelopment project has included both banks of the river. On the north waterfront, Jacksonville Landing serves as a visitors center and features outdoor entertainment, a variety of dining options and more than 40 specialty shops. A state-of-the-art, interactive museum aboard the *USS Charles F. Adams* was in the final planning stages at press time in summer 2018. This is part of a long-term vision for downtown Jacksonville. Stay tuned at waterwayguide.com for updates.

Across the water is the 1.25-mile wooden zigzag boardwalk known as Southbank Riverwalk. A highlight is the Friendship Fountain, a huge, circular fountain with jets of water that shoot as high as 120 feet into the air. The fountain glows with multi-colored lights at night.

The Jacksonville Maritime Museum (MOSH) is nearby and is well worth a visit, particularly if you have children aboard. The museum features interactive exhibits like the Currents of Time, which explores 12,000 years of Northeast Florida History, and the Florida Natural Center, where visitors can get up close and personal with Northeast Florida's native wildlife. MOSH is also home to the Bryan-Gooding Planetarium–the largest single-lens planetarium in the world (1025 Museum Cir., 904-396-6674).

EverBank Field (the Gator Bowl) is also located on the north side of the river. The stadium is home to the Jacksonville Jaguars, the college postseason Gator Bowl Classic and the annual Georgia–Florida football game, often described as the "world's largest outdoor cocktail party."

Also on the north shore near EverBank Field and the 78 free transient slips is Metropolitan Park (1410 Gator Bowl Blvd., 904-630-0837). This striking tent-like outdoor auditorium is a popular site for concerts and festivals. This park also hosts the Jacksonville Fire Museum built in 1902. The Museum of Contemporary

Art (333 N. Laura St.) is also on the north side of the river.

Shopping/Dining: Restaurants and shopping can be found on both banks of the river–at Jacksonville Landing on the north side and at Southbank Riverwalk on the south side. For provisioning, Harveys Supermarket (777 N. Market St., 904-353-6810) is located about 10 blocks north of the waterfront, and the trolley will take you to a Publix (about a 10-minute bus ride).

River City Brewing Company & Marina on the south side overlooks the river and the downtown Jacksonville skyline. They are open for lunch and dinner plus offer a Sunday brunch. The deck of the Brew House is dog friendly (under 25 pounds and on a leash) so your 4-legged crew can join you while you enjoy a Red Rooster Ale or Mad Monkey Mango Wheat (seasonal beer).

clearance), followed by the green **Hart-Commodore Point Bridge** at Mile 16.6, (135-foot fixed vertical clearance at center; also known as Isaiah D. Hart Bridge). Note that tugs and barges cross the river channel at all hours of the day and night, so be cautious.

Do not call the Coast Guard directly for navigation information; listen to the *Local Notice to Mariners* broadcast on VHF Channel 22A at 8:15 a.m. and 6:15 p.m. daily or go online to navcen.uscg.gov. Navigation alerts are also updated daily on the Waterway Explorer at waterwayguide.com.

After the Hart-Commodore Bridge, the four remaining Jacksonville bridges are less than 1 mile apart. From east to west the bridges are the unmistakable blue **Main Street Lift Bridge** (Mile 18.5, 35-foot closed vertical clearance), the **Acosta Bridge** (Mile 18.9, 75-foot fixed vertical clearance), the **FEC Railroad Bascule Bridge** (Mile 18.9, 5-foot closed vertical clearance) and the **Fuller-Warren Bridge** (Mile 19.7, 75-foot fixed vertical clearance). Construction on the Main Street Lift Bridge was completed in April 2018 and it opens on signal, except from 7:00 a.m. to 8:30 a.m. and from 4:30 p.m. to 6:00 p.m., Monday through Saturday (except federal holidays), when the draw need not open for the passage of vessels. The railroad bridge is usually open, unless a train is expected. Trains cross relatively frequently, all at slow speed.

⚠ The Fuller Warren Bridge will be under construction through fall 2020. Expect floating equipment in the vicinity of the bridge to include barges, cranes and other work vessels. Future waterway restrictions may be necessary for the replacement of the bridge fender system and girder erection.

Barge traffic is common in the area of these bridges; contact the tugboat skippers on VHF Channels 13 or 16 so they can tell you how to stay out of their way. After you pass the Fuller-Warren Bridge, the river widens. The next bridge is the **Buckman (I-295) Bridge** (Mile 29.1, 65-foot fixed vertical clearance), a twin-span structure that carries eight lanes of I-295 traffic.

Dockage: Mind the current when docking in this area, as it is strong. The first facility you encounter when headed to Jacksonville is Arlington Marina, Inc. (before the Mathews Bridge), which has transient space for vessels up to 60 feet at floating concrete docks. They also sell all fuels. Next, on the north bank of the river, The City of Jacksonville operates the 78-slip

St. Johns River, FL

		Dockage				Supplies		Services					
ARLINGTON		Largest Vessel Accommodated	VHF Channel Monitored	Transient Berths / Total Berths	Approach / Dockside Depth (reported)	Floating Docks	Groceries, Ice, Marine Supplies, Snacks	Gas / Diesel	Repairs: Hull, Engine, Propeller	Lift (tonnage), Crane, Rail	Min/Max Amps	Laundry, Pool, Showers, Courtesy Car	Pump-Out Station	Nearby: Grocery Store, Motel, Restaurant
1. Arlington Marina, Inc. 🖥 WiFi 904-743-2628		60	16/68	6/30	16/5	F	GD	IMS	–	L30,R	30/50	LS	–	GR
JACKSONVILLE														
2. Metropolitan Park Marina WG 904-630-0839		80	72	78/78	30/15	F	–	–	–	–	30/50	–	P	GMR
3. The Jacksonville Landing WiFi WG 904-353-1188		–	–	–		F	–	IS	–	–	–	–	–	R
4. River City Brewing Co. & Marina 🖥 904-398-7918		120	16	10/62	18/13	F	GD	IS	–	–	30/50	LS	–	GMR

🖥 Internet Access   WiFi Wireless Internet Access   WG Waterway Guide Cruising Club Partner   🖥 onSpot dockside WiFi facility

See WaterwayGuide.com for current rates, fuel prices, web site addresses, and other up-to-the-minute information. *(Information in the table is provided by the facilities.)*

ARLINGTON, NOAA CHART 11491

JACKSONVILLE, NOAA CHART 11491

I-95

South Jacksonville

Jacksonville

St. Johns River

Metropolitan Park Marina, located adjacent to TIAA Bank Field (formerly EverBank Field), home of the Jacksonville Jaguars football team and the tent-like pavilion of Metropolitan Park. This facility is intended for public use and does not charge for dockage except during special events such as football games and concerts. The marina has no showers or laundry facilities, but shore power is available via a kiosk on the dock (for a small fee) as well as a pump-out station. Water is also available at each dock. Transients may tie up here, on a space-available basis, for up to 72 hours. You may pick up the delightful aroma of roasting coffee, coming from the Maxwell House Coffee Co. upriver where one of their three U.S. roasting plants is located.

The Jacksonville Landing, a busy public marketplace located on the north waterfront, offers 72-hour complimentary dockage on a first-come, first-served basis. There is no electricity or water and storms have reduced the dock space, but rafting is permitted. Recreational craft must stay out of the way of the sightseeing boats or the busy water taxis. Across the river, River City Brewing Co. & Marina has dockage and sells gas and diesel fuel. Courtesy slips are available for guests who are dining with them.

Anchorage: You can anchor near the Matthews Point Bridge, between Exchange Island and the Arlington waterfront, behind the City Limits Range. Holding ground is best to the east and north of the bridge in 9- to 11-foot MLW depths. With the wind out of the north, you might elect to anchor in 8 to 20 feet at MLW on the southern side of the Matthews Point Bridge, in the lee of Exchange Island. (Expect some bridge traffic noise here in a north wind.) Traffic in the main channel might jostle you on either side of the bridge; just north of the anchorage is a dock for tugs. Note that local folks may party late on the island during weekends. You may also see college rowing teams honing their skills against the swift current.

■ ORTEGA RIVER–MILE 22

Heading due south from the Fuller-Warren (I-95) Bridge, delay your westward turn until you pass flashing red buoy "2" and the orange-white daybeacon marking the shoal extending south off Winter Point. In summer 2018 there were buoys off the mouth of the Ortega River but that seems to be variable, so be sure your charts are up-to-date. If in doubt, follow a local boat in and mind

Ortega River, FL

ORTEGA RIVER		VHF Channel Monitored	Approach / Dockside Depth (reported)	Transient Berths / Total Berths	Floating Docks	Groceries, Ice, Marine Supplies, Snacks	Gas / Diesel	Repairs: Hull, Engine, Propeller	Lift (tonnage), Crane, Rail	Min/Max Amps	Laundry, Pool, Showers, Courtesy Car	Pump-Out Station	Nearby: Grocery Store, Motel, Restaurant
			Dockage				**Supplies**			**Services**			
1. The Marina at Ortega Landing 🖥 📶 WG	904-387-5538	130	16/08	20/192	6/6	F	–	I	–	–	30/100	LPS	P	GR
2. Ortega River Marina 🖥 📶	904-389-1199	60	16/08	4/99	7/6	F	–	IS	–	–	30/50	LPS	P	GR
3. Sadler Point Marine Center 🖥	904-384-1383	50	16/08	0/65	6/8	–	–	IMS	HEP	L35	30/50	S	P	GR
4. Huckins Yacht Corp. 📶 WG	**904-389-1125**	**80**	–	**call/20**	**6/6**	**F**	–	**M**	**HEP**	**L77**	**30/50**	–	–	**GR**
5. Cedar Point Marina	904-384-5577	80	–	5/24	12/6	F	–	–	–	–	30/50	LS	–	GMR
6. Lamb's Yacht Center 🖥 📶 WG	904-384-5577	120	16/08	12/240	8/7	–	GD	IMS	HEP	L100, R40	30/100	LSC	P	GR
7. Florida Yacht Club-PRIVATE	904-387-1653	70	16/68	call/73	8/6	F	–	IS	–	–	30/50	PS	–	GR

🖥 Internet Access 📶 Wireless Internet Access WG Waterway Guide Cruising Club Partner 🌀 onSpot dockside WiFi facility
See WaterwayGuide.com for current rates, fuel prices, web site addresses, and other up-to-the-minute information. *(Information in the table is provided by the facilities.)*

ORTEGA RIVER, NOAA CHART 11491

the charted obstructions and pilings north of Sadler Point; large local yachts use the entrance regularly. Depths here are 5 to 8 feet at MLW in the river (with shallower spots), so watch the depth sounder, and proceed slowly, especially if you have a draft of 5 feet or more. The tidal range is about 1 foot.

For deepest water, give a wide berth to the shoal off Sadler Point and line up for the **Ortega River Bridge** (9-foot closed vertical clearance) after you are clear

of the shallow water. The 1920s-vintage classic bridge opens on request. Because of its low clearance in an area of high marine traffic, this is the most frequently opened drawbridge in Florida (about 15,000 openings per year).

The water is relatively consistent beyond the fixed **Roosevelt Blvd. Bridge** (45-foot vertical clearance), with 5- to 8-foot MLW depths. A busy **CSX Railroad Bascule Bridge** (2-foot closed vertical clearance, opens on signal) crosses the Ortega River just past the Roosevelt Blvd. Bridge.

Dockage: The Ortega River (known as "Jacksonville Marina Mile") has an almost solid wall of yards, marinas and boatbuilders on the northwest bank. The Marina at Ortega Landing is the first marina to starboard when heading upstream and is part of a residential development. This marina has full cruiser amenities, including a pool and loaner bikes. Next upstream is the Ortega River Marina with transient slips on floating docks. It is close to shopping, a West Marine, restaurants and rental cars. Advance reservations are required.

Just before the railroad bridge is Sadler Point Marine Center, which offers a full service and do-it-yourself boatyard with a 35-ton lift. They do not have transient slips.

Immediately to starboard past the railroad bridge is Huckins Yacht Corp., known for its beautiful custom yachts. Frank Pembroke Huckins was instrumental in designing the famous PT boats of World War II. The company was originally located in what is now the Maxwell House Coffee Co. near the Jacksonville waterfront but after the war, it moved to its present location. They offer slips, sell diesel from a truck (with 24-hour notice) and have 77-ton lift for large repairs. Call ahead for slip availability.

Nearby Cedar Point Marina has dockage to 80 feet and some reserved transient space. To the south, the large full-service Lamb's Yacht Center has transient slips, all fuels and extensive repair capabilities. They are capable of hauling power cats. (Sailors Exchange, which used to be located here, closed in 2016.)

The southwest shore is entirely residential, with private docks and wooded plots. The only problem in finding a berth here may be choosing among the yards and marinas, many of which welcome transients. All of the marinas are close to Roosevelt Square, which is four or five blocks from the waterfront. It has a large variety of shore amenities (restaurants and shops, a pharmacy, a West Marine and a large grocery store). There is also convenient city bus service here that runs to downtown Jacksonville.

If you are planning on continuing south on the St. Johns River, this is the last place to conveniently provision the boat. There are stores along the St. Johns, but you will need ground transportation to get to most of them, which could be a problem in some of the small, out-of-the-way places you'll encounter.

Anchorage: A few boats can anchor, with care, in the open spaces between the various boatyards and marinas. This is a busy area, so minimizing your swinging room will be important. Keep clear of the channel and set an anchor light at night. Naturally, you should get permission from the marinas before you tie up your dinghy. A better anchorage is on the south shore between the Ortega River Bridge and the Roosevelt Blvd. Bridge in 6- to 7-foot MLW depths with good holding in mud.

■ TO GREEN COVE SPRINGS

The St. Johns River seems to transform itself into a lake immediately beyond the Ortega River, with widths averaging a couple of miles or more for most of the 54 miles to Palatka. This section is great for sailing, although strong winds out of the north or south can kick up quite a chop. Deep water stretches from shore to shore, providing plenty of room for a sailor to make long, pleasant reaches.

Ortego River Bridge

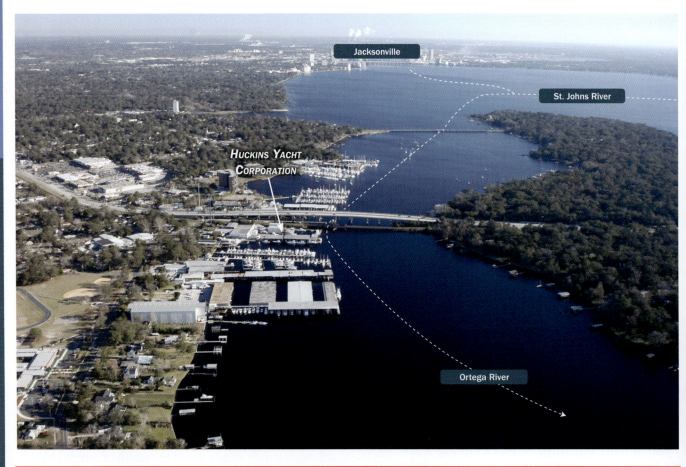

Jacksonville

St. Johns River

HUCKINS YACHT CORPORATION

Ortega River

To the Buckman (I-295) Bridge

NAVIGATION: Use Chart 11492. Even when the going is tranquil, it is wise to run compass courses for each lengthy reach between the daybeacons and lights, making sure you always have a good idea of your position. This country is great for fishing and crabbing, but the bobbing floats of the commercial crabber's pots–some of which are dark and difficult to see–are numerous enough to warrant close attention. All along the St. Johns River shoreline, remnants of old docks, some submerged, can be hazardous and warrant a lookout.

Dockage: About 2 miles past the entrance to the Ortega River, at Pirates Cove on the western shore, is the Florida Yacht Club. It is one of the country's oldest yacht clubs and is open only to its members and members of clubs that belong to the Florida Council of Yacht Clubs or by approval in advance by the Board of Directors.

Anchorage: Beyond Goodbys Creek, on the eastern side of the river, you can anchor in Plummers Cove between Beauclerc Bluff and the Buckman Bridge, also known locally as **Three Mile Bridge** (65-foot fixed vertical clearance). The entrance is straightforward. Just avoid the shoal off Beauclerc Bluff, which is marked by green daybeacon "9." Go in at the approximate middle of the "entrance," dodging the pot markers that sometimes pepper both the entrance and interior. Note shoaling along the shoreline and sound your way in. Choose your weather carefully, as this anchorage has no protection from the west, should a thunderstorm blow through. Anchor in depths of 6 to 8 feet at MLW. The holding is good in mud. You will hear some noise from the naval air station across the river at Piney Point.

Doctors Lake–Mile 32

About 2 miles south of the Buckman Bridge, on the west side of the St. Johns River, is Doctors Lake, 4 miles long and in many places deep (7- to 10-foot MLW depths) almost to the banks. The lake is beautiful and protected, and its wooded shores are dotted with homes, many with their own docks.

NAVIGATION: Use NOAA Chart 11492. The entrance to Doctors Lake, spanned by the **Park Ave. (Hwy. 17) Bridge** (37-foot fixed vertical clearance), is off Orange Point and marked by red daybeacon "2," which has been moved farther away from shore toward the channel. Stay

St. Johns River, FL

		Largest Vessel Accommodated	VHF Channel Monitored	Approach / Dockside Depth (reported)	Transient Berths / Total Berths	Floating Docks	Groceries, Ice, Marine Supplies, Snacks	Gas / Diesel	Repairs: Hull, Engine, Propeller	Lift (tonnage), Crane, Rail	Min/Max Amps	Laundry, Pool, Showers, Courtesy Car	Nearby: Grocery Store, Motel, Restaurant	Pump-Out Station
DOCTORS LAKE				**Dockage**			**Supplies**		**Services**					
1. Doctors Lake Marina WiFi	904-264-0505	70	–	2/100	7/6	–	GD	GIMS	HEP	–	30/50	LS	P	GR
JULINGTON CREEK														
2. Mandarin Holiday Marina	904-268-1036	50	16/68	5/150	6/6	–	GD	GIMS	HEP	L15	30/30	S	P	GMR
3. Julington Creek Marina	904-268-5117	40	16/09	call/326	6/5	–	G	IMS		L12	30/30	–	P	GR

🖥 Internet Access WiFi Wireless Internet Access WG Waterway Guide Cruising Club Partner onSpot dockside WiFi facility
See WaterwayGuide.com for current rates, fuel prices, web site addresses, and other up-to-the-minute information. *(Information in the table is provided by the facilities.)*

DOCTORS LAKE, JULINGTON CREEK, NOAA CHART 11492

clear of the shoaling on both sides of Doctors Inlet and steer toward the middle of the entrance.

Dockage: Doctors Lake Marina is located just inside the bridge on the south shore of Doctors Inlet with slips and gas and diesel. Eight miles of paths for walking and bicycling provide access to restaurants, laundry, pharmacies and a grocery. Additional slips were installed in 2018; call ahead for availability.

Fleming Island Marina on the south side of Doctors Inlet was closed at press time in summer 2018.

⚠ Note that fuel may not be available between Doctors Lake and Monroe Harbor (where diesel can be delivered as needed by truck with a two-day advance notice).

Anchorage: If you can clear the 37-foot fixed vertical clearance bridge and decide to anchor in Doctors Lake, do so with care because the holding in some places is poor, with very fine, soft silt.

In west through northwest winds, anchor above Peoria Point in Sugarhouse Cove; in strong northerly winds, try close in to the shore, between Macks Point and Indigo Branch; in heavy easterly weather, try the mouth of Mill Cove. In all places, be certain to power down on your hook and check it frequently. You will find 7 to 12 feet at MLW here; respect the charted submerged piling areas. Do not anchor in the middle of the lake except in an emergency; it is far too exposed.

Julington Creek–Mile 35

Almost directly across the St. Johns River from Doctors Lake is Julington Creek, with a fixed bridge (**Julington Creek Bridge**) with 15-foot vertical clearance and shallow depths beyond the bridge.

Dockage: Mandarin Holiday Marina is located before the fixed bridge, while Julington Creek Marina is after the bridge. Both accept transients. Gas and repairs are available at both; diesel is also available at Manderin Holiday.

Anchorage: Julington Creek is shoaling, so sound your way in, and check the depth of your swinging arc if you choose to anchor here. Above the opening, the creek shoals quickly to 4-foot MLW depths or less, especially on the north side. For larger boats, the more exposed Old Bull Bay at Julington Creek's mouth is a good anchorage with shelter from north through southeast winds. This attractive area is especially good for dinghy exploration. You will find 7- to 8-foot MLW depths on a line between the points of land and 4 to 6 feet at MLW closer to the bridge. South of Mandarin Point, there is 11 feet at MLW. It is protected from the north and northeast but should be used only in stable weather.

Black Creek–Mile 40

Black Creek empties into the St. Johns River just north of Green Cove Springs on the western bank of the St. Johns River at Wilkies Point. The creek is deep, placid, unspoiled and offers a microcosm of the world's subtropical rivers. If you make the trip in late spring or summer, don't be surprised if you disturb a slumbering alligator along the banks.

The **Black Creek (US 17) Twin Bridges** at the entrance have a fixed vertical clearance of 30 feet, and upstream is another bridge with a fixed vertical clearance of 20 feet. An overhead cable with an authorized vertical clearance of 47 feet also crosses the creek about 2 miles above the first bridge. If you can get under all of these (or have your mast unstepped at a nearby marina), you can cruise upriver to the headwaters and the town of Middleburg, which rivals St. Augustine as one of the

nation's oldest settlements. A grocery store is a pleasant walk from the Middleburg waterfront, but there are no transient docks.

Anchorage: You can anchor in Black Creek in at least 15 feet at MLW with good holding in mud and all-around protection. Continuing on the St. Johns River upriver from Black Creek, both banks offer coves with safe overnight spots. Most of these are obvious on the charts. You need only select a cove on the east or west bank, depending upon the wind direction at the time of your arrival. Most of the bottom here is sticky black mud, good holding for a well-set hook. Usually a current sets with the tide as far as Lake George. South of the lake, the weak current sets downstream (northward).

Green Cove Springs–Mile 44

The town of Green Cove Springs is on a very shallow, pretty cove off the St. Johns River. Here, the long piers of a World War II Navy facility jut out into the river. These piers clearly show up on the chart for the area.

Green Cove Springs took its name from the sulfur mineral spring found here. Long reputed to have medicinal qualities, the waters attracted many famous visitors in the late 1800s and early 1900s. Today, visitors will find the spring in the midst of a city park fringed with fine old homes. St. Mary's Episcopal Church, built in the late 19th century, is an elegant riverfront structure. The town is home to St. Brendan's Isle, a well-known cruiser's mail forwarding service.

Dockage/Moorings: The 12 floating finger boat slips allow visitors to dock and explore the City of Green Cove Springs. The depth is 8 to 9 feet at MLW. All slips are available on a first-come, first-served basis. An envelope will be available for leaving the payment in the drop box at the pier.

The next three facilities are in a row: Holland Marine (a boatyard that does not accept transients); Reynolds Park Yacht Center (may have transient space and also offers repairs); and Green Cove Springs Marina (with deep water slips on floating docks for vessels to 100 feet). If Green Cove Springs does not have space available at the dock, a mooring may be available; call ahead for details. Green Cove Springs Marina is a well-protected spot popular for long-term storage. The marina also has on-site approved contractors for painting, mechanical, electrical repair, bottom work and canvas, as well as a marine supply store.

You won't find fuel here, but what you will find is a bank, pharmacy and several eateries within six blocks of the dock. Provisioning can be done at a supermarket located about 1.25 miles north of town. Home Depot, Target, Walmart, Publix and other amenities are another 12 or so miles north (transportation required).

Anchorage: Governors Creek, just north of the town, has a boat ramp and fishing pier with a dinghy dock. Watch for the charted overhead power lines (30-foot vertical clearances) and fixed bridges (8- and 11-foot vertical clearances, respectively) heading upstream as you enter. Boats may anchor at the mouth of Governors Creek in 8 feet at MLW with fair holding in mud. This is open from the north through southeast. There is quite a bit of highway noise here.

Across the river, between Popo Point and the Shands Bridge at Orangedale (Mile 41.5) is another anchorage. Note the shoal water south of Hallowes Cove, as well as the 3-foot MLW spot northeast of flashing red "20." Enter well southeast of flashing red "20," avoiding the charted cable area. Protection is good only from the northeast, but holding is excellent in 7 to 10 feet at MLW.

■ GREEN COVE SPRINGS TO PALATKA

....

NAVIGATION: Use NOAA Charts 11487 and 11492. It is a 28-mile journey along the river's wooded and narrow banks from the Shands Bridge at Green Cove Springs to Palatka. Fish weirs (stakes) and numerous pot

markers populate the river hereabouts. At Mile 47.9 the **Shands Bridge** (45-foot fixed vertical clearance) sets the overhead clearance for the upper St. Johns River and runs across the river between Red Bay and Smith Points. (Construction of a new replacement 65-foot bridge will not begin until 2023.) When transiting the Green Cove Springs area, stick to the marked channel to avoid both charted shoals and possible submerged obstructions.

Beam winds, particularly from the west, can be very strong here, so mind the chart plotter or remain lined up on the visual ranges if you have a deep draft. Palatka's high and low tides happen about 7.25 and 8.5 hours, respectively, after Mayport's tides. The water depth in the channel ranges from 8 to 12 feet at MLW. The tidal range is about 1 foot.

Heading south from Green Cove Springs, the first of four ranges starts about 10 miles past the Shands Bridge. Align flashing white "29" and flashing white "31" as a back range if you need the deep channel to fixed green "33." This one leads into the second, which takes you past Ninemile Point and leads into the third range, which passes south of Verdiere Point. After rounding Forrester Point, you can pick up a range for the commercial channel to Hog Eye Point near Palatka.

Dockage: Trout Creek Marina may have space for you on their floating docks and they sell all fuels.

Anchorage: To the south of the Shands Bridge, Trout Creek enters the St. Johns River on the north side of Palmo Cove, around the east end of Jack Wright Island (Mile 48). Trout Creek is a popular anchorage, but note

Doctors Lake

that there is a fixed bridge about 0.5 miles up the creek. The official listed vertical clearance is 14 feet at high water, but locals report a few feet more. Trout Creek is a deep and gorgeous stream.

Navionics Sonar depths indicate depths of 6 feet at MLW in Palmo Cove and some underwater humps approaching the creek, where depths immediately increase to 9 feet or more, then 6 feet or more on the midline above the bridge.

About 4 miles upriver (south) from the Shands Bridge on the St. Johns River, there is a scenic cove on the west side of the river south of Bayard Point and north of another unmarked shoal northeast of Clark Creek. Depths are 9 to 10 feet at MLW in this cove, which is protected from the northwest and offers good holding in sandy mud. Sound your way in while dodging the pot markers that are often set here.

Four miles farther south and on the east side of the St. Johns River is Solano Cove, with 6- to 7-foot MLW depths and good holding. It is open to the northwest through south. To the south at Mile 64 is an excellent, remote, quiet anchorage at Deep Creek with all-around protection and good holding in mud. It has a tricky entrance, however, best navigated with the Navionics Sonar Chart.

Palatka–Mile 76

Palatka retains the ambiance of an old river town. A city park along the riverfront has picnic shelters, boat ramps and restrooms, and brick-paved residential streets run beneath grand old oaks hung with Spanish moss. A long walk from the marinas south of the bridge is Ravine Gardens State Park at 1600 Twigg St. The 59-acre state park was built in 1933 around natural ravines. The nature trails wander among thousands of azaleas and other ornamental plants growing near streams and ravines. There are picnic grounds and jogging trails. The park is open daily from 8:00 a.m. to sundown (386-329-3721).

Dockage: North of Palatka, about 1 mile west of flashing green "41," is Crystal Cove Resort Marina. This marina's docks were totally refurbished in the spring of 2018. The Quality Inn & Suites Riverfront, just to the north of **Palatka Memorial Bridge** (65-foot closed vertical clearance), has berths reserved only for guests staying at the hotel.

Past the bridge to starboard is the Palatka City Dock. Space is available on a first-come, first-served basis for boats up to 50 feet. There is no power, water or other amenities. At Mile 77.5 there are other city docks with shore power and water. A ship store, restrooms, showers and a coin-operated laundry are also provided. There is a minimal fee for overnight dockage. Shopping and restaurants are a few blocks away.

Boathouse Marina, south of the town dock, offers slips with full amenities. Transient dockage is available. You should head for the dock approximately midway between flashing green "1" and flashing red "2." Approach and dockside depths of 8 feet at MLW are reported. The town is just 3 blocks away. It is advisable to contact the marina in advance for reservations.

St. Johns River, FL

			Dockage					Supplies		Services				
		Largest Vessel Accommodated	VHF Channel Monitored	Transient Berths / Total Berths	Approach / Dockside Depth (reported)	Floating Docks	Gas / Diesel	Groceries, Ice, Marine Supplies, Snacks	Repairs: Hull, Engine, Propeller	Lift (tonnage), Crane, Rail	Min/Max Amps	Laundry, Pool, Showers, Courtesy Car	Pump-Out Station	Nearby: Grocery Store, Motel, Restaurant
GREEN COVE SPRINGS														
1. Green Cove Springs City Pier	904-297-7060	–	–	12/12	8/8	F	–	–	–	–	30/50	–	–	GR
2. Holland Marine	904-284-3349	65	–	0/15	10/10	F	–	M	HEP	L65,C	30/50	–	–	GMR
3. Reynolds Park Yacht Center 🖥 WiFi	904-284-4667	400	16/68	10/70	12/6	F	–	M	HEP	L60	30/200+	LS	P	MR
4. **Green Cove Springs Marina** 🖥 WiFi	**904-284-1811**	100	16/68	5/21	14/11	F	–	IM	HEP	L30,C	30/50	LS	P	GMR
TROUT CREEK														
5. Trout Creek Marina	904-342-2471	–	–	12/13	7/	F	GD	GIMS	–	–	30/30	–	–	G
PALATKA, SAN MATEO														
6. Crystal Cove Resort Marina WiFi	386-325-1055	–	–	call/45	5/5	–	G	IS	HEP	–	30/50	PS	–	MR
7. Quality Inn & Suites Riverfront 🖥 WiFi	386-328-3481	100	–	21/21	25/8	–	–	IS	–	–	30/50	LPS	–	GMR
8. Palatka City Dock	386-329-0100	50	–	14/14	9/6	F	–	–	–	–	30/30	–	P	MR
9. Boathouse Marina 🖥 WiFi	386-328-2944	60	16	10/40	8/8	–	–	IS	–	–	30/50	LS	P	GMR
10. Gibson Dry Docks 🖥 WiFi	386-325-5502	49	–	0/20	6/6	–	–	–	HEP	L30	30/30	S	–	GMR

🖥 Internet Access   WiFi Wireless Internet Access   WG Waterway Guide Cruising Club Partner   onSpot dockside WiFi facility

See WaterwayGuide.com for current rates, fuel prices, web site addresses, and other up-to-the-minute information. *(Information in the table is provided by the facilities.)*

GREEN COVE SPRINGS, TROUT CREEK, NOAA CHART 11492

PALATKA, SAN MATEO, NOAA CHART 11487

South of Palatka, just east of flashing red "12" at San Mateo, is Gibson Dry Docks, a repair facility that allows owners to do their own work. They have a 30-ton lift but no dockage for transients.

Corky Bells' Seafood at Gator Landing (386-325-1094) is at Devils Elbow in East Palatka (across from flashing red "6"). They have a dock and will let you do some nearby shopping if you eat a meal there. Nearby is a large hardware store, a drugstore and an independent grocery store.

Anchorage: At Mile 73 you can anchor north of Palatka along the east shore near the power cables below Cow Creek. This has good holding in 9 to 11 feet at MLW. Carman Cove at Maritoni Point, just east of flashing green "47," is another option. Sound your way in. The holding is good in mud and silt. Note that both of these anchorages are wide open to northwest through southeast winds.

There is some anchoring room south of the bridge, on the west side of the river between the bridge and the city dock. There is good depth here (12 to 15 feet) with good holding in mud and silt. Sound your way in and use an anchor light at night, making sure to stop well off the channel to clear tug and barge traffic. Stay to the north to avoid shoal areas. Avoid Wilson Cove, which is situated south of the bridge on the west side of the river. An old sawmill here was removed years ago, but the abandoned wrecks, stumps and sunken logs make passage treacherous.

Porters Cove, approximately 3.3 miles upriver from the Palatka Bridge at Mile 76.5, has good protection from the west and fair protection from the northwest and southwest. The cove, with wooded banks, is between the overhead power cables at River Crest and flashing red "12" on the west side of the river. Sound your way in to anchor in 8- to 10-foot MLW depths. Keep an eye out for the plentiful osprey nests here, which have Spanish moss woven in with the usual twigs and sticks.

■ PALATKA TO LAKE GEORGE

Past the Palatka Memorial Bridge, the St. Johns River puts on its most beautiful face, reminiscent of the quiet, winding Waccamaw River, just north of Georgetown, SC. For 80 miles, the scenery varies, and you can enjoy an array of villages, towns and anchorages. Use the most current charts for marks at shoals and other hazards, and note that bird nests change the apparent shape or obscure the numbers of some markers. All the way to Lake Monroe, osprey architecture (nest building) on the daybeacons grows more profuse, so look carefully.

Much of the area is undeveloped and excellent for bird watching. Anhingas (snakebirds) can be seen sitting on logs and drying their wings, and you may spot a bald eagle. All types of wildlife call this home, including playful otters, lazily swimming manatees and sleepy alligators sunning along the shore.

This part of Florida has a unique hazard: Blind mosquitoes. An invasive species that is neither blind nor a mosquito, these non-biting insects swarm and mate into permanent flying unions for a short period in springtime. They can cover your boat with their fiberglass-staining carcasses. Ask before you get here if the annual hatch of these pests has occurred.

Fishing is good, but remember that you need a Florida license if you are between 16 and 65 years old. This is part of the St. Johns River that you will be glad you did not miss.

NAVIGATION: Use NOAA Charts 11487 and 11495. From here upriver to Welaka, about 20 miles away, the relatively narrow St. Johns River has navigational aids and adequate depths for barge traffic. Many of the boats you will encounter here are fishing skiffs and rented pontoon boats. Use caution around the rental boats, as their skippers may not be highly skilled in the art of boat handling. Fish traps, stakes, submerged pilings and shoaling, usually along the banks, require your attention at all times, so follow the markers carefully, cruise slowly and take no shortcuts.

At the foot of Murphy Island is winding Dunns Creek, a wilderness stream with a controlling depth of 5 feet. It leads through 8 miles of untamed country to Crescent Lake (about 10 miles long with depths of 7 to 13 feet). The creek itself has several very sharp turns, but both Dunns Creek and Murphy Creek make for lovely gunkholing.

Once past the common mouths of Murphy and Dunns Creeks, proceed marker to marker. Two hard sand shoals extend from Murphy Island almost into the south side

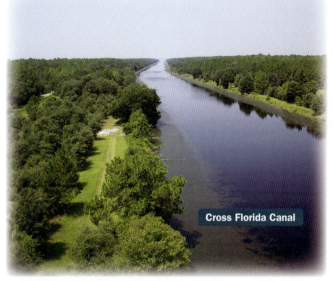

Cross Florida Canal

of the channel. Favor the north side of the river just before and at flashing green "23" to avoid shoaling and submerged pilings. Near green daybeacon "27" at Mile 86.5, the **Buffalo Bluff Bascule Railroad Bridge** (7-foot closed vertical clearance) is normally open, but closes 20 to 30 minutes before trains arrive, several times a day. The bridgetender responds on VHF Channel 09 and is usually on duty during the day.

When approaching Welaka from red daybeacon "42A" to flashing red "52," check your chart, and watch the depth sounder carefully for shoals in mid-river; some are marked, but many are not.

Dockage: There is a free dock at Murphy Island with over 20 feet at MLW. It is somewhat exposed to the southwest and southeast and wakes.

Anchorage: Browns Landing, which is approximately 7.5 miles south of Palatka, has a good anchorage. Leave the channel between flashing red "16" and red daybeacon "18" and head north. Holding is good in 10- to 14-foot depths. Watch for the shoal marked by red daybeacon "18." There is a dock and boat ramp located here for shore access for your four-legged crewmembers.

A snug anchorage is in Murphy Creek where it crosses Dunns Creek. Enter in the middle of the Dunns Creek mouth at Rat Island between pilings and pot markers. Watch the depth sounder and proceed slowly; you should find at least 5- to 7-foot MLW depths in the channel, but depths are far less outside. Murphy Creek is to starboard about 0.5-mile ahead and has pilings on both sides. Anchor anywhere past the pilings in 7- to 20-foot MLW depths. Crab pots are the only signs of civilization here among the pristine wooded banks.

St. Johns River, FL

			Largest Vessel Accommodated	VHF Channel Monitored	Approach / Dockside Depth (reported)	Transient Berths / Total Berths	Floating Docks	Gas / Diesel	Groceries, Ice, Marine Supplies, Snacks	Repairs: Hull, Engine, Propeller	Lift (tonnage), Crane, Rail	Min/Max Amps	Laundry, Pool, Showers, Courtesy Car	Pump-Out Station	Nearby: Grocery Store, Motel, Restaurant
WELAKA AREA					Dockage				Supplies		Services				
1. Acosta Creek Marina (WiFi)	386-467-2229		80	16/68	4/40	16/12	–	–	M	HEP	L25	30/50	LPS	P	MR
2. Welaka City Dock-Bryants Landing (WiFi)	386-467-9800		–	–	10/10	15/10	F	–	IS	–		–	S	–	GMR
GEORGETOWN															
3. Georgetown Marina, Lodge & RV Park ☐ (WiFi)	386-467-2002		70	16/68	7/7	12/5.5	–	G	IMS	–		30/50	LS	P	M

☐ Internet Access　(WiFi) Wireless Internet Access　**WG** Waterway Guide Cruising Club Partner　⊙ onSpot dockside WiFi facility

See WaterwayGuide.com for current rates, fuel prices, web site addresses, and other up-to-the-minute information. *(Information in the table is provided by the facilities.)*

WELAKA AREA, NOAA CHART 11495

GEORGETOWN, NOAA CHART 11495

About 1.5 miles south of Dunns Creek, a good spot lies in the first bend of the S-turn leading to the **Buffalo Bluff Railroad Bridge** (7-foot closed vertical clearance). When headed south, the half-mile sign (small, white and illegible) is between green daybeacon "25" and flashing red "26." You must make the northwest turn before you see the bridge. You have to get closer still before you will spot the draw, on the southeast (port) side close to shore. You will find 14 to 17 feet at MLW and plenty of swinging room in the space between the daybeacon and the southeast shore. Keep clear of the fish traps just inshore to the south and set an anchor light.

A comfortable anchorage lies between the land and the northeast side of the most northern of the Seven Sisters Islands at Mile 87 past the Buffalo Bluff Railroad Bridge. Enter opposite flashing red "28," favoring the landward side. Watch the depth sounder and stay away from the shoal area off the islet's upper tip. This anchorage is well protected and quiet, despite the houses along the northeast shore. Note the charted 6-foot spot at the entrance to this creek. The Seven Sisters area provides many anchoring possibilities; however, shore access for pets may be difficult to find.

Just before the Cross-Florida Barge Canal entrance (see sidebar) is Stokes Landing and Stokes Island. Stokes Landing features several boatyards, one of which maintains small ships. From time to time, handsome mega-yachts are hauled for repairs here, looking out of place in the isolated, jungle-like setting. Behind Stokes Island, you will find 8- to 9-foot MLW depths.

Welaka–Mile 96

Between the Buffalo Bluff Railroad Bridge and Welaka, the early morning sun and ground fog might make it difficult to see the markers. Also, the bird nests built on the pilings obscure some marker numbers along the way and can change the shapes of triangles into squares.

Now a sleepy hamlet, Welaka was once a bustling steamboat depot for the transportation of wood, produce and tourists. Ulysses S. Grant was a passenger on the steamboat that made the trip from Welaka up the Ocklawaha River to its headwaters at Silver Springs, one of Florida's early tourist attractions. Nowadays, elegant antique steamboats rendezvous here. Welaka is also home to one of the river's upscale fishing, vacation and conference resorts, the Floridian Sports Club.

Welaka is a good stopover area about halfway up the river. You might want to visit the Welaka National Fish

Side Trip: Cross-Florida Canal

A couple of miles beyond the Buffalo Bluff Railroad Bridge (NOAA Chart 11495), the entrance to the Cross-Florida Greenway (officially named the Marjorie Harris Carr Cross Florida Greenway) is to starboard and marked by red-green "C" opposite Trout Island. A series of historic events transformed this corridor from one of the nation's largest uncompleted public works project to a 110-mile greenway. It offers hiking, biking, equestrian and paddling trails, boat ramps, fishing spots and campgrounds. If you fancy a bit of real exploring in Old Florida and have a fast dinghy, it can make an fine side trip.

Before going through the canal (located west of green daybeacon "33A"), call ahead for depths and the operating hours of the Buckman Lock (386-329-3575). In June 2018, the lock was tended on Thursday through Sunday from 7:00 a.m. to 3:00 p.m. on a posted schedule. The channel from the St. Johns River has been dredged to 12 feet MLW but can be a few feet less.

On the other side of the lock is Rodman Reservoir, also known as Lake Ocklawaha, created from the Ocklawaha River. While many small fishing and pontoon boats use the lake, depths of 5 to 7 feet MLW and numerous snags make anchoring a cruising vessel outside the channel impractical. Although the upper river was cleared after Hurricane Irma in 2017, the lock tender echoes local consensus when he says, "There's no way I'd take a bigger boat up the Ocklawaha." That's a long way from a hundred years ago when big passenger and freight steamboats plied the river up to Lake Eustis.

This section and a 9-mile canal on the west coast at Yankeetown were the only two portions of the Cross-Florida Barge Canal completed before public opposition–caused by environmental concerns and right-of-way problems–halted the project in 1971.

Numerous navigational aids mark the completed section of the canal from the St. Johns River to the Ocklawaha River and through the Rodman Reservoir.

Every few years, in winter, the water is drawn down to a much lower level. Contact the Office of Greenways and Trails at 352-236-7143 for the latest canal conditions and bridge and cable clearances.

Hatchery and Aquarium, where striped bass are hatched and grown for reintroduction to other rivers.

NAVIGATION: Use NOAA Chart 11495. In this section of the St. Johns River, crabbers are about as likely to set their traps (also called "pots") in the channel as out of it. Just south of Welaka, at flashing red "52," the Ocklawaha River flows into the St. Johns River, carrying water that originally surfaced at Silver Springs.

South of Welaka to Lake George, a good part of the channel is dredged. Pay attention to markers, watch for lateral drift and keep the depth sounder on because it is easy to get out of the channel. In spots, depths are only 2 to 3 feet at MLW on both sides. Follow the channel carefully from red daybeacon "54" to flashing red daybeacon "58" and again between red daybeacon "60" and flashing green daybeacon "65," as it is narrow with shoaling on both sides.

Two ferries cross the channel in this area and deserve your attention. The Fort Gates Ferry is about 4 miles south of Welaka at Mile 101; it crosses just south of the overhead power cable between Buzzards Point and Mount Royal at flashing green "61." It is the oldest operating ferry in Florida. The second ferry is 8 miles south of Welaka at Mile 105 (Georgetown), south of flashing red "70." It provides the only vehicular connection between the mainland and Drayton Island. These antique ferries serve unpaved roads.

Dockage: Acosta Creek Marina, near red daybeacon "42A," is built around a charming old Florida river house and offers transient and long-term dockage. The marina also has dry storage and a do-it-yourself yard. Several restaurants dot the river within a couple of miles of the marina. There is a city dock in Welaka (Bryant's Landing) with good water depths but no services.

Anchorage: Several places around Turkey Island have good holding and 8- to 17-foot MLW depths, but watch for shoals near green daybeacon "43," flashing green daybeacon "45" and around the islets at the entrance. Anchor inside, past the islets; Navionics Sonar Charts are useful here.

A good secluded anchorage where, if you are lucky, you can see deer feeding on water hyacinths, is in the curve of the St. Johns River, east and behind Buzzards Point, in 13 feet at MLW. Entering from the west, turn off the channel halfway between flashing green "59" and red "60," avoiding the charted 6-foot shoal. Leaving the anchorage, follow the water's edge in 13 feet of water until a course due south brings you to flashing

green "61A," avoiding the 3-foot shoal to starboard. The anchorage is protected in northerly and easterly winds but is also prone to wakes from local fishing boats.

Another pretty spot to drop the hook is 1.5 miles south of Little Lake George in Fruitland Cove, on the eastern shore of the St. Johns River. You will find good shelter here from north through east winds, and the many houses along the shore prevent any feelings of isolation. Watch the depth sounder and you can anchor out of the channel by flashing green "63" in 8 to 11 feet at MLW but avoid the cable area shown on the chart.

Lake George—Mile 107 to Mile 118

NAVIGATION: Use NOAA Chart 11495. The first of the large lakes in the St. Johns River, Lake George is 75 miles south of Jacksonville. This 11-mile-long lake is 5 miles wide with a straight, deep channel that can be rough when winds are strong up or down its length. The lake is the site of a Navy bombing range. As the charts show, the range runs parallel to the channel along three sets of pilings and encompasses much of the eastern half of the lake. The rim is marked by tall pilings, while shorter pilings mark the target area. Avoid it!

Markers for the channel across the lake are easy to see. A hyacinth fence at the south end of the lake looks like a long set of bridge fenders; the channel across the Volusia Bar is between the fenders, while outside it are rocks and declining depths. The area is posted as a Slow-Speed/Manatee Zone. All the range markers for Lake George have been removed.

Two beautiful springs in the Ocala National Forest on the west shore of Lake George draw many visitors by boat and by road: Salt Springs and Silver Glen Springs. In settled weather, you can anchor a short distance offshore and dinghy into the shallow creeks that lead to the springs. Go on a weekday to avoid crowds.

Salt Springs is at the head of a long, winding creek west of green daybeacon "3" just after you enter the lake from the north. Silver Glen Springs (a state park) is farther south, west of green daybeacon "9." Both have marked entrances but not much water depth.

These two springs feature crystal-clear water at a constant 72 degrees year-round. Bring a mask and snorkel and enjoy watching the underwater wildlife.

Dockage: In Georgetown on the north side of Lake George, the Georgetown Marina, Lodge & RV Park has a few transient slips, gas and a pump-out station.

Astor Hwy. Bascule Bridge

■ ASTOR TO LAKE MONROE

Once through Lake George, you will enter yet another beautiful part of the river, continuing toward Lake Monroe. Much of the area is undeveloped and part of a wildlife sanctuary.

The river deepens towards Astor, about 4 miles south of Lake George. Fishing camps and waterside restaurants surround the Astor Hwy. Bascule Bridge. Waterfront homeowners with docks and boat slips in the Astor area have rigged various devices–PVC pipes, float lines, fences, etc.–to keep water hyacinths from building up and choking access to the river. Without such devices, the docks become surrounded by plant life and look as if they were constructed inland.

Manatee regulations upriver from Astor are strictly enforced. From here to Lake Monroe, keep an eye out for bald eagles, anhingas, ibises, herons and egrets. In the cool months, alligators migrate south to Lake Harney, but if the winter is warm, chances are you will find many of them in the river.

NAVIGATION: Use NOAA Chart 11495. Astor enforces its no-wake law strictly, so be sure to slow down between the signs. At Mile 123, the **Astor Hwy. Bascule Bridge** (20-foot closed vertical clearance) monitors VHF Channels 09 and 16 and opens on signal. Note that the bridge span hangs over the channel when open at a height of 72 feet. The overhead power cable north of the bridge has been reported by the Coast Guard to have less than its charted 50-foot vertical clearance but an exact measurement was not provided.

Dredged cuts have eliminated many turns in the St. Johns River channel. Bars block entrance to many of the oxbows that show deep water inside. Overhanging foliage sometimes obscures daybeacons here, adding confusion to some of the cuts where the natural course of the river makes abrupt turns off the channel (with some turns actually wider than the channel itself). The markers are there, however, so go slow, pay attention and enjoy the beauty of this special place.

As the crow flies, Lake Dexter is 4.5 miles south of Astor and less than 20 miles from Lake Monroe. On the river, however, it is more like 30 miles through a wilderness broken only by a few marinas. The route is well marked but losing concentration will put you aground quickly.

There are No-Wake Zones on both sides of the **DeLand/Whitehair (SR 44) Bascule Bridge** at Mile 140.2 (15-foot closed vertical clearance, opens on signal). A Manatee Zone, enforced year-round, begins just downriver of flashing green day-beacon "53" and extends all the way to flashing green daybeacon "81" south of Blue Springs. Please use common sense and common courtesy when passing through this area.

Dockage: The Astor Bridge Marina accepts transients and has 8-foot MLW approach depths. They have a fuel dock with gas only. Astor Landing Campground & Marina at the north end of Lake Dexter has deep-water (17-foot MLW) slips; call ahead for availability. For seafood, locals recommend the Blackwater Inn (352-759-2802), just south of the bridge on the west side.

St. Johns River, FL

		Largest Vessel Accommodated	VHF Channel Monitored	Dockage			Supplies		Services					
				Transient Berths / Total Berths	Approach / Dockside Depth (reported)	Floating Docks	Gas / Diesel	Groceries, Ice, Marine Supplies, Snacks	Repairs: Hull, Engine, Propeller	Lift (tonnage), Crane, Rail	Min/Max Amps	Laundry, Pool, Showers, Courtesy Car	Pump-Out Station	Nearby: Grocery Store, Motel, Restaurant
ASTOR														
1. Astor Bridge Marina ▭ WiFi	386-749-4407	–	–	20/70	8/	–	G	IS	–	–	30/50	S	P	GMR
2. Astor Landing Campground & Marina	352-759-2121	55	–	call/54	17/17	–	–	–	–	–	30/50	S	P	–
HONTOON LANDING AREA														
3. St. John's Marina & Resort ▭ WiFi	386-736-6601	70	16	12/170	12/10	–	–	GIMS	HEP	L35	30/50	S	P	GMR
4. St. Johns Marina South	352-589-8370	50	–	call/53		–	G	IMS	E	–	30/30	–	–	R
5. Holly Bluff Marina ▭ WG	386-822-9992	–	12	2/74	8/6	–	G	IMS	HEP	L30	30/50	LSC	P	R
6. Hontoon Landing Resort & Marina ▭ WiFi	386-734-2474	60	88	45/50	12/6	–	G	GIMS	–	–	30/50	LPS	P	GMR
7. Hontoon Island State Park	386-736-5309	50	–	40/40	17/6	F	–	IS	–	–	30/50	S	–	M

▭ Internet Access   WiFi Wireless Internet Access   WG Waterway Guide Cruising Club Partner   onSpot dockside WiFi facility

See WaterwayGuide.com for current rates, fuel prices, web site addresses, and other up-to-the-minute information. *(Information in the table is provided by the facilities.)*

ASTOR, NOAA CHART 11495

HONTOON LANDING AREA, NOAA CHART 11498

The restaurant dockage can handle vessels in the 40-foot range, but dock bow-in to get depths at your stern of 4 to 5 feet at MLW. They are closed on Mondays.

Flanking the Whitehair Bridge, St. Johns Marina & Resort has slips and offers repairs, while St. Johns Marina South sells gas but has no transient slips.

Anchorage: On the south side of Lake George is Zinder Point. Near flashing green daybeacon "19" you will find all-around protection in 5 to 10 feet of water. Just 2 miles south is a nice spot by Morrison Island which has excellent holding in mud in 5 to 6 feet.

Farther south there are two unnamed loops with anchoring options. The first, between red daybeacons "30" and "32," has good holding in mud and 8 to 20 feet at MLW. The second, known locally as Catfish Bend, is located between red daybeacons "36" and "38" and just north of Crows Bluff. This has good holding and protection in up to 17 feet at MLW. Sound your way in. If you do not have time for the entire trip to Sanford, Crows Bluff is a good place to turn around and start back downriver (i.e., north).

An anchorage at Drigger Island at flashing green "41" is shallow (5 to 7 feet at MLW) but has excellent holding in mud and all-around protection

Hontoon Landing to Lake Monroe

Real wilderness lies on the Hontoon Dead River, about 3 miles from the Whitehair Bridge and just opposite the end of Beresford Peninsula. Be sure to bring along a camera and fishing gear because you may not find a prettier place and the fishing is fantastic. This is a busy area on weekends, as the state park is popular.

NAVIGATION: Use Chart 11498. The winding river from Hontoon Landing to Lake Monroe has narrow channels, land cuts, water hyacinths and snags, but there are good navigational aids. This waterway is extremely beautiful, with an abundance of birds, turtles and manatees.

Blue Springs State Park is just south of flashing green daybeacon "71." The springs are worth exploring. Hontoon Island Park and Blue Springs State Park are independent of each other, but share a common manatee area that is carefully monitored by the marine patrol. If you are moving too fast (and even auxiliary sailboats sometimes do), you could get a ticket or a warning.

At flashing red daybeacon "96," the narrow entrance to the Wekiva River is almost totally obscured by water hyacinths. Although a boat with a 5-foot draft can be taken several miles up, the Wekiva River's entrance is tricky; explore it only with local knowledge.

Dockage: At Hontoon Landing (Mile 143.5), Holly Bluff Marina has limited transient dockage, but nearby Hontoon Landing Resort & Marina reports 45 reserved transient slips. They both sell gas (no diesel), and you can rent a houseboat, pontoon boat or runabout at the latter.

Flashing green daybeacon "53" at the apex of the curve marks Hontoon Island State Park. The park offers picnic tables, grills, spotless showers, a nature trail and an observation tower. The park docks are on the north end of Hontoon Island, along the St. Johns' western shore next to the river's marked entrance. The dock must be approached from the south; head for the face dock. The water is reported to be 6 feet at MLW on the approach. (Larger boats will have to dock on the dock T ends.) There is water and shore power at the docks for a nominal fee. This spot is especially popular on summer weekends.

Fishermen, campers and picnickers frequently use the free pedestrian ferry, which crosses the river from the island to the mainland. The park has a leash law, ostensibly to prevent your pet from falling prey to an alligator. You will also see a lot of manatees in the

Lake Monroe, FL

LAKE MONROE		Largest Vessel Accommodated	VHF Channel Monitored	Dockage Transient Berths / Total Berths	Approach / Dockside Depth (reported)	Floating Docks	Gas / Diesel	Supplies Groceries, Ice, Marine Supplies, Snacks	Repairs: Hull, Engine, Propeller	Services Lift (tonnage), Crane, Rail	Min/Max Amps	Laundry, Pool, Showers, Courtesy Car	Pump-Out Station	Nearby: Grocery Store, Motel, Restaurant
1. Boat Tree Marina ☐ ⊜onSpot	407-322-1610	70	16	call/245	13/10	F	G	IMS	HEP	L25	30/50	LPS	P	R
SANFORD AREA														
2. Monroe Harbour Marina ☐ WiFi	407-322-2910	80	-	5/236	6/5.5	F	G	IM	HEP	L35	30/50	LS	P	GMR
3. Sanford Boat Works & Marina, Inc. ☐	407-322-6613	70	16	10/140	8/5	F	GD	S	-	L25	30/50	LPS	P	R

☐ Internet Access WiFi Wireless Internet Access WG Waterway Guide Cruising Club Partner ⊜onSpot dockside WiFi facility
See WaterwayGuide.com for current rates, fuel prices, web site addresses, and other up-to-the-minute information. *(Information in the table is provided by the facilities.)*

LAKE MONROE, SANFORD AREA, NOAA CHART 11498

area. There are signs for "Idle Speed Only" due to the number of manatees.

Anchorage: There is plenty of room to drop your hook for a night or two. Hontoon Dead River is a deep-water oxbow. Leave the St. Johns at red daybeacon "50" and proceed as far into the river as you like. Anchor in 10- to 15-foot MLW depths with mud, silt and good holding. The protection is very good from all directions with almost no current.

Starks Landing Loop at Mile 146.8 near red daybeacon "70" is a little-used river loop behind the island off the western bank. Enter at the north end by flashing green daybeacon "69" and proceed slowly, as this is a manatee refuge. An area charted as having 23-foot MLW depths may have less than 5 feet of water. The bottom is soft mud. Our Cruising Editor has seen numerous boats anchored in this spot. Be sure to show an anchor light. You can dinghy to the beach just past the entrance of the springs. Sanford is only a few hours run from here, even for slow boats.

More oxbows are at Emanuel Bend and Butchers Bend. Emanuel Bend, a favorite anchorage for locals, is at Mile 153 across from the Wekiva River, between green daybeacons "95" and "97." Both ends are navigable, but the south end should be avoided as it is very narrow and may be full of hyacinths and overhanging trees plus other debris on the bottom. Campers may be on the island. Depths are less than the chart indicates.

Enter Butchers Bend at Mile 156 at either end, with 7.5-foot MLW depths at the north entrance at flashing green daybeacon "109" and 6-foot MLW depths at the south at green daybeacon "111." This pretty spot is popular with locals and fishermen. Eagles, manatees and turtles like it, too.

LAKE MONROE–MILE 160

Broad and shallow, Lake Monroe can vary greatly in depth with summer rainfall or winter drought. The charted values are correct for a low-water season but up-stream runoff from a wet summer or a hurricane may raise the water level as much as five feet.

NAVIGATION: Use Chart 11498. The St. Johns River continues to meander 6 miles from the Wekiva River to the three bridges before Lake Monroe. Just before the bridges is a power plant with multiple overhead cables crossing the river. The last two cable crossings, significantly lower than the others, have vertical clearances of 48.9 feet, according to the latest NOAA chart (Edition 17 in 2018).

The first bridge before the lake is **Port of Sanford Railway Bascule Bridge** at Mile 158.8, with a 7-foot closed vertical clearance. Call the tender on VHF Channel 09 for an opening. Adjacent is the **U.S. 17/U.S. 92 Bridge** (45-foot fixed vertical clearance) at Mile 158.8. The boat ramp immediately after this

Soundings in **Lake Monroe** are at mean lower low water, which are typical at the end of a dry winter. Rainfall controls the depth, which typically rises almost 4 feet above the charted values after a wet summer.

old bridge is very active and can generate significant congestion in the river channel. The **St. Johns River Veterans Memorial Twin Bridges** at Mile 159.2, (45-foot fixed vertical clearance) are the last bridges before the lake.

Be sure to use the latest charts for the new Lake Monroe buoyage. From the St. Johns River Twin Bridges, follow the markers carefully to the channel junction at flashing red daybeacon "8." A now-unmarked channel leads toward the north to the power plant at Enterprise while the one to the southeast goes to Sanford. Stay out of the area to the northeast between the two channels; the spar buoys mark where sunken trees were placed to attract fish. Red daybeacon "10" is next, followed by red daybeacon "12" and, finally, flashing green "13" and red daybeacon "14" at the

Sanford turning basin. Monroe Harbour Marina's west entrance and the Veterans Memorial Park are here.

To reach the east entrance of the marina, turn to port to red daybeacon "4," the green and red unnumbered daybeacons, and red daybeacon "6." To continue up to the headwaters of the St. Johns River, go from the unnumbered red daybeacon directly to flashing red daybeacon "2" south of Grassy Point.

Dockage: The Boat Tree Marina is located in the large basin on the western shore just before the bridges. Primarily a small-boat facility, the marina has limited transient dockage, sells gas (no diesel) and offers some repairs.

Sanford–Mile 164

At one time, Sanford was an important river port and the largest celery-producing area in the nation, but it is now a pleasure boat center. Here, you enter civilization again with businesses, stores, motels and accommodations for cruising boats. Sanford now boasts the Riverwalk, a 2-mile paved walking and bike path that meanders along Lake Monroe. It is a great way to spend a day. Historic Sanford has a number of good restaurants along 1st Street that sponsor street parties and other public social events most weekends, while large shopping malls are 5 miles west of the marina.

Dockage: Sanford's municipal marina, Monroe Harbour Marina, is two blocks from downtown. The marina places short-term transients in either the east or west basin; you will not see the entrance to the west basin until you are almost on it. They do not monitor VHF, so call 407-322-2910 to get docking instructions. The marina offers a well-stocked store and a friendly staff ready to assist you. They also have a pump-out boat that comes to your slip.

Indian Mound Slough

A straight line at the Sanford waterfront from daybeacon "6" to flashing red "2" at what locals call the "Government Cut" south of Mothers Arms will keep you in the deepest water to Indian Mound Slough. Our Cruising Editor found 5 feet in the dry, low-water season of spring 2018, except for a soft mud 3.5-foot shoal at flashing red "2," just as charted. Stay close to "2" and to red daybeacon "4" and head straight for green daybeacon "5." Depths of at least 5 feet at MLW hold from "5" to Sanford Boat Works if you stay quite close to the west shore once you have passed through the cut.

Beyond Sanford Boat Works and the **Osteen Bridge** (25-foot fixed vertical clearance), the St. Johns River system is wild, natural and unimproved, and cruising is restricted to small skiffs with shallow drafts and airboats. Numerous cattle ranches are here, and the area is excellent for bird watching.

Dockage: Sanford Boat Works & Marina, Inc. has some transient dockage, as does Gator's Riverside Grille (407-688-9700). Call ahead to be sure there is space for you.

■ NEXT STOP

From Sanford, we return you coastward to Jacksonville Beach and the ICW leg south to Daytona Beach and Ponce de Leon Inlet.

St. Johns River to Ponce de Leon Inlet

 ICW Mile 740–Mile 843

((VHF)) FL Bridges: Channel 09

CHARTS NOAA 11485, 11489

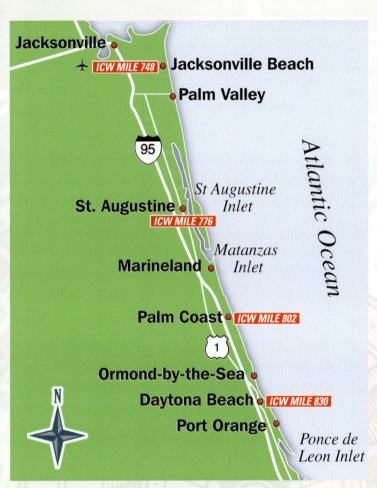

Jacksonville
✈ ICW MILE 748 • Jacksonville Beach
• Palm Valley

95

St Augustine Inlet
St. Augustine • ICW MILE 776

Matanzas Inlet
Marineland •

Atlantic Ocean

Palm Coast • ICW MILE 802

1

Ormond-by-the-Sea •
Daytona Beach • ICW MILE 830
Port Orange •

Ponce de Leon Inlet

N

⚠ Mariners transiting in vicinity of Pablo Creek and Mile Point at Mile 740 should be wary of a shoal that is forming on the northeast side of Pablo Creek. The shoal extends from east of Pablo Creek flashing green "5" to southeast of green "7" and is encroaching to the south and west of Pablo Creek. Minimum depths of 7.5 feet have been observed. Mariners transiting this portion of Pablo Creek with draft concerns are advised to navigate with caution while passing through this area. See the Waterway Explorer at waterwayguide.com for new alerts and updates.

Small boats often anchor in the land cut just beyond the river crossing on weekends and holidays. The current in the cut flows toward the St. Johns River on the ebb and can be very strong–up to 3 knots on the ebb and 2.5 knots on the flood, even without spring tides.

Eddies between red nun buoy "2" and flashing green buoy "1" at the entrance to Pablo Creek require close attention to the helm. When entering the channel, favor the green markers until you reach red daybeacon "8." This area is also a "No Wake Zone" up to the first bridge (Wonderwood Drive Bridge), which is enforced. Going slow can be difficult with the strong current. Be sure to look behind you to verify that you are staying in the channel.

⚠ The **Wonderwood Drive Twin Bridges** at Mile 742.1 typically has slightly less than the charted 65 feet of vertical clearance at high tide. However, ongoing construction on the bridge will reduce the vertical clearance to 61 feet MHW over one-half of the navigational channel until completion (estimated January 2019).

■ TO ST. AUGUSTINE INLET

The Jacksonville Beach region is part of what Floridians call the "First Coast" because it was settled first. It vigorously competes with the Gold Coast, the Sun Coast and the Treasure Coast for developer and tourist dollars. The area begins a parade of shoreside communities such as Atlantic Beach, Neptune Beach, Jacksonville Beach and Ponte Vedra Beach.

NAVIGATION: Use NOAA Chart 11489. After crossing the St. Johns River at Mile 740, the ICW continues along Pablo Creek toward Jacksonville Beach. Follow the markers carefully to stay on the narrow, dredged channel's centerline and be prepared to squeeze over for tugs with barges.

Jacksonville Beach, FL

JACKSONVILLE BEACH AREA		Largest Vessel Accommodated	VHF Channel Monitored	Transient Berths / Total Berths	Approach / Dockside Depth (reported)	Floating Docks	Gas / Diesel	Groceries, Ice, Marine Supplies, Snacks	Repairs: Hull, Engine, Propeller	Lift (tonnage), Crane, Rail	Min/Max Amps	Laundry, Pool, Showers, Courtesy Car	Pump-Out Station	Nearby: Grocery Store, Motel, Restaurant
		Dockage						**Supplies**			**Services**			
1. Palm Cove Marina 🖥 📶 WG 747.4	904-223-4757	90	16/69	25/221	6/6	F	GD	IS	HEP	L35	30/50	LPS	P	GMR
2. Beach Marine 747.6	904-249-8200	125	16/68	40/350	6/6	F	GD	IMS	–	–	30/100	LS	P	GMR
3. MarineMax Jacksonville	904-338-9970	–	–	–	–	–	–	–	HEP	–	–	–	–	R

🖥 Internet Access 📶 Wireless Internet Access WG Waterway Guide Cruising Club Partner 😊 onSpot dockside WiFi facility
See WaterwayGuide.com for current rates, fuel prices, web site addresses, and other up-to-the-minute information. *(Information in the table is provided by the facilities.)*

JACKSONVILLE BEACH AREA, NOAA CHART 11489

The **Atlantic Beach Twin Bridges** (Mile 744.7) mark the gateway to the Jacksonville Beach region. The bridge has charted 65-foot vertical clearance but expect slightly less on higher tides. Note that the current can be strong here. The large enclosed basin on the west side, just south of the Atlantic Beach Bridges, is a private marina for the surrounding condominium owners.

Shoaling continues on the east side of the channel at green can buoy "19," just north of the Atlantic Beach Bridges at Mile 744.7. Green can buoy "19" is sometimes difficult to locate, as often it is pulled under by the current.

After passing under the bridges, hug the west side of the channel close to the private marina, where depths should be around 15 feet. Eddies sometimes form above, under and below the bridges. The narrow, well-marked channel at the Atlantic Beach Bridges has ebb currents up to 6 knots at new and full moons, in synchrony with the St. Johns River. Attention at the helm is mandatory. It is easy to lose control here, and there is not much horizontal clearance. A number of fishermen work this area in small boats.

The *Coast Pilot* describes this area as: "On the flood, the current in the channel flows southward and at right angles to the bridges at an average velocity of 3.4 knots at strength. On the ebb, the current flows northward and sets about 15 degrees to the right of the axis of the channel at an average velocity of 5.2 knots at strength. The currents at a distance of 100 yards either side of the bridges are much weaker with practically no turbulence and give no warning of the strong current at the bridge."

Near the **McCormick (U.S. 90) Twin Bridges** (65-foot vertical clearance) at Mile 747.5 watch for strong currents, especially on the ebb (although they are not as strong as the currents through the Atlantic Beach Bridges).

Anchorage: On the east side of the ICW at Mile 744.2, between flashing green buoy "17" and green can buoy "19," is a wide and surprisingly deep stream. If you choose to try to anchor here, enter only from the north, with an eye out for shoaling on the south side and anchor behind the island. There is plenty of water after you pass the bar. Leftover mooring anchors may still be on the bottom so be wary of snags and set the hook well against the swift current. The current will keep you away from the shore, unless there is strong side wind at tide slack. This is not a great anchorage but will do in a pinch.

Jacksonville Beach

Ponce de Leon landed here in the 1500s in his search for the Fountain of Youth, and Jacksonville Beach has been a lively resort community ever since. This popular stopover has beautiful beaches and offers a full range of services, stores and restaurants. It is also a convenient central base for side trips to Fernandina Beach, Fort Clinch and Fort Caroline, Kingsley Plantation and the City of Jacksonville.

The proximity of the airports at Jacksonville and Daytona makes this a fine layover and fitting-out port. Many mariners cruise south to this point in the fall, leave their boats and fly home. When the cold weather arrives up north, they return to their boats and continue their journeys southward. The renowned Mayo Clinic has an extension here (904-953-2000).

Dockage: North of the McCormick Twin Bridges, at flashing red "32," is a small creek on the west side leading to Lake Cusic, which is unnamed on the chart. Stay to the middle of the privately marked entrance, which has 6 feet at MLW. Palm Cove Marina has competitively priced fuel (gas and diesel) and wet and dry storage. This 221-slip marina also features clean restrooms with showers, a pool, a ship store, electronics service, a 35-ton boat lift, pump-out station and transient dockage at floating docks for boats up to 90 feet. Also on site is the Marker 32 Restaurant (904-223-1534) with great views and first-class dining. Extensive shopping is just a very short walk (about one-half mile), including a grocery/pharmacy, West Marine, Target, drug store and various other stores, plus some fast food eateries. Rental cars and public transportation to explore the nearby Jacksonville area are readily available.

Family-owned and -operated Beach Marine (across the bridges on the east side of the ICW) has transient slips on floating docks, gas and diesel fuel and a repair yard in a large enclosed basin. There is a restaurant on the premises called Big Dawg's Pierside (904-372-4100). The other nearby restaurant is Safe Harbor Seafood (904-479-3474), open daily until 9:00 p.m., serving a wide variety of seafood items in a casual atmosphere. In the same basin, past Beach Marine, is MarineMax Jacksonville, a full-service repair yard (with no transient space).

The beach is about 2 miles away, shopping is over the bridges to the west (less than a 1-mile walk) and rental cars and public transportation to Jacksonville are also nearby.

Palm Valley Cut–ICW Mile 749 to Mile 759

NAVIGATION: Use NOAA Chart 11489. From the McCormick Twin Bridges, the channel is well marked, and the tidal range is about 5 feet. South of the **Butler Blvd. (Pablo Creek) Twin Bridges** (65-foot fixed vertical clearance) at Mile 749.5, the route enters 10-mile-long Palm Valley Cut. There is a high-rise condominium development with a private boat basin just south of the Butler Blvd. Bridges on the west side

of the ICW. The current may give your vessel a strong sideways push, and shoals are encroaching from the west side just south of Mile 750 at the intersection of Pablo and Cabbage Creeks.

The only marker in Palm Valley Cut (red daybeacon "2") is just before the bridge; stay in the middle of the channel or favor the east side if depths start to decrease suddenly. There are numerous pot markers along Palm Valley Cut that appear to be near the centerline. The deeper water is to the east of these floats.

Skippers, as always, are responsible for their own wakes. The narrow Palm Valley Cut is a Slow-Speed/Minimum-Wake Zone from the Marsh Landing area to just south of the Palm Valley Bridge. Proceed with appropriate caution. The east side of Palm Valley Cut is residential. Watch for debris, manatees and alligators in this popular fishing spot and mind the depth sounder.

Pass flashing red "48" within 100 feet for 12 feet at MLW. There is a shoal coming into the channel from the green side.

Near the south end of the cut, the ICW passes under the fixed 65-foot high-rise **Palm Valley (SR 210) Bridge** at Mile 758.8. Just past this bridge are the headwaters of the Tolomato River (Mile 760), which leads to St. Augustine.

Tolomato River–ICW Mile 760 to Mile 776

NAVIGATION: Use NOAA Charts 11489 and 11485. At Mile 760, the ICW enters the headwaters of the Tolomato River, which flows south to meet the Matanzas River at the St. Augustine Inlet. The dredged channel between Mile 760 and Mile 765 provides a deep water route through the marshes and side waters.

The river deepens below Pine Island (just north of Mile 765), and the ICW begins to follow its natural deep channel. From Mile 765 to Mile 770, pay close attention to the chart, as shoaling extends into the channel at flashing green "27." Give the marker a wide berth and stay toward the west bank.

Although problems have diminished recently, there is occasional shoaling near Capo Creek. Between green daybeacon "29" and red daybeacon "30" it is best to favor the east side of the channel. Above green daybeacon "33" a shoal extends toward the channel; give that marker a wide berth. South of green daybeacon "33" keep to the western side and give a wide berth to flashing red "44" and "44A" just before Mile 770. (NOAA Chart 11485 picks up here.) Beware of the shoal that extends from flashing green "45" below Mile 770; it juts out from the upper point of the Guana River and extends northward along the east bank.

Be alert for strong sideways currents at the junction of the Guana River and the ICW, which also may drag pot markers underwater. About 1 mile south of the Guana River on the west side, you will pass an airport. The route is well marked, wide and deep to the **Usina (Vilano Beach) Bridge** (Mile 775.8, fixed vertical clearance of 65 feet), except for a shoal that extends into the channel at flashing green "49." Keep a sharp eye out for this marker and the next green marker (flashing green "51") because they both have a tendency to blend in with the buildings and docks on the eastern side of the ICW channel.

There may be strong currents at an angle at the Usina Bridge, and some cruisers report that the clearance may be less than the posted 65 feet at high tide. A dredged private basin at a condominium development south of flashing red "54" on the Tolomato River has two entrances on the east side of the river.

Dockage: Several restaurants with dockage for patrons are north of the Usina Bridge on the east side of the ICW. Tying up at Cap's on the Water, the popular restaurant in the vicinity of flashing green "51," can be very rough, especially on busy summer weekends. Call the restaurant (904-824-8794) ahead of time to check on the approach and dockside depths as well as dock availability. Pass this area with no wake, as there are usually boats at the dock, sometimes rafted several deep.

Anchorage: At Mile 765 is the entrance to the Pine Island Loop anchorage, which is a fine place to drop the hook and enjoy a pleasant evening or two. Enter just south of green daybeacon "25" and favor the north bank, as there is a shoal extending out from the south bank. Mind the depth and allow for the full range of

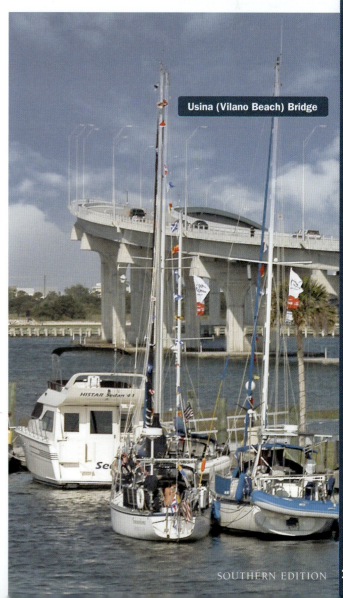

Usina (Vilano Beach) Bridge

For a little adventure, take a dinghy ride up the **Guana River** at Mile 770 to a dam about 3 miles upstream that is part of the Guana-Tolomato-Matanzas Rivers National Estuarine Research Reserve, a network of 55,000 acres of protected marsh, waters and wetlands. Anchor your vessel at the mouth of the river, off the ICW, taking care to avoid the charted submerged piling, but do not leave it unattended. Once at the dam, the beach is just across the highway.

tide in your entire swinging circle. There is a line of crab pot markers that indicates the shoal line on the southern side of the anchorage; it is deeper toward the north shore. The current is minimal and holding and protection are excellent; however, it can be very buggy when there is no wind. Shoals and submerged obstructions make the entrance north of the island between green daybeacon "21" and flashing green "23" almost impassable.

Another anchorage is at Mile 769. When abeam of red daybeacon "42" turn northeast toward shore. Go about halfway between mid-channel and shore and turn northwest into the pocket behind the charted shoal until roughly abeam of green daybeacon "41."

The farther you anchor from the ICW, the less you will be affected by wakes of passing boats. This is a fine area to do some exploring with your dinghy. You can see alligators and a huge variety of birds and other wildlife.

St. Augustine Inlet

NAVIGATION: Use NOAA Chart 11485. When entering the St. Augustine Inlet and heading northbound on the ICW, it is important to run a sufficient distance past the tip of the beach on the north side of the inlet channel before turning into the ICW channel. (See the Inlet listing in the front of this guide for more information.) Commercial and sportfishing boats use the St. Augustine

Inlet regularly; get local information but avoid this spot in rough conditions.

The inlet is frequently surveyed at around 12 to 15 feet deep at low tide at the outside bar; however, remember that this channel is subject to change at any time. Shoaling is common and the markers are frequently moved and may not be accurate, although the inlet is dredged on a regular basis.

Waves break dangerously close to the dredged channel, especially at low tide with ebb current against an onshore wind. There are nearly always breakers on the shallows on each side of the inlet, which looks intimidating even when the channel is flat calm.

Camachee Cove Yacht Harbor and the local towing services (SeaTow and TowBoat U.S.) have updated information on possible shoaling and will be very accommodating if called on for "local knowledge."

St. Augustine

NAVIGATION: Use NOAA Chart 11485. Use the Fernandina Beach Tide Tables. For high tide, subtract 20 minutes; for low tide, subtract 5 minutes. Between Mile 775 and Mile 780 there is continuous shoaling, as well as frequent changes to the marking system in the area. Study the chart before you get to the Usina Bridge and note that this is a very changeable area because of the currents and the close proximity to the inlet.

Bridge of Lions

The ICW channel south of the bridge is deceptively close to the beach (east) side as it approaches St. Augustine Inlet. Honor all markers in place south of the bridge at the time of your arrival. In summer 2018, these markers included flashing green buoy "57A," quick-flashing red buoy "60" and flashing green buoy "59," which is opposite and very close to the beach.

After passing between flashing green buoy "59" and quick-flashing red buoy "60," the ICW channel turns sharply to the west to pass between the first set of Matanzas River markers (flashing green buoy "1" and red nun buoy "2") just inside St. Augustine Inlet. Be careful to distinguish the inlet markers from the ICW markers. Also be careful not to confuse the marked channel into Salt Run for the ICW channel. Call one of the local towing services for advice if you are unable to sort out the numerous markers. Always remember that the ICW markers have either a yellow square or a yellow triangle.

Heading south, before you reach the **Bridge of Lions (SR A1A)** at Mile 777.9, you will see a tall white cross and then the fort Castillo de San Marcos (charted). Closer to town, the twin spires of the Catholic cathedral appear, making an interesting skyline. Beyond the inlet, on the Conch Island (east) side, the ICW channel turns sharply west, sweeps wide around Anastasia Island's northern tip and then turns up the Matanzas River and under the Bridge of Lions. This bridge, one of the most attractive on the ICW, was originally completed in 1927. The bridge has been rebuilt in recent years with the goal to improve the bridge's safety while preserving its historic value.

The Bridge of Lions opens on signal, except between 7:00 a.m. and 6:00 p.m., when the draw only opens on the hour and half-hour; however, the draw need not open at 8:00 a.m., 12 noon or 5:00 p.m., Monday through Friday (except federal holidays). On weekends and holidays, it opens only on the hour and half-hour between 7:00 a.m. and 6:00 p.m. Although charted with 18-foot closed vertical clearance, our Cruising Editor has observed an additional 4 feet of clearance in the center. Be aware that the bridge sometimes closes for special events (e.g., Blessing of the Fleet, 4th of July celebrations and various 5K walk/run events). These closures are usually well publicized and reasonably short in duration. Stay tuned for updates at waterwayguide.com.

Dockage: The number of berths available to transients in St. Augustine reflects its long-standing popularity as a port of call. Several elaborate marine complexes cater to

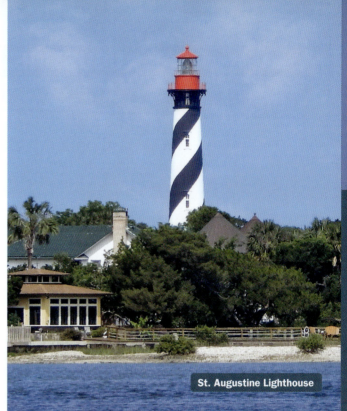
St. Augustine Lighthouse

cruising boats. Immediately north of the Usina Bridge on the west side of the ICW, Camachee Cove Yacht Harbor is the center of the huge Camachee Island Marina Village complex. Bulkheads and jetties on both sides of Camachee Cove's entrance help prevent shoaling and protect the outside slips. The entrance channel provides adequate depths for cruising boats of all sizes and the enclosed basin offers excellent protection.

Camachee Cove Yacht Harbor has two boater lounges, three laundry facilities and a well-stocked ship store. The complex boasts six fueling stations, and some fueling can be done from individual slips. The marina is surrounded by 20 businesses offering every imaginable service for boaters, including Camachee Yacht Yard, where trained on-site technicians can handle most any repair (50-ton lift and crane). First Mate Yacht Services is also on site offering full-service maintenance and repairs. Dessert First Bistro (904-417-0468), Kingfish Grill (904-824-2111) and Vinny's New York Style Pizza (904-342-8859) are on site as well as an inn, a canvas shop, yacht sales and TowBoat U.S., among others. Downtown St. Augustine is a couple of miles away, and the marina provides two courtesy cars for exploring or provisioning.

South of the inlet, on Salt Run, is the Conch House Marina. The marina has a tropical motif and full amenities. The popular Conch House Restaurant is on site, offering seafood and Caribbean fare.

ST. JOHNS RIVER TO PONCE DE LEON INLET

SERVICES		
1	Post Office	
2	Visitor Information	
ATTRACTIONS		
3	Castillo de San Marcos	
4	Colonial Quarters Living History Museum	
5	Flagler College/Ponce de Leon Hotel	

6	Lightner Museum
7	National Greek Orthodox Shrine
8	Pirate & Treasures Museum
DINING		
9	A1A Ale Works
10	Columbia Restaurant
11	Costa Bravo

12	Sangria's Wine and Tapas Piano Bar
13	San Sebastian Winery
MARINAS		
14	St. Augustine Municipal Marina

Founded in 1565 as a Spanish military outpost, St. Augustine is the oldest continuously occupied European settlement in the United States. Traces of the city's Spanish heritage are everywhere, and a Spanish Quarter where conquistadors once strolled is recreated for the 21st-century visitor.

Attractions: Tourists can explore the battlements and dungeons of Castillo de San Marcos National Monument, built in 1672, and wander the narrow old streets of San Agustin Antiquo, which depict Spanish Colonial life. Walking from the old town gates across from Castillo de San Marcos, you will encounter the oldest wooden schoolhouse in the United States, the Colonial Quarter's Living History Museum and the National Greek Orthodox Shrine.

Superb examples of 19th-century Spanish Renaissance architecture can be seen here. Flagler College occupies the buildings and grounds of Henry Flagler's luxurious Ponce de Leon Hotel, built in 1888. Tours are scheduled several times a day to view the original Tiffany stained glass windows, fountains, mosaics and sculpture in the beautifully restored building, which now serves as the college offices and main dormitory. Across King Street from Flagler

College is the Lightner Museum (built by Henry Flagler, 1887). This museum of antiquities is housed within the historic Hotel Alcazar building.

Of course, Ponce De Leon's Fountain of Youth is here. It's part of a 15-acre archaeological park and there is a fee to enter the grounds ($15 at press time in 2018). The Spring House is the site of the original spring that was recorded in a 17th-century Spanish land grant. It is a beautiful 60-year old coquina building. (The fountain itself is not much to look at.)

For a bit of fun, the Pirate & Treasures Museum at 12 S. Castillo Dr. is dedicated to pirate artifacts (877-467-5863). This was formerly known as the Pirate Soul Museum and was relocated from Key West.

If you happen to be in town on Palm Sunday, you can participate in the St. Augustine Blessing of the Fleet Festival, a tradition that goes back hundreds of years.

Shopping: The full length of St. George Street (just three blocks from the city marina) is a diner's and shopper's paradise. On Rt. 1 south just about 1.5 miles from downtown you will find West Marine (1030 S. Ponce De Leon Blvd., 904-810-5353) and a Winn-Dixie supermarket (1010 S. Ponce De Leon Blvd., 904-829-5509) in the same shopping center. If you need transportation, try the Sunshine Bus Company, which operates six lines and a connector route in and around St. Augustine. Check with the marina office as to where the closest bus stop is as it changes frequently.

On Rt. 1 south just about a 1.5 miles from downtown you will find West Marine and a supermarket in the same shopping center. If you need transportation, try the Sunshine Bus Company, which operates six lines and a connector route in and around St. Augustine. Check with the marina office as to where the closest bus stop is as it changes frequently.

Dining: There are restaurants to suit any taste in downtown St. Augustine. One of the favorites of cruisers is A1A Ale Works (1 King St., 904-829-2977), which has a large selection of beer and serves "New World" cuisine. For more upscale dining, visit Costa Brava, located in the Casa Monica Hotel (built in 1888) across from the college at 95 Cordova St. (904-810-6810), or Columbia Restaurant (904-824-3341) at the corner of St. George and Hypolita Streets. Columbia is one of the oldest and best-regarded Cuban restaurants in Florida and has been owned and operated by the same family for 110 years. Start with the black bean soup (served over white rice) and move on to the mixto, a traditional Cuban sandwich made of ham, salami, roast pork, swiss cheese, pickle and mustard. You will dine among hundreds of hand-painted tiles and Spanish-style fountains. See menus at columbiarestaurant.com.

For something a little different, be sure to try Sangria's Wine and Tapas Piano Bar (35 Hypolita St., 904-827-1947). They have indoor and outdoor seating and live music most nights.

Don't miss a tour and wine tasting at the San Sebastian Winery (157 King St., 904-826-1594), where they produce table, sparkling and dessert wines. "The Cellar Upstairs" is a wine, jazz and blues bar located on the rooftop of the winery. Call for reservations, as the bar is only open on Friday, Saturday and Sunday.

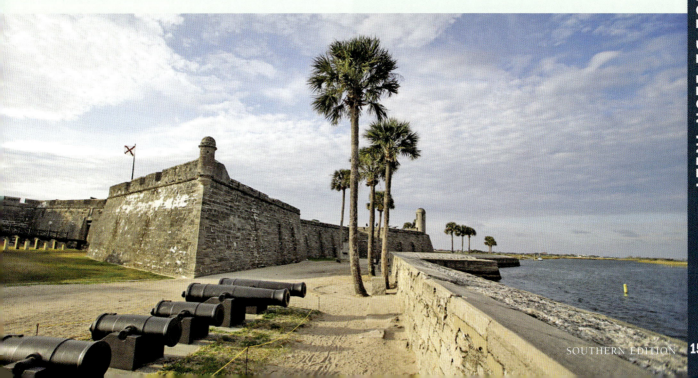

St. Augustine Inlet, St. Augustine, FL

	Phone	Largest Vessel Accommodated	VHF Channel Monitored	Transient Berths / Total Berths	Approach / Dockside Depth (reported)	Floating Docks	Gas / Diesel	Groceries, Ice, Marine Supplies, Snacks	Repairs: Hull, Engine, Propeller	Lift (tonnage), Crane, Rail	Min/Max Amps	Laundry, Pool, Showers, Courtesy Car	Pump-Out Station	Nearby: Grocery Store, Motel, Restaurant
TOLOMATO RIVER — *Dockage / Supplies / Services*														
1. Camachee Island Marina Village 🖥 WiFi WG 775	904-829-5676	135	16/68	40/260	6/7	F	GD	GIMS	HEP	L50,C5	30/100	LPSC	P	GMR
2. Camachee Yacht Yard 775.7	904-823-3641	65	16	–	–	F	GD	IMS	HEP	L50,C	30/50	LPS	P	GMR
SALT RUN														
3. Conch House Marina 🖥 WiFi .65 W of 776.7	904-824-4347	200	16/69	45/200	8.5/8.5	F	GD	GIMS	HEP	–	30/100	LPS	P	GMR
MATANZAS RIVER														
4. St. Augustine Municipal Marina 🖥 777.7	904-825-1026	280	16/71	call/100	20/15	F	GD	GIMS	–	–	30/100	LS	P	GMR
5. Marker 8 Hotel & Marina 🖥 WiFi 777.7	904-829-9042	103	16/72	24/24	9/7	F	–	IS	–	–	30/100	LPS	–	GMR
6. Fish Island Marina 779.8	904-471-1955	150	16	20/20	20/20	F	D	–	–	–	30/50	LS	P	GMR
SAN SEBASTIAN RIVER														
7. Cat's Paw Marina	904-829-8040	40	16	–	–	–	GD	IMS	H	L9	30/30	–	–	GR
8. St. Augustine Marine Center 🖥 WiFi .8 NW of 780	904-824-4394	150	16	call/50	10/6	F	–	IM	HEP	L110,C20	30/100	LPS	P	MR
9. Xynides Boat Yard 🖥	904-824-3446	55	–	call/20	16/10	F	–	M	HEP	L50	–	LS	–	GMR
10. Oasis Boatyard & Marina WiFi 1.2 NW of 780	904-824-2520	65	–	call/45	16/16	F	–	IMS	HEP	L50,C	30/50	LS	–	GMR
11. St. Augustine Shipyard	904-342-5159	120	–	call/300	–	F	GD	IMS	HEP	L	30/30	S	P	R
12. English Landing Marina WiFi	904-669-7363	–	–	call/23	20/15	F	–	–	–	–	30/30	S	–	GMR
13. Rivers Edge Marina 🖥 WiFi WG 1.7 NW of 780	904-827-0520	150	16/72	5/106	12/10	F	GD	IMS	EP	–	30/100	LS	P	GMR
14. The Marine Supply & Oil Company 1.8 NW of 780	904-829-2271	200	–	–	/12	–	GD	M	–	–	–	–	–	G
15. Hidden Harbor Marina – St. Augustine 🖥 WiFi 780	904-829-0750	–	68	2/45	8/15	F	–	–	–	–	30/50	LS	P	GR

🖥 Internet Access WiFi Wireless Internet Access WG Waterway Guide Cruising Club Partner onSpot dockside WiFi facility

See WaterwayGuide.com for current rates, fuel prices, web site addresses, and other up-to-the-minute information. *(Information in the table is provided by the facilities.)*

Dockage is also available south of the Bridge of Lions, and these facilities are convenient to the city's many restaurants and historic attractions. The St. Augustine Municipal Marina, on the west side, offers transient dockage and convenient fuel. Consider the direction of the current when docking here. You will need to make reservations early to reserve a slip here. Across the river on the east shore is a totally renovated hotel and marina. Marker 8 Hotel & Marina has a few transient slips. They also offer a complimentary breakfast and an afternoon social hour. They do not monitor the VHF radio so you will need to contact them by phone (904-829-9042). A little farther south, on the east side, is Fish Island Marina (Mile 779.8), which usually has some transient space available but you may want to check with them ahead of time. They also sell diesel fuel.

The San Sebastian River, which branches off the Matanzas River at Mile 780, is a better spot for provisioning and has a number of marine businesses and associated docks. You should exercise caution when docking anywhere on this river, as the current is swift. The Cat's Paw Marina is located past red day beacon "8" on the west shore of the San Sebastian River. This is a dry-storage facility with gas and diesel plus a 9-ton lift.

The channels are subject to continual changes. Entrance bouys are not charted because they are frequently shifted in position. Mariners are advised to seek local knowledge.

TOLOMATO RIVER, SALT RUN, MATANZAS RIVER, SAN SEBASTIAN RIVER NOAA CHART 11485

St. Augustine Marine Center is located near green daybeacon "13." This is a full service yard with a 110-ton lift and a cat crawler capable of hauling catamarans with up to 35-foot beam. This 23-acre yard has long and short-term storage and welcomes do-it-yourself boaters. What they do not offer, however, is transient slips.

Continuing farther upriver is Xynides Boat Yard, and next door is the Oasis Boatyard & Marina. Both have a 50-ton lift, and Oasis also has a 20-ton crane. Both are strictly repair/service facilities and do not offer overnight dockage to transients.

On the other side of the river is the St. Augustine Shipyard. This is a full-service yard with hull, engine and prop repairs as well as a dry-storage facility. Some wet slips were scheduled to be completed in December 2018.

English Landing Marina and Rivers Edge Marina are just one-half mile south of downtown St. Augustine at green daybeacons "29" and "33," respectively. The marinas are a short walk away from a supermarket and a West Marine, as well as stores offering beer, wine and spirits. Both marinas have transient slips, and Rivers Edge sells all fuels (via a fuel truck). Rivers Edge is a full-service marina with all the regular cruiser

amenities, including cable, WiFi, laundry and an on-site restaurant (Hurricane Patty's). The Marine Supply & Oil Company is less than 2 miles away with diesel. Call for delivery options.

Hidden Harbor Marina–St. Augustine is located just before the low **King Street** fixed bridge (2-foot vertical clearance) and has limited transient dockage.

Moorings: The City of St. Augustine-owned mooring field consists of approximately 175 moorings, which are managed by the Municipal Marina. There are four different mooring fields: Salt Run has two fields (north and south) with a total of 80 moorings, while the downtown area has two different fields (Menendez with 70 moorings and San Marcos with 28 moorings). The Menendez field is south of the Bridge of Lions and San Marcos is north of the Bridge of Lions. All of the moorings have access to a free pump-out boat that operates daily between the hours of 9:00 a.m. and noon, the dinghy dock, a shuttle boat and use of all of the facilities at the marina. The moorings can accommodate vessels up to 120 feet.

When entering the Menendez mooring field, you should enter just west of red daybeacon "8" on the ICW. Do not enter the field between daybeacons "8" and "10A" as it had shoaled and has less than 4 feet at MLW. Shoaling to 3 feet at MLW has also been observed near and below some of the moorings. Ask the marina when you call for a mooring, and get advice on where to enter the mooring field.

The Salt Run mooring fields (Mile 777 just off the St. Augustine Inlet) can be reached by following the private channel markers of the Conch House Marina and Resort. Once past the marina, you will see the mooring fields (north and south). The two mooring areas have a total of 80 moorings. Both have a pump-out boat and dinghy dock; however, if you want to have access to the city of St. Augustine, Salt Run is a poor choice because of the distance to the city. It would be a very long dinghy ride and a very long walk just to get there. This area is used primarily for long-term mooring.

Anchorage: St. Augustine has passed an ordinance restricting anchoring outside mooring fields that essentially wiped out all previous anchorages. Specifically, no anchoring is allowed within 100 feet of mooring field boundaries, within 50 feet of maritime infrastructure, within 500 feet of shellfish areas and for no more than 30 consecutive days in any 45-day period. Fines are $100 to $500. This is a part of a pilot mooring field study in St. Augustine, Martin County,

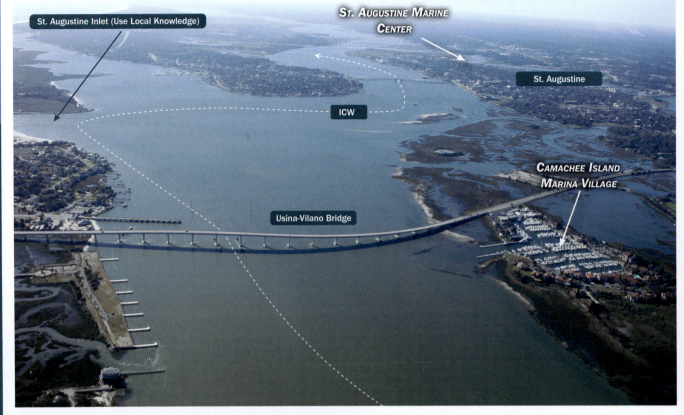

St. Augustine Inlet (Use Local Knowledge)

ST. AUGUSTINE MARINE CENTER

St. Augustine

ICW

CAMACHEE ISLAND MARINA VILLAGE

Usina-Vilano Bridge

St. Petersburg, Sarasota and the Florida Keys to help alleviate issues with anchoring.

In recent years, a few local and transient boats have been observed anchoring in the San Sebastian River, but this is not a good anchorage for a variety of reasons: the only deep water is directly in the narrow dredged channel, the reversing current here is very swift, and there is a sizable fleet of shrimp trawlers coming and going at all hours that use the commercial docks upriver as their base. Also, the swinging room is very limited.

ST. AUGUSTINE INLET TO DAYTONA BEACH

Matanzas River to Matanzas Inlet– ICW Mile 780 to Mile 796

NAVIGATION: Use NOAA Chart 11485. One nautical mile south of St. Augustine on the Matanzas River at Mile 780.3, **SR 312 Twin Bridges** (65-foot fixed vertical clearance) cross the river and the current is swift here. This area was dredged in spring 2017. The Matanzas River channel is deep but narrow, so follow the array of markers carefully until the dredged cut takes over south of Matanzas Inlet (closed to navigation).

Several markers along the stretch should be given a wide berth to avoid shoals. At red daybeacon "30," steer wide toward the east side of the channel to avoid the encroaching shoals from the west bank. Just north of Crescent Beach, at Mile 789, tides from St. Augustine and Matanzas inlets meet. From here, you run a dredged channel most of the next 80 miles to the Indian River.

At Crescent Beach, you will encounter the **Crescent Beach (SR 206) Bascule Bridge** (Mile 788.6, 25-foot closed vertical clearance), which opens on signal. The bridgetender is particularly helpful and accommodating. On both sides of the bridge for approximately 200 feet is an enforced No-Wake Zone.

⚠ At Mile 792.5, Matanzas River passage by the inlet has been dredged. Buoys have been moved and red can "80C" and red can "80D" have been removed. Just follow the buoys for a safe passage to 9 feet at MLW. Pass within 30 feet of red can "80A" for the best water. Elsewhere, just honor the buoys. This area is always evolving and filling in, check waterwayguide.com before transiting the area.

The current between the ICW crossing of Matanzas River (Mile 792) and Marineland (Mile 796) can be strong enough to pull pot markers underwater, but it decreases as you proceed toward Palm Coast.

⚠ Be aware of is a shoal coming in from the green side at Mile 796. Pass 50 feet off red daybeacon "86" for 11 feet at MLW. The channel north of red daybeacon "86" is very uneven with spots down to 7 feet at MLW. When in doubt, favor the red side.

Dockage: If you are looking to stop for the night, Marineland Marina at Mile 796 can accommodate boats up to 100 feet. After extensive renovation the marina now has new restrooms, showers, laundry facilities, pump-out service at each slip and a new marina office building. The marina provides direct access to the beaches and natural preserves. There is a Farmers' Market every Sunday from 10:00 a.m. to 2:00 p.m. right at the docks. Marineland Dolphin Adventure directly across the street offers hands-on exhibits and educational programs with Atlantic bottlenose dolphins (for a fee). Openings hours/days may vary; call first (904-471-1111).

Anchorage: A quiet anchorage can be found at Mile 781.2, south of flashing red "18" on the Matanzas River. This anchorage is easy to enter and offers deep water (at least 7 feet). Tide can be up to 5 feet. Several derelict boats are here so exercise caution.

An anchorage to the south at Butler Beach (Mile 786.2) offers good holding in 6 to 7 feet of water off flashing green "43" behind the spoil area. There are boat ramps nearby so this may get busy during the day.

Side Trip: Fort Matanzas

At the north end of Rattlesnake Island (Mile 792), you will see the stark remains of Fort Matanzas, once a Spanish outpost and now a national monument. Like its larger cousin, Castillo de San Marcos in St. Augustine, this fort was built of coquina, a rock made of tiny shells. You can reach the fort via a small National Park Service ferry that runs between Anastasia Island and Rattlesnake Island. Its terminal is just north of the inlet, and it is an easy drive from St. Augustine.

Anchorage: You will find good holding in 8 to 10 feet of water in front of Fort Matanzas by green can "81A." To enter the anchorage, turn between cans "80A" and "80B" and stay close to the north shore. Use extra caution at low tide. This is open to the north through southeast.

Palm Coast, FL

PALM COAST AREA	Largest Vessel Accommodated	VHF Channel Monitored	Transient Berths / Total Berths	Approach / Dockside Depth (reported)	Floating Docks	Gas / Diesel	Groceries, Ice, Marine Supplies, Snacks	Repairs: Hull, Engine, Propeller	Lift (tonnage), Crane, Rail	Min/Max Amps	Laundry, Pool, Showers, Courtesy Car	Pump-Out Station	Nearby: Grocery Store, Motel, Restaurant
			Dockage				**Supplies**			**Services**			
1. Marineland Marina 🖥 WiFi 796	904-814-9886	100	16/68	20/41	6.5/6	F	–	–	–	30/100	LSC	P	MR
2. Palm Coast Marina 🖥 onSpot WG 803	386-446-6370	165	16/69	25/80	8/8	–	GD	IMS	–	30/50	LS	P	MR
3. Marina At Hammock Beach Resort 🖥 WiFi 803	386-597-5030	125	16/10	150/209	8/7	F	–	GIMS	–	30/100	LPS	P	GR

🖥 Internet Access WiFi Wireless Internet Access WG Waterway Guide Cruising Club Partner onSpot dockside WiFi facility
See WaterwayGuide.com for current rates, fuel prices, web site addresses, and other up-to-the-minute information. *(Information in the table is provided by the facilities.)*

PALM COAST AREA, NOAA CHART 11485

Matanzas Inlet to Palm Coast– ICW Mile 797 to Mile 803

Marshland alternates with forests along the banks of the Matanzas River here as you pass through a part of the Guana-Tolomato-Matanzas National Estuarine Research Reserve, south of Marineland Marina on the east side of the ICW. You will likely encounter kayak tour groups here during warmer weather; give them a slow, no-wake pass out of courtesy.

This cut seems eerie and almost desolate in places, so it comes as a surprise when farther down the cut on the west side several wide, rip-rapped channels appear. This is part of the community of Palm Coast, accessible via its three canals. The large planned residential community includes 6 miles of beach and ICW frontage. Across from Palm Coast on the east side of the ICW is another cleared area, Ginn Hammock Beach, with residential lots and houses, canals, a large condominium building and a large marina basin.

NAVIGATION: Use NOAA Chart 11485. Locals report shoaling at Mile 797, on the west side of the channel just past flashing red "90" and additional shoaling from flashing red "94" to red daybeacon "104." Red daybeacon "92" has been repositioned to mark deeper water. There is a fixed, high-level toll bridge, **Hammock Dunes (Palm Coast Hwy.) Bridge** (Mile 803.0, 65-foot vertical clearance) just south of the entrance to the Palm Coast Marina.

Dockage: At Mile 803, a canal leads westward to the Palm Coast Marina. Once inside, favor the south side of the channel. The marina welcomes transients, and the dockmaster allows the office to serve as a mail drop. Gas and diesel fuels are available. Within walking distance from the marina (approximately one-half mile) is the European Village, which has numerous shops and dining options. There is also an urgent care center nearby; MediQuick Walk-in Clinic is located at 6 Office Park Dr. in Palm Coast (386-401-5470). No appointment necessary.

Marina at Hammock Beach Resort is in the large dredged basin directly across the ICW from the Palm Coast Marina, where the chart shows "Bon Terra." This marina offers transients the full range of amenities available through the Club at Hammock Beach. There is also a shuttle available to transport you to a market or elsewhere. This is a large private condominium and residential community, with its own dredged basin and private slips.

Palm Coast to Tomoka Basin–
ICW Mile 804 to Mile 818

If you leave the Palm Coast area marinas on a slow boat (less than 10-knot speed) at the start of the ebb tide, you can ride the current all the way to Ponce de Leon Inlet.

As a point of interest, between Mile 804 and Mile 807, you will notice a narrow interconnecting canal on the east side of the ICW. This was part of the original ICW and gives an idea of the size of some earlier sections.

NAVIGATION: Use NOAA Chart 11485. For several miles south of Palm Coast Marina, condominiums with community docks and boat lifts, golf courses and private homes line both sides of the ICW. At Mile 805, on the west side of the ICW, is Grand Haven, a country club community. The west side of the ICW down to Mile 809 is currently undergoing an increase in residential development, with many docks extending out toward the ICW. Not all of the docks are in deep water, however, and boaters should not assume that just because there is a dock that the water is deep enough. Stay in the center of the channel, especially south of the high-rise bridge at Palm Coast, near the long series of docks on the west side. If you see boats in the water at these docks, slow down out of courtesy and give them a "no-wake" pass. This area of the waterway is locally known as Smiths Creek.

Exposed rocks line both sides of the long Fox Cut from green daybeacon "1" to green daybeacon "5." Red daybeacons "2" and "4" and flashing green "3" mark rocks that extend to the edge of the channel. A ramp, dock and launch facility have been dug out of the west side of the ICW at flashing green "3" and red daybeacon "4." This is a Slow-Speed/No-Wake Zone. Stay to the center of the channel when passing the ramp. Rocks intermittently line the west side of the ICW close to shore at the residential construction, just south of the ramp, down to the entrance to the cement plant anchorage at Mile 809.

A dock development on the east side of the ICW, just north of the Flagler Beach Bridge, has been empty of boats since being built, and its entrance is roped off. This marina has been abandoned for a number of years, and there are prominent signs indicating "NO TRESPASSING/PRIVATE DOCKS."

Bulow (L.B. Knox) Bridge

The **Flagler Beach (Moody Blvd.) Bridge** (with 65-foot fixed vertical clearance) crosses the ICW at Mile 810.6. Expect shoals near the bridge along the edges of the channel. There is a busy ramp on the south side of the bridge; pass at idle speed. For the 5 miles between the Flagler Beach Bridge and the Bulow (L.B. Knox) Bascule Bridge, the channel is lined with pot markers on both sides, and some floats are in the channel itself.

At Mile 812.4, red daybeacon "20" has been moved to the bend in Smith Creek, and red daybeacon "20A" has been added at the previous location of red daybeacon "20." At Mile 814, a small, marked side channel leads to a state park and a ramp. This is the beginning of a Manatee Zone, with a 30-mph speed limit in the channel (25 mph at night), and slow speed required outside the ICW channel.

At Mile 816, expect congestion at the boat ramp at the **Bulow (L.B. Knox) Bascule Bridge**. Vertical clearance is only 15 feet, but the bridge opens on signal. South of the bridge, the channel shoals along the east side from flashing red "2" to flashing green "7." The ICW enters the headwaters of the Halifax River here, which gradually widens in its reach to Daytona Beach. The channel, is straight and well marked, and follows closely along the eastern bank and passes attractive homes. There is a negligible tidal range here.

Anchorage: At Mile 809, a side channel carrying less than 6-foot depths at its entrance, with 11-foot depths inside, leads west to a charted cement plant, which has been closed for some time. A Sea Ray factory that is located here generates a great deal of boat traffic at various times during the day; this activity is reported to begin early in the morning. Enter near the center of the channel; watch the depth sounder and ease toward the north shore. Once past the un-navigable side channels, you can move back to the middle. Anchor on the south side above the side channels or past the boat factory; "No Trespassing" signs make it clear that you may not go ashore. Holding is reported to be marginal here and the swing room is very limited. There are several homes with docks on the south side at the entrance, and the north side is undergoing residential and golf course development.

Tomoka Basin to Daytona Beach–ICW Mile 819 to Mile 829

Tomoka State Park, along the riverbanks of the Tomoka River, was once home to the Timucua Indians. Today, you can walk beneath the same ancient oaks that shaded their huts nearly 400 years ago or explore the marshes and tidal creeks by dinghy.

NAVIGATION: Use NOAA Chart 11485. For deeper-draft boats, the 5-mile-long passage from Tomoka Basin to the Ormond Beach Bridge calls for close attention to markers. Stick to the middle on this stretch because the east and west sides of the channel shoal and the water is shallow outside the channel. Depths are generally 8 feet at MLW at mid-channel in this area, although shoaling to 4 feet has been reported at the edge of the channel near red daybeacon "20" south of the bridge. The **Ormond Beach (SR 40) Bridge** at Mile 824.9 has 65-foot fixed vertical clearance.

Just north of the Ormond Beach Bridge, the channel gradually shifts toward the middle of the river. The open water of the Halifax River here is a popular windsurfing area. On a blustery day expect to see several windsurfers crisscrossing the channel. Slow speed is required in this area for the manatee zone.

Local festivals are often held on the nearby grounds of the Casements, the former summer home of John D. Rockefeller, which now houses museum exhibits and is owned and maintained by the City of Ormond. The city has developed extensive park lands along the banks of the Halifax near the Ormond Beach Bridge. These riverfront areas are pleasant spots for walkers and picnickers, but there are no docks.

Anchorage: Tomoka Basin at Mile 818.5 is too shallow for all but shoal-draft vessels. If you can follow the array of stakes and nudge your way in, the Tomoka River off the basin is deep quite a bit farther upstream.

Daytona Beach–ICW Mile 830

While the official tourist season for this northern Florida "summer resort" runs from Memorial Day to after Labor Day, Daytona Beach is popular all year long. In spring and fall, boats on the north-south run stop over, and in winter and summer, its mild climate attracts yachtsmen and tourists from other areas that are too hot or too cold. Skippers often stop at Daytona Beach either to have work done at one of the area's excellent repair yards or just to layover for a while to enjoy its many nearby attractions.

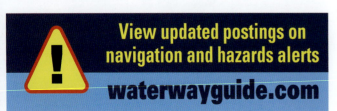

View updated postings on navigation and hazards alerts

waterwayguide.com

Soon after the invention of the automobile, Ormond became known as the **Birthplace of Speed**. Early auto owners were searching for places where they could drive on hard surfaces. Existing roads were no more than horse trails and posed problems for the cars. The broad, smooth beach at Ormond proved to be ideal. The first timed trials were held on March 26, 1903. Replicas of the winning cars can be seen at the Birthplace of Speed Park at the beach. Late in November, Ormond Beach hosts an antique car rally, featuring a gaslight parade of old cars to commemorate its place in the birth of auto racing.

NAVIGATION: Use NOAA Chart 11485. It's a straight 5-mile shot from Ormond Beach to the series of four bridges that welcome you to Daytona Beach: **Daytona Beach–Seabreeze Twin Bridges** (65-foot fixed vertical clearance); **Main St. (Daytona Beach) Bascule Bridge** (22-foot closed vertical clearance, opens on signal); **International Speedway Blvd. Bridge** (65-foot fixed vertical clearance); and **Veterans Memorial Bascule Bridge** (21-foot closed vertical clearance). The Veterans Bridge at Mile 830.6 is the only bridge with restricted openings. The bridge opens on signal, except from 7:45 a.m. to 8:45 a.m. and 4:45 p.m. to 5:45 p.m., Monday through Saturday (except federal holidays), when the draw opens only at 8:15 a.m. and 5:15 p.m. Both the Veterans and Main St. Bascule Bridges respond to sound signal as well as calls on VHF Channel 09. At press time (summer 2018), construction was underway for a fixed 65-foot vertical clearance replacement bridge for the Veterans Memorial Bridge. Anticipated completion was November 2018.

Dockage: Marinas and yacht yards line the shore on the west side of the ICW from north of the city all the way to Ponce de Leon Inlet. Just south of the Seabreeze Twin Bridges at Mile 829 is the 62-slip Coquina Marina, which offers transient dockage for vessels to 120 feet and many amenities, including laundry, a pool and a tennis court. Groceries are available within 1 mile.

To the south, Suntex Marina at Daytona Beach offers transient dockage on newly rebuilt docks and resort-like amenities. The on-site restaurant is Caribbean Jack's (386-523-3000), which is open daily with indoor and outdoor seating. (We prefer the swinging glider tables on the waterfront deck.)

The Halifax River Yacht Club is at Mile 830.7, in a basin just south of Memorial Bridge. They have some reserved transient space on their floating docks.

The municipal Halifax Harbor Marina is in a separate enclosed basin to the south. Enter the marina through the marked entrance channel just west of ICW green daybeacon "39A." The marina boasts 550 slips on a 60-acre property park, with excellent amenities, the Marina View Restaurant and Tiki Bar (844-383-6878) and nearby shopping. They also have gas and diesel fuel, a free pump-out service and a well-stocked ship store. The marina is convenient to downtown Daytona and the city bus stop is an easy walk away. In that same channel is Marina Point Marina, which only accepts long-term transients.

Daytona Marina & Boat Works is open 24/7 for fuel (both gas and diesel) and dockage and offers hull engine and propeller service and repair. The gold dome you see is the on-site Chart House Restaurant (386-255-9022).

Anchorage: There are anchorages both above and below the Seabreeze Twin Bridges. The anchorage south of the bridges is deeper, but there is scattered debris on the bottom. This area is a Slow-Speed/No-Wake Zone. The anchorage north of the Seabreeze Twin Bridges shallows up quickly and is in an area with submerged cables. Signs on each shore mark the location of the cables, but the signs are difficult to pick out from the water. The sign on the western shore is just south of the twin condos. This anchorage is also at one end of a 25-mph Manatee Zone, so wakes from passing boats can be a problem. This entire anchorage area seems to be generally shoaling, but it is still handy when you arrive late in the day from St. Augustine.

There is a cozy anchorage east of the ICW in the vicinity of the charted 11-foot depths at Mile 830.7. To reach this anchorage, turn east off the ICW immediately south of the Memorial Bridge. Using the yacht club's green daybeacons "3" and "5" as a back range, proceed east to within 100 to 150 feet of shore; if you stay on the range, you should find at least 6 feet of water over the bar. At this point, turn south along the shore to find a slot of water 9 to 13 feet deep about 100 feet from shore. The shoal on the channel side is less than 3 feet at MLW.

Many boats also anchor in the deep-water pocket northwest of red daybeacon "44," although depths are said to be less than the charted depth. Avoid the cable area if you stop here. This is a busy area with little wake protection. You can dinghy to the boat ramp from here but will need transportation to reach most amenities.

GOIN' ASHORE: DAYTONA BEACH, FL

SERVICES	
1	Library
2	Post Office
3	Visitor Information
ATTRACTIONS	
4	Brownie the Town Dog's Grave
5	Halifax Historical Museum

6	Jackie Robinson Memorial Baseball Park
SHOPPING	
7	Riverfront Shops
DINING	
8	McK's Tavern
9	Scuttlebutts Pub & Restaurant

10	Stavro's Pizza House
MARINAS	
11	Halifax River Yacht Club
12	Halifax Harbor Marina

Daytona Beach's 23 miles of beach were once a proving ground for automobile engines in the early 1900s. Automobile pioneers like Louis Chevrolet and Henry Ford found the hard-packed sand, gentle slope and wide expanse of beach to be the perfect venue for auto racing. Today, the beach remains popular with motorists, although they are restricted to a leisurely 10-mph pace and must pay an access fee. Automobile racing moved inland to Daytona International Speedway in 1959 as cars became faster and crowds of spectators grew larger.

Attractions: The Daytona Chamber of Commerce at 126 Orange Ave. (on City Island) can get your started on your exploration. They are open weekdays from 9:00 a.m. to 5:00 p.m. (386-255-0981). On the way, you will pass the Halifax Historical Museum (252 S. Beach St., 386-255-6976), which presents Daytona Beach from a historical perspective. Another intriguing stop is the gravesite of Brownie the Town Dog who was "owned by no one but loved by all." A large, brown, short-haired stray dog, Brownie lived on Beach Street for 15 years, during which time he was nicknamed Town Dog of Daytona Beach. Locals, merchants and tourists donated funds to keep Brownie well fed and cared for until he died on Halloween in 1954. The entire city mourned the dog's passing, and 75 people attended his funeral in Riverfront Park. The Mayor gave the eulogy. Brownie's grave is located on the corner of Orange and Beach Streets, should you care to pay your respects. You can't miss it; a full-size topiary shrub dog guards the grave.

The Main Street Pier, Oceanfront Boardwalk and the Coquina Clock Tower are historic landmarks on the waterfront in Daytona Beach.

On the western edge of town, Daytona International Speedway (the "World Center of Racing") is where the nation's top drivers and automobiles compete in the famous 24 Hours of Daytona endurance race every January and the world-famous Daytona 500 stock car race every February. Tour the grounds or take a lap around the speedway with the Richard Petty Driving Experience. If you aren't up for the drive, ride shotgun in a two-seat authentic NASCAR stock car driven by a professional instructor at speeds in excess of 160 MPH (daytonainternationalspeedway.com).

A flea and farmers market and 20 local golf courses are available year-round. Bus tours are also available, for a variety of Central Florida excursions. Three miles west of the waterway, Daytona Beach International Airport provides scheduled service to most cities.

The area hosts many impressive events throughout the year, including Bike Week, Spring Family Beach Break, the Coke Zero 400 and Biketoberfest.

The remainder of the year is peppered with a wide variety of art and music festivals, wine and chocolate walks, car shows and other delights. Minor league baseball at historic Jackie Robinson Ballpark (at Halifax Harbor) is a favorite, as is the free summer concert series at the open-air, oceanfront Daytona Beach Bandshell.

Shopping: Within walking distance of the marinas, the Riverfront Shops of Daytona Beach offers wide pedestrian walkways, riverfront parks and plenty of shops and restaurants. West Marine is located about 2 miles from the waterfront (1300 International Speedway Blvd., 386-255-2013). You also might find something you need at Surplus Unlimited Discount Marine (613 International Speedway Blvd., 386-252-5019). As in any city, this is an easy place to provision with numerous grocery, pharmacy and other such options.

Dining: There are many restaurants located in downtown Daytona along the waterfront. Caribbean Jack's (721 Ballough Rd., 386-523-3000) at Suntex Marina is one of our favorites, as are Scuttlebutts Pub Restaurant (114 S. Beach St., 386-872-2939); McK's Tavern (218 S. Beach St., 386-238-3321); and Stavro's Pizza House (262 S. Beach St., 386-258-5041). The Chart House Restaurant at the Daytona Marina and Boatworks (386-255-9022) is always a fine choice.

■ DAYTONA BEACH TO PONCE DE LEON INLET

ICW Mile 831 to Mile 839

NAVIGATION: Use NOAA Chart 11485. Stay in the channel between Daytona and Port Orange, as there are many shoals just outside the channel. At Mile 835.5, about halfway between Daytona Beach and Ponce de Leon Inlet, the high-rise **Dunlawton Ave. (Port Orange) Bridge** carries state Route A1A across the ICW. It is charted with a 65-foot fixed vertical clearance but tide boards at a full-moon high tide sometimes show a center-span clearance of 63 feet. Current is swift here, and the narrow channel can be congested, especially on weekends.

Just below the Port Orange Bridge, a small mangrove island on the west side of the ICW channel is a nesting ground for pelicans, egrets and cormorants during the spring. Confine your activity to watching only and do not disturb the nests.

The course south from Port Orange passes through a dredged cut that is usually crowded with fishermen in small outboard craft, so watch your wake. There was

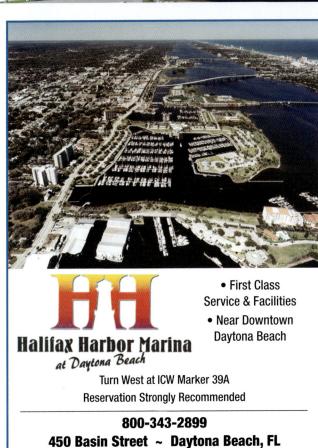

Daytona Beach to Ponce de Leon Inlet, FL

		Largest Vessel Accommodated	VHF Channel Monitored	Transient Berths / Total Berths	Approach / Dockside Depth (reported)	Floating Docks	Gas / Diesel	Groceries, Ice, Marine Supplies, Snacks	Repairs: Hull, Engine, Propeller	Lift (tonnage), Crane, Rail	Min/Max Amps	Laundry, Pool, Showers, Courtesy Car	Pump-Out Station	Nearby: Grocery Store, Motel, Restaurant
DAYTONA BEACH				Dockage				Supplies			Services			
1. Coquina Marina (formerly Sunset Harbor Yacht Club) 🖥 WiFi	386-317-0555	120	16	10/62	10/10	F	–	IS	–	–	30/100	LPS	P	GMR
2. Suntex Marina at Daytona Beach 🖥 onSpot	386-523-3100	75	16/79	10/85	6/6	–	–	GIMS	–	–	30/100	LPS	P	GMR
3. Halifax River Yacht Club 🖥 WiFi 830.7	386-255-7459	80	16/68	3/39	7/7	F	–	IS	–	–	30/50	LPS	P	GMR
4. Halifax Harbor Marina 🖥 WiFi WG 830.7	386-671-3601	100	16/71	55/550	8/8	F	GD	IS	–	–	30/100	LS	P	MR
5. Marina Point Marina 🖥 WiFi	386-239-7166	55	–	0/16	8/8	F	–	I	–	–	30/50	LS	–	GMR
6. Daytona Marina & Boat Works WiFi WG 831	386-252-6421	200	16/72	91/159	8/8	–	GD	IS	HEP	L55	30/100	LS	P	GMR
PORT ORANGE														
7. Seven Seas Marina & Boatyard 🖥 835.2	386-761-3221	44	16/72	10/30	6/9	–	GD	IM	HEP	L35,C	30/50	LS	P	GMR
8. Adventure Yacht Harbor 🖥 WiFi WG 836.8	386-756-2180	65	16/18	4/137	5/7	–	GD	IMS	E	–	30/50	LS	P	MR
9. Harbour Village Golf & Yacht Club–PRIVATE WiFi 839.6	386-316-9775	–	16	call/142	6/10	F	–	I	–	–	–	PS	P	GR
PONCE DE LEON INLET AREA														
10. Inlet Harbor Marina 🖥 WiFi	386-767-3266	180	06	12/84	9/15	F	GD	I	–	–	30/100	LS	P	GR
11. Sea Love Boat Works Inc. WiFi 1.3 SE of 839.5	386-761-5434	90	16/07	5/10	8/8	F	GD	M	HEP	L70	30/100	S	–	R

🖥 Internet Access WiFi Wireless Internet Access WG Waterway Guide Cruising Club Partner onSpot dockside WiFi facility
See WaterwayGuide.com for current rates, fuel prices, web site addresses, and other up-to-the-minute information. *(Information in the table is provided by the facilities.)*

a shoal reported to be in the channel on the west side between red daybeacons "68" and "70" in the vicinity of Tenmile Creek. Pass 50 feet off green daybeacon "69" for 16 feet at MLW. (Note there is only 5 feet at MLW by red daybeacon "68A," which was added to further define the deeper water.)

There is a condo with private docks on the east side of the ICW between green daybeacon "71" and red daybeacon "72." Its entrance channel is marked with a rather large red nun buoy and green can buoy. Do not confuse these for the floating ICW markers marking the beginning of the Ponce de Leon Cut just to the south after flashing green "1."

⚠️ This area is constantly changing. The numbering of the markers changes after daybeacon "72" (Mile 839) when you are going south on the ICW. Flashing green "1" is permanent, but red nuns "2" and "2A" and green cans "3" and "3A" are temporary and moved on a regular basis. Pass red "2" and red "2A" by 20 to 30 feet for 7 feet at MLW. This is an active shoaling area, so check for updates on the Waterway Explorer (waterwayguide.com) just before transiting.

Dockage: Seven Seas Marina & Boatyard is located above the Port Orange Bridge (east side). Pat's Riverfront Café (386-756-8070) is on the premises. Call ahead to check on dock availability. A short distance below the Port Orange Bridge on the east side of the ICW

past flashing green "59" is Adventure Yacht Harbor. They offer slips and sell gas and diesel. They mostly cater to sportfishing boats but are close to amenities and provisioning supplies. Look for the marked entry channel. Note that there is a tidal range here of 2.5 feet and the channel can be as low as 5 feet; call ahead for more exact depths.

Harbour Village Golf & Yacht Club is strictly private (members only) and does not accept transient boats at their docks.

Ponce De Leon Inlet Area–Mile 840 to Mile 843

The Ponce de Leon Inlet area (sometimes called New Smyrna Inlet) begins north of Mile 840. Just west of the inlet, the Ponce de Leon Cut portion of the ICW is protected but subject to shoaling, especially at its north and south ends. The historic Ponce de Leon Inlet Lighthouse is open to the public (daily except Thanksgiving and Christmas) and provides a stunning panoramic view of the area.

NAVIGATION: Use NOAA Chart 11485. From flashing green "1" to red daybeacon "6," on the north end of Ponce de Leon Cut, shoals are a constant problem. Our Cruising Editor observed 5- to 6-foot MLW depths here. Several buoys in this area are off station and may not match what is printed on your chart. Dredging was planned at press time in summer 2018. See the

DAYTONA BEACH, NOAA CHART 11485

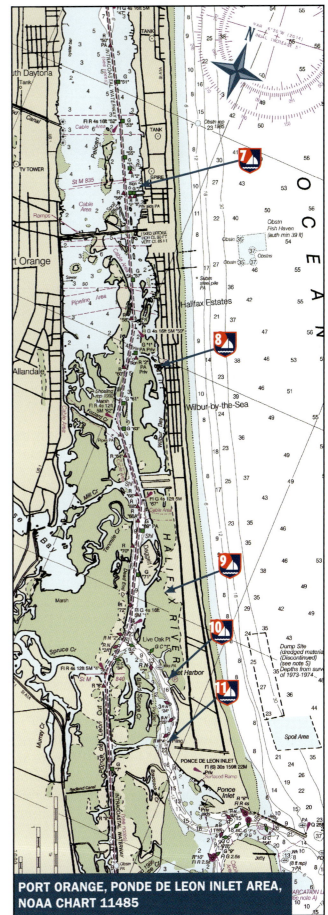

**PORT ORANGE, PONDE DE LEON INLET AREA,
NOAA CHART 11485**

ICW

Ponce de Leon Inlet

Waterway Explorer at waterwayguide.com for the latest information.

Ponce de Leon North Jetty Light is missing its foundation and due to Hurricane Matthew, the jetty has shifted. The area surrounding the structure is a hazard to navigation. Mariners are advised to use extreme caution while transiting the area. Stay to the center of the channel (or closer to the green side). The balance of the Ponce de Leon Cut up to marker "18" has 12 to 15 feet of water. Most of the cut sounded at 12 feet after the entrance at both ends.

The next opportunity going south to leave the ICW and go offshore is the Canaveral Barge Canal at Mile 894, east to Canaveral Inlet.

⚠️ South of the Ponce de Leon Cut on the ICW (Mile 843), there is a shoal of varying depths extending across the entire ICW channel between red daybeacon "18" and floating green over red (where the older chart showed green daybeacon "19") as well as at red nun "18A" and red daybeacon "20." Pass 50 feet off "18" and "18A" for 5 feet at MLW. Ponce de Leon Cut temporary buoy green "17A" has been added to mark deeper water. This is a very active shoaling area that is subject to change. Check for updates at Waterway Explorer at waterwayguide.com.

Dockage: Inlet Harbor Marina at the north end of the North Channel offers transient dockage, sells fuel and has laundry facilities. The on-site restaurant, Off the Hook (386-202-4490), is newly rebuilt and open.

Sea Love Marina & Boat Works, Inc. is 1 mile east of Mile 840 on the North Channel of the inlet. They offer transient berths, gas and diesel fuel and almost any type of repair. Their 70-ton lift can haul boats with up to a 23-foot beam. Down the Hatch Seafood Company (386-761-4831) is nearby. If you plan to stay a few days, check out the funky Hidden Treasure Rum Bar & Grill with a waterside tiki bar on the inlet (386-761-9271).

Anchorage: Note that all the side creeks in this area–North Channel, Spruce Creek, the unnamed side creek to the east and south of Spruce Creek, and Rockhouse Creek–are designated No-Wake Zones to protect the manatee population. All of the anchorages on these creeks have approximately 7 to 9 feet of water but are not included in the periodic dredging because they are not authorized federal channels.

Rockhouse Creek is a popular weekend anchorage and a congested small boat passage. Enter along the centerline of the cut from the ICW, as shoals are building from both the north and south shores. Once inside, 8- to 10-foot depths are easy to find and holding is good Provisioning opportunities are nearby.

The spoils island on the southeast side of Rockhouse Creek and adjacent to the ICW was scheduled to receive much of the spoil from recent dredging, which was instead used to refurbish the beach oceanside of the inlet.

■ NEXT STOP

At about Mile 840, the ICW begins its departure from the Halifax River and enters the Ponce de Leon Cut north of Ponce de Leon Inlet, joining with the Indian River north just below the inlet. Strong tidal currents often run up and down the land cut and occasionally may give your vessel a sideways push. For navigational information on the ICW south of the inlet, refer to the next chapter, "New Smyrna Beach to Vero Beach."

NAVIGATOR | JOURNEYS

Fernandina Beach to St. Simons Island

LEG 4 of 8

○ **START**

This leg of our yearlong journey by boat from Key West to Norfolk is full of island exploration. The adventure begins on Amelia Island, the northern Florida home of historic and colorful Fernandina Beach, and meanders north into Georgia's magical barrier islands, including Cumberland, Jekyll, and St. Simons. Make time for beachcombing, hiking, and scouting wild horses.

MILE 717
LEGENDARY BAR
Fernandina Beach

The Palace Saloon is Florida's oldest bar and the heart of this spirited little town. Order a Pirate's Punch and check out the mahogany bar and hand-painted murals. **TIE UP:** Leave the boat at anchor and dinghy to Fernandina Harbor Marina. Walk to **Florida House Inn,** a former boardinghouse dating from 1857. Rates start at $120.

MILE 710
NATURE BREAK
Cumberland Island

Crossing into Georgia waters, drop anchor at wild, wonderful **Cumberland Island** to explore 50 miles of trails through maritime forest, undeveloped beaches, and wide marshes. The island is home to about 150 wild horses.

MILE 684
HISTORY LESSON
Jekyll Island

Savor the social refinement that's held sway on this island gem by breakfasting at the **Jekyll Island Club Hotel,** a once exclusive club from the late 19th century. **TIE UP: Jekyll Harbor Marina's** dockage rates start at $2.25 per foot per day and include complimentary golf carts and bikes.

MILE 680
(5 NAUTICAL MILES WEST)
CULTURE ALERT
Brunswick

Built in 1899 as the Grand Opera House, the three-story **Historic Ritz Theatre** is a year-round cultural center that features films (including summer classics), live theater, concerts, and more. There's not a bad seat in the house!

MILE 677
TEE TIME
St. Simons Island

You can't always see the golf courses from the Intracoastal Waterway, but those who carry clubs on board could spend days course-hopping here, and the weather is golf-glorious year-round. **TIE UP:** Take a slip at **Morningstar Marinas/Golden Isles** for $2.25 per foot per day.

● **END**

NO BOAT (YET)? Sail the Golden Isles aboard a Catalina Yacht with your own skipper from **Dunbar Yachts.** Half-day, full-day, and sunset charters depart from St. Simons Island's Morningstar Marinas. Or step it up with **Taylor'd Yacht Charters,** which offers luxury yacht charters worldwide, including the East Coast.

40 MILES COVERED

8
NUMBER OF FLAGS
THAT HAVE FLOWN OVER
FERNANDINA BEACH

400+ SPECIES OF **BIRDS**

1
KENNEDY WEDDING
ON CUMBERLAND ISLAND

$50
PRICE TO ADOPT A
GEORGIA SEA TURTLE

READY TO SET SAIL? To order guidebooks and begin planning your boating adventures, visit **waterwayguide.com**

BY **JANI PARKER**

ST. JOHNS RIVER TO PONCE DE LEON INLET

FROM TOP: DANITA DELIMONT/GETTY IMAGES, COURTESY OF ATLANTIC CENTER FOR THE ARTS, ICON SPORTSWIRE/GETTY IMAGES, JASON GANSER/GETTY IMAGES, COURTESY OF THE COLUMBIA; MAP BY MATT CASERTA

NAVIGATOR | JOURNEYS

SAILS UP: THE ULTIMATE CRUISE UP THE INTRACOASTAL WATERWAY
Titusville to St. Augustine

○ START

LEG 3 of 8

ST. AUGUSTINE

FLAGLER BEACH

DAYTONA

NEW SMYRNA BEACH

TITUSVILLE

This sunny segment is an all-Florida cruise that begins on the Space Coast—home to Cape Canaveral—and makes its way north to the beautiful and historic city of St. Augustine, the oldest continuously occupied city in the country. Along the way, discover the laid-back surf town of New Smyrna Beach, hit the road for a break at Daytona, and enjoy the old-style fun of Flagler Beach.

MILE 878
BLAST OFF
Titusville
Kennedy Space Center Visitor Complex is the only place on Earth where you can check out a spacecraft launch pad, have lunch with an astronaut, see giant rockets, and experience what a rocket launch feels like.
TIE UP: Pick up a mooring at **Titusville Municipal Marina** for $20 per day.

MILE 846
ART AND EATS
New Smyrna Beach
NSB, as it's called by locals, is home to the **Atlantic Center for the Arts,** an artists-in-residence community that offers a wealth of workshops. Pull up for oysters and hush puppies at **JB's Fish Camp,** an old-school seafood dive with live music, kayaks for rent, and fishing off the dock.

MILE 829
DRIVING DAY
Daytona Beach
Take a few thrilling laps around the track on your own or with an instructor at **Daytona International Speedway's** Richard Petty Driving Experience.
TIE UP: At **Loggerhead Marina,** rates start at $2.25 per foot per day and include access to a heated pool and private cabanas.

MILE 778
CUBAN FEASTING
St. Augustine
Have cocktails on the boat and then dinner at **Columbia Restaurant,** a gorgeous Spanish-Cuban restaurant in this historic port city.
TIE UP: Grab a mooring operated by **St. Augustine Municipal Marina** in the shadow of Castillo de San Marcos, a landmark Spanish fortress built in 1695, for $20 per day.

MILE 810
TIME TO PLAY
Flagler Beach
Take the day off (the water)! Six miles of uncrowded beaches, great fishing spots (including the **Flagler Beach Municipal Pier),** fun shops, and oceanfront restaurants make Flagler Beach, which has been billed as "a retro town with salty style," well worth the shore leave.

● END

NO BOAT (YET)? St. Augustine Sailing offers bareboat (for experienced sailors) and captained (for the rest of us) charters aboard sailboats of up to 42 feet.

98 MILES SAILED

2 NUDE BEACHES

1 SURFING MUSEUM

1 ALLIGATOR FARM HISTORIC DISTRICT

55 YEARS BEFORE THE PILGRIMS ARRIVE, ST. AUGUSTINE IS ESTABLISHED

48 COASTAL LIVING *April 2017*

BY **JANI PARKER**

READY TO SET SAIL? To order guidebooks and begin planning your boating adventures, visit **waterwayguide.com**

New Smyrna Beach to Vero Beach

 ICW Mile 844–Mile 952   **VHF** FL Bridges: Channel 09

CHARTS NOAA 11472, 11476, 11485

Coming in from Ponce de Leon Inlet (detailed in the previous chapter), the safest route to the ICW is the South Channel leading to New Smyrna Beach, the Indian River North and Mosquito Lagoon farther south on the ICW.

■ NEW SMYRNA BEACH

ICW Mile 844 to Mile 846

NAVIGATION: Use NOAA Chart 11485. Use the Miami Harbor Entrance Tide Tables. For high tide at Ponce Inlet, add 5 minutes; for low tide, add 33 minutes. The charted floating markers for the North Channel from Ponce de Leon Inlet are on station, and the channel is always active with traffic. From the west side of North Channel to the **George E. Musson (Coronado Beach) Bascule Bridge** at Mile 845.0 is a strictly enforced No-Wake Zone, as is the intersection of the ICW and the South Channel.

The George E. Musson Bridge has 24-foot closed vertical clearance and is hydraulic and relatively slow in opening; a swift-moving current complicates the approach. The bridge opens on signal, except from 7:00 a.m. to 7:00 p.m. daily, when the draw opens only on the hour and half-hour.

South of the George E. Musson Bridge at Mile 845.0, continue to favor the eastern shore until the channel swings toward New Smyrna Beach. The area around red daybeacon "34" (Mile 845.5) has consistent issues with shoaling. It is easier and less stressful to just use the well-marked Sheepshead Cut at Mile 845.5 to bypass the shoaling.

Sheepshead Cut is a more direct, well-marked channel that runs south of Chicken Island and Bouchelle Island; a green-red junction daybeacon indicates the eastern tip of Chicken Island. The channel, which has 9- to 12-foot foot depths, meets the ICW and another green-red

junction daybeacon at the west end of Chicken Island. Stay to the center of the marked channel to avoid shoals.

Do not cut corners off the ICW where green daybeacons "37" and "39" and a white "Danger" daybeacon mark a shoal; also honor green can buoy "39A," which is not shown on current charts. Also note that the ICW channel has only 10-foot depths at low tide just off the New Smyrna Yacht Club close to flashing green "45." When passing the Smyrna Yacht Club, which borders the waterway, slow down and give them a "no-wake" pass.

New Smyrna Beach's harbor comes up suddenly beyond flashing red "38," which marks the turn toward

New Smyrna Beach, FL

NEW SMYRNA BEACH AREA			Largest Vessel Accommodated	VHF Channel Monitored	Transient Berths / Total Berths	Approach / Dockside Depth (reported)	Floating Docks	Gas / Diesel	Groceries, Ice, Marine Supplies, Snacks	Repairs: Hull, Engine, Propeller	Lift (tonnage), Crane, Rail	Laundry, Pool, Showers, Courtesy Car	Min/Max Amps	Pump-Out Station	Nearby: Grocery Store, Motel, Restaurant
					Dockage				**Supplies**			**Services**			
1. New Smyrna Marina dba The Fishing Store 🖥 📶		386-427-4514	125	16/80	6/31	12/10	F	GD	IMS	–	–	30/100	PS	–	GMR
2. North Causeway Marine 846.4		386-427-5267	60	16	2/35	8/10	–	GD	GIMS	HEP	L	30/50	–	–	GR
3. New Smyrna Beach City Marina 🖥 onSpot 846.5		**386-409-2042**	**65**	**16/68**	**7/43**	**8/10**	**F**	**–**	**I**	**–**	**–**	**30/100**	**LS**	**P**	**GMR**
4. River Deck Marina 846.6		386-428-7827	60	–	call/40	8/8	F	G	IMS	HE	L	30/50	–	–	GMR
5. Night Swan Intracoastal B & B 🖥 📶 WG 847		386-423-4940	32	–	3/6	12/9	F	–	–	–	–	30/30	LS	–	GMR
6. Smyrna Yacht Club 🖥 📶 847		386-427-4040	65	16	3/77	/4	F	–	IS	–	–	30/50	PS	P	R

🖥 Internet Access 📶 Wireless Internet Access WG Waterway Guide Cruising Club Partner onSpot dockside WiFi facility

See WaterwayGuide.com for current rates, fuel prices, web site addresses, and other up-to-the-minute information. *(Information in the table is provided by the facilities.)*

NEW SMYRNA BEACH AREA, NOAA CHART 11485

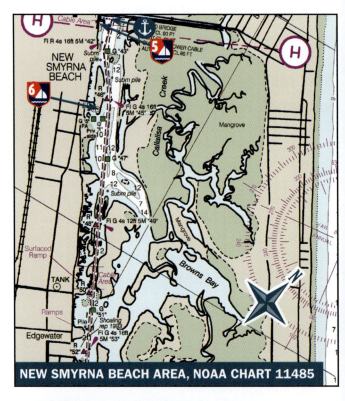

NEW SMYRNA BEACH AREA, NOAA CHART 11485

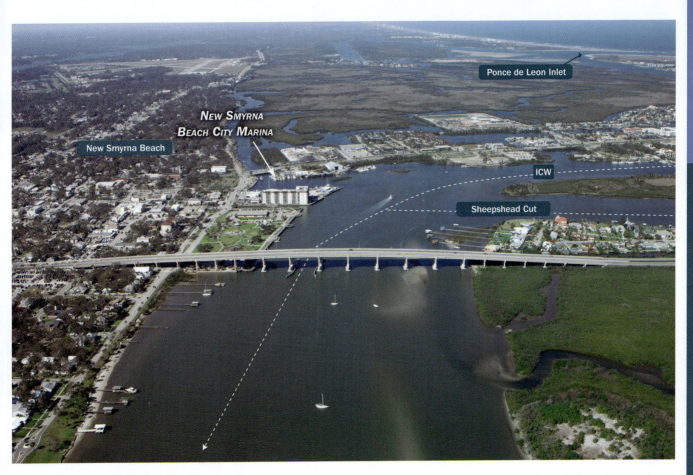

Ponce de Leon Inlet

New Smyrna Beach City Marina

New Smyrna Beach

ICW

Sheepshead Cut

the **Harris Saxon (New Smyrna) Bridge** at Mile 846.5 (with 65-foot fixed vertical clearance). The City of New Smyrna has built an attractive park at the northwest end of the bridge with a boardwalk, fishing pier and three small docking areas. Overnight docking is not allowed at the park docks. The park bulkhead takes up the entire area between the condominiums at the nearby marina and the bridge.

Dockage: Located just 2.5 miles from Ponce Inlet, the New Smyrna Marina (The Fishing Store) offers transient dockage on floating docks and fuel, both gas and diesel. A fleet of offshore and inshore fishing charters and daily pontoon boat rentals are available. The on-site Outriggers Tiki Bar and Grille offers lunch, dinner and Sunday brunch. North Causeway Marine to the south has limited space (two slips) reserved for transients, sells fuels and offers repairs.

At Mile 846.5, New Smyrna Beach City Marina offers slips on a first-come, first-served basis with full amenities, including cable TV, laundry and WiFi. It is close to the Canal Street Historic District, where you can find arts, history, shopping and dining. It is also across the street from the Old Fort Park historical site, which hosts a weekly Farmers' Market on Saturday. Nearby

River Deck Marina generally seeks to fill its slips with full-time renters, but they have some limited transient slips and sell gas.

Want to get off the boat? Night Swan Intracoastal Bed & Breakfast to the south has dockage if you stay with them. The Smyrna Yacht Club is beyond that, on an island west of the ICW and south of the Harris Saxon Bridge. They welcome members of clubs that are listed in the American Registry of Yacht Clubs. (They do not offer reciprocity to Florida Council of Yacht Club members.)

Anchorage: There is space in Sheephead Cut for three or four boats to anchor on the south side of the channel between green daybeacon "1" and just beyond green daybeacon "3" (between the markers and the condominium docks on Bouchelle Island). Show an anchor light and make sure that you will not swing into the channel or the docks at the tidal change; this is a very small, tight anchorage. The depths are 8 to 10 feet in MLW and the holding is good, but local boats use the channel at all hours.

It is possible to anchor south of the Harris Saxon Bridge at Mile 847 in 12 feet at MLW with good holding in mud. (Best water is found about 500 feet north of

SERVICES	
1	Library
ATTRACTIONS	
2	New Smyrna Museum of History
3	Old Fort Park

SHOPPING/DINING	
4	Save-A-Lot (groceries)
5	New Smyrna Brewing Company
MARINAS	
6	New Smyrna Marina

7	North Causeway Marine
8	New Smyrna Beach City Marina
9	Fishin' Cove Marina
10	Night Swan Intracoastal B&B
11	Smyrna Yacht Club

T he New Smyrna Sugar Mill ruins are located a few miles from the harbor. Built in the early 1800s with coquina stones (a natural limestone formed of broken shells and corals), the mill processed sugarcane into granular sugar that was shipped north. Molasses, a processing byproduct, went south for rum production.

Attractions: The historic Turnbull Ruins are located in Old Fort Park along Riverside Drive. The fort-like coquina ruins lead some historians to believe New Smyrna was originally the site of St. Augustine and that it could be even 500 years older than St. Augustine. Several paths and benches are scattered under a beautiful canopy of oak trees. This is the site of summer concerts and the annual Art Fiesta in February.

The Marine Discovery Center (located on the ICW at the North Causeway east of the marinas) is a nonprofit educational center that offers history and sunset tours as well as eco-tours of the New Smyrna area (386-428-4828). The nearby New Smyrna Beach Museum of History has interpretive exhibits of local culture and history (120 Sams Ave., 386-478-0052). The Atlantic Center for the Arts, a world-renowned artist-in-residence program, is based here. In addition to revolving exhibits, the Center features artist lectures, readings, demonstrations and presentations as well as workshops (atlanticcenterforthearts.org). Less than two miles away, the wide sandy beaches offer a relaxing day of sunbathing, swimming, water sports and surf fishing.

Shopping/Dining: There is a Save-A-Lot grocery store (720 S. Dixie Hwy., 386-847-8815) relatively close to the City Marina. The downtown area of New Smyrna Beach begins only a block away from the New Smyrna Beach City Marina where a variety of restaurants and shops line up and down the streets with local shoppers and visitors. Most of the restauarants are along Canal Street, including New Smyrna Brewing Company, with a taproom and brewery tours (386-957-3802). See more options at nsbfla.com.

green daybeacon "45.") This provides easy access to a dinghy dock and town. This location is, however, open to the south and passing boat wakes along with a lot of debris on the bottom. A trip line on your anchor is recommended.

■ TO INDIAN RIVER

ICW Mile 847 to Mile 859

NAVIGATION: Use NOAA Chart 11485. For about the next 10 miles, the ICW runs down a straight, dredged channel between the mainland and a jumble of small islets that support several fishing camps along with the usual Florida waterfront housing on the west side. Keep an eye out for kayaks and small fishing boats here; they frequently anchor in the channel or too close to the edge. Luckily for them, a good deal of this area is a Manatee Slow Speed, Minimum Wake Zone, from red daybeacon "64" at Mile 852.8 to green daybeacon "9A" at Mile 858.4. This is an area of frequent manatee sightings, so proceed cautiously anytime you see a circular disturbance on the surface of the water.

Staying in the center of the channel, you will see 11-foot to 14-foot depths. It shoals very quickly on the edges of the channel.

Mosquito Lagoon—ICW Mile 8609 to 869

Mosquito Lagoon is an open, shallow expanse of water that can only be explored by dinghy or shallow-draft boat. The same conditions that make this water popular for mosquitoes and deer flies also create an ideal feeding and breeding ground for sport and commercial fish, including redfish, sea trout and mullet. Crabs, clams and shrimp thrive among the dense aquatic grass beds. Flocks of white pelicans and the small fishing boats that fill Mosquito Lagoon attest to the abundance of fresh seafood. Swimming toward a common destination, the birds herd fish together by flapping their wings on the water. Before the fish can escape, the pelicans gobble them up.

NAVIGATION: Use NOAA Chart 11485. Eight-foot deep spots are numerous in the ICW channel, but depths decrease suddenly outside the channel. Stay on the green side of the channel but don't hug markers too closely, as some areas at the channel edges are shallow. Keep an eye on the depth sounder and watch your wake to avoid damaging other boats near the channel that could be fishing. Uncharted spoil banks line the outside of the dredged Mosquito Lagoon channel. Shoaling has been reported between green daybeacons "25" and "29" in Mosquito Lagoon. There also is shoaling near green daybeacon "35," which is just past Mile 865.

As you reach the middle of Mosquito Lagoon, you may be able to see a large building in the distance to the south. This is the Space Shuttle hangar, or vehicle assembly building (VAB) at the Kennedy Space Center. In clear weather, the giant VAB is visible for distances of 20 miles or more.

Anchorage: If you choose to exit the channel to anchor, seek local knowledge or do so carefully, so that if there is a spoil bank just outside the channel, you hit it at slow speed.

There are only a few places of Mosquito Lagoon deep enough for ICW travelers to anchor for the night in this stretch. Two anchoring areas are east of green daybeacon "19" at Mile 861.3 in the 6- to 7-foot deep area and southeast of red daybeacon "24" at Mile 862.8 in the 10-foot-deep charted area; however, the area of deeper water is quite small. Vessels report the best passage by entering the first anchorage from south of green daybeacon "19" and the second anchorage from north of red daybeacon "24." Be aware this anchorage is bouncy with any wind due to minimal protection and too much fetch between the anchorage and the land. This is best used in emergency situations only if there is any wind at all.

Haulover Canal—ICW Mile 870

NAVIGATION: Use NOAA Chart 11485. This 1 mile-long rocky cut (with jettied entrances) provides easy passage from Mosquito Lagoon to the Indian River on the opposite side of Merritt Island. The **Allenhurst (Haulover Canal) Bascule Bridge** (27-foot closed vertical clearance) crosses the canal at Mile 869.2 and opens promptly on request. If the bridgetender does not respond to VHF Channel 09, use a horn signal (one long, one short) to request an opening or call 321-867-4859. Be aware that there are shallow areas at both entrances to the Haulover Canal.

Although the current can run swiftly here, the tidal range is minimal. Strong winds may lower or raise the river and canal levels by as much as 2 feet. The ramp on the inside of the basin (southwest of the Haulover Canal Bridge) is always busy with small fishing boats. The entire Haulover Canal is a Slow-Speed/Minimum Wake

Zone, protecting the numerous (and usually visible) resident manatees that feed just below the surface. Wildlife abounds on shore, which is overgrown with vegetation. Keep a lookout for herons, egrets, alligators, manatees and small fishing boats.

On weekends, both Mosquito Lagoon and Haulover Canal are congested with small boats of every type and description. The small fishing boats often have as many as three people standing up to cast at the edge of the channel or under the bridge. Fortunately, much of the congested area is a Slow-Speed Manatee area, thus preventing wakes that could capsize these small boats.

Anchorage: The basin on the southwest side of the Haulover Canal Bridge is too small to even consider as an anchorage for most cruising boats, although a small boat with a shallow draft on a short scope may fit. There are reports of enough depth (8 to 10 feet at MLW) at one end of the dock for a tie up, but it is not recommended as an overnight spot.

Indian River–ICW Mile 870 to Mile 875

NAVIGATION: Use NOAA Chart 11485. A straight, dredged channel extends from Haulover Canal's western mouth across the flats of the upper Indian River. This channel tends to shoal along both sides, although depths are usually well maintained in the center and in the 10-foot range. Navigate cautiously and avoid being pushed out of the channel by beam winds.

Flashing green "1" and red daybeacon "2" are the first two aids to navigation you will encounter heading southwest out of the Haulover Canal. After reaching these markers, two huge white tanks on the Indian River's west bank line up with the less visible red markers on the channel's north side and may be used

In the past, the southern end of **Mosquito Lagoon** (on an imaginary line from Haulover Canal east to 3 miles out in the Atlantic Ocean) was off limits to all watercraft 72 hours before any Kennedy Space Center launches. Security boats from the Coast Guard and Kennedy Space Center patrolled these waters during this restricted time and levied fines to unauthorized boats entering this zone. This security zone did not, however, include the ICW route. All of this will probably change as the Space Center shifts to a commercial space port. As of summer 2018, no information was available about any of the above restrictions. Pay attention, ask local marinas for information and check waterwayguide.com for updates.

to aid in navigation. These tanks are charted as "TANK (NW OF TWO)." When steering for the tanks, keep an eye on the markers ahead and astern, watching for leeway. You do not want to stray out of the channel in this area as it shoals quickly.

Dredging took place near the Mims Boat Ramp (Mile 875) in the Indian River in winter 2017. Even off the marked channel, the lower Indian River is wide and deep for most of the 120 miles to the St. Lucie River and Inlet. There is 65 feet of vertical clearance at most of the fixed bridges across the Indian River but exercise care after periods of heavy rain. Observe the tide boards on the fixed high-rise bridges in the Indian River carefully, especially if your mast is close to the limit.

Several stretches allow sailboats to hoist their canvas in the right conditions and power boaters to relax (although you should still remain watchful for shoal areas and crab trap markers). The channel is dredged from Haulover Canal to past Cocoa, but outside the channel depths vary widely and there are numerous shoals.

■ SPACE COAST AREA– ICW MILE 876 TO 914

In what has come to be known as the Space Coast Area, the coastal topography changes from a slender barrier strip to a broad stretch of land, which forms Cape Canaveral. Inside the Cape area, the waters divide around Merritt Island, forming Indian River on the mainland side and Banana River on the east side. This section of the Indian River is a pleasure to navigate, although strong winds from the north or south may kick up an uncomfortable chop.

Watch closely for interesting sights along the banks of the river. In areas farther south, the Indian River is too wide to see much ashore.

NAVIGATION: Use NOAA Chart 11485. There are numerous bridges, both high span and restricted, that cross the Indian River. If a closed bridge delays your passage, you and the other waiting boats will probably have plenty of room to maneuver. You may even want to consider anchoring off the channel, as depths along the river accommodate most boats. In fall, when daylight is shorter, anchoring is preferable to entering a strange harbor at night.

Titusville–ICW Mile 876

Titusville is an important agricultural center for the Florida citrus industry. It is also a good port from which to visit Disney World and the other theme parks in the Orlando area. Titusville is also the most convenient location to visit the Kennedy Space Center, an excursion that should not be missed.

NAVIGATION: Use NOAA Chart 11485. North of Titusville, the **NASA (Jay-Jay) Railroad Bascule Bridge** at Kennedy Space Center crosses the ICW at Mile 876.6 with a 7-foot closed vertical clearance. The bridge is normally left in the open position unless a train is approaching, which is infrequent. When a train approaches the bridge, it stops and the operator initiates a command to lower the bridge. The lights go to flashing red and the draw lowers and locks, providing the scanning equipment reveals nothing under the draw. The draw remains down until a manual raise command is initiated, or will raise automatically 5 minutes after the intermediate track circuit is no longer occupied by a rail car. After the train has cleared, the draw opens and the lights return to flashing green.

About 2 miles south of the NASA Bridge, Titusville's **Max Brewer (Titusville) Bridge** with 65-foot fixed vertical clearance crosses the ICW at Mile 878.9. About 6 miles below Titusville, the **NASA Causeway Twin Bascule Bridges** (Mile 885.0, 27-foot closed vertical clearance) at Addison Point crosses the channel and has restricted hours. The bridge opens on signal, except from 6:30 a.m. to 8:00 a.m. and from 3:30 p.m. to 5:00 p.m., Monday through Friday (except federal holidays), when the draws need not open. Note that reports of closed vertical clearance as low as 21 feet has been reported.

Stay well inside the channel between the Max Brewer Bridge and the NASA Causeway Bridges; there is shoaling to depths as shallow as 7.5 feet at MLW in spots, especially from green daybeacon "33" to south of red daybeacon "34" where the channel narrows. If you do leave the channel, proceed carefully and use your depth sounder.

⚠️ At about Mile 888.5, there is a large power plant on the west side of the ICW from which power cables cross the ICW in a northeasterly direction. These cables have a charted height of 85 feet over the main channel. If you have a tall mast, be sure that you will have at least 12 feet of clearance when passing under power lines to avoid arcing.

Kennedy Space Center Visitor Complex

You will need a full day to tour the Kennedy Space Center Visitor Complex. "Must sees" include the U.S. Astronaut Hall of Fame, Astronaut Encounter (have lunch with a real astronaut), Shuttle Launch Simulator and Control Center tour. You will also want to visit the aptly named rocket garden as well as the final resting place of the Space Shuttle Atlantis. Complete your visit by visiting the inspiring tribute to America's fallen astronauts, The Astronaut Memorial.

Because the launch site itself is in a secured area, visitors must board buses for two-hour tours. The visitor complex opens daily at 9:00 a.m., closing only on Christmas Day. Admission includes a bus tour to the launch sites and two 3-D IMAX movies ($50/day). For more information, contact the Visitors Center at 866-737-5235. Purchase tickets at kennedyspacecenter.com.

For updated launch information, check the schedule at kennedyspacecenter.com.

GOIN' ASHORE: TITUSVILLE, FL

SERVICES		
1	Visitor Information & Bike Shop	
ATTRACTIONS		
2	American Space Museum and Space Walk of Fame	
3	North Brevard Historical Museum	

4	Pritchard House	
SHOPPING		
5	Downtown Art Gallery	
6	Save-A-Lot	
DINING		
7	Playalinda Brewing Co.	

8	Sunrise Bread Co.	
MARINAS		
9	Titusville Marina	
10	Westland Marina	

Titusville, FL, lives up to its slogan "Gateway to Nature and Space." Kennedy Space Center is within 20 minutes of the Titusville Basin. Kennedy Space Center Visitor Complex, located at NASA's launch headquarters, is the only place on Earth where you can tour launch areas, meet a veteran astronaut, see giant rockets or train in a spaceflight simulator. (See sidebar.) For more information, visit kennedyspacecenter.com.

Attractions: Your first stop should be the Titusville Welcome Center at 419 S. Hopkins Ave. (321-607-6216). They have all the information you need and will gladly rent you a bike for getting around. You won't need a bike, however, to visit the Historic Pritchard House, constructed in 1891 and a fine example of Queen Anne

architecture. It is located within easy walking distance of the marina basin at 424 S. Washington Ave. The North Brevard Historical Museum is also located within the historic downtown at 301 S. Washington Ave. The museum displays photographs, furniture, clothing and artifacts of the early Titusville area.

Don't miss the Space Walk of Fame Museum (308 Pine St., 321-264-0434). The items and displays have been donated by individuals, astronauts, space workers, NASA and space company contractors. On display are working consoles from Launch Pad 36A and a Model 4 Sequencer from Launch Pad 16. It is open Monday through Saturday from 10:00 a.m. to 5:00 p.m. Other places of interest (transportation required) include the American

Police Hall of Fame and Museum (6350 Horizon Dr.), and the Valiant Air Command (6600 Tico Rd.), featuring aircraft from World War I to Desert Storm.

For the more adventuresome, the coast-to-coast connector bike trail runs through Titusville (see more at fgtf.org) and kayak tours of the Indian River Lagoon are available from A Day Away Kayak Tours (321-268-2655). This is especially enjoyable during bioluminescence season. During the warm summer months, every movement in the water–from the swirl of your paddle to the ghostly glow of a slow moving manatee produces light.

There are numerous parks as well, including the Sand Point Park, Vietnam Memorial Park, Space View Park and even a special dog park for your cruising pooch.

The Merritt Island National Wildlife Refuge and Canaveral National Seashore are minutes away and provide many opportunities to enjoy natural Florida, including horseback riding, kayaking, nature walks and pristine beaches.

And, for those who love to fish, Titusville is known as the "Redfish Capitol of the World."

Shopping: Like all larger cities, you will have no problems provisioning here. Amenities such as groceries, pharmacies, hardware and other such shopping abounds. Save-A-Lot (groceries) is at 120 S. Hopkins Ave. The downtown area also offers a variety of outdoor-related stores.

Remember your trip with a memento from the Downtown Art Gallery. Five showrooms feature local art and photography of the Indian River Lagoon area (335 South Washington Ave., 321-268-0122).

Dining: The Town of Titusville appreciates and welcomes the boating public. A revitalized downtown district is within walking distance of the waterfront and offers a nice selection of dining opportunities and shops. Sunrise Bread Co. (315 South Hopkins Ave., 321-268-1009) offers homemade bakery items, coffee and free WiFi.

If you venture out of downtown, Dixie Crossroads (1475 Garden St., 321-268-5000) is famous for its shrimp and corn fritters, and just a few blocks south of the downtown area is Chef Larry's where exceptional low-priced meals are the norm (1111 Washington Ave., 321-368-9123). Call for hours of operation and be advised that they accept cash only.

Playalinda Brewing Company is nestled in a renovated, 100-year-old hardware store at 305 S. Washington Ave. In addition to craft beers, Playalinda offers cider, wine and non-alcoholic options, along with "brewery bites." Well-behaved dogs are always welcome at the outdoor tables in front of the brewery.

Indian River, FL

			Dockage				Supplies		Services					
TITUSVILLE														
1. Titusville Marina 🖥 📶 WG 878.3	321-383-5600	130	16/68	15/197	8/8	F	GD	IMS	–	–	30/100	LS	P	GMR
2. Westland Marina 🖥 onSpot 878.3	321-267-1667	55	16/71	call/70	7/8	–	–	M	HEP	L50	30/50	LS	P	GMR
INDIAN RIVER CITY														
3. Kennedy Point Yacht Club & Marina 🖥 📶 WG 883	321-383-0280	60	16/71	15/80	6/4.5	–	–	GIS	–	–	30/50	LPS	P	GMR

🖥 Internet Access 📶 Wireless Internet Access WG Waterway Guide Cruising Club Partner onSpot dockside WiFi facility
See WaterwayGuide.com for current rates, fuel prices, web site addresses, and other up-to-the-minute information. *(Information in the table is provided by the facilities.)*

TITUSVILLE, INDIAN RIVER CITY, NOAA CHART 11485

Haulover Canal Bridge

Dockage/Moorings: The protected harbor at Titusville has a well-marked entry channel that normally carries 7-foot MLW depths. As soon as you enter the harbor, depths increase. Two marinas are located in the Titusville basin. The first is the friendly Titusville Marina, which welcomes transients on both fixed and floating docks and can accommodate boats up to 130 feet. They also have a mooring field for vessels up to 60 feet. The mooring fee includes the use of the marina facilities, along with a pump-out boat that will come out to you.

The second facility in the Titusville basin is Westland Marina, with slips and an over 6-acre yard that is popular with "do-it-yourself" boaters. They have a 50-ton lift and offer bottom painting, diesel/gas mechanic, fiberglass/gelcoat repair and general refurbishing. Groceries, fast food, a pharmacy, a liquor store and other amenities are a short walking distance from the basin.

A few miles south on the Indian River, at green daybeacon "39," you will see a marked entrance channel leading to Kennedy Point Yacht Club & Marina (reporting 4.5 dockside depths). At press time the marina was being rebuilt after hurricane damage but should be open by the end of 2018. Call in advance for a possible reservation. A yacht club affiliation is not required for transient dockage.

Anchorage: Anchoring is restricted due to the proliferation of moorings. You must stay at least 150 feet from the mooring field, so you need to be aware of your swing room. Boaters anchored nearby (outside the mooring field) may tie up at the Titusville Municipal Marina and use the dinghy dock and showers for a nominal fee. This is a great spot to watch rocket launches.

Note that the spoil areas and shoals shown on the chart (and those not shown on the chart) seem to be expanding. At the Jay-Jay Bridge (Mile 876.6), for example, the west anchorage is shoaling at the entrance. The NASA Causeway Twin Bridges at Addison Point (Mile 885.0) and subsequent bridges that cross the Indian River can provide a better overnight anchorage from all wind directions. Simply choose the side that will be sheltered from the wind. If you leave the channel to seek out protection behind a bridge causeway, go slowly and keep an eye on your depth sounder.

Just south of Titusville, at about Mile 883 (opposite Indian River City on the mainland), you will see a large charted area of deeper water with depths of 7 to 8 feet at MLW to the east of the ICW. (This anchorage is another

excellent spot to watch the space center launches.) Give the charted spoils areas a wide berth, and then sound your way over toward Merritt Island. The holding is good near red daybeacons "38" and "40," but these offer no protection from wind or choppy water. If you sound your way in far enough, wakes from channel traffic are almost entirely eliminated, although other boats moving around in the anchorage may give you a good rolling. This spot is more than 1 mile from the ICW.

Side Trip: Canaveral Barge Canal– ICW Mile 894

The 8-mile journey from the ICW to the Atlantic Ocean includes a 3-mile cut through Merritt Island with one restricted bridge, a crossing of the Banana River and passage through Canaveral Lock and then twin bascule bridges with rush-hour closures. The cut through Merritt Island is very scenic with beautiful natural flora and an abundance of marine and wildlife.

NAVIGATION: Use NOAA Chart 11485. (NOAA Chart 11478 shows this route in detail; see the Inlet section at the front of this guide for more information on

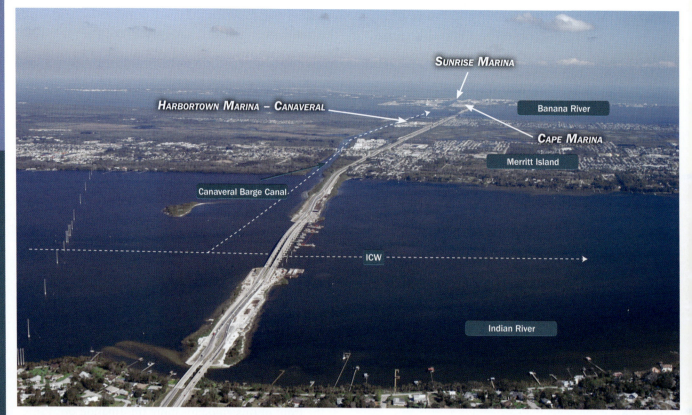

Cape Canaveral Inlet.) At Mile 894.0 the **Bennett Causeway (City Point) Twin Bridges** have a 65-foot fixed vertical clearance. East of the ICW channel, just north of the bridge, look for markers indicating the entrance to the Canaveral Barge Canal, which cuts through Merritt Island to the Banana River and Canaveral Inlet, and then leads on to the Atlantic Ocean.

Green daybeacons "13," "11A" (give these two wide berth due to possible shoaling) and green daybeacon "11," along with red flashing "12," provide the transition from the ICW to the barge canal entrance. Use caution transitioning through here, it has the minimum controlling depth for the route to the Atlantic. At press time in summer 2018, the shallowest area observed extended to the east from about 200 yards east of beacons "11" and "12" at 7.5- to 8-foot MLW depth (center channel with a typical river level). The canal itself is deep, 9 to 13 feet at MLW.

The **Christa McAuliffe Drawbridge** (26-foot closed vertical clearance) opens on the hour and half hour from 6:00 a.m. to 10:00 p.m. daily but is closed between 6:15 a.m. and 8:15 a.m. and from 3:10 p.m. to 6:00 p.m., Monday through Friday (except federal holidays). The bridge requires a 3-hour advance notice to open between 10:00 p.m. and 5:59 a.m. Call 321-452-5200 (daytime) or 321-213-2694 (after 10:00 p.m.).

Once you have transited Merritt Island via the Barge Canal, a fairly narrow channel maintains nearly the same course for 1.25 miles across the Banana River, carrying about 10-foot depths, to the Canaveral Lock. Be careful not to stray outside the channel and as always look behind you to be sure that you are not being laterally displaced by wind or current.

A north-south channel intersects this route prior to the Cape Canaveral Lock. A turn here to the north at daybeacons green "13" and red "14" puts you in the Saturn Barge Channel (Chart 11478). These waters are the backyard of Kennedy Space Center and provide unique vistas of the spaceport, cruise ship terminals and nature.

⚠️ Mariners must be aware that a Federal Manatee Sanctuary with a "No-Motor Zone" (NMZ) has been established in these waters. A wandering picket of advisory signs delineates the sanctuary. It crosses about 1.75 mile up this channel near green daybeacon "17." Vessels fitted with a propeller (even stowed) are not allowed into the Sanctuary.

Continue easterly for the **Cape Canaveral Lock** (321-783-5421). Hours of operation are from 6:00 a.m. to 9:30 p.m. year-round. It is the largest navigation lock in Florida and is designed to reduce tidal currents and prevent hurricane tides from entering the Banana River.

Canaveral Barge Canal & Banana River, FL

	Largest Vessel Accommodated	VHF Channel Monitored	Transient Berths / Total Berths	Approach / Dockside Depth (reported)	Floating Docks	Gas / Diesel	Groceries, Ice, Marine Supplies, Snacks	Repairs: Hull, Engine, Propeller	Lift (tonnage), Crane, Rail	Min/Max Amps	Laundry, Pool, Showers, Courtesy Car	Pump-Out Station	Nearby: Grocery Store, Motel, Restaurant
CANAVERAL BARGE CANAL			**Dockage**			**Supplies**		**Services**					
1. Harbor Square Marina ⌂ WiFi 1.5 E of 893.6 321-453-2464	60	16	7/120	13/7	–	D	IM	HP	–	30/50	LS	P	GMR
2. Harbortown Marina–Canaveral ⌂ WiFi 4E of 893.6 321-453-0160	–	16/10	50/275	6/6	–	GD	IMS	HEP	L70	30/50	LPS	P	GMR
CAPE CANAVERAL LOCK													
3. Ocean Club Marina at Port Canaveral ⌂ onSpot 321-783-9001	110	16	37/73	14/12	F	GD	I	–	L100	30/100	LPS	P	MR
4. Port Canaveral Marine ⌂ WiFi 0.6 E of 893.6 321-784-5788	110	16	–	15/15	F	GD	IMS	HEP	L110,C110	30/100	LPS	P	R
5. Cape Marina, Port Canaveral ⌂ WiFi 7 E of 893.6 321-783-8410	150	16/68	call/115	12/12	F	GD	IMS	–	L75	30/50	LPS	P	GMR
6. Port Canaveral Yacht Club ⌂ WiFi WG 6.9 E of 893.6 321-482-0167	60	–	call/50	40/10	F	–	IM	–	C	30/50	LS	–	MR
7. Bluepoints Marina 321-799-2860	47	16/10	call/26	40/15	F	GD	IMS	–	L25	–	S	P	GMR
8. Sunrise Marina 321-783-9535	98	16	3/21	20/8	F	GD	IMS	–	L12	30/50	–	–	MR
BANANA RIVER													
9. River Palms MHP ⌂ 321-452-8424	21	–	32/32	5/5			–	–	–	30/30	L	–	GM
10. Island Time Marina WiFi 321-613-4852	–	–	call/30	6/6			–	–	–	30/30	S	P	GR

⌂ Internet Access WiFi Wireless Internet Access WG Waterway Guide Cruising Club Partner onSpot dockside WiFi facility
See WaterwayGuide.com for current rates, fuel prices, web site addresses, and other up-to-the-minute information. *(Information in the table is provided by the facilities.)*

CANAVERAL BARGE CANAL, CAPE CANAVERAL LOCK, NOAA CHART 11476

BANANA RIVER, NOAA CHART 11476

The lift of the lock ranges from negligible to 3 to 4 feet at MLW, depending on the ocean tide stage.

Contact the lock tender on VHF Channel 13 for instructions and set your fenders in place before entering the lock. Have lines available fore and aft since they are not provided in the lock. There are synthetic rub rails with cleats spaced every 10 feet, making line control simple when locking through. The trip is worth the effort. Expect congestion around the two sets of boat ramps near the port.

East of the Cape Canaveral Lock, **State Route 401 Twin Bascule Bridges** (25-foot closed vertical clearance) at Mile 5.5 has a new schedule as of March 2018. The bridge opens on signal, except from 6:30 a.m. to 8:00 a.m. and 3:30 p.m. to 5:15 p.m., Monday through Friday (except federal holidays) and from 11:00 a.m. to 2:00 p.m. on Saturdays and Sundays, when the drawspans need not open for the passage of vessels. From 10:00 p.m. to 6:00 a.m., the draws will open on signal if at least 3 hours notice is given.

Dockage: The Canaveral Barge Canal contains two marinas that are considered "hurricane holes" by the locals, as the lock prevents any major tidal surge. Harbor Square Marina has recently been sold (at press time in summer 2018) and is expected to be fully renovated. The marina has good wind protection and offers slips. Harbortown Marina–Port Canaveral also have exceptionally good wind protection and is conveniently located in a basin 1 mile west of the Banana River. The marina offers gas and diesel, as well as a full-service restaurant and bar, along with a recreation area with grills, a fire pit, cornhole and horseshoes.

On the east side of the Canaveral Lock is a protected basin containing five marinas. Ocean Club Marina at Port Canaveral has floating transient slips and gas and diesel. Their 110-ton lift is wide enough for large catamarans. Nearby Port Canaveral Marine offers service, storage and sales at their 5-acre facility, but no wet slips.

The family-owned Cape Marina, Port Canaveral is a full-service marina and boatyard with a "do-it-yourself" area. They have high-speed fuel pumps (gas and diesel) on a 150-foot dock and a complete ship store that carries everything from "bait to batteries." Relax in the poolside lounge chairs or enjoy the on-site game room.

Port Canaveral Yacht Club accepts transients who are members of another yacht club. Be sure to call for reservations as they do get very busy. It is only a short walk from restaurants and gift shopping.

Indian River, FL

			COCOA		Dockage					Supplies			Services				
	Largest Vessel Accommodated	VHF Channel Monitored	Transient Berths / Total Berths	Approach / Dockside Depth (reported)	Floating Docks	Groceries, Ice, Marine Supplies, Snacks	Gas / Diesel	Repairs: Hull, Engine, Propeller	Lift (tonnage), Crane, Rail	Laundry, Pool, Showers, Courtesy Car	Min/Max Amps	Pump-Out Station	Nearby: Grocery Store, Motel, Restaurant				

COCOA

			Dockage			Supplies	Services				
1. Cocoa Village Marina 🖥️ 📶	897	321-632-5445	120	16/68	24/117	6.5/6.5	–	–	I	–	–	30/100	LS	P	GMR

🖥️ Internet Access   📶 Wireless Internet Access   **WG** Waterway Guide Cruising Club Partner   🔵 onSpot dockside WiFi facility

See WaterwayGuide.com for current rates, fuel prices, web site addresses, and other up-to-the-minute information. *(Information in the table is provided by the facilities.)*

COCOA, NOAA CHART 11485

To the east is Bluepoints Marina, which sells fuel and may have transient space but no shore power. Call in advance for dock availability. Sunrise Marina, closest to the inlet, welcomes transients with prior reservations are required. They offer full-service repairs and sell gas and diesel, have an on-site restaurant and provides easy ocean access.

The Cove, located near the marinas, is a waterfront dining area with numerous restaurants. The seven-story Exploration Tower is an architectural landmark with interactive exhibits and observation decks, plus a café and gift shop. Nearby Jetty Park and Cheri Down Park are recreational areas with beaches.

Anchorage: At the Bennett Causeway Bridges (City Point Bridge) just south of the entrance to the Canaveral Barge Canal, you can enter on the southwest side and anchor behind the causeway in 7 to 8-foot MLW depths

with good holding. Anchorage is also possible west of the Cape Canaveral Lock, just below the spoil island (7-foot MLW depths).

Additionally, a short run north in the Saturn Barge Channel offers access to anchorage possibilities near four spoil islands with 6 to 7-foot MLW depths just off the eastern side. These islands are before the previously mentioned "No-Motor Zone," but be aware the signage comes close to their eastern sides.

Side Trip: South on the Banana River

See the "Side Trip–North on the Banana River" section later in this chapter for more detailed information on this route.

NAVIGATION: Use NOAA Chart 11485. If heading south on the Banana River is your intention, approach flashing green "5," then turn for the high span of the Bennett Memorial Causeway Bridge (with a fixed vertical clearance of 36 feet). Proceed with caution keeping an eye on your sounder and the chart.

NOTE: When proceeding southbound in the Banana River keep red to port. The channel begins some 18 miles south, where it branches off of the Indian River (and the ICW at Mile 914.5) at Dragon Point, near Melbourne. There are some challenges on this route, and local knowledge is desirable. See the "Eau Gallie-ICW Mile 914" section for needed information.

Dockage: South of the fixed **Willard Peeble (SR 520) Bridge** (36-foot vertical clearance) are two marinas: The 32-slip River Palms MHP reports 5-foot dockside and approach depths. Call ahead for availability. Island Time Marina is also nearby and may have space for you. Call ahead.

Anchorage: Boats that can clear the **Bennett Memorial (A1A) Causeway Bridge** (36-foot fixed vertical clearance) can anchor in the Banana River, just south of the entrance to the Canaveral Barge Canal. Enter on the southwest side and anchor behind the causeway in 7- to 8-foot depths with good holding.

Cocoa Village–ICW Mile 897

NAVIGATION: Use NOAA Chart 11485. The **Merritt Island (Cocoa) Twin Bridges** (fixed 65-foot vertical clearances) cross the ICW at Mile 897.4. Cocoa Village is on the western shore and Merritt Island is on the eastern shore. Both offer numerous cruiser amenities.

⚠️ One vessel was lost and another severely damaged due to encounters with high voltage overhead cables that cross the Indian River south of the Merritt Island Twin Bridges at Cocoa, FL. While the cables are high at the ICW (charted at 88 feet authorized), they progressively descend towards shore and vertical clearance is substantially reduced (charted at 38 feet authorized). This is deceptive, and poses a serious risk for vessels operating near them, not just from physical contact but open-air arcing from the power lines to a mast. (We recommend a minimum mast-to-wire distance of 12 feet.) See the Waterway Explorer at waterwayguide.com for new alerts and updates.

The Army Corps of Engineers reports continuous shoaling between flashing green daybeacon "77" and green daybeacon "81" south of the Cocoa Twin Bridges. However, as of summer of 2018, this section all the way from the Twin Bridges to flashing "83" had an observed mid-channel controlling depth of 10 feet at MLW. Favor the western side of the channel but watch for pot markers. Do not attempt anchoring outside flashing green "83," due to shoaling.

There is essentially no daily tide range occurring from lunar tides in Cocoa since open passes to the ocean are far distant. However, strong currents (and some variation in level) are possible as the river responds to wind load and other factors.

Dockage: The ever-popular Cocoa Village Marina was undamaged by Hurricane Irma. It is a fully modern, clean facility with an exceptionally friendly and helpful staff. The well-marked approach channel is about a 0.25 mile north of the twin bridges and passes north of the marina's wave fence. This marina is convenient to the attractions, shops, and restaurants of Historic Cocoa Village.

As of press time in summer 2018, Cocoa Village Marina was the only dockage option in Cocoa. The City docks in Lee Wenner Park were fully destroyed by Hurricane Irma and have been removed. The rebuild for a greatly improved facility is scheduled to start in the fall of 2018. For current status on the project (including possible short-term day dockage), contact the Historic Cocoa Village Association (321-631-9075) or check "DOCKAGE INFO" at visitcocoavillage.com.

Anchorage: You can anchor west of the ICW and south of the bridges just off Cocoa Village in Cocoa Yacht Basin. The basin has been cleaned up from storm debris and is navigable as an anchorage. Enter with standard operating precautions and find 5 to 7-foot MLW depths with good holding. (Heed the warning signs for a submerged gas pipeline that runs out from Lee Wenner Park, then turns to parallel the causeway and crosses the river to Merritt Island. It comes ashore just south of the blue roofed building located south of the bridges.) Also note that this popular anchorage extends for about 0.5 mile down the river, along which you will find 6- to 9-foot MLW depths.

Most of the previous resident fleet has departed, so there is plenty of room. Until the new dock facilities are built in Lee Wenner Park, a temporary dinghy landing is being developed. To get the latest information on this, contact the Historic Cocoa Village Association, as noted above. Landing here puts you at the doorstep of Historic Cocoa Village and all that it offers.

The Merritt Island (east) side of the river offers the closest major provisioning, and there are now established anchorages on both sides of the Twin Bridges. For the north side, coming easterly off the ICW and paralleling the causeway will provide about 7-foot MLW depths all the way to the daybeacons "1" and "2" for Griffis Landing. This county park has six finger docks, a ramp, and a pump-out station; however, the approach/dockside depth is only 2 to 3 feet at MLW. Doc's Bait House (with a small-boat dock) and Ms. Apple's Crab Shack are on premises and unique enough to warrant a visit.

The south anchorage has grown into what is at times a sizeable community as a result of relocations due to hurricane damage at Cocoa. Approaching from the ICW, proceed with caution and be aware that the small island depicted on the chart has receded beneath the surface and is not visible, but it's there, as are it's shoals. Expect to find 5- to 6-foot MLW depths as depicted adjacent to the spoil area.

Note that there is easy shore access via dinghy from the south anchorage by passing under the feeder bridge on the causeway. This will bring you right to the Griffis Landing facilities.

A dinghy ride into this dock puts you within a 10-minute walk of West Marine, Publix, CVS, a UPS

GOIN' ASHORE: COCOA VILLAGE, FL

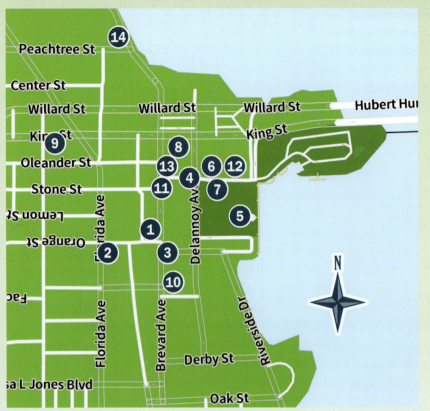

	SERVICES
1	Library
2	Post Office
3	Visitor Information
	ATTRACTIONS
4	Cocoa Village Playhouse
5	Cocoa Riverfront Park
	SHOPPING
6	S.F. Travis & Co. Hardware
7	Village Cycle Shoppe
	DINING
8	Cafe Margot
9	Dirty Oar Beer Company
10	Murdock's Southern Bistro
11	Ossorio Bakery and Cafe
12	Ryan's Pizza and Pub
13	Village Ice Cream & Sandwich
	MARINAS
14	Cocoa Village Marina

Settlers began arriving in the Cocoa area in the mid-1800s, and the City of Cocoa was chartered in 1895. Today, on the inland side of the ICW, a water tower with three large American flags painted on it serves as a well-known, and award-winning, landmark for Cocoa. Cocoa has a riverfront district known as Historic Cocoa Village.

Attractions: With well over 100 unique shops, businesses, and restaurants the Village is known for being dog-friendly and perfectly located for boating interests. A designated scenic drive runs through the Village as its 13-miles winds along the river's edge. With little vehicular traffic, it is very popular for biking, jogging, skating and walking. The state headquarters for the Florida Historical Society is located here and houses the Library of Florida History (425 Brevard Ave., 321-690-1971). The Cocoa Post Office has somewhat odd hours, so call before you go (600 Florida Ave., Ste. 101, 321-632-6846). Also in that building is the Historic Cocoa Village Association whose staff is available to provide current information for visitors on local attractions and events (600 Florida Ave., Ste. 104, 321-631-9075).

Riverfront Park, with a band shell and splash fountain for the kids, along with Lee Wenner Park (primarily a boat landing and ramp facility) and Taylor Park playground, form the Village's shoreline for Cocoa Yacht Basin. There are dozens of sponsored events and concerts, both large and small, throughout the year in the streets and the park. Check the local calendar for specifics at VisitCocoaVillage.com. The highly acclaimed Cocoa Village Playhouse has productions throughout the year (300 Brevard Ave., 321-636-5050).

Cocoa Beach, famous for surfing, is 8 miles away and is easily accessible by bus. Ron Jon Surf Shop is the world's largest surf shop (52,000 square feet) and is Ron Jon's flagship facility. Best of all, it's open 24 hours a day, seven days a week! The shop hosts the annual 3-day Beach 'N Boards Fest in March with live music and lots of surfing. (Caution: This coincides with Spring Break for many colleges.) See more at ronjonsurfshop.com.

The Kennedy Space Center Visitor Complex (20 miles away) is a major attraction. Check the schedule for the now common launches at kennedyspacecenter.com (855-433-4210). Orlando area theme parks are about 60 miles away and accessible by rental car.

Space Coast Area Transit bus service (Route 4) goes over to Merritt Island for provision shopping or to continue out to Cocoa Beach. Contact S.C.A.T (321-633-1878) for schedules. Nearby Enterprise Rent-A-Car provides pick-up and drop-off service (1750 W King St., 321- 633-7070).

Shopping: Cocoa Village is renowned for a multitude of truly unique shopping opportunities: art galleries, antique shops, art studios, boutiques, and more. As you walk around, look for "Cocoa Village Loves ICW Cruisers" anchor logos in store windows. Those establishments offer some type of perk to cruisers!

S.F. Travis & Co. (circa 1885) is a multi-building, old-style hardware store with an expansive inventory. This is a "must see" but they are closed on weekends (300 Delannoy Ave., 321-636-1441). If your boat bike needs repair, Village Cycle Shoppe offers bicycle service, rentals and new/used sales at 4 Harrison St. (321-806-3917).

West Marine is just beyond the ICW bridge on Merritt Island (320 W. Merritt Island Causeway, 321-452-4661). There are two Publix groceries (with adjacent CVS drug stores) within about 2 miles of the Village. One is on the mainland at Rockledge Square Shopping Center (1880 Rockledge Blvd., 321-639-1550). The other is across the ICW bridge at First Merritt Center (125 E. Merritt Island

Causeway, 321-452-0288). The latter Publix is larger and offers many more area shops, including Merritt Square Mall (777 E. Merritt Island Causeway), which is another mile to the east. This enclosed mall features many national chains and a 16-theater cinema complex.

Dining: The Village offers a variety of many desirable culinary choices ranging from fine dining to seafood raw-bar, vegan, Thai, pit Bar-B-Que, sushi, and more. A few of the dining establishments in the Village include Café Margot (220 Brevard Ave., 321-639-8343) for fine dining; Murdock's Southern Bistro (600 Brevard Ave., 321-633-0600) with great "southern comfort" food and live music; and Ryan's Pizza and Pub (4 Harrison St., 321-634-5550). Check on the boat from their second-story, open-air dining and bar area that overlooks Riverfront Park and the anchorage. Ossorio Bakery and Café (316 Brevard Ave., 321-639-2423) offers free WiFi and is a popular gathering place among boaters.

Also worth mentioning is Village Ice Cream & Sandwich at 120 Harrison St. (321-632-9808) with 30 flavors of ice cream plus yogurts, sugar-free, sherbets, and sorbets. Flavors change weekly. They also offer made-to-order sandwiches and cold drinks. If you're looking for a micro-brewery, try the Dirty Oar Beer Company (329 W. King St., 321-301-4306).

GOIN' ASHORE: EAU GALLIE, FL

SERVICES		
1	Library	
2	Post Office	
ATTRACTIONS		
3	Eau Gallie Square	
4	Foosaner Art Museum	
5	Intracoastal Brewing Company	
SHOPPING		
6	Eau Gallie Ace Hardware	
DINING		
7	Chef Mario's Café	
8	Joan's Perfect Pie	
9	Squid Lips	

Eau Gallie began as a small coastal town along the Indian River Lagoon in 1860. Incorporated in 1896, hardy souls settled in Eau Gallie and steamers, riverboats, and freighters plied the Indian River, transporting residents, cargo, and, in increasing numbers, tourists. Henry Flagler brought the railroad and Eau Gallie became a popular resort area and the railroad facilitated export of local products, causing Indian River Fruit to become famous nationwide and the citrus industry boomed. Eau Gallie, loosely translated as "rocky or gravel water."

Attractions: Eau Gallie today is a quaint, historical section that strives to retain its historical and cultural heritage while enhancing the area with new businesses and events that will grow Eau Gallie, yet preserve its distinct early Florida flavor. Historic buildings and churches remain in and around the downtown area, some dating back to the 1920s and 30s and earlier.

The Eau Gallie Arts District (EGAD) hosts many events in the Eau Gallie Square, at the corner of Eau Gallie Blvd. and Highland Ave. EGAD celebrates the First Friday of each month with a themed event featuring live entertainment in the band shell, beer and wine, arts and crafts vendors and food trucks around Eau Gallie Square, and shops and galleries are open late (5:30 to 8:30 p.m.). December's First Friday hosts Holiday Tree Lighting ceremony and an appearance by Santa. EGAD's signature events are Founders' Day, typically the first Saturday in February starting at noon, and a new event will begin in May 2017 that celebrates the waterfront. ArtWorks of Eau Gallie is a separate entity that has held the longest running outdoor art festival in Brevard County on the weekend before Thanksgiving every year.

The Foosaner Art Museum is located in the heart of Eau Gallie at 1463 Highland Ave. It is part of Florida Institute of Technology and has studio and gallery space. In addition to art exhibits, the museum offers classes and workshops and hosts an outdoor film festival. Open Wednesday through Saturday, 10:00 a.m. to 4:00 p.m. Call 321-674-8916 for details.

Intracoastal Brewing Company has a neighborhood taproom and features a rotating menu of original brews, plus growlers to take home (652 W Eau Gallie Blvd., 321-872-7395). Our favorite activity? "Namaste for one more" yoga and beer every Sunday at 11:30 a.m. ($15 or $10 without beer).

Shopping: Eau Gallie Ace Hardware (590 Eau Gallie Blvd., 321-254-3261) likely has whatever you need but if not, there are many more stores and specialty shops nearby.

Dining: Squid Lips (1477 Pineapple Ave., 321-259-3101) offers dockside dining and Floridian flare, while Chef Mario's Café (1437 Highland Ave., 321-241-4890) is an intimate and affordable Italian café with cappuccino and gelato bars. Joan's Perfect Pie was ranked the 12th best pie shop in Florida (1478 B Highland Ave., 321-610-7953). Local restaurants will deliver dinner to your table at Intracoastal Brewing Company (see above).

Visit eaugalliearts.com for more details on entertainment, shopping and dining.

store, and other businesses along SR 520. (Add about 1 mile to the distance if you walk across the bridge or dinghy over to Merritt Island from Cocoa Village. Note the bridge walkways are narrow and exposed. If you elect to cross, use the south bridge; its walkway is noticeably wider than the north span.)

Cocoa Village to Eau Gallie–ICW Mile 898 to Mile 914

NAVIGATION: Use NOAA Charts 11485 and 11472. The stretch from Cocoa to Palm Shores presents a few problems, including the ever-present pot markers that sometimes stray into the channel.

At Mile 909, the **Pineda Causeway (Palm Shores) Twin Bridges** (65-foot fixed vertical clearance) cross the ICW. South of the bridges, starting about Mile 910, the channel tends to shoal. The best water can be found along the western edge. A charted spoil area extends to the south from the bridge along the east side for approximately 2.5 miles. The only craft that may have problems are sailboats attempting to tack back and forth across the river.

Dockage: On the west side of the ICW several full-service marinas are located above and below the Pineda Causeway Bridges. Pineda Point Marina is on the west side, north of the Pineda Causeway Bridges, but is a dry-stack marina only and does not accept any transients.

The next facility south is a very popular dock-n-dine called Grills Riverside. The full-service restaurant will even cook your catch! They have 5-foot approach and dockside depths; you must call ahead about slip availability.

Note that SunDance Marina of Melbourne was fully destroyed by Hurricane Irma and has ceased operations.

Anchorage: At Mile 904.5, on the east shore of the Indian River, is "The Point." Just north is a residential stretch that provides a pleasant setting that is protected from northeast to southeast winds and good holding in 8- to 11-foot depths. This is open to wind and wakes; anchor accordingly. Don't be alarmed if you hear the cry of peacocks on shore. (It can sound like someone yelling "help.")

The anchorage above and below the Pineda Causeway Bridges (Mile 909) on the west side of the Indian River is an acceptable anchorage in a pinch. You will need to watch the depth here due to the charted spoil areas.

■ MELBOURNE AREA

On the mainland side of the ICW, two once distinct towns, Eau Gallie and Melbourne, have merged under the name of Melbourne to form a "metropolis." Each has its own harbor and facilities. Additionally, on the east side of the Indian River, there are more facilities on the Banana River as well that we include in this overview. Many skippers leave their boats in one of these areas for extended periods, catch a plane from Orlando Melbourne International Airport and then return later.

Eau Gallie–ICW Mile 914

NAVIGATION: Use NOAA Chart 11472. Eau Gallie, at Mile 914, is on the west side of the Indian River, although the NOAA chart doesn't mention it by name. A well-marked channel to the protected harbor is entered from south of the **Eau Gallie Causeway (SR 518) Bridge** at Mile 915. Just prior to ICW red flashing "2," the entry channel leads off to the west. Look for green daybeacons "1," "3," and "5" and flashing red "6" near shore. The controlling depth is reported as 6 feet at MLW, but deeper draft vessels utilize the channel. Beware of shoaling extending to the southeast of "6." Stay mid-channel or favor the green for the best water.

From here, the channel bends to the northwest as it enters the headlands and continues into the harbor and the Eau Gallie River. Favor the seawalled north shoreline after you enter into this narrow passage and be alert to increased traffic at a park and launch ramp on the south side.

Across the Indian River to the east, the mouth of the Banana River is located inside Dragon Point, north of the bridge and east of the ICW. To enter, round green daybeacon "1" off Dragon Point on the north side of the entrance but keep at least 100 feet south of that daybeacon.

⚠️ Groundings on Dragon Point's rocky rim occur frequently. Reports are that the charted shoal building up from the bridge is well south of green daybeacon "1." It is a sandy shoal, and it would be better to ground there than on Dragon Point's rocks. If you do hit the rocks, edge off backwards; do not try to go over them!

If the anchor or chain tangles and cannot be freed, Anchorage Yacht Basin can provide a diver to help you.

Indian River, Banana River, FL

		Largest Vessel Accommodated	VHF Channel Monitored	Transient Berths / Total Berths	Approach / Dockside Depth (reported)	Floating Docks	Gas / Diesel	Groceries, Ice, Marine Supplies, Snacks	Repairs: Hull, Engine, Propeller	Lift (tonnage), Crane, Rail	Min/Max Amps	Pump-Out Station	Laundry, Pool, Showers, Courtesy Car	Nearby: Grocery Store, Motel, Restaurant
PALM SHORES				**Dockage**				**Supplies**			**Services**			
1. ·Pineda Point Marina ⌨ 908.5	321-254-4199	60	16	0/60	8/8	–	–	IMS	–	L12	30/50	LPS	–	GMR
2. Grills Riverside 908.5	**321-242-8999**	–	–	call/12	5/5	–	G	–	–	–	30/30	–	P	MR
EAU GALLIE AREA														
3. Eau Gallie Yacht Basin ⌨ WiFi 915	321-242-6577	60	16	2/60	8/8	–	–	IMS	–	–	30/50	LS	P	GMR
4. Waterline Marina ⌨ WiFi 915	321-254-0452	80	16/68	8/92	8/8	–	–	–	HEP	–	30/50	LS	P	GR
INDIAN HARBOR														
5. Anchorage Yacht Basin 914.5	321-773-3620	60	–	10/80	6/10	–	G	IMS	HEP	L30	30/50	S	–	GMR
6. Telemar Bay Marina WiFi WG 1.8 E of 914.0	321-773-2468	120	16/68	20/205	9/8	–	GD	IS	–	L40	30/50	LS	P	GR

⌨ Internet Access   WiFi Wireless Internet Access   WG Waterway Guide Cruising Club Partner   ⏺ onSpot dockside WiFi facility

See WaterwayGuide.com for current rates, fuel prices, web site addresses, and other up-to-the-minute information. (*Information in the table is provided by the facilities.*).

PALM SHORES, INDIAN HARBOR, EAU GALLIE AREA, NOAA CHART 11472

PALM SHORES, NOAA CHART 11485

Dockage: Eau Gallie Yacht Basin is located on the west side of the Indian River in a basin south of the bridge and offers good protection with an easy-to-enter, well-maintained entrance. Favor the seawall to starboard as you enter, swing past the park and dock at the facilities ahead. It is a short walk from the Eau Gallie Yacht Basin through quaint streets to the historical restored downtown area of Eau Gallie, with its restaurants, shops, galleries and a Farmers' Market on Saturdays. Waterline Marina, associated with a condominium development, is at the head of the basin with some transient slips and repairs.

On the east side of the Indian River in the mouth of the Banana River, two marinas are available. On the south shore, just north and east of the Eau Gallie Bridge, is Anchorage Yacht Basin, which is a repair and dry stack facility only. They do, however, sell gas. Telemar Bay Marina is located just south of the **Mathers Swing Bridge** (7-foot vertical clearance, opens on the hour and half hour) and is located within (long) walking distance of shopping. The bridge will open on signal with a 2-hour advance notice. However, as of summer 2018, the U.S. Coast Guard has proposed implementing restricted openings. Stay tuned to the Waterway Explorer (waterwayguide.com) for any changes.

Anchorage: Boats anchor on either side of the Eau Gallie Causeway Bridge, depending on wind direction. This allows at least 9 feet at MLW but is exposed to wakes. Some vessels have been observed anchoring in the Eau Gallie Basin. There is little space outside the channel, and the holding is poor, so we do not recommend it.

Between Dragon Point and the Mathers Swing Bridge on the Banana River, you can anchor in 10- to 18-foot depths with good holding. You will find the most room north of the bridge. No tide will worry you here, but the current must be taken into account. Depths vary with wind and rain, and wakes can be considerable (although numerous "No-Wake" signs have resulted in

some improvement). Be careful not to interfere with the entrances to the yacht club or the marinas.

Anchorage Yacht Basin allows dinghy landings for cruisers between 8:00 a.m. and 4:00 p.m. for nearby provisioning (Publix, UPS, etc.). They require registering at the office and there is a $10 fee for dinghy landing only (no garbage drop, water service, etc.).

You can also anchor north 0.5 mile north of the Mathers Bridge in 8 feet at MLW. Nearby Telemar Marina does not allow dinghy landing, but if you continue east past the marina on that canal, you can take your dinghy all the way to the end and walk one-half mile south to a shopping center with Publix. You will pass a city facility with a dock called "Oars and Paddles Park" but don't stop here; there is "No Mooring" signage posted.

Side Trip: North on the Banana River– ICW Mile 914.5

See the "Side Trip–South on the Banana River" section earlier in this chapter for more detailed information on this route.

NAVIGATION: Use NOAA Chart 11472. The Banana River continues north up to Cape Canaveral. In about 18 miles it intersects the Canaveral Barge Canal near the Cape Canaveral Lock. This route can be tricky with distant navaids and skinny water. The controlling depth is 5 to 6 feet at MLW, but it is typically deeper. Oddly, if

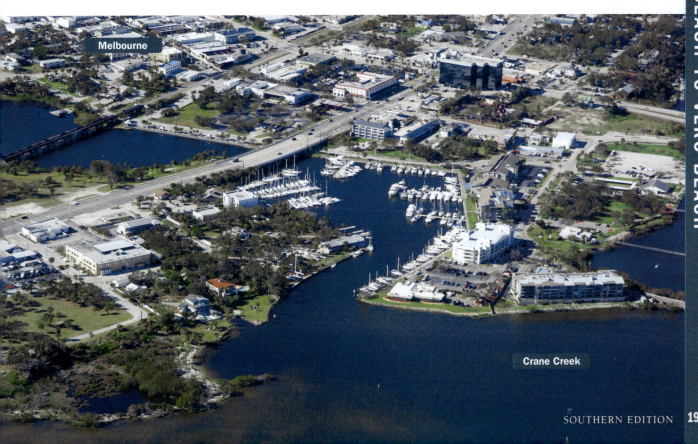

Melbourne

Crane Creek

Indian River, FL

MELBOURNE				Largest Vessel Accommodated	VHF Channel Monitored	Approach / Dockside Depth (reported)	Transient Berths / Total Berths	Floating Docks	Gas / Diesel	Groceries, Ice, Marine Supplies, Snacks	Repairs: Hull, Engine, Propeller	Lift (tonnage), Crane, Rail	Min/Max Amps	Nearby: Grocery Store, Motel, Restaurant Laundry, Pool, Showers, Courtesy Car Pump-Out Station
					Dockage				**Supplies**			**Services**		
1. Melbourne Harbor Marina ☐ (WiFi) 918.5		321-725-9054	130	16/68	10/85	8/8	–	GD	IMS	HEP	–	30/100	LS	P	GMR
PALM BAY														
2. Palm Bay Marina 921.2		321-723-0851	40	74	3/60	3/3	–	–	IMS	HEP	L5	30/30	S	–	GMR

☐ Internet Access (WiFi) Wireless Internet Access WG Waterway Guide Cruising Club Partner ⊙ onSpot dockside WiFi facility
See WaterwayGuide.com for current rates, fuel prices, web site addresses, and other up-to-the-minute information. *(Information in the table is provided by the facilities.)*

MELBOURNE, PALM BAY, NOAA CHART 11472

you follow the channel up to daybeacons red "8A" and green "9," what follows is 3-foot depths and no further course guidance. Local knowledge offers to leave the channel at daybeacon red "8" and proceed west, being careful to avoid the charted "Subm Piles" as shown. This cut-across provides about 7-foot MLW depths out into the adjacent deeper water. (This deeper water is the result of dredging for fill to extend the landmass for the runways of adjacent Patrick Air Force Base.)

Once into the deep water and around the submerged pilings, head north for 4.25 miles to pick up the marked channel at green daybeacon "11" and red daybeacon "12." Note that there is no daybeacon "10." The shallowest water observed on this route was 5.5-feet at MLW near daybeacons green "11" and the area approaching red "20." Fixed bridges at SR 520 and the fixed **Willard Peebles Bridge** at SR 528/A1A has a vertical clearance of 36 feet, establishing the air draft constraint for this route.

Melbourne–ICW Mile 917

The quiet, pleasant town of Melbourne sits midway between Jacksonville Beach and Florida's Gold Coast. It is home port to the Florida Institute of Technology's big research vessels, docked on the port side of the harbor entrance.

NAVIGATION: Use NOAA Chart 11472. The **Melbourne Causeway Twin (SR 516) Bridges** (65-foot vertical clearance) cross the ICW at Mile 918.2. Melbourne's landlocked harbor is easily approached just south of the bridges. To enter the basin from the ICW, turn west at red daybeacon "6," and then follow the markers until you are close to shore. The channel turns sharply to starboard, and then leads to the enclosed basin. The harbor and channel are dredged to a controlling depth of 8 feet at MLW, although the depth is reported to be between 6 and 7 feet at MLW between red daybeacon "6" and flashing green "7." Local knowledge advises favoring the red side.

Dockage: The Melbourne Harbor Marina is to starboard at the head of the basin. The marina offers all types of repairs and sells fuel (both gas and diesel). The harbor is also known for a springtime congregation of small bull sharks. They are fun to watch "finning" on the surface. It is a short walk from the marina to the quaint restored historical area with shops, restaurants, antiques stores and art galleries.

To the south at Mile 920, Palm Bay Marina is located in a basin between two fixed bridges (15-foot and 10-foot vertical clearance) on Turkey Creek. Palm Bay accepts transients and offers some repairs. This basin and creek were dredged in March 2018. Call ahead for exact depths.

Anchorage: Boats anchor on both sides of the high-rise Melbourne Causeway Bridge but the south side offers better protection from north and east. You can tie your dinghy up at a park to the east on the south side of the causeway and walk one-half mile to a beach. There are restaurants along the way but no groceries.

Because of the beaches on their west sides, the spoil island accessed by heading west off the ICW just north of red daybeacon "20" at Mile 925 and the one south of it are favorite local anchoring spots. On less crowded weekdays, ICW travelers often use this area for overnight anchorage. (It will be too crowded and noisy during "peak" season.) Depths are slightly less than shown on the chart (5 to 8 feet at MLW). Shoals extend westward from these islands and are usually marked with pipes or stakes. Transiting boats on the ICW will cause wakes here.

■ SEBASTIAN AREA

The Sebastian area includes the town of Micco, above the Saint Sebastian River and the City of Sebastian, below the river, as well as the Sebastian Inlet.

NAVIGATION: Use NOAA Chart 11472. Just past Mile 925, the channel slants a bit toward the west. You will enter a dredged channel with less than 6 feet at MLW on both sides in most places, so stay in the middle. The spoil islands are eroding on the north side. The one nearest North Rocky Point is a pelican rookery.

The spoils islands shown on the chart west of the ICW from Melbourne down to red daybeacon "18" have receded below the surface. The spoils island between red daybeacons "18" and "20" is very small with a long sandy shoal spit to its west. With frequent bends, the ICW channel passes west of Grant Farm Island (Mile 930), the only inhabited spoils island in the Indian River, which is accessible only by boat. There is a "slow-speed minimum-wake" zone from green daybeacon "37" to red daybeacon "42." From here on, proceed cautiously and be careful not to stray outside the channel, where the water may be only a few feet deep at MLW. You may have to strain to make out the markers, which seem to blend into the shoreline.

Also be alert for uncharted oyster beds and pot markers on both sides of the ICW. The lower part of Grant Farm Island is a rookery used mainly by ibis and egrets. From green daybeacon "49" to "61" be sure to favor the red side of the channel in 10 to 12 feet at MLW, as opposed to 8 feet or less on the green side.

Note: At press time (summer 2018), the sign boards on red daybeacon "54A" at Mile 933 were damaged.

Dockage: Several marinas welcome cruising boats in this area. At Mile 934 is the well-regarded Sebastian River Marina & Boatyard, a full-service boatyard offering service and repairs. They have a 40-ton lift and also offer dry storage. Both gas and diesel are available as well as transient dockage. It is in a seawall-protected basin close to a grocery store and restaurants. Sebastian Inlet Marina is just to the south with transient dockage, fuel and repairs.

Farther south at Mile 937.5, there are two entrance channels to the marinas on the west side: one on the north side of the spoil island and one to its south. Use only the southern entrance channel upon approach. Most of the northern channel has shoaled in. The northern entrance leading to Capt'n Butchers Marina and to Fins Marina is reported to carry somewhat less than the charted 6-foot MLW depths from the ICW to the marinas. Capt'n Butchers reports 5-foot MLW dockside depths. The southern entrance leads to Capt. Hiram's Sebastian Marina, which can be identified by its colorful rooftops. This is also a shallow (5-foot depth) channel. Before using either entrance channel, it would be highly advisable to call and ask for depth information as this area is continually changing.

Anchorage: Shallow-draft vessels (less than 5 feet at MLW) can anchor off Capt. Hiram's Sebastian Marina, with approximately 5-foot MLW depths.

GOIN' ASHORE: MELBOURNE, FL

SERVICES	
1	Post Office
2	Visitor Information
3	Downtown Yoga
ATTRACTIONS	
4	Crane Creek Promenade
5	Henegar Center for the Arts
6	Melbourne Civic Theatre
7	Strawberry Art League Gallery
SHOPPING	
8	West Marine
DINING	
9	Ichabod's Dockside Bar & Grille
10	Meg O'Malley's Restaurant & Irish Pub
11	Nomad Café
MARINAS	
12	Melbourne Harbor Marina

Melbourne has long been a destination for cruisers transiting the ICW. For those heading south in the fall and winter, it feels like you have finally arrived in sunny Florida. For the most part, you have left the cold north winds behind you, and palm trees start becoming more the rule and not the exception.

Settlers began to arrive in the Melbourne area in the late 1800s. Peter Wright, the area's most noted settler, used to sail regularly up and down the Indian River to deliver mail to other settlers living along the river between Titusville and Malabar. This area provided the best of both worlds to folks looking for a place to call their own—fertile land and water access.

Melbourne and its sister, Eau Gallie, grew up side-by-side, each on either side of the Indian River. They remained as individual cities until voters decided in 1969 to consolidate them into what is now the City of Melbourne.

Attractions: Need to stretch out after being on the boat all day? Try Downtown Yoga (532 E. New Haven Ave., 321-676-4600). Or, take a walk along the manatee and wildlife observation area at Promenade Park, located in historic downtown Melbourne along Crane Creek.

Downtown Melbourne is ripe with opportunities to engage in the arts. You can visit the Strawbridge Art League Gallery (819 E. Strawbridge Ave., 321-952-3070) or catch a show at either The Henegar Center for the Arts (625 E. New Haven Ave., 321-723-8698) or the Melbourne Civic Theatre (817 E. Strawbridge Ave., 321-723-6935). You can't stroll around the historic district without noticing the vibrant murals. There are currently six murals with a goal of completing 15 to 20. Subjects of existing murals include a blue bird, a sea turtle, a VW bus and a mermaid.

In April, you can find some fabulous fine art at the Melbourne Art Festival (melbournearts.org) and in the fall, there is the Downtown Melbourne Food & Wine Festival (melbournefoodandwine.com). On the second Friday of each month from 6:00 to 10:00 p.m., there is a street festival with live music, arts and crafts vendors and food called Friday Fest. The festival is located along E. New Haven Ave. between Depot Dr. and Waverly Place. To find other local events visit the Melbourne Regional Chamber at 1005 E. Strawbridge Ave. (321-724-5400) or check out DowntownMelbourne.com.

We would be remiss not to mention the Brevard Zoo, which is a short distance from the downtown area off I-95 at 8225 N. Wickham Rd. (Transportation is required.) See over 500 animals, feed giraffes or try zip-lining. Open 9:30 a.m. to 5:00 p.m. daily (321-254-9453).

Shopping: There are many wonderful shops and boutiques downtown selling clothes, shoes and accessories. You might, however, care more about West Marine (1001 W. New Haven Ave., 321-837-1113). Melbourne Shopping Center at 1355 S. Babcock St. has a grocery store (with a pharmacy) and a bank.

Dining: No matter what you crave, the downtown area has a restaurant to satisfy your hunger (or thirst). The upscale Chart House Restaurant serves "seafood with style" in an intimate waterfront setting. This is a chain restaurant but doesn't feel like one. (2250 Front St., 321-729-6558). Nearby is the more relaxed Ichabod's Dockside Bar & Grille with simple seafood fare at 2210 Front St. (321-952-9532).

For something altogether different, try the Nomad Café for delicious farm to table eats with an international flare (2002 S. Harbor City Blvd., 321-327-2996) or, further inland, Meg O'Malley's Restaurant & Irish Pub at 812 E New Haven Ave. (321-952-5510).

Indian River Inlet, FL

SEBASTIAN AREA		Dockage					Supplies		Services					
		Largest Vessel Accommodated	VHF Channel Monitored	Transient Berths / Total Berths	Approach / Dockside Depth (reported)	Floating Docks	Gas / Diesel	Groceries, Ice, Marine Supplies, Snacks	Repairs: Hull, Engine, Propeller	Lift (tonnage), Crane, Rail	Min/Max Amps	Laundry, Pool, Showers, Courtesy Car	Pump-Out Station	Nearby: Grocery Store, Motel, Restaurant
1. Sebastian River Marina & Boatyard WiFi **934**	**772-664-3029**	70	16/68	4/60	5/5	–	GD	MS	HEP	L40	30/50	S	–	GR
2. Sebastian Inlet Marina ☐ WiFi 934.3	772-664-8500	45	16	4/25	5/5	F	GD	GIMS	EP	L16	30/50	S	P	GMR
3. Capt'n Butchers Marina WiFi 937.2	772-589-2552	60	16	5/25	5/6	–	GD	I	–	–	20/50	L	–	GMR
4. Fins Marina WiFi 937.5	772-589-4843	80	16	10/78	6/6	–	–	I	–	–	30/50	S	–	GMR
5. Capt. Hiram's Sebastian Marina WiFi 937.7	772-589-4345	50	16/68	14/46	5/5	–	–	IMS	–	–	30/50	LPS	P	GMR

☐ Internet Access WiFi Wireless Internet Access WG Waterway Guide Cruising Club Partner onSpot dockside WiFi facility

See WaterwayGuide.com for current rates, fuel prices, web site addresses, and other up-to-the-minute information. *(Information in the table is provided by the facilities.)*

SEBASTIAN AREA, NOAA CHART 11472

Vero Beach Area, FL

			Dockage					Supplies		Services					
			Largest Vessel Accommodated	VHF Channel Monitored	Transient Berths / Total Berths	Approach / Dockside Depth (reported)	Floating Docks	Gas / Diesel	Groceries, Ice, Marine Supplies, Snacks	Repairs: Hull, Engine, Propeller	Lift (tonnage), Crane, Rail	Min/Max Amps	Laundry, Pool, Showers, Courtesy Car	Pump-Out Station	Nearby: Grocery Store, Motel, Restaurant
WABASSO															
1. Suntex Marina—Vero Beach ⌨ onSpot 948.5	772-770-4470		75	16/68	20/130	6/7	F	GD	IS	–	–	30/50	LPS	P	GMR
VERO BEACH															
2. Vero Beach City Marina ⌨ WiFi 952	772-231-2819		160	16/66	18/88	8/10	F	GD	GIMS	HEP	L3	30/50	LS	P	GMR
3. Vero Marine Center Inc. 952	772-562-7922		30	16	call/40	3/3	–	–	M	E	L3	30/30	–	–	–

⌨ Internet Access   WiFi Wireless Internet Access   WG Waterway Guide Cruising Club Partner   onSpot dockside WiFi facility
See WaterwayGuide.com for current rates, fuel prices, web site addresses, and other up-to-the-minute information. *(Information in the table is provided by the facilities.)*

VERO BEACH AREA, NOAA CHART 11472

There are a number of permanently moored vessels here. This is close to several pubs and restaurants and can get crowded. Enter through the marked channel. Only anchor here on a low wind day as it is exposed in all directions.

Sebastian Inlet–ICW Mile 936

NAVIGATION: Use NOAA Chart 11472. Sebastian Inlet, at Mile 936, is crossed by the fixed **A1A Bridge** (37-foot vertical clearance) and is used by local boats to reach the ocean. Constant shoaling necessitates careful piloting and current local knowledge. This is a local knowledge, fair-weather inlet.

Swift crosscurrents and the resulting shifting channel make navigation difficult in Sebastian Inlet, even with up-to-date local information. A 3,000-foot-long by 100-foot-wide and 9-foot-deep channel provides access to the ocean, but as with all ocean inlets, a cautious approach is warranted, as shoaling is ever present and continuous. The currents in this area can also affect travel on the ICW. See the Inlet section at the front of this guide for more information on Sebastian Inlet.

Anchorage: It is possible to anchor at Sebastian Inlet State Park near the northeast side of the inlet in 8 to 10 feet at MLW. There is only a 6-inch tide at this spot but a strong current. Only anchor here on a low wind day, as it is exposed in all directions.

It is a short dinghy ride to the basin to the north side of the inlet, just after the fixed bridge over the inlet, for snorkeling and swimming. Visibility for snorkeling is fair and the beach is excellent and not crowded. Great for a picnic and dog run. Park the dingy on the sand beach prior to the "lagoon." You will be joined by a lot of fishers and small boats.

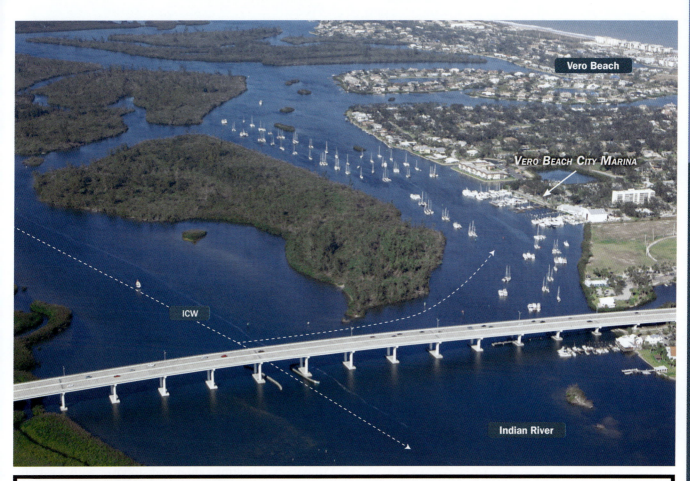

Vero Beach

VERO BEACH CITY MARINA

ICW

Indian River

◼ VERO BEACH AREA

Wabasso–ICW Mile 943

NAVIGATION: Use NOAA Chart 11472. The dredged ICW channel runs straight for 10 miles to Wabasso. At Mile 938, near red daybeacon "66A," beware of shoaling into the east side of the ICW that extends out to mid-channel. Due to a very sharp drop off from "dry land" to an observed 13-foot depth on the western side of the ICW, it is recommended you strongly favor the red side. At Wabasso, 25 miles south of Melbourne, small wooded islands suddenly crowd the narrowing river and create a maze through which the channel twists and turns. Observe markers carefully. Expect sporadic spots of shoaling between the Sebastian area and Vero Beach. The heavily congested areas are temporarily behind you as you enter one of the Indian River's most attractive stretches.

The **Wabasso Bridge** crosses the ICW at Mile 943.3. The bridge is charted with a 65-foot fixed vertical clearance; however, 64-foot vertical clearance was observed on the tide boards by our Cruising Editor in summer 2018. There is a private basin associated with a residential community on the northwest side of the Wabasso Bridge. More and more developments and private homes are springing up along the stretch between Wabasso and Vero Beach, including new condominiums.

Be on the lookout for manatees and other wildlife. Some of the islands in this area are rookeries for a variety of bird species. South of the Wabasso Bridge, on the west side of the ICW, at Mile 943.4 are the docks of the Environmental Learning Center, a 64-acre habitat for birds, fish, crustaceans and mammals of many kinds. The museum here is home to a 145-gallon touch tank, plus three other aquariums, several hands-on exhibits and a life-size replica of a manatee's head, from which you can experience how a manatee eats seagrass from the lagoon floor. See details at discoverelc.org.

At Mile 944.6, be alert for green can "91," marking the end of a shoal extending from the adjacent spoil island.

Dockage: At Mile 948.5, north of Vero Beach, on the west side of the ICW, a charted, marked channel with 6-foot MLW depths observed at the centerline leads to the docks of Suntex Marina–Vero Beach, an elaborate development with condominiums, golf, tennis and handsome waterfront homes. The marina can accommodate transients (including catamarans) up to

75 feet with 7-foot dockside depths. They also sell all fuels. There is a new shopping center approximately one mile away for provisioning, and the marina has loaner bikes available.

Anchorage: Vessels have been observed anchored in a small pocket between the Wabasso Bridge and the Learning Center with 10- to 12-foot depths. You can dinghy to the Environmental Center where depth at the dock is approximately 5 feet. Beware of charted underwater cables close to the bridge.

Shoal-draft boats have been observed at anchor behind the spoils island near Mile 946.4, south of Pine Island. The entrance to this anchorage is reported to be between that spoil island and flashing red "112." Enter from south to find 8 feet at MLW. After proceeding in a northwesterly direction, anchor between the spoils island and Hole in the Wall Island. This anchorage provides protection from ICW wakes. You can dinghy ashore but beware the live oysters that may cut your inflatable and your dogs feet! This may be your last secluded anchorage when southbound.

Vero Beach–ICW Mile 952

Just past some sizable islands, you will see Vero Beach (Mile 952), a boating center and stopover with a variety of facilities on both sides of the Indian River, above and below the **Merrill P. Barber (Vero Beach) Bridge** at Mile 951.9 (66-foot fixed vertical clearance). This is the beginning of the more densely populated areas of Florida, and the number of boats increases accordingly. Keep well inside the marked channel when passing through the bridge and maintain a firm hand on the helm, as winds and current can be strong here.

A little more than 1 mile below the Vero Beach Bridge is another high-rise bridge, the **Alma Lee Loy (17th St.) Bridge**, with a 65-foot fixed vertical clearance at Mile 953.2. Between the bridges on the west side is a power plant, which is a favorite spot for manatees to lounge. You must maintain a posted slow speed from November 15 through April 30, except when in the channel.

NAVIGATION: Use NOAA Chart 11472. Use the Miami Harbor Entrance Tide Tables. For high tide, add 2 hours 56 minutes; for low tide, add 3 hours 41 minutes. There is shoaling into the channel between red daybeacons "128" and "130" north of Vero Beach. Red daybeacon "128A" has been placed to help guide mariners through this area. Stay mid-channel to avoid shoals. Just north of the Vero Beach Bridge, markers to the east

SAILS UP: THE ULTIMATE CRUISE
Stuart to Port Canaveral

LEG 2 of 8

○ **START**

Cruise a fun-loving string of Florida Atlantic Coast playgrounds rich with activities worth a dropped anchor—from fishing in Stuart to strolling the sand in Vero Beach, from exploring Melbourne to surfing the break off Cocoa Beach. Get ready to find yourself dallying much longer than the easy long weekend this sunny segment of the Intracoastal Waterway inspires: It's just that much fun.

MILE 988 + 7 nautical miles west
GO FISH
Stuart
This warm-hearted town that is neighbor to beach-blessed Hobe Sound and Jensen Beach is proud to call itself the "Sailfish Capital of the World," so soak up the fishing life (and lore), including charters out of **Port Salerno.**

MILE 952
BEACH AND SHOP
Vero Beach
Take a free shuttle from the marina to the beach or to fun shops along the waterfront on Ocean Drive. Outdoor concerts and plays make for free year-round fun at **Riverside Park.** **TIE UP:** Dockage rates start at $1.60 per foot per day at cruiser-friendly **Vero Beach City Marina;** covb.org.

MILE 918
FESTIVALS AND FOOD
Melbourne
Plan to hit this town on the second Friday of each month for **Friday Fest,** a lively street festival full of food and music. Don't-miss photo ops: the historic district's vibrant murals.

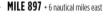

MILE 897 + 6 nautical miles east
SURF'S UP
Cocoa Beach
Catch your fill of waves at this surf-savvy hometown of legend Kelly Slater, with surfing and SUP lessons at **Ron Jon Surf School.**

MILE 893 + 7 nautical miles east
BEACH BAR? BINGO!
Port Canaveral
For a pure Florida night, hit the beach-sand dance floor beneath palm trees and tiki torches at **Milliken's Reef.** Have a signature Beach Babe cocktail at one (or all) of Milliken's three bars. **TIE UP:** Dockage rates are $2.25 per foot at **Cocoa Village Marina** in historic **Cocoa Village,** home to art galleries, boutiques, and fun eating.

● **END**

NO BOAT (YET)? Treasure Coast Sailing Adventures offers morning discovery, afternoon adventure, and romantic sunset sails on the **schooner *Lily,*** which is also available for private charters. *Lily* departs daily from Shepard Park in downtown Stuart.

135 MILES SAILED

IN 1895, JENSEN BEACH WAS THE **PINEAPPLE CAPITAL OF THE WORLD**

52k **SQUARE FEET OF SURFBOARD SHOPPING** AT RON JON SURF SHOP

72.7

AVERAGE YEAR-ROUND HIGH TEMPERATURE IN VERO BEACH

AREA CODE FOR CAPE CANAVERAL IS 321 (GET IT?)

3,2,1

BY **JANI PARKER**

READY TO SET SAIL? To order guidebooks and begin planning your boating adventures, visit **waterwayguide.com**

GOIN' ASHORE: VERO BEACH, FL

SERVICES	
1	Post Office
ATTRACTIONS	
2	Riverside Theatre
3	Vero Beach Museum of Art

DINING	
4	Lemon Tree Restaurant
5	Mulligan's Beach House
6	Ocean Grill
7	Riverside Café

MARINAS	
8	Vero Beach City Marina

Vero Beach is a favorite with cruisers. Many who plan to leave, don't; hence the nickname "Velcro Beach." This affluent resort community is known for its immaculate ocean and riverfront amenities. The historic downtown is part of a flourishing walkable community boasting many cultural amenities, great shopping and dining opportunities that rival Gold Coast cities to the south. Located in Indian River County, the area is known for its citrus shipped all over the world.

The Vero Beach area was first settled in the mid-1800s. The construction of Flagler's railroad in the late 1890s helped the local fishermen and farmers get products north to the East Coast. In the early 1900s, Drainage Districts were created to drain the wetlands and make them habitable. Citrus became a bumper crop, as well

as cattle ranching and timber farming. The town of Vero was planned, canals were dredged and a power plant was installed in 1918. The town continued to grow. Then a bridge was built to connect the island to the mainland in 1919 and to this day the town has been attracting tourists.

Attractions: The impressive Vero Beach Museum of Art (3001 Riverside Park Dr., 772-231-0707) and the Riverside Theatre (3250 Riverside Park, 772-231-6990) are within walking distance of the City Marina next to the Vero Beach Yacht Club (3601 Rio Vista Blvd., 772-231-2211). Gallery Strolls, outdoor concerts and productions and many eco-adventures await the visitor. A popular farmers market is held each Saturday morning on Ocean Dr.

Shopping: If you are in need of outboard engine parts or repairs, try Vero Marine Center (12 Royal Palm Pointe, 772-562-7922), which has a well-stocked parts department.

Village Beach Market on Hwy. A1A offers shopping and delivery services (for a fee). You would be hard pressed to not find what you need at this upscale market (772-231-2338).

On the Orchid Island side of Vero Beach there is an abundance of trendy little shops along the waterfront on Ocean Drive as well as the surrounding side streets; they are too numerous to mention here. Be sure to take your time strolling around and enjoying what the town has to offer.

One of the pluses to Vero Beach is the excellent free bus system, the GoLine (772-569-0903). The bus stops hourly in front of the captain's lounge at the Vero Beach City Marina. The bus will take you to the Oceanside business district, with its unique shops and restaurants, and guarded beaches and it also makes stops at major supermarkets, West Marine, liquor stores and other shops. The bus continues to a transfer station where you can connect to other routes taking you to Walmart, Target, pharmacies, a mall and a large outlet mall. All in all, it is a great service to boaters.

Dining: A great many dining choices await you in Vero Beach. The Riverside Café (3341 Bridge Plaza Dr., 772-234-5550) has food, music, a "Happy Hour" seven days a week and overlooks the Indian River Lagoon. This is a very popular spot for boaters and locals. It is located just south of the mooring field and has a dinghy dock for tie-ups.

Along Ocean Dr. is the popular Lemon Tree Restaurant (3125 Ocean Dr., 772-231-0858) serving breakfast and lunch, or for oceanfront dining pleasure, try Ocean Grill (772-231-5409) or Mulligan's Beach House Bar & Grill (772-492-6744), both located in the Sexton Plaza on Ocean Dr.

Many of Vero's restaurants serve fresh local fish that you may not recognize but will never forget, including pompano, cobia, unicorn filefish, snook, fresh water crappie, or any one of 15 species of grouper. Our on-the-water cruising editors provide the locations listed here. To assist you in enjoying all Vero Beach and the surrounding area has to offer, a mobile app is available for free download from the Apple Store and through Google Play Store. Key word searches for the app are "Vero Beach," "Sebastian" and "Fellsmere." The app is usable on Apple and Android technology and incorporates an "Eat, Stay & Play" directory with comprehensive information to enhance your stay including turn-by-turn directions, integrations with Yelp and OpenTable, and a community calendar featuring major festivals and events.

lead up the old ICW route past the city park to Vero Beach City Marina.

Enter the harbor by turning between flashing green "139" and the bridge, and then go in parallel to the bridge until you have lined up the channel markers. Be mindful of the strong current and compensate for the set. There is shoaling off of the mangrove island to the north at the entrance so do not get too close or cut the corner while compensating for the effects of the current. Outside of the channel that leads into the marina and mooring field, you will encounter 4-foot depths or less.

As you continue south along the ICW and pass under the two bridges, stay in mid-channel as the edges of the channel shoal quickly for a mile or so south of the bridges. From north of Vero Beach at red daybeacon "120" to green daybeacon "149," the Manatee Speed Zone is enforced year-round.

Dockage: Vero Beach's popular north basin offers tranquility in a crowded area. No-Wake signs are posted, improving comfort. Vero Beach City Marina is situated in a park-like setting, offering transient dockage, gas and diesel fuel, laundry and a free pump-out boat twice weekly. Free bus service is available to all shopping. The ocean and beach district is only 1 mile away and is serviced by the bus system or is a very pleasant walk. The marina hosts a "cruisers" BYOB/appetizers party every Thursday in the north pavilion around 4:00 p.m. (weather permitting). Located just south of the marina, but still part of the same area, is a large dog park where your pet can get out and stretch its legs.

Vero Marine Center Inc. is across the ICW (on the west shore) with sales and service. The channel leading to their facility is very shallow (3 feet or less at MLW) but can be accessed by dinghy. There are several restaurants nearby.

Moorings: Inexpensive and well-maintained city-owned moorings are available in both the north and south basins, on either side of Vero Beach City Marina. Protection from stormy weather is very good in this basin. These moorings are very popular, and it can get quite crowded in the busy season. Each mooring is assigned by the dockmaster of the municipal marina (reservations recommended).

Be aware that even if moorings are reserved, boaters may still be expected to share them; boats traveling together are encouraged to make arrangements to raft together. Otherwise, the first boat at a mooring is asked to put out fenders and accept whatever raft is assigned. It is well protected in this area and rafting is rarely a problem. Crews of moored boats enjoy the use of showers, a comfortable lounge, laundry facilities and a picnic area. Trash disposal and use of the dinghy dock are complimentary for moored boats.

Anchorage: Most of the areas outside the channel and near the mangrove islands above and below Vero Beach are shallow. Boats can anchor between the little islands but need to stay clear of the moorings and watch for shoals, which can be difficult in this area. Anchored boats are allowed to use the facilities but must register at the office and pay a fee on a daily basis.

■ NEXT STOP

Boaters proceeding south will next encounter Fort Pierce. It has a number of marine facilities, and its deep ocean inlet provides access to run outside to points south or as a gateway east to the Bahamas Islands.

Fort Pierce to St. Lucie Inlet

ICW Mile 952–Mile 988

VHF FL Bridges: Channel 09

CHARTS NOAA 11428 , 11472

Once you pass Vero Beach, you are positioned midway between the upper and lower reaches of the Indian River. As the river widens, the dredged ICW channel begins to straighten out for the 13 miles south to Fort Pierce. The project depth along this stretch is 12 feet at MLW, but the actual controlling depth is 8 feet or less.

Some of the spoil islands scattered along this stretch are blanketed in the spring by nesting pelicans, cormorants, herons and egrets. Enjoy watching them, but do not disturb their nests. In winter, the area from the Vero Beach Bridge south to the high-rise 17th Street Bridge becomes a protected area for manatees. They like the warm water discharged by the neighboring power plant. You will see the plant's three stacks near the bridge on the west side. You can also keep a lookout for manatees farther south at the Fort Pierce South Bridge; this is another favorite lounging area for the gentle creatures. It's not uncommon to see several manatees entertaining people on the docks and walkways in the Fort Pierce City Marina.

■ FORT PIERCE AREA

Vero Beach to Fort Pierce—ICW Mile 952 to Mile 965

NAVIGATION: Use NOAA Chart 11472. Use the Miami Harbor Entrance Tide Tables. For high tide, add 49 minutes; for low tide, add 1 hour 1 minute. From Vero Beach to Fort Pierce, the ICW continues south along the Indian River. In Vero Beach, shoaling exists in spots from flashing green "139" to red daybeacon "142," and from green daybeacon "149" to flashing green "153," reducing water depths to 8 or 10 feet at MLW along the edges of the channel. Watch the depth sounder and stay in the middle of the channel to avoid shallow water and spoil banks outside the channel. Shoaling has also been observed in spots from flashing green "157" to green daybeacon "165," with depths of less than 8 feet at MLW.

From green daybeacon "155" to green daybeacon "173," the Manatee Speed Zone varies from seasonal to year-round. The zones are posted on the markers. The stretch past Harbor Branch at Mile 960 is a strictly enforced Idle-Speed/No-Wake Zone.

At Mile 964.8, the **North Fort Pierce (SR A1A) Bascule Bridge** (26-foot closed vertical clearance) opens on signal. One-half mile south of Taylor Creek (Mile 965.1) is the intersection of the ICW and Fort Pierce Inlet. Just beyond the intersection, at Mile 965.8, is the **Fort Pierce (SR A1A) Bridge** (65-foot fixed vertical clearance), sometimes referred to as South Bridge. Watch for shoaling between red daybeacon "184" and red daybeacon "186" on the eastern edge of the channel between the North Fort Pierce Bridge and the inlet. Use caution and follow the aids to navigation closely in this area. Shoaling has also been reported on the west side of the channel just to the north of the bridge at the edge of the turning basin.

Dockage: Just north of the North Fort Pierce Bridge (on the west side) is Riverside Marina Fort Pierce, with a large yard with some transient dockage. Call ahead for slip availability. They have a new 70-ton lift for hauling vessels and a newly rebuilt 22-foot-wide boat slip. They have a mechanic on site and are also one of the few remaining self-service boatyards in south Florida.

Immediately south of the North Fort Pierce Bridge is Taylor Creek. This well-marked creek is the home of Harbortown Marina–Fort Pierce, a large full-service marina and boatyard in a tropical atmosphere. The island-themed Harbor Cove Waterfront Restaurant (772-429-5303) is located here, as is Sunnyland Canvas, specializing in marine canvas and upholstery. Also located on Taylor Creek is Cracker Boy Boat Works–Fort Pierce, with a do-it-yourself repair yard, and Taylor Creek Marina, with slips and gas (no diesel). Be sure to call in advance to check on their depths, as dockside MLW depths of 3 feet have been reported by the marina.

Anchorage: You can drop the hook at Mile 961.7 at Garfield Point in 4 to 5 feet at MLW with excellent holding. This is open to the north. Anchor south of the channel. More convenient to Fort Pierce is the anchorage between the Fort Pierce North Bridge and the Taylor Creek channel, to the west of the ICW channel off Harbortown Marina at red daybeacon "184." Depths are reported to be less than the charted 8 feet at MLW. (Depth is shallow near the bascule bridge but deeper near the entrance channel to Harbortown.) From here you can dinghy to Harbortown Marina and if you pay for dinghy dock, that fee may be applied towards marina services, gas or ice.

Fort Pierce Inlet–ICW Mile 965

NAVIGATION: Use NOAA Chart 11472. Use the Miami Harbor Entrance Tide Tables. For high tide, subtract 31 minutes; for low tide, subtract 18 minutes. The Fort Pierce Inlet is wide and deep with two stone jetties, an inner channel (30-foot MLW depths) and a turning basin (28-foot MLW depths). The channel is marked with ranges and buoys (both lighted and unlighted). Tidal currents in the inlet are strong, averaging 3 to 4 knots. Where the inlet channel crosses the ICW down to the Fort Pierce South Bridge (Mile 965.8), strong crosscurrents exist with a set to the south on the flood and to the north on the ebb.

Note: Tidal ranges are 3 feet at the inlet jetties and 1.5 feet in the Indian River near the city marina. In the entrance channel, the large shallow area inside the north jetty is a popular weekend hangout for local boaters. In the area of Fort Pierce (South) Bridge (Mile 965.8), the Idle-Speed/No-Wake Manatee Zone is poorly marked but strictly enforced.

Many cruising boats make Fort Pierce Inlet their exit or entry point for an outside run. It is 65 nm south of Cape Canaveral Inlet and 45 nm north of Lake Worth Inlet. Deep-sea fishing is a big attraction here because of the safe, deep inlet and its proximity to the Gulf Stream. See the Inlet section at the front of this guide for more information.

Dockage/Moorings: Inside the Fort Pierce Inlet, east of Mile 965.6, is Dockside Marina & Resort, with ample dockage for vessels to 130 feet, and Pelican Yacht Club, which has some reserved transient slips and sells fuel (gas and diesel). In the same basin is Fort Pierce Inlet Marina, which may have space. Call ahead for slip availability.

South of the Fort Pierce (South) Bridge (65-foot fixed vertical clearance) is Fort Pierce City Marina's dredged marked entrance channel. There are four man-made rock islands to help protect the marina entrance during storms. Consult new charts that show the relocated entrance and call the City Marina on VHF Channel 16 for information and docking and fueling instructions. They have ample transient space on their floating docks and sell all fuels.

Up a marked channel just 0.5 miles east of Mile 966 Causeway Cove Marina & RV Park is the newest marina facility in the Fort Pierce area. They have fixed docks and moorings for boats to 60 feet. Restrooms, showers and laundry facilities are among the many amenities. They can arrange to have a truck deliver fuel to the docks if you require refueling.

Harbour Isle Marina, which is also on the south side of Causeway Island, sells limited groceries and marine supplies. Amenities include a pool, fitness center, tennis courts, bocce ball court and an outdoor kitchen.

Anchorage: There are several anchorage areas on the east side of the ICW south of the Fort Pierce (South) Bridge. This channel branches off the ICW at Mile 967, near red daybeacon "188." The shallowest place in this channel is at the entry where the chart shows 7- to 8-foot MLW depths. Note that the spoil island at red daybeacon "2" on the south side of the privately marked channel was reduced to a broad shoal during hurricanes of the past few years.

The first anchorage on this channel, which runs along the south shore of Causeway Island, is south of red daybeacon "4." There is also room just south of green daybeacon "9" in the privately marked entrance channel to Faber Cove. Both of these anchorages offer at least 6 feet at MLW with excellent holding in north or east winds. If the anchorage area south of green daybeacon "9" is crowded, you may want to sound around the edges with the dinghy first because the boundary of deep water to the south is different than shown on the chart.

Beware as you round green "13" where the water becomes shallow as shown on chart. Continue on past green daybeacon "15" to Faber Cove, which is very protected and quiet with good depths of around 8 to 10 feet at MLW. In the summer of 2018 there were no anchoring restrictions for Faber Cove. This area is lined with homes so be respectful of private property. No shore access..

Side Trip: Hutchinson Island

Hutchinson Island stretches 22 miles between Fort Pierce Inlet and St. Lucie Inlet, on the ocean (east) side of the ICW. Visitors can reach Hutchinson Island via three long causeways that connect the mainland to the beaches. The first is the 65-foot fixed Fort Pierce (A1A) Bridge (Mile 965.8), and farther south is the 65-foot fixed **Jensen Beach Causeway (SR 707A) Bridge** at Mile 981.4. The third route to the beaches on Hutchinson Island is the 65-foot vertical clearance

Indian River, FL

FORT PIERCE AREA		Dockage					Supplies		Services					
		Largest Vessel Accommodated	VHF Channel Monitored	Transient Berths / Total Berths	Approach / Dockside Depth (reported)	Floating Docks	Gas / Diesel	Groceries, Ice, Marine Supplies, Snacks	Repairs: Hull, Engine, Propeller	Lift (tonnage), Crane, Rail	Min/Max Amps	Laundry, Pool, Showers, Courtesy Car	Pump-Out Station	Nearby: Grocery Store, Motel, Restaurant
1. Riverside Marina Fort Pierce 💻 WiFi 964.1	772-464-5720	105	16	5/70	6/6	–	–	M	HEP	L70	30/50	S	P	GMR
2. Harbortown Marina–Fort Pierce 💻 WiFi 965	772-466-7300	160	16/68	40/342	9/7	F	GD	IMS	HEP	L150	30/100	LPS	P	GR
3. Cracker Boy Boat Works–Fort Pierce WiFi 965.1	772-465-7031	–	16/68	–	8/7	–	–	M	HEP	L75,C	–	S	–	GMR
4. Taylor Creek Marina 965.1	772-465-2663	40	68/05	5/600	8/3	F	G	IMS	HEP	L9	30/30	–	–	GMR
FORT PIERCE INLET														
5. Dockside Marina & Resort WiFi	772-468-3555	130	–	58/58	16/12	–	–	IMS	–	–	30/200+	LPS	P	GMR
6. Pelican Yacht Club 💻 WiFi 1 E of 965.6	772-464-1734	95	16	5/93	6/6	–	GD	IMS	–	–	30/50	LPS	P	GR
7. Fort Pierce Inlet Marina 0.8 E of 965.6	772-236-3675	90	–	call/39	12/12	–	–	–	–	–	30/30	LS	P	GMR
8. Fort Pierce City Marina 💻 onSpot WG 966.5	772-464-1245	150	16/78	40/237	7/8	F	GD	IMS	–	–	30/50	LS	P	GMR
9. Causeway Cove Marina & RV Park onSpot 966.3	772-242-3552	60	16	25/198	5.4/6	–	–	IS	–	–	30/50	LS	P	GMR
10. Harbour Isle Marina WG 0.8 E of 966.2	772-461-9049	120	16/69	10/63	9/9	F	–	–	–	–	30/100	–	P	GMR

💻 Internet Access WiFi Wireless Internet Access WG Waterway Guide Cruising Club Partner onSpot dockside WiFi facility

See WaterwayGuide.com for current rates, fuel prices, web site addresses, and other up-to-the-minute information. *(Information in the table is provided by the facilities.)*

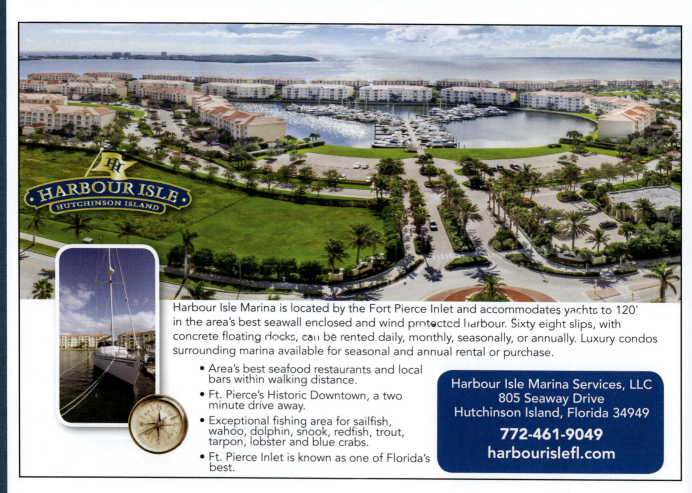

HARBOUR ISLE · HUTCHINSON ISLAND

Harbour Isle Marina is located by the Fort Pierce Inlet and accommodates yachts to 120' in the area's best seawall enclosed and wind protected harbour. Sixty eight slips, with concrete floating docks, can be rented daily, monthly, seasonally, or annually. Luxury condos surrounding marina available for seasonal and annual rental or purchase.

- Area's best seafood restaurants and local bars within walking distance.
- Ft. Pierce's Historic Downtown, a two minute drive away.
- Exceptional fishing area for sailfish, wahoo, dolphin, snook, redfish, trout, tarpon, lobster and blue crabs.
- Ft. Pierce Inlet is known as one of Florida's best.

Harbour Isle Marina Services, LLC
805 Seaway Drive
Hutchinson Island, Florida 34949

772-461-9049
harbourislefl.com

FORT PIERCE AREA, FORT PIERCE INLET NOAA CHART 11472

GOIN' ASHORE: **FORT PIERCE, FL**

SERVICES	
1	Library
2	Visitor Information
ATTRACTIONS	
3	Manatee Observations and Education Center
SHOPPING	
4	ACE Hardware/East Coast Lumber & Supply
5	P.P. Cobb General Store & Deli
DINING	
6	Cobbs Landing
7	Original Tiki Bar & Restaurant
MARINAS	
8	Fort Pierce City Marina

Founded as a military base during the Seminole War, Fort Pierce today is the center of the Indian River citrus industry. During World War II, its wide, gently sloping beaches provided the perfect grounds for U.S. servicemen training for amphibious assaults. Today, the beaches are still sometimes used for training Navy SEALS, but they mostly attract vacationers intent on relaxing. Within the city limits, visitors can wander through the Savannas, a large wilderness recreation project. Just north of the Fort Pierce Inlet, swimming, surfing and picnicking draw tourists and locals alike to the state recreation area.

Attractions: Fort Pierce has several notable attractions. A good place to start is at the Seven Gables House (Visitor Information Center) at 482 N. Indian River Dr. (772-468-9152), across the Ft. Pierce (A1A) Bridge. The Manatee Observation and Education Center next door features hands-on exhibits and boat tours to explore the manatees, Florida's "Gentle Giants," and other sea creatures such as dolphins, pelicans and terns (772-429-6266). The on-site Vanishing Mermaid Gift Shop is worth a look.

The St. Lucie County Aquarium, featuring the Smithsonian Marine Ecosystems Exhibit, features more than 8,000 gallons of marine life. The Aquarium's six aquarium displays and touch tank accurately reflect the habitats typically found in the Indian River Lagoon, which extends 156 miles from Ponce de Leon Inlet to Jupiter. It is located across the A1A Bridge at 420 Seaway Dr. (772-462-3474).

Downtown services, such as the public library, the Post Office, banks, a general store, a deli, cafés, a bakery and art galleries, are all located near the City Marina.

Every Saturday (year-round), a farmers' market is held at the improved waterfront park adjacent to the marina and features fresh produce, baked goods, arts and crafts and live entertainment. Our Cruising Editor claims it is the best he has seen. There is also a smaller farmer's market each Wednesday.

Shopping: Within walking distance of the City Marina, there is an ACE Hardware /East Coast Lumber & Supply Co. (308 Ave. A, 772-461-5950); D&L Supermarket (823 Orange Ave., 772-468-1881); P.P. Cobb General Store and Deli (100 Ave. A, 772-465-7010); and bit further, Save-a-Lot Grocery at 605 Delaware Ave. (772-467-1077). Inlet Hardware (1105 Seaway Dr., 772-468-8588) is located near Pelican Yacht Club on Causeway Island.

Publix and Winn Dixie Supermarkets and West Marine are a short cab or bus ride away. There is also a bus system, Treasure Coast Connector, which can get you around town and to a lot more shopping.

Dining: Harbor Cove Bar & Grill (772-429-5303) at Harbortown Marina offers casual, island-themed waterfront dining with short-term tie-up for dinghies and small boats. The Original Tiki Bar & Restaurant is a local favorite at the Fort Pierce City Marina (772-461-0880), offering fresh seafood, great hamburgers, full bar service and live music on weekends. If you would prefer more upscale yet casual dining, try Cobb's Landing, also adjacent to the marina's docks (772-460-9014).

Indian River

Hutchinson Island

HUTCHINSON ISLAND MARRIOTT
BEACH RESORT & MARINA

Ernest Lyons (SR A1A) Bridge at Sewalls Point at Mile 984.9. A large pier, a park, a picnic area and a playground lie on the northwest side of the Jensen Beach Causeway. Currents along this run will be affected by whichever inlet is nearer–Fort Pierce Inlet to the north or St. Lucie Inlet to the south.

Dockage: Just past the Ernest Lyons Bridge (65-foot fixed vertical clearance), the Hutchinson Island Marriott Beach Resort & Marina offers short- and long-term transient dockage, a laundry and three pools, along with full use of the resort facilities, including tennis courts, a golf course, a restaurant and two tiki bars. It is just 1 mile from the beach and 2 miles from the St. Lucie Inlet, making it a very good jumping off spot for the Bahamas.

Fort Pierce to St. Lucie Inlet– ICW Mile 965 to Mile 988

Below Fort Pierce, the Indian River is deceptively wide; you will see many birds walking along the shoals outside of the channel. The ICW route, which follows the deep natural channel, continues to narrow here, so be sure to keep markers lined up ahead and astern.

NAVIGATION: Use NOAA Chart 11472. Shoaling to 8 feet or less at MLW may occur along this stretch, first on both sides of green daybeacon "189" in the channel and

at about Mile 973.5, where private markers to Big Mud Creek head off to the east. (Do not mistake private green daybeacon "1," located in shallow water up Big Mud Creek, for an ICW marker.)

Shoaling has extended from red daybeacon "198" to the area past the overhead power cables (90-foot authorized overhead clearance at main channel) near green daybeacon "205." As always, the channel shoals along the edges off to the side, so stay in the center of the channel.

At Mile 975, the St. Lucie Power Plant stands on Herman Bay Point at Big Mud Creek, on the east side of the Indian River. Here, several high-level cables cross to the mainland (with 90-foot authorized vertical clearance at channel crossing). Four nautical miles farther, on the east side at Mile 979, you should spot Nettles Island (the skinny part of the island is at Mile 977), with a neighborhood and marina complex built around canals. The charted depth off the ICW here is 5 to 6 feet at MLW with shallow, unmarked spoil banks.

Another chronic shoal spot is near the Jensen Beach Causeway Bridge (65-foot fixed vertical clearance) at Mile 981.4. Finally, there is shoaling on either side of the channel from north of red daybeacon "228" to "230" at Mile 985.5. Stay in the middle for 7 feet at MLW.

Indian River, FL

				Largest Vessel Accommodated	VHF Channel Monitored	Transient Berths / Total Berths	Approach / Dockside Depth (reported)	Floating Docks	Gas / Diesel	Groceries, Ice, Marine Supplies, Snacks	Repairs: Hull, Engine, Propeller	Lift (tonnage), Crane, Rail	Min/Max Amps	Laundry, Pool, Showers, Courtesy Car	Pump-Out Station	Nearby: Grocery Store, Motel, Restaurant
HUTCHINSON ISLAND						**Dockage**				**Supplies**			**Services**			
1. Nettles Island Marina 🖥 WiFi WG 979.5		772-229-2811		115	16	10/65	7/10	–	GD	GIMS	HEP	L13	30/100	LS	P	GMR
JENSEN BEACH																
2. Sun Dance Marine Jensen Beach/Stuart 982.2		772-334-1416		45	16/10	8/10	8/4	–	G	GIMS	HEP	L8	30/30	–	–	GMR
3. Four Fish Inn & Marina 982.8		772-334-0936		90	16	15/35	8/6	F	GD	GI	HEP	L50	30/50	S	P	GMR
4. Hutchinson Island Marriott Beach Resort & Marina 🖥 WiFi 772-214-7063				125	16/10	20/77	7/6	–	GD	GIS	–	–	30/50	LPS	P	GMR

🖥 Internet Access   WiFi Wireless Internet Access   WG Waterway Guide Cruising Club Partner   🔵 onSpot dockside WiFi facility
See WaterwayGuide.com for current rates, fuel prices, web site addresses, and other up-to-the-minute information. *(Information in the table is provided by the facilities.)*

HUTCHINSON ISLAND, JENSEN BEACH, NOAA CHART 11472

Martin County begins just south of Mile 980, north of the Jensen Beach Bridge. Except for hospitals, zoning restricts buildings to a maximum of four stories. Local captains returning from the Bahamas are said to locate St. Lucie Inlet by merely aiming midway between the high-rise buildings of St. Lucie County to the north and Palm Beach County to the south.

Dockage: Nettles Island Marina is located on the east side of Nettles Island. Its entrance channel (8 to 10 feet at MLW) leads easterly from the ICW at Mile 979.2 between flashing red "214" and green daybeacon "215" and is marked by private green daybeacon "1." Some of the markers are difficult to see. There is a restaurant, grocery store, boutique and more on the premises.

Around the Jensen Beach Causeway Bridge, the first of the many marine facilities in and around Stuart start to appear. Thatched-roof Conchy Joe's Seafood Restaurant (772-334-1130) is located just north of the Jensen Beach Causeway on the west side of the ICW. Call for dockage availability for dinghies and boats drawing less than 2 feet. (Dockage is for dining patrons only.) Follow the well-marked channel carefully; the bottom is soft.

Sun Dance Marine Jensen Beach/Stuart is just south of the bridge on the mainland (Mile 982.2) and offers floating docks, fuel and some boat repairs. Call ahead for slip availability. Directly to the south (at Mile 982.8) is the Four Fish Inn & Marina, situated off a marked channel with transient slips, all fuels and some supplies.

Anchorage: Directly north and south of the Jensen Beach Causeway, you will find two good, although unprotected, anchorages on the west side of the ICW. Pick your anchorage according to the wind. Tidal range here is only 1 foot. The area of deep water in the north anchorage is fairly small, as there are less than the charted depths. There is a waterfront park

SLIP INTO AN EXCITING ISLAND RESORT TODAY.

Pull up to our 77-slip marina and immerse yourself with unspoiled beaches, pastel sunsets and more waterfront activities than you can count. At the Hutchinson Island Marriott Beach Resort & Marina, you can spread out, dive in and truly cut loose.

Relax on more than 200 acres of lush Florida coast. Hit the links for 18 holes of challenging golf at The Ocean Club. And dive into waterfront thrills with jet skiing, kayaking, paddle boarding and much more.

Kick back and unwind at one of our two on-site tiki bars. The refreshing Sandpiper Tiki Bar serves up tasty frozen drinks, while the Latitudes Tiki Bar offers poolside bites and lively weekend entertainment. With so much to do once you dock, you'll have everything you need all in one fantastic location.

AN UNFORGETTABLE ISLAND DESTINATION AWAITS. CALL 800.775.5936 OR VISIT MARRIOTTHUTCHINSONISLAND.COM.

HUTCHINSON ISLAND MARRIOTT® BEACH RESORT & MARINA
555 NE OCEAN BOULEVARD, STUART, FL 34996
PHONE 800.775.5936 FAX 772.225.0003
MARINA DOCK OFFICE 772.225.6989
MARINA CELL PHONE 772.214.7063
MARRIOTTHUTCHINSONISLAND.COM

© 2014 Marriott International Inc.

MARRIOTT RESORT
HUTCHINSON
ISLAND

area, as well as Conchy Joe's Seafood Restaurant (with a dinghy dock) adjacent on the northwest side of the Jensen Beach Causeway.

You will find depths of at least 7 feet at MLW in the south anchorage, but it is often crowded with boats, some of which are permanent residents. Keep clear of the charted pipeline and cable areas on both sides of the bridge. The adjacent county park (with a boat ramp) is good for dog walking. To reach the south anchorage, make your turn westward midway between red daybeacon "220" and green daybeacon "221," and then double back toward the Jensen Beach Causeway. Protection is good only in westerly to northwesterly winds and gets quite bumpy in winds from the south.

■ THE CROSSROADS

At the St. Lucie Inlet, Mile 988, the intersection of the ICW and the St. Lucie River (Mile Zero on the Okeechobee Waterway route to Florida's West Coast) is locally referred to as The Crossroads. Here, you have a choice of three routes:

1. Continue down the ICW to the resort areas of southern Florida;
2. Move outside via the St. Lucie Inlet and cruise down the Atlantic Ocean; or
3. Travel along the St. Lucie River and down the South Fork through the Okeechobee Lake and Waterway to Fort Myers and Florida's West Coast.

Note that you can traverse the Okeechobee Waterway only if your draft is shallow enough to do so and you can pass under a 49-foot fixed vertical clearance bridge. (See the "Okeechobee Waterway" chapter in this guide for more information and check the Waterway Explorer at waterwayguide.com for the latest lake depths.)

NAVIGATION: Use NOAA Chart 11472. When crossing the St. Lucie River on the ICW, be careful of crosscurrents, which can result in westerly or easterly sets depending on flood or ebb tides. Allow for the crosscurrents when turning from the ICW into the St. Lucie River or vice versa. Pay close attention to all of the boat traffic in this area. You will most likely encounter numerous boats heading for the inlet to go fishing.

The 16-foot-high flashing red buoy "240" (ICW marker) at The Crossroads channel marks the beginning of the St. Lucie River and the Okeechobee Waterway westbound. Red daybeacon "2" and flashing green "3," about three-tenths of a mile south, marks the continuation of the ICW south. You will find them past the white daybeacon on the west side of the ICW reading DANGER–SHOAL, which should be left well to starboard (red-right-returning) when southbound.

St. Lucie Inlet / ICW / To Manatee Pocket / St. Lucie River

St. Lucie Inlet

NAVIGATION: Use NOAA Chart 11428. St. Lucie Inlet is 1 mile from the ICW and is primarily used by the many sport fishermen in the area. It is conveniently located but requires a great deal of caution when entering due to problematic shoaling. A jetty to the north and a small breakwater to the south offer protection once inside, although protection from the south is marginal in east to southeast winds. .

St. Lucie Inlet is frequently dredged. Local knowledge should be obtained before using this inlet. Depths between the inlet and the ICW range from 7 to 20 feet at MLW. Markers are frequently moved to mark shifting shoals. Fort Pierce or Lake Worth Inlets would be better choices for smaller boats. See the Inlet section in the front of this guide for details.

◼ ST. LUCIE RIVER

NAVIGATION: Use NOAA Chart 11428. For Stuart, use the Miami Harbor Entrance Tide Tables. For high tide, add 2 hours, 13 minutes; for low tide, add 3 hours, 30 minutes. From its intersection with the Atlantic ICW at Mile 987.8 and Mile Zero of the Okeechobee Waterway, the St. Lucie River heads westward before turning to the north for a few miles at Okeechobee Mile 0.5. Aids to navigation are often relocated and additional ones established to mark the best water in this area. Take time to observe all aids and do not become confused if they do not match your chart.

If turning west toward Stuart and the Okeechobee Waterway, flashing red buoy "2" and green can buoy "3," (located southwest of flashing red "240") are the first markers in the St. Lucie River. Shoaling between 5 and 7 feet at MLW has been observed over a bar between these

GOIN' ASHORE: PORT SALERNO, FL

SERVICES	
1	Post Office
ATTRACTIONS	
2	Fish House Art Center
3	Geoffrey C. Smith Galleries
SHOPPING	
4	Chapman School of Seamanship

5	Stuart Angler Bait & Tackle
DINING	
6	Manatee Island Bar and Grill
7	Shrimpers Grill & Raw Bar
8	The Twisted Tuna
9	Pirates Loft Restaurant

MARINAS	
9	Pirate's Cove Resort & Marina
10	A&J Boat Works
11	Hinckley Yacht Services Stuart
12	Manatee Marina
13	Port Salerno Marine
14	Stuart Corinthian Yacht Club

Founded in the 1920s, Port Salerno was initially a commercial fishing village. It now has become world famous for its bill fishing tournaments. If you are in need of service, practically any marine service or specialty can be found here. Other attractions, shopping and facilities can be found in Stuart, only a short cab ride away.

The village of Port Salerno has a designated working waterfront dock area where commercial fishermen continue to work from the town docks. You can see them heading out each morning, but the village is now known for its resorts and marinas and marine repair facilities. It has all of the boat repair facilities any yacht owner might need. A visit to one of these facilities makes an interesting diversion, and the boats are magnificent.

Attractions: The town of Port Salerno and all its resources are easily accessed from the local marinas. While you are here you might want to visit one of the

local art galleries within easy walking distance of the town landing. The famous bronze sculptor Geoffrey Smith has a gallery in downtown Stuart that is open to the public at 47 SW Osceola St., (772-221-8031) and also a studio at 4545 SE Dixie Hwy. (772-283-8336, by appointment only). The waterfront Fish House Art Center at 4745 SE Desoto Ave. is a former working commercial fish processing facility that has been transformed into an eclectic center for working artists and crafters with studios where visitors can purchase freshly completed works of art. There is also a popular outdoor coffee, beer & wine café with live entertainment and a fantastic view of Manatee Pocket.

Sandsprit Park is a convenient landing point to take your pets ashore for some exercise. You can land at the floating piers of the ramp, or on the beach next to the launching ramps. If you have more time to explore the area in your dinghy, you will want to go to St. Lucie Inlet State Park. This park is only accessible by boat. The entrance pier is about 0.75 miles south of the St. Lucie Inlet. This park is one of the very few preserved Atlantic Coast barrier islands. Whether it is beach combing, snorkeling or bird watching, this park will fascinate you.

Shopping: Stuart Angler Bait & Tackle (4695 SE Dixie Hwy., 772-288-1219) is within walking distance to the marinas if you need fishing supplies or ice. Provisioning options further afield include Publix Supermarket at Cove Shopping Center (5893 SE Federal Hwy., 772-287-9355) and Walmart Supercenter (4001 SE Federal Hwy., 772-288-4749). There is also a Bealls Department Store (5803 SE Federal Hwy., 772-223-8205). Harbor Freight (3424 SE Federal Hwy., 772-220-9414) has a wide assortment of tools and hardware. Transportation will be required to access any of these businesses.

A light industrial park located just 0.75 mile from Manatee Pocket hosts a wide assortment of marine businesses. Here you will find carpentry shops, prop shops, metal fabricators, fiberglass repairs, marine electronics and hardware, and canvas shops, many of whom have moved here from locations further south. Well-known names such as Scopinich, Whiticar, Hinckley, Rupp, Jim Smith and Bonadeo call Stuart home, helped establish the Stuart area as a major boating manufacturing and service center.

Bargain hunters looking for a good used boat may want to check out Chapman School of Seamanship's collection of 75 to 100 boats donated to the school (4343 SE St.

Lucie Blvd., 800-225-2841). The Chapman website (chapman.org) contains course offerings and a list of the donated boats offered for sale, plus information about the maritime library and maritime artifacts collection.

Dining: With Port Salerno's reputation as a commercial fishing center it is not surprising that the local eateries specialize in seafood. They are all a short walk from most marinas, and they can be accessed from the anchorage if you take your dinghy to the public pier at the town dock.

For a tropical atmosphere with outdoor dining, a dock and great views, you have many choices: Pirate's Loft Restaurant (at Pirate's Cove Resort & Marina, 772-223-5048); Shrimpers Grill & Raw Bar (4903 SE Dixie Hwy., 772-220-3287); and Manatee Island Grill (4817 SE Dixie Hwy., 772-872-7288). Many of these venues offer live music various nights throughout the week.

The largest family owned and operated waterfront restaurant in Martin County is The Twisted Tuna (772-600-7239). Lunch and dinner are served seven days a week. The restaurant is situated directly on Manatee Pocket (4290 SE Salerno Rd.) and has several outdoor waterfront dining areas that are both smoking and pet friendly. They use only local produce and bake their own breads. They offer complimentary dockage with your meal.

If you are here in late January, be sure to attend the Port Salerno Seafood Festival. Most of the fish cooked and served during the festival are caught and cleaned by the local watermen.

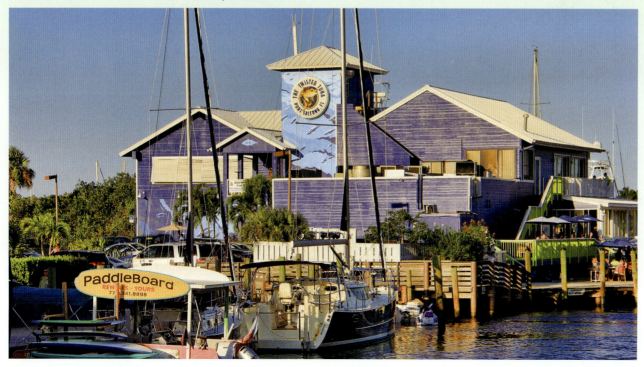

Manatee Pocket, FL

MANATEE POCKET		Largest Vessel Accommodated	VHF Channel Monitored	Dockage — Transient Berths / Total Berths	Dockage — Approach / Dockside Depth (reported)	Dockage — Floating Docks	Supplies — Gas / Diesel	Supplies — Groceries, Ice, Marine Supplies, Snacks	Services — Repairs: Hull, Engine, Propeller	Services — Lift (tonnage), Crane, Rail	Services — Min/Max Amps	Services — Pump-Out Station	Services — Laundry, Pool, Showers, Courtesy Car	Services — Nearby: Grocery Store, Motel, Restaurant
1. Whiticar Boat Works Inc. 1.5	772-287-2883	70	09	call/15	6/6	–	D	M	HEP	L75	15/50	–	–	MR
2. Sailfish Marina of Stuart 🖳 onSpot WG .8	**772-283-1122**	85	16	6/55	12/10	–	GD	IMS	HEP	L50	30/50	LS	P	GR
3. Mariner Cay Marina 🖳 WiFi WG 1.1	**772-287-2900**	80	16	5/48	6/6	–	GD	I	–	–	30/50	LPS	P	MR
4. Pirate's Cove Resort & Marina 🖳 WiFi WG 1.8	772-287-2500	100	68	10/50	7/6	–	GD	GIMS	E	–	30/100	LPS	P	GMR
5. Hinckley Yacht Services Stuart 🖳 onSpot	772-287-0923	115	16/09	4/78	10/6.5	F	GD	IM	HEP	L150	30/100	S	P	GMR
6. Stuart Corinthian Yacht Club 1.9	772-221-1900	45	16	2/25	8/5	–	–	S	–	–	50/50	S	–	R
7. A & J Boat Works 2.2	772-286-5339	60	–	call/13	/6	F	–	M	HEP	L50	30/50	S	–	GMR
8. Manatee Marina 2.2	772-283-6714	53	16	4/40	7/5	–	GD	IMS	EP	L	30/50	–	–	GMR
9. Port Salerno Marina	772-223-5022	–	16	call/19	6/6	–	–	–	–	L25	30/50	–	–	R

🖳 Internet Access WiFi Wireless Internet Access WG Waterway Guide Cruising Club Partner onSpot dockside WiFi facility

See WaterwayGuide.com for current rates, fuel prices, web site addresses, and other up-to-the-minute information. *(Information in the table is provided by the facilities.)*

MANATEE POCKET, NOAA CHART 11472

MARINER CAY MARINA

SAILFISH MARINA OF STUART

Manatee Pocket

two markers. The nuns and cans are moved regularly to mark the deeper water, which is on the green side. Always honor the markers, but especially in this area.

Be particularly alert for large wakes when traveling between The Crossroads area and the entrance to Manatee Pocket. This short but narrow stretch is often crowded with powerboats speeding to or from the ocean via the St. Lucie Inlet.

Deep water in the channel starts past Manatee Pocket. Tidal range is only about 1 foot, but the strong current bears watching, although it loses strength as you proceed up the St. Lucie River.

Manatee Pocket

Manatee Pocket is little more than one-half mile from the ICW and is often visited by cruisers traveling north and south on the ICW. Considered an all-weather anchorage, it is a delightful boating area where you can usually find dockage.

NAVIGATION: Use NOAA Chart 11428. There is a channel straight up the middle of Manatee Pocket of approximately 100 feet wide with a 10- to 12-foot MLW depth. Remember, the entire Manatee Pocket is an Idle-Speed/No-Wake Zone, which also includes dinghies.

Port Salerno, a small town at the head of Manatee Pocket, features several restaurants, a Post Office, a marine electronics store, a bank, a barbershop and a grocery store. Manatee Pocket is also home to the Chapman School of Seamanship, which has courses and programs for recreational boaters, along with vocational offerings in the maritime field.

Dockage: North of Manatee Pocket, on Willoughby Creek, is Whiticar Boat Works Inc., which is a repair/service facility with a 75-ton lift and diesel fuel.

The family-owned and -operated Sailfish Marina of Stuart is the first marina on the right when entering Manatee Pocket and the closest marina to the St. Lucie Inlet. They offer transient dockage, gas and diesel fuel, a well-stocked bait and tackle shop, fishing charters and a full-service boatyard (50-ton lift).

Farther in on the right, Mariner Cay Marina accepts transients and has gas and diesel fuel, as well as pump-out service, laundry facilities and a pool. Their fixed docks are set in a gated community.

To the south is Pirate's Cove Resort & Marina with slips and fuel (both gas and diesel) and offering engine repair. Hinckley Yacht Services Stuart, on the opposite shore, offers fuel and repair service (150-ton lift). They have on-site experts in painting, fiberglass, electronics, rigging and canvas and upholstery.

At the split in the pocket is Stuart Corinthian Yacht Club (eastern branch), which will accept transients if space is available (only two reserved spots reported). Both A&J Boat Works (western branch) and Port Salerno Marine on the western shore are repair/service yards and do not accept transients. Nearby Manatee Marina has a seawall for transients, sells fuel and has an on-site restaurant.

Anchorage: Except in a few spots near shore, depths are a uniform 5 to 6 feet at MLW, with a soft mud bottom. Take care that your anchor sets well in the mud. The most popular anchorage is in the bay between Mariner Cay Marina and Pirate's Cove Resort & Marina. Anchoring in Manatee Pocket is limited to 72 hours and the restriction is enforced. If anyone approaches you, make sure you have a copy of Florida Statute 327.02 on board which defines "liveaboard."

Just beyond the Pirate's Cove Resort & Marina docks is a tiny waterfront pier distinguished by a sign that says, "MOORING LIMITED TO ONE HOUR." It can be used by dinghies or by craft up to about 40 feet if dinghies are not blocking the end of the pier. There are plenty of good restaurants/tiki bars nearby but we are told it is tough to get groceries from here.

Stuart

Stuart, tucked back along the St. Lucie River, is barely visible, yet it is as well equipped as almost any port on the Atlantic coast and contains a sizable winter boat colony. Marine facilities and shore activities are a vital part of the community and protection is good. Beyond that is the St. Lucie Canal and Lock, leading to the Okeechobee Waterway (detailed in the next chapter).

NAVIGATION: Use NOAA Chart 11428. Where the St. Lucie River opens up and the long finger of Sewalls Point stretches downstream on the east side, the high ground is heavily wooded, with estates, both large and small, along the landscaped terrain.

The west side is equally attractive, residential and fronted by many private docks where property owners berth their vessels. Additional navigational aids, red daybeacons "6A" and "12A," were added within the last few years to better mark the shoaling along the natural channel and are not shown on older charts.

Note the shoal area shown on the chart between the ICW and the St. Lucie River's Hell Gate (at flashing green "17"). The dredged channel splits these extensive shoals inside Sewalls Point (where tides, incidentally, run about 1 hour behind Stuart), so follow the markers carefully as you enter.

One bridge crosses the St. Lucie River along the 6 miles between Manatee Pocket and downtown Stuart. The **Evans Crary (SR A1A) Bridge** (65-foot fixed vertical clearance) at the town of Sewalls Point is also called the St. Lucie River Bridge. The channel runs just west of the highest point on the bridge.

Continuing upriver, green daybeacon "23" and flashing green "23A," just east of the 65-foot fixed vertical clearance **Roosevelt (U.S. 1) Bridge** (also called the New Roosevelt Bridge), can be difficult to locate. Skippers should take special care to locate these markers before getting too close to the bridge.

Beyond Stuart, the Roosevelt (U.S. 1) Bridge is one of three that are clustered together within a distance of 800 feet. The other two are the **Florida East Coast (FEC) Railroad Bridge** (with a 7-foot closed vertical clearance) and the **Old Roosevelt (Dixie Highway) Bascule Bridge** (with a 14-foot closed vertical clearance).

The FEC Railroad Bridge is normally open but closes automatically when a train approaches. It works in concert with the Old Roosevelt Bridge, which open on signal, except from 7:00 a.m. to 6:00 p.m., Monday through Friday (except federal holidays), when the draw need open only on the hour and half hour. The draw will not open, however, during the daily rush hours between 7:30 a.m. and 9:00 a.m. and 4:00 p.m. and 5:30 p.m., except at 8:15 a.m. and 4:45 p.m. On Saturdays, Sundays and federal holidays, from 8:00 a.m. to 6:00 p.m. the draw need open only on the hour, 20 minutes after the hour and 40 minutes after the hour.

© 2003 Geoffrey C. Smith Galleries

To complicate matters, the FEC Railroad Bridge has a horizontal clearance (width) of only 50 feet, compared to the Old Roosevelt Bascule Bridge horizontal clearance of 80 feet. With little in the way of a turning basin prior to the Old Roosevelt Bascule Bridge, and with marine traffic and currents running, passage through the two bridges can be tricky, especially from the wider Roosevelt to the narrower railroad bridge. Exercise care.

A turn to the north, after passing through the old Roosevelt Bridge, takes you off the Okeechobee Waterway and up the North Fork of the St. Lucie River. This can be a very pleasant side trip if your cruising schedule allows you the time.

A turn to the south and past the **Palm City (SR 714) Bridge** (54-foot fixed vertical clearance) and the **Indian Street (SW Martin Hwy.) Bridge** (55-foot fixed vertical clearance) takes you on a cross-Florida journey on the Okeechobee Waterway. Note that the Indian Street Bridge is also called SW Martin Highway Bridge.

Dockage/Moorings: Just before the New Roosevelt Bridge are Central Marine Stuart (at Mile 7) and Harbourage Yacht Club and Marina (at Mile 7.2), located across the river from Stuart. Central Marine is a boat dealer and repair/service yard that does not offer transient dockage. Space is available for long-term rentals on the floating docks at the 300-slip Harborage

GOIN' ASHORE: **STUART, FL**

	SERVICES
1	Post Office
	ATTRACTIONS
2	Arts Council of Martin County
3	Lyric Theatre
4	Road to Victory Military Museum

5	Stuart Heritage Museum
	SHOPPING
6	Downtown Stuart Shopping Center
	DINING
7	Black Marlin
8	Osceola Street Cafe

9	Pelican Café
10	Riverwalk Café
11	Sailor's Return
	MARINAS
12	Sunset Bay Marina & Anchorage

The countryside surrounding Stuart provides a little bit of everything for which Florida is noted: citrus, winter vegetables, flowers and cattle. As the Martin County seat, Stuart has most of the facilities found in an urban center, including Martin Memorial Hospital, which accepts emergency patients at its own dock (4-foot dockside depths).

The region's agricultural importance notwithstanding, the emphasis throughout the area has gradually shifted from farming to sportfishing. Although Stuart's claim to being the "Sailfish Capital of the World" is sometimes disputed by other Florida cities, no one would deny that both its outside and inside waters provide outstanding fishing. Charter boats sail daily out of Stuart, Manatee Pocket and other nearby ports. Stuart has gained further prominence as a center of custom sportfishing boatbuilding. Several yards still build fine wooden yachts. A visit to one of these facilities makes an interesting diversion, and the boats are magnificent.

Attractions: Along with fishing and other water-intensive pleasures, Stuart is famed for its historic and pedestrian-friendly downtown. In historic downtown, a fountain in the shape of a sailfish marks the start of a group of unique galleries, cafés, restaurants, and shops on Flagler and Osceola Streets. One street over is the 2-mile-long wooden Riverwalk, where you can enjoy free concerts on the weekends, fishing off the pier and access to waterfront restaurants and shopping.

Start with an overview of the area at the Stuart Heritage Museum at 161 SW Flagler Ave.

(772-220-4600). Built in 1901, the museum celebrates the town's history with more than 10,000 artifacts that stretch back to 1880, when Stuart was first settled. Located in the Stuart Feed Store, the free museum is open daily from 10:00 a.m. to 3:00 p.m. Another interesting museum is the Road to Victory Military Museum at 319 E. Stypmann Blvd. (772-334-2990). This modest museum is dedicated to those who have served in the uniformed services and includes displays including dioramas, flags, weapons and vehicles.

For performance art, the restored Lyric Theatre (59 SW Flagler Ave., 772-286-7827) features shows and concerts, as well as movies and art cinema (a continuing series of art films, documentaries, independent films and hard to find international cinema). The Barn Theatre at 2400 SE Ocean Blvd. (transportation required) performs comedies and musicals, year-round (772-287-4884).

At 80 SE Ocean Blvd. is the Arts Council of Martin County (772-287-6676), which keeps an active calendar of events. ArtsFest, held annually in February at Memorial Park, is both the biggest celebration of the arts and the largest fundraiser for the Council.

If you are visiting on a Sunday, the Stuart Green Market and Live Music event is held from 9:00 a.m. until 1:00 p.m. near City Hall at 121 SW Flagler Ave.

Shopping: Publix Supermarket is at 746 SW Federal Hwy. (772-221-3922) for provisioning. They have groceries, a deli and bakery. Stuart Ace Hardware at 975 SE Federal Hwy. stocks tools, supplies and more (772-287-3664). Visit the web site historicdowntownstuart.com for complete shopping suggestions in the downtown area.

Dining: Local favorites here include Pelican Café (351 SW Flagler Ave., 772-283-3133) and Osceola Street Café (26 SW Osceola St., 772-283-6116). Sailor's Return is a good and popular waterfront restaurant located in the Sunset Bay Marina (772-872-7250). Riverwalk Café and Oyster Bar is located at 201 SW St. Lucie Ave. (772-221-1511) in the Historic District. Reservations are highly recommended. Black Marlin (53 SW Osceola St., 772-286-3126) is also popular.

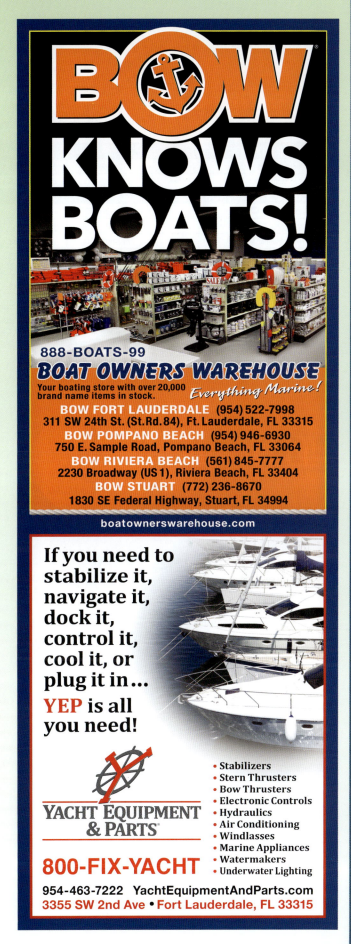

St. Lucie River, FL

		Largest Vessel Accommodated	VHF Channel Monitored	Transient Berths / Total Berths	Approach / Dockside Depth (reported)	Floating Docks	Gas / Diesel	Groceries, Ice, Marine Supplies, Snacks	Repairs: Hull, Engine, Propeller	Lift (tonnage), Crane, Rail	Min/Max Amps	Laundry, Pool, Showers, Courtesy Car	Pump-Out Station	Nearby: Grocery Store, Motel, Restaurant
				Dockage			**Supplies**		**Services**					
ST. LUCIE RIVER														
1. Central Marine Stuart 7.0	772-692-2000	50	–	call/20	6/5	–	–	IM	HP	L50	30/50	–	–	GMR
2. Harbourage Yacht Club and Marina 🖥 onSpot WG 7.2	772-692-4000	90	16/68	24/300	8/6	F	GD	IS	–	–	30/100	LPS	P	MR
ST. LUCIE RIVER – NORTH FORK														
3. Apex Marina–Stuart WiFi 7.5	772-692-7577	120	–	call/53	7/7	–	–	M	HEP	L60	30/100	–	–	R
4. Waterway Marina 7.7	772-220-2185	65	–	51/51	7/6	–	–	–	–	–	30/50	S	P	GMR
5. Harbor Inn & Marina 🖥 WiFi 7.8	772-692-1200	60	16/68	call/80	10/8	–	–	–	–	–	30/50	PS	–	MR
6. Sandpiper Bay Marina WiFi	**772-335-7875**	**150**	16/72	6/65	8/8	–	GD	IMS	HEP	–	30/100	LPS	P	GMR
ST. LUCIE RIVER – SOUTH FORK														
7. Sunset Bay Marina & Anchorage 🖥 WiFi 8	**772-283-9225**	**120**	16/69	60/198	8/8	F	GD	GIMS	–	–	30/50	LS	P	GMR
8. Meridian Marina & Yacht Club	772-221-8198	40	05	2/2	6/5	F	G	IM	HEP	L11	30/30	LS	–	–
9. Riverwatch Marina and Boatyard 9.6	772-286-3456	80	–	4/28	6/5	F	GD	IM	HEP	L60	30/50	S	–	GMR

🖥 Internet Access WiFi Wireless Internet Access WG Waterway Guide Cruising Club Partner onSpot dockside WiFi facility
See WaterwayGuide.com for current rates, fuel prices, web site addresses, and other up-to-the-minute information. *(Information in the table is provided by the facilities.)*

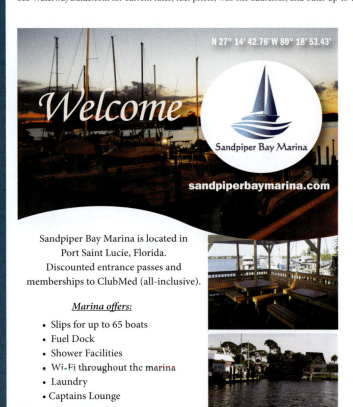

N 27° 14' 42.76' W 80° 18' 53.43'

Welcome

Sandpiper Bay Marina
sandpiperbaymarina.com

Sandpiper Bay Marina is located in
Port Saint Lucie, Florida.
Discounted entrance passes and
memberships to ClubMed (all-inclusive).

Marina offers:

- Slips for up to 65 boats
- Fuel Dock
- Shower Facilities
- Wi-Fi throughout the marina
- Laundry
- Captains Lounge

Yacht Club & Marina (formerly Loggerhead Marina). They have a ship store and on-site restaurant, along with the usual cruiser amenities.

Just inside Britt Point (due east of green daybeacon "5"), are three facilities: Apex Marina–Stuart, Waterway Marina and Harbor Inn & Marina. Call ahead for slip availability. (Harbor Inn has slips for hotel guests only.)

Located 3.7 miles northwest of the Old Roosevelt Bridge on the North Fork of the St. Lucie River is the Sandpiper Bay Marina, where transients are welcome. They offer fuel both gas and diesel, WiFi, a laundry, and some supplies (including beer and wine) and can accommodate vessels to 120 feet. They also offer discounted entrance passes and memberships to the all-inclusive Club Med, which has several restaurants, bars, swimming pools, golf, a spa and water sports rentals, including jet skis, tubing, fishing, sailing, water skiing and wake boarding.

Immediately past the Old Roosevelt Bridge on the south shore, you will find the Sunset Bay Marina & Anchorage. The very modern marina offers 60 transient slips as well as 69 moorings. The facilities ashore are top notch with a fuel dock, marine store, laundry facilities and a well-appointed captain's lounge. There is a popular restaurant on the premises called Sailor's Return (772-872-7250). It has a wonderful menu, and you can dine

ST. LUCIE RIVER – NORTH AND SOUTH FORK, NOAA CHART 11428

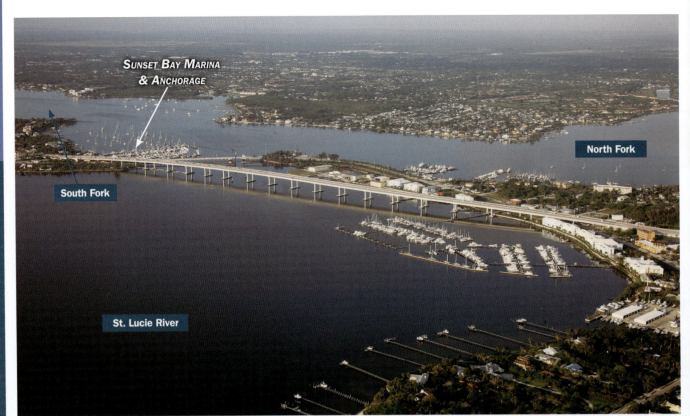

Sunset Bay Marina & Anchorage

South Fork

North Fork

St. Lucie River

either inside or outside. The marina also offers loaner bikes and a shuttle van, which runs twice weekly (on Tuesday and Friday). The shuttle takes you to a supermarket, Harbor Freight, West Marine and Walmart.

Before reaching the Palm City Bridge (54-foot fixed vertical clearance) on the South Fork, a channel on the western shore marked by private daybeacons leads to Meridian Marina & Yacht Club. It has gasoline but extremely limited dockage (two slips) and is primarily a repair and storage facility. Across from Palm City, just south of the Palm City Bridge, a marked channel leads into Riverwatch Marina and Boatyard, with 6-foot MLW depths in the approach channel and 5-foot MLW depths in the docking basin. Transient dockage and fuel is available but be sure to call in advance.

While in Stuart, the pump-out boat *M.S. Poop* will come to you. Call 772-260-8326 or use VHF Channel 16 to arrange a time to receive your free pump-out.

Anchorage: Boats anchor on the southwest side of Sewalls Point, at Hooker Cove near green daybeacon "19" in 7- to 8-foot MLW depths. Make sure that your anchor is set; currents tend to run swiftly here. Just north of the St. Lucie River Bridge, in Hoggs Cove, protection is good from northerlies and easterlies. Watch the charted rocky shoal off Pisgah Hill, and set the anchor in 7 to 9 feet at MLW.

In Stuart, Riverside Pier offers free dockage for up to 4 hours with 5-to 6-foot depths. It is possible to anchor most anywhere in the North Fork but the best anchorage is by red daybeacon "6A." Kitching Cove, past Sandpiper Bay Marina, provides a fine anchorage in 6 to 7 feet at MLW. At the north end of the anchorage, you can take a scenic dinghy trip to the headwaters of the river.

Beyond the bridges, on the South Fork, you will find very good holding in Pendarvis Cove. There is an excellent dinghy dock just inside Frazier Creek, just a one-half mile walk from Publix, laundry, restaurants and hardware. You can tie your dinghy to the wall at Frazier Creek Park and walk the dogs. There is water at the fish cleaning station and a dumpster in the park. This anchorage has reportedly gotten more crowded recently due to boats displaced at the new mooring field in Sunset Bay.

■ NEXT STOP

Those wishing to continue their journey on the Okeechobee Waterway should refer to the "Okeechobee Waterway" (next chapter). If you wish to return to the Atlantic ICW for the trip south, skip to Chapter 7: "St. Lucie Inlet to Pompano Beach."

SUNSET BAY
MARINA & ANCHORAGE

WELCOME HOME

- Transient and Long Term Dockage
- 69 Moorings & Dinghy Dock
- Floating & fixed docks
- 24 hour security
- Laundry & Shower Facilities
- Waterside patio with BBQ grill
- Salty's Ship Store
- Concierge Services & Shuttle Bus
- Free Wifi Marina-wide
- Pump-out facilities
- Protective Breakwater
- Boater's lounge/meeting room with HDTV & DVD
- High-speed fueling with Diesel & Non-ethanol Gas
- Pet-Friendly
- Walking distance to Downtown & Grocery Store
- Dock side lifts available up to 24k pounds
- Sailor's Return Restaurant on site 772.872.7250

sunsetbaymarinaandanchorage.com
615. SW Anchorage Way | Stuart, FL 34994
Latitude 27°12' N | Longitude 60°15' W
772.283.9225

Okeechobee Waterway

OCWW — Mile 986–Mile 1057   VHF — FL Bridges: Channel 09

CHARTS — NOAA 11427, 11428

The Okeechobee Waterway (OCWW) is considered by many to be the dividing line between Central Florida and South Florida. When traveling from the north, this is where you will begin to see greater changes in the climate and vegetation.

Opened in 1937, the Okeechobee Waterway offers a chance to see rural Florida, with small towns much as they were early in the last century. The scenery varies as the passage progresses from east to west from river to canal, to lake, to canal and back to river again. On the Okeechobee Waterway, ranches and big commercial farms alternate with moss-hung wilderness, while bustling boomtowns coexist alongside sleepy villages that popped up long before Miami was built.

The Caloosahatchee River was once the only way to get from the Gulf of Mexico to Central Florida, via small steamers and freighters. Some still consider the 76.6-mile-long Caloosahatchee the most scenic part of the OCWW, thanks to the backwaters and "bywaters," islands and coves, and flora and fauna. For the boater, the Okeechobee Waterway and Lake Okeechobee provide quite a transition from the pace of busy coastal cities to the tranquility of Florida's heartland.

The OCWW is also a tremendously efficient route from the east coast to the west coast of Florida, the only alternative being the long trek down around the Keys and up across Florida Bay. The OCWW is 154 or 165 statute miles (134 or 144 miles), from the Atlantic Ocean to the Gulf of Mexico, depending on whether you take Route 1 across Lake Okeechobee or the Rim Route (Route 2) along the lake's southern shore. Use the latter at your own risk due to the commonly present debris and low water depths.

The OCWW can be divided into three sections:

1. From Mile Zero (the intersection of the OCWW and the ICW at St. Lucie Inlet) down the South Fork of the St. Lucie River to the St. Lucie Canal to Lake Okeechobee.

2. Lake Okeechobee (either the "open-water route" directly across the lake, or the "rim route" along the lake's south shore).

3. From Clewiston through the Caloosahatchee Canal and down the Caloosahatchee River to the end of the OCWW in San Carlos Bay, at Mile 0 of the Gulf Intracoastal Waterway (GIWW) heading north.

As mentioned before, on Lake Okeechobee you have a choice of two routes for crossing. Route 1 is a 34-mile open-water crossing of the lake with 7.5-foot controlling depths (in summer 2018), while Route 2– which is also referred to as the Rim Route–follows the shoreline south from Port Mayaca Lock, on the eastern shore, before entering the tree-protected rim canal and running past Clewiston to the City of Moore Haven. Route 2 is 44 miles and requires a very shallow draft (4 feet or less). Be aware of the challenges of this route before proceeding. It is our suggestion that you call the Army Corps of Engineers in Clewiston (863-983-8101) and check the Waterway Explorer (waterwayguide. com) to get the latest information about the lake levels and the different routes. The lake levels vary depending on wind direction and rainfall.

Cruising Characteristics

NOAA Chart 11428 covers the area from the intersection with the Atlantic ICW to Fort Myers, while NOAA Chart 11427 continues down the Caloosahatchee River to the GIWW and the Gulf of Mexico. From that point, cruisers have the option of moving north on the GIWW to the Sun Coast, outside in the Gulf to the Big Bend or the Panhandle, or south to southwest Florida and the Keys.

Note that much of NOAA Chart 11428 is at a scale of 1:80,000, which is different from the charts adjoining at either end, NOAA Charts 11472 and 11427, both of which are at 1:40,000, or the usual ICW scale. NOAA Chart 11428 has two insets at its eastern end and one where it reaches Lake Okeechobee, plus an extension at its western end; all of these are at various larger scales.

Navigating Locks

The water level in Lake Okeechobee is higher than anywhere on the Atlantic Ocean or Gulf ICW. Whether you are headed east or west, you ascend through the locks to Lake Okeechobee and then descend after you leave. The OCWW has five modern, spacious and well-handled locks and more than 20 bridges, ranging from electronic controlled to hand operated. Typically locks operate between 7:00 a.m. and 5:00 p.m. Check in advance for current lock-through instructions. Visit the Waterway Explorer (waterwayguide.com) for detailed

information on locks before you go. Please note that the lockage schedule varies depending on lake levels.

Locking through here is simple compared to procedures necessary in the northeastern U.S. canal systems. Lock personnel furnish all necessary lines and regular boat fenders will suffice when locking through. Allow approximately 15 minutes once inside a lock. The OCWW locks are easier to transit when you are the only boat locking through, and the lock attendant will give you the windward dock line first when winds are strong. Gusty winds can set up a surge in the locks, so use caution. The attendant also might warn you that you could be locking through with a manatee or an alligator.

Also, note that the Army Corps of Engineers requires boat operators to turn off radar units during lockage to avoid exposing lock personnel to possible radiation risks. It is recommended, however, that engines be left running.

When you reach the mooring dolphins and the sign Arrival Point before each lock, contact the lockmaster on VHF Channel 13. Give your vessel's name and direction and request lockage. At that time, they will inform you of the current lockage status and estimate your wait time. It could be as long as 45 minutes to an hour in the unusual case where they have just started locking through from your side. The lockmaster will also instruct you "port-to" or "starboard-to," indicating which side of the lock to steer to and how to arrange your fenders; the lockmaster will then indicate for you to enter when the traffic light is green.

If you receive no response on VHF, sound two long and two short blasts. (Clewiston Lock is used to leave the waterway and reach the facilities at Clewiston and Roland Martin Marina & Resort; it is the only lock without a VHF radio.) At each lock, for the smallest

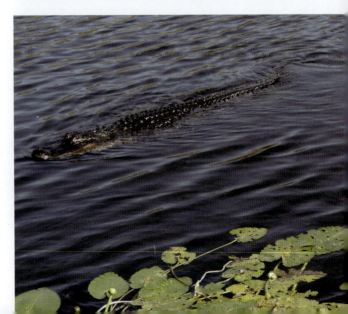

of craft, there is a pull-cord hanging down by a sign marking its location. The green light is your signal to enter the lock. The lockmaster will then hand or drop down to you (depending on the water level), a bow line and a stern line, or the lines will be hanging down from the top of the lock's sidewall, and you will have to steer to them and pick them up. (Keep a boathook handy.) Remember that the first boat into the lock should be the first boat out of the lock. Don't be too anxious.

Be prepared for moderate turbulence as water rushes in or out of the lock. Two people can safely handle a small or medium-sized boat, but an extra pair of hands is always useful on large boats. Single-handing through the locks is not safe and is strongly discouraged.

Check during your pre-cruise planning and again at the first lock to make sure the entire OCWW is open before proceeding. Maintenance on the locks is normally conducted each summer, and through-passage from the East Coast to the Gulf Coast may not be possible for as long as several months. During such times, Lake Okeechobee may be accessible from one side or the other, but not both. During a drought, lockage may be restricted depending on water supply. Call the Army Corps of Engineers at Clewiston (863-983-8101) for information or go to saj.usace.army.mil and select "Coastal Navigation" and then "Navigation Projects and Studies." Closures are usually well publicized and, as always, the Waterway Explorer (waterwayguide.com) is a very good source.

Depths and Clearances

Lake Okeechobee can be likened to a saucer full of water; it is shallow, with normal depths from 7 to 11 feet, depending on the season and annual rainfall onto the drainage area to the north and the lake itself. As a result of an ongoing drought, the level fell to a record low of 3.36 feet in mid-2007–the lowest level ever recorded. The Army Corps of Engineers and the South Florida Water Management District manage the level of the lake. There are a variety of ecological, environmental and economic reasons for various levels, and some of them conflict with others.

The depths charted in Lake Okeechobee are based on a datum of 12.56 feet. If skippers know the lake level, they can determine the difference between the datum and the current level and modify the charted depths accordingly. Depths in the sections between dams on either side of the lake vary slightly with lake level changes, but the differences are seldom enough

to affect navigation. The lake levels can also be affected by strong southerly winds, which will lower the water level.

⚠️ Lake levels are updated weekly on the Waterway Explorer (waterwayguide.com). Look for the Nav Alert labeled "Lake Okeechobee Lake Stage and Marine Weather Forecast" on the Lake Okeechobee planning chart.

The Florida East Coast (Port Mayaca) Railroad Lift Bridge, Mile 38.0, sets the 49-foot controlling vertical clearance (when open) of the OCWW. If you have any questions about clearance, call the Army Corps of Engineers at Clewiston (863-983-8101). Sailboaters can have their mast unstepped at Stuart, or wait and have it done at the Indiantown Marina, which is closer to the Port Mayaca Bridge.

Navigating the Okeechobee Waterway

With the exception of a lake crossing in less than perfect weather, passage along the OCWW is easy, piloting is simple and navigational aids are adequate for daytime running. Aids to navigation are numbered in several sequences from east to west all the way across; even-numbered red aids are on the starboard side (as they are southbound along the Atlantic ICW). Conversely, leave red aids to port eastbound on the OCWW, as you would when northbound on the ICW. Yellow squares and triangles are shown on daybeacons and buoys.

Nighttime navigation is not recommended as shoals and deadheads (partially submerged objects) are obscured. Fortunately, ample facilities and occasional anchorages make after-dark travel unnecessary. Some of the bridges operate daily from 6:00 a.m. to 10:00 p.m. and require a minimum of 3 hours notice to open at other times. Phone numbers are posted on each bridge; calls are best made during normal office hours. You can use adjacent dolphins for tie-ups. Make note that tying up to the dolphins can be tricky, and the dolphins are there for commercial boats and tugs with barges to use in case of any delays. They have priority.

Currents are not a problem on the OCWW, except for the turbulence that occurs when locks are opened. Average tides at the mouth of the St. Lucie River are 1.1 feet; 1.3 feet at Fort Myers; and 2.4 feet at Punta Rassa (at the western end of the waterway) near Mile Zero of the GIWW heading north. There is no tide in the lake itself.

Dockage & Anchorage Restrictions

Reservations are recommended at marinas on the OCWW. Anchoring in approach areas to some of the locks is also possible, and the lockmasters can provide local knowledge concerning depths and conditions.

In the last few years, many boats cruising the OCWW have found anchoring limits are being enforced by the Army Corps of Engineers. Officers have been instructed to enforce a "one-night-only" policy for anchoring. You may anchor for 24 hours, but the following day your vessel needs to show one day's travel distance before anchoring again. This applies to the OCWW between the St. Lucie Lock and the W. R. Franklin Lock, including all of Lake Okeechobee (OCWW Miles 15 to 121.4).

The ordinance does not allow for weather delays, rest days or maintenance needs, although it does make an exception "in case of emergency." The necessity for that exception would be up to a Park Ranger. The penalties associated with a citation are not outlined in the *Local Notice to Mariners*; however, we have heard reports of $100 per day fines.

If your vessel is left unattended at anchor for more than 24 hours, it is subject to impoundment, according to the notice. Meanwhile, expect to be asked to "move along" after anchoring along the OCWW; officers are telling boaters that they must continue down the OCWW or find a marina or other facility or risk a citation and fine. For updates on this somewhat contentious issue, stay tuned to navigation updates at waterwayguide.com.

Weather

Central Florida weather is generally mild. In winter, the prevailing wind is north to northeast, as opposed to summer, when wind is normally east to southeast, with very little rain except when cold fronts from the north pass through. Summer days are calm in the mornings, with occasional patchy fog, winds pick up at about 10:00 a.m. Afternoons often bring showers and thunderstorms, particularly late in the day, so it is a good idea to plan on getting in early. Hurricanes do occur in season–June through November–as well as other times and can affect the lake.

Since Lake Okeechobee is the second largest freshwater lake located wholly in the continental U.S. (Lake Michigan is the largest), it can get nasty. You should know the forecast before you leave port. The continuous NOAA marine weather comes from West Palm Beach and Fort Myers on VHF Channel WX-3 and from Belle Glade on WX-2. In the last few years, weather has gotten substantially easier because of cell phones and tablets. A good place to start is the National Weather Service Marine Forecast at forecast.weather.gov.

■ ST. LUCIE CANAL

NAVIGATION: Use NOAA Chart 11428. The OCWW departs the South Fork of the St. Lucie River near this point and continues as the start of the St. Lucie Canal with the St. Lucie Lock at Mile 15 of the OCWW. Check for local information regarding the OCWW if you plan to proceed through any of the locks.

In summer 2018, the lake levels provided channel depths across the lake (Route 1) of approximately 7.5 to 8.5 feet. The depth on Route 1 is shallowest just after leaving the Port Mayaca Lock for about 0.5 mile, then you will encounter 10 to 14 feet across the lake. At daybeacon "9" approaching Clewiston, the depth will come up to 8 feet at MLW and remain there until you turn into the channel heading toward Moore Haven.

Route 2 was open in summer 2018 with approximately 6.5 to 7.0 feet. The shallowest water our Cruising Editor has encountered on Route 2 is right at the beginning of the route when heading west. After about 1.5 miles, the water gets deeper (10-plus feet), but the Army Corps of Engineers warned that those who take this route do so at their own risk.

You can find navigation and lock schedule information at saj.usace.army.mil and on Waterway Explorer at waterwayguide.com. Conditions can change rapidly, especially if tropical storms or hurricanes pass over Lake Okeechobee. Call the Army Corps of Engineers in Clewiston (863-983-8101) for the latest conditions.

The canal carrying the OCWW up to Lake Okeechobee itself is deep and easy to traverse. You will pass under the **Indian St. (SW Martin Hwy.) Bridge** (55-foot fixed vertical clearance) at Mile 10.9, the **I-95 Twin Bridges** (56-foot fixed vertical clearance) at Mile 14 and the **Florida Turnpike Twin Bridges** (55-foot fixed vertical clearance) at Mile 14.5.

Dockage: American Custom Yachts, Inc., a full-service boatyard and custom builder, is located on the south shore between the bridges. It has limited space for transients and specializes in repairs or other services. They have a 150-ton lift and a crane and sell all fuels.

St. Lucie South Campground & Marina has 6-foot dockside and approach depths and some amenities. Call ahead for slip availability.

River Forest Yachting Center is located west of the St. Lucie Lock and offers transient dockage as well as a full range of on-site repair, maintenance and installation services. Be sure to call well in advance for availability of transient dockage. They have two freshwater locations with climate-controlled indoor storage buildings for 200 vessels from 20 to 90 feet. The marina offers a members-only Hurricane Club to offer boat owners safe harbor during hurricane conditions in both Stuart and LaBelle.

St. Lucie Lock–OCWW Mile 15.1

NAVIGATION: Use NOAA Chart 11428. The **St. Lucie Lock** at Mile 15.1 operates on request from 7:00 a.m. to 5:00 p.m. (Last lockage is at 4:30 p.m.) Radio ahead or call the lock (772-287-2665) prior to your departure for current schedules.

This first lock of the system lifts you approximately 13 feet. When approaching the No-Wake Zone entrance area, check the light system. If the light is red and a call on VHF Channel 13 or 16 does not get a response, give two long and then two short blasts, then wait well downstream in the standby area to avoid the discharge

from the dam and lock. Many boats arrive at the lower side of this lock and then turn around and go back without locking through, so the lockmaster does not assume, even if he sees you arrive, that you wish to lock through. You must call him via VHF or horn.

On each side of each lock, there is a sign marked "Arrival Point." Enter slowly on the green signal and be prepared to accept lines fore and aft from the lockmaster. As the water level rises, maintain your position with care. Remember that the Army Corps of Engineers requires boat operators to turn off radar units during lockage to avoid exposing lock personnel to possible radiation risks. It is recommended, however, that engines be left running. Additional information may be obtained from the lockmaster for the route ahead.

> **A note of caution:** The OCWW plays host not only to many varieties of fish but also to manatees (an endangered species), alligators and turtles of all sizes. The manatees frequently are "locked through," so take extra care if they are reported in the area.

Dockage: Immediately west of the St. Lucie Lock is a group of 8 slips for boats up to 35 feet, offering picnic and playground areas and nature trails. Four of the slips are first-come, first-served, and advance reservations can be made for the other four slips with the Army Corps of

St. Lucie Lock

St. Lucie Canal, FL

ST. LUCIE CANAL		Dockage					Supplies		Services					
		Largest Vessel Accommodated	VHF Channel Monitored	Transient Berths / Total Berths	Approach / Dockside Depth (reported)	Floating Docks	Gas / Diesel	Groceries, Ice, Marine Supplies, Snacks	Repairs: Hull, Engine, Propeller	Lift (tonnage), Crane, Rail	Min/Max Amps	Laundry, Pool, Showers, Courtesy Car	Pump-Out Station	Nearby: Grocery Store, Motel, Restaurant
1. Stuart Yacht Basin 💻 📶 13.8	772-286-9800	80	–	8/	7/7	–	–	M	HEP	L50	30/100	S	P	–
2. American Custom Yachts Inc. 📶 14.5	772-221-9100	135	16/68	6/25	8/8	–	GD	M	HEP	L150,C	50/100	S	–	MR
3. St. Lucie South Campground & Marina	772-287-1382	38	–	6/6	–	–	–	–	–	–	30/50	S	P	–
4. River Forest Yachting Center - Stuart 📶 16	772-287-4131	150	16	–	10/9	–	–	–	HEP	L66	30/100	S	P	–
INDIANTOWN														
5. Indiantown Marina 💻 📶 29	772-597-2455	120	16	10/34	8/8	F	GD	GIMS	HEP	L50,C	30/50	LS	P	GMR

💻 Internet Access   📶 Wireless Internet Access   🅦🅖 Waterway Guide Cruising Club Partner   📶 onSpot dockside WiFi facility

See WaterwayGuide.com for current rates, fuel prices, web site addresses, and other up-to-the-minute information. *(Information in the table is provided by the facilities.)*

ST. LUCIE CANAL, NOAA CHART 11428

INDIANTOWN, NOAA CHART 11428

Engineers (877-444-6777). Reservations must be made at least 72 hours before arrival. Stays are limited to two weeks. If you do stay at these slips, be sure to go to the Visitor Center just east of the lock for interesting and instructive exhibits.

Anchorage: Directly across the OCWW from the Army Corps of Engineers slips at Mile 15, at the entrance to a narrow bay, is a quiet overnight anchorage for one boat with 8 foot at MLW and good holding in mud.

Indiantown–OCWW Mile 29

The small community of Indiantown, less than 1 mile north of the river, has a Post Office, medical center, markets, banks and casual restaurants. Indiantown has lots of citrus groves and the historic Cracker House, a Florida pioneer farm home can be toured. It is also the home of Payson Park, a premiere horse racing facility (happyhorseswin.com).

The Seminole Inn and Restaurant was built in 1925 by S. Davis Warfield, a railroad executive, and was used by his niece, Wallis Warfield Simpson, on her honeymoon with the Duke of Windsor, explaining why Main Street in Indiantown is named Warfield Boulevard. If you want to eat at the Seminole Inn, you need to make arrangements ahead of time. They are open for lunch on Monday through Saturday and brunch on Sundays. Reservations are definitely required (772-597-3777). Ask at the Indiantown Marina for suggestions on transportation to get there; it is well worth the effort. For dinner, try the more casual Cracker's Cafe (772-597-3388), serving Wednesday through Sunday nights.

NAVIGATION: Use NOAA Chart 11428. Approaching Indiantown from the east, you will first pass under the fixed **SR 76A Bridge** (56-foot vertical clearance) at Mile 17.1, then the **Indiantown (SR 710) Bridge** (55-foot vertical clearance) at Mile 28.1. At Mile 28.2 is the **Seaboard (Indiantown) Railroad Swing Bridge** with a 7-foot closed vertical clearance. The operator may anticipate you, but if it is closed, call on VHF Channel 09. If a train is approaching, you may be delayed, as the train always has the right-of-way. The bridge opens on signal, except between 10:00 p.m. and 6:00 a.m., when a 3-hour notice is required. (Call 772-597-3822). Less than 1 mile east of these bridges, on the north side of the canal, is a park with a boat ramp and a posted No-Wake Zone.

Dockage: A short distance beyond the railroad bridge in Indiantown is Indiantown Marina. For those intending to cross Lake Okeechobee via the direct route,

this is the last marina until Clewiston, which is 35 miles away. The 43-slip Indiantown Marina is a well-protected hurricane hole offering transient slips as well as long-term boat storage. They have a do-it-yourself and full service boat yard and sell all fuels. The staff is very accommodating and friendly. Skippers planning to overnight here should call ahead for availability.

Port Mayaca–OCWW Mile 38

NAVIGATION: Use NOAA Chart 11428. At Mile 38.0, the **Florida East Coast (Port Mayaca) Railroad Lift Bridge** (49-foot open vertical clearance) sets the controlling overhead clearance for the OCWW. Elsewhere, at least 54 feet of overhead clearance can be carried. The bridge has 7-foot closed vertical clearance but is usually open.

Be sure to stay south of red daybeacon "52," as a ledge of rocks and submerged pilings runs from the marker to the northern bank of the canal. The **U.S. Hwy. 98 & 441 Bridge** (Mile 38.8) has a 55-foot fixed vertical clearance, and the **Port Mayaca Lock** is just a short distance ahead, serving as the entrance to the lake. Mooring dolphins provide the only place

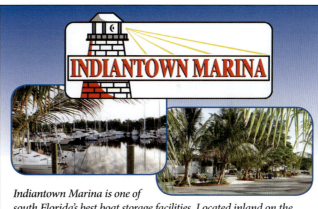

to make fast before reaching the lock, but they may be in use by barges.

At certain water levels, the Port Mayaca Lock is open at both ends, and on the flashing (or steady) green (or yellow) light, you may proceed through cautiously. You should contact the lockmaster on VHF Channel 16 or 13 before entering or if you have any questions. Eastbound boats may experience some difficulty with adverse winds and resulting seas. Under these conditions, entering the lock and making fast can be tricky. Until the lock is closed, waves tend to ricochet from wall to wall. Heading westbound is considerably easier, but if the winds are brisk, be prepared for a choppy exit. Operating hours are 7:00 a.m. to 5:00 p.m. with a last lock opening at 4:30 p.m. (561-924-2858).

Anchorage: Be warned that anchoring beyond the lock is precarious. A layover elsewhere would be a better plan. The mooring dolphins before the lock are a possibility for tie-up if not occupied by barges. The east side is reportedly better. This is exposed to wind but if tied properly this won't be an issue: Tie a very long bow line to forward piling cluster, back down to aft piling cluster and tie long line to it. Then take in slack on forward line and your boat will be tied between the two dolphins, with no drift, drag or swing. There is no current or tide here. There is also no shoreside access.

It might be possible to anchor in the mouth of the Port Mayaca Overflow Canal before the lock at OCWW Mile 36.6. You will find 7 feet of water here and all-around protection; however, there is only room for one to two boats here.

■ CROSSING LAKE OKEECHOBEE

Originally the headwaters of the Everglades, which author Marjorie Stoneman Douglas called "the river of grass," Lake Okeechobee is now the centerpiece of South Florida's water resource system. The lake is completely enclosed by an impressive levee system, officially named the Herbert Hoover Dike. The dike's construction began during the Hoover administration as a result of two disastrous hurricanes in the 1920s, when the lake was literally blown out of its banks. During periods of strong winds, the lake becomes choppy and turbulent with short, steep seas typical of shallow water.

Bass fishermen and their specialized boats frequent the known "holes" and wrecks of the lake. Pan fishermen

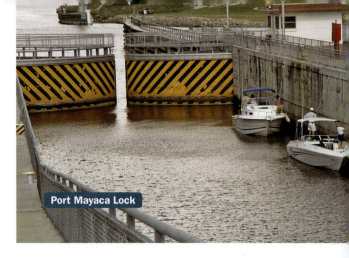

Port Mayaca Lock

are along the edges, in drainage canal entrances, near the locks and in the crannies of the many spoil islands along the southern rim. Seasonal tournaments bring out hordes of amateurs and professionals.

Be sure you have all needed provisions with you before you start the trek across the lake, as you will have few options once on the lake (on either route).

Route 1: The Open Water Route–OCWW Mile 40 to Mile 65

The Open Water Route is normally an enjoyable run, and Clewiston (at Mile 65) is a worthwhile stopover point. If the lake level and season are right, expect to see hundreds of beautiful white pelicans bunched together on the half-dozen offshore spoil islands that line the Clewiston approach channel. Unlike brown pelicans, which plunge-dive from high above the water for their meals, white pelicans scoop up fish by merely submerging their heads and necks while swimming.

NAVIGATION: Use NOAA Chart 11428. Crossing the southern portion of Lake Okeechobee, this 25-mile-long passage departs from the Port Mayaca channel in a southwesterly direction. The first run of 15 miles has just one aid to navigation, flashing red "6," which is located about 7 miles out to help you compensate for a slight magnetic anomaly in this area, which might affect your compass. About 3 miles out from the Port Mayaca Lock, there is a visible wreck to starboard. Do not be led off course. Your GPS chartplotter or radar could be useful on this stretch if visibility is compromised.

As you approach flashing green "7" on the eastern edge of Rocky Reef, note what appears to be a cluster of markers and the remains of a platform. Sort things out beforehand and follow the chart's magenta line carefully. After clearing the cut through the reef, stick to the charted course. The apparent shortcut due west, an auxiliary floodway channel, is shoaled in and

Fort Myers

Caloosahatchee River

WP Franklin Lock

Alva Drawbridge

Ft. Denaud Swing Bridge

La Belle

Hwy. 29 Drawbridge

Ortona Lock

Moore Haven

RR Swing Bridge & Hwy. 27 Bridge

Moore Haven Lock

Clewiston

Miami Canal

South Bay

North New River Canal

Hillsboro Canal

Belle Glade

Torry Island Swing Bridge

West Palm Beach Canal

Canal Point

West Palm Beach

Lake Okeechobee

Lakeport

Harney Pond Canal

Indian Prairie Canal

Kissimmee River

Fisheating Creek

Okeechobee

Taylor Creek

Route 1

Route 2

Port Mayaca

RR Lift Bridge

Hwy. 441 Bridge

Port Mayaca Lock

Indiantown

St. Lucie Canal

Hwy. 710 Bridge & RR Swing Bridge

Arundel Bridge

St. Lucie Lock

Stuart

St. Lucie River

Charlotte Harbor

Punta Gorda

N

Waterway Distances

Atlantic Intracoastal to St. Lucie Lock	15.1 miles
St. Lucie Lock to Port Mayaca Lock	23.9 miles
Port Mayaca Lock to Moore Haven Lock	
via open lake, Route 1	39.0 miles
via rim canal, Route 2	50.0 miles
Moore Haven Lock to Ortona Lock	15.5 miles
Ortona Lock to WP Franklin Lock	27.9 miles
WP Franklin Lock to Gulf Intracoastal	33.2 miles
St. Lucie Lock to WP Franklin Lock	
via Route 1	106.3 miles
via Route 2	117.3 miles

Locks operate on Marine VHF radio channel 13
Bridges operate on Marine VHF radio channel 9

★ = Major Clearance Obstacles

Note: Waterway minimum clearance is 49 feet at Port Mayaca railroad lift bridge (with St. Lucie Canal at 14.5 feet).

Okeechobee Waterway

5 4 3 2 1 0   5   10
Scale in Miles

obstructed with large boulders (particularly noticeable at low lake levels). This cut should not be attempted by cruising boats.

Entering the Clewiston approach channel, marked by a private concrete cylinder and numerous lights and daybeacons, is simple. Westbound, green daybeacon "1" is difficult to spot. If the water level is low or the winds are brisk, pay strict attention to course keeping; this is where the controlling depth for Route 1 applies. The channel is lined on both sides with rocks and spoil areas here. Exercise special care in the area between red daybeacons "4" and "6." This is another area in which the use of your GPS chartplotter will come in handy.

Close in to Clewiston, be aware that fishnets and traps are a way of life here, and their small markers are sometimes difficult to see. Some of the fishermen in high-speed bass boats or skiffs also add to the annoyance, but Clewiston, which bills itself as the "Sweetest Town in America" (due to its role in sugarcane production) is a real pleasure to visit.

Directly before reaching the Clewiston Lock, the channel makes a hard 90-degree turn to the northwest. There are no nearby channel markers on this northwesterly stretch, and a sign on the levee pointing to Moore Haven is difficult to read. *The intersection can be confusing, but don't go through the lock unless you wish to visit Clewiston.*

The Clewiston Lock is not technically part of the OCWW and is not equipped with a VHF radio, but if lake levels are not unusual, the lock is left open. If the traffic light is green, proceed through. If you wish passage and the lockmaster does not wave to you, use two long and two short blasts of your horn or whistle. The Army Corps of Engineers in Clewiston (863-983-8101) has more information on scheduled maintenance and lock operations.

On an eastbound trip from Clewiston, heading toward Indiantown, the Port Mayaca entrance markers may be hard to pick out. On the charted course, power company stacks are clearly visible at the port from many miles out, and a heading directly toward them will bring you almost directly to the channel entrance.

Route 2: The Rim Route–OCWW Mile 40 to Mile 75

⚠️ At the time of publication (summer 2018), the Rim Route was open (with a depth of just over 6 feet at MLW), but the Army Corps of Engineers warns that boaters use this route at their own risk.

Note that strong southerly winds can cause lower than charted depths. While the channel is marked, there are submerged obstructions and uncharted shoals with which to contend.

NAVIGATION: Use NOAA Chart 11428. If you are not pressed for time, or if the lake crossing is questionable due to weather, the Rim Route (10 miles longer), can be an interesting alternative, if the water level allows it. While open to Lake Okeechobee for about 15 miles, the exposure is from west through north. Unless winds are from this quadrant (and in the small craft advisory category), this part of the passage should be a pleasant one.

From Mile 55 on to Clewiston, where it joins the previously described route (Route 1), and farther to the Caloosahatchee Canal entrance, the course stays between the mainland levees surrounding Lake Okeechobee and the regular and spoil islands lining the rim. Depths vary according to lake levels and wind conditions. The shallowest stretch has been observed in the easternmost 4 miles; depths increase significantly beyond that.

Other than Pahokee and Clewiston, the only stopping points along the way are Slim's Fish Camp at Torry Island (which can only accommodate very small boats with shallow draft) and possibly pilings or dolphins.

Pahokee–OCWW Mile 50.6

The local harbor can be reached from red entrance daybeacon "2," which is opposite red channel daybeacon "62." If the wind is strong from the northwest or north, waves from Lake Okeechobee will be reflected back from the breakwater and, when combined with the incoming waves, can result in an uncomfortable, or even dangerous, situation for boats in the channel as they pass the breakwater. Near red daybeacon "78" (Mile 54), there is a charted, straight, well-marked channel that leads out through the shallows bordering the Rim Route to the "deep" water of the lake.

Dockage: The City of Pahokee owns the Pahokee Marina and Campground, which can accommodate cruising boats that can navigate the shallow approach depths. When the lake water levels fall below 12.5 feet the water depths in the marina entrance become extremely shallow, less than 6 feet at MLW. Vessels that draw greater than 4 feet should exercise extreme caution until water levels rise. The marina is a nice facility, but it is quite a hike to markets or restaurants.

Torry Island/Belle Glade to Clewiston–OCWW Mile 60.7 to 75.7

This section of the OCWW from Mile 55 to Mile 75.7 (Clewiston) has always been one of the more interesting stretches on the trip; however, hyacinths and water lettuce grow in profusion, sometimes even clogging the channel. If you must pass through them, do it slowly. Should you clog your prop and rudder, back down and then push ahead. Occasionally, the Rim Route will be closed to navigation because of vegetation in the water. These closures will be announced in the *Local Notice to Mariners* and on the Waterway Explorer (waterwayguide.com).

The **Torry Island (Belle Glade Dike) Swing Bridge** has only an 11-foot closed vertical clearance at normal lake levels. The fixed span just west of the swing span has a vertical clearance of 13 feet, which may be an advantage if you only require 12 feet of clearance. This bridge is hand-operated, and it takes awhile for the operator to get in place to open the span, so be sure to call ahead on VHF Channel 09 and give the operator an estimate as to the time of your arrival. Hours are from 7:00 a.m. to 6:00 p.m. Monday through Thursday, and 7:00 a.m. to 7:00 p.m. Friday through Sunday (fishing days). The bridge remains closed at night. It also need not open if winds are in excess of 20 mph. Call 561-996-3844 for details.

> ⚠ Note that the U.S. Army Corps of Engineers has identified a low hanging fiber optic cable at the Torry Island Bridge that is estimated to be 35 feet above the water. High masted vessels are encouraged to use Route 1 until the cable is raised to the required 52 feet. Recreational and commercial boaters are asked to use caution when navigating through these sections of waterway.

From Belle Glade, the OCWW first heads south for several miles, and then angles northwest past such communities as Bean City and Lake Harbor. A road parallels the OCWW most of the way, but you will not see it since it is behind the ubiquitous levee.

Hurricane Gate 3 at about Mile 67 (behind Ritta Island) is usually closed. There are markers along the way: Red daybeacon "94" is at Mile 70, and the channel is narrow and straightforward. As you approach Clewiston (Mile 75.7), be alert for small fishing boats anchored off and in the channel.

Dockage: Nearby you might find a very limited number of docks for small boats, including Slim's Fish Camp and Marina at Torry Island, which have some provisions. The water is extremely shallow (in the 2- to 3-foot range at MLW). You can probably find a way to get into the town area proper (nearly 2 miles distant), where you will find a community golf course, a small airfield and numerous stores.

Anchorage: Some anchoring room is west of the Torry Island Swing Bridge if you want an early start, but note that early risers also include many small-boat fishermen who rarely show concern for anchored craft. There is also a town dock at Point Chosen but overnight dockage is not allowed. A better bet is to anchor in South Bay Basin at Mile 63. To reach it, leave the OWW just west of the launch ramp and head north into the kidney-shaped basin shown on NOAA Chart 11428 in blue. Here you will find over 8 feet at the entrance and 10 to 25 feet in the basin. Islands, both natural and spoil, offer protection from winds off the lake along this route, although if the water level is high, it can get a bit unpleasant. There is room for several boats, plus lots of birds, alligators and bugs. From here you can easily dinghy back to the boat ramp.

The west side of Hurricane Gate 4, outside the immediate channel, is also a possible anchorage. The "gate" is normally closed.

Clewiston–OCWW Mile 75.5

Clewiston–OCWW Mile Route 1 (open-water route) joins Route 2 (Rim Route) at Clewiston, a point about halfway between Stuart and Fort Myers. Mileage from this point on is based on the lesser "cross-lake" figure of Mile 65; the rim mileage of 75.7 stops here.

A hurricane gate and the 50 feet wide by 60 feet long **Clewiston Lock**, operated by a contractor for the South Florida Water Management District (SFWMD), allow access through the levee into Clewiston Harbor. This lock is not equipped with a VHF radio, so contact

Clewiston Lock

Lake Okeechobee— Rim Route, FL

PAHOKEE		Dockage					Supplies		Services				
	Largest Vessel Accommodated	VHF Channel Monitored	Transient Berths / Total Berths	Approach / Dockside Depth (reported)	Floating Docks	Gas / Diesel	Repairs: Hull, Engine, Propeller	Groceries, Ice, Marine Supplies, Snacks	Lift (tonnage), Crane, Rail	Laundry, Pool, Showers, Courtesy Car	Pump-Out Station	Min/Max Amps	Nearby: Grocery Store, Motel, Restaurant
1. Pahokee Marina and Campground (WiFi) 50.5 561-924-7832	70	16	call/100	5/8	F	–	GIS	–			30/50	LPS	P	GMR
CLEWISTON													
2. Roland and Mary Ann Martins Marina & Resort ▢ (WiFi) 800-473-6766	130	16/68	12/15	8/7	F	GD	IMS	EP			30/50	LPS	P	GMR

▢ Internet Access (WiFi) Wireless Internet Access **WG** Waterway Guide Cruising Club Partner ◉onSpot dockside WiFi facility

See WaterwayGuide.com for current rates, fuel prices, web site addresses, and other up-to-the-minute information. *(Information in the table is provided by the facilities.)*

PAHOKEE, NOAA CHART 11428

CLEWISTON, NOAA CHART 11428

with the lockmaster must be made visually (waving is the method of choice) or by whistle signals, two long and two short. As mentioned before, if the lake is at normal levels, the lock is usually left open and clear for traffic; watch the traffic light to see if it is green or red.

After entering the lock grab a couple of the lines hanging from the top of the chamber and hold on. Lock personnel may help with the lines, but the change in water level as the lock opens and closes usually will not cause excessive turbulence. The schedule calls for an open lock if the water level is low, and the Clewiston Lock is usually open for direct passage. Otherwise, the hours are: 7:00 a.m. to 5:00 p.m. NOAA Weather is on WX2/Belle Glade.

Dockage: Roland and Mary Martin's Marina & Resort is a popular spot for transients and boat clubs to spend a weekend or more, particularly bass fishing groups. They sell gas and diesel fuel and have a popular tiki bar and restaurant as well as a courtesy car. Also, if you want some time off of the boat, the marina has rooms to rent. Reservations are a must. The main street of this town is only 3 blocks away and includes a small grocery store 0.5 mile from the marina and a pharmacy is 1.5 miles away. The famous Clewiston Inn Motor Lodge (108 Royal Palm Ave., 863-983-8151) offers lodging and dining to visitors. You may want to call a taxi, although it is a comfortable walk there.

Anchorage: Several mooring dolphins on the channel's edge northwest of Clewiston can be used for making fast.

Clewiston to Caloosahatchee Canal– OCWW Mile 75.5 Mile 78

From Clewiston to Moore Haven and the entrance to the Caloosahatchee Canal, Mile 78, the OCWW is fairly wide and deep. Fast boats frequent this route and small-boat fishermen anchor or drift-fish in the cuts and channel.

The variety of growth ranges from grass to scattered clumps of bamboo, melaluka and cypress, plus a few small trees with a crown of lobulated leaves and melon-like fruit. This last is the female papaya with edible fruit. If it is a sunny day, have your camera ready because this canal is probably one of the best places to see alligators sunning themselves on shore.

Be aware that strong southern winds can significantly lower water depths between Clewiston and Moore Haven. This is more sever during droughts.

CALOOSAHATCHEE CANAL

NAVIGATION: Use NOAA Chart 11428. The rim canal continues on well up the west side of Lake Okeechobee and provides some sheltered anchoring areas (again with limited swinging room and shallow water). Several facilities for small fishing boats are along the way, and at times, fishing activity is intense. As noted previously, hyacinths and water lettuce can clog the channel, as well as your prop and rudder here.

Moore Haven–OCWW Mile 78

After transiting the 13-mile Caloosahatchee Canal, the the entrance to the **Moore Haven Lock** (Mile 78) is directly to port and easy to see and negotiate. Because it is in a protected canal, it is even easier to pass through than the St. Lucie Lock, with equally capable lock tenders. It has smooth walls that do not catch rails and fenders as the old timbered walls did for many years. However, if Hurricane Gate 1 is in use during discharge of high water, turbulence on the "down" side of the lock can be considerable.

Stay well back from the lock until the green light comes on and enter carefully. Information about conditions farther on can usually be obtained from the lockmaster (863-946-0414). Remember, you are now being lowered with the water level, so do not tie off your bow or stern lines and be prepared for some surge as you drop. Wait for the gates to open completely before releasing the lines and then proceed slowly out of the lock. The lock operates from 7:00 a.m. to 5:00 p.m. with a last lock opening at 4:30 p.m.

Immediately beyond the Moore Haven Lock are two bridges. The first, the **Seaboard (Moore Haven) Railroad Swing Bridge** (Mile 78.3, 5-foot closed vertical clearance) is usually open; if closed, it opens on signal, except from 10:00 p.m. to 6:00 a.m., when it will not open. Signal before you leave the lock. The bridge is hand-operated, and the delay can be considerable. Use the eastern draw. The **Moore Haven (U.S. 27) Twin Bridges** has a fixed vertical clearance charted at 55 feet, but there are no clearance gauges or a fendering system.

Dockage: On the west side of the Caloosahatchee Canal (where the OCWW runs nearly north to south), the Moore Haven City Docks has provided alongside dockage for 3 or 4 (depending on size) visiting yachts. Normally, space is available, but during peak travel seasons, the early bird scores. The dock has a substantial

Caloosahatchee Canal & River, FL

		Largest Vessel Accommodated	VHF Channel Monitored	Transient Berths / Total Berths	Approach / Dockside Depth (reported)	Floating Docks	Groceries, Ice, Marine Supplies, Snacks	Gas / Diesel	Repairs: Hull, Engine, Propeller	Lift (tonnage), Crane, Rail	Min/Max Amps	Pump-Out Station	Nearby: Grocery Store, Motel, Restaurant / Laundry, Pool, Showers, Courtesy Car
MOORE HAVEN AREA				**Dockage**			**Supplies**			**Services**			
1. Moore Haven City Docks 78.4	863-946-0711	–	–	–	6/6	–	–	–	–	–	30/50	S	–	GMR
2. River House Marina 78.5	863-946-0466	–	16/68	6/6	5/5	–	–	–	–	–	30/50	PS	–	GMR
LAKE LICOPOCHEE													
3. The Glades Marina 🖥 WiFi 89	863-673-5653	90	16	4/23	8/8	F	–	IS	–	–	30/50	LPS	P	MR
4. Glades Boat Storage, Inc. 🖥 WG	863-983-3040	–	16/68	–	–	–	–	–	–	L40	–	LS	–	–
LA BELLE AREA													
5. River Forest Yachting Center - LaBelle WiFi 92.8	863-612-0003	150	16	20/20	9/8	F	–	–	HEP	L82	30/100	S	P	–
6. Port LaBelle Marina WiFi 100	863-675-2261	70	–	2/100	6/6	F	GD	I	–	–	30/30	LS	P	MR

🖥 Internet Access WiFi Wireless Internet Access WG Waterway Guide Cruising Club Partner 🔵onSpot dockside WiFi facility

See WaterwayGuide.com for current rates, fuel prices, web site addresses, and other up-to-the-minute information. *(Information in the table is provided by the facilities.)*

MOORE HAVEN AREA, NOAA CHART 11428

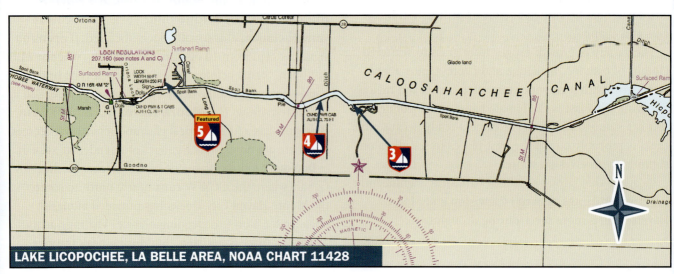

LAKE LICOPOCHEE, LA BELLE AREA, NOAA CHART 11428

LA BELLE AREA, NOAA CHART 11428

rub rail on the outside of the pilings; fenders will be needed, of course, to protect your boat from black marks. Use minimum space for tie-up so that the next boat will have room. Dockage fees may be paid at City Hall across the street, or to the dockmaster who calls in the early evening (and is a good source of local information). Showers are available behind City Hall during regular operating hours. You can get a key from the dockmaster.

The Post Office, a Dollar General (with some limited groceries), a few small restaurants, a liquor store and other convenience stores are about a on-half mile walk on U.S. Route 27. The public library, with free WiFi, is across the street from the wharf, next to City Hall.

Just beyond the City Dock is the River House Marina with slips. Dockage fees are collected on the "honor system." In the morning, you will find an envelope on your deck, or where your power cord is plugged in, with information on the dockage rate. Put cash or a check in the envelope and deposit it in the marked locked box near the gate that allows access to the dock. At the far edge of these docks, there is an overhead telephone or television cable (not a power line) crossing; clearance seems quite adequate, but specific height is not charted or known.

Anchorage: If you arrive at the east side of the Moore Haven Lock late in the day and would prefer not to lock through until morning, you can proceed on past the turn into the lock and anchor in the canal, or you can make fast for the night between the mooring dolphins located on the lake side of the OCWW, just before the canal turns into the lock. If you plan to anchor, mind the overhead power cable (reported to have only an 18-foot vertical clearance) that crosses the creek to the north.

Be sure to show an anchor light and also be aware of the limited swing room.

Lake Hicpochee–OCWW Mile 82.5

Early morning fog and mist sometime curtail an early departure, but normally the Caloosahatchee Canal is straightforward, wide and deep, with no surprises. At about Mile 82.5, the channel passes through shallow Lake Hicpochee, where again you may encounter small fishing boats anchored along the shore. Watch your wake as a matter of both prudence and courtesy.

Dockage: Just past Lake Hicpochee and the bend in the Caloosahatchee Canal, on the south bank is The Glades Marina. The basin is small and dockage is limited. Glades Boat Storage, Inc. is nearby with a 40-ton lift (no transient space).

A little farther along, at approximately Mile 93, is River Forest Yachting Center–LaBelle, which is owned by the same people who own the River Forest Yachting Center on the St. Lucie River. This facility is very similar to the one on the eastern side of the lake, except it is twice as large (at over 100,000 square feet). They also boast an 82-ton lift. This marina has been constructed to withstand hurricane winds. Transients are welcome with amenities that include showers and pump-out service. Be sure to call in advance for dockage availability.

Anchorage: At Mile 92.5, just before Turkey Creek, there is a narrow canal that leads into Lollipop Lake anchorage. It is small, but if you go all the way into the lake, you will find ample room for anchoring in very protected water. The water in the canal is 8- to 9-feet at MLW, and our Cruising Editor reports that it is much deeper (30-plus feet) once inside the basin. There is a lot of wildlife to see; you will be joined by eagles, osprey and owls to name a few. This is a nice out-of-the-way spot to spend an evening on the hook.

Ortona Lock–OCWW Mile 93.5

Before you get to Ortona Lock, several small canals lead off to the north into the Turkey Creek community. Most of its residents are boaters, and their docks usually are full of cruising boats of all descriptions.

NAVIGATION: Use NOAA Chart 11428. Like the Moore Haven Lock, Ortona Lock's smooth concrete walls are a vast improvement over timbered sides that invariably catch fenders and rub rails. Tie-up dolphins are located outside both ends of the locks; boats normally make fast to the south wall. The **Ortona Lock** operates the same way as the others; again, be prepared for some surge as the water is let out. The change in level varies, but 8 to 10 feet is normal depending on lake level. The lock operates from 7:00 a.m. to 5:00 p.m. with a last lock opening at 4:30 p.m. (863-946-0414).

Dockage: At Mile 100, an entry channel leads off to the south into the Port LaBelle Marina, with two reserved transient slips, fuel and some other amenities. Just east of the marina, there is another cove (known to some cruisers as Tranquility Cove), which is an extension of the marina.

La Belle–OCWW Mile 103

This quiet old river town of La Belle dates back to the early 1800s. The Swamp Cabbage Festival is held in La Belle during the last full weekend in February. Swamp cabbage, also known as hearts of palm, is the growing part of the sable palm. (Another local delicacy is alligator.) La Belle is also known as the "Honey Capital." The Harold P. Curtis Honey Company (355 N. Bridge St., 863-675-2187) is located near the beginning of the business district on the south side of the bridge. The company maintains about 1,000 beehives and will permit you to sample different types of honey.

The **La Belle (SR 29) Bascule Bridge** (Mile 103.0, 28-foot closed vertical clearance) opens on signal, except from 7:00 a.m. to 9:00 a.m. and 4:00 p.m. to 6:00 p.m., Monday through Friday (except federal holidays), when the bridge need not open. The bridge will open on signal between 10:00 p.m. and 6:00 a.m. if at least a 3-hout notice is given. Call 866-335-9696 for an opening during these hours.

Dockage: Just beyond the bridge, La Belle City Dock (863-673-1191) on the south side has free dockage with a 3-day limit, after which you must leave and not return for at least 8 days. These docks are usually full on the weekends and are on a first-come, first-served basis. They have mooring posts, making it more difficult to

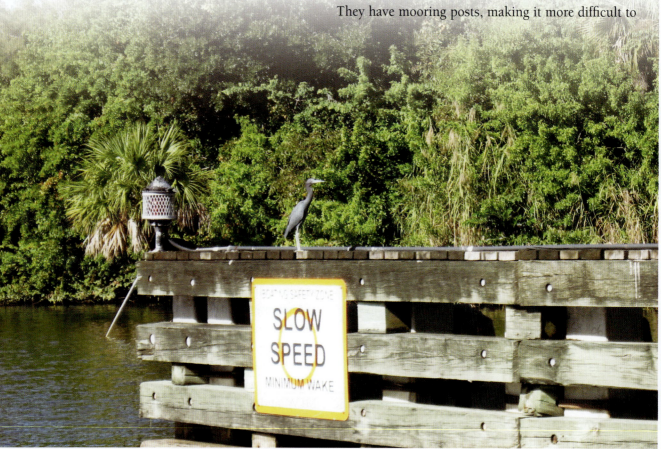

off-board for smaller boats. They are also exposed to the wake of passing boats and are noisy from bridge traffic. Note that some docks are not usable due to vegetation.

South along Bridge Street (within four blocks) are a library, bank and Post Office. A Save-A-Lot at 71 S Lee St. (863-675-8080) is within walking distance for your provisioning needs. There is a Dollar General Market on the way. A number of fast food restaurants are nearby as well.

To the west of the Town Dock is a Hendry County Boat Ramp with a pier for small boats. The municipal Bob Mason Town Park on the same side of the canal offers free dockage in 10 slips.

Anchorage: There is a fair anchorage at Mile 103 just east of the Bob Mason Park dock. It is deep (15 to 20 feet at MLW) but open to wakes.

■ CALOOSAHATCHEE RIVER

The Calusa Indians used the Caloosahatchee River as a highway. So did early settlers to Fort Myers. Today, powerboats and sailboats traverse the 67-mile-long river, which is an important link the OCWW. The river is wide enough to accommodate everyone, including the abundant wildlife. The Caloosahatchee River and its meandering tributaries are bordered by lush, towering leather ferns, stately oaks dripping with moss and verdant vegetation along every shore.

La Belle to Franklin Lock– OCWW Mile 103 to Mile 121

NAVIGATION: Use NOAA Chart 11428. These are the scenic headwaters of the Caloosahatchee River, once a major transportation artery in the settling of Florida. Today, you will rarely encounter tugs and barges, as over-land trucking has diminished the commercial importance of the river.

Where the Caloosahatchee River once wandered, it is now a series of straight sections punctuated by gentle turns and numerous intriguing oxbows and streams. Still a beautiful waterway, the water runs quite deep to the banks. Swinging room on the river, even at its widest points, is limited and anchoring is not recommended unless you can keep your vessel from swinging into the channel. Some of the oxbows are deep enough if you feel adventurous, but snags or shoals and even low-hanging power cables are prevalent. At about Mile

106.6, well out from the northern bank, red daybeacon "2" marks a shoal.

Two bridges cross this section of the Caloosahatchee River. The **Fort Denaud Swing Bridge** (Mile 108.2) has a 9-foot closed vertical clearance. The bridge opens on request, and arrows indicate which side of the draw to use. It is closed from 10:00 p.m. until 6:00 a.m. and requires a 3-hour notice to open during those hours; call 863-675-2055. The **Alva Bascule Bridge** (Mile 116) has a 23-foot charted closed vertical clearance and likewise opens on signal, except from 10:00 p.m. until 6:00 a.m. when a 3-hour notice is required. Use VHF Channel 09 or call 239-278-2704.

Anchorage: Boats are not permitted to anchor on the north side of the Caloosahatchee River in the wide spot across from the entrance to the former Rialto Harbor Docks. However, you may be able to anchor in nearby Hickey Creek at Mile 119.5 behind an unnamed island. Here you will find all-around protection from wakes in 7 feet at MLW. Be aware that this anchorage has poor holding in mud; check your holding!

W.P. Franklin Lock–OCWW Mile 121.4

NAVIGATION: Use NOAA Chart 11428. The final lock on the Okeechobee Waterway is at Olga. The **W.P. Franklin Lock** normally operates on request from 7:00 a.m. to 5:00 p.m. daily. (Last lockage at 4:30 p.m.) Enter on the green light, and remember not to tie off your lines tightly, as the level will drop about 3 feet. Wait until the lock is fully open before casting off and exit slowly. Sometimes eastbound boats are waiting nearby to enter. Please note that low water levels in Lake Okeechobee may result in lock schedule changes at the W.P. Franklin. Be sure to call in advance to check schedules (239-694-5451).

Dockage: Immediately east of the lock and dam, on the north shore, is a small, but attractive Army Corps of Engineers marina (W.P. Franklin Campground-Boat-in Docks), which can accommodate boats not more than about 40 feet long. Call ahead for reservations at least 72 hours before arrival (239-694-8770).

Anchorage: A protected anchorage is just below the Franklin Lock at Mile 121.5, next to the Army Corps of Engineers campground, with ample room and 10-foot depths. Anchoring is also available adjacent to the launch ramp above the lock near the slips. Here you will find 10 feet at MLW, good holding in mud and good protection.

Caloosahatchee River, FL

OLGA		Dockage						Supplies	Services					
		Largest Vessel Accommodated	VHF Channel Monitored	Transient Berths / Total Berths	Approach / Dockside Depth (reported)	Floating Docks	Gas / Diesel	Groceries, Ice, Marine Supplies, Snacks	Repairs: Hull, Engine, Propeller	Lift (tonnage), Crane, Rail	Min/Max Amps	Laundry, Pool, Showers, Courtesy Car	Pump-Out Station	Nearby: Grocery Store, Motel, Restaurant
1. W.P. Franklin Campground-Boat-In Docks 122	239-694-8770	40	–	8/8	–	–	–	–	–	–	30/50	LS	–	–
2. Calusa Jacks Marina □ WiFi 124.2	239-694-2708	200	16/68	3/15	23/8	–	GD	IMS	–	–	30/50	S	–	GMR
3. Owl Creek Boat Works 125.5	239-543-2100	125	–	6/48	7/7	–	–	M	HEP	L150	50/50	S	–	GMR
4. Sweetwater Landing Marina □ WiFi 126	239-694-3850	200	16	10/65	9/5	–	G	IS	HEP	–	30/50	LPS	P	GMR

□ Internet Access WiFi Wireless Internet Access WG Waterway Guide Cruising Club Partner onSpot dockside WiFi facility

See WaterwayGuide.com for current rates, fuel prices, web site addresses, and other up-to-the-minute information. *(Information in the table is provided by the facilities.)*

OLGA, NOAA CHART 11428

OWL CREEK
BOAT WORKS & STORAGE INC.

Southwest Florida's Finest Yacht Refinishing

- 3 Lifts for Hauling up to 150 Tons
- Awlgrip & Imron Refinishing - 6000 sq. ft. Spray Booth
- Custom Fiberglass fabrications
- Custom Woodworking, Alterations and Modifications. Specializing in older wood yacht hulls
- Bottom Painting, Gelcoat & Blister repair
- Complete Gas & Diesel Engine Sales & Service
- B&L Marine Electronics - Complete Sales & Service

BEST BOTTOM PAINT PRICING!

SINCE 1953
WWW.OWLCREEKBOATWORKS.COM
Ft. Myers, FL
239-543-2100

ASK ABOUT OUR SPECIAL DOCKAGE & STORAGE RATES

Did You Know?

Manatees only breathe through their nostrils, since while they are underwater their mouths are occupied with eating! A manatee's lungs are two-thirds the length of its body. Manatees take up residence primarily in Florida's coastal waters during winter. but some individuals migrate as far north as the Carolinas or as far west as Louisiana in summer. Manatees have swum as far north as Cape Cod, MA, in recent years..

Franklin Lock to Fort Myers– OCWW Mile 121.5 to Mile 135

NAVIGATION: Use NOAA Chart 11428. Use the St. Petersburg Tide Tables. For high tide, add 1 hour 56 minutes; for low tide, add 2 hours 23 minutes.

⚠️ The Caloosahatchee River has many aids to navigation, beginning with red daybeacon "2" just downriver from the W. P. Franklin Lock. Although this is a navigable river coming in from the Gulf of Mexico, it is not marked with the conventional "red-right-returning" system with numbers increasing as one proceeds inland. The daybeacons, lights, and such are a continuing part of the Okeechobee Waterway system; numbers increase as you cruise westward, and the "reds" are on your right side even though you are going downriver. This can be confusing if you do not understand the system.

From here to Fort Myers, you have several bridges to consider. The first, **Wilson Pigott (Olga) Bascule Bridge** at Mile 126.3, has a 27-foot closed vertical clearance. The bridge opens on signal, except between 10:00 p.m. and 6:00 a.m., when it requires at least a 3-hour notice to open. Call 866-335-9696.

At Mile 127.5, the scale of Chart 11428 changes to 1:40,000 for its final section, an inset marked "Fort Myers Extension." A Manatee Speed Zone here is strictly enforced; specific restrictions vary in the channel and outside, and also during different seasons. Beginning at Mile 128, signs near the overhead power cables, and the large power plant adjacent, mark the zone. Manatees can be found all along the OCWW, but as usual, they seem to congregate most often near the warm water outflows of power plants.

The **I-75 Bridge** crosses the OCWW at Mile 128.9 with a 55-foot fixed vertical clearance. At Mile 129.9 the **SCL Railroad Lift Bridge** at Beautiful Island is normally open unless a train is due. The closed vertical clearance is only 5 feet, so signal or call, and then hold well off until the train has passed and the bridge is fully opened. (Note that the overhang is 55 feet when the bridge is open.) Beautiful Island lives up to its name, but do not get in too close due to depth concerns. There are some areas, particularly on the south side, where you can leave the channel, but do so very cautiously after examining your chart.

Dockage: At Mile 124.2, Calusa Jacks Marina has transient space and sells gas and diesel and offers some

repairs. They experienced a lot of hurricane damage in 2017, but stated that they should be fully operational by the end of 2018. Approaching Mile 125.5, just before the Olga Bascule Bridge, a channel leads off to the north and the Owl Creek Boat Works, a full-service yard with a covered freshwater storage area. They have three lifts for hauling up to 150 tons and can handle all types of repairs. Transient dockage is possible if you call in advance. Owl Creek Boat Works has been around since 1953.

A little farther on is Sweetwater Landing Marina, a full-service facility that accepts transients, has gas available and offers some repairs. (An on-site restaurant was planned at press time in summer 2018.) Call ahead for slip availability. If you need to re-step a mast, this is a good time to do so, although this can also be done in Fort Myers.

Anchorage: Because the Caloosahatchee River is more than a mile wide, it can get rough in nasty weather, so anchoring, although possible, could be unpleasant.

At Mile 124.3, an oxbow on the south side of the waterway offers 5 feet at MLW and some protection. Leave the OWW west of the oxbow and head southeast into loop.

Across from flashing green "13," at Mile 128, is the last good anchorage before Fort Myers. Locally known as Power Plant Slough, the western channel is reached

Caloosahatchee, FL

FORT MYERS AREA

	Phone	Dockage						Supplies		Services					
Marina		Largest Vessel Accommodated	VHF Channel Monitored	Transient Berths / Total Berths	Approach / Dockside Depth (reported)	Floating Docks		Gas / Diesel	Groceries, Ice, Marine Supplies, Snacks	Repairs: Hull, Engine, Propeller	Lift (tonnage), Crane, Rail	Min/Max Amps	Laundry, Pool, Showers, Courtesy Car	Pump-Out Station	Nearby: Grocery Store, Motel, Restaurant
1. Prosperity Pointe Marina 🖥📶 WG 134	239-995-2155	56	16/06	10/53	6/4.5	F		–	IS	–	–	30/50	LS	P	GMR
2. Marinatown Yacht Harbour 🖥📶 135	239-997-7711	68	–	40/135	6/5	–		–	IS	EP	–	30/100	LPS	P	GMR
3. City of Fort Myers Yacht Basin 🖥 onSpot WG 134.5	239-321-7080	300	16/68	25/241	10/7	–		GD	GIMS	–	–	30/100	LS	P	GMR
4. Legacy Harbour Marina 🖥 onSpot 135	239-461-0775	120	16/12	10/131	7/7	F		–	I	–	–	30/50	LPS	P	GMR
5. The Marina at Edison Ford 🖥📶	239-895-7703	80	16/73	25/45	7/5	–		–	IS	–	–	30/50	LS	P	GR

🖥 Internet Access   📶 Wireless Internet Access   WG Waterway Guide Cruising Club Partner   onSpot dockside WiFi facility

See WaterwayGuide.com for current rates, fuel prices, web site addresses, and other up-to-the-minute information. *(Information in the table is provided by the facilities.)*

FORT MYERS AREA, NOAA CHART 11428

City of Fort Myers Yacht Basin

Stay & play in the heart of historic Fort Myers River District!

Conveniently located on the south bank of the Caloosahatchee River in downtown Fort Myers with direct access to the ICW.

- 241 slips & 7 moorings
- Welcoming vessels up to 300'
- Walking distance to great restaurants & shopping
- ValvTect diesel & ethanol-free fuel
- Well-stocked ship & convenience store
- Remodeled shower/restrooms, laundry and customer lounge
- Free pumpout & Wi-Fi

10% off transient dockage & 5 cents off per gallon of fuel for: Waterway Guide Cruising Club, BoatUS & SeaTow members

(239) 321-7080
www.cityftmyers.com/yachtbasin

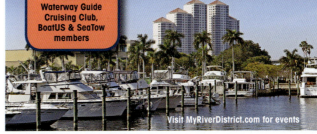

Visit MyRiverDistrict.com for events

LEGACY HARBOUR MARINA

131 Slips, Floating Docks
Length to 100' +, 7' Draft
Daily, Weekly, Monthly, Annual
Live Aboard Facilities
TV, Laundry
Showers & Restrooms
Heated Pool, onSpot wifi
Legacy Harbour Hotel & Suites
Close to Shops & Restaurants

239.461.0775

legacyharbourmarina.com
info@legacyharbourmarina.com

2044 West First Street
Fort Myers, Florida 33901

Caloosahatchee River • Channel Mark #49   26° 38.6' N • 81° 52.5' W

CHAPTER 6

OKEECHOBEE WATERWAY

by entering southwest of the manatee sign, about halfway between the sign and shore. Continuing in, the deepest water (8-foot plus depths) is about 100 feet off the western shore. The eastern channel of the slough is narrower, shallow and more difficult to follow.

Manatees love it here too, so be mindful that you are likely sharing this space.

Fort Myers–OCWW Mile 135

While Fort Myers is not actually the western end of the OCWW, most cruisers consider it to be. Like most of Florida, the city boasts a growing population, especially if you include the Cape Coral area, which is across the river on the north shore.

There are two high-level bridges here–the **Edison Twin Bridges** (56-foot fixed vertical clearance) at Mile 134 in North Fort Myers and the **Caloosahatchee Bridge** (55-foot fixed vertical clearance) at Mile 135.

⚠ Note that in summer 2018, two navigation markers east of the Editon Twin Bridges were posing potential hazards to navigation. Green daybeacons "39" and "41" were both reported destroyed with wreckage just above the waterline Exercise caution in this area.

Dockage/Moorings: Before the Edison Twin Bridges on the north bank of the river is Prosperity Pointe Marina, which may have transient space. Be cautious when approaching their very shallow entrance channel. Depths are reported as 3.5 feet at MLW. They also report 5-foot MLW dockside depths. Call the marina in advance for depth information.

On the north bank, south of the Caloosahatchee Bridge at Mile 135 is Marinatown Yacht Harbour. The flashing green "1" and red daybeacon "2" for the beginning of the well-marked channel to Hancock Creek are beside the Caloosahatchee River flashing red "52." The marina is around the first bend above green daybeacon "25." Within Hancock Creek, there is 5- to 7-foot MLW depths. In the section of the channel that parallels the shore, between green daybeacons "17" and "21," the channel carries only 4 to 4.5 feet at MLW with a soft mud bottom. Marinatown Yacht Harbour has plenty of transient space on their docks, but you should still call in advance for reservations. From the marina it is a relatively short walk to a CVS, large liquor store, several banks and a number of other stores, including a grocery.

The City of Fort Myers Yacht Basin, situated on the south shore of the Caloosahatchee River between the western-most span of the Edison Twin Bridges and the Caloosahatchee River Bridge, is within walking distance of supplies. The full-service facility can accommodate vessels both large and small, but reserve your slip ahead to make sure space is available when you arrive. They also sell all fuels.

Across the river are 10 moorings administered by the City Yacht Basin; access across the shallows is by a marked channel. These are available to smaller sailboats.

Legacy Harbour Marina's entrance is on the east side of the marina. Look for the piling with a white marina flag by the OCWW. Turn at that piling, leaving it to starboard and head for the south shore. You will be headed toward a restaurant with a green roof

Edison Twin Bridges

(Joe's Crab Shack). Make a right into the marina basin. Legacy Harbour Marina has concrete floating docks that can accommodate vessels up to 120 feet. One of the largest floating breakwaters in the Gulf of Mexico protects the marina from the wakes of the river traffic. The marina has cable TV, laundry, air-conditioned showers, metered-at-the-slip electric, WiFi and an in-slip pump-out station. A well-equipped and very pleasant boaters' lounge is available in the harbormaster's building. Adjacent to the marina is a hotel with well-appointed waterfront suites and standard hotel rooms (reservations recommended). Grocery, shops and restaurants are within walking distance in the Historic Downtown River District.

The family-owned and -operated Marina at Edison Ford is located about 1 mile beyond the Caloosahatchee River Bridge. The marina maintains a well-marked channel on the south shore. Pinchers Crab Shack (239-245-7049) is on site, as is a coin-operated laundry. It is only a short walk to groceries and plenty of shopping and dining.

Anchorage: There is a former mooring field at Lofton Island that has fallen into disrepair. It is unclear if you have to pay to anchor here but the Ft Myers Municipal Marina has dinghy docks nearby and you can walk pets or go shopping. This is between the bridges with rush hour traffic and car noise but a good place to position yourself to cross Lake Okeechobee if you are coming from the west.

Cape Coral–OCWW Mile 142

The second largest city in Florida was once swampland known as Redfish Point. Cape Coral is 114 square miles, and it numerous canals total more mileage than those of Venice, Italy. This is a boating-oriented area, and the traffic is reminiscent of downtown Fort Lauderdale.

NAVIGATION: Use NOAA Charts 11428 and 11427. Southwest of Fort Myers, the Caloosahatchee River continues somewhat circuitously for another 15 miles. At Mile 138.6 is the **Veterans Memorial (Mid-Point) Bridge**, with a 55-foot fixed vertical clearance. At Mile 142, the OCWW passes under the **Cape Coral Twin Bridges** (charted at 55 feet, but do not count on more than 54 feet of fixed vertical clearance). Note that water levels in the lake will affect bridge heights.

⚠ Frequent groundings occur in the Caloosahatchee River west of Cape Coral. Be sure to use front and rear ranges. See the Waterway Explorer at waterwayguide.com for alerts and updates.

Exercise some care in transiting the remaining miles of the OCWW. Numerous shoal areas are outside the channel.

Dockage: Between flashing red "70" and "72" on the south side of the river, a marked channel near shore leads into the private The Landings Marina, with gasoline and diesel fuel but no transient dockage. MarineMax Fort Myers is nearby, on a channel off Deep Lagoon, for fuel and repairs (75-ton lift).

GOIN' ASHORE: **FORT MYERS, FL**

	SERVICES
1	Library
2	Post Office
3	Visitor Information
	ATTRACTIONS
4	Burroughs Home & Garden
5	Edison's Estate
6	Henry Ford Estate
	SHOPPING
7	Franklin Shops
8	Publix
	DINING
9	Bennett's Fresh Roast

10	Firestone Grille, Martini Bar & Sky Lounge
11	Fords Garage
12	Los Cabo's Cantina
13	United Ale House
	MARINAS
14	City of Fort Myers Yacht Basin
15	Legacy Harbour Marina
16	The Marina at Edison Ford

Fort Myers is named for a fort established during the Seminole Indian War of 1841. The fort briefly saw action as a union fort during the Civil War. The town remained a small but important winter resort until the Tamaimi trail bridged the Caloosahatchee in 1924. This sparked the first real estate boom and the town grew rapidly. It became the winter home of Thomas Alva Edison in 1884 and remained so for almost 50 years. In 1911, Henry Ford purchased property adjacent to Edison and lived there for several winters.

Attractions: The side-by-side Edison and Ford Winter Estates are open to the public (239-334-7419). Edison's 14-acre riverfront estate is situated along McGregor Boulevard, which is lined for 15 miles with 2,000 royal palms (the reason Fort Myers is known as the "City of Palms"). When enjoying the gardens, visitors should note the tropical plants given to Edison by friends. The immense Australian fig tree was tiny when Henry Ford sent it, and the 400-foot banyan (a gift from Harvey Firestone) was only 2 inches in diameter when planted. There is a laboratory where Edison created several of his many inventions, and both homes have been restored to their original grandeur. The grounds are spectacular.

This is a must-see tour when visiting Fort Myers. The stately Burroughs Home at 2505 First St. (239-337-0706) overlooks the Edison Bridge. Built in 1901, this Georgian Revival Mansion offers guided tours (Tuesday through Thursday at 11:00 a.m., reservation required). Contact tera@burroughshome.com or call 239-337-9505 for a reservation.

Strolling through the downtown area and all its shops and restaurants is a great way to spend an afternoon or evening. Just seeing how the 20th-century buildings have been refurbished is well worth the time.

Art lovers are sure to find events of interest throughout the year, with the premier event being Art Fest Fort Meyers, held along the waterfront in early February each year. Theatre fans will find the plays, shows, and performances at the Florida Repertory Company at the Arcade, located right on the waterfront, to be greatly entertaining. On the first Friday of each month all year long, the city sponsors an Art Walk in the downtown River District area. It's very popular and well attended. Also, each Thursday morning from 7:00 a.m. to 1:00 p.m., there is a farmers market located at Centennial Park (Heitman and First Streets).

Nature lovers will find plenty to do; whether you are a bird lover or a manatee watcher, opportunities to experience the local flora and fauna abound in the Fort Meyers area.

Shopping: There are several boutiques and gift shopping opportunities downtown. For provisioning, a Publix Market is at First Street Village at 2160 McGregor Blvd. The Franklin Shops at 2200 First St. (239-333-3130) are close to the marinas. Being a small city, all sorts of big name shops are within a short cab ride from the waterfront.

Dining: There are several dining options within easy walking distance from the waterfront and marinas. Ford's Garage (2207 First St., 239-332-3673) is one of the most popular for lunch or dinner. They specialize in hamburgers and beer, with over 100 types of beer from which to choose. Cabo's Cantina & Tequila Bar (2226 First St., 239-332-2226) is an outstanding choice if you are interested in a great Mexican meal in a lively atmosphere. Next door is United Ale House (2236 First St., 239-362-1831), a London pub for beer and grub. For fantastic views, visit Firestone Grille, Martini Bar & Sky Lounge (2224 Bay St., 239-334-3473) with four floors of food and fun.

Start your day at Bennett's Fresh Roast at 2011 Bayside Pkwy. with fresh house-roasted coffee and donuts made on-site (239-332-0077).

Caloosahatchee River, FL

CAPE CORAL AREA		Dockage					Supplies		Services					
		Approach / Dockside Depth (reported)	VHF Channel Monitored	Transient Berths / Total Berths	Largest Vessel Accommodated	Floating Docks	Gas / Diesel	Groceries, Ice, Marine Supplies, Snacks	Repairs: Hull, Engine, Propeller	Lift (tonnage), Crane, Rail	Min/Max Amps	Laundry, Pool, Showers, Courtesy Car	Pump-Out Station	Nearby: Grocery Store, Motel, Restaurant
1. The Landings Marina-PRIVATE 142.5	239-481-7181	60	16	call/193	5/	–	GD	GIMS	HEP	–	–	S	–	GR
2. MarineMax Fort Meyers at Deep Lagoon ⌗ WiFi 143	239-481-8200	90	16	call/75	6/6	F	GD	IM	HEP	L75	30/100	S	P	GR
3. Gulf Harbour Marina ⌗ WiFi WG 143.5	239-437-0881	101	16/11	10/186	6/5	F	GD	–	–	–	30/50	LS	P	GMR
4. St. Charles Yacht Club WiFi 146	239-466-4935	78	16/68	call/65	5/5	–	GD	–	–	–	50/50	LPS	P	R
5. Cape Coral Yacht Basin ⌗ WiFi 144	239-574-0809	50	16/78	4/89	5/5	–	GD	IMS	EP	–	30/50	LPS	P	GMR
6. Tarpon Point Marina ⌗ WiFi 147	239-549-4900	120	16/18	15/225	7/8	F	GD	GIMS	–	–	30/100	PS	P	GMR
7. Cape Harbour Marina WiFi 147	239-945-4330	60	16	16/76	6/6	–	GD	IS	–	L11	30/50	LPS	P	GMR

⌗ Internet Access   WiFi Wireless Internet Access   WG Waterway Guide Cruising Club Partner   onSpot dockside WiFi facility
See WaterwayGuide.com for current rates, fuel prices, web site addresses, and other up-to-the-minute information. *(Information in the table is provided by the facilities.)*

CAPE CORAL AREA, CHART 11427

Near quick-flashing green "73," a well-marked channel leads southward to the Gulf Harbour Marina, a full-service facility that welcomes transients. East of flashing green "85," a marked channel (starting with green daybeacon "1") leads southward to the St. Charles Yacht Club, a member of the Florida Council of Yacht Clubs that recognizes reciprocity.

At Redfish Point (on the north shore), the municipal Cape Coral Yacht Basin offers daily, monthly and annual rentals on a first-come, first-served basis. It is located north of red daybeacon "78" off a marked channel. Individuals who rent slips in the marina have access to amenities within the nearby Yacht Club

Meet the Burrowing Owl

Cape Coral is home to Florida's largest population of Burrowing Owls. One of Florida's smallest owls, the Burrowing Owl averages 9 inches in height with a wingspan of 21 inches. It lives in open, treeless areas and spends most of its time on the ground, where its sandy brown plumage provides camouflage from potential predators. While it lacks the ear tufts of the more familiar woodland owls, it has distinctive bright yellow eyes and a white chin. It also has unusually long legs for additional height from its ground-level perch.

Aptly named, the owls either create new or make use of abandoned burrows to live in and nest. They are active both during day and night, and their nesting season starts mid-February and extends to mid-July. The owls first showed up in Cape Coral when the land was clear-cut for development. The sandy soil provides a suitable habitat for the owls.

If you don't understand what all the fuss is about, read the book *Hoot* by Carl Hiaasen. Visit capecoralburrowingowls.com for more information or to book a tour.

Community Park, including a public beach, tennis courts, a pool and a restaurant.

At red daybeacon "92," a channel leads behind Cattle Dock Point to the north, where markers guide you into the well-appointed Tarpon Point Marina. The resort-style facilities include a pool, a fuel dock with both gas and diesel, four on-site restaurants and access to boutique shopping at the nearby resort. They can accommodate vessels to 120 feet. Once again, reservations are a must.

Located just past Cattle Dock Point and Tarpon Point, signs will guide you to a small lock that provides access to the Cape Harbour Marina. The marina offers transient dockage in a condominium setting. A laundry, pool and competitive fuel pricing make this a popular stop. Be sure to call well in advance as this marina is usually full.

Anchorage: At red daybeacon "84A," there is a well-marked channel off to starboard that will lead you into Bimini Basin. You need to stay in this channel, and make a 90-degree turn to port when you get to green daybeacon "25." Then keep the red markers on your port side (we know that this is different, but it is very important) until you come to the canal that will lead you into the anchorage. It is well protected and is a handy spot to get to a couple of supermarkets and West Marine, plus a very large hardware store, as well as a variety of other services. There is also a dinghy dock at the park. You can anchor in 10 feet at MLW for up to 30 days.

Glover Bight, just behind Cattle Dock Point at Mile 147, is another excellent, all-weather anchorage. You will find good protection from all points with 10 to 12 feet at MLW with good holding in mud. There is also a restaurant and tiki bar at the water's edge along with a number of boutique shops.

■ NEXT STOP

Should you choose to continue your journey westward to the Gulf, our coverage continues in Chapter 13: "San Carlos Bay to Sarasota." Otherwise, we will return to the ICW traveling south in Chapter 7: "St. Lucie Inlet to Pompano Beach."

Florida's Lower East Coast

■ ST. LUCIE INLET TO POMPANO BEACH
■ FORT LAUDERDALE TO HOLLYWOOD ■ MIAMI & BISCAYNE BAY

ATLANTIC OCEAN

ICW MILE 917 Melbourne

ICW MILE 935 Sebastian

Vero Beach ICW MILE 952

Fort Pierce ICW MILE 965

ICW MILE 986 Stuart
St. Lucie Inlet

Lake Okeechobee

Okeechobee Waterway

ICW MILE 1005 Jupiter

Palm Beach

Lake Worth ICW MILE 1027

Ft. Myers

Pompano

Ft. Lauderdale ICW MILE 1063

Hallandale

ICW MILE 1085 Miami

Gulf of Mexico

ICW MILE 1094 Key Biscayne

Biscayne Bay

ICW MILE 1142
Flamingo Key Largo

Channel Five

N

Visit Waterway Explorer at waterwayguide.com

Florida's Lower East Coast

Below St. Lucie Inlet, the coastline becomes truly tropical, with a profusion of palm trees and exotic flowers. Here, the bustling Gold Coast comes into its own, with burgeoning development and fewer anchorages than you might wish.

You will also notice an increase in population–both on and off the water–as well as an increase in boat and home size. Large estates with manicured lawns line the waterways in Hobe and Jupiter Sounds, and they get more opulent in Palm Beach, where there are more "yachts" than "boats." The "water highway" widens at Lake Worth and continues past Boynton and Delray Beaches. Upscale shopping and art galleries define the Boca Raton area, and Pompano Beach offers harness racing and poker tournaments in addition to great fishing.

More than 300 miles of mostly navigable inland waterways carve through the Fort Lauderdale area, making it the "Venice of America." It is well known as a yachting center and boating amenities and services are readily available. The area boasts more than 800 marina-related businesses and this is the place to get that

Palm Beach is the easternmost town in Florida, known for its posh estates and the long, sandy Palm Beach Municipal Beach. In 2018, Bloomberg ranked Palm Beach as the 27th-wealthiest place in the U.S.

needed refit or repair. The craftspeople are some of the best in the business. This is also where "megayachts" become more prolific.

There is also access here to the Everglades National Park and the alligators, colorful birds and other wildlife that call this home.

If Miami is your destination, you will find easy access but expect increased boat traffic and an abundance of bridges. Note that the Julia Tuttle Causeway Bridge with 56-foot vertical clearance will necessitate an outside run for some vessels.

Florida Weather

Before you assume every day is paradise, it's good to know a bit more about southern Florida's weather patterns. The primary factors that determine the weather patterns of warm, humid summers and mild, cool winters are latitude and inland lakes. Florida is known as the thunderstorm capital of the U.S. These typically occur June through September in the afternoons and early evenings. Of course, hurricane season begins June 1 and ends November 30, with the highest storm probability from August through October. See more about the weather in the *Skipper's Handbook* section in the front of this guide.

Manatees

West Indian manatees, also known as sea cows, are enormous aquatic mammals. The average adult male is about 10 feet long and weighs around 1,000 pounds. Manatees live in shallow, slow-moving waters, such as quiet rivers, peaceful saltwater bays and calm coastal canals from spring to fall. In the winter, they search for warmer waters, heading to inland springs or even the heated outflow of power plants. Since manatees usually travel together with their bodies mostly submerged, they can resemble drifting coconuts. Also look for concentric circles in the water, a signal that manatees are about to surface.

Manatees are protected by the Marine Mammal Protection Act of 1972, the Federal Endangered Species Act of 1973 and the Florida Manatee Sanctuary Act of 1978. Many manatees are wounded and killed by watercraft and their propellers. Because of this, there are Manatee Zones posted along the waterways with restricted, no-wake speed limits. Some are seasonal (winter months) while others are year-round. Pay attention to these signs or risk fines.

Florida Clean Marina Program

The Florida Clean Marina Program is designed to bring awareness to marine facilities and boaters regarding environmentally friendly practices intended to protect and preserve Florida's natural environment. Marinas, boatyards and marine retailers receive clean designations by demonstrating a commitment implementing and maintaining a host of best management practices.

The Florida Clean Boater Program, in turn, encourages boaters to use the designated clean marinas, boatyards and marine retailers. Boaters are also encouraged to adopt their own environmentally friendly efforts such as practicing proper trash management, using bilge socks and fueling collars and recycling.

Visit dep.state.fl.us/cleanmarina for more information and to sign the clean boater pledge.

Source: Florida Dept. of Environmental Protection

St. Lucie Inlet to Pompano Beach

ICW Mile 986–Mile 1057 **VHF** FL Bridges: Channel 09

CHARTS NOAA 11467, 11472

■ ST. LUCIE INLET TO JUPITER INLET

Manatee speed zones occur with increasing frequency south of St. Lucie Inlet. From green daybeacon "13" to green daybeacon "15" you will encounter a Manatee Zone for approximately 1 mile. If you pay attention, you will see a lot of manatees swimming around. (They may look like floating coconuts.)

Most commonly, speed zones in the ICW channel will be 25 mph; outside the channel, speed zones will read "Slow-Speed/Minimum-Wake to Shore." Be alert, however, to whether the posted speed zone includes or excludes the channel and if it is seasonal. See the Inlet section at the front of this guide for more information.

NAVIGATION: Use NOAA Chart 11472. On the east side of the ICW, the incoming St. Lucie Inlet markers end with green daybeacon "17" near the junction with the ICW. (Leave those to port as you continue south on the ICW.) The first aid to navigation on the southbound continuation of the ICW is a daybeacon with white dayboards, reading DANGER–SHOAL, which should be left well to starboard (red-right-returning) when southbound. This is followed by red daybeacon "2" and flashing green "3."

St. Lucie State Park–ICW Mile 990

When entering Great Pocket past Horseshoe Point, watch for shoaling and use caution in the area. Long docks and piers are on both sides of Great Pocket that are not shown on the chart.

A bit of wilderness is preserved just south of the inlet in the St. Lucie Inlet State Park and adjoining Reed Wilderness Seashore Wildlife Refuge at the north end of Jupiter Island at Mile 990. An elevated boardwalk with restrooms and picnic pavilions at either end takes visitors from the docks across mangrove forests and hammocks of live oaks, cabbage palms, paradise trees, and wild limes to a neatly preserved Atlantic beach.

Hobe Sound, Jupiter Inlet Area, FL

		Dockage					Supplies		Services					
		Largest Vessel Accommodated	VHF Channel Monitored	Transient Berths / Total Berths	Approach / Dockside Depth (reported)	Floating Docks	Gas / Diesel	Groceries, Ice, Marine Supplies, Snacks	Repairs: Hull, Engine, Propeller	Lift (tonnage), Crane, Rail	Min / Max Amps	Laundry, Pool, Showers, Courtesy Car	Pump-Out Station	Nearby: Grocery Store, Motel, Restaurant
PECK LAKE														
1. Loblolly Marina 💻 WiFi WG 992.2	772-546-3136	110	16/10	5/74	7/7	-	-	I	-	-	30/100	LS	-	-
N. JUPITER AREA														
2. Blowing Rocks Marina 💻 WiFi 1002.2	561-746-3312	70	16	2/60	6/5	F	GD	IMS	HEP	L10	30/50	S	P	GMR
3. Jupiter Pointe Club & Marina 1002.8	561-746-2600	55	16	-	5/5	F	GD	IS	HEP	L	30/50	P	P	GMR
4. Black Pearl Marina and Gilbane Boatworks	561-744-2223	-	-	call/58	8/8	-	-	IMS	H	-	30/30	S	-	GMR
JUPITER AREA														
5. JIB Yacht Club Marina 💻 WiFi 1004.2	561-746-4300	70	16	4/40	8/8	-	GD	IMS	-	-	30/50	PS	P	GMR
6. Jupiter Yacht Club & Marina–PRIVATE 1006.5	561-741-3407	65	-	call/79	5/5	-	-	-	-	-	30/50	-	-	GMR
7. Suntex Marina at Jupiter WG 1006.8	561-747-8980	100	16	call/31	7/6	F	G	IMS	EP	-	30/50	LPS	P	GMR
8. Admirals Cove Marina 💻 onSpot 1007.8	561-745-5930	170	16/10	5/65	11/10	F	GD	GIMS	-	-	50/100	LPS	P	GMR
9. The Bluffs Marina onSpot 1008	561-627-6688	130	16	call/102	-	F	GD	-	-	L	50/100	S	-	R
10. Loggerhead Marina–Palm Beach Gardens 💻 onSpot	561-627-6358	120	16/10	10/136	8/8	-	GD	IS	-	-	30/100	LPS	P	GMR

💻 Internet Access WiFi Wireless Internet Access WG Waterway Guide Cruising Club Partner onSpot dockside WiFi facility

See WaterwayGuide.com for current rates, fuel prices, web site addresses, and other up-to-the-minute information. *(Information in the table is provided by the facilities.)*

THE CLUB AT ADMIRALS COVE

FLORIDA'S PREMIER YACHT & COUNTRY CLUB

GOLF • FITNESS • TENNIS • INN • DINING • SPA

A 5-Star Platinum Club of America
Distinguished Emerald Club

JUPITER, FL 33477
561-745-5930
CRAWLS@ADMIRALSCOVE.NET
WWW.ADMIRALSCOVE.NET

Distinguished Emerald Club *of the World* from BOARDROOM

Watch for shoaling between the dock and the ICW channel. There is a lot of shallow water in this area. Come out of channel right by the big dock sign that reads "St. Lucie Inlet Preserve Park" for the deepest water. On the way back out, be sure to turn into the channel right away. If you go too far west you will hit shoaling (especially at low tide). Dogs are allowed on the walkway but not on the beach.

Dockage: A small floating dock and a long pier with slips for smaller boats are near the north end of the St. Lucie State Park, which is accessible only by boat. There is an unmarked, shallow channel (4-foot MLW depths) that is best accessed by dinghy after anchoring in Peck Lake. Tie off carefully, as powerboats often pass without slowing, causing heavy wakes. A small charge is collected on the honor system for use of the park.

Peck Lake–ICW Mile 991

Low dunes, uninhabited beaches and sparkling ocean waters may beckon, and dredging of the lake and lake access has made anchoring in Peck Lake less of a challenge than in the past. Peck Lake, east of the ICW channel, has depths of 6 to 12 feet at MLW, from the ICW to close to shore.

⚠ There is shoaling on the west (red) side at flashing red "16" to red "18" to 5 feet at MLW or less. Favor the green side of the channel for 7 feet at MLW.

PECK LAKE, ICW, NOAA CHART 11472

N. JUPITER AREA, NOAA CHART 11472

N. JUPITER AREA, JUPITER AREA, NOAA CHART 11472

Loblolly Marina

Peck Lake

Location: situated at Loblolly, a distinguished private residential community on the west shore of Peck's Lake at Hobe Sound between Palm Beach and Stuart, Florida; forty minutes north of Palm Beach International Airport.

Convenience: close by Stuart offers complete marine services; the St. Lucie Inlet is only 3 bridgeless miles north for access in minutes to some of the world's greatest game fishing, cruising, and sailing waters.

LOBLOLLY MARINA

Facilities: secure, safe, and able to accommodate craft up to 110 feet in length. Surge protected 30, 50 and 100 amp electrical service, and softened water. Restrooms, showers, wireless internet service, and laundry facilities. We also offer a private beach shuttle to the adjacent Hobe Sound National Wildlife Refuge and over 3 miles of dedicated bike paths. A limited number of slips are available to transients and on an annual or seasonal basis.

7407 S.E. Hill Terrace, Hobe Sound, Florida 33455   Telephone (772) 546-3136 • marina@loblollyinfo.com

A Limited Number of Marina Memberships Are Available.

We monitor Channel 16 • ICW MM 992.2

There is an additional posted Manatee Zone from green daybeacon "21" in Peck Lake to the **Hobe Sound (SR 708) Bascule Bridge** (Mile 995.9), which includes areas both outside and inside the channel. North of green daybeacon "21," the Manatee Zone does not include the ICW channel and has a 25-mph speed limit in the channel only. This speed limit goes past the Peck Lake anchorage, at flashing green "19," which is very close to the ICW channel and can be subject to large wakes, although some boaters are usually courteous enough to slow for the anchored boats here.

Dockage: On the west side of the ICW, just across from Peck Lake, is Loblolly Marina. Do not be scared off by the two "Private" signs; transient and long-term dockage is available in this residential community in a very protected and pretty basin. Loblolly boasts "No bridges, no wakes, no worries." The marina is surrounded by lush mangroves and is adjacent to the Hobe Sound Wildlife Refuge. They offer complete marine services as well as full cruiser amenities and can accommodate vessels to 110 feet.

Anchorage: Deep water for entrance to Peck Lake is located close to flashing green "19," on the south side. Take it slowly, and head in on a course of 060 degrees toward the "Danger" sign. Watch for shoaling south of the sign. You will find 6 to 12 feet at MLW in a narrow strip with room for half a dozen boats or more. There is the possibility of debris on the bottom, so exercise caution when choosing an anchoring spot. Even though it is well protected on all sides and a no wake zone, you will still encounter wakes from some passing boats. The anchorage is often busy during the week and becomes even more crowded on weekends.

Once anchored, a dinghy ride to shore brings you to within a short distance over the dunes to a beautiful, unspoiled ocean beach. The park is for daytime use only, and the portion north of the crossover path is closed in the spring and early summer months to protect nesting Least Terns (*sterna antillarum*, the smallest of the American terns). This may be why dogs are not allowed on the beach (year round). South of this path, the beach is available for walking and swimming. When temperatures are above 60 degrees, with little or no wind, sand gnats (commonly called "no-see-ums") can be a problem.

Some **Manatee Speed Zones** are seasonal (winters), while others are year-round. Assume restrictions are year-round if no specific dates appear on the sign.

Hobe Sound—ICW Mile 996

The Jove Indians, whose name the Spanish pronounced "Ho-bay," gave Hobe Sound its name. A highly exclusive area, sometimes compared with Palm Beach, Hobe Sound shows off many of its grand mansions and manicured lawns along the eastern shore of the channel. The Hobe Sound National Wildlife Refuge dominates the western shore of the sound at about Mile 997, and its natural wilderness contrasts strikingly with the sculptured lawns on the eastern shore.

NAVIGATION: Use NOAA Chart 11472. At the northern end of Hobe Sound, the **Hobe Sound (SR 708) Bascule Bridge** crosses the ICW at Mile 995.9. The bridge has a closed vertical clearance of 21 feet at center and opens on signal. Both sides of the well-marked channel through Hobe Sound have good depths, but do not stray too far and give points a wide berth as there is some shoaling out of the channel.

Hobe Sound is heavily populated with both Slow-Speed/Minimum-Wake and Idle-Speed/No-Wake Zones to protect the manatees. Manatees frequent the area from November through March, so keep them in mind as you transit the sound. Much of the ICW channel itself is exempt from these speed restrictions, but check posted warnings to be certain. In one area, for example, signs on daybeacons cite different speed restrictions for craft larger and smaller than 35 feet.

Dockage: At Mile 1002, Blowing Rocks Marina sells both gas and diesel and has very limited transient space (two slips). Jupiter Pointe Club & Marina sells gas and diesel but does not have transient dockage. Groceries and restaurants are about 1.5 miles away.

To the south is Black Pearl Marina and Gilbane Boatworks. This is a repair/service facility that does not offer transient dockage.

Anchorage: Because there is a 25-mph speed limit in the Hobe Sound channel, almost all anchorages here are susceptible to annoying boat wakes. In easterly winds, craft drawing less than 5 feet will find an attractive anchorage just off the western shore of Harbor Island. Sound your way in and set the hook well. We received a report in summer 2018 that a privately marked channel is now in this location.

There are numerous anchorages with 8 to 9 feet at MLW west of the ICW channel between red daybeacon "38" and green daybeacon "49" north of Mile 999 on the west side of the channel. (See details on the Waterway Explorer at waterwayguide.com.) Follow your chart carefully. In the daytime, passing vessels and water skiers may throw some wake your way, but nights are generally peaceful. Do not be surprised by a routine boarding from local marine police and be sure to show an anchor light.

■ JUPITER SOUND TO LAKE WORTH

The ICW leads into Jupiter Sound at Mile 1002, where the estates of Hobe Sound give way to only slightly more modest homes. Nearby spoil areas and shoals demand careful attention; stay in the channel! Jupiter Inlet marks the confluence of Jupiter Sound to the north, Lake Worth Creek to the south and Loxahatchee River to the west. The inlet is known for its red brick lighthouse and aquamarine-colored waters.

Jupiter Sound

NAVIGATION: Use NOAA Chart 11472. Use the Miami Harbor Entrance Tide Tables. For high tide, subtract 10 minutes; for low tide, subtract 9 minutes. A submerged obstruction lies north of flashing green "53," but off the channel. Several small marinas and dry storage facilities are on the western shore of Jupiter Sound. The **Jupiter Island (CR 707) Bascule Bridge** (hail it as the "707 Bridge") at Mile 1004.1 has a 25-foot closed vertical clearance and opens on signal. If your vessel is lightly powered, do not get caught by the swift current here while waiting for the bridge. Contact the bridgetender prior to your arrival and allow for the set of the current.

Dockage: The JIB Yacht Club Marina is just south of the Jupiter Island Bridge on the east side of the ICW and offers gas and diesel fuel and some transient dockage.

Anchorage: Jupiter Sound, which is protected from boat wakes by a nearly continuous spoil bank, is just south of red daybeacon "54" at Mile 1002. This crowded anchorage is hard to enter and exit due to a proliferation of private moorings and derelict boats and is not a recommended anchorage. White spherical buoys mark the northern entrance, which carries 6.5-foot MLW depths. The former southern entrance has shoaled badly. On warm days you will have plenty of company. Small powerboats will pull right up on the spoils bank.

Jupiter Inlet

NAVIGATION: Use NOAA Chart 11472. Jupiter Inlet fights a constant battle with shifting sand and was last dredged in spring 2018. A short jetty protects the inlet entrance from the north, and a steel barricade extends halfway into the inlet from the south bank. The mouth of the inlet has strong currents, eddies, turbulence and breaking seas over sandbars that extend from the south side of the inlet offshore towards the northeast.

Jupiter Inlet has an average tidal range of 2.5 feet. Despite constant dredging, the inlet is cited by the Coast Guard as "not navigable without current local knowledge." The inlet channel is unsafe for all but small boats with local knowledge and very shallow draft. If you are tempted to try and run the inlet, be sure to refer to the Jupiter Inlet District Commission site at jupiterinletdistrict.org (561-746-2223). They have a live webcam that reports current weather and sea conditions and allows you to observe the inlet conditions at any time. (A second web cam is at evsjupiter.com.) Additional information on Jupiter Inlet is provided in the Inlet section at the front of this guide.

ICW Mile 1004 to Mile 1012

NAVIGATION: Use NOAA Chart 11472. Use the Miami Harbor Entrance Tide Tables. For high tide, add 28 minutes; for low tide add, 1 hour and 5 minutes. At Mile 1004, at the intersection of the ICW and Jupiter Inlet, the route south begins a sharp reverse S-curve, first to starboard (west) into the Jupiter Inlet/Loxahatchee River, then under the **Jupiter (U.S. 1) Bascule Bridge**, then to port (south) out of the Loxahatchee into Lake Worth Creek. The Jupiter Island Bridge at Mile 1004.8 has 26-foot closed vertical clearance and opens on signal.

There has been consistent shoaling over the years at red nun buoy "2" at the turn into Jupiter Inlet (Mile 1004). Give red nun buoy "2" a wide berth as the shoal extends well off the point. Always follow the buoys, watch inlet currents and make the final turn to port cautiously. You will not see the opening southbound into Lake Worth Creek until you are almost on it, and boats coming from the south will not be visible until after you have begun the final swing.

The **Loxahatchee River**, Florida's only designated wild and scenic river, is shallow beyond the bridges. It is virtually unnavigable for anything larger than a kayak or dinghy, but it is definitely worth exploring, if possible. It is marked by private aids to navigation. You may be able to dock at the Jupiter marinas and investigate by dinghy. DuBois Park, on the west side of the river at the inlet, has 17 day-use boat slips. You can also tour the 1898 DuBois Pioneer Home located here.

The route appears to dead end in a false lead created by the **Old Dixie Highway Bridge** (SR Alternate A1A Bridge), which has a 25-foot fixed vertical clearance, and the **Loxahatchee Railroad Bridge** that follows (4-foot closed vertical clearance, normally open except during train traffic), both crossing the Loxahatchee River.

The ICW, however, continues past green daybeacon "7," where the channel bustles with boats of all sizes, and the shore gleams with one-story condominiums and houses set among beautifully manicured lawns. Do not let your eye stray too far from mid-channel and check the depth and boat speed frequently. This patrolled stretch is a marked Idle-Speed/No-Wake Zone, channel included. Much of the length below Mile 1007 does not have speed restrictions.

The **Indiantown (SR 706) Bascule Bridge** (35-foot closed vertical clearance) crosses the ICW at Mile 1006.2 and has restricted openings. The bridge opens on the hour and half-hour 24 hours a day, 7 days a week. This is an enforced No-Wake Zone. The **Donald Ross Bascule Bridge** (35-foot closed vertical clearance) at Mile 1009.3 opens on the hour and half-hour.

Dockage: The Jupiter Yacht Club & Marina, on the east side at Mile 1006.5, is private. A little farther south on the west side at Mile 1006.8 is Suntex Marina at Jupiter, offering secure wet or dry storage, gas and pump-out service. Amenities include a pool and a well-stocked marina center. Call ahead for slip availability.

At Mile 1007.8, Admirals Cove Marina offers slips and resort-style amenities. The marina can accommodate boats up to 170 feet and is considered a natural weather refuge for yachts. They also offer repairs. The Bluffs Marina, at Mile 1008 is primarily a dockominium marina with limited transient slips.

Loggerhead Marina–Palm Beach Gardens, at Mile 1009, is just south of the Donald Ross Bridge in a well-protected basin off the ICW. Loggerhead can accommodate transient boats up to 120 feet and has pump-out service at each slip. They also sell fuel (gas and diesel) and some supplies and offer easy access to restaurants, shopping, golf, tennis and other social activities.

Anchorage: The shallow anchorage north of the Indiantown Bridge on the east side pass flashing green "11" is full of small boats permanently moored, along with a public boat ramp and a floating hot dog stand on weekends in season.

■ LAKE WORTH (PALM BEACH) AREA

A concentration of marinas offering all kinds of services and repairs is located on the ICW stretch from just north of the PGA Boulevard Bridge in North Palm Beach to Palm Beach. All are convenient to the area's famous shopping, from The Gardens Mall in Palm Beach Gardens to Worth Avenue in Palm Beach.

North Palm Beach–ICW Mile 1012 to Mile 1016

NAVIGATION: Use NOAA Chart 11472. At Mile 1012.6, the **PGA Blvd. Bascule Bridge** and the **Parker (U.S. 1) Bascule Bridge** are about 1 mile apart and both have restricted openings. The PGA Blvd. Bridge (24-foot closed vertical clearance) opens on the hour and half-hour, while the Parker Bridge at Mile 1013.7 (25-foot closed vertical clearance) opens on the quarter and three-quarter hour.

The well-developed area in the 1 mile or so between the PGA Blvd. and Parker Bridges, and including the North Palm Beach Waterway (a canal splitting off to the west of the ICW), is a well-justified Slow-Speed/Minimum-Wake Zone. The No-Wake Zone continues to the opening into Lake Worth at Mile 1014.2.

The PGA Bridge area of Palm Beach Gardens is a restaurant junction for boaters. Just north of the bridge on the east bank is Seasons 52 Restaurant (561-625-5852). Just south of the bridge on the west bank is Waterway Café (561-694-1700) featuring salads and seafood items. Traffic can be congested from boats docking at these restaurants.

At Mile 1014, just past the Parker Bridge, the ICW enters the open waters of Lake Worth. The lake is long and broad, but shallow, except for the ICW channel. Do not confuse the ICW markers leading south with those splitting off to the east and then north to Old Port Cove Marina and the extreme upper end of Lake Worth (and then to Little Lake Worth, a separate body of water). Lining both shores of Lake Worth are boating-oriented towns and cities with marinas that include all the usual resort amenities.

Some of Lake Worth is a Manatee Zone with Slow-Speed/Minimum-Wake restriction, but with a few exceptions, most of the ICW channel is exempt from these restrictions and enjoys a 25-mph speed limit. Limited stretches of Idle-Speed/No-Wake Zones appear at bridges and adjacent to marinas. Carefully observe restricted speed limits, where they prevail. Lake Worth is crowded with boats, marinas and private docks, so damage from wakes can be severe.

Dockage: North of the PGA Bridge, Ways Boatyard and Seminole Marine Maintenance both offer haul-out and repair services. Call ahead for slip availability. Next is the Soverel Harbour Marina, which welcomes transients on its floating docks. It is a well-known "hurricane hole" and is close to dining, shopping and entertainment. Gas and diesel fuel are available here and next door at PGA Marina, which also offers repairs.

Just south of the Parker Bridge (U.S. 1) to starboard is the North Palm Beach Marina. It is located in a secluded, sheltered keyhole-shaped harbor and can accommodate vessels to 150 feet. The marina features hardwood decked floating docks, a fully stocked ships store, fuel and pump-out service at every slip. They also have a full service concierge.

A short distance farther south, at green daybeacon "27," turn to port to enter Lake Worth and you will see Old Port Cove Marina on your port side, which has floating docks and a convenient fuel dock with pump-out facilities. On-site amenities include Sandpiper's Cove Restaurant & Bar (561-626-2280), Captain's Lounge, a fitness room and indoor laundry facilities. A West Marine and Publix are nearby. To reach Old Port Cove Marina, turn off the ICW to the east after entering Lake Worth proper, following the private green daybeacons, then head north around the Old Port Cove townhouses and condominiums. You will spot the entrance off to port shortly after passing green daybeacon "7." Hail Old Port Cove Marina on VHF Channel 16 to be directed to a slip.

Anchorage: Some cruisers have reported adequate depths for anchoring in the lagoons off the North Palm Beach Waterway. They are reached by turning to starboard at the bend just before Parker Bridge. The canal is charted at 7 feet at MLW with 6-foot MLW depths in the first basin and 8 feet at MLW in the second, both of which will be to starboard. This is a very nice residential community; landing is not permitted.

Another well-protected anchorage is located at the north end of Lake Worth in Turtle Cove. Just after clearing the Parker Bridge and passing North Palm Beach Marina to starboard, enter Lake Worth and immediately turn off the ICW to port. Follow the green and red daybeacons off to the east, then north around Old Port Cove Marina, and follow the daybeacons to

Lake Worth, FL

		Largest Vessel Accommodated	VHF Channel Monitored	Approach / Dockside Depth (reported)	Transient Berths / Total Berths	Gas / Diesel	Floating Docks	Groceries, Ice, Marine Supplies, Snacks	Repairs: Hull, Engine, Propeller	Lift (tonnage), Crane, Rail	Min/Max Amps	Laundry, Pool, Showers, Courtesy Car	Pump-Out Station	Nearby: Grocery Store, Motel, Restaurant
NORTH PALM BEACH				**Dockage**					**Supplies**			**Services**		
1. Ways Boatyard 1012	561-622-8550	80	16	call/10	10/5	–	–	MS	HEP	L70,C,R	30/50	S	–	GMR
2. Seminole Marine Maintenance 1011.9	561-622-7600	100	–	9/9	6/6	–	–	GIMS	HEP	L100,C	50/100	S	–	GMR
3. Soverel Harbour Marina ▭ ☺onSpot 1011.9	561-691-9554	100	16/08	10/146	12/8	F	GD	GIMS	–	–	30/50	LS	P	GMR
4. PGA Marina 1011.9	561-626-0200	90	16	5/30	8/8	F	GD	GIMS	HEP	L35	30/50	–	–	GMR
5. North Palm Beach Marina ☺onSpot WG 1013.7	561-626-4919	150	16/08	10/107	10/8	F	GD	IMS	E	–	30/100	LS	P	GMR
6. Old Port Cove Marina ▭ ☺onSpot WG 1014	561-626-1760	200	16/08	5/202	8/15	F	D	GIS	EP	–	30/200+	LPS	P	GMR
RIVIERA BEACH														
7. Lake Park Harbor Marina WiFi 1016.2	561-881-3353	80	16/08	10/112	6/5.5	F	GD	I	–	–	30/50	LS	P	GMR
8. Suntex Marina – Riviera Beach 1017	561-840-6868	47	–	call/300	6/6	–	GD	IMS	–	–	30/50	–	P	G
9. New Port Cove Marine Center ▭ ☺onSpot WG 1017.4	561-844-2504	80	16/08	10/49	5/5	F	GD	IMS	HEP	–	30/50	LS	P	GMR
10. Rybovich Marine Center ▭ WiFi 1017.8	561-863-4126	300	16/65	4/10	15/17	F	–	IMS	HEP	L150	30/200+	PS	P	GR
11. Riviera Beach City Marina ▭ ☺onSpot 1018	561-842-7806	150	16/11	70/140	8/7	F	GD	IMS	–	–	30/200+	LS	P	GR
12. Cracker Boy Boat Works – Riviera Beach WiFi 1018.1	561-845-0357	110	16/11		19/19	–	–	IM	HEP	L150,C	30/100	S	–	GMR
SINGER ISLAND														
13. Cannonsport Marina ▭ WiFi	800-627-8328	130	16/11	54/54	10/8	–	GD	GIMS	–	–	30/100	LPS	P	GMR
14. Buccaneer Marina ▭ WiFi 1017.6	561-842-1620	85	16/68	call/16	12/12	–	GD	I	–	–	30/50	LP	–	GMR
15. Sailfish Marina Resort ▭ ☺onSpot 1017.7	561-844-1724	110	16/68	40/94	8/8	F	GD	GIMS	–	–	30/200+	LPS	–	GMR

▭ Internet Access   WiFi Wireless Internet Access   WG Waterway Guide Cruising Club Partner   ☺onSpot dockside WiFi facility

See WaterwayGuide.com for current rates, fuel prices, web site addresses, and other up-to-the-minute information. *(Information in the table is provided by the facilities.)*

NORTH PALM BEACH, RIVIERA BEACH, SINGER ISLAND, NOAA CHART 11472

the extreme (northern) head of Lake Worth. You can drop the hook in 9- to 14-foot MLW depths and have plenty of swinging room. You will find a handy place to land the dinghy at the east abutment of the A1A Bridge (8-foot fixed vertical clearance) over the cut between Lake Worth and Little Lake Worth.

This anchorage is in a residential neighborhood, and there is only a small patch of sand on which to land. Cruisers tie up their dinghies to anything that will hold them. Be sure to chain and lock the motor. Also, be mindful of private property. Groceries, marine supplies and extensive shopping areas are nearby. There is a West Marine Superstore within a 20-minute walk from the dinghy landing.

Riviera Beach Area–ICW Mile 1016 to Mile 1018

NAVIGATION: Use NOAA Chart 11472. Lake Worth is broad in the first stretch leading to the **Blue Heron Blvd. (SR A1A) Bridge** at Mile 1017.2. Riviera Beach is on the ocean (east side) of the ICW.

⚠ The Blue Heron Blvd. Bridge has a charted clearance of 65 feet but actual clearance has been reported to be as low as 60 feet; check the tide boards mounted on the fender system to be sure.

The channel is narrow, but a 25-mph speed limit holds, with Slow-Speed/Minimum-Wake outside the channel to shore. A Slow-Speed/Minimum-Wake Zone was established in the ICW channel in the past, in the vicinity of the Lake Park Harbor Marina south to Blue Heron Bridge. In a strong crosswind, watch the set of your course.

Just through the bridge, you must make a decision. Directly ahead is Peanut Island. If you plan to continue south on the ICW, you will alter course to starboard, following the ICW around Peanut Island on the west side. (See sidebar.) If you plan to utilize Lake Worth Inlet, there are two channels.

After you pass under the Blue Heron Bridge, you can turn to port in a marked channel and reach the inlet. Be sure to stay to the north "red" side of the channel as that is where you will find the deeper water. There are marinas on the east side of this channel so watch your wake.

Dockage: Above the Blue Heron Blvd. Bridge at Mile 1016.2 is Lake Park Harbor Marina with slips and fuel. They can accommodate vessels to 80 feet on both floating and fixed docks and sell all fuels. Here you will

receive personalized service from a knowledgeable staff. (And they are dog friendly too!)

The Suntex Marina at Riviera Beach is on the west side just above the bridge (Mile 1017). It's easy to spot its two towers and huge (hurricane-rated) dry storage facility. The marina offer slips with club-type amenities and close proximity to waterfront restaurants, shopping, golf, beaches, tennis, and nightlife.

South of the Blue Heron Blvd. Bridge, marine facilities are abundant on both shores, north and south of Lake Worth Inlet. On the mainland western shore, beginning at Riviera Beach, are repair yards capable of handling boats of any size. New Port Cove Marine Center has a state-of-the-art dry stack storage system, 49 in-water slips for vessels up to 80 feet, fuel with high-speed pumps and engine repair services. They also have a fully stocked marine store and complimentary WiFi.

The next facility heading south, opposite Peanut Island, is Rybovich Marine Center. Their in-house tug fleet can escort you to their floating dry dock space for any service or refit. Transient dockage is available but call well in advance.

Continuing south is the Riviera Beach City Marina (Mile 1018), which offers dockage to 150 feet plus has

Lake Worth, FL

		Largest Vessel Accommodated	VHF Channel Monitored	Transient Berths / Total Berths	Approach / Dockside Depth (reported)	Floating Docks	Gas / Diesel	Repairs: Hull, Engine, Propeller	Groceries, Ice, Marine Supplies, Snacks	Lift (tonnage), Crane, Rail	Laundry, Pool, Showers, Courtesy Car	Min/Max Amps	Pump-Out Station	Nearby: Grocery Store, Motel, Restaurant
WEST PALM BEACH				**Dockage**				**Supplies**			**Services**			
1. Rybovich Marina 🖥 📶 1019.5	561-840-8308	330	16/65	20/60	18/18	F	GD	IMS	HEP	L660	30/200+	PS	P	GMR
2. Palm Beach Yacht Club & Marina ●onSpot 1022.9	561-655-8711	150	16/68	5/47	13/13	–	GD	IM	–	L15	30/100	LS	–	GR
3. Palm Harbor Marina 🖥 📶 1022	800-435-8051	250	16/68	25/200	11/11	F	GD	GIS	–	–	30/200+	LS	P	GMR
PALM BEACH														
4. Palm Beach Town Docks 🖥 📶 1024.5	561-838-5463	262	16/69	83/83	9/12	–	–	I	–	–	50/100	S	P	GMR

🖥 Internet Access 📶 Wireless Internet Access WG Waterway Guide Cruising Club Partner ●onSpot dockside WiFi facility
See WaterwayGuide.com for current rates, fuel prices, web site addresses, and other up-to-the-minute information. *(Information in the table is provided by the facilities.)*

WEST PALM BEACH, PALM BEACH, NOAA CHART 11472

catamaran slips. They boast floating concrete and Brazilian hardwood docks and pump-out service at every slip. The municipal marina is adjacent to Cracker Boy Boat Works–Riviera Beach, which has repair services and do-it-yourself facilities.

On the eastern shore, the resort area of Singer Island is crowded with houses, motels, docks and restaurants. There is a strong current at all the marinas on Singer Island, so exercise care while docking. The 54-slip Cannonsport Marina is the northernmost facility on Singer Island. It caters to sportfishing vessels, but all transients are welcome. They have a pool, spa, well-stocked ship store and sell both gas and diesel fuel. Cannonsport is "an intimate marina that's big on service."

Buccaneer Marina at Mile 1017.6 has slips and fuel, as does Sailfish Marina Resort, located just inside Lake Worth Inlet on Singer Island. Giant "jacks," a type of schooling fish, patrol the docks at Sailfish Marina. During the afternoon, while fishermen clean their catch, the school waits patiently for leftovers at the cleaning tables. It is quite a spectacle and worth watching.

Anchorage: Just northeast of the Blue Heron Blvd. Bridge, you can drop the hook in 8- to 13-foot MLW depths over the "Discontinued Spoil Area." There are a number of derelict boats and a few sunken ones here. Beware of wreckage on the bottom. There are several anchorages in the vicinity of Lake Worth Inlet (described in the next section). Anchor lights should be used in all Lake Worth anchorages.

Lake Worth Inlet–ICW Mile 1018

Wide, well-marked and jettied, Lake Worth Inlet (also known as Palm Beach Inlet) boasts a deep straightforward big ship channel that is one of the easiest to enter on the Atlantic coast. The meandering Gulf Stream is closer here than at any point in the U.S. (sometimes as close as 1 mile offshore, but usually out about 8 to 12 miles), and both commercial and recreational craft give the inlet heavy use. It is located approximately midway between Fort Pierce Inlet (45 nm north) and Ft. Lauderdale (Port Everglades) Inlet (40 nm south), making it popular with boaters who prefer to travel offshore.

NAVIGATION: Use NOAA Chart 11472. Use the Miami Harbor Entrance Tide Tables. For high tide, subtract 21 minutes; for low tide, add 4 minutes. To access the ocean, continue on the ICW around Peanut Island and pick up the official Lake Worth Inlet channel and follow it to the ocean. It is deep and well marked.

Inside the Lake Worth Inlet the Port of Palm Beach handles commercial cargo, ranging from construction supplies to seafood, to tropical fruit and cruise ships. The Coast Guard establishes fixed and moving security zones at the Port of Palm Beach for the protection of passenger vessels (cruise ships), vessels carrying cargoes of a particular hazard and vessels carrying hazardous gases. A moving security zone activates when such a vessel passes red and white buoy "LW" when entering the port and becomes a fixed zone when the ship is docked. These zones cover the waters within 100 yards all around the subject vessels, and no craft can enter without prior permission. Patrol craft may be contacted on VHF Channel 16 for the status of these security zones.

Some shoaling lies close in on the north side of the entrance channel, but it is frequently dredged.

Popular Peanut Island

Peanut Island was originally created in 1918 as a result of material excavated when the Lake Worth Inlet was created. Originally called Inlet Island, Peanut Island amounted to only 10 acres. Today, as a result of continued maintenance dredging of the inlet and the ICW, Peanut Island comprises approximately 80 acres.

Peanut Island is a public park that is popular with small powerboaters who anchor around its perimeter and party in the shallow, sandy-bottom water that extends out into the ICW. (There are also 18 boat slips available for day use only.)

Swimming areas, kayaking lagoons and terrific snorkeling are among the draws of Peanut Island. There are paved walkways with scenic outlooks. Island facilities include picnic shelters and restrooms, and a dredged boat basin on its northwest side for dinghy tie-up.

The former Coast Guard Station and JFK Bomb Shelter on the south side of Peanut Island are part of the Palm Beach Maritime Museum and open for tours. The shelter, about 1,500 square feet in all, was abandoned after JFK's assassination in 1963 and was close to ruin when the Palm Beach Maritime Museum took over in the 1990s.

Water taxi service is available from Palm Beach Water Taxi (561-683-8294) and Peanut Island Shuttle Boat (561-723-2028). Call the water taxi on VHF Channel 16.

⚠ Be aware that green daybeacon "1" (south of the charted turning basin) was reported to be destroyed in spring 2018. The steel pile may pose a hazard to navigation.

For additional details on Lake Worth Inlet, see the Inlet section at the front of this guide.

Anchorage: There are several anchorages in the vicinity of Lake Worth Inlet. Anchor lights should be used in all Lake Worth anchorages. When entering any of the following anchorages pay strict attention to your depthsounder as there are several areas of shallow water. Just southeast of the turning basin marked by flashing green "11" and "13" you will find 9 to 13 feet at MLW; avoid the "cable area" shown on the chart. This area is subject to tidal currents from the inlet, so observe proximity of other anchored vessels and their anchor set.

West Palm Beach–ICW Mile 1018 to Mile 1020

South of the inlet and Peanut Island, Lake Worth is open, the ICW channel is well marked and maintained, and patches of deep water appear along the eastern Palm Beach shore. Palm Beach remains a winter ocean resort of elegance and charm. Across Lake Worth from Palm Beach, the West Palm Beach shore is given over to marinas, boatyards and yachting amenities.

In other places, any one of these would be outstanding in size, quality of work and service; here, though, mariners can be overwhelmed by the choices. Not all the services available are confined to the waterfront. A phone call or a short walk can put you in touch with just about every known kind of boat specialist–sailmakers, electronic sales and services, boat designers, boat maintenance and cleaning and diving services. Supplies of all kinds are close at hand.

Downtown West Palm Beach and City Place, an upscale outdoor mall surrounding an open-air plaza, are near the marinas. City Place has live entertainment, shopping, theaters, restaurants, groceries and art galleries; this is a festive commercial and cultural district. A free trolley runs from Clematis Street in West Palm Beach to City Place.

West Palm is the home of the Palm Beach International Boat Show, held in March. The event includes hundreds of boats from inflatables to megayachts, plus tents full of the latest electronics and accessories, seminars and fishing clinics for kids.

Dockage: Just before Mile 1020, privately maintained green daybeacon "1" marks the entrance to Rybovich Marina, which is a megayacht service facility with a 660-ton lift. They can accommodate vessels to 330 feet and sell fuel, both gas and diesel.

North of the Flagler Memorial Bridge at Mile 1022.9 is Palm Beach Yacht Club & Marina with slips and all fuels. Just south of the bridge, also on the West Palm Beach side, is Palm Harbor Marina, which has transient berths and all the usual amenities plus all fuels.

Anchorage: One-half nautical mile south of the Lake Worth Inlet along the east shore of Lake Worth, you can anchor just southwest of Palm Beach at red daybeacon "6." Avoid the charted spoil and cable areas here. There are numerous permanently moored vessels in this area. Depths are 8 to 12 feet at MLW.

Palm Beach–ICW Mile 1021 to Mile 1028

Palm Beach's famous Worth Ave. deserves a visit, with its collection of boutiques, jewelers, art galleries, restaurants and antiques stores. Grand old hotels such as the Brazilian Court and the Breakers have been renovated and still set the standard for this historically significant resort. One pleasant way to see Palm Beach is to have lunch or dinner at one of the numerous fine restaurants, then, have a leisurely stroll around town to take in the sights.

NAVIGATION: Use NOAA Chart 11472. There are three bridges connecting the mainland to Palm Beach. At Mile 1021.8, you will come to the first, **Flagler Memorial (SR A1A) Bascule Bridge**. The old 17-foot bridge has been completely replaced with a 21-foot closed vertical clearance bascule bridge. The bridge opens at 15 minutes and 45 minutes past the hour, except Monday through Friday, when it does not open at 8:15 a.m. and 4:15 p.m. due to rush-hour traffic. There will be restricted openings during presidential visits.

The second crossing is the **Royal Park (SR 704) Bascule Bridge** at Mile 1022.6, which has a 21-foot closed vertical clearance and opens on the hour and half-hour. The third bridge is the **Southern Blvd. (SR 700/80) Bascule Bridge** (Mile 1024.7, 14-foot closed vertical clearance) opens at 15 and 45 minutes past the hour daily, 24 hours a day. Construction of a replacement 21-foot bascule bridge was under construction at press time in summer 2018. The project is planned to be completed sometime in 2021. Be aware that you could experience delays due to the construction.

Dockage: The Palm Beach Town Docks–at Clematis St. and Fern St.–offer complimentary dockage (83 slips) not to exceed 4 hours during the daytime hours of 8:00 a.m. to 5:00 p.m. There is no dockage after 5:00 p.m.

Anchorage: At Mile 1022 there is an anchorage between the municipal docks for day use only.

Palm Beach to Lantana–ICW Mile 1028 to Mile 1031

Lake Worth may be wide in this area, but south of Palm Beach, the water is shallow outside the ICW channel. Small islands (many of them originating as dredge spoil banks) break the open expanses and are overgrown with foliage. Estates border a large portion of the eastern shore, and tall condominiums appear with increasing frequency on both banks.

Small water-oriented communities, with many amenities for yachtsmen, are located all along Lake Worth. The first of these, the town of Lake Worth, has small shops, restaurants and art galleries. A large municipal beach and a 1,000-foot-long fishing pier provide recreational opportunities. The **Lake Worth-Lake Ave. Bridge** (35-foot closed vertical clearance) is at Mile 1028.8 and opens on signal. A public launch ramp on the mainland near the western end of this bridge has piers that can serve as dinghy landings.

Continuing south over the next 30 miles, the ICW alters its configuration and becomes a narrow land cut in the vicinity of Boynton Beach. Lined with residences and spanned by numerous bridges, the ICW truly looks like a water highway here. Two small, shallow lakes, Wyman and Boca Raton, and a brief stretch of the Hillsboro River are the only naturally formed bodies of water along this route. Even though the Atlantic Ocean is barely one-half mile away in places, you will find it hard to see among the proliferation of houses, motels, high-rise apartments and condominiums that line the route.

◼ LANTANA TO DELRAY BEACH

Lake Worth ends just north of the E. Ocean Ave. (Lantana) Bascule Bridge. The ICW becomes a canal, with concrete bulkheads lining its borders. Along this stretch, town follows town, and beautiful homes surrounded by subtropical growth add to the view.

Traveling south from Lake Worth, keep an eye out for the many Slow-Speed/Minimum-Wake Zones. They increase with greater frequency the closer you get to Fort Lauderdale. Be ready to call on VHF Channel 09 or whistle signal (two blasts: one prolonged, one short) for the opening of many of the 28 bridges that span the channel between Lake Worth and Government Cut at Miami Beach. Schedule a little extra time to allow for restricted openings, occasional bridge malfunctions and No-Wake Zones.

Lantana to Boynton Beach–ICW Mile 1031 to Mile 1038

NAVIGATION: Use NOAA Chart 11467. Lantana is the next mainland town on Lake Worth. The **E. Ocean Ave. (Lantana) Bascule Bridge** at Mile 1031 (21-foot closed vertical clearance) connects Lantana on the mainland with Hypoluxo Island and South Palm Beach on the ocean side. The bridge has scheduled openings on the hour and half-hour. South of the Lantana Bridge, the route enters the Boynton Inlet approach area. Four miles to the south of the Lantana Bridge is the **E. Ocean Ave. (Boynton Beach) Bridge** with 21-foot closed vertical clearance, which opens on the hour and half-hour. The **E. Woolbright Rd. (SE 15th St.) Bridge** crosses the ICW at Mile 1035.8 (with 25-foot closed vertical clearance, opens on signal). Bridge restrictions apply 24 hours a day, 7 days a week.

Beginning with red daybeacon "52" there is some shoaling both on the western shore and the eastern shore until you reach green daybeacon "53." Stay in the center of the channel. There is also some shoaling in spots along the channel just south of Lake Roger to the north side of Lake Wyman and again in the channel on the south side of Lake Wyman.

Dockage: North of the Lantana Bridge, on the west side, is Suntex Marina–Lantana (Mile 1030.2), with dry storage and wet slips for vessels up to 100 feet. They also offer repairs and have a well-stocked ship store. Nestled in what was once a tiny fishing village, this facility

Boynton Inlet Area, FL

		Largest Vessel Accommodated	VHF Channel Monitored	Transient Berths / Total Berths	Approach / Dockside Depth (reported)	Floating Docks	Gas / Diesel	Groceries, Ice, Marine Supplies, Snacks	Repairs: Hull, Engine, Propeller	Lift (tonnage), Crane, Rail	Min/Max Amps	Laundry, Pool, Showers, Courtesy Car	Pump-Out Station	Nearby: Grocery Store, Motel, Restaurant
LANTANA				**Dockage**				**Supplies**			**Services**			
1. Suntex Marina – Lantana ▱ onSpot	561-582-4422	100	16	25/83	6/8	–	G	IMS	EP	L8	30/50	S	–	GR
2. Murrelle Marine WIFI 1030.4	561-582-3213	55	16	2/36	4.5/5	–	–	IMS	HEP	L50,C	30/50	S	–	R
3. Suntex Marina – South Lantana ▱ onSpot 1030.5	561-582-4422	120	16	12/80	5/7	–	G	IMS	–	–	30/50	PS	–	GR
BOYNTON BEACH														
4. Palm Beach Yacht Center WIFI 1032.7	561-588-9911	80	16	10/100	6/6	–	GD	IMS	HEP	L80	30/50	S	P	GMR
5. Gateway Marina 1033.1	561-588-1211	35	68	2/211	6/6	F	G	IMS	HEP	L10	–	–	–	GMR
6. Boynton Harbor Marina 1035	561-735-7955	40	16/11	4/23	12/6	–	GD	IMS	–	–	50/100	–	–	GMR

▱ Internet Access WIFI Wireless Internet Access WG Waterway Guide Cruising Club Partner onSpot dockside WiFi facility
See WaterwayGuide.com for current rates, fuel prices, web site addresses, and other up-to-the-minute information. *(Information in the table is provided by the facilities.)*

LANTANA, BOYNTON BEACH, NOAA CHART 11467

reflects the quiet pace of Old Florida. To the south is Suntex Marina–South Lantana, which has transient dockage, including catamaran slips, a pool and a health club. This location is convenient to groceries and restaurants. Located between the two Suntex facilities is Murrelle Marine, offering repairs (50-ton lift and crane). Call ahead for slip availability.

On the west side of the ICW, two repair yards with transient dockage are co-located in a basin. The approach is marked and has depths to 6 feet at MLW. Palm Beach Yacht Center (Mile 1032.7) offers slips, fuel and repairs (with 80-ton lift). Gateway Marina is primarily a "dry stack" marina and has no shore power but water is available at the dock.

In Boynton Beach, Boynton Harbor Marina at Mile 1035 sells gas and diesel and may have a slip on a face dock. They offer a multitude of water activities including fishing charters, drift fishing, scuba diving charters, jet-ski rentals, boat rentals and waterfront dining at one of two restaurants. A shopping center and supermarket are within walking distance of the waterfront.

Anchorage: Just to the south and west of the Lantana Bridge is a good anchorage with 6- to 8-foot MLW depths and room for many boats. Anchoring here is limited to 18 hours. New dinghy docks are available at the boat launch ramp. Commercial fishing boats operate from a nearby pier, and Old Key Lime House Waterfront Grill & Bar is nearby (at 300 E. Ocean Ave.) with daily specials, happy hour (during the week) and live music (except Mondays). There is a dinghy dock, but you must dine at the restaurant to use it. They claim to be Florida's oldest waterfront restaurant (561-582-1889).

Boynton Inlet–ICW Mile 1034

NAVIGATION: Use NOAA Chart 11467. Boynton Inlet (also known as South Lake Worth Inlet) is popular with local fishermen, but it is narrow, shallow and crossed by the fixed **Boynton Inlet Bridge** with an 18-foot vertical clearance. The Coast Guard does not recommend passage through the inlet without complete local knowledge of all the hazardous conditions that exist. A seawall helps stabilize Boynton Inlet's shoreline, but currents run swiftly, and bad tidal rips develop in strong easterly winds. See the Inlet section in the front of this guide for more information on Boynton Inlet.

The ICW, where it passes Boynton Inlet, is narrow and shallow, inside and outside the channel. Shoaling in the ICW channel where the inlet current crosses the channel is a continuing problem, reducing depths in the vicinity of red nun buoy "46." This area both north and south of red nun buoy "46" has not been dredged in recent years, so check locally for information on depths and/or marking before you pass through. The shoaling seems to be worse on the western edge of the channel. It is about 7 feet at MLW or less; stay to the green side. Watch your course carefully and do not be confused by the green buoys (quite large) marking a channel leading in to the western shore. Follow the ICW channel markers carefully, as groundings are frequent here, usually resulting from the current at Boynton Inlet pushing vessels out of the channel.

Dockage: The county-operated Ocean Inlet Marina south of the inlet has 20 slips for boats to 45 feet; however, the marina is usually full of long-term rentals with a reported 5-year waiting list.

Delray Beach–ICW Mile 1039 to Mile 1044

Delray Beach is a first-class resort destination and a diverse, vibrant, community situated on the Atlantic Ocean between Boca Raton and West Palm Beach. The area has diverse restaurants, a great art museum housed in a 1913 schoolhouse (The Cornell) and the quirky Silverball Museum, which is dedicated to the preservation of the vintage arcade. In this arcade you pay by the hour, not with tokens or quarters, and play as much as you want in that hour. Games include favorites such as Pac-Man, Asteroids, Frogger and Space Invaders They also sell food. This is a great rainy-day diversion.

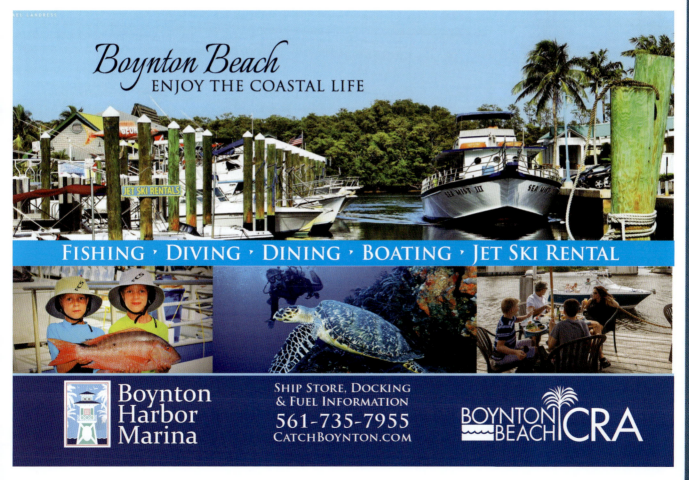

Hillsboro River, FL

		Largest Vessel Accommodated	VHF Channel Monitored	Transient Berths / Total Berths	Approach / Dockside Depth (reported)	Floating Docks	Gas / Diesel	Groceries, Ice, Marine Supplies, Snacks	Repairs: Hull, Engine, Propeller	Lift (tonnage), Crane, Rail	Laundry, Pool, Showers, Courtesy Car	Min/Max Amps	Pump-Out Station	Nearby: Grocery Store, Motel, Restaurant
DELRAY BEACH				**Dockage**				**Supplies**			**Services**			
1. Marina Delray 1038	561-276-7666	–	16	1/9	5/5	–	GD	IM	HE	L	30/50	PS	–	R
2. The Seagate Yacht Club 🖳 🌐onSpot 1039.8	561-330-3811	130	16	6/44	6.5/6.5	–	D	IS	–	–	30/100	LPS	–	GMR
3. Delray Beach City Marina 1039.8	561-243-7250	55	–	call/24	/10	–	–	I	–	–	30/50	LS	P	GR
4. Delray Harbor Club Marina 📶 WG 1040.5	561-276-0376	200	16/08	7/44	8/8	F	GD	IMS	HEP	L80	30/100	PS	–	GR
BOCA RATON														
5. Boca Raton Resort & Club 🖳 1048.2	561-447-3474	170	16	32/32	12/10	–	–	GIS	–	–	50/100	LPS	–	GMR
DEERFIELD BEACH														
6. Two Georges at the Cove Waterfront Restaurant and Marina 954-427-9747		65	16/09	5/31	7/7	–	GD	GIMS	–	–	30/50		–	GMR
HILLSBORO INLET AREA														
7. Lighthouse Point Yacht and Racquet Club 🖳 📶	954-942-6688	100	16/68	5/76	10/8	–	GD	I	–	–	30/100	LPS	P	GR
8. Lighthouse Point Marina Inc. 🖳 📶 1053.7	954-941-0227	80	16	10/100	7/7	–	GD	IMS	–	–	30/50	LPS	P	GR
9. Yacht Management Marina 🖳 📶 WG	954-941-6447	130	16	5/24	12/5	–	–	–	HEP	L	30/50	L	P	GMR
POMPANO BEACH														
10. Merritt's Boat & Engine Works 1054.8	954-941-5207	100	–	–	10/8	–	–	MS	HEP	L100	30/30	–	–	MR
11. Aquamarina Hidden Harbour 🖳 📶 1054.8	954-941-0498	43	–	3/3	–	F	GD	IMS	HEP	L75	30/30	–	P	R
12. Sands Harbor Resort & Marina 🖳 📶 1056.2	954-942-9100	100	16/10	30/50	10/10	–	GD	GIMS	HEP	L80	30/100	LPS	P	GMR
13. Taha Marine Center	954-785-4737	–	–	call/25	10/10	–	GD	MS	–	–	–	–	P	GMR

🖳 Internet Access 📶 Wireless Internet Access WG Waterway Guide Cruising Club Partner 🌐onSpot dockside WiFi facility

See WaterwayGuide.com for current rates, fuel prices, web site addresses, and other up-to-the-minute information. *(Information in the table is provided by the facilities.)*

DELRAY BEACH, NOAA CHART 11467

BOCA RATON, DEERFIELD BEACH, NOAA CHART 11467

HILLSBORO INLET AREA, POMPANO BEACH, NOAA CHART 11467

NAVIGATION: Use NOAA Chart 11467. Use the Miami Harbor Entrance Tide Tables. For high tide, add 1 hour 24 minutes; for low tide, add 2 hours 7 minutes. From Delray Beach south to Fort Lauderdale, smaller boats, and those bothered by the constant buffeting of the irregular, choppy sea caused by wakes, might consider traveling on weekdays when traffic is lighter. Wakes on this narrow channel retain their energy between opposing cement bulkheads, bouncing back and forth for some time after the passing of the craft that caused them. If the weather permits, you may just want to make the outside run from Lake Worth South to avoid the numerous bridges and boat wakes.

The first Delray Beach bridge you will encounter is the **George Bush Blvd. Bascule Bridge** (Mile 1038.7, 9-foot closed vertical clearance). This bridge opens on signal at all times. The second bridge in Delray Beach is the **Atlantic Ave. (SR 806) Bascule Bridge** (Mile 1039.6, 12-foot closed vertical clearance), which opens at 15 and 45 minutes past the hour. The **Linton Blvd. Bascule Bridge** (Mile 1041.0, charted 30-foot closed vertical clearance) opens on the hour and half-hour at all times. (Call ahead to verify as our Cruising Editors have observed an actual clearance of 27 feet: 561-278-1980.)

Approximately 0.6 miles south of this bridge, at Mile 1041.7, steer well clear of the white buoy marked "Rocks" well out from the western shore of the ICW.

Dockage: Boating amenities at Delray Beach range from restaurants with their own dockage and full-service marinas and repair shops. Just north of the Atlantic Ave. Bridge is a city park complex (lawn bowling, shuffleboard, etc.) on the mainland side of the ICW. At one time, complimentary daytime dockage was available at the park (2-hour limit, no overnight docking) but this dock was closed for repairs in 2018 with no anticipated opening date. (Note that a sign advises there are 4-foot MLW depths.)

Just south of the George Bush Blvd. Bridge is the small (9-slip) Marina Delray with only 1 reserved transient slip and 5-foot approach and dockside depths at MLW. Continuing south past the Atlantic Ave. Bridge are The Seagate Yacht Club and Delray Beach City Marina, both with transient space and gas. The Seagate Yacht Club also sells diesel fuel. To the south is Delray Harbor Club Marina. This full-service marina has slips, fuel and an 80-ton lift.

The free dock at Veterans Park at Mile 1039.5 north of the Atlantic Ave. Bascule Bridge was closed for repairs at press time in summer 2018.

ICW

Delray Beach

Boca Raton Inlet

Anchorage: At about Mile 1042, the round basin to the west of the ICW, known locally as Pelican Harbor, is a 24-hour only anchorage (by order of the town of Delray Beach). The basin has 5-foot MLW depths at the entrance and 6-foot depths inside. Poor holding has been reported due to a very soft bottom.

■ BOCA RATON AREA

NAVIGATION: Use NOAA Chart 11467. Use the Miami Harbor Entrance Tide Tables. For high tide, add 23 minutes; for low tide, add 1 hour 7 minutes. The **Spanish River Blvd. Bascule Bridge** at Mile 1044.9 has 25-foot closed vertical clearance and opens on the hour and half-hour, 24 hours a day. About 1 mile to the south, the ICW crosses broad, shallow Lake Wyman through a narrow, well-marked channel favoring the eastern shore. If you stray from the channel, unmarked shoals call for extra caution. Be on the lookout for water skiers and swimmers in the water.

About 5 miles south of Delray Beach, the ICW route leads into Lake Boca Raton through a cut lined with beautiful homes. Before entering the lake, the ICW passes under **Palmetto Park Bascule Bridge**

(19-foot closed vertical clearance) at Mile 1047.5. The bridge opens on the hour and half-hour. This bridge crosses a narrow opening through which strong currents stream. If your vessel is lightly powered, when running with the current be sure to avoid being carried into the bridge or being carried by eddies into the concrete walls and docks along the sides. During weekends and particularly in season, many small boats mill around the boat ramp next to the southwestern bridge abutment at Silver Palm Park, adding to the confusion. This is usually a very busy area and extra caution should be taken.

The ICW next passes through Lake Boca Raton on its western side and continues south through the **Camino Real Bridge** (Mile 1048.2, 9-foot closed vertical clearance). It opens on the hour, and at 20 and 40 minutes past the hour 24 hours daily. This is the only restricted bridge in Palm Beach County that opens more than twice an hour, attesting to the large number of boats passing through. This is also the southernmost bridge in Palm Beach County.

When heading south through the Palmetto Park and Camino Real bridges, keep in mind that the current usually reverses in the ICW as it passes the Boca Raton Inlet. It is nothing even a lightly powered vessel can't handle, but be aware of it, particularly on an incoming tide. The Camino Real Bridge can be quite busy, particularly on weekends in season.

The ICW channel through Lake Boca Raton is an Idle-Speed/No-Wake Zone, and the local marine police make a point to strictly enforce it. It is busy with tour boats and water taxis ferrying passengers between the Boca Raton Resort & Club and its private beach.

Dockage: The Boca Raton Resort & Club is located at Mile 1048.2 on Lake Boca Raton. The pink hotel is a local landmark and offers dockage with a 50-foot minimum charge. Nearby is Waterstone Resort & Marina, which may have transient space for daytime use only; no overnight docking is allowed.

Anchorage: Just south of the Palmetto Park Bridge (Mile 1047.5), a small anchorage is located at the northeastern end of Lake Boca Raton. Enter north of flashing green "65," and anchor in 8-foot MLW depths north and east of the charted shoal areas. An unmarked channel runs through the anchorage area and along the eastern shore to the Boca Raton Inlet. There is heavy traffic in the area, especially on weekends.

Boca Raton Inlet–ICW Mile 1048

The Boca Raton Inlet is not recommended for passage without local knowledge due to shoaling. The tall, pink Boca Raton Resort & Club is a landmark visible from many miles offshore. The inlet's entrance has short jetties marked by private lights, and depths change due to shoaling and shifting sandbars. The inlet channel and markers are not charted and transit is considered dangerous. The **Boca Inlet Bascule Bridge** (23-foot closed vertical clearance) crosses the inlet and opens on signal. See the Inlet section in the front of this guide for more information on Boca Raton Inlet.

■ DEERFIELD BEACH TO POMPANO BEACH

Deerfield Beach to Hillsboro Inlet– ICW Mile 1048 to Mile 1053

NAVIGATION: Use NOAA Chart 11467. The ICW leaves Lake Boca Raton through the Camino Real Bridge at Mile 1048.2, as described earlier. It then enters another straight section with many canals, followed at Mile 1050 by the Hillsboro River with its many bridges and speed restrictions.

Manatee Zones and Boating Safety Zones are frequent and often overlap. Where they do, the more restrictive limitation applies. Some are seasonal (November 15 through March 31), some are year-round, some are weekends only, some are for the full width of the water, and some are more restrictive within a specified distance from the shore. The official signs are well placed and

Hillsboro Inlet

GOIN' ASHORE: BOCA RATON, FL

The area now known as Boca Raton is shown on old Spanish navigational maps charts as Boca de Ratones, meaning "mouth of the harbor of the hidden rocks." It appears that the name was originally applied to Biscayne Bay near Miami Beach, but early mapmakers moved the name to the present location. The construction of the Florida East Coast Canal (today's ICW) and the Florida East Coast Railway in the 1890s brought pioneers and farmers to the area. In 1925, eccentric architect Addison Mizner was hired to design a world-class resort community. His exclusive hotel, known as the Cloister Inn, was completed in 1926, and remains a landmark as the Boca Raton Resort and Club. The ICW route through Lake Boca Raton hugs the western shore and passes within view of the resort Mizner designed and built, and the many other buildings that mimic his Mediterranean revival design.

Attractions: Want some culture? This is the place! The Boca Raton Museum of Art has more than 4,000 works ranging from pre-Columbian to the modern masters, as well as traveling exhibits (501 Plaza Real, 561-392-2500). The Boca Raton Historical Society and Museum (71 N. Federal Hwy., 561-395-6766) is located in the historic "Old Town Hall" and offers a wide range of exhibits and lecture series. The Wick Theatre &

Costume Museum (7901 N. Federal Hwy., 561 995-2333) produces current Broadway hits, musicals and revivals. In the north end of Downtown Boca, the Mizner Park Amphitheater (590 Plaza Real, 561-393-7890) is a public venue of community events and concerts. This is part of Mizner Park, a unique mixed-use development of shops, restaurants, a movie theater, offices, residences and public spaces.

Shopping/Dining: For provisioning, there's a Trader Joe's at 855 S. Federal Hwy. and a Publix Supermarket at 1001 S. Federal Hwy. These are within walking distance to Boca Raton Resort. At 75 SE 3rd St. is the small, family-owned 4th Generation Organic Market & Café (561-314-1341), which is open daily from 9:00 a.m. to 9:00 p.m. This organic food store sells produce, groceries and prepared dishes you can bring back to the boat to enjoy.

"Downtown Boca" along Federal Hwy. and East Palmetto Park Rd. features upscale shopping, restaurants, art galleries, events and festivals with something for everyone. Just south of Palmetto Road is Royal Palm Place, another center in downtown with dining, shopping and living. There are too many shopping and dining options to list here. Visit delraybeach.com or mydelraybeach.com for a complete listing.

repeated at intervals, and some vary in only small details. You must keep a sharp lookout and read each sign carefully. The speed and wake limits are enforced by state, county and municipal police boats.

Deerfield Beach is the next city, closely followed by the Lighthouse Point area, Hillsboro Inlet and Pompano Beach proper. A maze of manmade canals shoots off the ICW in all directions, and from here southward, virtually all land routes end up at the water.

Near Deerfield Beach, the Hillsboro Drainage Canal enters the ICW from the west at Mile 1049.9. During times of high flow from the canal, strong currents exist in the ICW about 100 yards from the **Hillsboro Blvd. (SR 810) Bascule Bridge** at Mile 1050.0. The bridge (21-foot closed vertical clearance) opens on the hour and half-hour at all times. Southbound boats approaching the bridge should not proceed past the canal until the bridge is fully open and should maintain adequate headway to avoid being pushed into the east bridge fender by the canal crosscurrents. From the bridge to Mile 1052 (south of red daybeacon "68") shoaling exists along the edges of the channel.

Dockage: Deerfield Island Park is on the west side of the ICW with picnic areas and nature walks. A short distance up the Hillsboro Drainage Canal, the park boat dock can accommodate dinghies and small runabouts up to about 16 feet. Marina One is located 0.6 mile to the north on the canal. It is a boat storage facility with fuel (no overnight dockage).

Back on the ICW, Two Georges at the Cove Waterfront Restaurant and Marina is just south of the Hillsboro Blvd. Bridge. They might have transient dockage with a 7-foot-deep approach (at MLW) and offer gas and diesel fuel. Call ahead for reservations.

Hillsboro Inlet–ICW Mile 1053

NAVIGATION: Use NOAA Chart 11467. Use the Miami Harbor Entrance Tide Tables. For high tide at Hillsboro Inlet Coast Guard Station, subtract 16 minutes; for low tide, add 3 minutes. Just south of Hillsboro Inlet, the ICW swings wide around a projecting point that builds out from the eastern shore. South from the inlet, for the next 1.5 miles shoaling occurs in spots along the edges of the channel.

The speed limit is Slow-Speed/Minimum-Wake to just before the next bridge, where an Idle-Speed/No-Wake Zone begins. Beyond that bridge, a sign lists the complex speed restrictions that prevail for the next 2.5 miles.

At Hillsboro Inlet, the 136-foot-tall lighthouse for which the area is named has one of the most powerful beacons on the coast (visible from 28 miles at sea). The fast-operating **Hillsboro Inlet Bridge** (13-foot closed vertical clearance), spanning the inlet approach from the ICW, opens on signal, except from 7:00 a.m. to 6:00 p.m., when it need only open on the hour and at 15, 30 and 45 minutes past the hour. (Note that this bridge is not on the ICW proper.) If you are planning on using the Hillsboro Inlet, be sure to get up-to-date information regarding the status of the bridge. The current runs swiftly beneath the bridge. Wait for the bridge to open completely before you start your passage.

Although Hillsboro Inlet's shoals shift rapidly, dredging is frequent, and local boats and the large fleet of charter fishing and head boats heavily travel the passage here. Swells and/or tidal rip on the ebb against an easterly wind will decrease the available depth.

Under good weather conditions, boats with 5-foot drafts or less can run the inlet safely by observing the constant flow of local boats going in and out. With any swell from the east, passage becomes hazardous. Local reports indicate to proceed all the way to the

Hillsboro Inlet

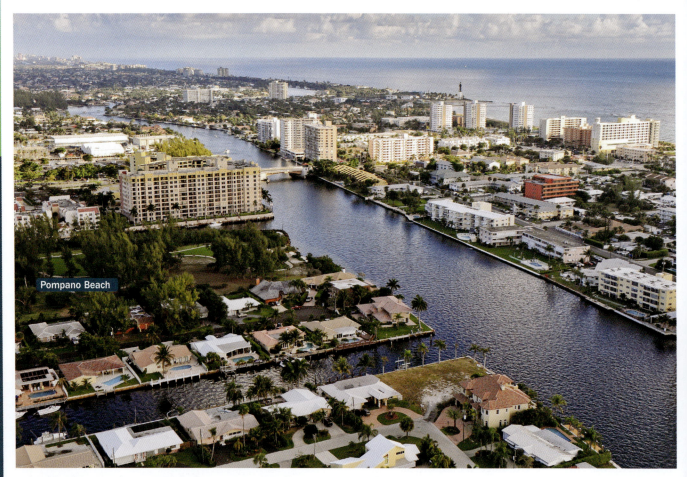

Pompano Beach

red-and-white sea buoy "HI" before turning south, to avoid shoals. A rock jetty extends southeast from the north side of the inlet and is submerged at the outer end. It is wise to seek local knowledge before running this inlet. See the Inlet section at front of this guide for more information on Hillsboro Inlet.

Dockage: Lighthouse Point Yacht and Racquet Club (Mile 1052.2) and Lighthouse Point Marina, Inc. (Mile 1053.7) have transient slips and sell fuel (both gas and diesel). Just past the Hillsboro Inlet is Yacht Management Marina, which may have space for you. Call ahead for docking availability and details.

Hillsboro Inlet to Pompano Beach– ICW Mile 1053 to Mile 1056

Pompano Beach means "fishing." Even its name was inspired by one of the more popular species found in its waters. When some native folks served a group of surveyors who were mapping the area the local game fish, they wrote the name of the pompano fish on their map, and the name has stuck to the spot ever since.

In April, the Pompano Beach Seafood Festival brings together arts and crafts, non-stop live entertainment and great seafood. During the summer, "Music under the Stars" sponsors a variety of free concerts throughout the city.

NAVIGATION: Use NOAA Chart 11467. Two bascule bridges cross the ICW in Pompano Beach, both with 15-foot closed vertical clearance. The northernmost, the **Pompano Beach (NE 14th St.) Bridge** crosses the ICW at Mile 1055. The bridge opens at 15 and 45 minutes past the hour. The **Atlantic Blvd. (SR 814) Bridge** at Mile 1056 opens on the hour and half-hour. Both bridges monitor VHF Channel 09.

Dockage: Pompano Beach has abundant boating services on protected side canals or in enclosed basins along the ICW. Almost anything the yachtsman might want in the way of service, supplies, convenience or outright luxury is available in the immediate area.

Just north of the Pompano Beach Bridge, Merritt's Boat & Engine Works is a major yacht yard. Transient dockage is not available, but they offer all types of repairs and have a 100-ton lift. Aquamarina Hidden Harbour (located at the end of a well-protected canal off the ICW) also does repair work (75-ton lift) and sells all fuels but does not have transient dockage.

Just before the Atlantic Boulevard Bridge, the Sands Harbor Resort & Marina is part of a large resort

Pompano Beach will be hosting the 29th annual nautical flea market on January 19 and 20, 2019. The event will be held at Community Park (820 NE 18th Ave.) on Saturday from 8:00 a.m. to 5:00 p.m. and Sunday from 8:00 a.m. to 3:00 p.m. Over 200 vendors will be selling new and used gear and boating equipment, plus fishing tackle, nautical antiques and artwork, scuba gear, beach attire, boat shoes, jewelry, motors, anchors, hard-to-find parts and manufacturer close-outs. Local dealers and private sellers will be on site with new and used boats, motors, trailers and jet-ski's. For details, visit nauticalfleamarket.net or call 954-946-6419.

complex and provides transient dockage and fuel, as well as all types of repairs (80-ton lift). Nearby Taha Marine Center sells fuel and has slips with 10-foot dockside and approach depths (at MLW). Call ahead for availability.

Anchorage: Anchoring in Lake Santa Barbara (approximately Mile 1057.0) on the west side of the ICW is still possible. The local marine police do not encourage it, but cannot forbid it. (Refer them to Florida Statute 327.02.) Remember to always stay apprised of the current Florida anchoring laws. They are challenged almost every year in the state legislature. Wakes from ICW traffic make this an uncomfortable anchorage and charted depths of 5 to 6 feet at MLW are not reliable.

Anchoring is also possible in Lettuce Lake on the east side of the ICW (7- to 12-foot MLW depths) but not recommended, as the lake (actually just a wide spot in the ICW) is exposed to heavy and fast ICW traffic and holding is notoriously poor in very soft mud.

◼ NEXT STOP

Ahead to the south lies a true yachting center, Fort Lauderdale, the Venice of America. Check our *Skipper's Handbook* in the front of this guide for headings from either Hillsboro Inlet or Port Everglades Inlet that will take you to Grand Bahama or Bimini.

Fort Lauderdale to Hollywood

 ICW Mile 1059–Mile 1073

VHF FL Bridges: Channel 09

CHARTS NOAA 11467, 11470

■ FORT LAUDERDALE AREA

Nearly 300 miles of canals, channels and waterways wind through the Fort Lauderdale area, and at least half are navigable by virtually any size recreational craft. Often referred to as the "Yachting Capital of the World," the city lies about halfway between the Palm Beaches and Miami. With the Atlantic Ocean surf to the east and the traffic-laden ICW running north and south, the city is conspicuously water-oriented. The New River and its tributaries cut through the center of town and artificial side canals run almost everywhere.

Well known as a yachting center, Fort Lauderdale harbors more recreational boats than any other port in Florida. Not surprisingly, the marine industry–marinas, boatyards and builders, yacht and charter brokers and marine services–ranks second only to tourism.

Although the entire city of Fort Lauderdale has the look of a huge yachting center, most boating amenities and services are concentrated in three main areas: the main ICW channel, the New River and the Dania Cut-off Canal. Jostling each other for room is a collection of marinas, yacht services, sailmakers, boatyards, sales organizations, dinghy manufacturers, marine supply stores and other useful facilities.

Lauderdale-by-the-Sea to New River Sound–ICW Mile 1059 to Mile 1064

Fort Lauderdale is an important commercial harbor. The straight, deep inlet at Port Everglades forms an excellent big-ship terminal and commercial port, handling millions of tons of ocean cargo each year. The cruise ship terminals in the port often accommodate cruise ships, tankers, freighters and military vessels.

NAVIGATION: Use NOAA Charts 11467 and 11470. Use the Miami Harbor Entrance Tide Tables. For high tide at Bahia Mar, subtract 5 minutes; for low tide, add 33 minutes. For the 8 miles from Pompano Beach to Port Everglades, the boater faces five bridges, scores of canals and rows of homes, small and large, on both sides of the

Ft. Lauderdale

17th Street Causeway

MILE 1067

Port Everglades

Dania

1

Hollywood

MILE 1072

Hollywood Beach

Hallandale

Atlantic Ocean

N

ICW. For all practical purposes, the Fort Lauderdale area begins at Mile 1059, 2 miles south of Pompano, just past Lauderdale-by-the-Sea.

Between Mile 1059 and Mile 1064 are four bridges, all with restricted schedules. The first, the **Commercial Blvd. (SR 870) Bascule Bridge** at Mile 1059.0 has 15-foot closed vertical clearance and opens on the hour and half-hour. The **Oakland Park Blvd. Bascule Bridge** at Mile 1060.5 has 22-foot closed vertical clearance and opens at 15 and 45 minutes past the hour. The **East Sunrise Blvd. (SR 838) Bascule Bridge** at Mile 1062.6 has 25-foot closed vertical clearance and opens on the hour and half-hour. The **East Las Olas Blvd. Bascule Bridge** at Mile 1064 has 25-foot closed vertical clearance and opens at 15 and 45 minutes past the hour.

> Special closures are in effect at the East Sunrise and Las Olas bridges during the first weekend of May each year during the annual Air and Sea Show. See the bridges listings in the front of this guide for specifics.

Speed restrictions in open stretches differ for weekends and weekdays, and there are a number of short Idle-Speed/No-Wake Zones. In one 3-mile segment, there are almost 60 side canals, many with offshoots of their own, and each is lined with gorgeous houses, some with large boats in front of them.

After Mile 1059, the ICW is straight (with no need for aids to navigation), densely populated and heavily traveled. To the east, on the ocean side of the ICW, 180-acre Hugh Taylor Birch State Recreation Area stretches for one-quarter mile north of the East Sunrise Boulevard Bridge, opposite the yacht club and marina. A pleasant, wooded oasis, the park provides the perfect spot for a sailor's holiday and offers rental canoes on a quiet lagoon and a swimming beach for a tropical picnic. Unfortunately, the park has no docks on the ICW. Local marine police frequently patrol the ICW here and vigorously enforce the speed limit.

South of the East Sunrise Boulevard Bridge, the channel zigzags past Coral Ridge Yacht Club and Sunrise Harbor Marina and associated condominiums to the west. Stay close to the western bank until you reach the first aid to navigation, flashing green "3," where the channel heads southeast. At the second navigation aid, flashing green "5," the channel turns back southwest. Be careful to give the mainland point opposite flashing

green "5" a wide berth. Before you make your turn, be sure to locate the next marker, flashing red "8."

An Idle-Speed/No-Wake Zone begins north of flashing red "8," north of the East Las Olas Boulevard Bridge.

Dockage: Numerous restaurants just above and below the Oakland Park Boulevard Bridge have docks for their customers. Mastro's Ocean Club (954-561-4800) and Shooters Waterfront (954-566-2855) are among them. On weekends, several of the livelier drinking and dining spots on the east side have boats rafted out into the ICW, six or more deep.

Just north of the East Sunrise Boulevard Bridge (Mile 1062.6) are the Coral Ridge Yacht Club (private) and the Sunrise Harbor Marina, which caters to megayachts (up to 200 feet). Amenities at the upscale Sunrise Harbor include a controlled-access garage, 24-hour valet parking, concierge service, Club Room, climate-controlled wine room, business center, health and fitness center, spa, tennis courts and two heated pools.

There is an area of privately rented slips about 0.5 mile north of the East Las Olas Bridge at Mile 1063.5. To reach the long-term dockage areas at Isle of Venice and Hendricks Isle, turn west off of the ICW at Middle River between flashing green "3" and "5." These canals are the last three straight north-south canals in the Nurmi Isles section. Hendricks Isle is the westernmost large isle; Isle of Venice is the next one east. Many properties rent slips on these two islands. Most are long-term rentals, but some properties rent slips on a daily basis. The various docks are different sizes, provide different shoreside amenities and are priced accordingly. The best way to find a slip here is to stop elsewhere temporarily, and then visit the area to check slip availability. During the winter season, slips here may be hard to find.

All liveaboard docks here are equipped with a direct pump-out hose to each slip, which must be hooked up to each vessel's holding-tank deck fitting. "Y" valves must be locked, and flow-through treatment devices cannot be used. With new condominium development in this area, there is considerably less liveaboard dockage space than in the past.

Anchorage: Florida legislation passed in 2016 bans overnight anchoring in the section of the Middle River at Mile 1063.4 from NE 21st St. to the ICW. It is illegal to anchor at any time during the period between one-half hour after sunset and one-half hour before sunrise. The revision to the anchoring laws in Florida in 2017 continued to include this restriction and also one for Miami's Sunset Lake.

East Las Olas Blvd. Bridge to Port Everglades–ICW Mile 1064 to Mile 1066

Between the East Las Olas Blvd. Bridge and the SE 7th St. Bridge there is a concentration of marinas close to the bridges. Canals branch off in all directions, lined by spectacular homes with yachts docked in their back yards. Many of these residences have been "remodeled" or expanded in size numerous times. Multimillion-dollar homes are often torn down here to make room for even more expensive homes.

Ashore, the Fort Lauderdale oceanfront between Bahia Mar and Sunrise Blvd. is limited to one-way

Fort Lauderdale, FL

FORT LAUDERDALE AREA		Largest Vessel Accommodated	VHF Channel Monitored	Transient Berths / Total Berths	Approach / Dockside Depth (reported)	Floating Docks	Groceries, Ice, Marine Supplies, Snacks	Gas / Diesel	Repairs: Hull, Engine, Propeller	Lift (tonnage), Crane, Rail	Min/Max Amps	Laundry, Pool, Showers, Courtesy Car	Pump-Out Station	Nearby: Grocery Store, Motel, Restaurant
				Dockage			**Supplies**		**Services**					
1. Coral Ridge Yacht Club – PRIVATE WiFi 1062.3	954-566-7886	100	-	3/58	10/8		-	-	-	-	30/50	PS	P	GR
2. Sunrise Harbor Marina 1062.3	954-667-6720	200	16/11	call/22	10/8.5	F	-	-	-	-	50/200+	P	-	GMR
3. Las Olas Marina 1063.4	954-828-7200	200	16	60/60	10/10	F	-	I	-	-	30/200+	LS	-	GMR
4. Hall of Fame Marina 1063.8	954-764-3975	150	16/08	40/40	9/9	-	-	IM	-	-	30/200+	LPS	P	GMR
5. Bahia Mar Yachting Center onSpot	954-627-6309	250	16/68	150/240	16/16	F	GD	GIMS	-	-	30/200+	LPS	P	GMR
6. Lauderdale Yacht Club 1066.0	954-527-2209	-	16/69	5/64	5/5	-	-	IS	-	-	30/30	PS	-	R
7. Lauderdale Marina/15th Street Fisheries 1066.2	954-523-8507	165	16	10/60	10/10	F	GD	IMS	HEP	L35	50/200+	S	P	GMR
8. Hilton Fort Lauderdale Marina 1066.5	954-463-4000	300	16/71	33/33	20/10	-	-	IS	-	-	30/50	LPS	P	GMR
9. Marina Boathouse of Fort Lauderdale	954-343-2470	200	-	10/10	14/12	-	GD	-	E	-	50/100	L	P	GMR
10. Cable Marine East 1066.4	954-462-2822	120	16/09	call/12	20/15	-	-	M	HEP	L40	50/50	-	-	GMR
11. Hyatt Regency Pier Sixty-Six Marina	954-728-3578	350	16	127/127	16/17	-	GD	GIMS	-	-	30/200+	LPS	-	GMR
12. The Sails Marina 1067	954-728-3578	500	16	15/20	45/24	F	GD	GIMS	-	-	30/200+	LPS	-	GMR

Internet Access   WiFi Wireless Internet Access   WG Waterway Guide Cruising Club Partner   onSpot dockside WiFi facility

See WaterwayGuide.com for current rates, fuel prices, web site addresses, and other up-to-the-minute information. *(Information in the table is provided by the facilities.)*

FORT LAUDERDALE AREA, NOAA CHART 11467

northbound traffic and features bike trails, sidewalks and landscaping, all creating an attractive setting. Beach Place, an oceanfront multilevel shopping and entertainment complex with a Marriott resort, is drawing crowds, as are the numerous restaurants and nightclubs both north and south of Las Olas Boulevard. A large number of high-rise luxury condominium resorts, quite conspicuous from offshore, line the strip between Sunrise and Las Olas Boulevards. Many of these offer upscale shopping and dining experiences on their lower floors.

NAVIGATION: Use NOAA Chart 11470. Between the Las Olas and SE 17th St. bridges, and farther south beyond the Dania Beach Boulevard Bridge, there are nearly continuous Slow-Speed/Idle-Speed Zones.

The **SE 17th St. (Brooks Memorial) Bascule Bridge** at Mile 1065.9 has a vertical clearance of 55 feet and opens on the hour and half-hour as needed for sailboats and large motor yachts. Vessels waiting on the south side for bridge openings should stay clear of the turning basin and cruise ship berths, as well as any government patrol boats. To the south, Port Everglades is a major cruise ship port, and traffic is heavy in the area. If approaching from the south, the ICW channel may be difficult to pick out along the east side of the turning basin.

Marine Police boats are active in the vicinity of the Lauderdale Marina and the SE 17th St. Bridge. It is necessary to maintain the slowest possible speed through

FORT LAUDERDALE AREA, NOAA CHART 11467

this area to avoid a warning or ticket. Do not be tempted to speed up to make the bridge.

Dockage/Moorings: Although jam-packed with permanent year-round or seasonal boats, most marinas reserve some space for transients, so the visiting cruiser is almost certain to find a berth at one place or another. At the height of the season, you must reserve a berth in advance of arrival.

The first concentration of marine facilities southbound begins at the Las Olas Bridge on the eastern side of the ICW. (The western side is residential except for the small anchorage and mooring area just south of the

bridge.) Going south, the marinas that appear are: Las Olas Marina (with slips north and south of the bridge); Hall of Fame Marina; and the large (240-slip) Bahia Mar Beach Resort and Yachting Center.

The municipal Las Olas Marina has slips on floating docks with an array of amenities, including a comfort station with clean restrooms, showers and a laundromat. This facility is just steps from the beach.

Hall of Fame Marina to the south offers slips and full amenities, including a pool, laundry service, car rentals, beach access and three adjacent restaurants. They can

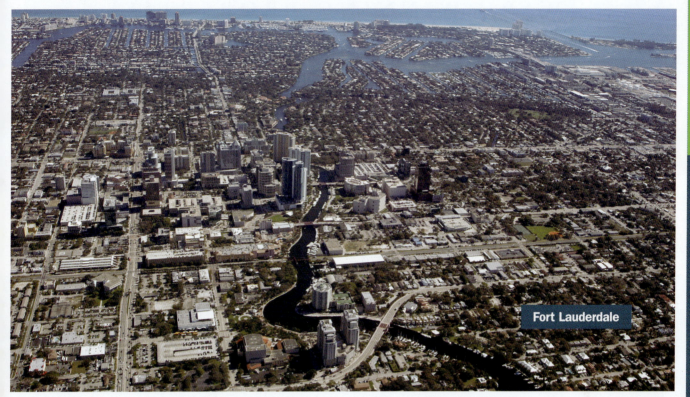

Fort Lauderdale

accommodate a wide variety of craft, with plenty of slips for year-round tenants and visitors.

Bahia Mar Yachting Center has dockage to 250 feet and sells gas and diesel (high-speed fueling) and some supplies. The property features a Doubletree Hilton, complete with restaurants, shops, swimming pool and tennis and directly across the street from a sand beach. Bahia Mar is also the home to the world-renowned Fort Lauderdale International Boat Show.

The Las Olas mooring area at Mile 1064 contains 10 city-owned moorings, which are available on a first-come, first-served basis. The city dockmaster, whose office stands by on VHF Channels 09 and 16, will come by to collect fees. Phone ahead at 954-828-7200 for more information about availability. Any one vessel may rent moorings for no more than 30 days during a calendar year. White and orange buoys have been placed along the south boundary of the moorings. All landing of dinghies is done at the Las Olas Marina on the opposite (east) side of the ICW from the anchorage. Showers, laundry and trash disposal are available for moored boats.

The second concentration of marinas begins just north of the SE 17th St. Bridge. Heading south on the west side of the ICW, the Lauderdale Yacht Club has a narrow marked entrance channel through shallows (5 feet at MLW). You must belong to a yacht club to dock here. (Call ahead for availability.) Next on the western side

is the Lauderdale Marina/15th Street Fisheries offering berths and some repairs. (They have a 35-ton lift on site.) The marina also sells all fuels. Boaters should try to come in against the current, take up as short a space as possible and fuel up quickly. There is often a line of boats waiting, especially on weekends. TowBoat U.S. boats are based here.

The Hilton Fort Lauderdale Marina can accommodate megayachts up to 300 feet with 10-foot dockside depths at MLW. This facility is at the head of a channel that leads to Marina Boathouse of Fort Lauderdale and Cable Marine East. Both facilities offer some repairs. On the east side of the ICW, the Hyatt Regency Pier Sixty-Six Marina has dockage for vessels to 350 feet and offers resort amenities and sells all fuels. Just south of the SE 17th St. Bridge is The Sails Marina with slips to 500 feet, plus repairs and gas and diesel.

Anchorage: There is little space in the harbor outside the Las Olas mooring area, and you must stay at least 500 feet from the moorings. Boats anchored on the outside close to the channel are subject to the current's effect. Anchored vessels are requested not to block access to the docks at private residences adjacent to the Las Olas mooring area. The dinghy dock is under the bridge.

Lake Sylvia is your best bet now for anchoring in this area. To reach the anchorage, head east past the southwestern corner of Bahia Mar Marina, cut well

Fort Lauderdale

inside flashing green "13," then hug the eastern sea wall when approaching the entrance channel into the lake. There is a 5-foot shoal that is building in the center of the channel so go slow until you enter the lake. You will pass a large condominium building and private residences with docks as you head south. Stay close to the docks on the east side until about two-thirds of the way into the entrance channel, then move into the middle of the channel and enter the lake. The last stretch of the entrance, where you head into the middle of the canal, has an uneven bottom and is about 7 feet at MLW. The lake has depths of around 12 feet at MLW. Luxurious homes surround the anchorage. On weekends, Lake Sylvia is full of local boats, many rafted for the night. It is frequented by water skiers.

There is not a dinghy landing in Lake Sylvia, but there is a space to land approximately 1 mile from the anchorage at Southport Raw Bar (954-525-2526). They will allow you to leave your dinghy for a $10 fee, which will be returned to you if you eat or drink at the restaurant. To reach the restaurant, go into the farthest side channel in the lake, run west to the ICW and cross over to the channel that is occupied by the boathouse-covered slips. Go to the very end of the channel. There is

a supermarket, liquor store and several other stores just a short walk away.

Water taxis stand by on VHF Channel 68 and will pick up or drop off passengers at locations throughout Fort Lauderdale, along both the ICW and the New River. A pass provides the passenger with unlimited stops and rides for the whole day. Details on fares, routes and stops are at watertaxi.com (954-467-6677).

⚠️ It is imperative that you stay up-to-date on the anchoring restrictions in these waters. As of summer 2018 the Florida Anchoring Laws included the following:
• You may not anchor or moor within 150 feet of any marina, boat ramp, boatyard, or other vessel launching or loading facility;
• You may not anchor within 300 feet of a facility that services or repairs a yacht with a water line of 120 feet or more in length;
• You may not anchor within 100 feet from the marked boundary of a public mooring field.
Check the Waterway Explorer at waterwayguide.com for updates as the State Legislature is continuously trying to change the anchoring restrictions.

GOIN' ASHORE: **FORT LAUDERDALE (PORT EVERGLADES), FL**

SERVICES	
1	Post Office
SHOPPING	
2	Harbor Shops
3	West Marine
4	Winn Dixie

DINING	
5	15th Street Fisheries
6	Boatyard Restaurant
7	Southport Raw Bar
MARINAS	
5	Lauderdale Marina

8	Hilton Fort Lauderdale Marina
9	Marina Boathouse of Fort Lauderdale
10	Cable Marine East

Fort Lauderdale is known for its beaches and boating canals. Some skippers travel only on weekdays to avoid the heavy weekend traffic between Pompano Beach and Miami. However, there isn't another harbor like Fort Lauderdale, and it would be a shame to miss it.

Shopping/Dining: Skippers can tie up at on-the-water restaurants and shopping centers for shoreside dining, shopping or strolling. Most shopping and services line the 15th St. Canal, the first canal on the west side of the ICW just north of the SE 17th St. Bridge. The canal runs parallel to the busy shopping strip along SE 17th St. The 15th Street Fisheries Restaurant (954-763-2777) at the Lauderdale Marina and the Boatyard Restaurant (954-525-7400) on the south side of the canal are popular eateries in this area. The Southport Raw Bar (954-525-2526) at the west end of the canal is a popular spot to visit by dinghy. Publix, Total Wine & More and various other shops and restaurants are located in the Harbor

Shops on the south side of SE 17th St. (on Cordova Rd.). There are also a hardware store, a Winn-Dixie and several dive shops nearby.

A relatively short land-taxi ride away from the marinas is a West Marine store. The "superstore" at 2401 S. Andrews Ave. (951-400-5323) is the largest West Marine in the country. Boat Owners Warehouse, located a few blocks west of South Federal Highway on SR 84, offers competitive prices, knowledgeable help and special ordering from an extensive network of local marine suppliers (954-522-7998). Sailorman at 3000 S. Andrews Ave. (954-522-6716) sells new and used boating equipment. You can buy, sell, trade or consign marine gear there. They specialize in hard to find items, marine surplus, scratch n' dent and used marine merchandise See more shopping and dining options at fortlauderdale.gov/visitors.

■ SIDE TRIP: NEW RIVER

The gently curving, meandering New River bisects the heart of Fort Lauderdale and serves as another major yacht service area. The New River is Fort Lauderdale's yachting center, with some of the finest facilities for building, repair, haul-out and storage on the entire East Coast. Even if you don't need anything, it is worth taking a trip–by boat, dinghy or one of the regularly scheduled sightseeing craft–just to see the contrast of the old and new Fort Lauderdale. In the past several years, there has been major construction of high-rise condominiums and apartment buildings near the river.

NAVIGATION: Use NOAA Chart 11470. Use the Miami Harbor Entrance Tide Tables. For high tide at the Andrews Ave. Bridge, add 15 minutes; for low tide, add 51 minutes. Entrance to the New River depends on the direction you travel. The mouth is forked, and its two openings merge obliquely with the ICW at two different points. Check your chart carefully.

Heading south, the route to the New River follows the ICW around a sharp turn to the west past flashing red "16." Just beyond, the channel splits. Care should be taken when you pass red and green junction daybeacon "A." To go up the New River, leave the marker to port; to continue down the ICW channel, leave it to starboard. The water is very shallow immediately behind this daybeacon, and boats going up the New River frequently run aground by passing it on the wrong side. Leave it to port and, heading west, watch for daybeacons "1" through "4." There is a white-and-orange DANGER daybeacon marking a charted shoal, as well as one marking a shoal on the opposite side of the ICW from the New River entrance.

When traveling the southern approach to the New River, watch the chart closely, and sort out the confusing transposition of buoys and colors before trying the entrance. Once inside the river's mouth, the buoy pattern is easy to follow.

> Depending on the tide, small boats with less than 10 feet of overhead clearance and drawing less than 2 feet can make the full circuit of the **New River, South New River Canal and the Dania Cut-off Canal** and rejoin the ICW just south of Port Everglades. The entire trip is 11.7 miles.

If heading north, the ICW is basically a straight line from the SE 17th St. Bridge to flashing red "20," where the ICW channel starts a turn to the east, but a secondary channel continues northward to the mouth of the New River. If bound for the New River from the ICW heading north, vessels should leave flashing red "20" to starboard. After passing the light, favor the bulkhead-lined western shore just opposite red daybeacon "2" until you have made the turn into the river's buoy system. Aids to navigation on the New River route, after passing red and green junction daybeacon "A" or flashing red "20," follow the normal red-right-returning rule for the river itself. (River aids to navigation do not have the yellow squares or triangles of ICW aids.)

Bridges

The strong tidal current should be considered when transiting the New River, because there is always congestion, especially at the bridges and along the Las Olas Riverfront dining and entertainment area.

- **SE 3rd Ave. Bascule Bridge** (16-foot closed vertical clearance): Opens on signal, except from 7:30 a.m. to 9:00 a.m., and from 4:30 p.m. to 6:00 p.m., Monday through Friday (except federal holidays), when the draw need not open.
- **Andrews Ave. Bascule Bridge** (21-foot closed vertical clearance): Opens on signal, except from 7:30 a.m. to 9:00 a.m., and from 4:30 p.m. to 6:00 p.m., Monday through Friday (except federal holidays), when the draw need not open. The bridge will not open if the FEC Railroad Bridge is closed.
- **FEC Railroad Bascule Bridge** (4-foot closed vertical clearance): Usually open unless train approaching. It is remotely operated. See details in bridge listing in the front of this guide.
- **William H. Marshall (7th Ave.) Memorial Bascule Bridge** (20-foot closed vertical clearance): The draw opens on signal except from 7:30 a.m. to 9:00 a.m., and from 4:30 p.m. to 6:00 p.m., Monday through Friday (except federal holidays), when the draw need not open.

The New River forks beyond the William H. Marshall Memorial Bridge into the North Fork and the South Fork of the New River. The North Fork is residential and has only one bridge (**11th Ave. Swing Bridge**) with 3-foot closed vertical clearance and a hand-operated swing that opens on signal.

New River, FL

NEW RIVER		Largest Vessel Accommodated	VHF Channel Monitored	Transient Berths / Total Berths	Approach / Dockside Depth (reported)	Floating Docks	Gas / Diesel	Groceries, Ice, Marine Supplies, Snacks	Repairs: Hull, Engine, Propeller	Lift (tonnage), Crane, Rail	Min/Max Amps	Laundry, Pool, Showers, Courtesy Car	Pump-Out Station	Nearby: Grocery Store, Motel, Restaurant
		Dockage						**Supplies**		**Services**				
1. New River Downtown Docks	954-828-5423	170	16/09	90/100	15/8	–	–	GM	–	–	30/100	L	P	GR
2. Riverfront Marina	954-527-1829	40	16	–	10/6	–	G	GIMS	HEP	L8	30/30	P	–	GMR
3. Cooley's Landing Marina 💻 WiFi	954-828-4626	50	09	call/30	10/6	–	–	GIM	–	–	30/50	LS	P	GMR
NEW RIVER – SOUTH FORK														
4. Riverbend at LMC 💻 WiFi	954-713-0333	80	–	call/89	12/10	F	–	IMS	HEP	L75	30/100	S	–	GMR
5. Lauderdale Marine Center 💻 WiFi	954-713-0333	200	16	call/180	10/12	F	–	IMS	HEP	L485,C	30/100	S	P	GMR
6. Fort Lauderdale Boatyard and Marina	954-895-8360	200	–	–	8/8	–	–	M	HEP	L70,C	–	–	–	–
7. Marina Mile Yachting Center 💻 WiFi	954-583-0053	150	–	10/35	12/10	F	–	–	HEP	L70,C25	50/100	–	–	GMR
8. Marina Bay Marina Resort 💻 WiFi WG	954-791-7600	150	–	10/168	12/45	F	–	–	–	–	30/200+	LPS	–	GMR
9. Yacht Haven Park & Marina WiFi	954-583-2322	120	–	–	10/6	–	–	I	–	–	30/100	LPS	–	MR
10. Cable Marine West Yard WiFi	954-587-4000	120	16	call/75	12/12	–	–	M	HEP	L100	50/50	–	–	GMR
11. Rolly Marine Service Inc. 💻 WiFi	954-583-5300	150	–	–	9/9	–	–	IM	HEP	L200,C40	50/100	S	–	–
12. Billfish Marina 💻	954-587-6226	130	16	45/45	14/9	F	–	–	HEP	L70	30/100	S	–	GMR
13. Yacht Management South Florida 💻 WiFi	954-941-6447	140	16	5/25	13/7	F	D	GM	HEP	L80	50/50	–	P	GMR
14. Bradford Marine Inc. 💻 WiFi	954-791-3800	180	78	60/105	10/8	F	–	–	HEP	L300	20/100	S	–	GMR
15. Roscioli Yachting Center 💻 WiFi	954-581-9200	140	–	75/75	10/10	–	–	MS	HEP	L250	30/200+	LS	P	GMR
16. Aquamarina Marina Road Boat Yard	954-793-4214	65	–	call/4	–	–	–	–	HEP	L30	30/30	–	–	MR
DANIA CUT-OFF CANAL EXTENSION														
17. Anglers Avenue Marine Center	954-962-8702	70	–	call/65	8/8	–	–	IM	HEP	L30	30/30	S	–	GMR
18. Sundance Marine WG	954-964-4444	–	–	–	–	F	–	I	–	L10	30/30	S	–	GMR
19. Thunderboat Marine Service Center-Dania Beach	954-924-9444	44	–	call/60	5/5	F	G	I	HEP	–	–	S	–	GMR
20. Cozy Cove Marina 💻	954-921-8800	100	–	call/59	–	F	–	MS	HEP	L30	30/30	–	–	GR

💻 Internet Access   WiFi Wireless Internet Access   WG Waterway Guide Cruising Club Partner   ⬤onSpot dockside WiFi facility
See WaterwayGuide.com for current rates, fuel prices, web site addresses, and other up-to-the-minute information. *(Information in the table is provided by the facilities.)*

The South Fork is residential for a distance but becomes commercial where it makes a sharp turn to the west at Pier 17 and River Bend Marina. Several bridges cross the South Fork:

- **Davie Blvd. Bridge** (21-foot closed vertical clearance): Opens on signal, except Monday through Friday from 7:30 a.m. to 9:00 a.m., and from 4:30 p.m. to 6:00 p.m. (except federal holidays), when the draw need not open.
- **I-95 Twin Bridges** (55-foot fixed vertical clearance). There is also a fixed 55-foot vertical clearance railroad bridge for Tri-Rail passenger trains running alongside the I-95 Twin Bridges.
- **SCL Railroad Bascule Bridge** (2-foot closed vertical clearance): Open except when trains are approaching.
- **SR 84 Bridge** (21-foot closed vertical clearance): Span opens only with 24-hour advance notice. This unmanned bridge is one of the few in Fort Lauderdale not equipped with a VHF radio. Call the bridge at 954-776-4300.
- **I-595 Bridge** (40-foot fixed vertical clearance).

New River (North Fork)

Just beyond its mouth, the New River wanders lazily through a short stretch edged by fine lawns and some of the area's older, grander and more gracious homes. Entering the commercial area, you pass over south Florida's only traffic tunnel, which carries U.S. Highway 1 beneath the river. This area was Fort Lauderdale's original business district and its first boating center. Long before World War II, the wooded riverbanks were lined with docks, much as they are today.

Spanning the north and south banks of the New River is the Riverwalk Park, a waterfront park in the heart of downtown with lush tropical landscaping and winding brick walkways linking attractions, restaurants and shops. Most cruisers thoroughly enjoy this stretch of river dockage. Water traffic is heavy on weekends, and extra fendering is desirable, although wake action is not nearly as noticeable as might be expected. The variety of watercraft is seemingly endless, and the sights and sounds of this traffic are fascinating. Las Olas Boulevard offers excellent restaurants, gourmet food shops, fashionable boutiques and specialty shops.

NEW RIVER AND DANIA CUT-OFF CANAL

The contolling depth was 6½ feet in New River from the daybeacon R "10" to the William H. Marshall Memorial Bridge; thence 6 feet 26° 05' 57.2" N 80°09'45.1" W; thence 10 feet to 26°05'42" N 10' 21.8" W; thence 3½ feet to Dania Cut-off Canal.

Dec. 1976 - Jan. 1995

In Dania Cut-off Canal, the last reported depths were 2 feet to the U.S.1 Highway Bridge; thence 5 feet to a point in 26°03'35"N 80°08'06"W

NEW RIVER, SOUTH FORK, DANIA, NOAA CHART 11467

DANIA CUT-OFF CANAL EXTENSION

SCALE 1:24,000

SERVICES			SHOPPING/DINING			MARINAS	

	SERVICES
1	Library

	ATTRACTIONS
2	Broward Center for the Performing Arts
3	Historic Stranahan House Museum
4	History Museum Fort Lauderdale
5	Museum of Discovery and Science

6	Old Fort Lauderdale Village & Museum
7	Riverwalk

	SHOPPING/DINING
8	Briny's Riverfront Pub
9	Himmarshee Historic District
10	DownTowner
11	Las Olas Riverfront

12	Pirate Republic Bar, Seafood & Grill

	MARINAS
13	Cooley's Landing Marina
14	New River Diwntown Docks
15	Riverfront Marina

The New River area of Fort Lauderdale is an important destination port on the ICW and has many onshore attractions and superb boating amenities. Spanning the north and south banks of the river is the Riverwalk Park, a waterfront park in the heart of downtown. The lush tropical landscape and winding walkways link attractions, restaurants and shops and is the epicenter for special events, including a Jazz Brunch, held the first Sunday of every month in the Bubier Park area of Riverwalk.

Attractions: Coming up the New River you will pass the historic Stranahan House, which looks a bit out of place among the high-rise buildings that flank it. The two-story structure was originally a 1901 trading post that was later converted to a residence. It is open for tours daily at 335 SE 6th Ave. (954-524-4736). You will have to "hoof it" as there is no dockage here.

The Broward Center for the Performing Arts is a commanding presence at the heart of historic Sailboat Bend. Located at 201 SW 5th Ave., the center is home of the Florida Grand Opera and also hosts ballet and dance performances, music, theater, family entertainment and more (954-462-0222). The downtown district is also home to the Museum of Discovery and Science (401 SW 2nd St., 954-467-6637). Hands-on exhibits and an IMAX 3D Theater are the big draws here. There is a long floating dock available to the public, for day use only, in front of the Museum of Discovery and Science. You can tie up your boat and walk a very short distance to all of the museums and attractions.

Continuing our museum tour, the History Museum Fort Lauderdale is housed in Broward County's oldest standing hotel at 231 SW 2nd Ave.(954-463-4431) and at Old Fort Lauderdale Village & Museum are several more historic buildings, including an inn, a schoolhouse and a library (219 SW 2nd Ave., 954- 463-4431).

The Sun Trolley offers inexpensive ($1.00 in exact change for each trip or you can purchase an all-day pass for $3.00) transportation around the downtown area and to the beach (every 10 minutes on weekends) as well as several other routes for similar fares (or free to the Tri-Rail). Information is available at 954-761-3543 and at suntrolley.com.

Adventuresome travelers can take the shuttle bus to the Tri-Rail Terminal just west of I-95 off Broward Boulevard, three miles from the New River dockage area. The Tri-Rail (800-874-7245) makes connections to towns with marinas from West Palm Beach to Miami. The city bus terminal, located near the river, provides excellent transportation anywhere in Broward County. Rental car agencies with competitive rates are also conveniently located.

Shopping/Dining: For convenient provisioning, Publix supermarket/pharmacy (601 S. Andrews Ave.) is just a short walk or bike ride away from the New River Downtown Marina.

The Himmarshee Historic District, inland and adjacent to this area, features numerous restaurants and shops in a restored historical setting. Nightly live entertainment at the gazebo, a 23-screen cinema with new releases, restaurants ranging from casual to fine cuisine and extraordinary martini bars are all part of this festive riverfront.

On the north side of the New River, just east of the FEC Railroad Bridge, is a large shopping and entertainment complex, Las Olas Riverfront, with a dazzling array of shops and restaurants. (Visit lasolasboulevard.com for a map and details.)

For riverfront dining, try the historic DownTowner (10 S. New River Dr., 954-463-9800) or Briny's Riverfront Pub (305 S. Andrews Ave., 954-376-4742), which is accessible by water taxi. The Pirate Republic Bar, Seafood & Grill, located across the river from the Broward Center, can accommodate vessels to 100 feet on their docks (first come, first served) if you dine with them (400 SW 3rd Ave., 954-761-3500).

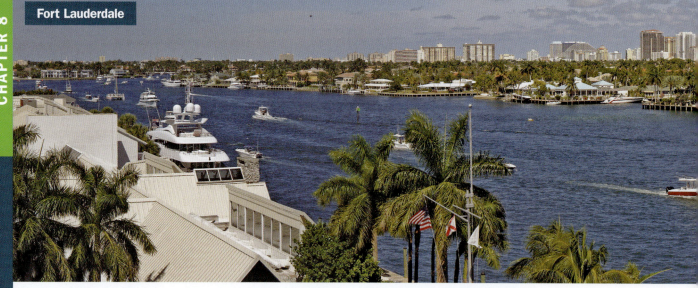

Fort Lauderdale

NAVIGATION: Use NOAA Chart 11470. A Slow-Speed/Minimum-Wake Zone is in effect along the New River between the ICW and Tarpon Bend, where the Tarpon River branches off to the south. The last New River marker, red daybeacon "12," marks a hard shoal extending into the channel at Tarpon Bend. Deep-draft vessels should not hug this too closely as they make the hard turn around it. The bottom is a rock ledge. After red daybeacon "12," keep to the middle of the river. Minimum depths are around 8 feet at MLW, but there are plans to dredge it to accommodate the megayachts needing to get to the facilities upriver. Above Tarpon Bend, the New River is an Idle-Speed/No-Wake Zone.

Beyond the William H. Marshall Memorial Bridge (20-foot closed vertical clearance), the river branches, and the principal channel takes the South Fork into another opulent residential section. The water is brown and murky, tinted by the Everglades' cypress swamps and drains into an inland link in the river. Floating water hyacinths, coconuts and other debris appear frequently. Occasionally, you will spot the broad back of a manatee or the bulging eyes of an alligator. Another Idle-Speed/No-Wake Zone on the New River extends about 500 yards on either side of the I-95 Twin Bridges.

Dockage: At the New River Downtown Docks, the city offers dockage along the river available on a first-come, first-served basis or by reservation a few days in advance. The docks (actually a seawall) are located in the heart of downtown, beginning a short distance upriver from the SE 3rd Ave. Bridge and extending intermittently to the William H. Marshall (7th Ave.) Bridge at Cooley's Landing. There is ample deep water dockage, two pump-out stations and grassy picnic areas. Be aware that the current in this area can be

swift. On the same side of the river, just above the FEC Railroad Bridge, is the Riverfront Marina, which does not offer transient dockage but offers repairs and sells gas. There is a supermarket just two blocks south of the bridge on Andrews Ave.

Cooley's Landing Marina, also city owned, is located on the north bank and is situated next to the Arts and Science District. The marina has slips and sells some supplies. The city dockmaster's office is on the south bank, just east of the Andrews Ave. Bridge and next door to the DownTowner (954-463-9800). The Himmarshee Historic District's shops and restaurants, as well as Las Olas Riverfront are within easy walking distance.

New River (South Fork)

NAVIGATION: Use NOAA Chart 11467. A 2-mile stretch of yacht yards, service shops and freshwater storage begins less than 1 mile above the Davie Blvd. Bridge, on the New River's South Fork. The channel accommodates deep-draft vessels to the storage and yacht-repair yards up to the I-95 Twin Bridges (55-foot fixed vertical clearance). You may encounter strong currents near the twin bridges and around the nearby railroad bridges; turning room is limited. Extra caution is needed here.

The South New River Canal continues to the southwest. Although narrow, it holds good depths, but a 50-foot-high cable south of the boatyards limits vertical clearance here. This is as far as most cruising boats go. The South New River Canal passes under the SR 84 Bridge (21-foot closed vertical clearance) and the I-595 Bridge (40-foot fixed vertical clearance) before joining the Dania Cut-off Canal, located 2 miles south.

Dockage: Most of the facilities on the South Fork of the New River offer repairs. For details on each facility, see the "New River" marina table in this chapter.

On the north side of the I-95 Twin Bridges is the 180-slip Lauderdale Marine Center and the smaller (89-slip) Riverbend at LMC. Both offer repairs. Lauderdale Marin Center has a 485-ton lift and can handle large repairs. Fort Lauderdale Boatyard and Marina was closed at press time 2018 due to demolition and construction. Marina Mile Yachting Center is located on the southern shore and is a service/storage facility only. Next is Marina Bay Marina Resort, which offers "country club style" amenities, including an expansive activity center with a resort pool, fitness and tennis facilities, private theater, racquetball court, sauna and spa and complete Captain's Lounge.

Nearby Yacht Haven Park & Marina is a combination RV park and marina. It is located in a gated 20-acre, park-like setting and welcomes long- and short-term boaters. Cable Marine West is in a basin to the south followed by Rolly Marine Service. Both offer repairs and services but no transient space.

The next group of marinas is about 0.5 mile south. Billfish Marina is first, followed by Yacht Management South Florida, Bradford Marine Inc., Roscioli Yachting Center and Marina Road Boat Yard (on the South Fork New River Canal). All of these facilities offer varying levels of repairs, sales and service.

Dania Cut-Off Canal Extension

NAVIGATION: Use NOAA Chart 11467 (New River Extension and Dania Cut-Off Canal Extension insets). Chart 11467 notes that in the Dania Cut-Off Canal, the latest reported depths were 2 feet at MLW west of the U.S. 1 Highway Bridge. This passage along the canal is surrounded by wilderness and swamp, has a 2-foot controlling depth at MLW and is suited for small-boat exploration only. East of this junction is a water-control gate that rises like a guillotine to allow vessels with less than 10-foot vertical clearance to pass beneath. Various fixed bridges have limited vertical clearances that are not shown on the chart, but 10 feet MLW is the controlling

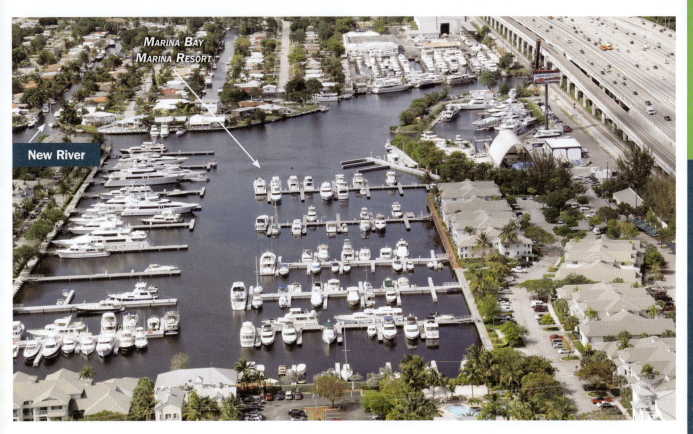

New River

MARINA BAY
MARINA RESORT

height west of Dania. For this reason, the Dania Cut-Off Canal is typically entered from the ICW, proceeding to the west. There are several large yards at Port Laudania, where small freighters and cargo ships dock. We cover the dockage at the east end of the Dania Cut-Off Canal in the Dania Beach section of this chapter.

Dockage: The route proceeds eastward past several marinas, including Anglers Avenue Marine Center, and Sundance Marine, which both offer repairs and services but no transient docking. Thunderboat Marine Service Center–Dania Beach sells gas and offers storage but no transient slips; Cozy Cove, however, offers transient dockage if space is available. Call first.

■ PORT EVERGLADES TO HOLLYWOOD

Port Everglades–ICW Mile 1066 to Mile 1069

Port Everglades is a modern deepwater harbor and the third of Fort Lauderdale's important boating areas. Ashore, expensive waterfront homes overlook the endless stream of cruise ships, recreational craft, tankers, freighters and warships constantly parading through the

inlet. Nearly 150 warships, both domestic and foreign, visit the port every year. Port Everglades is now off limits to private vehicular traffic, with police guards at each entrance.

⚠ Keep clear of large-vessel traffic in the busy inlets, especially Port Everglades, Government Cut and Lake Worth. The Coast Guard establishes a moving security zone for the protection of passenger vessels (cruise ships), vessels carrying cargoes of particular hazard and vessels carrying liquefied hazardous gas, when such a vessel passes buoy "PE" to enter the port. Approaching closer than 100 yards to such a vessel is prohibited without prior permission.

When such vessels are docked in the port, boat traffic may still proceed along the ICW, provided that they stay to the east of law enforcement craft and cruise ship tenders being used to mark the transit lane. When such vessels are not docked, boats may use the ICW without restriction. Occasionally, all traffic may be halted temporarily while ships are docking or undocking. Patrol craft may be contacted on VHF Channel 16 for the status of these security zones.

The Coast Guard has also established a Slow-Speed Zone in the Port Everglades Entrance Channel from the

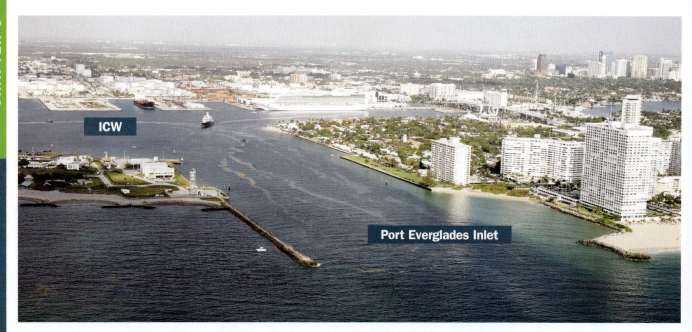

ICW

Port Everglades Inlet

outer end of the jetties to the turning basin and ICW. The Coast Guard strictly enforces this Slow-Speed Zone.

NAVIGATION: Use NOAA Charts 11470 and 11467. When approaching the port from offshore, the RACON sea buoy will be your best offshore waypoint. However, the air traffic into and out of the Fort Lauderdale airport will give you a visual aid from miles out to sea. The entire port area has deep water, with the exception of the northeastern corner outside the marked ICW channel. Deepwater docking extends to the south along the ICW to the Dania Cut-Off Canal. At the point where the ICW crosses the ship channel, keep the inlet and ICW buoys sorted out in your mind. Remember that ICW markers have a yellow triangle or square above the numerals.

Vessels southbound on the ICW follow the arrow-straight course on the chart across the turning basin into the channel leading south from the southeastern corner where the Fort Lauderdale Coast Guard Station is located. After passing close to the Coast Guard Station, be careful to avoid the mangroves and partially submerged rocks outside of the channel on the eastern side of the ICW, while keeping the required distance from the cruise ships usually berthed on the mainland side and paying close attention to the Slow-Speed/Minimum-Wake Zones.

Port Everglades Inlet

NAVIGATION: Use NOAA Chart 11467. One of the best and safest big ship inlets in Florida, Port Everglades Inlet (also called Fort Lauderdale Inlet) is well marked

with flashing buoys along the entrance channel. Currents average 0.7 knots with a tidal range of 3.1 feet in the turning basin. See the Inlets listing in the front of this guide for more information. The port and inlet may be crowded with both commercial and recreational traffic.

The inlet is a popular take-off point for cruisers heading to and from the Bahamas, fishermen heading out to the nearby Gulf Stream and skippers cruising north and south along the coast to escape the bridges and speed restrictions. It is also popular with ICW boaters hankering for different scenery.

⚠️ Vessels with mast heights over 56 feet that are headed south of Miami's Julia Tuttle Causeway Bridge (Mile 1087.2, 56-foot fixed vertical clearance) have no choice but to go outside at Port Everglades. These vessels can then rejoin the ICW via Miami's Government Cut at Dodge Island. (See sidebar: "The Outside Run to Miami.")

Dania Beach–ICW Mile 1069 to Mile 1070

Named for its early Danish settlers, the city of Dania Beach was once the "Tomato Capital of the World." Visitors today can enjoy the beach, the 800-foot-long fishing pier and a remarkable collection of antiques shops. The Dania Marine Flea Market is billed as the largest marine flea market in the world. It is held annually in March. Check online at daniamarinefleamarket.com for general information, dates and location, as it moves from year to year. Both commercial vendors and private sellers show their wares. Just about anything for a boat can be found at the event. If you love garage sales, this is the largest one of all and is worth visiting if you are passing through in March.

NAVIGATION: Use NOAA Chart 11467. The area from Port Everglades Inlet to the next bridge south along the ICW is a manatee protection Slow-Speed/Minimum-Wake Zone. Take special care opposite the power plant, where the warm discharge water frequently attracts manatees. The area is well marked with signs, and speed limitations are rigidly enforced, especially during weekends and the winter season.

Leaving Port Everglades observe the buoys and, if in doubt, favor the mainland. The eastern side is shallow and marshy with rocks outside the channel. The expanding port complex now extends to the Dania Cut-Off Canal south of the inlet at Mile 1069.4.

The Dania Cut-Off Canal area is a busy marine service center. Businesses here include well-equipped yards, modern marinas, boatbuilders and marine service specialists.

In addition to good protection, the canal offers a rare treat for this part of the coast: There are no bridges on

The Outside Run to Miami

In ordinary weather, the outside run—north or south—is easy, safe and pleasant. Proceeding out the wide, straight channel at Port Everglades Inlet, you will find good depths in waters that are reportedly clear of obstruction out beyond the jetties and inlet buoys. On the south side, the good water extends well inshore, so many boaters turn south just beyond flashing green buoy "5." On the north side, however, a submerged breakwater and a large spoil area parallel the ship channel can obstruct navigation. The local small craft that often run along the beach inside the spoil area (which sometimes surfaces at low tide) follow a hazardous course. Those aboard larger boats should stay clear of this area by standing offshore past the jetty and flashing red buoy "2."

Southbound boats can travel safely within a quarter to a half-mile of the beach, outside the breakers, all the way to Miami. This route keeps you inshore of the Gulf Stream, with its approximately 2-knot northerly set. Going north, stand out to sea to take advantage of the free push. Boats equipped with GPS will easily recognize the Gulf Stream by the increase in speed over the bottom or a sudden tendency to drift off course to the north.

The NOAA Weather Stations (Miami, WX-1, serves this area) broadcast the location of the inshore edge of the Gulf Stream from 4:00 p.m. to 8:00 p.m. on Mon., Wed. and Fri., and from 4:00 a.m. to 8:00 a.m. on Tues., Thurs. and Sat. in the fall and winter. NOAA Weather does not give Gulf Stream hazards and locations in periods of warm weather because satellite photographs do not adequately distinguish between water and air temperatures.

The western edge of the Gulf Stream ranges from as close as 1 nm offshore to more than 10 nm; the width of the Gulf Stream is also stated in the WX broadcasts. The Gulf Stream really moves water. A sailboat can travel along at a good clip going south in the stream and stay in the same place all day. Sometimes southbound boats are lucky enough to find a counter-current running close to the shoreline.

Hollywood Beach, FL

DANIA CUT-OFF CANAL		Largest Vessel Accommodated	VHF Channel Monitored	Transient Berths / Total Berths	Approach / Dockside Depth (reported)	Floating Docks	Gas / Diesel	Groceries, Ice, Marine Supplies, Snacks	Repairs: Hull, Engine, Propeller	Lift (tonnage), Crane, Rail	Min/Max Amps	Laundry, Pool, Showers, Courtesy Car	Pump-Out Station	Nearby: Grocery Store, Motel, Restaurant
				Dockage			**Supplies**		**Services**					
1. Dania Beach Marina WiFi	954-924-3796	–	16	call/92	4/4	F	–	IS	–	–	30/50	LS	P	MR
2. Harbour Towne Marina ▢ 1 W of 1068.6	954-926-0300	200	16/11	35/165	17/7	–	GD	GIMS	HEP	L100	30/200+	LS	P	GMR
3. Sun Power Diesel & Marine 1 W of 1068.6	954-237-2200	100	–	2/13	20/10	F	–	IMS	E	R	50/50	–	–	GMR
4. Playboy Marine Center WiFi 1 W of 1068.6	954-920-0533	86	16	3/3	17/15	–	–	IM	–	L88,C18	30/50	S	–	GMR
5. Royale Palm Yacht Basin WiFi 1 W of 1068.6	954-923-5900	80	78	30/60	7/7	–	–	–	HEP	L70	30/50	LS	–	GMR
6. Derecktor Shipyards ▢ WiFi 1 W of 1068.6	954-920-5756	210	–	1/49	17/14	F	–	–	HEP	L900,C35	30/200+	S	–	GMR
7. Marine Max East Florida Yacht Center 1 W of 1068.6	954-926-0308	112	16/71	call/11	6/6	–	–	M	HEP	L90	30/50	–	–	GMR
8. Seahaven Superyacht Marina	561-625-6443	200	–	call/20	–	–	–	–	–	–	–	–	–	GMR
HOLLYWOOD BEACH AREA														
9. Hollywood Marina WiFi 1072.1	954-921-3035	115	16/68	15/55	6/7	–	GD	I	–	–	30/50	LS	P	GMR
10. Suntex Marina at Hollywood ▢ onSpot 1072.5	954-457-8557	120	16	15/190	15/8	–	GD	GIS	–	–	30/100	LPS	P	GMR

▢ Internet Access   WiFi Wireless Internet Access   WG Waterway Guide Cruising Club Partner   onSpot dockside WiFi facility

See WaterwayGuide.com for current rates, fuel prices, web site addresses, and other up-to-the-minute information. *(Information in the table is provided by the facilities.)*

DANIA CUT-OFF CANAL TO HOLLYWOOD BEACH, NOAA CHART 11467

the ICW between the canal and Port Everglades so boats berthed on the canal have unimpeded access to the inlet and ocean. Moreover, it is the nearest dockage to the Fort Lauderdale–Hollywood International Airport for those arriving and departing by air.

The Dania Cut-Off Canal is an interesting waterway to explore. Consult the New River text earlier in this chapter for the North and South Forks to the Dania Cut-Off Canal. When approaching the canal from either direction along the ICW, keep a sharp lookout for high-speed traffic swinging out of the canal into the ICW.

Dockage: Dania Beach Marina, just off the ICW on the east side behind an 18-foot vertical clearance fixed bridge, offers transient dockage but reports 4-foot dockside depths at MLW; call ahead.

On the Dania Cut-Off Canal, Harbour Towne Marina has over 20 waterside businesses located on the property and is able to provide a wide range of services and amenities for professional captains as well as the weekend boater. They offer wet and dry storage, can accommodate transient vessels to 200 feet, sell fuel and offer repairs (100-ton lift). Sun Power Diesel & Marine is in the next basin to the west, with limited transient space and repairs.

Playboy Marine Center is a "Do-It-Yourself" boatyard but has highly qualified technicians should you decide to seek professional services. Each visiting boat receives a clean, spacious work space equipped with its own water connection plus electrical hook-ups. They also provide (at no charge) ladders and sturdy scaffolding for ease of access to elevated work areas. Their 88-ton lift can handle sail or power boats to 80 feet in length (with a maximum beam of 21 feet).

Royale Palm Yacht Basin has ample dockage and offers repairs, while Derecktor Shipyards and Marine Max East Florida Yacht Center are primarily repair/service facilities. Derector has a 900-ton lift and a 35-ton crane and handle most any large (or small) job.

The new Seahaven Superyacht Marina was scheduled at press time to open in fall 2018. They can accommodate vessels to 200 feet in deep water slips. Call ahead for details.

Hollywood–ICW Mile 1073

South of Dania Beach is an area that has become almost a suburb of Fort Lauderdale and Miami. Hollywood Beach's proximity to Fort Lauderdale makes it a fine alternative when berths are hard to find.

Just a short walk from the Hollywood Municipal Marina, across the Hollywood Blvd. Bridge, is beautiful Hollywood Beach and Oceanwalk, a 2-mile-long, brick-lined pedestrian promenade with lots of outdoor dining options. A few miles west (a 45-minute walk) on U.S. 1 in downtown Hollywood you will find extensive shopping and a historic, recreated old town with a new family-oriented park in the center of Hollywood Circle.

NAVIGATION: Use NOAA Chart 11467. The **Dania Beach Blvd. (A1A) Bascule Bridge** (Mile 1069.4) has 22-foot vertical clearance and opens on the hour and half hour. South of Dania Beach, the ICW cuts through several broad natural areas where the water is spread thinly, and the dredged channel is narrow. Pay careful attention to navigational markers and your depth sounder. The **Sheridan St. Bascule Bridge** (Mile 1070.5, 22-foot closed vertical clearance), which opens at 15 and 45 minutes past the hour, has a dogleg approach. The channel cuts across from the east close to the western shore before passing under the bridge. Be sure not to stray out of the charted, marked channel. Shoaling near green daybeacon "39" leaves depths at about 6 feet at MLW. Stay clear of the submerged pilings along the east shore at flashing green "39A."

The speed limit within the ICW channel is 25 mph (with a Slow-Speed/Minimum-Wake Zone buffer within 50 feet of shore) until reaching an Idle-Speed/No-Wake Zone about one-quarter mile south of the Sheridan Street Bridge, then continues past the next bridge, the **Hollywood Beach Blvd. (SR 820) Bascule Bridge** (Mile 1072.2, 25-foot closed vertical clearance), which

Broward County has placed buoys at locations of interest in the offshore waters for **divers and snorkelers.** To protect the coral from damage caused by anchoring, the buoys should be used as moorings. Buoy locations are:

Pompano Drop-Off: N 26° 13.034'/W 80° 05.028'
Hall of Fame: N 26° 11.581'/W 80° 05.00'
Anglin's Ledge: N 26° 11.338'/W 80° 05.246'
Oakland Ridges: N 26° 09.276'/W 80° 05.072'
The Caves: N 26° 07.631'/W 80° 05.354'
Barracuda Reef: N 26° 04.575'/W 80° 05.505'

The mooring buoys are maintained by the Natural Resources Planning and Management Division. For more information or to report a problem, call 954-519-1270.

opens on the hour and half-hour. Farther south, Slow-Speed/Minimum-Wake Zones will alternate with 25-mph limits within the ICW channel and more Idle-Speed/No-Wake Zones. Watch carefully for regulatory signs and read them carefully. In some areas, the ICW channel is exempt; in others, different speeds apply on weekends and/or seasonally, and other restrictions may apply.

⚠ Hollywood Beach flashing "39A" at Mile 1070.7 was reported to be destroyed in spring 2018. The steel pile wreckage is marked but may pose a hazard to navigation.

Dockage: South of the Sheridan Street Bridge, the eastern shore is lined with casual restaurants complete with tie-up locations on the bulkhead for dining customers. The municipal Hollywood Marina lies at the southeast corner of North Lake (Mile 1072.1) and maintains slips for transients plus sells gas and diesel fuel. Call ahead if you wish to dock here. Controlling depths in the middle of North Lake at large are reportedly as little as 1.5 to 2.5 feet at MLW. If docking at Hollywood Marina, stay close to the docks and follow the contour of the docks; minimum depth alongside is reportedly 7 feet at MLW.

At red daybeacon "42," just south of the Hollywood Blvd. Bridge, Suntex Marina at Hollywood offers a wealth of amenities. In addition to the conventional water and shore power, the facility offers slip-side cable TV (for a fee), a vacuum pump-out system for each slip and a lounge with Internet access, TV and daily newspapers. The Hollywood Beach boardwalk is just minutes away.

Anchorage: Near the Sheridan Street Bridge, anchorages are available both north and south of the bridge along the east shore. The little cove with the beach at the north anchorage is within the boundaries of a park where anchoring is prohibited. Therefore, be sure you drop your anchor a bit north of the cove for 7-foot MLW depths. On the south side, there is a snug anchorage for one or two boats north of the line of docks along the edge of the ICW in 9- to 11-foot MLW depths. Dinghy access to the adjacent park is prohibited.

A short distance south of the Hollywood Boulevard Bridge is South Lake. Although the chart still shows depths of 4 and 5 feet at MLW, dredging has increased controlling depths to 28 feet at MLW and as much as 40 feet; investigate with caution. There is room for a number of boats and the holding is good, but you may be rolled by the wake of passing boats on the ICW.

Next Stop

Next the *Waterway Guide* takes you to the Greater Miami Area, including North Miami, Miami Beach, the Miami River, Key Biscayne, Coconut Grove and Coral Gables.

Hollywood

Miami & Biscayne Bay

 ICW Mile 1074–Mile 1106

VHF FL Bridges: Channel 09

CHARTS NOAA 11451, 11465, 11467

Miami today is a top global city. It is a uniquely multicultural region with a large and diverse Hispanic population; the global headquarters for major multinationals, international trade, banking and tourism; and the cruise capital of the world. Year-round outdoor sports, theater and an abundance of hotels, restaurants and nightclubs provide visitors with a kaleidoscope of opportunities for entertainment and the shoreside facilities are excellent.

Our coverage of the Greater Miami area includes from the mainland to Miami Beach, Government Cut and the islands of Biscayne Bay, all of which could be considered part of the Florida Keys, but in reality are normally considered part of the approach to the Keys. Boca Chita is considered the official start of the Florida Keys by water and Key Largo by land. Visiting boaters may call the Marine Council at 305-569-1672 for information on the local marine and tourism industry.

■ NORTH MIAMI BEACH AREA

Hallandale to Bakers Haulover Inlet– ICW Mile 1074 to Mile 1080

South of Hollywood, the channel is well marked, relatively straight and bordered by high-rise condominium buildings leading through this growing suburban area to North Miami and Greater Miami.

NAVIGATION: Use NOAA Chart 11467. The **Hallandale Beach Blvd. (SR 858) Bascule Bridge** at Mile 1074.0 (26-foot closed vertical clearance) opens at 15 and 45 minutes past the hour. At this point to south of Sunny Isles, boaters must comply with the Idle-Speed/No-Wake (minimum steerage) and Slow Speed/Minimum-Wake (5 knots) signs (except for one brief passage in the middle of Dumfoundling Bay, where signs indicate a 25-mph speed limit in the channel).

Hallandale & North Miami Beach, FL

		Largest Vessel Accommodated	VHF Channel Monitored	Dockage: Transient Berths / Total Berths	Dockage: Approach / Dockside Depth (reported)	Supplies: Floating Docks	Supplies: Gas / Diesel	Supplies: Groceries, Ice, Marine Supplies, Snacks	Services: Repairs: Hull, Engine, Propeller	Services: Lift (tonnage), Crane, Rail	Services: Min/Max Amps	Services: Laundry, Pool, Showers, Courtesy Car	Services: Pump-Out Station	Services: Nearby: Grocery Store, Motel, Restaurant
HALLANDALE														
1. Hallandale Beach City Marina (WiFi)	954-457-1653	60	–	3/26	–	–	–	–	–	–	–	S	P	GMR
2. Suntex Marina at Aventura (internet)(onSpot) 1075.2	305-935-4295	120	16/68	call/99	20/10	–	–	GI	–	–	30/100	–	P	GMR
3. Turnberry Marina (internet)(WiFi)(WG) 1075.5	305-933-6934	225	16/68	30/60	30/20	F	–	IS	–	–	30/100	LPS	P	GMR
NORTH MIAMI BEACH														
4. Aquamarina Hi Lift 1077.3	305-931-2550	40	–	call/9		F	G	IMS	HEP	L	30/30	–	–	R
5. Williams Island Marina (internet)(WiFi) 1076.6	305-937-7813	160	16/10	15/106	10/8	F	–	IS	–	–	30/100	LPS	–	GMR
6. Marina Palms Yacht Club (WiFi)	786-707-2629	100	16	12/112	/9	F	GD	IS	–	–	30/200+	–	–	GR
BAKERS HAULOVER INLET AREA														
7. Bill Bird Marina at Haulover Park (WiFi) 1079.7	305-947-3525	90	–	call/150	8/8.5	F	GD	IMS	–	–	30/100	LS	P	GMR
8. Bal Harbour Yacht Club – PRIVATE (WiFi)	305-865-6048	140	–	call/35	8/8	–	GD	–	–	–	–	–	–	–
9. Keystone Point Marina 1.3 W of 1080.8	305-940-6236	110	16/09	10/26	8/8	F	GD	IMS	HEP	L	30/50	–	P	GMR

(internet) Internet Access (WiFi) Wireless Internet Access (WG) Waterway Guide Cruising Club Partner (onSpot) dockside WiFi facility
See WaterwayGuide.com for current rates, fuel prices, web site addresses, and other up-to-the-minute information. *(Information in the table is provided by the facilities.)*

The fixed **William Lehman Causeway (SR 856) Bridge** crosses the ICW at Mile 1076.3 with a 65-foot vertical clearance. South of Golden Beach, the ICW is especially well marked as it enters the Miami area. Dumfoundling Bay is a broad, open and generally shallow body of water with a few deeper patches along its eastern shore. (There is no anchorage room here; it is all a cable crossing area.) At Dumfoundling Bay's southern end, the marked route crosses over to the western shore. To the north of the Maule Lake entrance, there is a shoal marked by a privately maintained white daybeacon; give it a wide berth.

From Dumfoundling Bay, the ICW enters Biscayne Creek, home of the community of Sunny Isles (on the eastern shore). At Mile 1078.0, the **NE 163rd St. (Sunny Isles) Twin Bridges**, with a 30-foot charted closed vertical clearance, links that community to the mainland. The bridge opens on signal, except from 7:00 a.m. to 6:00 p.m., Monday through Friday (except federal holidays) and from 10:00 a.m. to 6:00 p.m., on weekends and federal holidays, when the draw need only open at 15 and 45 minutes past the hour.

Dockage: The Hallandale Beach City Marina is located at Mile 1074 on the west side of the ICW in the canal just north of the Hallandale Beach Blvd. Bridge. The marina has just three reserved transient slips. Be aware that there is a fixed bridge (**Three Islands Blvd. Bridge**) with 17-foot vertical clearance prior to reaching the marina. Call the marina for more approach details.

The Suntex Marina–Aventura, located across from Golden Beach, accepts transients in their large, protected harbor. They have numerous amenities including waterfront dining and great shopping (including groceries) adjacent to the property.

To the south, at Mile 1075.5, Turnberry Marina is a world-class hotel marina offering full amenities, including WiFi, laundry facilities and a dockside pool. Complimentary shuttle service is available between the marina, Turnberry Isle Miami Resort, the beach access and Aventura Mall. The marina also offers personalized dockside service.

Past the William Lehman Causeway Bridge on the western shore is Aquamarina Hi Lift on a canal cut at Mile 1077.3. They sell gas and offer some repairs but no slips (private).

Just to the south, a straight, narrow and deep canal cuts westward off the ICW to Maule Lake and Williams Island Marina, which offers full resort amenities and dockage in a well-protected harbor. Nestled on 84 lush acres, Williams Island offers an amenities-rich experience; you can go to the spa or gym, play tennis at one of the 16 courts or have a dip in one of the multiple pools. Afterwards, enjoy fine dining, an inviting café or the pool and bar grill.

Marina Palms Yacht Club is in a condominium complex in Maule Lake and has slips, along with gas and diesel fuel. They offer a full range of activities from jet skiing to kayaking and snorkeling. Reservations should be made in advance.

Anchorage: It is possible to anchor in Maule Lake west of red daybeacon "54" in 8 to 20 feet at MLW. Even though this provides all-around protection, the holding

HALLANDALE, NOAA CHART 11467

NORTH MIAMI BEACH, BAKERS HAULOVER INLET AREA, NOAA CHART 11467

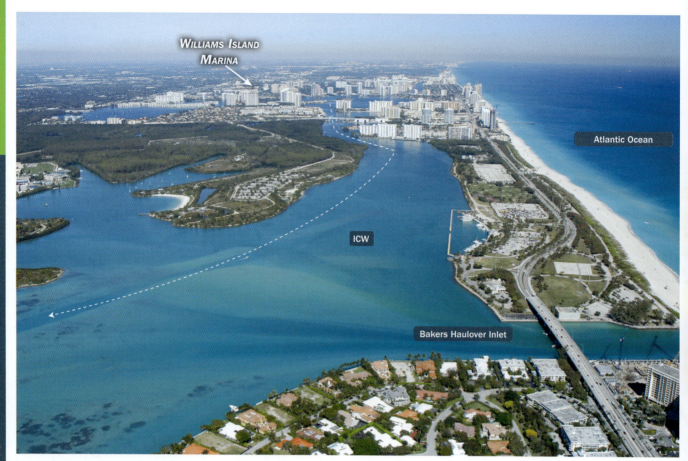

is just fair due to the mud and rock bottom. There is shore access at the launch ramp with plenty of shopping within walking distance.

Bakers Haulover Inlet

When you observe that the tidal current is speeding up along the ICW route, you are nearing Bakers Haulover Inlet. Northernmost of Miami's entrances from the Atlantic Ocean, Bakers Haulover Inlet is heavily used by fishermen and local boats.

NAVIGATION: Use NOAA Chart 11467. Coming in from the Atlantic, Bakers Haulover Inlet is marked by a quick-flashing white light on the south jetty and is spanned by the **Bakers Haulover Inlet Bridge** (32-foot fixed vertical clearance). Jetties are short here, and currents are strong (2.0 to 3.0 knots). The inlet can become especially nasty when wind and current oppose. Because of this, it is best to head just 8.3 miles south to Government Cut, a clear, well-marked Class A inlet.

If you are determined to use this inlet, turn to port out of the ICW at red daybeacon "4A" and take a bearing on the entrance to the inlet, a straight shot. The shoaling problem on the ICW channel west of Bakers Haulover Inlet, Mile 1080, south of red daybeacon "6A," is

legendary. Periodically it is dredged, and like clockwork, it fills back in.

Follow buoys "7," "7A," "7B" and "7C" even if it appears that they are leading you to one side of the normal channel. If the sun is at the proper angle, you can see the path through the shoal area.

⚠️ Severe shoaling exists in the vicinity of Biscayne Bay Buoy "7B." The shoal protrudes into the channel on the east side, which reduces the channel width by approximately half of the charted depths at press time in summer 2018. Buoy "7B" has been relocated to mark the best water. Watch for a strong set to the west with flood tide and to the east with the ebb. This is a very busy area of the ICW so you need to give it your undivided attention. See the Waterway Explorer at waterwayguide.com for news and navigational updates.

There is a Slow-Speed/Minimum-Wake restriction along this entire area. See the Inlet section at the front of this guide for more information on Bakers Haulover Inlet.

Dockage: North of the inlet on the east side of the ICW is Bill Bird Marina at Haulover Park with slips, both

Marina

Berths within Protected Harbour
10 foot Deep-Water Approach
Monitored VHF Channel 16
106 Yacht Berths | Max 160 Ft/8 Ft Draft
Parallel Docking for Larger Yachts
Three Phase Electric Dockage
North Marina Slips with Pump Out
Wi Fi Internet & Cable
24 Hour Monitored Security
Complimentary Club Membership

Marina Office

Staffed with over 30 years of Experience
Richly appointed Lobby & Reception
Fully Equipped Business Center
Spacious Conference Room
Boaters Lounge with Smart TV
Top-of-the-line Laundry Facility
Modern Showers & Lockers
Convenient Fitness Center

Club Amenities

27,000 Sq. Ft. Spa & Fitness Center
   with personalized programs
16 Hard & HAR-TRU Courts and Tennis
   Center with Pro Shop
Fully Refurbished Island Club
Three Dining Venues
   Island Club Prime | Fine Dining
   The Cafe | Overlooking Tennis
   Pool Bar & Grille | Informal Open Air

Welcome to Williams Island, The Florida Riviera, nestled on 84 acres in Aventura, Florida, mid-way between Miami and Fort Lauderdale. Close to both airports and seaports. Williams Island offers an exclusive, private way of life to those accustomed to the finest of things at one of South Florida's most prestigious addresses. This magnificent Marina worthy of those in its sister Rivieras enjoys a protected harbour with berth's up to 160 feet and depths of 10 feet approaching the marina and 8 feet within the marina itself, plus a Marine Basin area to help assure a calm, restful environment. Our 106 berths are as comfortable and convenient for our boaters as they are for their vessels.

Marina guests will be treated to an amenity-rich lifestyle that encompasses an all-new Marina office with richly appointed conveniences, and complimentary Williams Island Club membership. Williams Island Club Amenities include a newly renovated Spa and Fitness Center. The Grand Slam-inspired Tennis Center with 16 tennis courts is expertly staffed. Exquisite fine dining at the Island Club Prime, an inviting Cafe overlooking Center Court, and the Pool Bar & Grille offer relaxed pool side tropical favorites. Entertainment and Social events are offered in the recently refurbished Island Club.

The Marina is conveniently open daily from 9 am to 6 pm.

4100 Island Boulevard, Aventura, Florida 33160 | 305.937.7813 office | 305.936.5713 fax
WilliamsIslandMarina.com | dockmaster@WilliamsIslandMarina.com

gas and diesel fuel and repairs. Bal Harbour Yacht Club to the south in a basin off Indian Creek is private and does not accept transients for dockage or fuel.

On the mainland opposite Bakers Haulover Inlet is the start of North Miami. Here, in protected New Arch Creek, are a number of boating amenities, repair yards and stores that are eager to serve transient mariners, including Keystone Point Marina. There is a well-marked approach channel leading west from ICW red daybeacon "12." The marina is usually full so call in advance to check on the availability of a slip. Keystone is locally known for their very competitive fuel pricing.

Anchorage: One of the finest overnight anchorages along this section of the ICW is the basin across the ICW from Bakers Haulover Inlet at Mile 1080. The only drawback is its entrance. According to cruiser reports, at high tide you should turn northwest off the ICW, approximately 75 feet north of red daybeacon "6A," and then slowly head directly toward the large, green, rounded roof of the Florida International University athletic building (approximately 305 degrees magnetic). To pass safely between the 3-foot MLW bar to port and the 4-foot-deep spoils area to the north, use the large-scale inset on side B of Chart 11467. If you encounter depths of less than 8 feet at MLW within the first couple of hundred feet, you are beginning to stray out of the channel. Once you pass over the bar (soft mud and sand), you will find 8- to 12-foot MLW depths. Inside this virtually undeveloped deepwater basin are serene anchorages protected from all wind directions. The bottom is quite soft (there may be debris in some places); make sure that your anchor is set well. Visiting boaters are not permitted ashore on the University's property.

Bakers Haulover Inlet to Government Cut–ICW Mile 1080 to Mile 1090

A variety of routes wait south of Broad Causeway Bridge. While threading between markers, passing under or through various bridges and causeways, the mariner can opt to stay with the ICW to Miami and the Keys, or leave the ICW, via any of several routes, to explore Miami Beach.

NAVIGATION: Use NOAA Chart 11467. Use the Miami Harbor Entrance Tide Tables. For high tide at Baker's Haulover Inlet, add 57 minutes; for low tide, add 1 hour 37 minutes. The upper bay is extremely shallow, and the ICW cuts diagonally across it from northeast to southwest down to the 79th Street JFK Causeway. The

Offshore Run from Miami

Coming up on the outside from the south, northbound boats that want to enter inshore waters can take either Cape Florida Channel or Biscayne Channel, once they have passed Fowey Rocks Light, or they can continue on to Government Cut. The Miami GPS Differential Beacon (nominal range 75 miles) is located on Virginia Key near the west end of the fixed bridge across Bear Cut.

Coming down along the ocean side of Key Biscayne, southbound boats should stand offshore on the run from Miami. Take a heading due south from the entrance buoys off Government Cut's Outer Bar Cut to pick up Biscayne Channel Light (better known locally as Bug Light), the 37-foot-high spidery pipe structure (flashing white every four seconds) marking the seaward entrance of Cape Florida and Biscayne Channels. Coming in at flashing red "6," you have a choice of two channels leading to Biscayne Bay. Depths in the shared entrance channel to the Cape Florida Channel and the Biscayne Channel are charted at 7 feet at MLW over the bar.

From the sea, the right-hand, northern fork is the Cape Florida Channel leading past the prominent lighthouse and the lovely palm-fringed beach. The chart clearly identifies the deep-water passage along the curving shoreline, indicating also the two shoal spots situated between 0.1 and 0.2 mile southwest of the shore. Hug the shore along the curving concrete bulkhead of the park property to clear the charted shoals, marked by green daybeacon "1." At the inner end, bear off to leave red daybeacon "2" and flashing red "4" to starboard. From the outside, this is the easiest route to No Name Harbor, the area's most popular jump-off point for mariners awaiting favorable weather for a Bahamas passage.

The southern route, which is better marked and deeper than the unmarked Cape Florida Channel, is known as Biscayne Channel. It is wide, straight, well marked and easy to run. Depths in the channel range from 11 to 16 feet. Even so, the entrance depth from the ocean sometimes limits the channel. At its western end, the channel produces good fishing during flood tide.

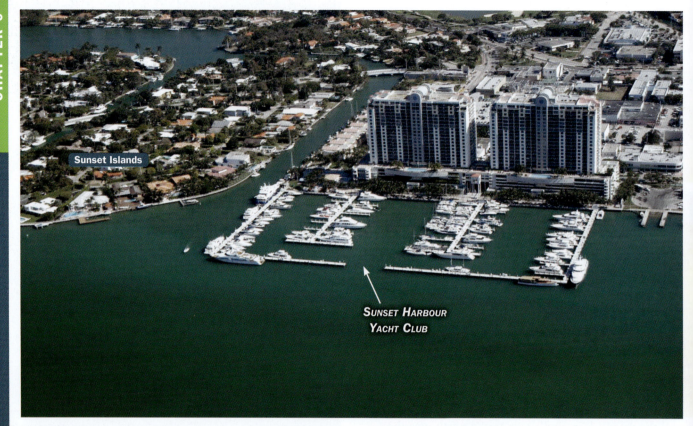

Sunset Islands

SUNSET HARBOUR
YACHT CLUB

channel is narrow but well marked, favoring the eastern shore until it passes under Broad Causeway. The **Broad Causeway Bridge** (Mile 1081.3, 16-foot closed vertical clearance) is the first of five restricted Miami spans. The span opens at 15 and 45 minutes past the hour, year-round, between 8:00 a.m. and 6:00 p.m.

Continuing south from Broad Causeway, follow your chart carefully. The channel runs diagonally across Biscayne Bay to the western shore and the west span of the **West 79th St. (JFK) Bridge** at Mile 1084.6 (25-foot closed vertical clearance, opens on signal). Be sure to indicate that you want the "western" span when calling the bridge on VHF Channel 09; there is another span of the 79th Street Causeway to the east.

To the south of the **East 79th St. Bascule Bridge** (25-foot vertical clearance, opens on signal), the Indian Creek is a narrow body of water that splits off Miami Beach proper and the beach. It skirts down across the road from many of the lavish hotels in Miami Beach's Bar Harbor area. Favor the eastern shore in Indian Creek; shoaling occurs along parts of the western bank of the creek.

Just south of the West 79th St. Bridge on the western shore is the marked entrance to Little River, which has facilities with various services for transients. South of Little River, the ICW–now narrow and surrounded by

shoals–continues relatively straight to the **Julia Tuttle Causeway (I-95) Bridge** at Mile 1087.2.

⚠️ The Julia Tuttle Bridge (56-foot fixed vertical clearance) sets the limiting overhead clearance for the inside passage from Fort Lauderdale to Miami. A few extra feet may be gained at low tide, but study the tide gauge before starting through because there is only a 2-foot tidal range.

The next pair of bridges are only a short distance apart. The **Venetian Causeway Bascule Bridge (West)**, at Mile 1088.6, has a 12-foot closed vertical clearance, and opens on signal, except from 7:00 a.m. to 7:00 p.m., Monday through Friday, when the draw need only open on the hour and half hour. The **MacArthur Causeway (A1A) Twin Bridges** at Mile 1088.8 have a 65-foot fixed vertical clearance.

Although well marked, it is wise to take particular care navigating the ICW at the MacArthur Causeway, as the markers here can be confusing. Just north of the causeway, channel markers lead off from the ICW to enter the Main Ship Channel of Government Cut. (No small-boat traffic is allowed when the cruise ships are in, and marine police diligently patrol the entrance.) Once through the MacArthur Causeway Twin Bridges, markers

Sunset Harbour Yacht Club

Sunset Harbour Yacht Club offers a unique equity club membership program where owners and shareholders share a piece of the prime waterfront real estate in Miami Beach. In addition, to their berths and a gated covered parking space, new buyers are granted membership privileges including private access to the equity members lounge, use of a private fitness centre, heated Olympic-size pool, high power electrical service, fresh water, phone, extremely fast internet, digital satellite TV and a personal dock box.

LOCAL POINTS OF INTEREST

- Ocean Drive and South Beach 1 mile away with Bal Harbour shoppes
- Le Gorce Golf Course, The Forge and Nobu Restaurant
- Art Basel International Art Show
- Annual Miami International Boat Show
- Located In Sunset Harbour Shops with 17 restaurants, 10 retail shops, 4 salons, 6 fitness/spa just across the street

Slip into South Beach

Slide into the lifestyle

TECHNICAL SERVICES

- Extremely fast hard wire internet and Wifi
- Private gym
- Olympic-size heated pool
- In-slip fueling and pump-out
- 24-hour security with CCTV and access control
- Private equity membership clubhouse
- Assigned private parking space
- Up to 480v 3 phase 200 amps

BERTHING DETAILS:

- 125 slips ranging in size from 40' up to 310'
- 8 slips over 120 feet
- Controlling draft at Mean Low Tide is 8 feet

Sunset Harbour Yacht Club

dmason@sunsetharbouryc.com

305-398-6800

www.sunsetharbouryc.com

1928 Sunset Harbour Dr.
Miami Beach, Fl 33139
USA

Did You Know?

Sunset Harbour Yacht Club is Miami Beach's only private yacht club that sells equity memberships with berths in perpetuity. The values of these berths have more than doubled in the past four years.

Upper Biscayne Bay, FL

TREASURE ISLAND AREA, INDIAN CREEK, MIAMI BEACH, GOVERNMENT CUT, NOAA CHART 11467

			Largest Vessel Accommodated	VHF Channel Monitored	Transient Berths / Total Berths	Approach / Dockside Depth (reported)	Floating Docks	Gas / Diesel	Groceries, Ice, Marine Supplies, Snacks	Repairs: Hull, Engine, Propeller	Lift (tonnage), Crane, Rail	Min/Max Amps	Laundry, Pool, Showers, Courtesy Car	Pump-Out Station	Nearby: Grocery Store, Motel, Restaurant
TREASURE ISLAND AREA					**Dockage**			**Supplies**				**Services**			
1. Grandview Palace Yacht Club 1.5 E of 1083.8	305-300-6828	120	16/68	call/118	8/8	–	G	GIMS	–	–	50/50	LPS	P	GMR
2. Gator Harbor West Marina 2 E of 1084.8	305-754-2200	45	–	call/20	6/6	–	–	I	–	–	30/100	S	–	GMR
3. Pelican Harbor Marina 1084.8	305-754-9330	50	16/68	10/112	6/6	–	GD	I	–	–	30/50	LS	P	GMR
4. North Beach Marina 1084.8	305-758-8888	43	–	call/6	–	–	–	GIMS	HEP	L9	30/30	–	–	GR
INDIAN CREEK															
5. Miami Beach Resort ☐ WiFi	305-532-3600	200	16/09	20/20	7/7	–	–	IS	–	–	30/50	LPS	–	MR
6. Fontainebleau Marina	305-538-2022	140	–	4/23	7/7	–	–	IS	–	–	30/100	PS	–	GMR
MIAMI BEACH															
7. Sunset Harbour Yacht Club ☐ WiFi 2 E of 1088	305-398-6800	210	16/11	call/125	8/8	–	D	IS	–	–	30/100	LPS	P	GMR
8. Bentley Bay Marina	305-674-0686	65	16/72	8/16	10/8	–	–	–	–	–	30/100	–	P	GMR
9. Miami Beach Marina ☐ ☁ onSpot 1089 3 E of 1089	305-673-6000	250	16/68	100/400	13/12	F	GD	GIMS	–	–	30/100	LPS	P	GMR
10. One Island Park - Miami Beach (IGY) WiFi 1089	754-701-4020	800	16/11	call/8	/40	–	GD	–	–	–	100/200+	–	–	GMR
GOVERNMENT CUT															
11. Sea Isle Marina & Yachting Center WiFi 1089	305-377-3625	132	16/11	call/220	13/10	–	GD	GIMS	–	–	30/100	LS	P	GMR
12. Island Gardens Deep Harbour Marina WiFi	305-531-3747	550	16/71	call/50	13/22	F	GD	IMS	–	–	50/200+	LSC	P	MR
13. Miami Yacht Club ☐ WiFi 1089	305-377-9877	40	–	2/40	6/6	F	–	IMS	–	L2	30/30	PS	–	GR

☐ Internet Access WiFi Wireless Internet Access **WG** Waterway Guide Cruising Club Partner ☁ onSpot dockside WiFi facility
See WaterwayGuide.com for current rates, fuel prices, web site addresses, and other up-to-the-minute information. *(Information in the table is provided by the facilities.)*

TREASURE ISLAND AREA, INDIAN CREEK, MIAMI BEACH, GOVERNMENT CUT, NOAA CHART 11467

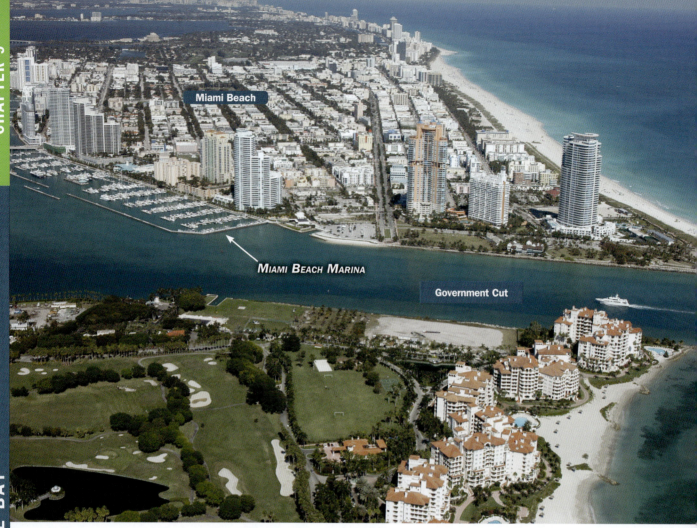

Miami Beach

MIAMI BEACH MARINA

Government Cut

indicate the route southeast to Fishermans Channel, south of Dodge Island.

Dodge Island railway and highway bridges cross the ICW at Mile 1089.3. The fixed **Dodge Island Hwy. Bridge** has a 65-foot vertical clearance, while the **Dodge Island Railroad Bascule Bridge** has a 22-foot closed vertical clearance; however, the railroad bridge is usually in the open position unless a train is approaching. Once you pass these bridges, you can access Fishermans Channel, the alternate route east to reach Government Cut (as well as Miami Beach Marina) when the Main Ship Channel is closed.

Dockage/Moorings: Grandview Palace Yacht Club is 1.5 miles east of the ICW at Mile 1083.8, before the 79th St. Bridge (East) between Treasure Island and Normandy Isle. Call in advance for slip availability. They also sell gas (no diesel). On the north side of the 79th St. Causeway are two facilities: Gator Harbor West Marina, which is private (does not accept any transients), and the municipal Pelican Harbor Marina. Pelican Harbor Marina sells fuel and accepts transients.

Miami-Dade County Parks and Recreation Department has a mooring field and dinghy dock at Pelican Harbor Marina. There are 27 moorings for boats up to 35 feet. There is also a dinghy dock. Farther south of the 79th St. Causeway on a marked channel of the Little River is North Beach Marina. They accept only long-term (6-month or longer) stays and offer some repairs.

Nearby Indian Creek is chock-full of hotel and condominium docks, such as Miami Beach Resort and Fontainebleau Marina. These marinas provide easy access to the bustling Collins Avenue.

Anchorage: It is possible to anchor near the NE 79th St. Bridge at North Bay Island (south side) in 6 to 8 feet at MLW with good holding in mud. This is open to the south through west and wakes. You can also drop the hook in 14 feet at MLW north of the Julia Tuttle Causeway. This provides minimal exposure and is open to ICW wakes. Anchoring in either of these is limited to 7 days; this ordinance is enforced. (See Anchoring Update in the Skipper's Handbook in the front of this guide.)

■ MIAMI BEACH

Whether you take the ICW or the well-marked Miami Beach Channel to Miami Beach, be sure to allow ample time for sightseeing once you get there. Essentially a creation of the tourism industry, Miami Beach and its islands are mostly manmade. Its hip, vibrant image thrives in the Art Deco District, with its numerous hotels and acclaimed restaurants, as well as the trendy South Beach area. So many people in the entertainment industry have moved here that it has been dubbed "Hollywood East."

Some of the world's most flamboyant hotels and residences grace the 9 miles of beach here, where visitors will find spectacular water views and thousands of graceful coconut palms. If you travel with a pet aboard, you will find that virtually all the sidewalk restaurants are extremely pet-friendly.

NAVIGATION: Use NOAA Chart 11467. A major commercial and recreational port, Greater Miami bustles with activity on land and water. Study your charts carefully before attempting to transit this busy and sometimes confusing area.

The relatively well-marked Miami Beach Channel runs south along the eastern coast of Biscayne Bay (the western shore of Miami Beach) all the way to Government Cut. Land for homes was created by pumping sand up from Biscayne Bay's bottom and depositing it behind bulkheads. As a consequence, MLW depths of 6 to 7 feet lie almost anywhere near the shore, except where indicated on the chart. The open bay outside the ICW channel, on the other hand, has MLW depths of only 1 to 3 feet. Visit the Waterway Explorer at waterwayguide.com for more information.

The northernmost crossover to Miami Beach appears just below Broad Causeway Bridge. At green daybeacon "15," south of the Broad Causeway Bridge, bear a bit east of south off the ICW toward flashing red "2" (leave it to starboard), which then leads to the short, marked channel at the tip of Biscayne Point. When passing through the narrow channel marked by green daybeacons "3" and "5" to port and red daybeacons "4" and "6" to starboard, steer for red daybeacon "8" at the western tip of Normandy Isle. You will come upon deep water at the East 79th Street Causeway. Do not try to circumnavigate the island unless you do so in a dinghy. The fixed **71st St. Bridge** with a 5-foot vertical clearance connects the island to the ocean beach.

The **East 79th St. Causeway** connects Normandy and Treasure Islands. The bridge has 25-foot closed vertical clearance and opens on signal. (Be sure to include "east" in your call for an opening.) Going south on the Miami Beach Channel, you can leave the route at red daybeacon "10" south of Normandy Isle and go east to the beginning of Indian Creek. Be sure to stay within the charted deep water and enter between La Gorce Island and Normandy Isle.

To access the Indian Creek marinas, head south on the eastern side of Allison Island through the **63rd St. Bascule Bridge**, which connects Allison Island with the beach island. This bridge has 11-foot vertical clearance and opens on signal, except from 7:00 a.m. to 7:00 p.m., Monday through Friday (except federal holidays), when the draw need only open on the hour and half-hour. From 7:10 a.m. to 9:55 a.m. and 4:05 p.m. to 6:59 p.m., Monday through Friday (except federal holidays), the draw need not open for the passage of vessels. In February of each year during the period 7 days prior to the City of Miami Beach Yacht and Brokerage Show and the 4 days following the show, from 10:00 a.m. to 4:00 p.m., the bridge need not open except for 10 minutes at the top of the hour. Make sure to check Waterway Explorer at waterwayguide.com for schedule changes.

To continue down the Miami Beach Channel, steer south between flashing green "11" to port and red daybeacon "12" to starboard to the 35-foot vertical clearance fixed **Julia Tuttle Causeway (East)** over the Miami Bridge Channel on the eastern shore of Biscayne Bay. Here a channel connecting back to the ICW runs just north along the causeway. The only aid to navigation identifying the channel is green daybeacon "25" just before the bridge. Be aware that there are a few 2- to 3-foot-deep shoal areas along the causeway.

Continuing south, the next two crossings between the ICW and Miami Beach are north and south of the Venetian Causeway. Both routes are safe and easy, with the one on the north being slightly deeper. The channel is relatively well marked, although some daybeacons may be missing. This causeway jumps over a series of small islands, starting with Belle Isle, the oldest island in Biscayne Bay and the closest to Miami Beach. The two cross-routes skirt the islands' northern and southern extremities.

The final cross-bay passage is along the main ship channel to the end of the MacArthur Causeway. The southernmost approach to Miami Beach is spanned by the 35-foot fixed **MacArthur Causeway East Bridge** near the U.S. Coast Guard base at the inner end of Government Cut at Meloy Channel.

Dockage: You will find many excellent, expensive marinas with substantial amenities. You will also find less fancy but somewhat more economical ones. For dockage information, visiting boaters may also call the Marine Council at 786-586-4688 for information on the Miami-Dade marine and tourism industry.

The Miami Beach Channel leads directly to Sunset Harbour Yacht Club on Biscayne Bay, which offers slips for lease or sale. Membership privileges include use of the private fitness center, and heated Olympic-size pool, as well as high power electrical service, fresh water, phone, Internet digital satellite TV and a personal dock box. Transient space is available but be sure to call ahead to check availability. The marina also sells diesel.

A major supermarket, drugstore, Post Office and a city bus stop are less than three blocks from Sunset Harbour. The Lincoln Road Mall, a pedestrian-only street mall on 16th St., has numerous art galleries, shops, restaurants and theaters, all within easy walking distance.

Farther south on Meloy Channel (the southern end of Miami Beach Channel), just opposite the Coast Guard base, the 400-slip Miami Beach Marina can accommodate vessels up to 250 feet and sells fuel. There is a dive shop on site as well as boat and jet ski rentals. The famous Art Deco District is nearby with shopping and the night life of trendy South Beach. The well-known Monty's Sunset (305-672-1148) is on site and offers excellent food and service, both in a swimming pool/raw bar setting and upstairs in a fine food restaurant.

One Island Park Marina–Miami Beach is located adjacent to the USCG station. The smallest yacht that is permitted to dock there is 100 feet (with 800 feet being the largest). Fuel and pump-out services are available. There are restrooms but no showers or laundry facilities

Anchorage: On the Miami Beach Channel, you can anchor at the Tuttle Causeway Bight, south of the east span of the bridge. Here you will find 8 to 9 feet at MLW with excellent holding and protection from all but the west. (Due to increased usage, this anchorage has recently expanded and spilled over into Biscayne Bay on the other side of the channel.)

Note that 2016 Florida legislation bans overnight anchoring in Sunset Lake. It is illegal to anchor at any time during the period between one-half hour after sunset and one-half hour before sunrise. You can, however, anchor just off the Sunset Harbour Channel

(privately maintained daybeacons and lights) on the northeast side of Belle Isle in 7- to 11-foot MLW depths. Wakes from passing vessels, particularly on weekends, can be disturbing.

A good anchorage is southwest of the small island with the Flagler Monument (south of the eastern span of the Venetian Causeway). Approach via the Miami Beach Channel or the cross-bay route south of the Venetian Causeway (on the northern side of the entrance channel with 6-foot MLW depths). It is also possible to anchor on the east side of Watson Island (7 to 8 feet at MLW).

As of summer 2018 there are only a couple of places to land your dinghy to go ashore at Miami Beach: the Marine Patrol dock and the city-owned dinghy dock up the Collins Canal. It is our suggestion that you check with locals or the Marine Patrol (305-673-7959) before using either of the docks.

> There is an enforced **7-day** anchoring limit on all the anchorages listed here. See details in the Skipper's Handbook in the front of this guide.

Government Cut and Fishermans Channel

NAVIGATION: Use NOAA Chart 11467. Use the Miami Harbor Entrance Tide Tables. A Class A big ship inlet, Government Cut (Miami Inlet) is wide, deep and free of hazards. It runs between Miami Beach (to the north) and Fisher Island (to the south). An alternate to Government Cut, Fishermans Channel is used by cruisers when Government Cut is closed for security reasons. Watch for frequent dredging operations in this area. Through the short passage from the west end of this channel to the ICW, controlling depth is about 10 feet at MLW, but make sure you identify the markers carefully.

Biscayne Bay pilots report that recent dredging in and around the Port of Miami has affected currents in the harbor. Both flood and ebb are stronger than published predictions. If outward bound, just follow the buoys. See the Inlet section at the front of this guide for more information on Miami Inlet.

Whenever there are cruise ships at the docks, Fishermans Channel must be used. Closures are announced on VHF Channel 16. It is similarly free of hazards, although when entering from the ICW heading south, one should leave green daybeacons "53A" and "55" well to port before turning in to the channel due to shoaling extending into the channel. The channel

Miami Harbor & Miami River, FL

		Dockage					Supplies		Services					
Facility	**Phone**	Largest Vessel Accommodated	VHF Channel Monitored	Transient Berths / Total Berths	Approach / Dockside Depth (reported)	Floating Docks	Groceries, Ice, Marine Supplies, Snacks	Gas / Diesel	Repairs: Hull, Engine, Propeller	Lift (tonnage), Crane, Rail	Min/Max Amps	Laundry, Pool, Showers, Courtesy Car	Pump-Out Station	Nearby: Grocery Store, Motel, Restaurant
MIAMI HARBOR														
1. Miamarina at Bayside [WiFi] 1089.5	305-960-5180	165	16/18	26/130	14/10	F	IS	–	–	–	30/100	LS	P	GMR
2. Epic Marina [icon][WiFi] 1090	305-400-6711	325	16/68	20/20	17/15	–	–	–	–	–	20/200+	PS	P	GMR
MIAMI RIVER														
3. 5th Street Marina [icon]	305-324-2040	240	–	–	15/13	–	–	–	HEP	L100	50/100	–	P	–
4. Norseman Shipbuilding Corp. [icon]	305-545-6815	90	–	call/25	15/10	–	–	–	HEP	L100,C	50/50	–	–	–
5. Anchor Marine of Miami	305-545-6348	50	–	–	–	–	M	GD	EP	L15	30/30	–	–	G
6. RMK Merrill-Stevens [WiFi][WG]	305-324-5211	250	–	10/20	16/15	–	IM	GD	HEP	L70,C30,R500	30/100	S	P	GMR
7. Hurricane Cove Marina & Boatyard	305-324-8004	85	–	call/150	12/10	–	M	GD	HEP	L80	30/30	–	–	GMR
8. River Cove Marina	305-545-5001	60	–	call/72	12/10	–	M	–	–	L14	30/30	S	P	GMR
9. Austral International Marina [WiFi][WG]	305-325-0177	40	–	5/35	6/6	–	M	–	HEP	L20,C18	30/50	S	–	G
10. Brisas del Rio Marina [WiFi]	305-392-1487	–	–	–	15/15	–	–	–	HEP	–	30/50	–	–	GR
11. Jones Superyacht Miami Inc. [WiFi]	305-635-0891	300	–	call/11	15/15	–	MS	–	HEP	L950	50/200+	–	–	–

[icon] Internet Access [WiFi] Wireless Internet Access [WG] Waterway Guide Cruising Club Partner [onSpot] dockside WiFi facility
See WaterwayGuide.com for current rates, fuel prices, web site addresses, and other up-to-the-minute information. (*Information in the table is provided by the facilities.*)

Miami River's controlling depth is 14 feet at MLW up to the Northwest 27th Ave. Bridge and then 9 feet up to the 36th St. Dam. Boats proceeding upriver should lower outriggers and antennas for bridge clearance. If land traffic is heavy (and it usually is), bridgetenders will enforce the law.

The stated controlling depths hold on Miami River's more important side branches, South Fork (3 miles from the river's mouth) and Tamiami Canal (1 mile farther on). Both shoot obliquely off to the southwest and, like the main river, each has its own series of boatyards and marine installations. Tamiami Canal, a drainage ditch that parallels the Tamiami Trail to the northwest almost completely across Florida, is navigable for 6-foot draft vessels (8 feet at high tide) as far as a low limiting fixed bridge over Northwest 37th Ave.

In addition to the vast array of recreational craft and amenities to serve them, the Miami River carries considerable commercial traffic. Tugs working in pairs maneuver to place the big oceangoing vessels that line the last mile or so of the river. Give these ships plenty of room.

With the exception of two fixed bridges (with vertical clearances of 75 feet) all the bridges crossing the Miami River have restricted openings. They open on signal year-round, except from 7:00 a.m. to 7:00 p.m., Monday through Friday (except federal holidays), when the draw need open only on the hour and half-hour. However, from 7:35 a.m. to 8:59 a.m., 12:05 p.m. to 12:59 p.m. and 4:35 p.m. to 5:59 p.m., the draw need not open. Most Miami River clearance gauges show the clearance at the fenders instead of the center of the span; there may be a sign indicating the additional clearance available at the center.

Closed vertical clearances for the bridges in sequence up the Miami River are:

Brickell Ave. Bascule Bridge (23 foot clearance)
Metro Train Bridge (75 foot fixed clearance)
Miami Ave. Bascule Bridge (21 foot clearance)
SW 1st Ave. Bridge (75 foot fixed clearance)
SW 2nd Ave. Bascule Bridge (11 foot clearance)
I-95 Twin Bridges (75 foot fixed clearance)
SW 1st St. Bascule Bridge (18 foot clearance)
W. Flagler St. Bascule Bridge (35 foot clearance)
NW 5th St. Bascule Bridge (12 foot clearance)
NW 12th Ave. Bascule Bridge (22 foot clearance)
Dolphin Expressway Bridge (75 foot fixed clearance)
NW 17th Ave. Bascule Bridge (17 foot clearance)
NW 22nd Ave. Bascule Bridge (25 foot clearance)

There is one fixed bridge (8-foot vertical clearance) over the South Fork, and a swing bridge (erroneously charted as bascule) with 6-foot vertical clearance crossing the Tamiami Canal.

Whenever a big event takes place at Orange Bowl Stadium, home of the University of Miami Hurricanes football team, extra closures are usually imposed. All closures for the regularly scheduled events at the Orange Bowl, from August through January, are posted online

MIAMI HARBOR, MIAMI RIVER, NOAA CHART 11467

in the *Local Notice to Mariners* starting in late July; they are repeated a week or two before the event dates. These closures usually last only about two hours. Bridge schedules are always subject to change. If you plan to go upriver, check ahead of time for bridge restrictions.

Dockage: Miamarina at Bayside is south of the Dodge Island bridges at Bayfront Park and may have transient space; call ahead. Epic Marina is at the mouth of the Miami River, across the river from Brickell Point, before the bridge. This is a luxury destination directly on the Miami River with full amenities and two on-site restaurants. They can accommodate yachts over 300 feet in deep water slips.

There are many repair facilities for the cruising boater on the Miami River but few transient slips. Call ahead for slip availability. The 5th Street Marina has a seawall for dockage. Norseman Shipbuilding Corp. offers repairs but no transient slips. Anchor Marine of Miami and Hurricane Cove Marina & Boatyard sell both gas and diesel but have no transient slips. RMK Merrill-Stevens has slips for vessels to 250 feet and offers most any type of repair or service. (They have a lift, crane and railway.) River Cove Marina, Austral International Marina and Brisas del Rio Marina are also on the Miami River and offer repairs. Jones Superyacht Miami is located up the Miami Canal and caters to vessels to 300 feet. They have a 950-ton lift. All of these offer varying levels of repairs and services.

■ SOUTHERN BISCAYNE BAY

The **William M. Powell (Rickenbacker) Causeway Bridge** (65-foot fixed vertical clearance) will probably be referred to as "the Powell/Rickenbacker" or just "Rickenbacker" for some time to come. The older structure is dwarfed alongside its modern replacement and remains in use as a fishing pier.

South of the Rickenbacker Causeway, Biscayne Bay changes character, becoming broad, relatively deep (average 10 feet) and lovely. Sailing regattas are held in these waters nearly every weekend, while fishing, swimming, water skiing and cruising are everyday, year-round activities. Cruisers will find this part of Biscayne Bay especially inviting. The deep, open water makes a pleasant change from the narrow confines of the ICW.

Marine Stadium on Virginia Key was originally built in 1963 to promote powerboat racing. It was considered a modernist icon because of its cantilevered, fold-plate roof and construction of lightweight, poured-in-place concrete, popular in mid-century stadiums. At 326 feet in length (longer than a football field), it was the longest span of cantilevered concrete in the world when it was built. Its eight big slanted columns are anchored in the ground. It has been the site of the Miami International Boat Show since 2016.

Key Biscayne

NAVIGATION: Use NOAA Chart 11467. Cruising south of the Rickenbacker Causeway is easier if you use Chart 11465 (ICW–Miami to Elliot Key). Although the scale is the same on both charts, Chart 11465 covers a larger area (as far as Elliot Key) and makes navigation simpler.

Bear Cut is on the southeast side of Virginia Key, between it and Key Biscayne. It is unmarked at its northeastern end, except for red daybeacon "2," which provides an outlet to the ocean for smaller boats that can pass under the **Bear Cut Bridge** (16-foot fixed vertical clearance).

Skippers southbound along the main ICW channel should follow the chart closely and take time to sort out the buoys. On the ICW east of the mouth of the Miami River, several channels (described earlier), all with their own markers, meet and intersect. There are a couple of different marker numbering sequences; steer toward green daybeacon "59" and then make your turn to follow the ICW channel. Slow down, and take your time picking out the navigational aids for your particular course.

Dockage: Rickenbacker Marina Inc. is located in the Marine Stadium with limited reserved dockage for transients. There are restaurants and shopping within walking distance. Marine Stadium Marina has no wet slips, only dry storage. Both of these facilities sell gas (no diesel)

Just south of the Rickenbacker Causeway, on the mainland side, is an emergency dock belonging to Mercy Hospital. It has depths of 4 feet at MLW and 6 feet at high tide and provides a telephone, restricted to emergency use only.

Anchorage: You can anchor at the Miami Marine Stadium for 24 hours only. The anchoring provides good protection in 8- to 12-foot MLW depths with a mud and sand bottom. This anchorage offers a beautiful view of downtown Miami. Jet skis and wake boarders use this area on the weekends. There are signs that indicate no dinghy landing and our Cruising Editor said that they were being enforced. Please note: This anchorage is closed from mid-January until after the boat show (middle of February) each year.

Anchoring is also possible on the southeast side of Virginia Key in at least 7 feet at MLW with good holding in sandy mud. Drop the hook outside the basin north of the Miami Seaquarium.

Bill Baggs State Park

At the southern end of Key Biscayne is Bill Baggs Cape Florida State Park, named after the late Miami newspaper editor who championed the fight to designate this area a state park. With more than 1 mile of ocean beach, the park is set in a wilderness of tropical growth. There are bike paths and running trails in a beautiful tropical setting here; this is a great place to get off the boat and stretch your legs but will require a walk or bike from Hurricane or No Name Harbors. Don't forget your camera; there are numerous opportunities for beautiful shots.

The oldest structure in Miami-Dade County is the 95-foot-high Cape Florida Lighthouse. The original light was built in 1825 and has survived numerous hurricanes, an 1836 Seminole Indian attack that resulted in a fire, and the harsh effects of the environment. Refurbished that same year, its replacement was in service until 1878, when Fowey Rocks Light took over in a position 5 miles offshore, which enabled it to better guide deep-draft ships that had to stand far out to sea. The original structure was restored to its authentic 1855 condition and is now maintained and charted as a private aid to navigation, flashing a white beam that is visible 7 nm out to sea.

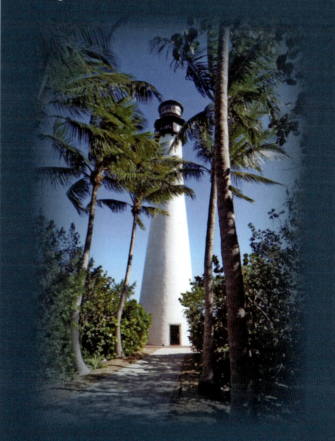

Key Biscayne, FL

KEY BISCAYNE AREA	Largest Vessel Accommodated	VHF Channel Monitored	Approach / Dockside Depth (reported)	Transient Berths / Total Berths	Floating Docks	Gas / Diesel	Groceries, Ice, Marine Supplies, Snacks	Repairs: Hull, Engine, Propeller	Lift (tonnage), Crane, Rail	Min/Max Amps	Laundry, Pool, Showers, Courtesy Car	Pump-Out Station	Nearby: Grocery Store, Motel, Restaurant
		Dockage				**Supplies**			**Services**				
1. Rickenbacker Marina Inc. 🖥 WiFi 1091.5 305-361-1900	100	16	2/200	8/9	-	G	IMS	HEP	L	30/50	S	P	R
2. Marine Stadium Marina 1091.5 305-960-5140	43	16/83	-	8/10	-	G	GI	HEP	L9	-	-	-	GMR
3. Crandon Park Marina 1094 305-361-1281	80	16/68	10/294	6/5	F	GD	GIMS	-	-	-	LS	P	GMR

🖥 Internet Access   WiFi Wireless Internet Access   WG Waterway Guide Cruising Club Partner   onSpot dockside WiFi facility
See WaterwayGuide.com for current rates, fuel prices, web site addresses, and other up-to-the-minute information. *(Information in the table is provided by the facilities.)*

KEY BISCAYNE AREA, NOAA CHART 11465

Key Biscayne–ICW Mile 1094

Key Biscayne, site of southern Florida's first town, was founded in 1839. It was also headquarters for a band of renegades who lured ships onto the reefs and "salvaged" their cargo. Today, the key is made up of two parks: The northern end is taken up by Dade County's Crandon Park, while the southern is home to Bill Baggs Cape Florida State Park. Crandon Park occupies the northern end of Key Biscayne at Mile 1094. This county park boasts a marina (Crandon Park Marina), boat ramp, two miles of ocean beach and excellent picnic grounds; nearby is the International Tennis Center and an excellent golf course. Bus service is available to the city. At Key Biscayne's southern end is the restored Cape Florida Lighthouse.

NAVIGATION: Use NOAA Charts 11467 and 11451. Heading south, after passing beneath the Rickenbacker Causeway Bridge at Mile 1091.6 and Virginia Key to the east, you enter lower Biscayne Bay. Up to 8 miles wide and about 28 miles long, lower Biscayne Bay is a cleaner, different body of water than all the other bays along this coast.

Just below Key Biscayne to the east, you will see the remaining houses of Stiltsville, an eclectic group of homes on stilts that now belong to the National Park Service. Stiltsville has a colorful history that dates back to the 1930s. The remaining structures are visible along the reef.

Dockage/Moorings: The Crandon Park Marina complex includes gas and diesel fuel. (Note that the showers are cold water only.) It is best approached from Biscayne Bay by a privately marked natural channel that leads northeastward from the shoal light (flashing white, four seconds) off West Point. The marina also has moorings available to sailboats only in its protected cove with easy access to marina amenities. If you have to do any type of shopping, you will need to arrange for ground transportation, as there are no shops or restaurants for several miles.

Anchorage: Two of the most popular harbors among boaters waiting for favorable weather to cross over to the Bahamas are Hurricane Harbor, near the southwest corner of Key Biscayne, and No Name Harbor, around the point from Hurricane Harbor and in the Bill Baggs State Park. Hurricane Harbor does not have shore access but is a sheltered spot for inclement weather. Favor the port side as you come in; the starboard side of the channel shoals to 4 feet at MLW. Drop the anchor in 5 to 13 feet at MLW with excellent holding and some exposure to the northwest.

When the wind is out of the east, another option is to simply anchor in the lee of the west side of Key Biscayne, just north of Hurricane Harbor's entrance in at least 8 feet at MLW (exposed west to southwest). Leave the ICW Mile 1095 and head due east towards flashing green "3." Head into the small cove to the east located just south of yacht club. You will have plenty of swinging room and a great view of the Miami skyline here. Do mind the shoals off West Point and stay well south of them. Winds from the west (rare) can set up choppy conditions due to long fetch from mainland coast.

No Name Harbor has shore access and a fee for overnight anchoring. In 2018, overnight anchorage (and use of the facilities) was available for $20. Envelopes are provided for depositing the fees in an honor box ashore. There is room for about 25 boats. (Expect lots of company on weekends.) The bottom is hard mud in 11- to 12-foot MLW depths, and holding is good with wind protection from all directions except due west (and that is actually not too bad).

There are clean restrooms, inexpensive showers and a laundry (although not always operational). Cleats along the seawall make going ashore much simpler. There are no fenders along the raw concrete seawall, so you should rig your own fenders in advance.

A pump-out station is located on the southern side of the harbor, near the entrance, but it is not always working. There is no seawall protection here either, so rig your own fenders in advance. There is a small fee for daily tie-ups ($8), but overnight stays along the wall are prohibited.

At the head of the harbor, the highly recommended Boaters' Grill (305-361-0080) offers a menu of appetizers, light meals, deli take-out, along with beer and wine.

Coconut Grove Area–ICW Mile 1095

Across Biscayne Bay from Bear Cut is Dinner Key, the major center of boating activity for the southern sector of Biscayne Bay, which is served by a 1.5-mile-long, well-marked channel on the western mainland shore. It was once a seaplane base–first for the enormous Pan American clippers flying to the Caribbean and South America and later for the U.S. Coast Guard. The Coconut Grove area includes a cluster of friendly marine services, including yacht clubs, marinas, a boatyard, restaurants and a mooring field.

SERVICES	
1	Library
2	Post Office
3	Visitor Information
ATTRACTIONS	
3	Miami City Hall (original PanAm terminal)

SHOPPING	
4	CocoWalk
5	Fresh Market
DINING	
6	Atchana's East West Kitchen
7	Grove Bay Grill

MARINAS	
8	Coral Reef Yacht Club
9	Dinner Key Marina
10	Grove Harbour Marina
11	Prime Marina Miami

Part of the City of Miami, Coconut Grove is known to locals as "The Grove." It is one of the hippest, most energetic and most inviting corners of South Florida. Unlike the rest of Miami, low-key and restful Coconut Grove preserves much of the ambiance of traditional Florida. All the usual daily necessities—laundries, supermarkets, restaurants, Post Office, library, bank, drugstores—are only a short distance from the marinas, as are art galleries, antiques and gift shops, boutiques and craft shops catering to tourists.

Coconut Grove was once a seaplane base for the enormous Pan American clippers flying to the Caribbean and South America. Known as the "Air Gateway between the Americas," the Pan Am Seaplane Base and Terminal Building at Dinner Key linked the United States with Latin America. The inaugural flight from Dinner Key to Panama took place on December 1, 1930. The original Pan Am complex was designed to look like an airplane when viewed from above: Pan Am Drive and Circle were designed to be the body of the plane; the Terminal Building the cockpit, and the hanger buildings representing the wings. (See more at coconutgrovevillagecouncil.com/history.) The original building now serves as Miami City Hall, where you can pick up visitor information.

The giant, 3.5-ton revolving world globe once located in the lobby of the Pan Am terminal greeted visitors to the old Miami Museum of Science for 55 years. The museum relocated to The Patricia and Phillip Frost Museum of Science in the Grove is now located in the Museum Park area of downtown Miami (1101 Biscayne Blvd.). This hands-on facility offers exhibits on weather and technology, a planetarium and wildlife centers. Call 305-434-9600 for details. On the Bay at 3251 S. Miami Ave. is Vizcaya Museum & Gardens, housed in a 1914 mansion with 34 period decorated rooms and

10 acres of formal gardens with sculptures and grottos (305-250-9133).

Many special events are held here throughout the year, although the most special might be the annual Coconut Grove Arts Festival, scheduled each February to occur during President's Day weekend. The three-day event is one of Florida's most vibrant outdoor art festivals, highlighting works of hundreds of artists.

For years, the U.S. Sailing Winter Sail Training Center has been at Coconut Grove's Kennedy Park. Equipped with a 40-foot-wide ramp and a pair of 2-ton capacity hoists, as well as good weather and good winds virtually all winter long, the Center proves invaluable to those training for the Olympics and for the various one-design classes holding mid-winter regattas here.

Shopping: The Grove is home to CocoWalk, a popular shopping and dining district. First Flight Out is located here, featuring a collection of Pan Am merchandise, luggage, travel apparel, aviation collectibles and gifts.

For provisioning, a Fresh Market is conveniently located near the marinas at 2640 S. Bayshore Dr.

Dining: There are numerous places in which to dine, from simple fare to the more elegant. The Grove Bay Grille (3381 Pan American Dr., 305-285-1366) is the closest, with a great waterfront view and a bar-type menu. It's popular with the locals and always busy.

Next to Prime Marina Miami is Monte's Raw Bar, a funky bayside hangout with drinks, a raw bar, live music and weeknight happy hour (2550 S. Bayshore Dr., 305-856-3992). For great pizza or other Italian dishes, try Spartico at the Mayfair Hotel & Spa (3000 Florida Ave., 305-779-5100). For a Thai and American food dining experience be sure to try Atchana's East West Kitchen (2951 S. Bayshore Dr., 305-774-0409) which is located inside the Mutiny Hotel.

Biscayne Bay West Shore, FL

		Largest Vessel Accommodated	VHF Channel Monitored	Approach / Dockside Depth (reported)	Transient Berths / Total Berths	Groceries, Ice, Marine Supplies, Snacks	Gas / Diesel	Floating Docks	Repairs: Hull, Engine, Propeller	Lift (tonnage), Crane, Rail	Min/Max Amps	Laundry, Pool, Showers, Courtesy Car	Pump-Out Station	Nearby: Grocery Store, Motel, Restaurant
COCONUT GROVE AREA				**Dockage**					**Supplies**		**Services**			
1. Palmeiras Beach Club at Grove Isle ▭ 1093	305-858-8300	120	16	85/85	8/12	F	–	IS	EP	–	30/100	PS	P	MR
2. Coral Reef Yacht Club 1094	305-858-1733	65	71	call/104	7/7	F	–	IS	–	C	30/100	PS	P	GMR
3. Prime Marina Miami (WiFi) 1094	305-854-7997	100	16/68	call/114	5/6	F	–	I	–	L20	30/100	LS	P	GMR
4. Grove Harbour Marina ▭ 1094	305-854-6444	150	–	call/58	18/8	F	GD	GI	HP	L90	30/100	–	P	GMR
5. Dinner Key Marina ▭ 1095	305-329-4755	110	16/68	50/582	8/7	F	–	IS	–	–	30/100	LS	P	GMR
6. Matheson Hammock Marina 3.6 W of 1098	305-665-5475	55	–	call/243	5.5/5	F	GD	IS	–	–	30/50	PS	P	R
HOMESTEAD AREA														
7. Suntex Marinas – South Miami 1106	305-258-3500	38	16/08	1 /299	5/9	F	GD	IMS	HEP	L	30/30	–	–	GR
8. Black Point Park & Marina 1106	305-258-4092	55	16/09	20/200	4.9/5.5	F	GD	IMS	–	–	30/50	–	P	GMR
9. Herbert Hoover Marina at Homestead Bayfront Park (WiFi)	305-230-3033	50	16/72	174/174	3.5/5	–	GD	GIMS	–	L	30/50	PS	P	GMR

▭ Internet Access (WiFi) Wireless Internet Access WG Waterway Guide Cruising Club Partner onSpot dockside WiFi facility
See WaterwayGuide.com for current rates, fuel prices, web site addresses, and other up-to-the-minute information. *(Information in the table is provided by the facilities.)*

> Note: **Hurricane Irma** left a trail of damage across South Florida in September 2017. Some marinas in the area were still rebuilding at press time in summer 2018. It would be a good idea to call ahead prior to your arrival.

Dockage: Palmeiras Beach Club at Grove Isle at Mile 1093 is private. One nautical mile south is the Coral Reef Yacht Club, which uses the same entrance channel from Biscayne Bay as the marina. Members of other yacht clubs may be able to arrange brief transient dockage; call ahead before reaching the club. Next, still heading south, are Prime Marina Miami and Grove Harbour Marina, which have very limited transient dockage. The 582-slip Dinner Key Marina provides accommodations in a park-like setting to transients and long-term renters. Note that the docks were closed at press time (summer 2018) due to major hurricane damage. Call ahead for updates.

Most of the private marinas and yacht clubs in the area offer reciprocal agreements for members of other recognized yacht clubs. Be sure to call ahead because space may be tight.

Moorings: Dinner Key Marina offers a mooring field with 225 mooring balls. All of the moorings are available on a first-come, first-served basis. Call the marina for your mooring assignment. Included in the cost of the mooring are pump-out service and a dinghy dock next door at the launching ramp. A water taxi will take you into the marina, which is very close to the attractions of Coconut Grove. You can also come in to take on water. Trash pickup and recycling are available as well. This is a popular spot to wait for favorable weather to cross to the Bahamas.

For your provisioning needs, The Fresh Market (2640 S. Bayshore Dr., 305-854-7202) is just one block away from the marina area. Dinner Key's location puts boaters within walking distance of the popular Coconut Grove area with it galleries and cafés and numerous restaurants.

Anchorage: Anchoring is still possible outside of the mooring field to the north (on the opposite side of the channel) and to the east in 7 to 8 feet at MLW. This is open and exposed to the east through southeast. The anchorage is usually crowded so look carefully before dropping your hook.

Coral Gables–ICW Mile 1096

NAVIGATION: Use NOAA Charts 11467 and 11465. Located directly south of Coconut Grove, Coral Gables has its own waterway with a well-marked entrance and a 5-foot MLW controlling depths. Since bridges on both branches of this waterway are fixed (most offer about a 12-foot vertical clearance), you will likely have to explore by dinghy. The canals interconnect, wind through residential sections and finally exit to the bay just north of Coral Gables' wide Tahiti Beach.

Dockage: About 4 miles south of Coconut Grove is Matheson Hammock Park, a county park, beach and marina. Matheson Hammock Marina was damaged in Hurricane Irma but at press time in summer 2018 there were plans to reopen before the end of the year. It is one of South Florida's few remaining natural areas, with native forest and a lagoon-type atoll beach. This marina has slips for transients, a sandy beach and other amenities, including fuel.

COCONUT GROVE AREA, NOAA CHART 11451

COCONUT GROVE AREA, NOAA CHART 11451

COCONUT GROVE AREA, NOAA CHART 11451

HOMESTEAD AREA, NOAA CHART 11451

Farther south, in the Homestead Area, is Suntex Marinas–South Miami, which provides dry storage as well as transient dockage and a well-stocked ship store. They also have both diesel and gas and an on-site restaurant (Black Point Ocean Grill, 305-258-3918), which has live bands on weekends. Kayak and canoe rentals are available as well.

Located in the same protected basin is Black Point Park & Marina with transient dockage, bike trails and fishing as well as gas and diesel fuel. Continuing south is Herbert Hoover Marina at Homestead Bayfront Park offering transient dockage and fuel. It is in a beautiful tropical setting with a natural atoll pool and a pristine beach. Approach depths, however, are reported by the facility as 3.5 feet at MLW; call ahead for actual depths.

■ NEXT STOP

Cruisers are now in an ideal position to head east to the Bahamas or continue south into the fabled Florida Keys. The run north, outside from Government Cut, is spectacular and offers the best available view of the Miami Beach skyline. The run south from Government Cut offers some interesting coastline as well, leading past Virginia Key and Key Biscayne to the next entry from the ocean at Cape Florida.

If headed to the Keys via Hawk Channel, bear east between Mile 1097 and 1098, setting a course for flashing green "21" and flashing red "20."

The Florida Keys

■ FLORIDA UPPER & MIDDLE KEYS ■ FLORIDA LOWER KEYS

Key Biscayne

ICW MILE 1094

Biscayne Bay

ICW MILE 1130 Key Largo

Flamingo

ICW MILE 1155 Islamorada

Cape Sable

ICW MILE 1165 Lower Matecumbe

Channel Five

ICW MILE 1194 Marathon

ICW MILE 1205 Big Pine Key

Seven-Mile Bridge

Boca Chica Key

ICW MILE 1235

Key West

ICW MILE 1240

The Marquesas

N

Visit Waterway Explorer at waterwayguide.com

The Florida Keys

Extending in a sweeping southwesterly curve from Miami and the mainland, the Florida Keys offer the cruising mariner an environment unlike any other waterway area. In many ways, the Keys resemble the islands of the Bahamas, except for the main highway and 42 bridges (a total of 18.94 miles of bridges) that tie them together. West of Marathon, Moser Channel (Seven Mile) Bridge–which is actually 6.77 miles–is the longest, while the Harris Gap Channel Bridge at 108 feet is the shortest. The highway runs from the tip of the Florida peninsula to Key West, the nation's southernmost city and one with a year-round carnival atmosphere. Farther west, the Marquesas and the Dry Tortugas provide the challenge of remote and unconnected islands, accessible only by water or air. Tourism and fishing support the numerous communities lining U.S. 1 South, known as the Overseas Highway.

Geologically the Florida Keys are mainly the exposed parts of coral reefs. Some of the islands have been exposed for so long that sand has built up around them, creating barrier islands, while other smaller islands remain as coral atolls. With outstanding natural and artificial underwater reefs, fishermen, snorkelers and divers have found a tropical paradise along the southeastern (ocean side) of the Keys. The northern and northwestern sides are a fisherman's heaven and the gateway to the Everglades National Park.

Below Miami, two different, but equally interesting, routes are available for the cruise along the Keys to Key West and beyond to the Dry Tortugas. One follows

Islamorada is a village surrounding 6 of the Florida Keys, known for their coral reefs and also known as the "Sportfishing Capital of the World".

(encompassing all of the Keys) see cruisers as more of a bother than a benefit. Incidents of nudity, drunkenness, environmental violations, property destruction and theft have been noted. While it is unlikely that readers of this guide contribute in large part to these problems, we each should be mindful that we need to consistently show respect to the environment, boating regulations and the local community. Indeed, by being good citizens in this way we strengthen the cause for cruisers generally, enriching our own community of cruisers.

During the winter season (November through April), lobster or crab pots marked by floats of all descriptions are found in all areas surrounding the Keys. Cruisers should be prepared to dive to check and clear their own props. Generally fishermen lay their traps in a line. So if you see one, it's wise to determine the orientation of the line to help locate others. Most pots are painted with a contrasting colors but some are black or even "sea blue." The risk of fouling is relatively low but given the tight maneuvering space often encountered in the Keys, a close lookout is warranted. Keep in mind you are most likely to snag if you are in a cross-wind and making significant leeway. In this scenario you can easily snag a pot between your skeg and rudder, and once jammed, unfouling can be a tiresome effort. Remember to shift to neutral if a snag is feared.

the ICW "inside" through Florida Bay. The other, deeper passage, which traverses the "outside," is the Hawk Channel route.

Note: Throughout the Florida Keys, marine sanctuaries are marked by yellow buoys. Do not enter these areas!

Cruising Notes

The Florida Keys are more than a waterway for many cruisers; they are a destination. Many make extended stays and are truly more than visitors, becoming temporary members of the Keys community, contributing not only to commerce but also as community members. While some cities in the Keys embrace the cruising community and provide excellent services, it should be noted that some members of the Monroe County Council

Also consider that night-time operation is much like Russian-roulette. In Florida Bay lobster pots can be found 20 miles or more from shore. This hazard requires constant vigilance.

Hawk Channel Offshore

The deepest and most viable route for vessels with a draft of 5 feet or more is Hawk Channel, running from Miami to Key West. Not "officially" part of the ICW, it lies southeast and south of the Keys, taking the form of a somewhat protected "channel" running between the line of Keys and the Florida Reef (actually a series of reefs paralleling the islands).

With a controlling depth of 9 feet MLW, and in the lee of the Keys themselves, it is generally rather well protected from winter northerlies and affords even more protection the farther down the Keys you go. In ordinary weather, it is a pleasant sail or an easy run for the entire length of the Keys.

The prevailing southeasterly winds can provide a nice boost for a long reach under sail. With numerous breaks in the outer reef, however, it can offer its share of rough water should the wind be strong from the southern or southwestern quarter.

As for navigation, GPS and radar are both extremely useful, but a reliable compass and an accurate depth sounder are just as necessary. An autopilot has its place, particularly along the Hawk Channel route, but you still must watch for and dodge the crab traps, as well as other vessels.

Connections Between the Inside and Outside Route

There are only three major routes between the ICW and Hawk Channel. The first, the Cape Florida/Biscayne Channels at ICW Mile 1096, is the northern crossover from Biscayne Bay to the Atlantic. The others–Channel Five at ICW Mile 1170 and Moser Channel at ICW Mile 1195–pass under bridges with 65-foot vertical clearances along U.S. Route 1. Several other channels with mixed limitations exist but are not recommended. For detail, see the Inlet section in the front of this guide.

Prevailing Winds

A mariner needs to be particularly aware of the winds while navigating in the Keys. There are, for example, a number of marinas located along the "top" of the Keys; by that, we mean the Florida Bay side. These marinas will have higher water readings when the wind blows out of the north and lower depths when the wind is southeasterly. For marinas on the Hawk Channel side of the Keys, the opposite is true. If it is windy, and you are not sure how the depths are going to play out for you, stay put.

ICW to Florida Bay

The well-marked but shallow ICW channel down to Florida Bay, northwest and north of the main chain of islands, is well protected in all but the worst weather.

While a hard chop built up from strong winds can provide a wet ride, most cruising boats should experience no difficulties making this passage. Along some stretches, the channel markers are widespread and careful attention is required to stay in the controlled channel. Also, the tidal flow through the keys tends to clear material from the natural channels between the keys. This material is typically deposited at the approach both on the bay-side and the ocean-side. Near these channels, the charted depths are suspect and prudent boaters reduce speed and keep a close watch on their depth sounder. Shoaling in these areas is common. Because of numerous shallow areas and the possibility that a strong northerly or easterly wind can literally blow the water out, pay strict attention to navigational aids and your course. Better yet, pay more attention to the weather you expect to encounter. If it is going to be bad, stay put.

Many boats will leave "tracks" somewhere along this route. This is usually just stirred-up, powdery sand. Should you go aground, it is generally not too difficult to regain deeper water unless, of course, you plow your way in at fairly high speed. There are towing services available; both the Coast Guard and its Auxiliary monitor VHF Channel 16 and have stations along the way. They are not permitted to tow except in a life-threatening situation, but they can provide assistance, such as contacting a commercial towing service (e.g., BoatU.S. or SeaTow) should you have trouble making direct contact.

Be advised that if you run aground in the Keys and hit coral heads, coral reefs or sea grass beds, you could be levied a large fine for your transgression. And that is in addition to what it costs to get your boat out of trouble and repaired. Take care not to damage this fragile ecosystem.

Florida Upper & Middle Keys

ICW Mile 1094–Mile 1197

VHF FL Bridges: Channel 09

CHARTS NOAA 11449, 11451, 11453, 11463, 11464, 11465, 11467, 11468

If continuing further on to Key West from Miami, there are two options: (1) Stay in the ICW on the Florida Bay side, cross over to the Hawk Channel in the Atlantic at either Cape Florida Channel/Biscayne Channel, Channel Five or Moser Channel (outside route); or (2) cross over to the Big Spanish Channel, southwest of Marathon, into Florida Bay and run down the northern edge of the remaining keys on the ICW (inside route). For boats that draw over 4.5 feet, cruising through the keys will require you to stay on the ocean-side of the Keys, in Hawk Channel.

Often cruisers will try to visit both "sides" on their return trip. As the Keys offer so many inviting attractions, it is likely you'll want to take your time and enjoy the experience. Cultural activities, snorkeling, fishing and birdwatching are all world renowned. Careful planning of anchorages and provisioning stops can also influence your routing decisions. Depth and clearance restrictions will make some harbors and marinas inaccessible, particularly to sailboats.

If winds are blowing from the northwest to the northeast at more than 10 to 15 knots, Hawk Channel (outside route), on the south and sheltered side of the Keys, will be the more comfortable route heading southwest, as the westerly curve of the keys can provide more protection. The route through Big Spanish Channel (inside route) involves navigating shifting shoals and will take a bit longer, but in southerly or southeasterly winds, it will be the more protected route heading southwest.

The Keys are unique in that there are many different, distinct areas requiring a great variety of charts. We will refer to charts with their appropriate titles and the most current edition numbers for a given cruising area. We then refer to the proper chart by number only when discussing specific locations within that area.

⚠️ Hurricane Irma left a trail of damage across South Florida in September 2017. The Middle Keys were particularly affected. At press time in summer 2018, some navigational aids were still missing or off station. Additionally, marinas in the area were still rebuilding. It would be a good idea to call ahead prior to your arrival and stay tuned to Waterway Explorer at waterwayguide.com for daily updates.

A word to the wise: There are no marine facilities on the Florida Bay side (inside route) between Big Spanish Channel (Marathon) and Key West. Also, when you

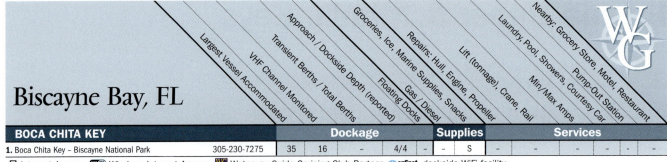

Biscayne Bay, FL

BOCA CHITA KEY		Dockage					Supplies		Services					
		Largest Vessel Accommodated	VHF Channel Monitored	Transient Berths / Total Berths	Approach / Dockside Depth (reported)	Floating Docks	Gas / Diesel	Repairs: Hull, Engine, Propeller	Groceries, Ice, Marine Supplies, Snacks	Lift (tonnage), Crane, Rail	Min/Max Amps	Laundry, Pool, Showers, Courtesy Car	Pump-Out Station	Nearby: Grocery Store, Motel, Restaurant
1. Boca Chita Key – Biscayne National Park	305-230-7275	35	16	–	4/4	–	–	S	–	–	–	–	–	–

💻 Internet Access 📶 Wireless Internet Access WG Waterway Guide Cruising Club Partner 🔵 onSpot dockside WiFi facility
See WaterwayGuide.com for current rates, fuel prices, web site addresses, and other up-to-the-minute information. *(Information in the table is provided by the facilities.)*

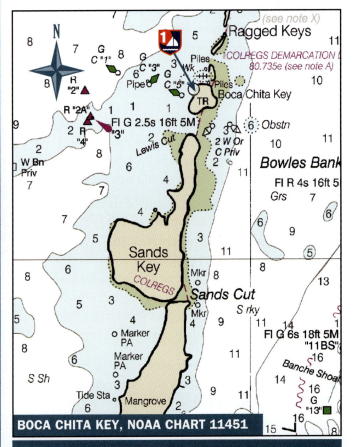

BOCA CHITA KEY, NOAA CHART 11451

Distances
Inside Route: ICW (Miles from Miami)

LOCATION	STATUTE MILES	NAUTICAL MILES
Miami (Mile 1090)	0	0
Angelfish	30	26.1
Jewfish Creek	43	37.4
Tavernier	60	52.1
Islamorada	69	60.0
Channel Five	80	69.5
Marathon (Sisters Creek)	102	88.6
Moser Channel	107	93.0
Harbor Key Bank Light	128	111.2
Northwest Channel	147	127.7
Key West	154	133.8

(Moser Channel to Key West via Hawk Channel is 40 statute miles.)

are in the Florida Keys, your travel is totally weather dependent. There is plenty of good weather here and a lot to enjoy. Remember that strong winds can reduce charted depths, particularly on the Florida Bay side. Be prepared to adapt your plans or simply stay put until conditions improve. Carrying a supply of canned food and some extra water is part of good cruising practice and waiting for good travel weather is smart boating, especially in the Keys.

■ UPPER KEYS–INSIDE (ICW) ROUTE

For boats that draw no more than 4.5 feet and that can take the occasional short, hard chop of shallow water, the inside (ICW) route provides a relatively protected and interesting passage to Islamorada, Marathon, Bahia Honda and beyond to Key West. This route is clearly marked; however, the daybeacons in certain stretches are often far apart. It is essential to pay attention to your course as you do not have to drift too far out of the channel to find yourself hard aground. This inside route has a wide variety of marinas and shore facilities, plus a variety of anchorages for different wind and weather conditions. Be aware that some of the northern keys are privately owned and getting to shore can be a problem

Biscayne National Park–ICW Mile 1107 to Mile 1120

NAVIGATION: Use NOAA Charts 11451 and 11463. After a straight run from the Miami area, the ICW route passes through the well marked, but narrow channel at Featherbed Bank (Mile 1108). Biscayne National Park boundary flashing yellow light "C" lies exactly on the ICW route and serves as a helpful intermediate checkpoint on this long run. East of the

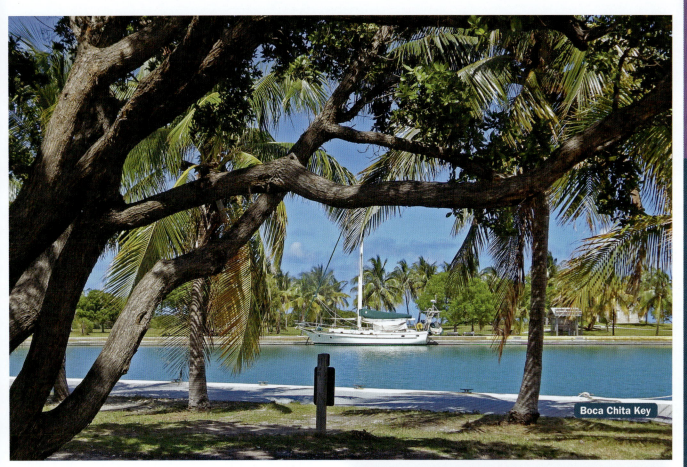

Boca Chita Key

ICW channel near Mile 1107 is a side channel marked by daybeacons and lights, with 6-foot controlling depths. It runs past several small islands and past Boca Chita Key, then close in to Sands and Elliott Keys. Be aware that both channels are prone to shoaling. Maintain low speed and a watchful eye on your depth sounder as you pass through this area. Tiny Boca Chita Key is considered the official start of the Florida Keys by water. The 65-foot Boca Chita lighthouse, built in the 1930s, guides boats to the park.

Elliott Key, about 3 miles east of ICW Mile 1113, is part of Biscayne National Park and is open to the public. Graced with a hardwood jungle and a shell-laden ocean beach, Elliott Key is the largest of the 25 keys encompassed by Biscayne National Park. Campsites and picnic grounds are available through the park rangers at the visitor center. Pets must be on an attended leash that is no longer than 6 feet in length. Be sure to bring lots of bug spray because you

Mooring buoys are available throughout the park but use is limited to 4 hours by any one boat for snorkeling and diving. Visit nps.gov/bisc for a complete listing of moorings.

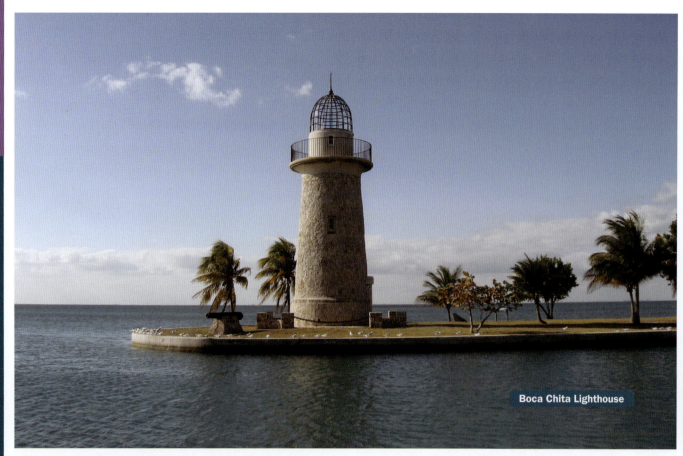

Boca Chita Lighthouse

SHHHH! Personal watercraft ("jet skis") are prohibited in Biscayne National Park, as are generators (after 10:00 p.m.).

will encounter mosquitoes and no-see-ums. Visitors are requested not to feed the wildlife. The rest of the 181,500-acre park (including much of Biscayne Bay) includes portions of the ocean reef and numerous shipwreck sites.

At the southeastern end of Elliott Key is Caesar Creek (southeast of Mile 1116), with a shallow entrance marked by Park Service buoys. The creek meanders past Elliott Key and out toward Hawk Channel and is a pretty passage for boats with less than a 4-foot draft.

⚠️ Be aware that Caesar Creek flashing green "29" was reported to be destroyed in summer 2018. The concrete wreckage is 3 feet below the waterline at high-tide and is marked with a flashing green marker.

Dockage: The National Park Service operates a facility to the north at Boca Chita Key that is more suitable for cruising boats. A channel with at least 4-foot MLW depths begins 0.5 mile north of Sands Key Light (flashing green "3") and runs straight in toward the middle of Boca Chita Key. The channel is marked with three pairs of daybeacons. Alongside dockage for 25 to 30 craft is available but there is neither drinking water nor showers, although there are restrooms ashore. Boats with pets onboard are *not* permitted to dock, even if the animal remains on the boat!

Showers and restrooms are located in a building a short distance from the boat basin at Elliott Key and have only non-potable water; drinking-quality water is available from a faucet there. There is no approach channel to the boat basin, which has slips for small boats (less than 20 feet). Depths may be as little as 2 feet at MLW, making it strictly dinghy territory. There are two dinghy landings. Cruising vessels typically anchor well offshore.

Anchorage: Anchoring is available anywhere in Biscayne National Park except over coral or sponge beds. Ragged Keys, located 3 miles east of Mile 1106, has 7 to 8 feet at MLW with good holding in grass and mud. This is exposed northwest through southwest. The inner anchorage at Sands Key (two miles south) has excellent holding in 6 to 7 feet at MLW and all-around protection, but for all but shoal draft boats the approach can be a little tricky (with spots as shallow as 4 feet at MLW), so you might have to wait for high tide to either enter or exit. There are a few rocks but you should find a place to drop your hook. If you can't manage the inner anchorage, you can anchor outside on the west side of Sands Key in 5 to 6 feet at MLW with good holding in grass and mud. This is exposed, however, north through southwest.

During summer months with prevailing winds from the southeast, Elliott Key plays host to hundreds of boats. You will have to stay about one-half mile offshore and keep an eye out for storm systems during the summer. During the winter, far fewer boats will visit this beautiful area because frequent northerlies make anchoring here risky and downright uncomfortable. It is possible to anchor off Coon Point on the northwest side of Elliot Key in 4 to 6 feet at MLW with good holding. This is protected from the east.

Caesar Creek winds around tiny Adams Key (7- to 12-foot MLW depths and facilities ashore for day use only) and has a southern spur leading to an anchorage between Rubicon and Reid Keys. There are only about 3-foot MLW approach depths; however, you should have up to 12 feet at MLW once inside.

See more on anchoring in the Keys in the Skipper's Handbook in the front of this guide.

Card Sound–ICW Mile 1120

NAVIGATION: Use NOAA Charts 11451 and 11463. After traversing Featherbed Bank and altering course to approximately 192 degrees magnetic for about 7 miles, you will find flashing red "8." At this point, you will alter course to about 221 degrees magnetic (just to the west of Rubicon Keys and Caesar Creek) for the straight, 2.6-mile, well marked, but narrow channel run through 3- and 4-foot shoals to the pass through Cutter Bank and into Card Sound (at about Mile 1119).

Once in Card Sound, you will pass numerous fishing channels between the adjacent keys to the east. One is Angelfish Creek, heavily used for passage between the ICW and Hawk Channel. For vessels wanting to utilize the Gulf Stream's power for a transit to Bimini Island in the Bahamas, 1.8-nm-long Angelfish Creek provides a more southerly approach than Miami, albeit 14 nm longer (56 nm versus 42 nm). The channel is a fair weather proposition only, with 4-foot MLW depths on both ends. See more on Angelfish Creek on the Waterway Explorer at waterwayguide.com.

Dockage: On Key Largo, the Ocean Reef Club (305-367-2611) once welcomed transients, but now has a "members and sponsored guests only" policy.

Anchorage: In a north wind, some protection can be found behind Long Arsenicker Island between Biscayne Bay and the northeast corner of Card Sound at Midnight Pass (Mile 1120). To the south, just past Mile 1120, the entrance to Angelfish Creek from Card Sound is a well-known rendezvous and anchoring spot under the lee of small Pumpkin Key. ICW cruisers frequently congregate here, some waiting to cross the Gulf Stream to the Bahamas by exiting the bays via Angelfish Creek and others just to enjoy a quiet stop en route. Drop the anchor in 7 to 9 feet at MLW with excellent holding in grass and mud. (No shore access.) Little Pumpkin Creek is another "locals spot" and can get busy on weekends. It is popular with locals as a hurricane hole.

The southernmost anchorage in Card Sound is at Jew Point, about 1.5 miles east of the mouth of Steamboat Creek (Mile 1125). There is 7 to 9 feet at MLW with good holding in grass and mud but poor protection in north winds.

Barnes Sound–ICW Mile 1126

NAVIGATION: Use NOAA Charts 11451 and 11463. From Cutter Bank Pass set a course of 233 degrees magnetic for about 4.7 miles to flashing green "17," which leads to the pass through Card Bank to Little Card Sound (Mile 1125). The **Card Sound Bridge** (65-foot fixed vertical clearance bridge) at Mile 1126.9 serves as the next landmark. This is the first of two highway bridges leading to the Keys from the mainland.

The channel under the bridge is marked and dredged, but it shallows rapidly upon entering Barnes Sound, so follow your markers closely. Once you are through the channel to flashing red "26" in Barnes Sound, good depths (6 to 8 feet at MLW) run the straight 4.5 miles or so to the end of Barnes Sound and the Jewfish Creek channel leading to Blackwater Sound. Depending on wind direction, the chop can build and Barnes Sound can get sloppy.

During the winter season, you will likely encounter commercial stone crabbing or lobster boats, in addition to the usual menagerie of sportfishermen and ICW cruisers.

Dockage: Inside Manatee Bay, where Manatee Creek was dead-ended by construction of the Overseas Highway (U.S. Route 1) decades ago, Manatee Bay Marine Inc. operates a working yard. The facility normally reserves dockage for repair customers. Transients looking for dockage in this laid-back and

Upper Keys, FL

		Largest Vessel Accommodated	VHF Channel Monitored	Transient Berths / Total Berths	Approach / Dockside Depth (reported)	Floating Docks	Gas / Diesel	Groceries, Ice, Marine Supplies, Snacks	Repairs: Hull, Engine, Propeller	Lift (tonnage), Crane, Rail	Min/Max Amps	Laundry, Pool, Showers, Courtesy Car	Pump-Out Station	Nearby: Grocery Store, Motel, Restaurant
KEY LARGO AREA: INSIDE ROUTE		Dockage					Supplies			Services				
1. Manatee Bay Marine Inc. 3.4 NW of 1131.5	305-451-3332	50	16/72	call/45	4.5/5	F	–	M	HEP	L60,C50	30/30	S	P	R
2. Gilbert's Resort and Marina WiFi 1134	305-451-1133	105	16	call/50	6/15	–	GD	IMS	–	–	30/50	LPS	P	GMR
3. Anchorage Resort & Yacht Club WiFi 1134	305-451-0500	180	16/09	6/20	6/8	–	–	I	–	–	30/50	LPS	–	MR
4. The Marina Club at BlackWater Sound WiFi	305-453-0081	40	16	–	4/4	F	G	GIMS	HEP	L	30/50	S	–	GMR
KEY LARGO AREA: OUTSIDE ROUTE														
5. Garden Cove Marina WiFi	305-451-4694	45	16/78	6/14	4/14	–	G	IM	EP	L10,R2	30/30	S	–	GMR
6. John Pennekamp Coral Reef State Park	305-451-6325	50		9/9	–	–	–	–	–	–	30/30	S	P	–
7. Key Largo Harbor Marina WiFi 1.7 E of 1141.3	305-451-0045	65	16	–	4/10	–	GD	GIMS	HEP	L80,C	30/50	LS		G
8. Ocean Divers	305-451-1113	50	16	–	5/20	–	GD	–	–	–	–	–	–	GR
9. Marina Del Mar Resort and Marina WiFi	305-453-7171	60	16	50/77	4.5/18	–	–	GI	–	–	30/50	LPS	P	GR
10. Pilot House Marina WiFi	**305-747-4359**	85	16	25/55	4.5/10	F	GD	IMS	HEP	L20	30/100	LPS	P	GMR
PLANTATION KEY AREA: INSIDE ROUTE														
11. Mangrove Marina WiFi 1.3 S of 1150.0	305-852-8380	50	–	call/111	5/5	–	GD	I	–	L7	30/50	LPS	P	GM
12. Tavernier Creek Marina 1.4 SE of 1151.7	305-852-5854	36	–	call/21	5/5	–	G	GIMS	HEP	L10	30/30	S	–	GMR
13. Plantation Yacht Harbor Marina WiFi	**305-852-2381**	80	16/10	7/85	5/5	–	GD	I	–	–	30/100	LPS	P	MR
14. Smuggler's Cove Marina WiFi 1157	305-664-5564	60	79	10/33	5/6	–	GD	GIMS	HEP	L8	30/50	PSC	–	GMR
PLANTATION KEY AREA: OUTSIDE ROUTE														
15. Curtis Marine Inc. WiFi 1.3 SE of 1149.7	305-852-5218	60	–	1/20	4.5/14	–	–	M	–	–	30/50	LS	P	GMR
16. Blue Waters Marina WiFi 1.3 SE of 1149.7	305-853-5604	60	–	call/20	4.5/20	–	–	I	–	–	30/50	LS	–	GMR
17. Treasure Harbor Marine WiFi	800-FLA-BOAT	50	16/09	5/23	4/7	F	GD	–	–	–	30/50	LS	P	MR
18. Snake Creek Marina WiFi	305-396-7724	40	09	10/20	3.5/3.5	F	G	IS	HE	L9	30/50			MR

⌨ Internet Access WiFi Wireless Internet Access WG Waterway Guide Cruising Club Partner onSpot dockside WiFi facility

See WaterwayGuide.com for current rates, fuel prices, web site addresses, and other up-to-the-minute information. *(Information in the table is provided by the facilities.)*

INSIDE ROUTE

OUTSIDE ROUTE

PLANTATION KEY AREA, NOAA CHART 11451

KEY LARGO AREA, NOAA CHART 11451

HOME   MARINA   RESTAURANT   GLASS BOTTOM BAR   THINGS TO DO   CONTACT US   BLOG   WEBCAM

Welcome to Paradise! Pilot House Marina, In the heart of Downtown Key Largo, FL

Secure Port

On Site Dining

Diving/Fishing

Pilot House Marina is a full service Marina centrally located in the heart of beautiful downtown Key Largo, FL just 50 miles south of Miami and 50 miles west of the Bahamas. Amenities are many so please visit our website for photos, charts and much more.

www.pilothousemarina.com or call 305-747-4359

out-of-the-way location may find it at one of the smaller marinas just east of Manatee Bay Marine.

Anchorage: At the northeast end of Barnes Sound, near Steamboat Creek is a fairly protected cove with 7 to 9 feet at MLW. It offers protection from the north through east only. (It is more protected inside where there is just 4 to 5 feet at MLW.) There is good fishing here and you can dingy through the mangroves. There are 5-foot MLW depths with good holding in mud in Manatee Creek located north of Mile 1132. This is open to the north.

Jewfish Creek–ICW Mile 1134

At about Mile 1133, you enter the well-marked, deep Jewfish Channel. From here on, you really are in the Keys. Key Largo lies to the east and offers many sites of historical, geological and romantic interest in its 30-mile length. Some sites are close to the marinas, but if this is a first visit, it is best to arrange for land transportation. Private watercraft are rented locally, so be prepared to navigate carefully and defensively here. The local radio station in this area is WCTH-FM 100.3, offering up-to-date local weather information and music.

NAVIGATION: Use NOAA Charts 11451 and 11463. Jewfish Creek itself is a favorite fishing spot and small boats often congregate in the area. The numerous anchored or slow-trolling small fishing boats occupying this narrow channel require a close watch and a fast hand on the throttle to slow to Idle-Speed/No-Wake. The route leads to the **Jewfish Creek (U.S. 1) Bridge** at Mile 1134.1 (65-foot fixed vertical clearance).

Dockage: Immediately south of the bridge, on the western side, is the well-known Gilbert's Resort and Marina, with a long wooden wharf along the channel for easy access to the gasoline and diesel pumps. Their lively tiki bar has music nightly. On the east side of the channel, the Anchorage Resort & Yacht Club also has slips for transients.

Anchorage: Just before the entrance to Jewfish Creek is Thursday Cove with excellent holding and protection from all but the north and west. It is possible to anchor in Jewfish Creek at the junction with Cross Key Creek at red daybeacon "32." Space is limited but there is 8 feet at MLW and all-around protection. Boats are often seen anchoring just to the south of the Jewfish Creek Bridge near green daybeacon "37." Charted depths outside of the channel in the immediate vicinity are 6 to 8 feet at MLW. Our Cruising Editors have always found this area to be full of local boats with very limited room to anchor

on the east side of the channel. However, there is room to anchor on the west side, just pay attention to your depth sounder. This anchorage is exposed to wakes and winds from any westerly quadrant and promises to be very buggy. Be sure to have plenty of bug spray at all times of the year!

Blackwater Sound–ICW Mile 1135

NAVIGATION: Use NOAA Charts 11451 and 11464. Leaving Jewfish Creek at flashing red "38" and setting a course of 224 degrees magnetic will take you the 2.6 miles to the entrance to Dusenbury Creek, which leads to Tarpon Basin (Mile 1139). To the west of Blackwater Sound lies the Everglades National Park with its vast expanses of water and mangrove forests.

All of the keys within the **Everglades National Park** are restricted from landings except where specifically designated and charted by park authorities.

The fishing on the expansive shallow flats here is outstanding, but catch and licensing regulations are in effect here and enforcement is strict.

Dockage: The Marina Club at Blackwater Sound is located just north of a dredged canal, which leads to Largo Sound on the ocean side. This facility is storage only (no transients), sells gas and offers repairs.

Anchorage: There are numerous anchorages on the eastern side of Blackwater Sound. Sexton Cove at the northeast end (Mile 1135) has 6- to 7-foot MLW depths and a grassy bottom with fair holding. (Lake Surprise to the north is not a viable anchorage, despite its size, unless you can traverse the 3-foot MLW entrance channel.)

To the south, you can snug up to the south of Stellrecht Point in 6 to 7 feet at MLW with good holding in grass and mud. At the southeast end of Blackwater Sound, you can drop the hook in 6 to 7 feet at MLW with good holding and protection from the south.

Tarpon Basin–ICW Mile 1139

NAVIGATION: Use NOAA Charts 11451 and 11464. From Blackwater Sound, the ICW snakes through mangrove-lined Dusenbury Creek (Mile 1138), where roseate spoonbills occasionally can be seen. The birds look for food by making sweeping motions with their flat bills. They are pink in color and rather pretty. Tarpon Basin is at the end of the creek.

Plantation Yacht Harbor Marina

Plantation Key

If you draw more than 3 feet, pay close attention to channel markers through Tarpon Basin and take it slowly. Our Cruising Editor draws 4.5 feet and found plenty of depth when in the channel. Pay particular attention to red daybeacon "42" through flashing red "48" and hug them closely while making the hard turn to starboard. The water here is clear most of the time, so keep your head up, out of the cockpit. Although charts show 5- to 6-foot MLW depths, depth sounders may register 2.5- to 3-foot MLW depths in certain spots just outside the curve of the channel. At flashing red "48," steer directly for red daybeacon "48A" and then on to flashing red "50."

Narrow Grouper Creek is marked by red daybeacon "52" and exits between green daybeacon "53" and red daybeacon "52A." Flashing red "54" leads into Buttonwood Sound. Quite often fast boats will travel through this area at high speeds with no regard for other boats. Caution should be taken if this occurs.

Anchorage: With its small reach, Tarpon Basin offers some good anchoring opportunities. Just be aware that holding is just fair due to the grassy bottom (some rock has been reported). The most popular area is just south of the large shoal in the center of the basin; proceed to red daybeacon "48A" before turning and then head south while watching your depth. There is a large community of liveaboards here but there's lots of room. If you drop a hook here, be sure to seek local knowledge about the mangrove tunnels that you can explore from the comfort of your dinghy.

Good dinghy docks and picnic tables can be found in the Nelson Government Center Park, behind the Monroe County Nelson Government Center in Tarpon Basin. Cruisers can use the restrooms in the Government Center during office hours, but be respectful; this is a public facility, not a marina. The Government Center does not offer water but garbage can be placed in their dumpsters. The park is less than a mile east of the Trade Winds Plaza Shopping Center, which has a very good Publix and a large Kmart, and 0.8 miles west of a West Marine. There are several restaurants and other shopping within one mile of the dinghy dock.

Buttonwood Sound–ICW Mile 1140

NAVIGATION: Use NOAA Charts 11451 and 11464. Buttonwood Sound (Mile 1141) starts the area of 5-foot controlling depths along the ICW. Deeper water is sometimes inexplicably found to either side of the channel. Nevertheless, adhere strictly to the marked channel on the chart unless you maintain constant watch of your depth sounder or you have obtained local knowledge. Pay close attention to your exact location in relation to ICW markers, both forward and astern. Groundings are frequent for unwary boaters. Although the normal 1-foot tidal range may not warrant concern, strong winds can create considerable alterations in depth, making the water difficult to read, and may blow a boat just enough off course to make a difference.

Anchorage: At Mile 1140 in Tarpon Basin, you can anchor north of red daybeacon "48A" in 7- to 8-feet MLW depths. There are good dinghy docks at the Nelson Government Center Park (which also offers restroom facilities during office hours). There are picnic tables, along with a bike rack where cruisers can leave their bikes ashore for short periods. There is a 24/7 police presence so the park and dinghy dock are safe. There are several restaurants and shopping (including groceries and a West Marine) within 1 mile of the dinghy dock. You can explore the nearby mangrove tunnels in your dinghy from here.

To the east of Baker Cut lies Sunset Cove. If you turn to port between daybeacons red "54" and green "55" and proceed towards the beach, you can anchor in 4 to 6 feet at MLW with good holding. Snook's Bayside Restaurant and Bar (305-453-5004) is located here. They have an excellent "happy hour" and great food. The anchorage is exposed to the north and west and is shallow (5 feet at MLW), but it is a very flat bottom with almost no tide. You will not be alone; there are always numerous boats anchored here.

The Upper Keys Sailing Club is to the northeast at Point Pleasant. This is a private sailing club, but if you get permission, you may be able to stop here for a short time and wander down to town, which isn't more than a half-mile walk. Nearby is a liquor store, some good restaurants and several stores including a Publix supermarket. Passing through Baker Cut, you can anchor by Butternut Key (Mile 1146) in 5 to 6 feet at MLW with fair holding. This will provide some protection from the northeast winds.

Pigeon Key to Cowpens Cut– ICW Mile 1149 to Mile 1155

NAVIGATION: Use NOAA Charts 11451 and 11464. Leaving Buttonwood Sound, the ICW continues its shallow course through a well-marked, but narrow channel (Baker Cut) into Florida Bay at Mile 1144. Shoal spots lie on either side of the channel. After you pass Pigeon Key and swing to starboard to avoid a little (unnamed) island that will be to your right, you will pass red daybeacon "64A" to starboard. Pay careful attention to your chart and your depth sounder; there have been several reports of grounding here. Our Cruising Editor hugged the markers and had no problems. Once past

Note: **Cowpens** was named for the pens used to hold manatees, which were once used for food.

Upper Keys, FL

WG

	Largest Vessel Accommodated	VHF Channel Monitored	Transient Berths / Total Berths	Approach / Dockside Depth (reported)	Floating Docks	Gas / Diesel	Groceries, Ice, Marine Supplies, Snacks	Repairs: Hull, Engine, Propeller	Lift (tonnage), Crane, Rail	Min/Max Amps	Laundry, Pool, Showers, Courtesy Car	Pump-Out Station	Nearby: Grocery Store, Motel, Restaurant
MATECUMBE KEYS: INSIDE ROUTE			**Dockage**				**Supplies**			**Services**			
1. Islamorada Yacht Basin Lorelei Restaurant 🖥 WiFi 1160.2 305-664-2692	45	16	3/15	4.5/4.5	–	–	I	–	–	30/50	LS	P	GMR
2. Coral Bay Marina WiFi 1160.2 305-664-3111	62	16	10/35	5/6	–	–	M	HEP	L50	50/50	LS	P	GMR
3. Caribee Boat Sales & Marina 1160.2 305-664-3431	32	–	–	5.5/5.5	–	G	IM	HEP	L	30/30	–	–	GMR
4. World Wide Sportsman/Bayside Marina 305-664-3398	40	16/68	20/43	3/4	–	GD	IMS	–	–	30/50	S	P	GMR
5. Islamorada Marina 1161.0 305-664-8884	50	–	2/18	8/4.5	F	GD	I	HEP	L10	30/50	S	–	GMR
6. Angler House Marina 305-664-5247	45	–	–	8/4	–	GD	I	–	–	30/50	S	–	GMR
MATECUMBE KEYS: OUTSIDE ROUTE													
7. Islamorada Resort Co. ~ Post Card Inn Marina at Holiday Isle 🖥 WiFi 305-664-2321	100	16/73	19/56	4.5/8	–	GD	IMS	–	–	30/50	P	–	MR
8. Whale Harbor Marina 305-664-4511	–	–	call/22	5/6	–	–	IS	–	–	30/30	S	–	GMR
9. La Siesta Resort & Marina WiFi 305-250-0755	45	–	5/20	3.5/6	–	G	I	–	–	30/50	LPS	–	GMR
10. Bud'n Mary's Fishing Marina 1162.1 305-664-2461	45	77	10/35	4.5/4.5	–	GD	GIM	HP	L	30/50	–	–	GMR
11. Caloosa Cove Marina & Resort WiFi 1169.5 305-664-4455	65	16	5/32	5/4	–	GD	GIMS	E	L6	30/50	LS	–	GMR

🖥 Internet Access WiFi Wireless Internet Access WG Waterway Guide Cruising Club Partner onSpot dockside WiFi facility

See WaterwayGuide.com for current rates, fuel prices, web site addresses, and other up-to-the-minute information. *(Information in the table is provided by the facilities.)*

INSET 7 PAGE F

INSIDE ROUTE

OUTSIDE ROUTE

MATECUMBE KEYS, NOAA CHART 11451

"64A," you can head south to a little bay with private markers. The water depths just off the channel are 6 feet at MLW, and then shallow to 4 feet as you get closer to shore.

The main ICW route continues westward from daybeacon "64A" through Ramshorn Cut, which is well marked. Approaching Travemier Creek things get confusing as the markers for both channels are placed close together. Also the exit of Travernier Creek is prone to shoaling and finding your way here requires heightened attention. Slow down and pick your way carefully. If it starts getting shallow, veer north to gain better depth.

The area just beyond Cowpens Cut can also be confusing when you arrive at flashing red "78" (Mile 1153.7). It appears as if the ICW ends here; the yellow squares and triangles no longer appear on aids to navigation, and the daybeacons and lights appear in a different section of the *Light List* published by NOAA (navcen.uscg.gov). On the other hand, NOAA considers the ICW to continue on to Key West. The magenta line continues on charts, and the mileage continues to increase. Coverage in the *Coast Pilot* chapter on the ICW also continues to Key West.

Dockage: Mangrove Marina is a popular marina and transient slips must be reserved in advance. Call Mangrove Marina for specific navigation. Dockside and approach depths are 5 feet at MLW. If you are in need of supplies, there is a shopping center with a supermarket close by. In the area labeled "Community Hbr" on the chart is the Old Tavernier Restaurant and Tavern (305-852-6012) with an active local crowd. This Italian and Greek restaurant is open for dinner only.

Tavernier Creek Marina, north of the fixed **Tavernier Creek Bridge** bridge (15-foot vertical clearance), is primarily a dry-stack marina that sells gas only.

Anchorage: The Cowpens anchorage at Mile 1155 has 5- to 6-foot MLW depths with good holding in grass and mud. This anchorage is open and exposed to the northwest.

Plantation Key Area–ICW Mile 1156

NAVIGATION: Use NOAA Charts 11451 and 11464. Cowpens Cut through Cross Bank (at Mile 1153) leads into the Plantation Key area. At Mile 1156, Snake Creek leads off to the southeast. Its channel is marked with flashing red "12" at the northern end; note that the aids here are numbered from the ocean side. The **Snake Creek Bascule Bridge** has 27-foot closed vertical

clearance and opens on signal, except from 7:00 a.m. to 6:00 p.m., when it will only open on the hour. The Snake Creek channel provides very shallow access to Hawk Channel on the ocean side. The channel on the ocean side of the bridge has shoaled, and the passage is not recommended. Coast Guard Station Islamorada may be able to provide depth information.

⚠ From Cotton Key at ICW red daybeacon "78A" (Mile 1155) to Steamboat Channel, the ICW passes through what is perhaps the shallowest part of the entire route. In addition, the wide spacing of makers in this area makes following the channel difficult. Remember, touching a sandy bottom at slow speeds is rarely dangerous but, at high speeds, can do considerable damage to your props.

Marker floats for lobster and stone crab traps fill the channel and surrounding water in season so be careful about fouling your propeller shaft. During the off-season (May 15 to October 15), all traps and floats are supposed to be removed. Navigation is much simpler then, but some stray traps do remain, requiring a sharp lookout.

Dockage: Plantation Yacht Harbor Marina offers protection from all but hurricane-force winds. If westbound from flashing red "78," continue toward red daybeacon "78A" for 1 mile, then alter course to about 150 degrees magnetic and continue about 1 nm toward shore. You will spot a red and white horizontally striped lighthouse at the end of the marina's breakwater. Leave it to starboard, make a sharp starboard turn around the lighthouse and follow the marked channel.

The village of Islamorada owns the 42-acre park in which Plantation Yacht Harbor Marina is located. In addition to the slips and the regular cruiser amenities, it has a soccer pitch, tennis courts, a swimming pool, a dog park, basketball courts, a saltwater swimming beach, a baseball diamond and a place to jog. Good restaurants are nearby. Smuggler's Cove Marina is to the south, with slips, hotel rooms and all fuels.

Anchorage: The charted Cowpens anchorage at Mile 1155 has 5 to 6 feet at MLW with good holding in grass and mud. This anchorage is open and exposed to the west. You can anchor in 5 to 6 feet at MLW south of Cotton Key at Mile 1158 in Barley Basin. This provides protection from the east through southeast with excellent holding in at least 5-foot MLW depths.

GOIN' ASHORE: **ISLAMORADA, FL**

SERVICES	
1	Library
ATTRACTIONS	
2	Hurricane Monument
3	Keys History & Discovery Center
4	Redbone Gallery
SHOPPING	
5	Hooked on Books

DINING	
6	Trading Post Market and Deli
7	Worldwide Sportsman
DINING	
7	Islamorada Fish Company Restaurant and Seafood Market/ Zane Grey Long Key Lounge
8	Lorelei Restaurant and Cabana Bar
9	Morada Bay Beach Cafe

MARINAS	
7	World Wide Sportsman/Bayside Marina
8	Islamorada Yacht Basin
10	Caribee Boat Sales & Marina
11	Coral Bay Marina

Islamorada is made up of four islands. The first one you would come to from the north is Plantation Key, then Windley Key, Upper Matecumbe Key and Lower Matecumbe Key. Indian Key and Lignum Vitae are islands just off the highway only accessible by boat and belong to the State of Florida. They are now state parks. Note that the highway Mile Markers (or MM) do not correspond to the waterway statute miles. Also, addresses are given as "bay side" or "ocean side," depending on which side of Overseas Highway (U.S. 1) they fall.

Attractions: The Islamorada Chamber of Commerce and Visitors Center is located at MM 87 (305-664-4503) and is a perfect first stop for information about the area. Another good stop is the Keys History & Discovery Center, located on the property of the Islander Resort (MM 82). Here you can see a model of Indian Key the way it looked in 1840, a "legends of the line" fishing

exhibit and numerous historical photos of the area. Open Thursday through Sunday from 10:00 a.m. to 5:00 p.m. (305-922-2237).

The Matecumbe Historical Trust has a self-guided tour brochure that can be downloaded from their web site at MatecumbeHistoricalTrust.com. There are markers on historic sites throughout the islands of Islamorada, including many located by the water. One to look for is the 1935 Hurricane Memorial, located at MM 81.5, across from the library. It was dedicated November 14, 1937, as The Florida Keys Memorial and memorializes the World War I veterans and civilians who perished in the 1935 hurricane.

The Redbone Gallery at 200 Morada Way at MM 81.5 specializes in fine original angling and island art. The Gallery is run by a fund raising organization supporting a cure for Cystic Fibrosis. Portions of all original art sales benefit The Cystic Fibrosis Foundation. Unique paintings, sculptures and jewelry (much of which is related to saltwater fishing) are among their offerings. Open daily except Sunday (305-664-2002).

Along U.S. Route 1 (Overseas Highway), you will find paved pedestrian/bike paths that make walking and biking on the Key pleasant, easy and safe. On foot or by bicycle, Upper Matecumbe Key is a manageable 4.8 miles.

Shopping: For provisions, the 24-hour Trading Post Market and Deli (305-664-2571) at MM 81.8 is a small, well-stocked supermarket and deli. (The nearest full-size supermarket is the Winn Dixie in Tavernier at MM 92. Worldwide Sportsman at MM 81.5 on the Bay side (305-664-4615) carries fishing tackle and some boating supplies. Caribee Boat Sales (305-664-3431), located next to the Trading Post at MM 81.5 (also Bay side), is a Yamaha dealer and has a marine supply store, complete with a Parts Department.

Just for fun, at MM 81.9 on the ocean side is Hooked on Books (305-517-2602), a small, independent book seller with a collection of new and used books about the Keys, the Everglades and Florida, as well as a fiction section.

Dining: The Islamorada Restaurant and Bakery (also known as "Bob's Bunz") is at MM 81.6 for breakfast and lunch (305-664-8363). There are several excellent restaurants at the top of the Keys, including Wahoo's Bar and Grill (305-664-9888) at the Whale Harbor Inn on Upper Matecumbe Key. At MM 82 on the Bay side (at the large mermaid sign) is the Lorelei Restaurant and Cabana Bar (305-664-2692) with good food (breakfast, lunch and dinner), reputedly the best happy hour on the Key, live entertainment seven nights a week and, for boaters, a marina and dinghy dock. It's the place to be at sunset, when it is crowded and alive. In the same area is Morada Bay Beach Café at MM 81.6 (305-664-0604), which offers Mediterranean cuisine, weekend entertainment and a small boat/dinghy dock on the Little Basin (Bay side).

Adjacent to the Worldwide Sportsman (owned by Bass Pro Shop) at MM 81.5 is the excellent Islamorada Fish Company Restaurant and Seafood Market (305-664-9271). Be sure to check out the tarpon swimming in the pen alongside the dock. Zane Grey Long Key Lounge (305-664-4615) is located upstairs in the Worldwide Sportsman building. Visit the Islamorada Visitors Center at MM 87; they can provide more options.

Upper Matecumbe Key–ICW Mile 1160

Plantation Key and Upper Matecumbe Key are separated by Whale Harbor Channel. The channel to Hawks Channel is crossed by a 10-foot fixed **Whale Harbor Channel Bridge**. Islamorada (Spanish for "Purple Island") is located on Upper Matecumbe Key, the third largest island in the Keys.

NAVIGATION: Use NOAA Charts 11451 and 11464. Use the Miami Harbor Entrance Tide Tables. For high tide, add 2 hours 45 minutes; for low tide, add 4 hours. Islamorada may be reached on a southeasterly course from red daybeacon "84" prior to entering Steamboat Channel. At the south end of Upper Matecumbe Key is **Upper Matecumbe Key Bridge**, crossing a shallow (not navigable) channel to the Hawk Channel side. It has 7-foot fixed vertical clearance.

Dockage: From red daybeacon "84," steering a course of 150 degrees magnetic and keeping your eye dead ahead on the charted tall radio tower, you will come to Islamorada Yacht Basin & Lorelei Restaurant. There is a tight, well-protected yacht basin (4.5-foot controlling depth at MLW) beside the casual outdoor bar and restaurant. To the south, a set of white stakes mark the entrance to Coral Bay Marina, which has a 50-ton lift and on-site mechanics. Caribee Boat Sales & Marina is nearby with gas (no transient slips). Farther south are Worldwide Sportsman/Bayside Marina, Islamorada Marina and Angler House Marina. All three offer transient slips and various amenities, including fuel.

Anchorage: A local anchorage area is located offshore from Lorelei's Restaurant and Cabana Bar. This is a magnet for locals, cruisers and land-based tourists and the place to be at sunset. Dinghies from anchored boats are welcome at the restaurant's dinghy dock (for a fee if not dining with them), and at The Worldwide Sportsman dock and the Morada Bay Beach Café's small boat dock. The Coral Bay Marina does not have a dinghy dock; when the office is open dinghies can, with permission and space permitting, tie up in front of the office for an hour or two.

Indian, Lignumvitae & Lower Matecumbe Keys–ICW Mile 1161 to Mile 1165

At just 18 feet above sea level, Lignumvitae Key is the highest of the Keys; it is named for one of the hardest woods in the world, "the tree of life." A visit to the Lignumvitae State Botanical Site is worthwhile. Rangers conduct tours at 10:00 a.m. and 2:00 p.m. except on Tuesdays and Wednesdays, when the site is closed. As a historical aside, Indian Key was the first county seat of Dade County. Now Indian Key doesn't have a soul living on it.

NAVIGATION: Use NOAA Charts 11451 and 11464. Lying between Steamboat Channel (Mile 1161) and Bowlegs Cut (Mile 1165), Lignumvitae Basin offers good depths for substantial keels and fair-weather anchorages in the lees of Shell Key and Lignumvitae Key to the south. These two keys, bordered by the three navigable channels between Upper and Lower Matecumbe Keys and historic Indian Key (at the south end of Indian Key Channel), are all now a part of the Lignumvitae Key Management Area.

All channels in the management area are well marked, but only **Indian Key Channel Bridge**

Channel Five Bridge

The **Village of Islamorada** is actually a group of islands that stretches 18.2 miles, from the Tavernier Creek Bridge to the Channel Two Bridge and includes Plantation, Upper Matecombe, Indian, Lightnumvitae and Lower Matecombe Keys.

offers significant fixed vertical clearance (27 feet). **Teatable Key Channel Bridge** has just 10 feet of fixed vertical clearance, the same as **Lignumvitae Channel Bridge**.

⚠️ The shallow turtle grass flats in this area are clearly marked. The flats are all closed to boats with internal combustion engines (gas or diesel, inboard or outboard). State law enforcement officers police the area, and violators (particularly those who have damaged the grass with their props) are subject to stiff fines.

Dockage/Moorings: Indian Key has small boat docks, and the pier at Lignumvitae Key can accommodate medium-size cruising craft (4-foot MLW depths) at both locations, although no docking is permitted after 5:00 p.m., and pets are not allowed ashore. One mooring (complimentary for up to 1 week) may be available at Shell Key. The mooring pick-up line was reported to be in poor condition at press time (summer 2018).

Anchorage: Matecumbe Bight in Lower Matecumbe offers 6 to 7 feet at MLW with excellent holding in mud. (This is not a good place to be when wind is out of the north.)

Distances
Outside Route: Hawk Channel
(Miles from Miami)

LOCATION	STATUTE MILES	NAUTICAL MILES
Miami (Government Cut)	0	0
Miami (Cape Florida)	8	6.9
Fowey Rocks Light	14	12.0
Angelfish Creek	28	24.0
South Sound Creek	51	44.0
Tavernier	63	54.7
Islamorada	70	60.8
Channel Five	82	71.0
Duck Key	92	79.9
Marathon (Sisters Creek)	102	88.6
Moser Channel	109	94.7
Key West	151	131.0

(Moser Channel to Key West via Hawk Channel is 40 statute miles.)

■ UPPER KEYS: OUTSIDE (HAWK CHANNEL) ROUTE

For boats that draw over 4.5 feet, cruising through the keys will require you to stay on the ocean side of the Keys, in Hawk Channel. For deep draft vessels this is the only route, save for an ocean leg bucking the Gulf Stream outside of the reefs. In westerly through northerly winds of 15 knots or more, Hawk Channel may provide a more protected passage along the Keys than the ICW route.

Access to Hawk Channel from Miami and Miami Beach is through Government Cut. From just below Miami in Biscayne Bay, the Florida Channel/Biscayne Channel (treated as one) provides a more protected route. In winter, northerlies frequently become northeasters (20 knots or more) for several days and give Hawk Channel a lumpy, irregular following sea. It only abates where the Keys bend to the west.

Well-found and appropriately crewed sailboats will get a great sleigh ride. Powerboats, depending on size, may find it a wet and uncomfortable passage. Obviously, knowledgeable skippers with larger boats equipped with stabilizers and autopilots should not have difficulties.

Hawk Channel is relatively wide; nevertheless, navigation should be precise because the aids to navigation are frequently far apart and difficult to spot. Unlike on the ICW, NOAA charts show no magenta line or mile markers on Hawk Channel. Compass courses should be the rule, as well as following prudent piloting practices. GPS will be extremely useful in this passage, particularly during times of poor visibility, as numerous shoals line this route. You should take a cautious attitude when planning daily runs and plan to complete each day's run well before dark. As in the Bahamas, night passages are not recommended. Fortunately, both anchorages and marinas can be found at reasonable intervals throughout the Keys.

 Note that fines for damaging the bottom here can be significant. Anchor in designated areas only.

In heavy easterly weather, beam seas are the rule, amplified by current and counter-current in the stretches abeam the numerous gaps in the Florida reef. Sailboats might like this weather, but powerboats may wish to sit it out or move inside to the ICW.

Middle Keys, FL

		Largest Vessel Accommodated	VHF Channel Monitored	Transient Berths / Total Berths	Approach / Dockside Depth (reported)	Floating Docks	Gas / Diesel	Groceries, Ice, Marine Supplies, Snacks	Repairs: Hull, Engine, Propeller	Lift (tonnage), Crane, Rail	Min/Max Amps	Laundry, Pool, Showers, Courtesy Car	Pump-Out Station	Nearby: Grocery Store, Motel, Restaurant
MARATHON AREA: INSIDE ROUTE				Dockage			Supplies		Services					
1. Blackfin Resort and Marina [WiFi]	305-743-2393	40	–	20/27	8/10	–	–	I	–	–	30/30	LPS	P	GMR
2. Banana Bay Resort & Marina [WiFi] 1193	305-743-3500	60	16	34/34	5/7	–	–	IS	–	–	30/50	LPS	P	GMR
3. Keys Boat Works	305-743-5583	67	–	–	5/7	–	–	M	HEP	L50,C	30/30	S	–	MR
4. Marlin Bay Yacht Club [WiFi]	**305-731-2207**	60	16/17	24/99	6/10	–	–	I	–	–	30/100	P	P	GMR
5. Faro Blanco Resort & Yacht Club [WiFi]	**305-743-9018**	130	16/09	74/74	7/8.5	–	GD	IMS	–	–	30/100	LPSC	P	GMR
6. Capt. Pip's Marina & Hideaway	305-743-4403	–	16	–	5/5	–	–	IS	–	–	–	S	–	GMR
DUCK KEY: OUTSIDE ROUTE														
7. Hawks Cay Resort Marina ⌨ [WiFi] [WG] 1180	**888-974-8469**	110	16/10	52/85	5/5	–	–	GIMS	–	–	30/50	LPS	P	GMR
MARATHON AREA: OUTSIDE ROUTE														
8. Driftwood Marina & Storage 1187.3	305-289-0432	60	–	–	4/18	F	–	M	HP	L60	–	–	–	GMR
9. Outta The Blue Marina 1187.3	305-289-0285	48	–	5/10	8/12	–	–	IM	HEP	L60	30/30	S	P	GMR
10. White Marlin Marina [WiFi]	305-481-6721	80	–	27/27	6.5/12	–	–	I	–	–	20/50	LS	–	MR
11. Shelter Bay Marine	305-743-7008	38	–	call/20	8/12	F	GD	M	HEP	L	–	–	–	GMR
12. Key Colony Beach Marina [WiFi] 1187.0	305-289-1310	120	16	8/35	12/8	–	GD	IMS	–	–	30/100	–	P	GMR
13. Skipjack Resort & Marina ⌨ [WiFi]	305-289-7662	65	16	10/54	10/15	–	–	I	–	–	30/50	LPS	P	GMR
14. Sombrero Marina Dockside [WiFi] 1192.0	305-743-5663	85	16	20/57	7/9	–	–	IS	–	–	30/50	LS	P	GMR
15. Boot Key Harbor City Marina ⌨ [WiFi] 1193	**305-289-8877**	60	16	12/12	10/20	F	–	IS	–	–	30/50	LS	P	GMR
16. Marathon Boat Yard Marine Center ⌨ [WiFi] 1193	**305-743-6341**	80	16	5/20	8/20	F	–	M	HEP	L75	30/50	LS	P	GMR
17. Burdines Waterfront Marina 1193	305-743-5317	120	16	21/21	10/7	F	GD	GIMS	–	–	30/50	LS	P	GMR
18. Pancho's Marina and Fuel Dock [WiFi] 1193	305-743-2281	90	16	3/20	8/6.5	–	GD	GIMS	–	–	30/50	LS	P	GMR
19. Marathon Marina & Resort ⌨ [WiFi] [WG] 1193	**305-743-6575**	130	16/10	60/118	9/11	F	GD	IMS	HEP	L75	30/100	LPS	P	MR

⌨ Internet Access [WiFi] Wireless Internet Access [WG] Waterway Guide Cruising Club Partner onSpot dockside WiFi facility

See WaterwayGuide.com for current rates, fuel prices, web site addresses, and other up-to-the-minute information. *(Information in the table is provided by the facilities.)*

Hawks Cay Resort Marina

Toms Harbor

Duck Cay

DUCK KEY, NOAA CHART 11451

MARATHON AREA, NOAA CHART 11451

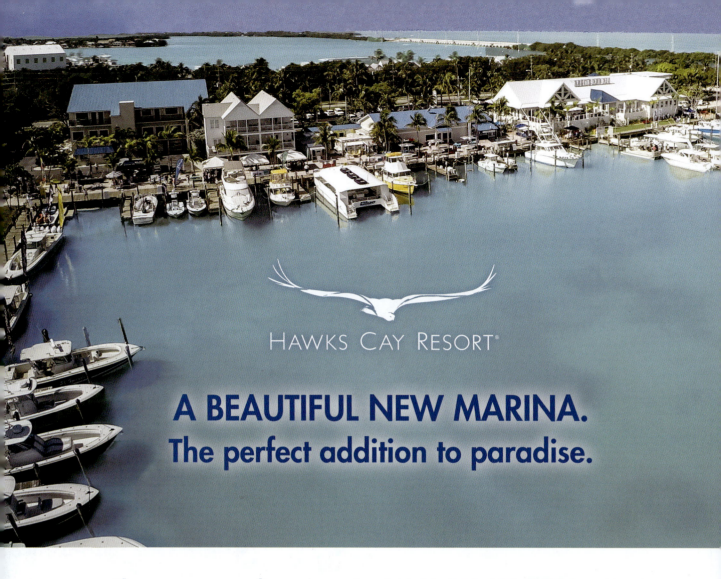

HAWKS CAY RESORT®

A BEAUTIFUL NEW MARINA.
The perfect addition to paradise.

Chart a course for waypoint N24° 45′ 48′ W80° 54′ 40′ and slip into the best spot to tie up in the Florida Keys.

Hawks Cay Marina recently reopened after a complete renovation and accommodates boats up to 110 feet. Stay aboard boaters are welcome to enjoy full access to the restaurants and amenities of Hawks Cay. Steps from your boat, Angler & Ale is serving up daily Captain's Hours specials and the best seafood around. The chefs will even prepare your catch while you relax and watch the sun set over some of the greatest fishing grounds in the world. **It just doesn't get any better than this!**

MENTION THE
WATERWAY GUIDE
AND **SAVE 10%**
ON YOUR DOCKAGE!

LIFESTYLE™
Preferred
HOTELS & RESORTS

Visit **HawksCay.com/Marina**
or call **(888) 974-8469**

AAA
Four Diamond
Award

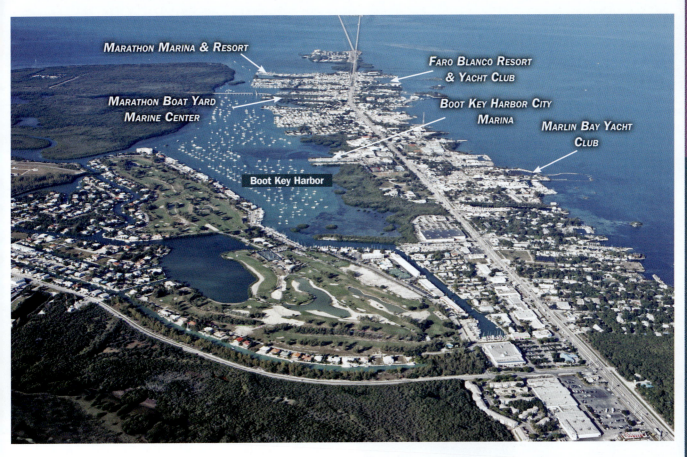

Marathon Marina & Resort

Faro Blanco Resort & Yacht Club

Marathon Boat Yard Marine Center

Boot Key Harbor City Marina

Marlin Bay Yacht Club

Boot Key Harbor

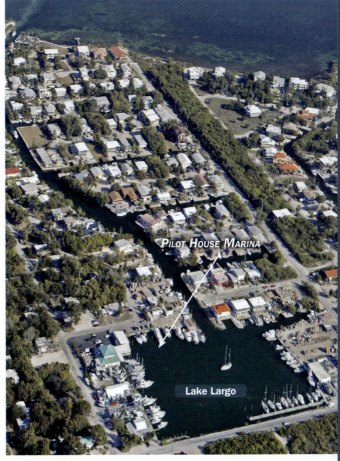

Pilot House Marina

Lake Largo

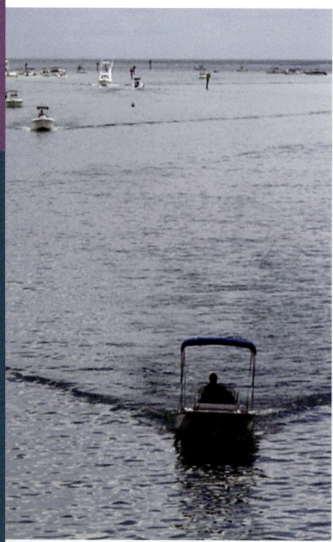

When winds slacken and veer to the southeast and south, conditions quiet down. With slack winds, sailboats may motorsail or make short close-hauled runs. Powerboats may still roll, but the journey will be generally enjoyable.

Biscayne Bay to Lower Matecumbe Key

NAVIGATION: Use NOAA Charts 11451, 11463, 11465 and 11468. (The charts listed provide different perspectives on the navigation routes discussed.) To enter Hawk Channel from Miami you will depart through Government Cut, or if you are in the Coconut Grove area you will depart through the more southerly openings of the Cape Florida Channel/Biscayne Channel. If you are departing from the Miami area, remember that when there are cruise ships docked at the Port of Miami the main channel is closed to recreational boats. This restriction is strictly enforced.

You will access the cut through the channel on the south side of Dodge Island and Fisher Island.

As you exit Government Cut, you must go seaward through Outer Bar Cut past the spoil areas. Or, if you are familiar with the area, cut between the range markers just south of the jetty. Either way, bear in mind there is a 3-foot shoal area extending out from Cape Florida. Keep red daybeacon "2," outside of Bear Cut just past Virginia Key, well off to starboard. You might do well to set a southeasterly course to pass about 1 mile inside Fowey Rocks Light (flashing white every 10 seconds) and the red daybeacon "2" and green daybeacon "3" marking the start of Hawk Channel. The channel markers, as with the ICW, generally follow red-right-southbound.

⚠️ Some variation in channel markers has resulted from recent storms, so navigate carefully using the latest charts. (The latest edition of Chart 11451 is the 36th from January 2017.)

The route from the Coconut Grove area gives a choice of the Cape Florida or Biscayne Channels. Both of these converge at 12-foot flashing red "6" south of Cape Florida's lighthouse. Vessels using Biscayne Channel from the west must pass between the two daybeacons (green daybeacon "7" and red daybeacon "8") just before flashing red "6." There is a well-marked channel, but you will need to pay attention to some shallow areas (7 to 9 feet at MLW). Current charts and local knowledge should be obtained before entering for the first time. For more details, see the Inlet section in the Skipper's Handbook at the front of this guide.

The cluster of houses amidst the reefs south of Biscayne Channel is Stiltsville, whose landmark homes are part of Biscayne National Park. When going to seaward in either channel, remember that green markers are to starboard until you reach flashing green "1."

From here to Hawk Channel, between red daybeacon "2" and green daybeacon "3," at ICW Mile 1098 west of Fowey Rocks, swing well east of the shoals south of Biscayne Channel flashing green "1," flashing red "2" and the flashing white light on a 37-foot skeleton tower. From this point to Channel Five is approximately 74 miles.

Slower boats may want to plan short runs between anchorages or marine facilities along the way. If you are sightseeing, you may want to do the same. To the west, as you pass Fowey Rocks Light, you will see the first of the small keys projecting above the ancient reef between the ocean and Biscayne Bay. About 3 miles on, the Ragged Keys appear, followed closely by Boca Chita, Sands and Elliott Keys. At Bowles Bank Light (flashing red "8"), the channel narrows and bends to the south-southwest as the westward curve of the Florida Keys commences. Sailboats that are close-hauled will want to plan their course carefully in this area.

Caesar Creek

NAVIGATION: Use NOAA Charts 11451 and 11463. At the southwest end of Elliott Key, Caesar Creek is the first crossover to the ICW. It is open to shallow-draft vessels only due to the shallows on the western end of the cut. The channel is well marked, but narrow and bounded by 1- to 2-foot depths at low tide; use extreme caution when transiting this area. Try to obtain local knowledge before using this as a crossover.

Flashing red "20" is at the entrance to the Park Service's marked channel. The channel is charted with at least 7 feet at MLW and has a low point of 4 feet at MLW on the Bay side. Pay attention to the wind direction as it will affect depths. Enter in the early morning when the water is easy to read. Caesar Creek provides a tight little anchorage at its western end.

Angelfish Creek

NAVIGATION: Use NOAA Charts 11451 and 11463. Local skippers use well-marked Angelfish Creek, about 3 nm south of Caesar Creek, to cross over from ocean to the Bay and back. (Study your chart carefully and avoid Broad Creek to the north, which is shoal at the entrance.) There are shoals at both the east and west ends of Angelfish Creek but for boats that draw 5 feet or less, it is fairly simple. If you draw over 5 feet, you can use the channel on a rising tide. The tidal range in this area is approximately 1 foot. Stay well out until the channel markers line up before you enter. Just inside the entrance from Hawk Channel is a rocky ledge with 5-foot MLW depths.

Keep dead center in Angelfish Creek at low tide and maintain enough speed to prevent leeway. Do not enter if another boat is coming out; you need to stay on the centerline. Once inside, the controlling 5-foot depth creates no problem, and you can often find deeper water. Depths of at least 7-feet at MLW along this passage are the rule rather than the exception. Side creeks offer anchorages, but the bottom is rocky and currents are strong. For more details, see the Inlet section in the Skipper's Handbook at the front of this guide.

Dockage: South of the ocean-side entrance to Angelfish Creek is the private Ocean Reef Club. It accepts only members and sponsored guests. Other facilities along the Hawk Channel side cater to transients, although many are oriented primarily to charters and sport fishermen. Average approach depths are 5 feet or less to many of these privately marked channels. Be sure to call ahead for channel depths.

A little over 10 nm to the south, Garden Cove Marina's well-marked channel begins at red daybeacon "32." Turn to starboard and sound your way into their channel. The approach depth is around 4 feet at MLW. There is plenty of water once you get into their basin, where you will find slips, gas and some repairs.

John Pennekamp Coral Reef State Park

The John Pennekamp Coral Reef State Park offers glass-bottom boat tours, Scuba gear rentals and instruction, boat rentals, a campground and a visitor's center with a 30,000-gallon saltwater aquarium. There are 50 miles of natural mangrove trails to explore via kayak or paddleboard, and the underwater park contains 178 square miles of coral reef, sea grass beds, mangrove swamps and the larger of two living reefs that lie in Florida waters. Tropical fish live around the coral, and there are shipwrecks, making an underwater paradise for divers and snorkelers. Only hook-and-line fishing is permitted here.

NAVIGATION: Use NOAA Charts 11451 and 11463. At green daybeacon "23," you cross the northwest boundary of the State Park. To reach the park's land attractions by boat, enter through South Sound Creek on the southwest side of Largo Sound, about midway down Key Largo and less than 2 miles to the north of Mosquito Bank flashing green "35." Flashing red "2" marks the entrance. *Do not cut this mark!* The channel carries 6-foot depths, but 5-foot depths have been reported in Largo Sound.

⚠️ Some variation in channel markers has resulted from recent storms, so navigate carefully using the latest charts. (The latest edition of Chart 11451 is the 36th from January 2017.)

Dive and sightseeing boats use this channel frequently, so be prepared to move, but not too far, because 3-foot depths have been reported out of the channel. Because of the narrow channel and blind turns, commercial vessels make a Sécurité call on VHF Channel 16 before entering it. Listen for such calls and make your own if appropriate.

Vessels with drafts of 4 feet or less and overhead clearances of 14 feet or less can cross over from Largo Sound to Blackwater Sound via a rock cut (charted as Marvin D. Adams Waterway) that connects the southernmost corner of Blackwater Sound with the western shore of Largo Sound. (The shallowest water lies at the beginning and end of the cut.) If you cannot get your big boat through here, it makes a great dinghy trip. Bear in mind that a strong current runs through here.

Dockage/Moorings: The John Pennekamp Coral Reef State Park's marina offers nine full-service slips. It is highly recommended to call the dockmaster on VHF Channel 16 to check availability and the current depths.

Although overnight anchoring is prohibited in Largo Sound, about a dozen white mooring balls are located in the southwest corner of the sound, near the park headquarters. Simply tie up to an empty one and dinghy over to the dockmaster's office (in the dive center) to check in.

Key Largo to Tavernier Key

NAVIGATION: Use NOAA Charts 11451 and 11463. To the south of John Pennekamp State Park is Port Largo Canal with more dockage options. Make your approach to the canal starting at green daybeacon "7" on a northeasterly course and watch your depth as the approach is only around 5 feet. Continue a short distance down the Hawk Channel to marker "8" and turn to starboard to enter the canal leading to Lake Largo and the Pilot House Marina.

Dockage: Key Largo Harbor Marina on Port Largo Canal offers slips, fuel and repairs (with an 80-ton lift). A bit farther into the canal is Marina del Mar Resort and Marina, also offering dockage and some amenities. On the same canal is Ocean Divers, a charter company that offers fuel.

About 7 nm south at Long Point, you will find two additional marinas–Curtis Marine Inc. and Blue Waters Marina. There is a channel leading to both, but it is very shallow (4.5 foot reported depths at MLW). It is strongly recommended that you call ahead for the latest information and slip availability as well as the current depth of their channel.

Anchorage: Only a short distance (2 nm) from the entrance of Largo Canal you will find Rodriguez

The reception of weather information in the Middle Keys has improved with the establishment of a transmitter on **Teatable Key** on Channel WX-5 (162.450 MHz). The local radio station is WCTH-FM 100.3. On TV, Channel 17 is the NOAA Channel, repeating the same weather reports available on VHF weather channels.

Key, a favorite anchorage. Be aware of which way the wind will be blowing, as it is fairly open to wind and wakes. Watch for tidal shifts. Boats have been observed grounded after arriving earlier at high tide Depths behind Rodriguez Key average 7 to 8 feet at MLW, and the holding is good over grass and sand.

About 1 mile north of Rodriguez Key is the Rock Harbor anchorage with 5 to 6 feet at MLW and good holding in sand and grass. There are several small marinas and a boat ramp in and around Rock Harbor where you might land in your dinghy. Several restaurants and a Publix Market are a short cab ride away. Straight out from the anchorage is Molasses Reef for easy snorkeling. This is a good stop for boats preparing to cross to the Bahamas or heading on to Marathon. (See more at "Crossing the Gulf Stream" in the Skipper's Handbook in the front of this guide.)

Tavernier Key to Lower Matecumbe Key

NAVIGATION: Use NOAA Charts 11451 and 11464. Below Rodriguez Key, Hawk Channel leads from the charted Triangles, marked by green daybeacon "39" (equivalent to about ICW Mile 1150) west of Molasses Reef, about 9 miles southwest to Hen and Chickens flashing red "40." The unmarked shoal known as "The Rocks," with depths of 3 feet MLW, lies northwest of flashing red "40." Take care in navigating as these rocks have created problems for daydreaming sailors.

Tavernier Creek (ICW Mile 1150) is crossed by the fixed **Tavernier Creek Bridge** bridge (15-foot vertical clearance). There are charted 3-foot depths at MLW at the entrance, but you can anchor outside in the harbor at Tavernier Key.

Seven miles to the south, Snake Creek is a limited crossover to the ICW that leads off to the northwest below "The Rocks." The marked channel is reportedly shallow, with 4-foot MLW depths or less at the entrance, even though small boats and the Coast Guard use it. Windley Key to the west is home to Windley Key Fossil Reef Geological State Park, which has self-guided trails, including one along an 8-foot high quarry wall. It is open Thursday through Monday from 9:00 a.m. to 5:00 p.m. See more at floridastateparks.org/park/Windley-Key.

At the western end of Windley Key is Whale Harbor Channel, a privately marked and maintained channel that leads into a basin with 5-foot approach depths just before the **Whale Harbor Channel Bridge** (10-foot fixed vertical clearance).

Next is tiny and picturesque Teatable Key (ICW Mile 1162). Once a navy base and now a private island, it lies on the Hawk Channel side of the southwest end of Upper Matecumbe Key. Between Teatable and Indian Keys lie two channels to the Bay side: Teatable Key Channel and Indian Key Channel. The fixed **Teatable Key Channel Bridge** with a 10-foot vertical clearance limits access to Teatable Key Channel. Indian Key Channel is also a simple run all the way to ICW Mile 1163 northwest of the Lignumvitae Key State Botanical Site. This would be considered a major crossover if it were not for the 27-foot fixed vertical clearance **Indian Key Channel Bridge**. Be sure to follow the numerous navigational aids marking the channel between Upper Matecumbe and Lower Matecumbe. Lower Matecumbe Key is the midpoint in the run from Fowey Rocks to Key West. At its western tip, Channel Two, with the 10-foot fixed vertical clearance bridge (**Channel Two Bridge**) makes this a restricted crossover.

Dockage: Treasure Harbor Marine is in a protected harbor on the ocean side. They welcome transients, as well as short- and long-term boaters. Nearby Snake Creek Marina (to the west of Snake Creek Bridge) has 3.5-foot MLW approach and dockside depths and sells gas and offers some repairs.

At the north end of the Whale Harbor Channel Bridge, Islamorada Resort Co.~Post Card Marina at Holiday Isle offers sportfishing activities and sells fuel. There are motel rooms, restaurants and many bars here, including a popular tiki bar. A nearby sandbar is a gathering spot for locals on the weekends. At the south end of the Whale Harbor Channel Bridge is Whale Harbor Marina, which may have slips; call ahead.

Less than 4 nm to the west is a privately marked channel that leads to La Siesta Resort & Marina. Before entering this channel, you would be well advised to call for instructions due to reported 3.5-foot MLW depths. Behind Teatable Key to the east, a privately maintained channel (controlling depth of 4.5 feet at MLW) leads to Bud n' Mary's Fishing Marina, one of the oldest and most active sportfishing/charter centers in the Keys. Rental

skiffs and guided fishing charters are available, as well as transient dockage. Call ahead for reservations. There are a number of retail shops, art galleries and restaurants to the north of the marina.

Caloosa Cove Marina & Resort is located at Lower Matecumbe Key with slips and sells both gas and diesel fuel. Expect approach depths of 4.5 to 5 feet at MLW.

Anchorage: The harbor at Tavernier Key has 4 to 7 feet at MLW with good holding in sand and grass. This is open and exposed from the northeast through the east.

In calm conditions or with light winds from the west through to the north-northeast, it is possible for vessels drawing up to 5 feet to anchor on the sand off the Whale Harbor Inn (Mile 1158). This is not a particularly good or a recommended anchorage, but if you do anchor here, you and your dinghy are welcome at the Whale Harbor Inn. Whale Harbor Channel continues under the 10-foot fixed Whale Harbor Channel Bridge to the ICW side.

The designated Indian Key anchorage has at least 7 feet of water with good holding in sand and grass. This anchorage is open and exposed to the south–southwest.

■ CHANNEL FIVE BRIDGE

NAVIGATION: Use NOAA Charts 11451. Hawk Channel is reached through the second major crossover point: deep, well-marked Channel Five, crossed by the fixed **Channel Five Bridge** with a 65-foot vertical clearance. To reach Channel Five from green daybeacon "97" on the ICW (near Mile 1165), steer about 210 degrees on a course to the south-southwest for 5 miles. This will bring you to a point just north of the bridge.

⚠ There are no marks indicating the best water to the north of the Channel Five Bridge. Pay attention! Heading straight for the center span should keep you out of trouble.

The current NOAA chart shows at least 8 feet at MLW in the marked Channel Five, but out of the channel it shallows very quickly. The channel itself is sparsely marked. There are a couple of marks south of the Channel Five Bridge–red daybeacon "4," flashing red "2" and green "1." After passing under the bridge, take those marks in the order given if heading for

Hawk Channel. There is a prominent shoal to port south of the bridge. The red aids mark its westernmost edge.

From the bridge, if you are heading south, plot your course southwesterly to flashing red "44" which, when left to starboard, puts you into Hawk Channel. At that point, alter course westerly to 247 degrees magnetic.

To continue on the ICW inside from Mile 1165 and Bowlegs Cut, steer a course of 246 degrees magnetic to flashing green "1," about 6 miles west, just north of Old Dan Bank. There are no navigation aids on this span but the Everglades National Park markers to the north should keep you on course.

■ MIDDLE KEYS: INSIDE (ICW) ROUTE

Long Key to Moser Channel–ICW Mile 1168 to Mile 1196

NAVIGATION: Use NOAA Charts 11449, 11451 and 11453. The ICW passes west of Old Dan Bank on a course of 246 degrees magnetic for about 5 miles in good depths to Channel Key Pass, the passage between the shoals of Channel Key Bank (Mile 1179). **Long Key Viaduct Bridge** (23-foot fixed vertical clearance) lies to the southeast at Mile 1176 before passing through Channel Key Pass. Power boaters with local knowledge frequently use it en route to Duck Key and the marina at Hawk's Cay Resort on the Hawk Channel.

Grassy Key Bank (Mile 1182) projects northerly from long, low Grassy Key. At this point, if you plan to stop at one of the marinas on the Bay side of Marathon, you can take the shortcut that parallels the ICW but is closer to the keys. Plot a course between Bamboo Key and the shoal to its northwest. Skirt Stirrup Key and then take a bearing on Rachel Key, passing between Rachel Key and the marked shoal on Rachel Bank. Thereafter, you should have depths of at least 7 feet at MLW until quite close to shore.

Dockage: There have been some turnovers in the yacht docking business in Marathon, but names and facilities have not changed much. The marinas that line the western entrance to Boot Key Harbor are all intact. As conditions change with the seasonal hurricanes, you can get up-to-date information on all the marinas in the Marathon area by visiting the Waterway Explorer at waterwayguide.com.

At Mile 1193, Blackfin Resort and Marina has slips and good (8-foot) MLW approach depths. Those with drafts of less than 5 feet may want to try the nearby Banana Bay Resort & Marina. It has been reported to us that this small marina has a great seasonal community of boaters. Restaurants, grocery stores and a Home Depot are all within easy walking distance. Nearby Keys Boat Works offers repairs and has a 50-ton lift and a crane (no transient slips).

The newest marina in the area is Marlin Bay Yacht Club with 24 slips for vessels to 60 feet with boutique resort-style amenities, including a clubhouse lounge and game room, fitness center, heated pool and hot tub, a pool bar and concierge service. This is a great place for a crew change or for visiting friends who can stay at one of the on-site accommodations. (Advance reservations required.)

The well-regarded Faro Blanco Resort & Yacht Club has state-of-the-art facilities and world-class amenities including fuel, pump-out service, 24-hour security, marine concierge services, WiFi, a marine store, pool and fitness center and first-class room accommodations on site. This is another fine location for a crew change or friend and family visits.

Capt. Pip's Marina & Hideaway is before the Seven Mile Bridge. Dockage is reserved for charter boats.

Anchorage: Tiny Rachel Key at Mile 1195 offers some protection if you anchor on the southwest side. There is good holding in sand and 6 to 7 feet at MLW. The area just east of Pretty Joe Rock offers the best protection. Holding is fair in sand and grass.

Boot Key Harbor

NAVIGATION: Use NOAA Chart 11453. From the north shore of Marathon, you can round Knight Key and head south through the **Knight Key Channel Bridge** (19-foot fixed vertical clearance) to find flashing green "1," marking the entrance to the channel to Boot Key Harbor, between Knight Key and Boot Key. Although frequently used by small power boaters, this route is not well marked. Currents run swiftly with either tide, and the monofilament lines of numerous anglers dangle from the old bridge. If you do choose this route, once through to the ocean side, keep well clear of the shoal extending west of Knight Key. This is not the preferred route for cruising-size boats.

Our Cruising Editor suggests that cruising boats follow the ICW to Moser Channel, passing under the

65-foot fixed side-by-side **Seven Mile Bridge** and the **Old Seven Mile (Moser Channel) Bridge** and then enter Boot Key Harbor going west to east. Cruisers with deep-draft vessels (up to 8 feet) will want to overlook the shortcut and remain on the ICW route.

Once under the bridge and past Moser Channel red daybeacon "2," you should turn east and head to the red daybeacon "2" at the entrance to Boot Key Harbor. (Boot Key Harbor, which is more easily accessed from the Hawk Channel, is described in detail in the following section.)

MIDDLE KEYS: OUTSIDE (HAWK CHANNEL) ROUTE

Long Key to Marathon

NAVIGATION: Use NOAA Charts 11449, 11451 and 11453. Opposite Channel Five in Hawk Channel, at flashing red "44," your course to Vaca Key and the City of Marathon is relatively clear in the range of 247 to 258 degrees magnetic to East Washerwomen Shoal at flashing green "49." To the west of Duck Key (NOAA Chart 11453) you will find Grassy, Crawl, Little Crawl, Deer and Fat Deer Keys. Fat Deer Key is fronted by Coco Plum Beach, which is well marked by a 14-story-high condominium tower, an excellent landmark from Hawk Channel (and the highest building in all of the Florida Keys).

Dockage: On Hawk Channel, abeam of Channel Five, it is about 10 nm to Hawk's Cay Resort Marina on Duck Key. Heading south in Hawk Channel, at flashing red "44," follow a heading of about 255 degrees magnetic to the 8 entry daybeacons that guide you into the Duck Key moat. Once inside the Duck Key moat entrance, turn to the right and, at Idle Speed/No Wake, enjoy the deep water on your way to the marina at Hawk's Cay Resort. The area in front of the dolphin and seal pens has shoaled somewhat; call ahead for exact depths. If your assigned slip lies across the marina, skirt the slips clockwise and avoid the center shoals. A swift crosscurrent can test your docking skills; check with the marina staff and use caution.

Hawks Cay Resort Marina was being completely renovated at press time in summer 2018. The facility features 85 boat slips, can accommodate vessels up to 110 feet in length and offers boat in/boat out service and

Two routes are available to leave the ICW in the Keys and traverse Florida Bay westward for Cape Sable and points north along Florida's west coast. These routes-one at Mile 1173 and one at Mile 1190-are detailed in Chapter 12, "Flamingo to Fort Myers Beach."

dockage for resort guests who wish to trailer their boat to the Keys. All overnight boaters have access to Hawks Cay's pools, restaurants and attractions, including diving and watersports–with free shuttle service between the marina and the resort.

To the south on Fat Deer Key, Driftwood Marina & Storage has repair (with a 60-ton lift) and storage facilities in a protected basin with a dredged channel (reported 4-foot MLW approach depths but with plenty of water once inside).

Bonefish Towers lie at the eastern edge of the deep channel leading to the Key Colony Beach Basin. In the basin are several facilities, including Outta the Blue Marina, White Marlin Marina, Shelter Bay Marine and Key Colony Beach Marina. Here you can find slips, repairs and fuel; see the marina table in this chapter for details. This location puts you in the heart of the city of Key Colony Beach. Shops, restaurants, hotels and some of the Keys' best ocean beaches are within walking distance. Within a short cab ride are restaurants regarded as among the best in the middle keys. Some are situated on nearby Grassy Key. The Key Colony Inn is just down the street from the marina and has great seafood and Italian dishes (305-743-0100).

Anchorage: Long Key is the home of Long Key State Park (305-664-4815), a 300-acre wild area with a campground, numerous picnic tables and grills. You can drop the hook in Long Key Bight in 4- to 6-foot MLW depths with good holding in sand and grass. It is open and exposed to the northeast.

Marathon Area

NAVIGATION: Use NOAA Charts 11451 and 11453. Continuing west in Hawk Channel past Key Colony Beach, Vaca Key lies off to starboard. The closest gateway to it and the community of Marathon lies where Vaca Key and Boot Key Harbor meet at Sister Creek, just northwest of East Washerwoman Shoal, marked by flashing green "49."

Boot Key Channel is approached from Hawk Channel by a turn due north once Sombrero Key Light is directly

Welcome Cruisers To Boot Key Harbor & Your One Stop Boating Center!

Boot Key Harbor City Marina is a modest community of liveaboards, ranging from year-round residents to transient loopers to cruisers from all over the world. With the City Park located just next door, you can enjoy bocce ball, tennis, basketball, or one of the several events hosted there throughout the year...and walk back to your boat when you're done. We hope to welcome you soon!

Boot Key Harbor City Marina
(305) 289-8877
VHF Channel 16 for Dock or Mooring Assignment
www.cityofmarathonmarina.com

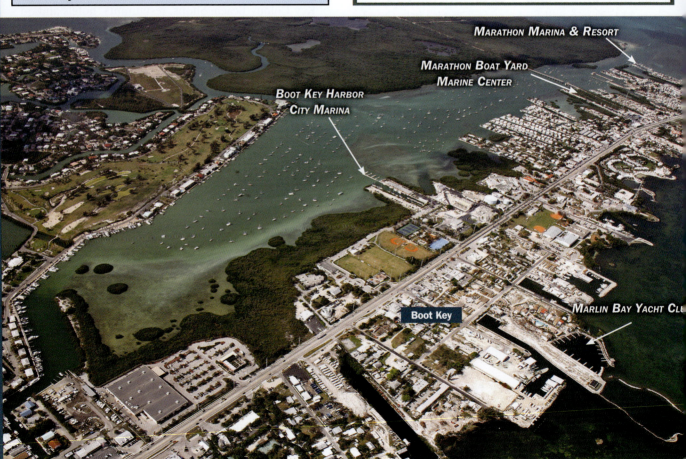

MARATHON MARINA & RESORT

MARATHON BOAT YARD MARINE CENTER

BOOT KEY HARBOR CITY MARINA

Boot Key

MARLIN BAY YACHT CLUB

abeam to port. Four nautical miles north of Sombrero Key, you will find red daybeacon "2," situated just south of Knight Key.

 Be aware that Boot Key flashing green "1" was reported to be destroyed at press time in summer 2018.

Additional daybeacons lead to an abundance of marine facilities along Boot Key Channel and in the harbor beyond. This channel carries 7 feet at MLW. The creek entrance, however, may be as low as 5-foot MLW depths. The bascule portion of **Boot Key Harbor Bridge** has been removed (even though your chart may not show this).

Strictly observe the posted "SLOW-SPEED/MINIMUM-WAKE ZONE" in this busy area. Boot Key Harbor, one of the best and most heavily populated harbors in the Keys, lies just beyond the head of the creek.

 Caution: There are charted overhead cables on either side of the Boot Key Bridge with 65-foot clearance.

Dockage/Moorings: A turn to starboard (coming from Hawk Channel) when entering Boot Key channel will take you to Skipjack Resort & Marina, at the end of Boot Key Harbor. They have transient slips, as does the nearby Sombrero Marina Dockside. Sombrero Marina also offers useful services geared toward the liveaboard population of Boot Key.

The friendly Boot Key Harbor City Marina manages 211 moorings for boats up to 45 feet and 15 moorings for boats to 60 feet, as well as slips and a designated anchorage. They do not take reservations, but if you appear in person, you can go on a waiting list if they are full. The mooring rates are on a daily, weekly or monthly basis and include showers and weekly pump-out service, plus they provide a large dinghy dock adjacent to their facility and offer free loaner bikes (if you bring a secure lock). More information is available from ci.marathon.fl.us (search "moorings"). The marina is located next to a beautiful park and sports complex and provisions and repairs are all available within 1 mile of the marina. Public bus service connects to Key West and the mainland.

GOIN' ASHORE: **MARATHON, FL**

SERVICES		
SERVICES		
1	Library	
2	Post Office	
ATTRACTIONS		
3	Crane Point Museum & Nature Center	
4	Turtle Hospital	
SHOPPING		
5	Publix	

6	Seamark Electronics	
7	West Marine	
DINING		
8	Burdines Waterfront	
9	Keys Fisheries Restaurants	
MARINAS		
8	Burdines Waterfront Marina	
10	Banana Bay Resort & Marina	

11	Blackfin Resort and Marina	
12	Boot Key Harbor City Marina	
13	Capt. Pip's Marina & Hideaway	
14	Faro Blanco Resort & Yacht Club	
15	Keys Boat Works	
16	Marathon Boat Yard Marine Center	

17	Marathon Marina & Re:
18	Pancho's Marina and Fuel Dock
19	Skipjack Resort & Mari
20	Sombrero Marina Dock

The islands of Marathon boast some of the best boating and fishing activities anywhere, plus waterfront restaurants, kayaking and paddleboarding, and access to world-class diving and snorkeling. A bike ride on Sombrero Beach Road leads to one of the finest public beaches in the Keys.

Attractions: For diversions ashore, consider the Crane Point Museums & Nature Center. The complex has a natural history museum, marine touch tanks and a bird rescue center (5550 Overseas Hwy., 305-743-3900). Also enjoy the nature trails that wind through a tropical palm forest, canopied with thatch palms and loaded with trees and shrubs native to the area. Or the longer (0.5-mile) trail that leads to the Crane House, surrounded by exotic trees and with spectacular views of the Gulf of Mexico.

There are lots of opportunities nearby for interacting with the local marina life. The Turtle Hospital is located in a 1940s-era motel at 2396 Overseas Hwy. The hospital is dedicated to the rehabilitation of endangered sea turtles and offers 90-minute guided tours with proceeds directly benefiting the program. At the end of each program guests are invited to feed the permanent residents. Call for hours and fees (305-743-2552). At the north end of Marathon is the

Florida Keys Aquarium Encounters at 11710 Overseas Hwy. (305-407-3262), an interactive place to see sharks, stingrays, bonefish, barracuda, turtles and more. For interactive dolphin encounters, swimming with the dolphins, dolphin demonstrations and more, visit the Dolphin Research Center, located on Grassy Key (7 miles east of Marathon), a not-for-profit organization that provides education about dolphins (305-289-1121).

Shopping: Provisioning possibilities abound, most clustered along U.S. Route 1 within walking distance of the Boot Key City Marina dinghy docks. The marina also loans out bikes to guests that have a lock. To the east of the docks, you will find a Publix Supermarket & Liquor Store, Home Depot, pharmacy, bank (with ATM), Post Office and Marathon Liquor & Deli (MM 50), with a huge selection of beers, wines and liquor and perhaps the best gourmet deli selection in the Keys. Just a bit further east is a Kmart, a Winn-Dixie supermarket and the Marathon Airport (MM 52). Several car rental services operate from the airport.

To the west of the dinghy dock is a West Marine and Seamark Electronics at 2994 Overseas Hwy. (305-743-6633) offering a full range of marine electronics.

There are several good dive shops in Marathon but you may find better selection and prices in Key West.

Dining: Oceanside at the foot of the Seven Mile Bridge is one of the best places to see the sunsets: Sunset Grille and Raw Bar (305-396-7235). For a unique Lobster Reuben sandwich, eat at the Keys Fisheries Restaurant (305-743-4353). Burdines Waterfront is another very popular waterfront restaurant (305-743-5317). All three have dinghy docks for dining patrons.

Continuing to work "outward" from Boot Key Harbor, immediately before the remnants of the Boot Key Bridge, you will see the entry channel to the very well protected Marathon Boat Yard Marine Center. The full-service boatyard has a 75-ton lift and a paint tent. They have earned a "Clean Boat Yard" designation and are known for quality workmanship. Boaters will also have access to their service team of certified technicians and master craftsmen. A large West Marine is next door. Marine supplies are also available at Home Depot (with boating supplies) and the local NAPA auto parts store, which stocks a large variety of marine engine parts. If you can pay with cash, NAPA will deliver parts dockside.

Pancho's Marina and Fuel Dock are next to Burdines Waterfront Marina. Both offer gas and diesel fuel and the store at Burdines stocks a professional fishing tackle inventory. The Chiki Tiki Bar and Grille (305-743-9204) on site here is one of our favorites for a simple menu with good food and a great view.

Marathon Marina & Resort has deep-water slips, as well as a great restaurant, Lazy Days South (305-289-0839), with a fun happy hour and spectacular sunset views. Another dining option is a 0.5-mile stroll to the end of Knight Key. Here, you will find the 7-Mile Grill (305-743-4481) close to the old trestle bridge. It is open 7 days a week for breakfast, lunch and dinner. Breakfast here, on a warm winter's day, is not to be missed.

Anchorage: You can anchor outside of the Boot Key Harbor in the lee of Boot Key in 8 to 9 feet at MLW on a line between red daybeacon "2" and Sombrero Key Light. Shoal-draft vessels can work their way closer to shore in the charted 5-foot area. This anchorage is comfortable in northeast through southeast winds, but you will want to move around to the north side of Marathon for any strong winds out of the south or southwest. This anchorage offers excellent holding in sand and grass but the downside is the near constant wakes from powerboats taking a shortcut out of the harbor.

Finding a place to anchor inside Boot Key Harbor can be a challenge from Thanksgiving through March. You can anchor on either side of the shore west of the Boot Key Harbor Bridge. Boats also anchor east of the bridge in the harbor. Remember that by Florida law you must stay 100 feet from a designated mooring field, including the one in front of Boot Key Harbor City Marina.

Boot Key Harbor City Marina has pump-out facilities and a pump-out boat. They will provide pump-out services for $5 either at their dock or at your anchored boat in Boot Key Harbor or in Sister Creek.

For a fee, you can have dinghy tie-up privileges (nearest to complete shopping), a bike rack, message services and water at Sombrero Marina Dockside at the east end of the harbor, or alternately at the City Marina for $20 per day and get full access to their facilities.

Side Trip: Sombrero Key Reef

NAVIGATION: Use NOAA Charts 11451. All manner of tropical fish, southern stingrays, nurse sharks and the occasional barracuda will swim with you at Sombrero Reef, adjacent to the 142-foot Sombrero Key Lighthouse. About 4 miles out from the Knight Key Channel Bridge, look for the bog tower. Pick up a mooring ball on the outside (deep side).

Be sure to swim through the natural coral limestone arch for an amazing photo opportunity. The reef is in a strictly regulated sanctuary area. Divers are reminded to look but not touch so this spectacular reef will be preserved.

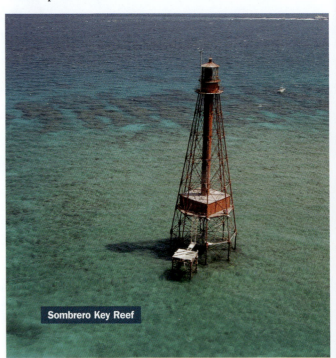

Sombrero Key Reef

■ NEXT STOP

From here, we will continue to the Lower Keys, where the pace will pick up the closer you get to the "Conch Republic" (Key West), an extremely walkable and exceedingly fun place to visit. And make sure you have some snorkel gear, as the reefs just get better and better.

Florida Lower Keys

ICW Mile 1197–Mile 1243   (VHF) FL Bridges: Channel 09

CHARTS NOAA 11420, 11434, 11441, 11442, 11445, 11447, 11448, 11451, 11453, 11464

If continuing farther on to the Lower Keys, there are three options: crossing over to Hawk Channel in the Atlantic at either Cape Florida Channel/Biscayne Channel, Channel Five or Moser Channel (outside route), or going through Big Spanish Channel, southwest of Marathon, into Florida Bay and running down the northern edge of the remaining keys on the ICW (inside route).

For boats that draw over 4.5 feet, cruising through the keys will require you to stay on the ocean side of the Keys, in Hawk Channel. Regardless of boat size, you will want to be on Hawk Channel, on the south and sheltered side of the Keys, if winds are blowing from the north or northeast at more than 10 to 15 knots.

If you are continuing on to Key West from Marathon, the ICW will take you through Big Spanish Channel into Florida Bay and running down the northern edge of the western keys. The route through Big Spanish Channel will take a bit longer to traverse, but in southerly or southeasterly winds, it will be the more protected route.

There are no marine facilities on the Florida Bay side between Big Spanish Channel and Key West. Also, when you are in the Florida Keys, your travel is totally weather dependent. There is plenty of good weather here and a lot to enjoy. Waiting for good travel weather is a smart boating decision, especially in the Keys.

■ LOWER KEYS–INSIDE (ICW) ROUTE

NAVIGATION: Use NOAA Charts 11445, 11448, 11451 and 11453. The famous **Seven Mile (Moser Channel) Twin Bridges** (65-foot fixed vertical clearance) begins its passage to Key West at the western end of Vaca Key, immediately crossing Knight Key Channel. Although frequently used by skiffs and center consoles, the passage to the north through the spans at **Knight Key Channel Twin Bridges** (19-foot fixed vertical clearance) is not well marked. Currents run swiftly with either tide, and the monofilament lines of numerous anglers dangle in profusion from the old bridge above for about half the distance into Knight Key Channel from shore. If you do choose this route, once through to the ocean side, keep well clear of the shoal extending west of Knight Key.

The preferred passage is Moser Channel (Mile 1197), the primary passageway and the last major crossover to the inside route from Hawk Channel. Here, about 1 mile west of Pigeon Key, the channel is deep and well marked, and as you head into Florida Bay set a course towards red daybeacon "24" and rejoin the ICW.

The ICW route to Key West from Bethel Bank continues past Bahia Honda into the National Key Deer

Lower Keys, FL

		Largest Vessel Accommodated	VHF Channel Monitored	Transient Berths / Total Berths	Approach / Dockside Depth (reported)	Floating Docks	Gas / Diesel	Groceries, Ice, Marine Supplies, Snacks	Repairs: Hull, Engine, Propeller	Lift (tonnage), Crane, Rail	Min/Max Amps	Laundry, Pool, Showers, Courtesy Car	Pump-Out Station	Nearby: Grocery Store, Motel, Restaurant
BAHIA HONDA KEY AREA				**Dockage**			**Supplies**			**Services**				
1. Sunshine Key RV Resort & Marina 🖥 📶	305-872-2217	50	/16	14/172	/5	F	GD	GIMS	–	–	30/50	LPS	P	GMR
2. Bahia Honda State Park & Marina 📶 1205	305-872-3210	50	16/10	19/19	3.5/4.5	–	–	GIS	–	–	30/30	S	P	GMR
NEWFOUND HARBOR AREA														
3. Dolphin Marina & Cottages WG 1215	305-872-2685	50	16/09	call/5	4/10	–	GD	IS	–	–	–	S	P	GMR

🖥 Internet Access 📶 Wireless Internet Access WG Waterway Guide Cruising Club Partner 📶 onSpot dockside WiFi facility

See WaterwayGuide.com for current rates, fuel prices, web site addresses, and other up-to-the-minute information. *(Information in the table is provided by the facilities.)*

BAHIA HONDA KEY AREA, NOAA CHART 11445

NEWFOUND HARBOR AREA, NOAA CHART 11445

Wildlife Refuge. The route, shown best on NOAA Chart 11448, then bends north just past green daybeacon "29" at about Mile 1204, steering a course of about 300 degrees magnetic. At this point, you are in the well-marked Big Spanish Channel route to the Gulf and then to Key West via the Northwest Channel. Markers have been changed and added to this area, requiring use of only the most recent chart editions (Edition 15, Jan. 2017).

On the ICW, prior to reaching Seven Mile Bridge, at Bethel Bank (Mile 1194), you will note a split in the chart's magenta track, which is clearly shown on NOAA Chart 11451. The southern route leads closer to Moser Channel, and then continues west past Little Money Key and the massive RV resort on Ohio Key. It then bends southward, following the northern shore of Bahia Honda Key, leading to the **Bahia Honda Twin Bridges** (20-foot fixed vertical clearance) at Mile 1205, the last possible crossover from the ICW to Hawk Channel. If you are cruising the Florida Keys in a boat that can get under a bridge with 20-foot vertical clearance, you have a few more options than most.

The other ICW route shown on the chart continues on a more northerly route to Big Spanish Channel heading for Florida Bay, the Gulf of Mexico and the Northwest Channel to Key West. Head for red daybeacon "32" south of Little Pine Key, being sure to regard red daybeacon "26" at Mile 1200, which marks a dangerous shoal to the north. Turn northwest and proceed about 8 miles to red daybeacon "42" leaving all navigational aids to the correct side. (You are returning to Florida Bay so red navigational aids are to be passed to starboard.)

As you pass red daybeacon "42" at Cudjoe Key and head for green daybeacon "43" the channel shoals to 5 feet at MLW for about 0.5 mile. At this point, the channel deepens again to 10 feet at MLW. The channel is deep but narrow for the next 0.25 mile; follow the marks and be aware of a submerged pile near green daybeacon "49." Bear north at red daybeacon "52" and in 2.5 miles you will turn to port at green daybeacon "57" for the 28-mile run to Key West.

Just 8 miles west from green daybeacon "57" is Cudjoe Channel with 7 feet at MLW with a deeper channel cutting back to the southeast through the flats. This

Bahia Honda Twin Bridges

might be a nice place to hang out when the weather is good and forecast to stay that way. You are off the beaten track, but close enough to it to get underway again with no trouble. The fishing in the deeper channel could be great. There really aren't a lot of places to anchor when traveling from Florida Bay to Key West. It is a very shallow bank (4 to 4.5 feet at MLW) with mangrove islands most of the way along the ICW route. (See more on anchoring in the Keys in the Skipper's Handbook in the front of this guide.)

At this point, you should shift to NOAA Chart 11442. From Harbor Key Bank Light, a course of 250 degrees magnetic will carry you to flashing bell buoy "1," marking the Northwest Channel to Key West (N 24° 38.880'/W 081° 53.960'). In navigating to the marker, be sure to avoid low keys located about 2 nm offshore in depths up to 26 feet at MLW. There is no reason to stray from your course as you must reach bell buoy "1" before turning south to Key West; the semi-submerged East Jetty blocks the way and there is no viable shortcut. Without current local knowledge, the Calda Channel and various other shortcuts are not recommended.

Dockage: On tiny Ohio Key, the Sunshine Key RV Resort & Marina might have transient space, although they primarily cater to small, trailerable boats.

■ LOWER KEYS–OUTSIDE (HAWK CHANNEL) ROUTE

As this edition is being prepared, many of the facilities providing services along this route are rebuilding after Hurricane Irma. Many are only partially open or completely closed. It is best to contact service providers prior to arrival to verify that services are available. This is wise in any case, as channel depths change regularly in the Keys and local knowledge is always helpful.

Bahia Honda to Sugarloaf Key

NAVIGATION: Use NOAA Chart 11445. You will see the Seven Mile Bridge as you head southwest, once you pass Sombrero Key Light to port. The old Bahia Honda Bridge (Mile 1207), at Bahia Honda Key's western end, is a national historic monument that is slowly disintegrating into the water. The old bridge has a section removed so that sailboats can pass through to the cove between the old bridge and the newer Bahia Honda Twin Bridges (20-foot fixed vertical clearance). Do not make your approach from the southeast; stay west and well off the

Seven Mile Bridge

little island 0.5 mile off the tip of Bahia Honda Key to avoid the shifting sand shoals. There are no aids here except for a dead tree on the island; this can be a tough entrance in poor visibility, so caution is advised. There is plenty of water (9-plus feet at MLW), but be aware of the currents under the bridge.

Dockage: Transients can find dockage in the well-protected boat basin at the Bahia Honda State Park & Marina (entrance from the cove between the old and new bridges). There is plenty of water in the harbor, but the entrance is shallow (controlling depth of 3.5 feet at MLW with an average tidal range of a little over 1 foot; favor the east side of the channel on entry).

On the west side of Pine Channel, the canal nearest the Overseas Highway leads directly to Dolphin Marina & Cottages, with a controlling depth of 4 feet at MLW. Both gasoline and diesel fuel are available here. Dolphin Marina is the departure point for the Little Palm Island ferry service.

Little Palm Island Resort, a secluded and very luxurious resort on Little Palm Island (westernmost of the Newfound Harbor Keys and called Little Munson on some charts), was closed at press time (summer 2018) due to damage from Hurricane Irma. They are undergoing a total restoration and plan to reopen in late 2019.

Anchorage: The cove between the bridges, immediately west of Bahia Honda State Park, provides a popular anchorage. Be warned that the holding here is only fair in sand and grass and the currents are strong. It is wise to check your position after a turning tide to avoid a closer look at one bridge or the other. This is a good place to let out extra scope. Once securely anchored, you can go ashore to the park and enjoy two of the nicest beaches in the Keys. The palm-rimmed Calusa Beach on the western edge is sheltered and roped off for swimming and snorkeling. (If you choose to swim off the boat, drop a line to counter the sometimes strong current.) A park concession stand that sells snack and ice is nearby. Mile-long Sandspur Beach across the road looks out on Hawk Channel. Bring shoes or aqua socks to hike one of the three nature trails, including one that winds along the shore of a tidal lagoon; you will see tropical plants and beautiful birds here. The old Bahia Honda Key Bridge is a great place for spotting rays and the occasional shark.

Continuing west past Bahia Honda Key, you will see the Newfound Harbor Keys, about 4.5 miles due north of the superb diving sites of Looe Key National Marine Sanctuary (an excellent snorkeling site). The relatively well-marked and well-protected Newfound Harbor Channel has become an increasingly popular anchorage area. The channel has depths of 8 to 16 feet at MLW but the approach is quite shallow, particularly in a strong north wind when depths can be reduced by over 1 foot. In normal conditions you should have 7 to 8 feet at MLW. On entry, give flashing red "2" a wide berth to starboard to avoid shoaling that extends about 100 yards south and west of this mark but don't go too far west as the channel has shoaled there as well. Use the American Shoal Light as a stern reference and head just off the Little Palm Island Resort docks. Once adjacent to the docks aim for each daybeacon, getting quite close to red "4" before turning for green "5." Once inside, the holding is good in sand and grass. Most anchor in the cross-bar of the "H" etched by the deeper channels in 7 to 8 feet at MLW. Shoal-draft boats can anchor in 5- to 6-foot MLW depths just east of the main channel.

With some ingenuity, you may be able to locate a dinghy landing on Big Pine Key near the east end of the **Little Torch Key (Pine Channel) Bridge** (15-foot fixed vertical clearance). This may mean just tying to a mangrove tree. From here, complete provisioning is possible about 1 mile east at the island's full-sized Winn-Dixie store. If you can locate transportation (and decent directions), No Name Pub (305-872-9115), just west of the bridge crossing Bogie Channel on Big Pine Key, is a funky and unique classic, considered a Florida Keys landmark since 1935. The ceilings are covered with thousands of fluttering dollar bills but the pizza is the main event, and folks drive miles for it. There is good reason....It is fantastic!

About 2 nm to the west, Niles Channel (crossed by the fixed 40-foot vertical clearance **Niles Channel Bridge**) offers a reasonably well-protected anchorage between Ramrod Key and Summerland Key. Anchor between red daybeacons "4" and "6" in 7 to 10 feet at MLW. Be careful to avoid a couple of 2- and 3-foot MLW shoals here. The area is also not well protected from southerlies.

Farther west, before Loggerhead Keys and due north of flashing red "50A," a marked shoal-draft channel with the entrance marked by green daybeacon "1" leads to sheltered, though relatively shallow Kemp Channel, between Cudjoe and Summerland Keys. This channel only carries 4 to 5 feet at best at MLW. Be sure to watch your depth sounder.

Saddlebunch Harbor, about 10 nm to the south, has fair holding in 7 to 8 feet at MLW with a grassy and mud bottom. It offers good protection from the east but only limited protection from the south. In east winds, snug-in close to shore just north of daybeacon red "8." The current is strong here but the depth holds quite close to land.

Boca Chica Key to Key West

NAVIGATION: Use NOAA Charts 11441, 11442 and 11445. Hawk Channel narrows past the marked and lighted Ninefoot Shoal and passes safely north of West Washerwoman Shoal to Key West. From the western end of Sugarloaf, the Saddlebunch Keys extend for about 3 miles to the start of the Boca Chica Key complex. Here, about 2 miles past flashing red "56," the deep, well-marked Boca Chica Channel leads into the basin and mooring area of the Boca Chica Naval Air Station. This facility is open to retired and active-duty members of the armed forces. Rental moorings, ice, showers and limited snacks are available. An overhead power cable with an authorized vertical clearance of 60 feet restricts access to the basins for both Boca Chica and the Stock Island anchorage.

 At press time in summer 2018, several aids to navigation were missing in Boca Chica channel.

Dockage: Immediately west of Boca Chica Channel is an unnamed, but charted channel leading to the Stock Island service facilities. (The previously mentioned overhead cable does not restrict access to these facilities.) Several boat builders, boat storage and fishing docks are here. Provisioning from this location, however, requires ground transportation. Check with marinas, as some offer a shuttle service into Key West.

The first marina you will encounter on Stock Island is Florida Marina Clubs–Key West Harbor, which has transient slips and fuel, both gas and diesel. The on-site restaurant here offers Cuban- and Caribbean-inspired cuisine accompanied by incredible views of the Atlantic Ocean. Nearby the newly renovated Oceanside Marina

MAIN SHIP CHANNEL

MALLORY SQUARE

OLD TOWNE AREA

PIER HOUSE

HYATT HOTEL & RESTAURANT

MARKER 24

GALEEON RESORT AND MARINA

ENTRANCE

RED MARKER 4

Key West's Luxurious Resort Marina

The Galleon MARINA

Marina guests enjoy the pool, fitness center, sauna, outdoor spa, sundecks and the harbor view tiki bar.

The Galleon's breakwater shielded floating docks have been engineered for maximum protection and security (24 hrs.) for your vessel. The Galleon provides Old Towne Key West's finest accommodations for yachts up to 150 ft. Guests not staying on board may find luxurious two bedroom, two bath suites with complete kitchens at the dockside Galleon Resort . . . all near the exciting nightlife of famous Olde Towne Key West. A full watersports program . . . small boat and jet skis, as well as mopeds and bicycles. Our Harbourmaster is on duty 24 hours, 7 days a week monitoring channel 16. Plenty of fresh water at no extra charge, 50 amp electricity, cable TV, telephones and 9 ft. of water dockside. A warm welcome awaits you!

619 Front Street, Key West, FL 33040. For additional information call Toll free: 1-800-6MARINA or 305-292-1292

www.galleonmarinakeywest.com

Stock Island, Key West, FL

		Largest Vessel Accommodated	VHF Channel Monitored	Transient Berths / Total Berths	Approach / Dockside Depth (reported)	Floating Docks	Gas / Diesel	Groceries, Ice, Marine Supplies, Snacks	Repairs: Hull, Engine, Propeller	Lift (tonnage), Crane, Rail	Min/Max Amps	Laundry, Pool, Showers, Courtesy Car	Pump-Out Station	Nearby: Grocery Store, Motel, Restaurant
				Dockage			**Supplies**		**Services**					
STOCK ISLAND														
1. Florida Marina Clubs-Key West Harbour 💻 📶	305-292-3121	110	16/11	20/100	8/10	F	GD	IMS	HEP	–	30/100	LPS	P	GMR
2. Oceans Edge Key West Resort Hotel & Marina 💻 📶	786-862-6315	140	16	50/125	20/12	–	GD	IS	–	–	30/50	LPS	P	GMR
3. Robbie's of Key West LLC 📶 1237	305-294-1124	400	–	–	/15	F	–	GI	HEP	L125,C50	30/100	S	–	GMR
4. Stock Island Marina Village 💻 📶 WG	305-294-2288	300	16/10	125/215	15/20	F	GD	GIS	–	–	30/200+	LPS	P	GMR
5. Sunset Marina Key West 1239	305-296-7101	55	16	25/120	6/9	F	GD	GIMS	–	–	30/50	LS	P	GMR
KEY WEST														
6. Margaritaville Resort & Marina 💻 📶 1243	305-294-4000	160	16	25/37	37/14	F	–	IS	–	–	15/100	LPS	P	GMR
7. Galleon Marina 📶 1243	305-292-1292	150	16	80/91	12/9	F	–	GIMS	–	–	30/100	LPS	P	GMR
8. A & B Marina 💻 📶 1243	305-294-2535	190	16/10	40/50	14/12	F	GD	GIMS	–	–	30/100	LS	P	GMR
9. Key West Bight Marina 💻 onSpot 1243	305-809-3984	140	16/17	33/145	20/12	–	GD	GIMS	–	–	30/100	LPS	P	GMR
10. Conch Harbor Marina 💻 onSpot 1243	305-294-2933	195	16	20/40	30/9	–	GD	IMS	–	–	30/100	LPS	P	GMR
11. Spencer's Boat Yard 1243	305-296-8826	45	–	–	4/6	–	–	M	HEP	L25	30/50	–	P	GMR
12. Garrison Bight Marina 1243	305-294-3093	40	–	10/280	4/6	–	G	GIMS	EP	L	–	–	–	GMR
13. City Marina at Garrison Bight onSpot 1243	305-809-3981	70	16	30/245	7/6	F	–	I	–	–	30/50	LS	P	GMR
14. Key West Yacht Club 📶 1243	305-896-0426	58	16	3/67	6/9	–	–	IS	–	–	30/50	S	–	MR

💻 Internet Access 📶 Wireless Internet Access WG Waterway Guide Cruising Club Partner onSpot dockside WiFi facility

See WaterwayGuide.com for current rates, fuel prices, web site addresses, and other up-to-the-minute information. *(Information in the table is provided by the facilities.)*

STOCK ISLAND, KEY WEST, NOAA CHART 11441

The Conch Republic

On April 23, 1982, the U.S. Border Patrol established a military-style roadblock on U.S. 1 at Florida City. The Border Patrol stopped all northbound highway traffic at a place motorists know as The Last Chance Saloon and searched for illegal aliens and drugs. The ensuing well-publicized traffic jam—traffic stretched back for 19 miles—supposedly stymied the Key's tourism industry.

This spurred a movement in which citizens of the Keys (called "Conchs") elected to secede from the Upper 48. With tongue in cheek, but with a serious gleam in their eyes, they selected a flag, designated their boundaries and became the "Conch Republic." They proclaimed their independence, declared war on the United States and then immediately surrendered, applying for foreign aid. The roadblock was discontinued after several days, and the economy was saved.

Today, the tradition of the Conch Republic revolution continues with a yearly celebration in April and appointment of various Conch Ambassadors. To many Key West locals, both natives and transplants alike, the event symbolizes both the intense individualism of the island's people and the keen sense of humor that they enjoy.

at Oceans Edge Key West Resort Hotel has slips to 140 feet and sells all fuels. The marina caters to sportfishing boats with all new docks, pump-out service and a fully-covered and secure dry-rack storage facility. A little farther west on Stock Island is Robbie's of Key West LLC. Traditionally, Robbie's is heavily involved in the repair and refurbishing of large, commercial vessels, as well as megayachts, and has a 125-ton lift and 50-ton crane.

Stock Island Marina Village can accommodate vessels up to 300 feet and sells fuel. With 220 slips and state-of-the-art floating docks, every type of boat can be accommodated. Every reservation includes dockage, water, pump-out service and other amenities. There is new (in 2018) restaurant on the premises, Deluna's Bar & Grill (305-204-4294), which serves up true Cuban-inspired cuisine with fresh, locally caught fish and homemade recipes. You can even walk right off your boat with your catch and DeLuna's will prepare it for you.

Sunset Marina Key West is at the northwest end of Stock Island with transient slips, fuel and laundry facilities. It is a short walk from here to The Key West Golf Club, a public golf course. Between the west side of Stock Island and the east side of Key West on Cow Key Channel, Hurricane Hole Restaurant and Marina (305-294-0200) has slips for dining patrons, serving excellent conch and calamari dishes. Fresh catches of tuna, wahoo, grouper and mahi-mahi are served alongside traditional non-seafood meals.

We can't talk about Stock Island and not mention The Hogfish Bar and Grill (305-293-4041), a *Waterway Guide* staff favorite. The open-air restaurant and bar is famous for its hogfish sandwich, cold beer, local flavor and live music on the weekends. Hogfish has an "old Florida" laid-back style and a lot of character.

Anchorage: The Stock Island anchorage provides good all-round protection but access is restricted to vessels requiring 60 feet or less vertical clearance. Some use the local boat ramp to provide shore access by dinghy.

■ KEY WEST

Key West is the sunny, end-of-the-line destination for tourists and travelers of all descriptions. Lots of them come down U.S. 1. Thousands more make their way via cruise ships that dock at the Key West waterfront.

Casual sailing duds substitute for more formal attire almost anywhere on this island. Jimmy Buffett tunes, smoke from handmade cigars and frangipani blossoms fill the air; tourist shops and raucous bars are juxtaposed to what are surely some of the finest open-air restaurants and most tastefully preserved period architecture in America.

Key West is difficult to categorize. It is a unique and irresistible magnet to yachtsmen, long-distance cruisers and sportfishermen. For them, Key West offers amenities and attractions of virtually every level and description.

NAVIGATION: Use NOAA Charts 11441 and 11447. Past Stock Island, the towers and radar domes of Key West International Airport appear to starboard, along with many waterfront hotels and condominiums. Once past the range marker off Whitehead Spit (Mile 1241)– the southwesterly tip of Key West–you can cut inside, leaving to port flashing red "12," which marks the eastern side of the Main Ship Channel from the ocean. Turn to starboard towards flashing green "13," leaving it to port as you turn northwestward up the well-buoyed Main Ship Channel.

The entrance to Key West from the Atlantic Ocean side is relatively straightforward, yet the abundance of buoys in the area can confuse a first-time visitor, particularly at night. We strongly recommend that first-timers do not attempt a night passage, particularly through the Northwest Channel Entrance from the Gulf of Mexico.

The Main Ship Channel guides the deepest-draft commercial vessels in from the Atlantic Ocean on a well-marked path leading just west of north from lighted red-and-white whistle buoy "KW" on a range to the prominent (and lighted) red-and-white water tank on the western end of the island. The channel takes an abrupt dogleg to the northwest at quick flashing red "8," and then another dogleg (about 1 mile farther), this time to the north, between flashing green "9" and quick flashing red "12." Entrance for boats southbound on Hawk Channel should be made at the first elbow in the Main Ship Channel.

⚠ It is important to monitor VHF Channel 16 in the Main Ship Channel. Larger vessels will issue a Sécurité call before they enter the channel; this is particularly important when the massive cruise ships are on the move (usually in the morning and early evening). The channel has good width and depth but the current and wind can be significant factors here, and there is lots of vessel traffic. It's prudent to have a "Plan B" in case of traffic conflicts or possible breakdowns in this area.

The Northwest Channel (shown best on NOAA Chart 11441, Edition 41) begins at flashing green bell buoy "1." At this point, steer a course for red nun buoy "2," leaving it to starboard and continuing between quick-flashing green "3" to port and red nun "4" to starboard. Both are located to bring you safely inside between two submerged jetties, east and west. (The eastern jetty is awash at high tide.) Then, continue on down the well-marked channel to the Main Ship Channel at flashing green "19." Continuing on NOAA Chart 11447, a sharp turn to the northeast here will bring you to flashing red "24" and the Key West Bight. Again, only highly experienced navigators should attempt this channel at night. To avoid the jetties, you must pass green bell buoy "1" on entry or leaving. This is not a place to attempt shortcuts.

Take the well-marked channel around the north end of Fleming Key to access Garrison Bight. If you stay centered in the channel you should carry at least 7- to 8-foot MLW depths. Note that the chart depicts 50-foot-high power lines at the opening of Garrison Bight, but the yacht club and others there claim it is closer to 60 feet of vertical clearance. North of the channel inside the basin its closer to 34 feet. If vertical clearance is a consideration, call ahead, wait for low tide and then make your own decision. Very few cruising sailboats enter the bight; also be advised that overnight anchoring in the Bight is prohibited for all vessels.

In the past three decades, the City of Key West has undergone a noticeable transformation from a tiny tourist and fishing curiosity into a luxurious, moneyed resort. Nowhere is this more evident than in the aggressive but controlled development of quality hotels, Key West-styled condominiums, proudly restored wooden homes, historic sites and inventive new restaurants.

Within an easy walk from the major marinas the city operated dinghy landing in Key West Bight, Old Town serves up a savory variety of provisioning and dining possibilities, along with shops, watering holes, dives and other local color. Pick up a free Key West map before you start out, available at most marinas and many shops. The free "Duval Loop" bus is a great way to get around. With the exception of a few resort hotels, the architecture in Old Town is largely "Conch Island" style and worthy of a walking tour between stops.

Attractions: Tourist attractions abound (although most charge fees). Consider a bundled pass, if you plan to visit a few. Some buildings operated by the historical society accept donations and the wonderful ECO-Discovery Center operated by NOAA is free (35 E Quay Rd, 305-809-4750).

There are numerous other historic structures here and not enough space to list them all. Noteworthy are the Ernest Hemingway House at 907 Whitehead St. (305-294-1136), Tennessee Williams House at 1431 Duncan St. and President Harry S. Truman Little White House at 111 Front St. (305-294-9911). Other popular stops include the Mel Fisher Maritime Museum (200 Greene St., 305-294-2633) with a collection of treasure from 17th-century shipwrecks; the Key West Butterfly & Nature Conservatory (1316 Duval St., 305-296-2988); the Key West Shipwreck Museum (305-292-8990) with an observation tower; and Key West Aquarium (305-296-2051). (The latter two–in true Key West style–both claim 1 Whitehead St. as their address.) Another option is the tourist-laden, but highly informative, Conch Tour Train (305-294-5161). In service since 1958, the train itself is part of Key West history. It has four stops near attractions and is a great way to get around. (Tickets are good for the entire day of purchase.)

The sunset celebration at Mallory Square is always worth a visit, whether it is your first or 100th visit to Key West. In the waterfront square just north of the cruise ship dock, buskers perform nightly in the light of the setting sun. Wander through the crowd and enjoy performances of fire eaters, jugglers, acrobatic musicians, mimes, contortionists, sword swallowers, bicycle tricksters and other oddities. There are always tempting concoctions (such as chocolate-dipped cheesecake) to snack on while waiting for the sunset.

On your way to or from Mallory Square, don't miss the Key West Historic Memorial Sculpture Garden on the corner of Wall Street and Tifts Alley. Bronze busts of the island's historic figures portray a colorful and intriguing past. The tour is financed entirely by individual memorials etched in the bricks of the garden walkway (more than $700,000 worth).

Be sure to take the obligatory photo at the popular Southernmost Point in the Continental United States. This multi-striped buoy at the end of Whitehead Street is just "90 Miles to Cuba." Another good photo-op is from the top of the Key West Lighthouse (88 steps), located across the street from the Hemingway House, at 938 Whitehead St. (305-294-0012).

Shopping: Within a block or two of Harbor Walk in Key West Bight is Key West Marine Hardware (818 Caroline St., 305-294-3519) with an unusually well-stocked chandlery; West Marine at 951 Caroline St. (305-296-0953) in a large facility; and Lost Reef Adventures with dive gear sales, service and rentals at 261 Margaret St (305-296-9737). Just east is Ace Hardware at 1101 Eaton St. (305-296-9091). Also within an easy walk is Fausto's Food Palace (522 Fleming St., 305-296-5663). It's a convenient place to do some provisioning and has reasonable prices. They have a wonderful meat and seafood selection, a full grocery department, as well as produce, beer, wine and prepared foods.

Dining: The restaurant selection in Key West rivals that of any major American port city. Local residents from as far away as Key Largo will travel the full length of the Overseas Highway for lunch in Key West in preference to a shorter run to Miami. One such draw is Louie's Backyard, which is actually a backyard that is right on the Atlantic Ocean (700 Waddell Ave.). Indoor and spectacular outdoor seating is arranged in a series of terrace levels, descending to the sea. Louie's is widely regarded as having the best and most innovative cuisine in the Florida Keys; prices are high, but customers come away satisfied. Reservations are advised (305-294-1061).

The Harbor Walk connects virtually all marine facilities, restaurants, bars, shops and an excellent market that cluster around Key West Bight. If you're on a budget, keep in mind that many establishments offer an extended happy-hour.

Starting at the end of Margaret Street, the Half Shell Raw Bar (305-294-7496) has seafood selections in tempting variety. Across the small square, Turtle Kraals (305-294-2640) is famous for its colorful seafood preparations, Floribbean-style and its tower bar. Bahamian or blues music fills the air here nightly. The next stop along the Harbor Walk is the Conch Republic Seafood Company (305-294-4403), famous for its Baked Oysters Callaloo and featuring indoor and outdoor dining. Where Front Street meets the Bight are the co-located Alonzo's Oyster Bar and the A&B Lobster House, serving up Florida's famous crustacean and plenty of steak (305-294-5880). Reservations are recommended for A&B.

Close to the inner harbor, the oldest restaurant in Key West is Pepe's Café (806 Caroline St., 305-294-7192). Pepe's was established in 1909 and has served everyone from Ernest Hemingway and Harry Truman to Carl Hiaasen and Bob Dylan. Open for three meals daily.

For a complete change of pace, try Blue Heaven (729 Thomas St., 305-296-8666), serving three meals Monday through Saturday and lunch and dinner on Sundays; limited reservations for dinner. Most of the seating is outside under a tropical canopy. Two friends at 512 Front St (305-296-3124) serves a light menu on their patio. For seriously authentic and inexpensive Cuban cuisine, El Siboney (900 Catherine St., 305-296-4184) is consistently recommended as the place to go (lunch and dinner).

We would be remiss to not mention the active bar scene in Key West. Up on the corner of Greene and Duval, Sloppy Joe's Bar has been in the same location since 1937. Capt. Tony's Saloon is just around the corner, as is The Hog's Breath Saloon, a biker favorite, which serves the saloon's own medium-weight beer on tap, along with lunch and dinner daily. Nearby, at 505 Front St., is the Island Dogs Bar with a slogan of "Come as you are." Margaritaville at 500 Duval St. is awash in Jimmy Buffett memorabilia, and you can buy the famed cocktail along with Buffett clothing, CDs and other items. This is but a sampling of the purported 650 or so bars on the 4-mile-long and 2-mile-wide island!

For more options, visit fla-keys.com/keywest.

Dockage: The Margaritaville Resort & Marina (formerly the Westin Key West) is located just off the main channel to starboard as you enter the harbor. The resort has multiple restaurants, a pool surrounded by tropical native plants and lush trees and a private spa. Access to the marina may be limited because cruise ships dock on the outside pier. If the wind and waves are up, you may want the greater protection of docking opportunities within Key West Bight.

To reach Key West Bight, continue in the Main Ship Channel until just before flashing red "24," then turn right, heading to flashing red "2" and quick flashing red "4" to starboard at the end of the seawall. The spacious floating docks (finger piers port and starboard) of the Galleon Marina lie immediately to starboard on rounding the seawall. Adjacent to the Historic Seaport Harbor Walk, which extends all the way to the restaurants and shops on the southeast side of the Bight, the Galleon Marina is a popular spot. Reservations are recommended far in advance during high season, and especially for regatta weeks and Fantasy Fest. Take advantage of all of the resort amenities including a pool, private beach, sauna and exercise room. The marina is breakwater shielded and provides specially engineered docks for maximum protection. They also have bicycle, moped and Jet Ski rentals on site. The Harbor Master is on site 24/7. A & B Marina is A & B Marina is home to the Harbor Walk and offers transient slips and fuel. There are several good restaurants in this immediate area, connected by the Harbor Walk. (See "Key West: Goin' Ashore.")

On the south side is the Historic Seaport at Key West Bight (a.k.a. Key West Bight Marina), identified by the Chevron sign at the easily accessible fuel dock, as well as the cluster of schooners available for harbor cruises. This friendly marina can accommodate vessels to 140 feet in its deep water (12 feet at MLW) transient slips.

Key West Marine Hardware is within easy walking distance at 818 Caroline Street (305-294-3425) and has a complete selection of marine paint and hardware.

At the southeast end of the inner harbor, Conch Harbor Marina is dead ahead as you enter the Bight, rounding flashing red "4" at the end of the breakwater, and easily identified by the large TEXACO sign (both gasoline and diesel fuel available). Most slips are reserved well in advance and reservations must be made via a faxed form.

A bit farther afield, Spencer's Boat Yard in Garrison Bight has a 25-ton lift and repair capabilities (no transient slips). *Remember that access to Garrison Bight is controlled by the 50-foot authorized power line at the entrance.* Additional transient dockage may be available at Garrison Bight Marina, which is primarily used by local small-boat fishermen, many of them utilizing the marina's ample dry storage capability. (Note 4-foot approach depths at MLW.) Also in this inner harbor is City Marina at Garrison Bight, which has dockage on both sides of the 19-foot vertical clearance fixed **Garrison Bight Bridge**. Limited transient slips are also available at the Key West Yacht Club at the east end of Garrison Bight.

> Key West is a federal **No-Discharge Zone**, meaning no waste, even that which has been treated, should be discharged overboard. A pump-out service for boats on moorings, anchored or in marinas is provided by City Marina Pump-Out (305-809-3981 or VHF Channel 16), with service available Monday through Saturday, 8:00 a.m. to 4:00 p.m. Check our Waterway Explorer at waterwayguide.com for updates.

Moorings: The City of Key West has a mooring field east of Fleming Key with daily and monthly rates. Key West City Marina at Garrison Bight administers these. For reservations call 305-809-3981. To the west of Fleming Key (north of the Key West Historic Harbor) is a second mooring field that is free but be advised that mooring integrity is questionable. The east side has significantly less traffic (and wakes) and is much less bumpy than the west side. It's a short dinghy ride under the Fleming Key Bridge and into the tourist area of Key West Bight if we want to go downtown.

Anchorage: If you are short on money, and time spent going to and from your boat is not a consideration, Key West abounds with anchorage possibilities, although

A cruiser essential in the clear water of the Keys is a **"Lookie Bucket"** or an underwater viewer. Bascially, it is a bucket with a clear plastic bottom. When placed on top of the water, it acts like a snorkeling mask allowing you to see what is underwater.

many locations afford only modest protection from fast-shifting winds and swift currents. The holding southwest of Wisteria Island (known locally as Christmas Tree Island), for example, is poor. The exposure from north through east can be a problem in unsettled weather.

West of Fleming Key, there is a strong reversing current, making careful watches during the first turn of the tide a virtual necessity. Remember to take into consideration the number of anchors, swinging radius and windage of surrounding vessels. Fresh winds against the tides regularly make for some interesting float patterns; keep an eye out for other vessels that may wander too close to your vessel. You will find 7 to 10 feet at MLW and lots of boat traffic.

Both the Wisteria Island and Fleming Key anchorages are relatively close to Old Town and the Key West Bight Marina dinghy dock. (It's about a 1-mile walk from Garrison Bight to downtown.) Just inside the breakwater protecting the Bight, turn to starboard in front of the Marathon fuel sign, pass the first dock, and then turn to port toward the Waterfront Market. Turn again to port as you approach the seawall. The dinghy dock is located immediately in front of Turtle Kraals Restaurant for vessels up to 13 feet. The fee for tying up your dinghy is payable to the Key West Bight Marina; lower daily rates are available for longer stays. The dinghy dock has two sections–one with reserved spots and another (more chaotic) one for everyone else. You can expect shenanigans if you tie up in the wrong space.

An alternative to the first two anchorages is in the area just to the north of the mooring field and Sigsbee Park.

There are good depths of 7 to 10 feet at MLW and good holding. Make sure you are outside of the mooring field buoys. From here, you can access the second dinghy dock at Garrison Bight and pay your fee to the Garrison Bight Marina. (Remember to bring your pump-out receipt.) This anchorage is exposed to the north, but has much less current and boat wakes than the others. Even in strong northerly winds, the shallow water between here and the Gulf cuts down most of the swells, just leaving you with wind waves. Note in a strong northerly a significant chop can build up. Some cruisers have been unable to dinghy back to this anchorage under some conditions; be sure to monitor the weather when you do go ashore.

Side Trip: Sand Key

NAVIGATION: Use NOAA Charts 11441. If you decide to explore the wonders of the water, you can take a leisurely 6-mile-long boat ride southeast of Key West to Sand Key. All the Marine Sanctuary sites in this region offer excellent snorkeling. Mariners should be aware that the U.S. Coast Guard extinguished Sand Key Light because it was structurally compromised. A temporary light has been established in its place. Exercise caution when transiting this area. At Sand Key, you can secure your boat to one of 21 mooring balls made available at this natural shallow reef. If no mooring buoy is available and you are outside a no-anchor zone; you may anchor in sand (but not on the coral).

■ TO THE DRY TORTUGAS

Seventy nautical miles from the nearest settlement in Key West, the Dry Tortugas are the westernmost of the Florida Keys, the most remote and, in some respects, the most fascinating and beautiful. The beautiful Marquesas Keys lie in the path to the Tortugas, only 24 nm west of Key West. Some also stop at Boca Grande Key, about 5 nm closer to Key West. This site offers less protection but can accommodate boats with deeper drafts. Either site make an excellent stop to break up the trip to the Dry Tortugas. Other than these, there are no intermediate anchorages and there are no facilities or supplies of any kind once leaving Key West.

Because of erratic, and sometimes severe, weather in the area (unpredicted fronts packing high winds are not that unusual), passage to the Dry Tortugas requires planning for the unexpected and packing everything–water, food, fuels, clothing and all other supplies–for a trip of substantially longer duration than anticipated. Schedules are not recommended. Weekend trippers, Caribbean-bound cruisers and fishermen alike frequently find themselves holed up for a week or more in the modestly protected harbor off Garden Key in persistent 25- to 35-knot winds attending stalled fronts in the Gulf of Mexico or off the Cuban coast.

If weather conditions are less than ideal, a trip to the Dry Tortugas should be postponed. In all conditions, boats bound for the Dry Tortugas should be equipped, at a minimum, with a VHF radio, depth sounder and GPS unit. Careful checking with NOAA radio forecasts before and during such a trip is essential for your safety. Once at Garden Key, the National Park Service posts daily NOAA weather reports at its docks. Before departure from Key West, skippers should also check with the Coast Guard for the current *Local Notice to Mariners*, available online at navcen.uscg.gov. In addition to changes in aids to navigation in the area, you should check on any military operations in the restricted area west of the Marquesas Keys. The Coast Guard can be reached on VHF Channels 16 and 22A in Key West. With careful preparation, a voyage to the Dry Tortugas can be most rewarding.

NAVIGATION: Use NOAA Charts 11420 and 11434. One route to the Dry Tortugas runs south of the Marquesas and the other to the north. The southern route, via West Channel, then west past Man Key and then Boca Grande Key, permits easy access to the best anchorage in the Marquesas. Check your charts for shoal areas and stay clear of both keys.

Anchorage: If you choose to take the southern route, stop off and anchor to the west of Boca Grande Key near green daybeacon "17" in 10 to 16 feet at MLW. Choose your location based on wind direction.

The Marquesas

An interesting stopover with a fairly well-sheltered lagoon, the Marquesas are made up of numerous small keys arranged in the shape of a South Seas atoll. Use binoculars to locate a suitable entrance. If you have a shoal-draft boat, a high tide and an overhead sun, then you might want to try it; otherwise, forget it!

NAVIGATION: Use NOAA Charts 11420 and 11464. Some promising-looking entrances might be between the two large islands to the southeast marked "mangrove" on the chart. Two other potential entrances on the south side to the west of Mooney Harbor Key might provide enough depth. A third possibility exists on the western side of the atoll. Only very shoal-draft vessels should attempt entry, and be prepared to get yourself off the bottom if you run aground. You are likely out of VHF range for assistance here.

Fort Jefferson

FLORIDA LOWER KEYS

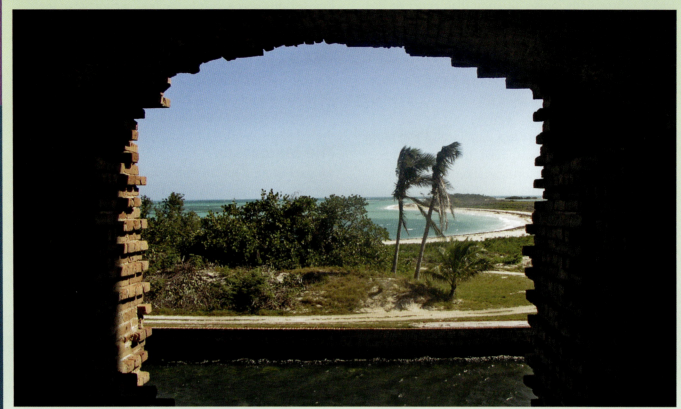

First charted by Spanish explorer Ponce de Leon and named for the turtles gathering there, the Dry Tortugas became U.S. territory in 1821 with the purchase of Florida from Spain. Situated on the rim of the Gulf Stream at the pivot point of trade routes to the Mississippi River and Gulf Coast, the Dry Tortugas were quickly recognized for their navigational and strategic importance. Garden Key soon became the site of a substantial lighthouse. A quarter-century later, construction began on a mighty fortress there. But the technologies of seamanship and national defense changed before the fort was completed. Chief among them was the invention and use of rifled cannon shot, which went through the sides of masonry forts like they were made of cookie dough.

Today, the eerie presence of massive, but never-finished Fort Jefferson still dominates Garden Key, but its importance is historical. The working lighthouse, long since moved to Loggerhead Key to the west, also appears as a sentinel from the past. Contemporary value of this island group is found in its pristine natural beauty, including the unpolluted clarity of its waters and sparkling live reef systems, and the raucous wonder of thousands of nesting seabirds.

In 1992, the entire area, bound by an elliptical circuit of 10 large yellow buoys, was dedicated as the Dry Tortugas National Park. For park info check nps.gov/drto/index. htm or call 305-242-7700. Touring Fort Jefferson on your own is an option, but you will learn much more if you take one of the ranger-guided tours. The rangers share many interesting and unusual facts that will enhance your visit and understanding of life at the fort. The largest of the forts of last century's American coastal defense perimeter (8-foot-thick brick walls, standing 50 feet high to support three gun tiers and surrounding a 17-acre quad), it is also one of the most well preserved.

On arrival at the Dry Tortugas, you must first check in at the National Park Service Visitor Center in Fort Jefferson. You will receive a copy of the park's brochure with maps and regulations and the latest weather report. The Park Service has restrooms at its docks and beach space for dinghy landings. The park is a No-Discharge Zone and, time permitting, park rangers may check your vessel's Y-valve. There are picnic tables, a few charcoal grills and a beautiful sandy beach at the fort's south end. Everything you require must be brought with you, and all trash must be carted back to your boat. Visit drytortugas. com for more information on this fascinating area.

Approach the Mooney Harbor Key from the southeast. The northern route, via the Northwest Channel, leads out past Harbor Key Bank and then to the west. You can switch channels if you change your mind and head through the north-south Boca Grande Channel, approximately 2 nm west of Boca Grande Key and identified by green daybeacon "1" to the north and red daybeacon "2" to the south.

Anchorage: NOAA Chart 11439 shows Mooney Harbor as having room for several boats, but that is deceiving. At the Marquesas, try to figure out the winds and then anchor in the lee of the islands An anchorage on the southwestern side of the atoll is comfortable in winds from an easterly quadrant. Depths of 8 to 13 feet at MLW can be found fairly close to shore. Shallow draft boats can snug up due west of Mooney Harbor Key in at least 4 feet at MLW with exposure from the south. You will find excellent holding here.

Enjoy a dinghy ride through the maze of passages in the atoll, but do not go ashore. This is a marine sanctuary and signs on the shore prohibit you from landing. This area is known for the famous Spanish treasure ship, the *Atocha*, which sank just to the west of the Marquesas in the Quick Sands. Many boat captains from Key West bring their clients here to bonefish or angle for tarpon.

Marquesas to Dry Tortugas

NAVIGATION: Use NOAA Charts 11420 and 11464. Heading west from either the anchorage or the lagoon, after clearing the shoals to the west of the Marquesas, use Halfmoon Shoal and Rebecca Shoal Light as waypoints. Mind your depth sounder as you leave the shallows east of the light. On the northern route, the same suggestion applies, but you do have some markers along the shallows south of your course. The marker on the western edge of New Grounds Shoal (flashing four second, 19 feet high) can also serve as a waypoint before passing Rebecca Shoal. From the light, you pass over deep water. As you approach the eastern edge of the Dry Tortugas, you can pick out Bush Key and Garden Key with Fort Jefferson dominating the island landscape.

The approach for long-distance cruisers from the north is best made due south on the meridian W 082° 52.00, passing immediately abeam of lighted boundary buoy "I" (yellow) to a point about 0.25 mile east of the red and green daybeacon at Middle Ground. From there, head

to red daybeacon "6" and the Northwest Channel. Skip the eastern channel, as you cannot count on it. Vessels approaching from the south are advised to use Southwest Channel east of Loggerhead Key and marked initially by green can buoy "1." At red daybeacon "6," Garden Key's southerly entry channel requires an abrupt turn to starboard to follow the closely spaced markers on both sides of the deep channel into the anchorage.

A solid isthmus between Bush Key and Garden Key was observed in spring 2018. The latest corrected NOAA Chart 11438 (Edition 14, dated January 2017) indicated the presence of the isthmus. We would suggest that you buy print-on-demand charts if you are interested in the latest information on the channels in and out of the Garden Key anchorage beside Fort Jefferson.

Anchorage: Best anchorage is found in front (to the east) of the deteriorated steamship docks at Garden Key's southern end. There is variable holding here in 15 to 20 feet at MLW. Be careful; outside the channel, charted depths are about 1 foot at MLW. It is best to search out a sandy spot, and then make sure your anchor is set well and securely buried with either a "lookie bucket" or an anchor dive. In this relatively confined and exposed area, there are nearly always at least half a dozen boats, often more than twice that number during a blow. Park regulations restrict overnight anchoring to within 1 mile of Garden Key Harbor Light. During nesting season, you may want to anchor away from Bush Key to avoid the nighttime noise of the sooty terns.

Prior to making the passage, you should carefully the latest weekly *Local Notice to Mariners* from the Coast Guard, available online at navcen.uscg.gov/lnm for changes to navigation aids. Also check the interactive Waterway Explorer at waterwayguide.com for the latest navigational updates.

■ NEXT STOP

Next up is the eclectic West Coast of Florida, where the alligators, fish camps and seagrass of the Everglades give way to the face-paced urban life of the Tampa Bay area to the north. Take your time and consider a stop in Everglades National Park on the way. The scenery and wildlife are spectacular and you can eke out some solitude as this coastline is only accessible by boat.

SAILS UP: THE ULTIMATE CRUISE
Key West to Key Largo

LEG 1 of 8

○ START

See America's glorious Southeast coastline the best way possible: by boat. All year, we're collaborating with Waterway Guide Media to bring you the best segments of the 1,243-mile-long Intracoastal Waterway on a journey from Key West, Florida, to Norfolk, Virginia, at the end of the (watery) trail. This issue: a sun-drenched passage from Key West to Key Largo.

MILE 1243
SUNSET KICKOFF
Key West

Start the journey with a sunset at **Mallory Square** surrounded by the nightly pageant of tightrope-walking cats and acrobats. (Watch for the green flash.) **TIE UP:** Dockage rates at the **Westin Key West Resort & Marina** are $4 per foot. (Room rates start at $279.)

MILE 1209
DIVE-BAR MUST
Big Pine

No Name Pub may look like an old wooden cottage on the outside, but venture inside and you will see that the walls and ceilings are covered with thousands of fluttering dollar bills, many with personal messages. Locals know the pizza is the best around.

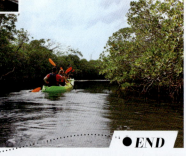

MILE 1194
SNORKELING ADVENTURE
Boot Key

Join tropical fish, stingrays, and the occasional barracuda at the magnificent coral reef adjacent to **Sombrero Key Light.** Grab Instagram snapshots at the natural coral limestone arch. **TIE UP:** Dockage rates at **Faro Blanco Resort & Yacht Club** on **Marathon Key** start at $3.50 per foot. (Room rates start at $139.)

MILE 1160
FISHING PILGRIMAGE
Islamorada

Of course the **Worldwide Sportsman/ Bass Pro Shop** sells a huge selection of fishing gear and apparel, but it's the saltwater aquarium and the full-size 1933 inspiration for Hemingway's yacht, the *Pilar,* that make this angler's bazaar worth a port stop.

MILE 1140
PADDLE THE MANGROVES
Key Largo

At **John Pennekamp Coral Reef State Park,** you can explore 50 miles of natural mangrove trails via kayak, paddleboard, or canoe, or take a guided diving or snorkeling tour. **TIE UP:** If you have a shallow-draft boat, overnight at a mooring in **Largo Sound,** which you will share with the resident pelicans.

● END

NO BOAT (YET)? It's easy to rent or charter any type or size with or without a captain in the Keys. Get hooked up with the right vessel from family-owned **Vacation Boat Rentals** (866/420-1515 or vacationboatrentals.com) or **Boatsetter** (844/262-8738 or boatsetter.com).

103 MILES SAILED

42 BRIDGES YOU DON'T HAVE TO DRIVE OVER!

600+ SPECIES OF FISH IN THE FLORIDA KEYS

1,700 TOTAL ISLANDS IN THE FLORIDA KEYS

9 SHIPWRECKS TO EXPLORE

BY **JANI PARKER**

READY TO SET SAIL? Order guidebooks and begin planning your boating adventures at **waterwayguide.com**

FROM TOP: TRINA DOPP PHOTOGRAPHY/GETTY IMAGES, ROBBIE CAPONETTO, MIKE THEISS/NATIONAL GEOGRAPHIC CREATIVE, TYPHOONSKI/GETTY IMAGES, PETER PTSCHELINZEW/GETTY IMAGES; MAP: MATT CASERTA

Florida's West Coast

- ■ FLAMINGO TO FORT MYERS BEACH
- ■ SAN CARLOS BAY TO SARASOTA ■ TAMPA BAY AREA TO TARPON SPRINGS

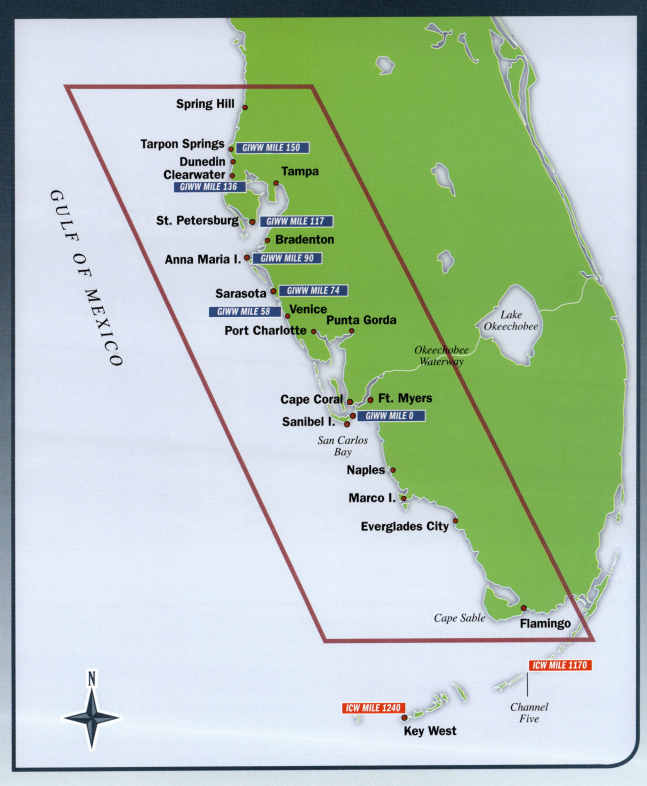

Spring Hill

Tarpon Springs   *GIWW MILE 150*

Dunedin
Clearwater   Tampa
GIWW MILE 136

St. Petersburg   *GIWW MILE 117*

Bradenton

Anna Maria I.   *GIWW MILE 90*

Sarasota   *GIWW MILE 74*

GIWW MILE 58   Venice
Port Charlotte   Punta Gorda

Lake Okeechobee

Okeechobee Waterway

Cape Coral   Ft. Myers

Sanibel I.   *GIWW MILE 0*

San Carlos Bay

Naples

Marco I.

Everglades City

Cape Sable

Flamingo

GULF OF MEXICO

N

ICW MILE 1170

ICW MILE 1240

Channel Five

Key West

Visit Waterway Explorer at waterwayguide.com

Florida's West Coast

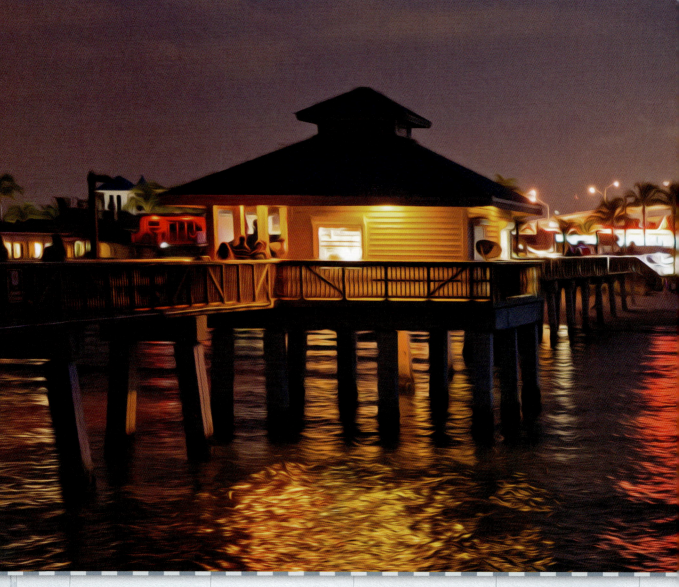

Sugar sand beaches and shells or tropical hardwoods and Everglades swampland, Florida's lower west coast provides a greater diversity of experiences than the east. Instead of being packed with crowds, cultures and glamour, cruising the west coast brings opportunities for relaxation and the kind of casual luxury that appears in isolated high-end resorts. The cruising, too, is entirely different. The amenities are more limited and spaced farther apart, but Florida's southwestern waters give access to the swampy wilderness of the Everglades, the long sweep of Sanibel and Captiva Islands, picturesque fishing villages, bustling Tampa Bay and the history- and restaurant-rich Greek sponge center of Tarpon Springs.

The lower half of the coast is alternately wild and developed. At the bottom of the peninsula, the Ten Thousand Islands guard the swampland of the Everglades. Up the coast, the shoreline develops into sandy beach backed by a solid wall of pine and tropical hardwood jungle.

At San Carlos Bay, the tropical barrier islands emerge. Deep water moves in closer toward shore, and resort communities begin to appear. Mile Zero of the Gulf Intracoastal Waterway (GIWW) whets the appetite for travel at the mouth of the Caloosahatchee River, where the Okeechobee Waterway ends (or begins, depending on the direction you are traveling).

From Fort Myers north, the west coast sees increased boat traffic, houses, marinas and shore activity and, from as far

Fort Myers is a gateway to the southwest Florida region and a major tourist destination within Florida. It was founded on February 21, 1866, by Capt. Manuel A. Gonzalez.

south as Naples up the coast to Clearwater, the mangroves increasingly give way to extensive shoreside development.

Cruising Conditions

Cruising waters through much of the lower half of Florida's west coast are part of the areas vast conservation areas. These include 14 aquatic preserves, 40 state parks, 14 national wildlife refuges, 2 national parks and the over 100,000-acre Rookery Bay National Estuarine Research Reserve–one of the few remaining undisturbed mangrove estuaries in North America. The GIWW, which is for the most part either a dredged channel behind barrier islands or a passage shielded from the Gulf of Mexico, begins at the mouth of the Caloosahatchee River and runs 150 statute miles north to Anclote Keys through a narrow channel. Outside the marked route, shoals are everywhere, similar to the ICW on Florida's east coast.

Though they might seem worse to the inexperienced, most tidal currents are less than 2 knots here. At 1 to 3 feet, the tidal range is relatively small, and water depths tend to be governed more by wind than by tide. When winds blow from the northeast, the water is driven out of the bays, while strong winds from the southeast and southwest push water in. Under northeast wind conditions, there is generally less water in the bays than the chart shows. Be especially wary when a spring low tide combines with a fresh northeast breeze.

From time to time, navigational skills will be tested as you follow the course offshore into the Gulf proper. The occasionally capricious weather may surprise you with a severe and sudden storm. Be prepared with the latest charts and weather advisories, and make sure your boat and equipment are in top shape.

Florida's West Coast: The Gulf Intracoastal Waterway (GIWW)

The GIWW runs 150 statute miles north to Anclote Keys through a narrow channel. Outside the marked route, shoals are everywhere, similar to the ICW on Florida's east coast. For the most part, the GIWW is either a dredged channel behind barrier islands or a passage shielded from the Gulf of Mexico that begins at the mouth of the Caloosahatchee River. This west coast waterway provides the same type of protection from inclement weather as the Atlantic ICW and, like its East Coast counterpart, the GIWW varies in nature with location. In some areas, the GIWW is serpentine with many sharp bends and turns; in other places, it runs in open straightaways. No matter its course, the GIWW still requires navigational vigilance, so keep the following precautions in mind:

- Look astern as often as ahead and keep markers lined up fore and aft to maintain your course in-channel.

- Stay to mid-channel as often as possible and be alert to side currents that may cause lightly powered or high-windage vessels to drift off course and out of the channel.

- Slow down in any area where shoaling is likely, especially if your boat draws more than 3 feet. West coast bottoms tend to commonly consist of soft mud or sand. Grounding at slow speed will do less damage than barreling full-tilt onto a shoal.

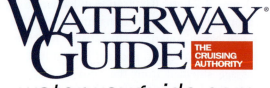

Flamingo to Fort Myers Beach

CHARTS NOAA 11427, 11429, 11430, 11431, 11432, 11449, 11451, 11452 FL Bridges: Channel 09

■ TO FLORIDA'S WEST COAST

NAVIGATION: Use NOAA Charts 11449 and 11452. Two routes are available to leave the ICW and traverse Florida Bay westward for Cape Sable and points north along Florida's west coast.

Route 1: Long Key to Flamingo via Yacht Channel

The first route begins at ICW Mile 1173, north of Long Key and skirting shoals on and surrounding Old Dan Bank. The so-called "Yacht Channel" is well marked and protected. However, it abounds in charted, but otherwise unmarked, shoal patches of 5- to 6-feet at MLW (less in a significant blow from the north and less still for vessels straying even marginally off course). This route is not recommended for boats drawing over 4 feet or for travel in poor light.

Route 2: Vaca Key to Flamingo via Moser Channel

A second route begins just west of ICW Mile 1190, due north of Vaca Key (City of Marathon). Vessels will need to look out for shoals surrounding Rachel Bank for the first 4 miles of the Moser Channel north of the Seven Mile Bridge and then begin a course of 003 degrees magnetic in 7- to 11-foot depths direct to flashing red "2," located 2.2 miles south of East Cape Sable.

The best-marked route to the north consists of six markers along Moser Channel between the bridge and Bullard Bank. Note that older chart editions do not show these markers. When traveling in this area, be sure to use the latest charts available and check Waterway Explorer at waterwayguide.com for navigational updates.

Please consider what your final destination is before you pick a route to use. If you have a vessel big enough to cruise along offshore, then heading for East Cape is just adding extra miles to your trip. Basically, if the weather is right, and you are seriously heading north from the Seven

Mile Bridge (over Moser Channel), you may not want to go anywhere near the tip of Florida. In that case, we suggest that you consider a course of 337 degrees magnetic and a distance of 136 miles that will bring you in proximity of land up around Boca Grande Channel.

⚠ Due to numerous hazards in marine waters resulting from Hurricane Irma, boaters are advised to use extreme caution. Hazards include sunken vessels, missing/broken channel markers and submerged debris. Clean up and repair efforts will continue throughout 2018.

Don't rely on a cell phone to call for **assistance** in this area. There is no service.

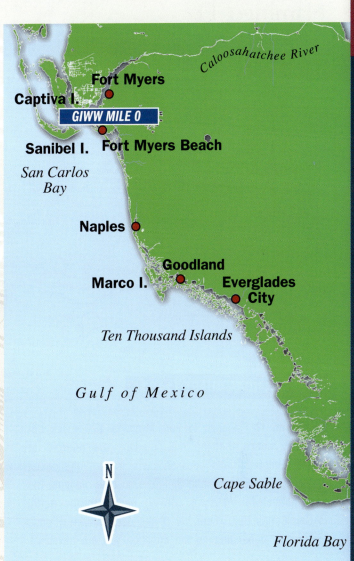

Flamingo, FL

FLAMINGO		Largest Vessel Accommodated	VHF Channel Monitored	Approach / Dockside Depth (reported)	Transient Berths / Total Berths	Floating Docks	Groceries, Ice, Marine Supplies, Snacks	Repairs: Hull, Engine, Propeller	Gas / Diesel	Lift (tonnage), Crane, Rail	Nearby: Grocery Store, Motel, Restaurant	Laundry, Pool, Showers, Courtesy Car	Min/Max Amps	Pump-Out Station		
				Dockage				**Supplies**			**Services**					
1. Flamingo Marina	239-695-3101	–	16/71	50/50	1/3.5	–	G		GIS	–	–		30/30	S	P	G

⌨ Internet Access   📶 Wireless Internet Access   **WG** Waterway Guide Cruising Club Partner   🔵onSpot dockside WiFi facility

See WaterwayGuide.com for current rates, fuel prices, web site addresses, and other up-to-the-minute information. *(Information in the table is provided by the facilities.)*

FLAMINGO, NOAA CHART 11433

Where Am I? Flamingo to Fort Myers is 120 miles but you may notice that no mile markers are referred to in this chapter. That's because there is no "Intracoastal Waterway" in this area, and therefore no mile markers. The Gulf Intracoastal Waterway (GIWW) begins to the north, in San Carlos Bay, where the Okeechobee Waterway ends (or begins, depending on the direction you are traveling).

Flamingo to Fort Myers Beach

For approximately 130 miles from Flamingo to Fort Myers Beach, the cruising skipper first travels off Cape Sable's East, Middle and Northwest Capes, along the edge of the wild, primitive and beautiful Ten Thousand Islands region, and then through the unofficial continuation of the ICW behind the green mangrove curtain from the Ten Thousand Islands region to the Goodland/Marco Island area. At that point, the cruising skipper with a shoal draft has the choice of moving offshore at Marco Island or following the winding 8-mile stretch of the Gordon Pass Channel from Marco Island to Naples and finally out to the Gulf of Mexico. Any

boat drawing more than 4 feet will need to take the outside route. From there, the skipper runs the shoreline to San Carlos Bay and the official start, Mile Zero, of the Gulf Intracoastal Waterway (GIWW) at its juncture with the Okeechobee Waterway, crossing Florida to the east.

■ FLAMINGO TO TEN THOUSAND ISLANDS

The wild and undeveloped Everglades swampland, beginning at Flamingo, envelope you in the power of nature and teach you a thing or two about respect at the same time. Heading north toward the desolate Ten Thousand Islands, cruisers will wonder if they are still in Florida, and it is this very diversity that makes cruising the west coast of Florida such a draw for the adventuresome.

NAVIGATION: Use NOAA Chart 11451. The combination of several hurricanes set Flamingo back substantially as the unique overnight stopover it had become. This is small boat territory only. Before you venture into

Flamingo, we suggest that you call ahead for up-to-date information and conditions. Taking it slow and easy is recommended when exploring this area.

⚠️ The key to reaching Flamingo, either for a daytime visit or an anchorage, is locating flashing red "2," which is 1.95 nm on a course of 178 degrees magnetic from East Cape, on Cape Sable. The approaches to flashing red "2" are either from the Keys, via Yacht Passage, directly from Key West across Florida Bay or from the north, skirting the edges of Everglades National Park on the west coast of Florida. For activity schedules, trail guides, a backcountry trip planner, natural history and more, visit the home page of the Everglades National Park website at nps.gov/ever or call 305-247-7700.

To reach Flamingo, you will travel approximately 8 miles east-by-northeast from flashing red "2," passing four more daybeacons to flashing green "9," which starts off the marked entry to Flamingo proper. You will then turn north-northeast for a little over 1 mile in the narrow but well-marked channel to the Flamingo basin.

⚠️ Daybeacon "18" was reported destroyed in December of 2017 and the wreckage shows approximately 1 foot above the surface at mean low water. Follow the buoys and daybeacons carefully; depths outside the channel are 1 to 2 feet at MLW. Play the tides if your draft is over 3 feet; the chart shows 4.5 feet at MLW in the entry channel, but the date of the sounding data is quite old. Refer to the Waterway Explorer (waterwayguide.com) and NOAA online charts for the most up-to-date information.

Dockage: Flamingo Marina is open year-round and can accommodate more than 50 boats with electric and water hookups. Fuel is available and there is a marina store with a limited variety of snacks, drinks and ice.

Anchorage: It is possible to anchor in Flamingo Basin in 4 to 5 feet at MLW with good holding in mud. This provides all-around protection.

North from East Cape Sable

NAVIGATION: Use NOAA Charts 11429, 11431 and 11451. From Flamingo, retrace your entry route and round East Cape Sable heading north. You will encounter thousands of lobster and crab pot markers if you leave the marked boundaries of Everglades National Park.

Refer to the Waterway Explorer (waterwayguide.com) and NOAA online charts for the most up-to-date information during planning and then pay close attention to your chart and the depth sounder while underway. Enter the appropriate waypoints into your GPS, and plot your course around Middle and Northwest Capes inside the park boundaries. If you are planning to head for Cape Romano, Marco Island or Naples, set your course to remain well offshore. Remember to stay well south of the finger shoals, about 12 miles below Cape Romano. This entire area is riddled with shoals and spots of very shallow water (2 to 3 feet at MLW). Your depth sounder and your chartplotter will be your friend.

Heading toward Cape Romano and its long shoals, your exposure is from the entire northern sector. "Holing up" in a blow is recommended. Even in the summer, squall lines and even high winds from the prevailing southeasterlies can stir things up. NOAA weather reports on VHF Channel WX2 or WX3 should keep you informed so you can make the passage safely.

Anchorage: If the winds are light and the weather pleasant, you can anchor off the beach between East and Middle Capes and dinghy ashore. There is 6 to 8 feet at MLW here with good holding in sand and grass. This is open northwest through south. The area provides excellent beach combing opportunities, and you will have little competition as few people anchor here. The Middle Cape Canal just north of Middle Cape is reported to be a good fishing spot, but you will need a freshwater license if you intend to dip the rod in Lake Ingraham.

■ TEN THOUSAND ISLANDS

Passing Cape Sable 0.25 nm offshore and then paralleling the coast inside the occasional Everglades National Park beacons brings you into the Ten Thousand Islands. This area stretches for about 56 nm to Cape Romano. Primitive, remote and uninhabited, these islands form the coastline of the Everglades National Park.

Little Shark River

NAVIGATION: Use NOAA Charts 11431 and 11432. About 6 miles above the Northwest Cape, pick up the marked entrance to the Little Shark River off the point just south of Ponce de Leon Bay.

Little Shark River is a gateway to the inner regions of the Everglades National Park and can provide access

Everglades Harbor, Gullivan Bay, FL

				Dockage			Supplies		Services					
		Largest Vessel Accommodated	VHF Channel Monitored	Transient Berths / Total Berths	Approach / Dockside Depth (reported)	Floating Docks	Gas / Diesel	Groceries, Ice, Marine Supplies, Snacks	Repairs: Hull, Engine, Propeller	Lift (tonnage), Crane, Rail	Min/Max Amps	Laundry, Pool, Showers, Courtesy Car	Pump-Out Station	Nearby: Grocery Store, Motel, Restaurant
EVERGLADES CITY														
1. Everglades Rod & Gun Club ⌨	239-695-2101	100	16	17/17	5.5/6	–	–	IS	–	–	50/50	PS	–	GMR
2. Everglades Isle Marina (WiFi)	239-695-2600	60	–	call/100	–	F	G	I	–	–	20/100	LPS	P	GMR
GULLIVAN BAY														
3. Port of the Islands Marina ⌨ (WiFi)	239-389-0367	65	16	20/175	5/6	F	G	GIMS	–	–	30/50	LPS	P	GMR
4. Walker's Coon Key Marina	239-394-2797	60	16	5/40	8/6	F	GD	IMS	HEP	L35	30/30	–	–	GMR
5. Calusa Island Marina (WiFi)	239-394-3668	70	16/05	25/84	5/6	F	GD	IMS	HEP	L50	30/50	LS	P	MR

⌨ Internet Access   (WiFi) Wireless Internet Access   WG Waterway Guide Cruising Club Partner   ☁ onSpot dockside WiFi facility
See WaterwayGuide.com for current rates, fuel prices, web site addresses, and other up-to-the-minute information. (*Information in the table is provided by the facilities.*)

EVERGLADES CITY, NOAA CHART 11429

GULLIVAN BAY, NOAA CHART 11429

to the Everglades Wilderness Waterway connecting Flamingo and Everglades City. This route is not recommended for vessels requiring more than 18 feet of clearance nor those that have high cabins and/or windscreens because of the narrow channels and overhanging foliage in some areas. However, if you are looking to wait out nasty northerly weather, getting a hook down in Little Shark River and out of the waves is good for anyone. The water is deep (10 to 15 feet at MLW), and the scenery is beautiful. Mariners have been waiting out bad weather here for many years.

Marked channels lead into coffee-colored wide and shallow bays, or up narrow rivers through and past hundreds of islands and winding waterways. Remember, navigating this type of course requires knowing where you are at all times; it is easy to get lost.

Anchorage: Many cruising boats anchor in the first mile or so of the Little Shark River, which is protected by a 60-foot-high mangrove forest. It has been reported to us that the anchorage at the mouth of the river has shoaled in with mud/shell from the charted depth of 4 to 12 feet at MLW. Since the bottom is so soft, you can slowly feel your way to anchor. There is a strong current, so make sure your anchor is well set. If staying for several days likely use a Bahamian moor to keep the anchor from fouling with the rode. Boats have also been observed anchored along the river near the south shore.

If your boat is not screened in, keep plenty of bug repellent handy. (On second thought, keep some handy even if you do have screens.) Those with keen eyes can spot alligators along the banks or in the water. At night, a flashlight shone into the wilderness will usually reveal dozens of little red eyes that belong to alligators. This is a definite "no swimming" area!

The pelicans work this area quite often and are fun to watch. A crab line dropped overboard and carefully hauled in will supply the galley with a magnificent meal. Fishing is good, but licenses are required and limits must be carefully observed. Leave the area as you found it. There are no shoreside facilities in this area.

Weather caveat for this area: The winter season's stronger winds and frontal storms arrive with ample warning from the northwest through north and finally the northeast. When you clear the East Cape, if the winds are strong from the northwest, seas can increase rapidly. The farther out into the Gulf of Mexico you go, the worse it will get. A closer-to-shore, but slower route will provide many rewards.

Everglades City

Everglades City

Everglades City's history, dating back more than 1,000 years to the age of the coastal mound dwellers, was based on trade, fishing and shellfishing. With the arrival of early settlers, it gradually evolved into a shipping port for produce and seafood. Seafood is still a major economic factor in the area but is following the decline of the produce market.

Unique to Everglades City is the Rod and Gun Club. Once a rambling, private, wood frame home, it is now a delightful hotel right on the Barron River, and it is worthy (if you have the time) of a trip all the way in from Indian Key just to see it, dine here and maybe stay overnight. You will be in touch with another era entirely. Lots of people whose names you may recognize have been here: Presidents Roosevelt, Truman, Eisenhower, Hoover and Nixon, as well as actors John Wayne, Burt Reynolds, Sally Field, Sean Connery, Danny Glover and Joe Pesci. Novelist Ernest Hemingway was a frequent guest here as well.

Everglades City has the basics: a very limited market, a museum, a hardware store and a Post Office. There are also good restaurants, including Camellia Street Grill (202 Camellia St. W., 239-695-2003) with creative southern cuisine and City Seafood (702 Begonia St., 239-695-4700), which specializes in fresh Gulf seafood. Triad Seafood Market and Café (401 W. School Dr., 239-695-0722) is a small, family-owned restaurant at the water's edge, which also has a fresh seafood market. If all-you-can-eat stone crab sounds good, this is the spot. The city is the northern terminus of the Everglades Wilderness Waterway and offers water-based tours of all types, including airboats, kayaks, canoes and swamp buggies.

Since heavy insecticide spraying has been virtually eliminated in the Everglades National Park, **mosquitoes** have become almost as important a consideration as weather. They swarm continually in warm weather. If you plan to anchor in this area, opt for spots that garner what breeze there is and keep plenty of bug spray on hand.

NAVIGATION: Use NOAA Charts 11429 and 11430. North of the Little Shark River, it is advisable to follow the markers out and farther offshore to transit the wide and shallow mouth of Ponce de Leon Bay. Prudence would indicate staying outside the Three Nautical Mile Line. For about 33 nm, only channels among the islands break the coast. Some are deep enough to attract shoal-draft boats and increasing numbers of skippers seeking more remote anchorages and good fishing.

These unmarked channels require careful, experienced navigation. A remote ranger station can be spotted on the north shore of one channel, but no other sign of civilization will be evident beyond Everglades National Park boundary signs until you reach a mark offshore of Everglades City. At this point, you find the 16-foot-high flashing white light "IK," about 3.5 nm off flashing green "1" at Indian Key, which leads into the marked channel to Everglades City. Flashing green "1" is difficult to pick out from offshore; try using GPS coordinates to guide you in.

⚠ Between the flashing red "22" and the red "30," where the channel crosses the Chokoloskee Bay, there is a strong lateral current from the south during the ebb and to the north during the flood. The channel is deep but narrow, and you need to watch the marks ahead and behind as it is easy to drift into 2 to 3 feet at MLW and out of the channel.

In Everglades City, between the red daybeacons "44" and "46" (past the Everglades Rod and Gun Club) the marked channel cuts off a natural bend in the river. Depths at the bend are charted at 7 to 8 feet at MLW but it has shoaled to less than 4 feet at MLW. Be sure to stick to the marked channel. Refer to the Waterway Explorer (waterwayguide.com) and NOAA online charts for the most up-to-date information.

Seven miles west (as the crow flies) of Everglades City is the shallow Faka Union River, home of the Port of the Islands Marina. After exiting Indian Key Pass (the entry you followed into Everglades City from the Gulf), turn northwest to find green daybeacon "3" off Gomez Point at the tip of Panther Key. This marks the entrance to the 5-mile-long mangrove-fringed channel on the Faka Union River to the marina.

Most of the passes and waterways in this area, other than Indian Key Pass, have numerous sandbars and shoals. The small-boat operator can be a good source of information for side trips and excursions off the main channels.

Dockage: Up the Barron River, The Everglades Rod & Gun Club, built by the late Barron G. Collier, has dockage with limited facilities. Water is available but is not potable. The old clubhouse is well worth a visit, and a bike ride to nearby Chokoloskee Island is a good diversion. The general store and Post Office is out of another age entirely. Everglades Isle Marina is 0.5 mile further up the Barron River. The marina is situated in a "Class A" motor home facility and sells gas. Call ahead for approach and dockside depths.

Those desiring the amenities of a full-service resort in a primeval setting will find it at Port of the Islands Marina, located at the head of the Faka Union River. The straight channel to the marina is well marked by daybeacons, beginning with green daybeacon "3" and red "4." Charted depths in the channel are 5 to 6 feet at MLW. Call ahead on VHF Channel 16 to verify available space and for advice on tide and channel conditions. (Tides in this area are from 1 to 3 feet.) This is a year-round manatee zone so proceed at idle speed only.

Anchorage: If you do not want to go all the way to Everglades City and would rather drop the hook, you can do so behind New Turkey Key (Mile 75). Depths are 3 to 6 feet at MLW so only shallow draft boats will find refuge here. You can also anchor shortly after entering Indian Key Pass, just northwest of flashing green "7" in Russell Pass where you will have at least 7-foot at MLW. For more wind protection, you can proceed farther up Russell Pass to where it opens up to the south and find 7- to 8-foot MLW depths. Make sure you avoid the uncharted pocket or you could find yourself on the bottom at low tide. Make sure you set your anchor well as the currents in this area are strong.

Capri Pass

Collier Bay

Marco Island

Factory Bay

◼ TO MARCO ISLAND

Two routes are available to travel from the Ten Thousand Islands area to Marco Island and beyond: the Inland Passage and the Outside Passage.

Ten Thousand Islands to Goodland–Inland Passage

Situated on a small peninsula of a large island and marsh complex, the village of Goodland is a laid-back fishing village with good but unpretentious restaurants, fishing supplies and some very limited groceries.

NAVIGATION: Use NOAA Chart 11430. If your draft is 4 feet or less and height above water is less than 55 feet, you may save some time by taking the inside and protected route to Marco Island. Vessels with slightly deeper drafts may take this route if they have the flexibility to schedule their trip at high tide.

The route begins about 6 miles west of Faka Union Bay at the head of Gullivan Bay off Coon Key where Coon Key Light, a 22-foot-high flashing white light, marks the entrance to Coon Key Pass. Stay well east of the light (400 to 500 yards) and head north up the east side of Coon Key to pick up red daybeacon "2" (on the

west side of Tripod Key), and then through well-marked Coon Key Pass (heading north, leave red markers to starboard) to the village of Goodland, which is east of Marco Island. The route is a bit lean in spots, but fortunately, the bottom is reported to be soft mud. Local boats frequently use this passage (some at high speed), so ask for latest channel conditions, and then make your own decision. The fixed Goodland Bridge (55-foot vertical clearance) sets the bar as the lowest bridge for the rest of this route.

Dockage: Walker's Coon Key Marina does not accept transients, but they do have a fuel dock with gas and diesel and offer some repairs. The Calusa Island Marina (west of Coon Key Pass red daybeacon "6") welcomes transients to its docks and sells all fuels. They also have a boatyard with repair facilities.

While in the area, be sure to experience Stan's Idle Hour Restaurant (239-394-3041). This waterfront seafood fixture has a festive vibe, lots of outdoor seating and frequent live music.

Anchorage: Panther Key north of West Pass has 7 to 10 feet at MLW with good holding in soft mud. At Tripod Key to the north, you can anchor at the intersection of Sugar Bay at Coon Key Pass in 5 feet at MLW. You can also anchor at Blue Hill Creek in

Marco Island, FL

GOODLAND TO MARCO ISLAND		Largest Vessel Accommodated	VHF Channel Monitored	Transient Berths / Total Berths	Approach / Dockside Depth (reported)	Floating Docks	Gas / Diesel	Groceries, Ice, Marine Supplies, Snacks	Repairs: Hull, Engine, Propeller	Lift (tonnage), Crane, Rail	Min/Max Amps	Laundry, Pool, Showers, Courtesy Car	Pump-Out Station	Nearby: Grocery Store, Motel, Restaurant
Dockage							**Supplies**		**Services**					
1. Pelican Bend Restaurant & Marina	239-394-3452	60	16/14	3/18	5/7	–	GD	IS	–	–	30/30	–	–	R
2. The Tarpon Club Marina	239-417-6802	36	16	call/140	4/5	F	G	M	–	–	50/50	–	–	R
3. Snook Inn	239-394-3313	60	–	10/20	15/6	–	–	S	–	–	–	–	–	GMR
4. Marina at Factory Bay ⌨ 📶	239-389-2929	107	16/06	call/72	12/10	F	–	I	–	–	30/100	LS	P	GMR
5. Rose Marina ⌨ 📶	239-394-2502	160	09	20/109	7/8	F	GD	GIMS	HEP	L75	30/100	LS	P	GMR
6. Walker's Hideaway Marina of Marco Island 📶	239-394-9333	–	–	–	–	–	G	IMS	HEP	L,C	–	C	–	GM
7. Marco Island Marina ⌨ onSpot	239-776-2986	110	16/14	25/121	7/6.5	F	–	I	–	–	30/100	LPS	P	GMR
8. Esplanade Marina ⌨ 📶 onSpot	**239-394-6333**	**60**	**16/11**	**11/77**	**6/6**	**F**	**–**	**IS**	**–**	**–**	**50/50**	**LS**	**P**	**GMR**

⌨ Internet Access   📶 Wireless Internet Access   [WG] Waterway Guide Cruising Club Partner   onSpot dockside WiFi facility
See WaterwayGuide.com for current rates, fuel prices, web site addresses, and other up-to-the-minute information. *(Information in the table is provided by the facilities.)*.

Goodland (to the west at red daybeacon "6") in 7 to 10 feet at MLW, or across the channel from green daybeacon "7" in 8- to 10-foot MLW depths and dinghy to town. There are 4-foot MLW approach depths here; pay close attention to your instruments and stay in deep water.

Goodland to Marco Island–Inland Passage

NAVIGATION: Use NOAA Chart 11430. This section of the ICW and the Big Marco River requires considerable care, even for those who have traveled it before. Local knowledge, which is available at Goodland or over the VHF radio, can help. Markers are moved when necessary to reflect shifting shoals and may not be exactly where the chart shows them. Many prefer a rising tide for obvious reasons.

After you have passed Goodland, you may notice that daybeacon "8" is missing. At red daybeacon "10," you will need to make a sharp turn to the north, staying close to the marker and pass under the **Goodland Bridge** (55-foot fixed vertical clearance). Maintain a close watch on the depth sounder, and use a pre-set alarm, if available. It is also a good idea to study your charts and GPS carefully after you have gathered some local knowledge. It is very doable; just pay close attention to your depth sounder and charts. Refer to the Waterway Explorer and NOAA online charts for the most up-to-date information.

After passing under the Goodland Bridge, you will find deeper water for a short time. Just beyond daybeacon "16," there is a very shallow area when approaching daybeacon "18." Once past "18," the water deepens again. When you pass green daybeacon "25," make sure you do not head straight for the bridge open span. You will need to veer further west and head for daybeacon "26." Don't be fooled by what the smaller boats are doing because it gets extremely shallow if you go straight. It looks as though you are going completely off track because daybeacon "26" is almost to shore on the west side of the river. Turn north just after red daybeacon "26" and run parallel to the **Marco Island Bridge** (55-foot fixed vertical clearance) a short distance until you can turn west through the center passage span.

To the east, as you pass under the bridge, a string of small islands that are bird sanctuaries for thousands of pelicans, egrets and cormorants. Be sure to have the binoculars and camera handy.

⚠ Just past the Marco Island Bridge, the channel markers reverse; northbound boats will now have green to starboard and red to port until you reach the Gulf of Mexico. Pay attention and sort them out.

The next green daybeacon for the main channel, "15," is directly across from green daybeacon "1," which starts the channel into Factory Bay. Continue north and then west if heading out to the Gulf.

If you plan to continue into the Gulf, be aware that the charted Coconut Island is now a sand bar that is sometimes visible. The area is well marked, so just pay close attention to the markers. Big Marco Pass is too shallow for passage; Capri Pass just to the north is marked and tricky but usually passable.

GOODLAND TO MARCO ISLAND, NOAA CHART 11430

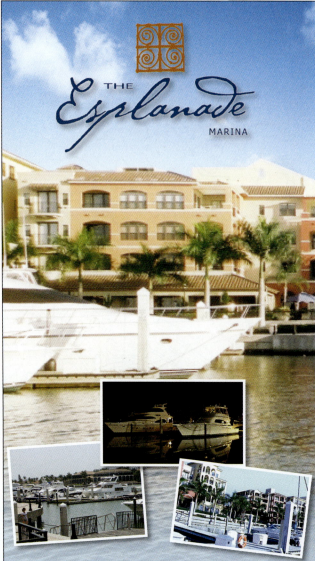
Ten Thousand Islands to Marco Island– Outside Passage

NAVIGATION: Use NOAA Chart 11429. To reach Marco Island from Everglades City, or farther south outside in the Gulf, you must pass outside the shoals of Cape Romano and well offshore of the Cape itself. Charts record isolated spots with depths of as low as 1 to 3 feet at MLW as far out as the Three Nautical Mile Line. Your course should take you at least 3 to 4 miles west of Cape Romano if coming from the south or north. Use your GPS and enter a good standoff waypoint south of the finger shoals. If using radar, Cape Romano will be prominently displayed as you run offshore to avoid it.

The shoals extend out from Big Marco Pass and the southern end of Marco Island. If you are heading south, or if you are approaching Capri Pass from the south, make sure you chart a course to 16-foot-high flashing red buoy "2" and the 16-foot flashing white light to stay clear of the shoaling near Big Marco Pass. As mentioned above, the charted Coconut Island is no longer visible. However, it lies just under the surface, so pay attention when you get to red daybeacon "6" and continue into the pass with caution. There is plenty of room, but it does get busy on weekends.

Dockage: If you continue on the Isle of Capri Pass, you will find the Pelican Bend Restaurant & Marina, which has slips and sells fuel. The Tarpon Club Marina is located on Tarpon Bay, accessible from the Big Marco River, and has slips and sells gas and some marine supplies.

Snook Inn, a landmark for more than 30 years, offers dockage for patrons and waterfront dining inside or out at the tiki bar. They have live entertainment 7 days a week and offer daily specials. Snook Inn can accommodate vessels up to 60 feet. (They also offer free transportation from other marinas.)

Marina at Factory Bay is the closest and deepest marina upon entering Capri Pass heading up the Big Marco River past Collier Bay. Past flashing red "14" and the Snook Inn Restaurant, pick up the side channel at green daybeacon "1." The Marina at Factory Bay is between green daybeacons "3" and "5." Hail the dockmaster for assistance tying up and to arrange a long-term or transient stay.

The full-service Rose Marina is in the southwestern corner of Factory Bay and may be hailed on VHF Channel 16 for reservations and directions. Their highly qualified team of technicians can haul vessels (75-ton lift) and offer as array of services. Their floating and

Marco Island

fixed docks can accommodate a variety of vessels, including catamarans.

Walker's Hideaway Marina of Marco Island is primarily a service and repair center and dry storage facility. They do not have transient slips but they do have a deli and a ship store and sell gas.

If you are looking for quiet surroundings, Marco Island Marina, on the south side next to the Marco Island Bridge, is a very nice stop. The well-marked entrance is approximately 3 miles from Capri Pass, past the stanchion of power lines, and has 7-foot approach depths at MLW. They have the usual amenities, plus slip-side pump-out service. Stay here and you will receive a guest card for the full-service restaurant at the adjacent yacht club. From the facility, a walk of less than 1 mile leads to a Publix, a Walgreen's Pharmacy and other shopping amenities.

Esplanade Marina is tucked inside Smokehouse Bay, which is tricky to get into, but once inside, is well protected (360 degrees). Between red daybeacons "12" and "14," turn south and follow the shallow but well-marked channel to Collier Bay, then continue southwest to red daybeacon "6" and make a sharp eastward turn, leaving green daybeacon "7" to the

north and heading into Smokehouse Bay. Esplanade Marina has 6-foot MLW approach and dockside depths alongside their floating docks. Each slip has water, shore power, pump-out service and a dock box, as well as cable TV. There are numerous restaurants, markets and West Marine just a short walk away.

Anchorage: Protected anchorages and good holding are available in both Smokehouse Bay and Factory Bay. Just follow channel markers closely, stay nearer docking side of channel for more depth. Once you work your way into Collier Bay, proceed to daybeacon "7" and then enter the anchorage. There is 10 feet at MLW here and very good holding. Grocery shopping is easily accessed by going through the low bridge at the end of the anchorage, then east to the convenient dinghy dock that is located beside the Winn-Dixie Supermarket. This anchorage is located in a residential neighborhood.

Factory Bay also has good holding with 10 to 12 feet at MLW. A sand bar splits the bay, but there is plenty of water around the edge. Anchor in the southeast side by red daybeacons "2" and "4" for good protection. You can also anchor in Capri Pass to the northwest of flashing green "15" in 10 to 12 feet at MLW.

Naples Bay, FL

NAPLES		Dockage					Supplies			Services				
		Largest Vessel Accommodated	VHF Channel Monitored	Transient Berths / Total Berths	Approach / Dockside Depth (reported)	Floating Docks	Gas / Diesel	Groceries, Ice, Marine Supplies, Snacks	Repairs: Hull, Engine, Propeller	Lift (tonnage), Crane, Rail	Min/Max Amps	Laundry, Pool, Showers, Courtesy Car	Pump-Out Station	Nearby: Grocery Store, Motel, Restaurant
1. Hamilton Harbor Yacht Club	239-775-0506	60	16	call/36	7/7	F	GD	IMS	–	L27	–	–	P	R
2. South Pointe Yacht Club and Marina	239-774-0518	72	16/12	call/72	5/5	–	–	S	–	–	–	PS	–	R
3. Naples Yacht Club 🖥 📶	239-262-7301	130	16/09	5/88	8/6	F	GD	I	–	–	30/200+	PS	P	GR
4. Naples City Dock	239-213-3070	200	16/06	10/79	9/9	F	GD	IS	–	–	30/100	LS	P	GMR
5. Olde Naples Seaport 📶	239-643-0042	100	16	10/30	8/7	F	–	I	HEP	–	30/50	LS	P	GMR
6. Naples Boat Club Marina 📶 WG	239-430-4994	110	16/14	20/47	8/8	F	GD	GIMS	HEP	L70, C70	30/100	LPS	P	GMR
7. MarineMax Naples Yacht Center	239-262-1000	65	16	–	6/6	–	–	M	HEP	L70	50/50	–	–	MR
8. Naples Sailing & Yacht Club 📶	239-774-0424	65	16/68	7/75	6/6	F	GD	I	–	–	30/100	PS	–	MR
9. Marina at Naples Bay Resort 🖥 📶 WG	239-530-5134	90	16/68	call/97	5.5/5.5	F	G	GIS	–	–	30/50	LPS	P	GMR
10. Gulf Shores Marina	239-774-0222	35	16	3/110	4/4	F	G	M	HEP	L	50/50	–	–	–
11. Walker's Hideaway Marina of Naples 🖥 📶	239-213-1441	–	–	call/25	–	F	GD	IMS	HEP	L	–	PS	–	GMR

🖥 Internet Access 📶 Wireless Internet Access WG Waterway Guide Cruising Club Partner onSpot dockside WiFi facility
See WaterwayGuide.com for current rates, fuel prices, web site addresses, and other up-to-the-minute information. *(Information in the table is provided by the facilities.)*.

■ TO NAPLES

To Naples–Inland Passage

NAVIGATION: Use NOAA Chart 11430.

⚠ NOAA Chart 11430 bears the warning "This area is subject to continual change" referring to the area from Capri Pass to just past Little Marco Island.

There are spots, particularly at daybeacon "30A," where the water gets very shallow. Pay strict attention to the channels and don't stray. This is a very pretty pass and shouldn't be missed if your draft allows. Reports indicate that a boat drawing 4 feet can make the trip.

About halfway along (red daybeacon "46"), you pass Rookery Bay, a major wildlife sanctuary and will likely encounter local fishing boats. The Gordon River used to be a "no wake" zone from Gordon Pass to the **Route 41 Bridge** (10-foot fixed vertical clearance). The "no wake" zone now extends from flashing red "34" (south of the Naples Yacht Club) to the bridge and is frequently ignored by "weekend warriors."

Naples is a good place to pick up or discharge crew. The airport (or a rental car) is a quick cab ride away.

To Naples–Outside Passage

NAVIGATION: Use NOAA Chart 11430. If you choose to go outside for this 8.2-mile-long stretch, it is a fairly straightforward passage along the face of Marco Island to the well marked, but slightly tricky channel entrance to Gordon Pass.

A rock jetty on the south side of Gordon Pass extends 100 yards into the Gulf of Mexico. Favor the south side of the channel along the jetty. With onshore winds and outgoing tide, it can be challenging for slow or underpowered vessels. Once inside, do not run green daybeacons "7" to "7A" as a straight line. Take it wide to the right to avoid the shoal off the northern spit (visible at low tide).

⚠ There is dangerous shoaling from Gordon Pass Channel daybeacon "1" to Naples Bay Channel Light "20." The Army Corps of Engineers is not currently maintaining the federal project channel depth of 12 feet MLW, but they have converted daybeacon "1" and lighted red "2" into buoys that can be moved to mark the best channel as conditions continue to change.

City of Naples

Naples is known for high-end shopping, sophisticated dining and an abundance of golf courses. The Naples Pier is a popular fishing and dolphin-spotting destination, and the miles of fine white "sugar" sand and calm waters make the beaches here especially desirable.

NAPLES, NOAA CHART 11429

Cocohatchee River, FL

W·G

WIGGINS PASS			Dockage				Supplies				Services			
		Largest Vessel Accommodated	VHF Channel Monitored	Transient Berths / Total Berths	Approach / Dockside Depth (reported)	Floating Docks	Gas / Diesel	Repairs: Hull, Engine, Propeller	Groceries, Ice, Marine Supplies, Snacks	Lift (tonnage), Crane, Rail	Min/Max Amps	Laundry, Pool, Showers, Courtesy Car	Pump-Out Station	Nearby: Grocery Store, Motel, Restaurant
1. Pelican Isle Yacht Club ⌨	239-566-1606	55	16/68	3/190	5/4.5	F	GD	IS		–	–	30/50	LPS	P	GMR
2. Cocohatchee River Park Marina	239-514-3752	30	16	15/39	6/6	–	GD	IMS		–	–	30/50	–	P	MR

⌨ Internet Access (WiFi) Wireless Internet Access W·G Waterway Guide Cruising Club Partner ⊙onSpot dockside WiFi facility
See WaterwayGuide.com for current rates, fuel prices, web site addresses, and other up-to-the-minute information. *(Information in the table is provided by the facilities.).*

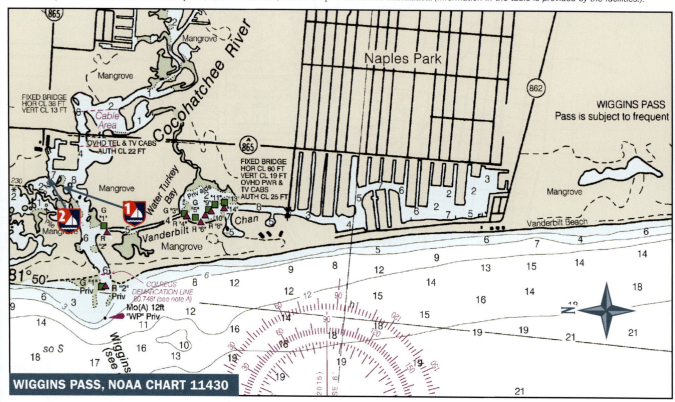

WIGGINS PASS, NOAA CHART 11430

Dockage/Moorings: Dock space is usually available at Naples' numerous marinas, but local marina operators recommend calling ahead for slip or mooring reservations, particularly during the peak periods (holidays and weekends). Hamilton Harbor Yacht Club and South Pointe Yacht Club and Marina–both convenient to Gordon Pass–are to the east as you head north for Naples. Call ahead to check on slip availability. Hamilton Harbor sells gas and diesel.

Farther north, after flashing red "32" is Naples Yacht Club, with slips (to 130 feet) and fuel. Naples City Dock, beginning just to the west of green daybeacon "35" and extending to the north, has 84 slips and also controls a total of 12 moorings in two well-protected coves. Rental of the moorings includes use of a public bathhouse and laundry facilities. If you rent a mooring,

it is mandatory that you receive a (free) pump-out service before picking up the mooring and every four days thereafter. The floating dinghy dock is on the same side of the pier as the mooring field.

If you continue north on the Gordon River (beware of the shoal 200 feet northwest of red daybeacon "36"), the next marina on the west bank is Olde Naples Seaport, a private "dockominium." When owners are away, the dockmaster rents slips to last-minute transients. In a convenient location on Naples Bay at red daybeacon "40" is the full-service Naples Boat Club Marina with transient slips, a fuel dock (both gas and diesel) and repairs. Both Naples Boat Club Marina and Marine Max Naples Yacht Center to the north have a 70-ton lift.

At the south end of the island in the Gordon River (before the 5th Ave. Bridge) is Naples Sailing & Yacht

Fort Myers Beach

Matanzas Pass

Club, which offers reciprocity to members of other recognized yacht clubs. Marina at Naples Bay Resort, on the east side of the river, has slips and gas; call ahead.

On the north side of the 5th Ave. Bridge are Gulf Shores Marina and Walker's Hideaway Marina of Naples. Call ahead to these facilities for slip availability, approach depths and bridge clearance.

Anchorage: After entering Gordon Pass, turn north between red daybeacons "10" and "12." A charted bar with 4-foot MLW depths crosses the entrance. Enter the first canal to the east and anchor in a well-protected cove in 9-foot MLW depths among beautiful homes. There is no place to land a dinghy.

A second option is to proceed into Gordon Pass to green daybeacon "21," turn northwest and then southwest into the first cove. You will be well protected from all sides in 7-foot depths. There is no shore access here but you may find beach access just east of red "22."

■ TO FORT MYERS BEACH

Naples to Big Carlos Pass– Outside Passage

NAVIGATION: Use NOAA Charts 11427 and 11430. There is no inside route directly between Naples and Fort Myers Beach, so to reach Fort Myers Beach, you must either exit at Gordon Pass or continue offshore if that is how you came from Marco Island. Plan to stay about 2 nm off the beach. In good weather, the Gulf of Mexico is calm and easy to transit. In winter months, when the winds are often out of the northwest or north, it can get rough. If the winds are northwest at more than 12 knots, you may want to wait it out in Naples. Pick your weather correctly, and it should be no problem.

For vessels drawing 4 feet or less, daybeacons lead from Wiggins Pass for a distance of just under 0.5 mile into the Cocohatchee River, where dockage is available.

⚠ Shoaling has been observed in Wiggins Pass between Safe Water Light "WP" and Wiggins Pass daybeacon "12." Mariners are advised to exercise extreme caution while transiting the area.

Fort Myers Beach, FL

		Dockage					Supplies		Services						
		Largest Vessel Accommodated	VHF Channel Monitored	Transient Berths / Total Berths	Approach / Dockside Depth (reported)	Floating Docks	Gas / Diesel	Groceries, Ice, Marine Supplies, Snacks	Repairs: Hull, Engine, Propeller	Lift (tonnage), Crane, Rail	Min/Max Amps	Laundry, Pool, Showers, Courtesy Car	Pump-Out Station	Nearby: Grocery Store, Motel, Restaurant
BIG CARLOS PASS														
1. Waterside at Bay Beach Marina – PRIVATE WiFi	239-765-6400	60	–	0/42	10/8	F	–	–	–	–	50/50	PS	P	GMR
2. Fish Tale Marina WiFi	239-463-3600	80	77	call/100	4/8	F	G	IMS	HEP	L37	30/50	LS	P	GMR
3. Snook Bight Yacht Club & Marina ▢ WiFi	**239-765-4371**	70	16/72	21/74	6.5/6.5	F	GD	GIMS	HEP	L30	30/50	LPS	P	GR
ESTERO ISLAND														
4. Pink Shell Beach Resort and Marina ▢ WiFi	**239-463-8620**	120	16/12	30/41	15/8.5	F	–	IMS	HEP	–	30/100	LPS	P	MR
5. Moss Marina ▢ WiFi	239-765-6677	180	16/14	35/40	–	F	GD	IMS	E	L	30/50	LS	P	GR
6. Matanzas Inn Bayside Resort and Marina ▢ WiFi	**239-463-9258**	60	16	16/16	12/8	–	–	–	–	–	30/50	LPS	P	GMR
7. Fort Myers Beach City Mooring Field	**239-463-9258**	70 MOORING BALLS MANAGED BY MATANZAS INN RESORT & MARINA												GMR
8. Diversified Yacht Service	239-765-8700	–	16	call/20	–	F	GD	IMS	HEP	L150	30/30	–	P	GMR
9. Gulf Star Marina ▢	239-463-9552	55	16/07	20/20	17/8	–	G	IM	H	L9	30/50	LPS	P	GMR
10. Olsen Marine Service Inc.	239-463-6750	55	16	–	6/6	–	–	M	HEP	L37,C	50/50	S	–	GMR
11. Gulf Marine Ways & Supply	239-463-6166	130	–	call/2	10/10	–	–	IMS	HEP	L150,C	50/50	–	–	GMR
12. Ballard Oil Company WiFi	239-463-7677	–	–	FUEL DOCK	–	–	GD	–	–	–	–	–	–	–
13. Salty Sam's Marina ▢ WiFi	239-463-7333	225	16/17	50/130	14/12	F	GD	IMS	HEP	L13	30/100	LS	P	GMR

▢ Internet Access WiFi Wireless Internet Access **WG** Waterway Guide Cruising Club Partner ◉ onSpot dockside WiFi facility

See WaterwayGuide.com for current rates, fuel prices, web site addresses, and other up-to-the-minute information. *(Information in the table is provided by the facilities.)*

BIG CARLOS PASS, ESTERO ISLAND, NOAA CHART 11427

FORT MYERS BEACH
CITY MOORING FIELD

Matanzas Pass

MATANZAS INN BAYSIDE
RESORT AND MARINA

PINK SHELL
BEACH RESORT & MARINA

The Only Thing We Overlook is the Beach

Treasure an exclusive beachfront escape. With sugary white sand, endless waves and breathtaking views from sunrise to sunset, Pink Shell Beach Resort & Marina invites you to bring your vacation fantasies to life across 12 lush acres of brilliant blue backdrop. Whether spurring romance or making a splash with the whole family, our full-service destination resort has everything you need to soak up the sights and sounds of the Gulf of Mexico at one of the premier Fort Myers Beach resorts.

- *Dockage for Boats up to 120 ft.*
- *30, 50 and 100 Amp. Electrical Service*
- *Water Hook-Up*
- *Pump-Out Available*
- *HD Direct TV and Wi-Fi*
- *Floating Docks*
- *ADA Accessible*
- *Full Access to Resort*
- *Two Restauarants*
- *Lunch Boats Welcome*
- *Overnight Dockage Entitles You to 10% Off Resort Rooms*

866-843-3253
PinkShell.com

LAT   26° 27.665N
LONG -81° 57.855W

275 Estero Boulevard
Fort Myers Beach, Florida

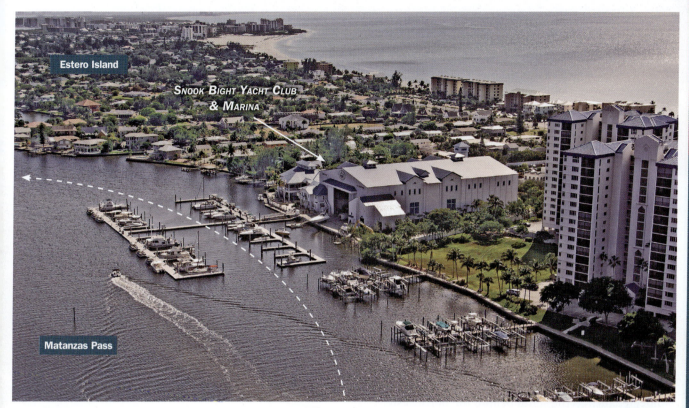

Estero Island

SNOOK BIGHT YACHT CLUB
& MARINA

Matanzas Pass

Controlling depths in the marked channel from New Pass to Big Carlos Pass are reported to be 4 feet at MLW with a 2.5-foot tidal range. New Pass is unmarked and impassable to the Gulf of Mexico. Shoal markers warn of 2-foot MLW depths. Keep a close watch for the numerous traps set for Atlantic blue crabs.

Dockage: Once through Wiggins Pass, controlling channel depths to the marina are 4 to 5 feet at MLW. Pelican Isle Yacht Club, located just inside Wiggins Pass, may have transient dockage and sells all fuels. Directly across from Pelican Isle is Cocohatchee River Park Marina, which has slips (for boats 30 feet or smaller) and sells gas and diesel.

Anchorage: About 5.7 miles north of Gordon Pass, narrow Doctors Pass can serve as a harbor of refuge. The area is well marked; favor the center. Once inside, Moorings Bay has 3 to 6 feet at MLW with good holding and all-around protection. There are no services for transients.

Big Carlos Pass to Fort Myers Beach– Inland Passage

NAVIGATION: Use NOAA Chart 11427. If you are hugging the coastline about 1 nm offshore from Naples, you should note where the shoal projects out on the north side of Big Carlos Pass. If you are trying to reach Estero Bay and Fort Myers Beach, you can enter here if you know the present location of the channel or can find a lead-in boat to follow. Although charts indicate controlling depths of 4 to 6 feet at MLW, the channel reportedly carries about 8 feet at MLW. Although constantly shifting, it reportedly follows the contour of Lovers Key on approach from the south. It is best to call ahead to nearby Estero Bay Boat Tours (VHF Channel 79) for an update on directions and controlling depths.

Once you are past Big Carlos Pass (dredged in May 2017), the inside route north to Fort Myers Beach is well marked from the Pass along the northeast side of Estero Island to Matanzas Pass and the north side of Fort Myers Beach.

Big Carlos Pass Bascule Bridge (23-foot closed vertical clearance) opens on signal except from 7:00 p.m. to 8:00 a.m. daily, when it is closed. Once you pass under the bridge, daybeacons guide your passage either north or south through the natural and historic beauty of Estero Bay. From here, it is a matter of carefully watching the many markers blazing the trail to Matanzas Pass and the facilities along the northern shore of Fort Myers Beach. It is very shallow in spots and a 5- to 5.5-foot draft vessel might have problems. Traveling at high tide would be wise.

Dockage: After passing Big Carlos Pass, the first marina you encounter will be Waterside at Bay Beach Marina, which is private. Fish Tale Marina is located a little farther up Estero Island in a channel behind Coon Key with slips, gas and some repairs. (Call ahead.)

Approximately halfway along Estero Island you will find Snook Bight Yacht Club & Marina. Away from the hustle and bustle of the harbor area, Snook Bight offers everything a boater could ask for in a marina, including an on-site service center, plenty of indoor, covered storage, waterfront dining (Bayfront Bistro with daily happy hours) and a well-stocked ship store. They also offer boats, kayaks and paddleboards for rent so you can explore the waters of Estero Bay up close. A Publix supermarket is right next door.

Big Carlos Pass to Fort Myers Beach– Outside Passage

NAVIGATION: Use NOAA Chart 11427. From Big Carlos Pass, chart a course for the Morse (A) 16-foot-high marker "SC." From that point, you should be able to pick out 16-foot flashing red buoy "2" approximately 1 mile to the north-northwest. (Be careful: Shoals move around here a bit.) From that point, you should be able to pick out the well-marked entrance channel leading off from San Carlos Bay into Matanzas Pass, making a 90-degree turn to the south behind the northwestern hook of Estero Island.

Currents are sometimes swift, depending on the tide, and an endless stream of fishing boats of all sizes utilize the channel that runs between Estero Island and San Carlos Island. About 2 miles after you enter the channel you will pass under the **Fort Myers Beach (Matanzas Pass) Bridge** (65-foot fixed vertical clearance).

Dockage/Moorings: Heading south after entering Matanzas Pass, the first marina you will find is the full-service Pink Shell Beach Resort and Marina, which is set on 12 lush acres. The marina can accommodate vessels up to 120 feet on floating docks. Guests at the marina are welcome to the resort's numerous amenities, including the pool and beach club, a fitness center and water sport rentals. (Be sure to ask about their grocery service.) As always, call in advance for reservations.

Moss Marina's complex of white buildings is highly visible to the south, adjacent to daybeacon "17." Transient berths are available, but make advance reservations, particularly during the winter months. They also have multiple fueling stations.

Soon after you pass under the Fort Myers Beach Bridge on the south shore is Matanzas Inn Bayside Resort and Marina with slips for boats up to 60 feet in length. They also manage the 70 mooring balls Fort Myers Beach City Mooring Field. The martina provides restrooms/showers and a dinghy dock for those who rent a mooring, and a pump-out boat is available. The on-site restaurant, Matanzas on the Bay, serves up seafood and pizza, delicious drinks and nightly entertainment on a waterfront patio.

Diversified Yacht Service maintains, repairs, and upgrades luxury yachts and vessels of all sizes. They do not have transient slips, but they do have a full-service fuel dock and well-stocked ship store.

On the north shore is Gulf Star Marina, which accepts transients and has a fuel dock (gas only). Olsen Marine Service offers some repairs and may have slips; call ahead. Gulf Marine Ways & Supply is close by with a 150-ton lift and a crane for larger jobs. A little farther up the channel is Ballard Oil Company, a fuel dock with gas and diesel fuel at great prices.

At the end of the harbor (beyond the shrimp fleet) is Salty Sam's Marina, where you can get gas and diesel fuel or tie up for a bite at the Parrot Key Caribbean Grill (239-463-3257). Overnight slips are also available.

Anchorage: Boats anchor east of the bridge in the south channel (not in the northern Matanzas Pass channel). You can also drop the hook in 5 to 7 feet at MLW east of red daybeacon "4" in Matanzas Pass, on the north side of the unnamed island.

■ NEXT STOP

Fort Myers Beach is a pivotal location for vessels making passages farther north up the west coast of Florida or south along the coast to Flamingo and the Keys. Or you can pick up the Okeechobee Waterway and cruise all the way to its east coast terminus at the ICW in Stuart. This is a genuine nautical crossroads. (The Okeechobee Waterway is covered in detail in Chapter 6 of this guide.)

San Carlos Bay to Sarasota

 GIWW Mile 0–Mile 87

 FL Bridges: Channel 09

CHARTS NOAA 11425, 11426, 11427

This 60-mile-long stretch from San Carlos Bay to Sarasota Bay is characterized by an almost-tropical climate and features the popular coastal barrier islands of Sanibel, Captiva, North Captiva, Cayo Costa, Gasparilla Island, Little Gasparilla Island, Don Pedro Key and Manasota Key, fertile fishing grounds and one of Florida's great bodies of water (Charlotte Harbor). While some summer days can get very hot, swimming is always an option.

Traveling north from Fort Myers Beach, a skipper can choose between two passages from San Carlos Bay: inside along the Gulf Intracoastal Waterway (GIWW) or outside up the Gulf of Mexico. Unless you must hurry to meet a deadline and are in a powerboat that can hit high double numbers, we suggest you take the protected and infinitely more interesting GIWW route inside.

The Army Corps of Engineers' project depth for the length of the 150-mile-long GIWW is purported to be 9 feet at MLW, but do not count on having that much water. Keep an eye on the depths here, especially in winter when northerly winds push the water out of bays and channels. Even under optimum conditions, in certain spots (noted in the text) shoaling is so chronic that boats must slow down and gently ease their way through.

Going north on the GIWW, leave red daybeacons to starboard, green to port. As with the Atlantic ICW, GIWW channel markers are green or red with small yellow triangles on red markers and squares on green markers (and an occasional yellow stripe), in addition to the numbers and/or letters. Another way to remember this is that the red marks delineate the mainland side of the GIWW channel.

A number of bridges cross the GIWW. See the Skipper's Handbook section in the front of this guide for bridge schedules, but to stay on the safe side, verify information locally or with the Coast Guard.

■ TO CHARLOTTE HARBOR: INSIDE (GIWW) ROUTE

Fort Myers Beach to Sanibel Causeway

NAVIGATION: Use NOAA Chart 11426 or 11427. At this junction, boats from Florida's east coast, the Keys and the southwest coast all meet. (See the "Okeechobee Waterway" chapter of this guide for coverage of the passage to and from Florida's east coast.) If you come out of the Okeechobee Waterway here, you will transition to the GIWW at Shell Point. Simply keep heading southwest between Merwin Key to the north and Big Island and Fisherman Key to the south, past St. James City and around York Island into Pine Island Sound.

To reach the GIWW from Fort Myers Beach, head west from Matanzas Pass. If your vessel requires more than 26 feet of vertical clearance, you will have to go through span "A" (70-foot fixed vertical clearance) on the Punta Rassa side of the bay.

You can use the fixed span "C" (26-foot fixed vertical clearance) otherwise.

To reach the high span ("A") of the **Sanibel Causeway** from flashing green "1" at Matanzas Pass, steer a course of 282 degrees magnetic to flashing red "6," indicating the start of the channel to the Caloosahatchee River and the Okeechobee Waterway. Follow the channel from flashing red "6," through the bridge and then to flashing red "14," leaving it to the east. Shortly past that red lighted aid, watch for the green daybeacon "15" to the southwest and flashing green "101" to the northeast, which mark the end of the Okeechobee Waterway and the beginning of the GIWW (Mile 0). Turn southwest at green can "1" and pick up the well-marked channel as described above.

If you plan on transiting span "C" from Matanzas Pass, set a course of 265 degrees magnetic from flashing green "1" when leaving the Matanzas Pass channel to flashing red "2" on the Sanibel Island side of the entrance to San Carlos Bay, a distance of about 2.75 nm. Once under the "C" span and about 2.5 nm up the well-marked channel, you will pick out the 16-foot high, quick flashing green "11" for the GIWW channel.

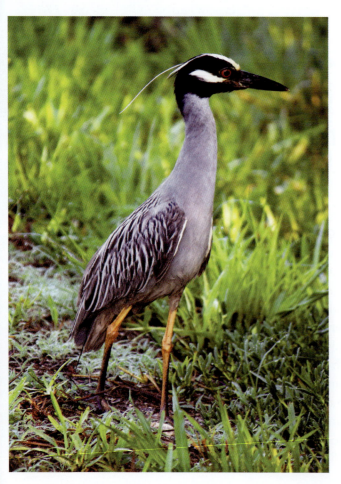

Dockage: Just north of the eastern end of the fixed bridge (span "A") west of Punta Rassa, you may find a berth at Port Sanibel Marina, which also sells gas and diesel. The nearby Sanibel Harbour Yacht Club is private.

Anchorage: Vessels have been seen anchored in the deeper water slot between Kitchel Key and Fisherman Key in 7 to 11 feet at MLW. Watch the shoal to starboard when entering from the waterway. Boats also anchor just north of Punta Rassa Cove in 8- to 13-foot MLW depths. Both anchorages are fairly exposed but will suffice during settled weather for those who want to make an early start in the morning through the Okeechobee or are heading north on the inside in the GIWW.

Pine Island Sound

Liberally dotted with small islands and protected from the open Gulf by a string of barrier islands, Pine Island Sound runs about 15 miles to the mouth of Charlotte Harbor at Boca Grande Pass. Many of the small islands in the sound are part of the Pine Island National Wildlife Refuge, closed to all public access to protect the wildlife. Along this stretch, you will see many ospreys tending their large nests.

NAVIGATION: Use NOAA Charts 11426 and 11427. Sailors in auxiliary-powered sailboats know the "Miserable Mile" well. Here, the tide sweeps in and out directly across the arrow-straight channel, and strong crosscurrents are likely. Allow for the set, and line up markers fore and aft. The channel is well marked and easy to follow. Be especially careful crossing south of Matlacha Pass (pronounced "Mat-la-shay"). The channel cuts off to the northwest just past flashing green "5" (when headed west). Do not stray too far to the west into 2- to 3-foot MLW. Around that same green daybeacons "5" and green daybeacon "9," the currents are very strong and the channel, running through shoals, is prone to silting. One nautical mile farther west, near where the channel bends to the northwest south of Pine Island, the problem worsens. Northerly winds tend to build up silt in the area.

The channel runs a jagged course, often at an angle to the swift current, through pools of relatively deep water interspersed with great shallow bays. Exercise caution. Stay to mid-channel, take navigational aids in order and do not try any shortcuts. In Pine Island Sound, between flashing green "23" and red daybeacon "24" at about Mile 8, power lines cross the channel with a charted vertical clearance of 95 feet at the main channel.

Matlacha Pass carries a marked, but shallow, crooked channel north between Pine Island and the mainland to Charlotte Harbor. Controlling depth is about 3 feet at MLW, and a 32-foot-high power cable and the **Matlacha Pass Bascule Bridge** (restricted schedule, with a 9-foot closed vertical clearance) cross the pass. This passage is not recommended, but can be safely explored from the northern entrance.

Anchorage: At the southern tip of Pine Island sits St. James City, the central point for fishing on the lower sound. Fishing camps and small boat marinas abound here, along with shallow water and numerous private markers that can be confusing to the stranger. You can anchor south of town by the mangroves in 8 to 9 feet at MLW and dinghy to shore. There are several waterside "Tiki-type" restaurants if you dinghy up the residential canals, and each one brings its own flavor to the area.

To the north, Chino Island in Pine Island Sound offers protection from easterly and northerly winds with good holding. Leave the GIWW at flashing green "23," and you will find 7- to 8-foot MLW depths almost to the shore. You may receive a few wakes from vessels traveling the GIWW and locals who use this area for fishing and a shortcut to nearby canals.

A number of anchorages are located off the Pine Island Sound to both the north and south, where deeper water is indicated, and in the deep pockets of Matlacha Pass to the north to the bridge.

Punta Rassa to Charlotte Harbor

A string of barrier islands, including Sanibel, Captiva, North Captiva and Cayo Costa, separate Pine Island Sound from the Gulf of Mexico. Together, the islands form a shallow crescent lying at an angle to the currents. That accident of shape and location causes what are said to be the world's most prolific shell deposits and the resultant "Sanibel stoop" of the island's visitors. More than 300 varieties of shells have been found on these beaches. A Sanibel Island law prohibits collectors from taking live shells, living starfish and sand dollars. The best shelling is at low tide after a storm, when winds and waves have washed a new supply up on the beaches.

Sanibel Island can have as many as four tides a day. In March, the annual Shell Show attracts collectors from all over the world.

Facilities for transient mariners on Sanibel and Captiva Islands range from rather simple overnight stops, to full-service marinas and resorts. Be careful making your approach, however. The sandy bottom is always shifting. You are best advised to enter these basins at half-tide or better and to call ahead for the latest local information.

Sanibel Island

The 6,354-acre J.N. "Ding" Darling National Wildlife Refuge takes up much of 12-mile-long Sanibel Island, mainly along the northern (Pine Island Sound) side. The refuge also serves as headquarters for several small wildlife refuges on nearby islands. During the nesting season, mariners are asked not to land on these rookery islands. If pelicans are frightened off their nests by human intruders, they leave their eggs exposed to fish crows. The refuge offers nature walks, canoe trips, a wildlife drive and an interpretive center. Even the most casual visitor here will inevitably see numerous alligators, anhinga ("snakebirds"), roseate spoonbills, snowy egrets, wood storks, turkey vultures and great blue herons. Pink flamingos are seen quite often as well. The park is open daily from 10:00 a.m. to 4:00 p.m. For more information, call the "Ding" Darling Wildlife Society at 239-472-1100.

Sanibel Island has miles of bicycle paths (rental bikes are readily available from numerous sources) for easy access to all parts of the island. Heading southeast from the marina, you will come to the historic Sanibel Lighthouse at Point Ybel (1884), the Lighthouse Beach Park and a fishing pier. Heading northwest from the marina, the tree-lined main thoroughfare, Periwinkle Way, takes you to the Sanibel Historical Village and Museum (950 Dunlop Rd., 239-472-4648), which showcases the island's history with pioneer-vintage island residents and 1920s versions of a general store, Post Office and tea room. The Bailey-Matthews National Shell Museum (3025 Sanibel-Captiva Rd., 239-395-2233) houses shells from around the world, as well as special Florida exhibits. An annual Shell Show held every March attracts collectors from all over the world.

The only public landing on the island, other than dropping the hook and landing by dinghy, is at Sanibel Marina. If you want to explore the island by land,

San Carlos Bay, FL

		Largest Vessel Accommodated	VHF Channel Monitored	Transient Berths / Total Berths	Approach / Dockside Depth (reported)	Floating Docks	Gas / Diesel	Groceries, Ice, Marine Supplies, Snacks	Repairs: Hull, Engine, Propeller	Lift (tonnage), Crane, Rail	Laundry, Pool, Showers, Courtesy Car	Min/Max Amps	Pump-Out Station	Nearby: Grocery Store, Motel, Restaurant
PUNTA RASSA				**Dockage**				**Supplies**			**Services**			
1. Sanibel Harbour Yacht Club–PRIVATE	239-333-4200	50	16	0/4	–	–	G	S	–	–	–	–	S	–	MR
2. Port Sanibel Marina 🛜	239-437-1660	65	16/68	10/104	5/5	–	GD	IMS	–	L35	30/50	LS	P	R
SANIBEL ISLAND														
3. Sanibel Marina 💻 🛜	239-472-2723	70	16	15/65	6/6	–	GD	IMS	EP	–	50/50	LS	P	R

💻 Internet Access 🛜 Wireless Internet Access **WG** Waterway Guide Cruising Club Partner ⬤ onSpot dockside WiFi facility
See WaterwayGuide.com for current rates, fuel prices, web site addresses, and other up-to-the-minute information. *(Information in the table is provided by the facilities.)*

SANIBEL ISLAND, PUNTA RASSA, NOAA CHART 11427

you will need to obtain permission to tie up your dinghy at the marina.

NAVIGATION: Use Chart 11427. Plot a course for flashing red "2" east of span "C" of the Sanibel Causeway and about .5 nm due east of the coast of Sanibel. A little less than 1 nm to the southwest, you will see red daybeacon "2" marking the entrance to the channel to Sanibel Marina. Enter the channel heading south and stay to the west side to avoid the obvious shoal at the first canal to the east. Continue south and you will arrive at Sanibel Marina's fuel dock.

Dockage: A snug harbor is available at the full-service Sanibel Marina, the only marina on the island. The marina monitors VHF Channel 16 and has transient slips for vessels up to 70 feet in an unhurried, palm-fringed setting. They have all the usual amenities, plus laundry, fuel (gas and diesel) and fishing tackle. There is a ship store on site with a large inventory of boat necessities and clothing. The award-winning Gramma Dot's Seaside Saloon (239-472-8138) is on site at Sanibel Marina. They serve seafood, chowder, gourmet burgers, specialty salads and famous desserts seven days a week at lunch and dinner. Check in with dockmaster for a lunch slip.

West of the marina, and within walking distance, is Huxter's Market & Deli (1203 Periwinkle Way, 239-472-2151), a complete deli with some fruits and vegetables, as well as an excellent beer, liquor and wine selection. Depending on direction, it is 0.5 mile to either one of the world's most famous shelling beaches or two supermarkets. Thanks to a reverse osmosis

Home of Award Winning Gramma Dot's Seaside Saloon and Ireland Yacht Sales!

Sanibel Marina is nestled near the lighthouse on the southern tip of Sanibel Island, on Florida's pristine Gulf Coast. It's ideal location grants boaters traveling up and down the Intercoastal Waterway direct access to the Gulf of Mexico and the Island's gorgeous beaches as well as Florida's fantastic fishing. The marina has 65 slips for boats up to 70'. Transients and Yacht Club cruises are always welcome.

While you are with us, be sure to make time to enjoy local fresh seafood at one of Sanibel's few waterfront resturants: our charming, award winning Gramma Dot's Seaside Saloon.

(239) 472-2723

www.sanibelmarina.com
sanibelmarina@gmail.com
634 N. Yachtsman Drive
Sanibel, FL 33957
We monitor VHF 16

Large inventory of 32' to 41' Back Coves

BACK COVE
Y A C H T S

water-treatment system, Sanibel Island has some of the best water in the area.

Anchorage: There is a nice day anchorage for a swim and lunch at the south end of Sanibel Island. It is exposed, so stay overnight only in settled weather.

J.N. "Ding" Darling National Wildlife Refuge offers an excellent anchorage possibility during settled weather in the cove due south of flashing red "16" (situated south of York Island). Easy access off channel; watch charts while entering for one shallow shoal. Holding is excellent in sand and mud close to Sanibel Island's mangrove shoreline in at least 6 feet at MLW. It's a very scenic anchorage and a great spot to explore.

You can anchor with good protection in San Carlos Bay. When you enter from the Gulf of Mexico, proceed to flashing red "6" northeast of Port Ybel and turn toward the fixed bridge to the west (span "C") on the Sanibel Island side of the Punta Rassa-Sanibel Causeway. Good holding is also available past the fishing pier on Sanibel Island, although the tidal current may call for a Bahamian moor.

Captiva Island–GIWW Mile 9

NAVIGATION: Use NOAA Chart 11427. Just to the north of Sanibel is Captiva Island, about 6 miles long and separated from Sanibel Island by Blind Pass, which is crossed by a 7-foot fixed vertical clearance bridge. Heading north up Pine Island Sound at red daybeacon "38," a course of about 215 degrees magnetic brings you back through shoal water to the little village of Captiva, where transients will find marinas and amenities.

Dockage: Honor the red markers (controlling depth is 6.5 feet at MLW) to reach Tween Waters Island Resort & Spa tucked in behind Buck Key. To reach the marina, turn west at red daybeacon "38" of the GIWW and proceed on a course of 215 degrees magnetic (for about 0.25 mile) to locate the channel. The resort is complete but unpretentious with beach access, a pool complex, tennis courts and lively pub-style bar (with entertainment on weekends). Farther up the channel is Jensen's Twin Palm Cottages and Marina, followed by McCarthy's Marina, located before Redfish Pass. Call ahead for slip availability.

A channel marked with daybeacons leads from the GIWW between red daybeacon "38" and flashing green "39" to South Seas Island Resort & Marina. The channel leading into the marina is well marked. All vessels must

announce entry upon arrival at the entrance marker on VHF Channel 16. It's a good idea to call ahead to the harbor master to ask for local conditions and guidance.

Anchorage: One anchorage is still available near 'Tween Waters Marina at green daybeacon "21." However, the marina does not offer dinghy docking privileges to anchored boats. Another anchorage area is located north of 'Tween Waters at green daybeacon "17" off the Green Flash Restaurant (15183 Captiva Dr., 239-472-3337) dock. The restaurant welcomes boaters who dinghy in for a meal, but call ahead to make arrangements if you want to dock there and eat.

North Captiva Island–GIWW Mile 14.5

NAVIGATION: Use NOAA Chart 11427. Shifting, shoaling Redfish Pass divides Captiva Island from North Captiva Island. This pass should only be used with current local knowledge. If you choose to exit or enter the Gulf of Mexico here, call the South Seas Island Resort Marina for advice. Remember that currents are strong in this area and shoaling persists.

North Captiva Island is accessible only by boat. There are many private and rental homes here and a few restaurants in the Safety Harbor area. Stilt houses guard the entrance. Boca Grande Pass, a good exit to the Gulf of Mexico, is the preferred pass and is only 6 miles to the north.

A marked channel runs north from Captiva Pass across the GIWW toward Charlotte Harbor, but do not use it as a shortcut unless yours is a very shallow-draft boat. This channel shoals in its upper reaches to about 5 feet at MLW. In the rest of the channel, depths run 7 to 13 feet at MLW with occasional spots for anchoring. The channel leads to Pineland, where there is a small marina with 3-foot controlling depths MLW that services North Captiva Island.

Although used by fishers with local knowledge, Captiva Pass–between North Captiva Island and Cayo Costa–is unmarked and subject to change.

Anchorage: The anchorage at the northern tip of North Captiva Island is a beautiful location in fair weather but is fully exposed from northeast through south-southeast. Off the southeast tip of Cayo Costa, an anchorage is within a dinghy-pull of the beaches at both North Captiva Island and Cayo Costa. Both anchorages have 7 to 10 feet at MLW.

Captiva Island

'TWEEN WATERS ISLAND
RESORT & SPA

Roosevelt Channel

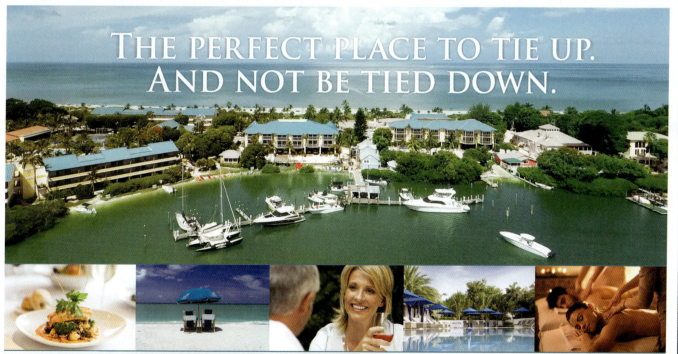

Pine Island Sound, FL

CAPTIVA ISLAND		Largest Vessel Accommodated	VHF Channel Monitored	Transient Berths / Total Berths	Approach / Dockside Depth (reported)	Floating Docks	Gas / Diesel	Groceries, Ice, Marine Supplies, Snacks	Repairs: Hull, Engine, Propeller	Lift (tonnage), Crane, Rail	Min/Max Amps	Laundry, Pool, Showers, Courtesy Car	Pump-Out Station	Nearby: Grocery Store, Motel, Restaurant
					Dockage		**Supplies**		**Services**					
1. 'Tween Waters Island Resort & Spa 11.0	239-472-5161	100	16/72	41/41	6/6	–	GD	GIMS	–	–	30/50	LPS	P	GMR
2. Jensen's Twin Palm Cottages and Marina 💻 📶 12	239-472-5800	25	16/14	call/20	5/5	–	G	IMS	–	–	–	–	–	GMR
3. McCarthy's Marina	239-472-5200	–	16	call/19	5/5	–	–	IS	–	–	–	–	–	GMR
4. South Seas Island Resort & Marina 💻 📶 13.6	888-777-3625	120	16	–	6/6	–	GD	GIMS	–	–	30/100	LPS	P	GMR
PINE ISLAND AREA														
5. Cayo Costa State Park	941-964-0375	–	–	–	6/6	F	–	–	–	–	–	S	–	–
6. Useppa Island Club 💻 📶 22	239-283-1061	110	16	call/50	10/10	–	–	IS	–	–	30/100	LPS	–	MR
7. Cabbage Key Inn 📶 21.4	239-283-2278	85	16	23/25	8/6	–	–	IS	–	–	30/50	LS	–	MR
8. Pineland Marina 💻	239-283-3593	38	16	4/30	5/7	–	GD	IMS	HEP	L	–	–	–	MR
9. Four Winds Marina 💻 📶 6 NE of 19	239-283-0250	40	16/14	call/89	3.5/4	F	G	IM	HEP	–	30/50	PS	–	MR
10. Jug Creek Marina	239-283-3331	30	16/12	35/35	/3	–	GD	IMS	–	L20	30/50	S	–	GMR
MATLACHA														
11. Olde Fish House Marina	239-283-0114	–	–	–	12/5	–	–	IS	–	–	–	–	–	R

💻 Internet Access 📶 Wireless Internet Access WG Waterway Guide Cruising Club Partner onSpot dockside WiFi facility
See WaterwayGuide.com for current rates, fuel prices, web site addresses, and other up-to-the-minute information. *(Information in the table is provided by the facilities.)*

Cayo Costa–GIWW Mile 18.5

Spanish fishermen from Havana gave 6-mile-long Cayo Costa its name (translated as "Coastal Key"). Located at the north end of Pine Island Sound on the south side of Boca Grande Pass, this almost-uninhabited island (home to a swine of feral pigs) is accessible only by boat.

Dockage: Both Punta Blanca Island and Cayo Costa are part of the Cayo Costa State Park (941-964-0375). The park headquarters are located on Cayo Costa, just inside Pelican Pass. Here you will find daytime dockage for small boats (25 feet and under) and some overnight dockage (no hookups). The park extends to the Gulf side of the island where there are not only beautiful beaches, but also cabins and camping. Transportation across the island is by foot, tram or rental bike. The beaches on the Gulf side are very popular shelling beaches.

Anchorage: At Mile 22.5, at the southern tip of Punta Blanca Island, is a slice of deep water that provides an attractive anchorage. The adventurous skipper can take up to a 6-foot draft vessel completely around the point where there is an exceptionally cozy anchorage. The downside of the equation is that this anchorage has poor ventilation and is best in winter months.

At Mile 25, at the northern end of Punta Blanca Island (between Punta Blanca and Cayo Costa), is Pelican Pass and Pelican Bay. Although the Pelican Pass entrance may at first appear a bit dicey, the anchorage beyond is well worth the effort. With caution, a little help from the tide and a reliable depth sounder, boats drawing up to 5 feet can normally get through Pelican Pass into Pelican Bay.

To reach the anchorage from red daybeacon "74," travel southwest toward the tip of the beach on Cayo Costa. Stay to within about 75 feet of the sand beach, and just past the little sign in the water, turn slightly east and follow the beach up into Pelican Bay. You will find 5 to 6 feet at MLW in the pass. When inside Pelican Bay, pay attention to your depth sounder as there are several very shallow areas. You can anchor in 7 to 8 feet at MLW with plenty of swinging room and really good holding. This is a very popular anchorage so it can get crowded on weekends.

If feeling adventuresome, take your dinghy and look for the unmarked small but deep creek that opens into a small lake of about 200 yards in diameter. The depth in the creek is more than adequate for dinghies. There is a small dock on the lake that was once used for loading supplies on the island. You can land your dinghy there and explore. It is very pretty and worth the effort! This is one of the best anchorages on the west coast of Florida and should not be missed.

Useppa Island–GIWW Mile 21

This lovely, 100-acre island stands 37 feet above the water due to the numerous shell mounds here. The dunes are covered with more than 200 varieties of tropical trees, plants and flowers. Barron Collier first built the cottages here in 1912 for his

CAPTIVA ISLAND, PINE ISLAND AREA, NOAA CHART 11426

Cabbage Key Cottage

tarpon-fishing friends; his mansion now serves as the clubhouse and restaurant.

Legend claims the pirate José Gaspar kept a Spanish noblewoman prisoner here, and the island's name is a derivation of her name, Joseffa de Mayorga. The Barbara Sumwalt Museum (239-283-9600) on Useppa Island, open for a few hours a day, presents the history of the island and surrounding area in wonderful detail. It is a must stop for all visitors, but it's a good idea to call ahead to make sure they are open. (A $5 donations is requested for entrance.)

NAVIGATION: Use NOAA Chart 11427. Opposite Cayo Costa, north of the GIWW at about flashing red "60," is the private island of Useppa.

Dockage: Accessible only by water, Useppa Island Club has been established as a private club that has preserved the authentic flavor of the past. They do not accept transients; you must be a member or a guest of a member. All vessels must announce entry upon arrival at entrance marker on VHF Channel 16.

Anchorage: A large, popular anchorage is available off the GIWW between flashing red "60" and red daybeacon "62" near the west side of Useppa Island. This anchorage can sometimes be uncomfortable from wakes of passing boats, especially on weekends, but the scenery is beautiful. It is also somewhat exposed to wind, so caution should be used when anchoring. The advantages of this anchorage far outnumber the disadvantages.

Cabbage Key–GIWW Mile 21

Just west of the GIWW channel, Cabbage Key lies in the lee of Cayo Costa. The delightful and unspoiled island of Cabbage Key (accessible only by boat) offers ample opportunity for observing nature in all its forms. For bird and nature enthusiasts, the bird watching and nature walk should not be missed. It is best to begin at the top of the inn's walk-up water tower for an overview of the island. Easily followed trails traverse Cabbage Key's connected shell mounds, revealing representative varieties of subtropical trees, shrubs, plants and bird life. Nesting ospreys are abundant, as are telltale signs of the Florida gopher tortoise.

The Calusa and their Pre-Columbian ancestors made mounds and causeways from millions of oyster and whelk shells. Canals and basins were created to hold and protect their fishing fleet of canoes. Several hundred lived in the town of Calos in the 16th century, conducting one of the most sophisticated North American societies of its day.

A great side trip by dinghy gives you access to the front beach of Cabbage Key by way of The Tunnel. If you are anchored northeast of flashing red "60," proceed south around Cabbage Key to Murdock Bayou. Go almost to the end of Murdock Bayou, and you will see a small, open area in the mangroves on the west side. There is enough room to tie a couple of dinghies to the mangroves. Walk through the tunnel of mangroves to the path that leads to the beach. (Watch for alligators.) It is a great place to picnic and enjoy the white sandy beach. In north winds, depths through The Tunnel and Murdock Bayou may be too shallow even for dinghies.

Dockage: Reached by the privately-marked entry channel just west of green daybeacon "61" is the classic old Florida island retreat, the Cabbage Key Inn, which sits upon a 38-foot-high Calusa shell mound. One hundred acres of tropical vegetation surround the historic restaurant, inn and rental cottages. The marina sits at the base with slips and some amenities.

For years, visiting fishers, passing to and from local tarpon-fishing hot spots, have taken rest and refreshment in the bar at the Cabbage Key Inn. The story goes that to guarantee a cold beer on their return, they started the tradition of posting signed dollar bills on the walls. The accumulated currency has piled up dollars deep over every square inch of wall and ceiling space, now adding up to more than $50,000. In addition to the expensive décor, the fresh shrimp, grouper and mahi-mahi are prepared to order and the burgers are well regarded. The "open air" restaurant serves breakfast, lunch and dinner 365 days a year (239-283-2278).

Pine Island–GIWW Mile 26

The largest island off Florida's Gulf Coast, Pine Island offers a small-town atmosphere amid mangroves, three aquatic preserves and acres of palm, tropical plants and fruit groves. The waters of Pine Island Sound provide not only some of the finest fishing in Florida, but are a haven for birdwatchers and nature lovers. The heart of Pine Island is a collection of homegrown shops, galleries, fish markets and residences.

As described earlier in this chapter, Matlacha Pass carries a marked, but shallow, crooked channel north between Pine Island and the mainland to Charlotte Harbor. Controlling depth is about 3 feet at MLW, and a 32-foot-high power cable and the Matlacha Pass Bascule Bridge (restricted schedule, with a 9-foot closed

vertical clearance) cross the pass. This passage is not recommended, but can be safely explored from the northern entrance.

Dockage: Olde Fish House is a restaurant and seafood market offering slips at a reasonable rate ($1/foot) on Matlacha Pass. At the northwestern end of Pine Island is Wilson Cut, which leads to Pineland Marina. Call ahead for approach depths. Before the Boca Grande Pass, on the north end of Pine Island is the small settlement of Bokeelia on Bokeelia Island. Bokeelia Island is home to Four Winds Marina with slips and gas, as well as the smaller 35-slip Jug Creek Marina, which sells all fuels and accepts limited transients. Be sure to call in advance for depth information as this area is very shallow (3 feet at MLW).

■ TO CHARLOTTE HARBOR: OUTSIDE (GULF) ROUTE

NAVIGATION: Use NOAA Charts 11425, 11426 and 11427. Mariners running the Gulf of Mexico to Charlotte Harbor or points north need only to choose their weather and go. The only complications along this route are the shoals and bars that extend out from many areas of the shoreline and form an integral part of virtually every pass and inlet on Florida's West Coast. Be sure you are standing sufficiently offshore to clear them, which may make the trip somewhat longer than cutting up Pine Island Sound. Staying 3 to 4 nm off the coastline should get the job done.

To reach the Gulf for the trip north, head south down the marked channel that goes underneath Sanibel Causeway Bridge. Well-charted shoals extend most of the way from Point Ybel south to the San Carlos Bay Morse (A) marker "SC," where it becomes safe to turn west as long as the weather and water won't sweep you into the shallow areas. Curve north with the sweep of Sanibel Island and lay a course that will take you to the Boca Grande flashing red bell buoy "2" (roughly 4.5 nm outside the entrance to Charlotte Harbor; GPS coordinates: N 026° 39.846'/W 082° 19.565'). Refer to the Waterway Explorer (waterwayguide.com) and NOAA online charts for the most up-to-date information.

If not planning to stop at Charlotte Harbor, entering a target waypoint just offshore of your target destination will provide the distance and, after a close double-check along the path, a "stay outside" line for quick visual reference. Venice provides a clean, well-marked inlet if visiting Sarasota, though the flashing red "2" was reported destroyed in September 2017. Refer to the Waterway Explorer and NOAA online charts for the most up-to-date information. Using the two passes closest to Sarasota (New Pass and Big Sarasota Pass) to enter Sarasota Bay definitely requires local knowledge.

Charlotte Harbor–GIWW Mile 25

About 60 miles southeast of Tampa Bay, Charlotte Harbor is a wide, elbow-shaped bay carrying 9-foot MLW depths to Punta Gorda at the mouth of the Peace River. Stretching 20 miles long and 10 miles wide, Charlotte Harbor offers a lot for the cruising boater.

Charlotte Harbor is formed by the confluence of the Peace and Myakka Rivers. Tidal range averages 2 feet, but winds from the west reportedly can increase water levels as much as 5 feet. The open sweep and relatively uniform depths of water in Charlotte Harbor provide a welcome change from the narrow, shoal-bordered GIWW. The high sandbars that protect the shoreline limit opportunities for gunkholing, but both the Peace and Myakka Rivers compensate for that weakness by offering opportunities for scenic dinghy trips.

It is a good place for daysailing and has variable winds. Yacht clubs in the area are involved year-round in sailboat racing and offer privileges to members of reciprocating clubs. When entering any marina in Charlotte Harbor be sure to stay inside the well-marked channels; the water can be very shallow outside of them.

When you leave Boca Grande for the northward push to Sarasota, or farther to Tampa Bay, you can choose to go outside to run north up the Gulf of Mexico or continue on the GIWW.

Dockage: Opposite Boca Grande Channel, and midway up the eastern shore of Charlotte Harbor, the large Burnt Store Marina is a very popular stop. Flashing red "6" leads off the approach from Charlotte Harbor and is then followed by flashing red "2" and a series of daybeacons into the protected harbor. Amenities include groceries and Cass Cay Restaurant & Bar (941-347-7148). Taxis are available for the relatively lengthy ride to Punta Gorda for extensive provisioning.

Side Trip: North on the Myakka River

Myakka State Park, in the upper reaches of the Myakka River, preserves a wilderness reminiscent of the Everglades. This is home to large alligators, feral hogs, eagles, deer, rattlesnakes and even the very rare Florida panther.

NAVIGATION: Use NOAA Chart 11427. Wandering through dense woodland, the Myakka River runs from the northwest from Myakka Lake to Charlotte Harbor. Boats drawing 3 feet or less and armed with local knowledge can travel about 17 miles up the Myakka River. Three nautical miles up the river the **SR 776 Bridge** with 25-foot fixed vertical clearance limits visitors; the railroad bridge just beyond is open and abandoned.

At the mouth of the Myakka River, past green daybeacon "9" on the south shore of the river, is a set of daybeacons that lead to an automated lock and the Santa Cruz Waterway, which has 6.5-foot MLW depths.

Dockage: A series of canals (6-mile long) lead to Placida Harbor where there are a few marine facilities, including Safe Cove Boat Storage and Charlotte Harbor Boat Storage. Safe Cove is primarily a dry storage facility but may have room for you; call ahead. Amenities include laundry facilities and WiFi. They allow do-it-yourself or you can choose from the full range of services. They also sell all fuels.

Anchorage: A protected anchorages lies at the beginning of the waterway leading to the marine facilities at green daybeacon "9" in the river. Here you will find 5 to 7 feet at MLW with protection from the west.

Punta Gorda, Peace River

At the foot of the Tamiami Trail Twin Bridges on the southern shore of the Peace River is Punta Gorda. This is a charming boating community made up of 60 miles of canals that meander through its neighborhoods and lead to Charlotte Harbor. The city has a historic district with 157 significant historical residential and commercial structures along its brick-lined streets. Its designation as a Florida Main Street Community has resulted in many new or renovated amenities now available to boaters. Along the Punta Gorda coastline of Charlotte Harbor is Harborwalk, a scenic pedestrian- and bicycle-friendly river walk lined with palm trees, brick pavers and park amenities.

Locations of over 2500 anchorages and free docks

waterwayguide.com

NAVIGATION: Use NOAA Chart 11427. The Peace River enters Charlotte Harbor from the northeast. It is very shallow (7 to 8 feet at MLW) and marked for only about 6 miles, but its channel is navigable to the town of Hull, 15 miles upriver. Offering 3-foot MLW depths, this stretch calls for local knowledge, and the snags and heavy growths of hyacinths in the upper river require caution as well. Two 45-foot fixed vertical clearance bridges (**Tamiami Trial Twin Bridges** and **I-75 Bridge**) and a 12-foot fixed vertical clearance bridge (**CR761 Bridge**) cross the Peace River. If you can get under the lower bridge, there is a lot of adventure ahead.

Dockage/Moorings: Fishermen's Village Marina is located on upper Charlotte Harbor with no bridges or other restrictions to the Gulf of Mexico and is within walking distance of Historic Punta Gorda. This is a very popular spot for transients to spend the winter and spring months. The marina has courtesy docks for day-trippers and a long dinghy dock. A supermarket/pharmacy is located approximately 1.5 miles away.

Laishley Park Municipal Marina has floating concrete slips and a mooring field. Be sure to call in advance for availability. They also have a day use-only dock. Laishley Park is the site of many festivals and activities throughout the year. The popular 16,000-square foot Laishley Crab House restaurant (150 Laishley Ct., 941-205-5566) is in the park as well, offering seafood classics and sushi and a breezy waterfront deck.

Farther along is the Punta Gorda Marina, which is strictly a repair/storage facility. (No transient dockage.) At the north end of the Peace River at Port Charlotte

is Charlotte Harbor Yacht Club, which recognizes reciprocity from other clubs. Call ahead for availability.

Anchorage: You need to be resourceful for this out-of-the-comfort-zone kind of travel, but if you travel beyond the 12-foot fixed vertical clearance **CR761 Bridge**, you will find plenty of anchorages in at least 4 feet at MLW and miles of unspoiled natural scenery. Be sure to stay in the channel.

■ TO SARASOTA: OUTSIDE (GULF) ROUTE

NAVIGATION: Use NOAA Chart 11425. From Boca Grande Pass, shoal-draft boats (5-foot draft or less) can use the shortcut route (known locally as "The Swash Channel"), according to local knowledge. The channel leads to deep water well inshore of the end of the big-ship route, the main ship channel. To follow The Swash Channel around the tip of Gasparilla Island, you should proceed west in Boca Grande Pass until you reach the end of the dilapidated commercial pier, bearing 340 degrees magnetic. Pass the old concrete pier about 50 to 100 feet out in 8- to 9-foot MLW depths, avoiding the long shoal that runs off to the south-southeast. Once clear of the shoal, you will find 10- to 11-foot MLW depths.

Note, however, that if you are returning to Charlotte Harbor from the Gulf of Mexico in a brisk northwesterly with an outgoing tide, the longest way around is the shortest way home. Under such conditions, Boca Grande Pass can appear reasonably docile until you are almost next to the piers, when you can be in breaking waves before you know it. (The waves break away from you and are hard to recognize.) It is wise to avoid The Swash Channel in such conditions because there is no "wiggle room" there. Current local knowledge is advisable.

The more prudent, safer approach, particularly if the water is rough, is to enter via the ship channel. The shoals along the ship channel, particularly on the northwest side, need to be monitored carefully as the charted channel runs very close to them. If entering Boca Grande Channel when coming from the north, take care to come all of the way to green buoy "3" and red nun buoy "4" to avoid the shoal entirely. You will be at about the Three

Charlotte Harbor, FL

PUNTA GORDA AREA			Approach / Dockside Depth (reported)	VHF Channel Monitored	Transient Berths / Total Berths	Dockage — Gas / Diesel	Floating Docks	Supplies — Groceries, Ice, Marine Supplies, Snacks	Repairs: Hull, Engine, Propeller	Lift (tonnage), Crane, Rail	Services — Min/Max Amps	Laundry, Pool, Showers, Courtesy Car	Pump-Out Station	Nearby: Grocery Store, Motel, Restaurant
1. Burnt Store Marina 💻 📶 WG	941-637-0083	100	16/14	30/525	8/8	F	GD	GIMS	E	L8	30/100	LPS	P	GR
2. Safe Cove Boat Storage 💻 WG	**941-697-9900**	**65**	**63**	**call/15**	**6/7**	**–**	**GD**	**M**	**HEP**	**L35**	**30/30**	**LS**	**P**	**–**
3. Charlotte Harbor Boat Storage 📶	941-828-0216	55	–	–	–	–	–	I	HEP	L30,C	–	LS	–	–
4. Fishermen's Village Marina 💻 📶 WG	941-575-3000	100	16/12	call/111	7/5	–	GD	IS	–	–	30/100	LPS	P	GMR
5. Laishley Park Municipal Marina 💻 📶 WG	941-575-0142	80	16/19	20/94	7/7	F	–	IS	–	–	30/50	LS	P	MR
6. Punta Gorda Marina	941-639-2750	60	–	–	5/5	–	–	–	HEP	L30, C5	–	–	–	–
7. Charlotte Harbor Yacht Club 📶	941-629-5131	60	16/68	4/18	4/6	–	GD	IM	–	–	30/50	S	P	GMR

💻 Internet Access 📶 Wireless Internet Access WG Waterway Guide Cruising Club Partner 📶onSpot dockside WiFi facility

See WaterwayGuide.com for current rates, fuel prices, web site addresses, and other up-to-the-minute information. *(Information in the table is provided by the facilities.)*

see our interactive charts

MARINAS

ANCHORAGES

FREE DOCK

BRIDGES

LOCKS

NAV ALERTS

FUEL

waterwayguide.com

PUNTA GORDA AREA, NOAA CHART 11426

Nautical Mile line and can then turn safely toward the northeast. Deeper water lies to the south side of the channel if you need to get out of the way of commercial vessels. Inexperienced skippers have lost their vessels on these shoals, so take heed.

Gulf Passes

- **Boca Grande Pass:** Well marked, deep and straightforward. If you follow the charts, you shouldn't have any problems.

- **Gasparilla Pass:** Not well marked and plagued with shoaling. Should NOT be attempted by cruising vessels.

- **Stump Pass:** The private navigational aids are relocated as channel conditions change. Do not enter without local knowledge.

- **Venice Inlet:** Well maintained, well marked and with plenty of depth. After passing the jetties, be aware of a "No-Wake Zone," which is strictly enforced.

- **Midnight Pass:** Closed. The adjacent beach is approachable by dinghy only.

- **Big Sarasota Pass:** Has reasonably good depths for most cruising boats. Follow the charted marks. (Note: Green daybeacons "15A" and "18" may be missing.) Be sure to call for local information. Towing services are really good about giving information, as is the Sarasota Yacht Club. Go to sarasotayachtclub.org on a mobile device and choose "Big Pass." Green daybeacon "15A" and red daybeacon "18" were reported missing in January of 2018. The Yacht Club updates information for the pass on a regular basis. Refer to the Waterway Explorer (waterwayguide.com) and NOAA online charts for the most up-to-date information.

- **New Pass:** The Coast Guard strongly recommends avoiding this channel if possible. There is also a bascule bridge (23-foot closed vertical clearance) to contend with at the opening of the pass. Call one of the towing services for local knowledge before attempting this pass.

- **Longboat Pass:** Previously well marked, the Coast Guard has discontinued the approach light and the quick-flasher marking the shoal after it was destroyed in Hurricane Irma. The channel had good depths (10 to 15 feet at MLW) previous to the hurricane but has a 17-foot closed vertical clearance bascule bridge (opens on request). A call to a towboat captain for local knowledge is wise. Refer to the Waterway Explorer and NOAA online charts for the most up-to-date information.

- **Passage Key Inlet:** Follow the charts closely and stay in deep water. Not marked, so be aware that there could be hazards. Should only be attempted with local knowledge. Better route is Southwest Channel.

- **Southwest Channel:** Well marked and deep, this is the inlet into Tampa Bay. It carries a lot of commercial traffic, so stay alert and pay attention. Remember, tonnage rules!

◼ TO SARASOTA: INSIDE (GIWW) ROUTE

The inside route from Charlotte Harbor to Sarasota Bay is well marked and not too heavily congested with manatee or boating safety areas. The 25-mph speed zone in the GIWW channel (Slow-Speed/Minimum-Wake within a specified distance from the shore) is more the rule than the exception. Pay close attention to posted signs in these slow-speed restriction areas.

Gasparilla Island (Boca Grande)– GIWW Mile 28 to Mile 34

The waters around Boca Grande Pass are one of the world's great tarpon fishing grounds. Boca Grande, on the south end of Gasparilla Island, located about halfway between Fort Myers and Tampa, makes a good stop. In a bygone era, Boca Grande was a winter resort and fishing retreat for Northern socialites and tycoons. For the most part, the gracious old homes they once occupied have been faithfully maintained, preserving the elegance of the past. Those in the entertainment business seem to favor the Gasparilla Inn for its privacy and good manners as well as the absolutely charming atmosphere. This is a wonderful stop and shouldn't be missed if time permits.

NAVIGATION: Use NOAA Chart 11425. Use the St. Petersburg Tide Tables. For high tide, subtract 1 hour 12 minutes; for low tide, subtract 1 hour 56 minutes. The Boca Grande Channel, one of the primary inlets from the Gulf, runs between Cayo Costa and Gasparilla Island, forming the entrance to Charlotte Harbor. Easy to navigate, deep, well marked and lighted, it is one of the primary, important passes on the stretch between Naples and Tampa.

To cross Boca Grande Channel from the GIWW inside, flashing red "76" (off the northeast point of Cayo Costa) and flashing green "1" (off the eastern shore of Gasparilla Island) are the important markers. If heading north, follow a bearing of about 350 degrees magnetic after leaving flashing red "76" to the east. The channel carries 10 to 12 feet at MLW and is well marked.

The Boca Grande yacht basin (not a business, but a designation on some charts), located about a quarter of the way up Gasparilla Island when you are headed north, offers secure berths, limited anchorage and a full range of amenities for visiting boaters. Sixteen-foot flashing green "1" lines you up to use red daybeacon "2" and green daybeacon "3" to enter the channel into the harbor. The channel carries 7 to 9 feet at MLW. On entering the Boca Grande Bayou, flashing green "7" should be given a wide berth because of the encroaching sandbar. Controlling depths are 6 feet at MLW in Boca Grande Bayou.

Dockage: Boca Grande Marina, located one-half mile from downtown and inside the yacht basin, has slips with dockage rate options (with or without shore power) and water hookups. Guests also enjoy friendly dockside assistance, a well-stocked ship store and the on-site Miller's Dockside with casual dining (inside or out). Open daily. Call or reservations (941-964-8000).

You must make a room reservation to dock at either the Gasparilla Inn & Club or The Innlet on the Waterfront (beyond the northern anchorage and past a bridge with 13-foot fixed vertical clearance). You cannot stay aboard your vessel at night.

Anchorage: You can go north from flashing green "7" and drop the hook in the small basin before the fixed 13-foot fixed vertical clearance bridge. If you go south into Boca Grande's yacht basin, be prepared to drop your anchor, back down on it and then tie off on the mangroves with a stern line to stop your swing in the tight quarters.

Little Gasparilla Island–GIWW Mile 35 to Mile 40

NAVIGATION: Use NOAA Chart 11425. Those running north on the GIWW will find the bays beginning to narrow somewhat. Shores are closer and more developed, and you should watch the markers carefully.

The channel from Boca Grande and Charlotte Harbor winds sufficiently to maintain interest. Channel depths

average 7 to 11 feet at MLW, although depths are extremely shallow outside the marked channel where the birds are often able to walk in the shallows.

When moving up the GIWW from the south and traversing Gasparilla Sound near the town of Placida at green daybeacon "19," the waterway channel doglegs farther west toward a pair of bridges.

Pass through the permanently opened railway bridge just past green daybeacon "21," then leave green daybeacon "1" to the south as you approach the **Boca Grande Swing Bridge** at GIWW Mile 34.3. The swing bridge (22-foot closed vertical clearance) opens on signal, except 7:00 a.m. to 6:00 p.m., Monday through Friday, when the draw need only open on the hour and half-hour. Saturdays, Sundays and federal holidays, the draw opens every 15 minutes. Vessels must request an opening. Be sure to check the Coast Guard *Local Notice to Mariners* or the Waterway Explorer at waterwayguide. com for schedule changes, or use VHF Channel 09 to get in touch with the bridgetender.

When approaching from the Gulf, Gasparilla Pass is not recommended. This is an access used by local fishers with a lot of local knowledge and very shallow-draft boats. The area around the pass is riddled with charted 2- to 3-foot MLW spots, and the entire north side of the pass has a 1-foot MLW bar on its border. Use Boca Grande Pass instead.

Dockage: Arriving at this northern tip of Gasparilla Island, along the GIWW from the south, transients can find dockage at Uncle Henry's Marina. Turn southwest between the open railroad bridge and the Boca Grande Swing Bridge. (Note that private green daybeacon "1" may be missing.)

This is a quiet, peaceful marina with all of the usual cruiser amenities plus fuel. The 58-slip marina can accommodate vessels up to 80 feet. The buildings are attractive southern contemporary Victorian structures. At the end of the dock, the marina building houses the laundry and showers. The entrance has 6 to 7 feet at MLW and a 1.5- to 2-foot tidal range. With a wind out of the north, depths will be less. Pay attention to the tide tables; deep-draft vessels should call Uncle Henry's for a current report. There has been some silting along both sides of this access passage, so honor all markers and stay as close to center channel as possible. Kappy's Market and Deli (941-964-2506) is adjacent to the marina for groceries and golf cart rentals.

At flashing red "20," a channel leads off to starboard past the mouth of Coral Creek to the Gasparilla Marina,

GOIN' ASHORE: BOCA GRANDE, FL

SERVICES	
1	Visitor Information
ATTRACTIONS	
2	Boca Grande Art Center
SHOPPING	
3	Hudson's Grocery
4	Railway Depot
DINING	
4	Loose Caboose Restauarant
5	Pink Elephant/The Gasparilla Inn & Club
MARINAS	
5	The Gasparilla Inn & Club
6	Boca Grande Marina
7	The Innlet on the Waterfront

The restored and upscale old Florida town of Boca Grande is at the south end of Gasparilla Island. It is a charming place, with some of the feel of old Key West in the 1950s and 1960s, before the tourist boom. As a point of interest, "Boca Grande" means "big mouth" in Spanish, referring to the deep Boca Grande Pass, one of Florida's deepest natural inlets.

Attractions: One of Gasparilla Island's prime attractions is the community bike path, which runs almost the entire length of this 7-mile island. It begins at Boca Grande's most famous landmark. The Boca Grande Lighthouse (880 Belcher Rd., 941-964-0060) was built in 1890 to mark the entrance to Charlotte Harbor. It is open to the public 10:00 a.m. to 4:00 p.m. daily from November through April, and Wednesday through Sunday from May through October. The lighthouse is closed in August and all major holidays.

Touring Boca Grande by golf cart is also popular and there are a few for rent at Kappy's Market & Deli (5800 Gasparilla Rd, 941-964-2506). Make a reservation for a cart well in advance unless you want to walk or take a cab into town. The beautiful vistas and accessible beaches along the way make this trek–whether by foot, bike or golf cart–well worth the effort. No tour of the island is complete without a walk along Banyan Street, south of the depot.

The Boca Grande Chamber of Commerce (471 Park Ave., 941-964-0568) can make sure you hit all the main attractions. The Boca Grande Art Center (236 Banyan St., 941-964-1700) was founded in 1986 by a small group of talented artists in search of a venue to show their art works to residents and visitors. The BGAC offers exhibits and classes.

Shopping: Hudson's Grocery (441 Park Ave., 941-964-2621) sells fresh produce, meat, fish, cheese and wine (closed on Sundays). The old railway depot in the center of town has been converted into a mini-mall with a variety of shops. Nearby are two banks, a hardware store, a health center, the post office (on Fourth Street), various boutiques and a bookstore.

Dining: The Gasparilla Inn & Club is home to the highly rated Pink Elephant (491 Bayou Ave., 941-964-4540), where lunch and dinner menus focus on imaginative regional cuisine, seafood and steaks. Other dining options at the Club include the upscale main dining room or the more relaxed Beach Club. A four-course, traditional heritage experience dinner is served in the evening from 6:30 p.m. to 9:00 p.m. in the main dining room (although there's a dress code), while the Beach Club serves beverages poolside or on their own beach, as well as hosting delightful daily luncheons.

The well-regarded Loose Caboose Restaurant (433 4th St. W., 941-964-0440) is located in the historic train depot. Dinner is served seasonally, and they close altogether for four weeks in September/October. Menu items include southern fried green tomato and crab cake combo, fresh grouper sandwich and seafood pot pie, but the homemade ice cream is an especially strong draw.

Gasparilla Sound, FL

BOCA GRANDE AREA		Dockage					Supplies					Services			
	VHF Channel Monitored	Transient Berths / Total Berths	Approach / Dockside Depth (reported)	Floating Docks	Gas / Diesel	Groceries, Ice, Marine Supplies, Snacks	Repairs: Hull, Engine, Propeller	Lift (tonnage), Crane, Rail	Min/Max Amps	Laundry, Pool, Showers Courtesy Car	Pump-Out Station	Nearby: Grocery Store, Motel, Restaurant			
1. Boca Grande Marina 📠 WiFi 28.5	**941-964-2100**	150	16/14	15/20	–	–	GD	GIMS	–	–	30/50	LS	P	GMR
2. The Gasparilla Inn & Club 29.5	941-964-4620	50	–	call/24	6/4.5	F	GD	IM	EP	L	50/50	S	–	GMR
3. The Innlet On The Waterfront WiFi 29.5	941-964-4600	35	–	call/23	6/5	–	–	IS	–	–	30/30	PS	–	GR
4. Uncle Henry's Marina WiFi 32.8	**941-964-0154**	90	16/14	40/58	6/9	–	GD	GI	–	–	30/100	LS	P	GMR
5. Gasparilla Marina 📠 WiFi	941-697-2280	100	16/14	10/225	7/6	F	GD	GIMS	HEP	L70	30/100	LS	P	GR

📠 Internet Access   WiFi Wireless Internet Access   WG Waterway Guide Cruising Club Partner   onSpot dockside WiFi facility

See WaterwayGuide.com for current rates, fuel prices, web site addresses, and other up-to-the-minute information. *(Information in the table is provided by the facilities.)*

BOCA GRANDE AREA, NOAA CHART 11426

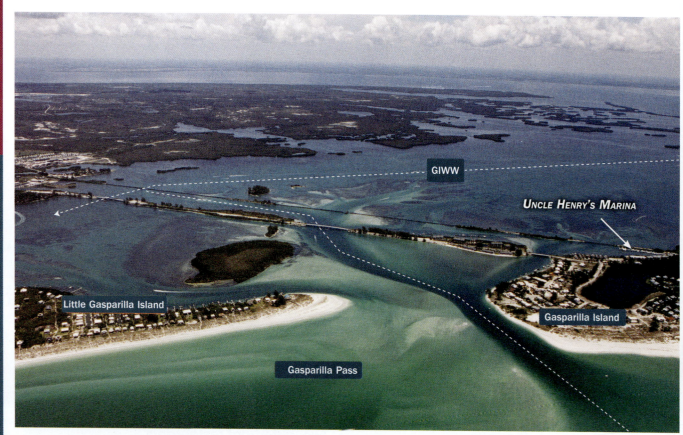

Little Gasparilla Island

GIWW

UNCLE HENRY'S MARINA

Gasparilla Island

Gasparilla Pass

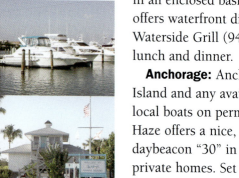
the largest marina in the area with deep water slips in an enclosed basin. The marina has a fuel dock and offers waterfront dining and live entertainment at Waterside Grill (941-697-0724), open for breakfast, lunch and dinner.

Anchorage: Anchorage is limited around Gasparilla Island and any available space is often filled with local boats on permanent moorings. At Mile 36, Cape Haze offers a nice, quiet anchorage northeast of red daybeacon "30" in 9-foot MLW depths surrounded by private homes. Set your anchor carefully as the bottom is soft mud. This is a pleasant anchorage with more protection from the GIWW than is evident from the chart. There is a small canal that leads to the north, and the tidal current may swing you more than the wind. There is only enough room for two or three boats to anchor comfortably.

Lemon Bay to Venice–GIWW Mile 40 to Mile 50

NAVIGATION: Use NOAA Chart 11425. Beyond Placida Harbor, the GIWW turns south and threads through a series of small islands to a narrow 2.25-mile straight stretch called The Cutoff, leading into Lemon Bay. At green daybeacon "7" toward the end of The Cutoff, watch for the car ferry that crosses the waterway.

Once into Lemon Bay, the GIWW swings to the northeast shore and opens up for a 7.5-mile narrow straightaway through shallow water to the end of the bay. Green daybeacon "17A" keeps you on the straight and narrow where other daybeacons indicate the channel leading to Stump Pass, which opens to the Gulf. Hurricane Irma created extreme shoaling in Stump Pass, which was already not navigable without very current local knowledge. At GIWW Mile 43.5 is the **Manasota (Tom Adams) Key Bascule Bridge** (26-foot closed vertical clearance), which opens on signal.

At Mile 49.9 is the **Manasota Bascule Bridge** (26-foot closed vertical clearance). This bridge also opens on signal. Past Lemon Bay, at Mile 53, the GIWW becomes a long, high-banked land cut, which runs through a corner of the Venice Municipal Airport. Watch for water-soaked debris in the cut; there is little tidal flushing action to move it out, and it can be a nuisance. Refer to the Waterway Explorer and NOAA online charts for the most up-to-date information

At GIWW Mile 54.9 the **Tamiami Trail (Circus) Twin Bridges** (25-foot vertical clearance) opens on signal. This is followed by the **Venice Ave. Bascule Bridge** at Mile 56.6 (30-foot vertical clearance), which opens on signal, except from 7:00 a.m. and 4:30 p.m., Monday through Friday, when it opens at 10, 30 and 50 minutes past the hour. (Note that it does not open between 4:35 p.m. and 5:35 p.m.).

Dockage: Marinas in Lemon Bay tend to be small, unpretentious and friendly but are geared to handle cruising boats. Two marinas are located near Mile 38 before the GIWW enters Lemon Bay at Englewood Beach or at Englewood on the mainland shore. The sheltered Aquamarina Palm Harbour, located on the mainland side near green daybeacon "7," is a boutique, resort-style marina with full amenities. The marina features dry stack storage for up to 40 feet and wet slips up to 65 feet. Johnny Leverock's Restaurant (941-698-6900) is in the marina basin with traditional seafood offerings.

From Leverock's, take the water taxi across the GIWW to Rum Bay (941-697-0566), a tropical-themed restaurant and bar on Knight Island. If your timing is good, you will arrive during one of the barbecues and enjoy the tangy ribs and sunset entertainment. "It's more than a restaurant...It's an experience" is their motto.

Just to the north is the Cape Haze Marina with a narrow, dredged channel. The friendly marina has transient dockage in a protected basin just off the ICW.

At green daybeacon "17A," right at the entrance to the Stump Pass Channel and just off the GIWW at Mile 40.8, is the large, full-service Stump Pass Marina with overnight dockage and some boat repair services. A towering rustic lighthouse identifies the marina.

Venice

Lemon Bay, FL

CAPE HAZE TO ENGLEWOOD		Largest Vessel Accommodated	VHF Channel Monitored	Approach / Dockside Depth	Transient Berths / Total Berths	Floating Docks (reported)	Gas / Diesel	Groceries, Ice, Marine Supplies, Snacks	Repairs: Hull, Engine, Propeller	Lift (tonnage), Crane, Rail	Min/Max Amps	Laundry, Pool, Showers, Courtesy Car	Pump-Out Station	Nearby: Grocery Store, Motel, Restaurant
		Dockage					**Supplies**		**Services**				
1. Aquamarina Palm Harbour ☐ WiFi 38.5	941-697-4356	65	16/14	27/90	7/6	–	GD	IM	HEP	L50	30/50	LPS	P	GMR
2. Cape Haze Marina ☐ WG 39	941-698-1110	70	16/71	4/105	6/9	F	GD	I	HEP	L14	30/50	LPS	–	GR
3. Stump Pass Marina 40.8	941-697-4300	50	66	call/300	4.5/4		GD	GIMS	HEP	L	30/50	–	–	GMR
4. Skip's Marina	941-460-8157	25	71	call/80	3/4		G	IMS	HEP	L	–	–	–	GMR
5. Harbor at Lemon Bay–PRIVATE	941-475-7100	50	08	0/15	6/6	F	GD	I	HEP	L20	30/50	S	–	G
6. Royal Palm Marina ☐ WiFi 45.8	941-475-6882	80	16/14	20/160	5/9	–	GD	GIMS	HEP	L50	30/50	S	P	GMR

☐ Internet Access   WiFi Wireless Internet Access   WG Waterway Guide Cruising Club Partner   ☺onSpot dockside WiFi facility

See WaterwayGuide.com for current rates, fuel prices, web site addresses, and other up-to-the-minute information. *(Information in the table is provided by the facilities.)*

CAPE HAZE TO ENGLEWOOD, NOAA CHART 11425

Just before the Tom Adams Bascule Bridge is Skip's Placida Marina, which sells gas and may have transient space for smaller shallow-draft boats. North of the bridge at about Mile 43.5 is Harbor at Lemon Bay, which is private.

Royal Palm Marina is tucked away at Mile 45.8 and has "old Florida charm." They offer transient dockage, wet and dry storage, a well-stocked ship store and pontoon rental boats. The on-site Snook's Bayside Bar & Grill (941-475-6882) with panoramic views and a waterfront Tiki bar. The restaurant is open daily for lunch and dinner. They also frequently have live entertainment.

Anchorage: Anchorages in the area include one at the north end of Thornton Key (Mile 40.9) and one on the south side of Peterson Island (mile 43.3). Both offer good holding and protection.

At Mile 43.5, on the west side of the GIWW, is a large, quiet anchorage with 7- to 10-foot MLW depths at Englewood Beach. The anchorage is reached by heading southwest between lighted red daybeacon "22" and the Tom Adams Bascule Bridge. Buildings around the anchorage help to protect visiting yachts from buffeting winds. If you continue south, hugging the mangroves, you will be sheltered from all directions. Watch depths closely. You can dinghy to a nearby dock and restaurant. You can tie up your dinghy, but you will be required to have either a drink or a meal. A convenience store and souvenir shop, dive shops, restaurants and the beach are across the street. To the north is an anchorage with 6 feet at MLW and excellent holding at Mile 44.5 east of red daybeacon "26."

Venice to Siesta Key–GIWW Mile 50 to Mile 65

Warm Mineral Springs Park (941-426-1692) is located 12 miles south of Venice. Known as Florida's Fountain of Youth, its waters are 87 degrees year-round. They do allow re-entry on the daily passes and have added spa services.

About 15 miles south of Sarasota, Venice is one of Florida's younger towns. Around a central green, which was planned in the 1920s with a Mediterranean theme, you will find boutiques for shopping, a theater and a variety of dining options. As you can imagine, there are several good Italian restaurants here as well. You shouldn't leave Venice feeling hungry.

From the marinas, it is a short walk to one of the widest and loveliest beaches on Florida's west coast.

Venice Inlet, FL

WG

	Phone	Largest Vessel Accommodated	VHF Channel Monitored	Approach / Dockside Depth (reported)	Transient Berths / Total Berths	Floating Docks	Gas / Diesel	Groceries, Ice, Marine Supplies, Snacks	Repairs: Hull, Engine, Propeller	Lift (tonnage), Crane, Rail	Min/Max Amps	Laundry, Pool, Showers, Courtesy Car	Pump-Out Station	Nearby: Grocery Store, Motel, Restaurant
				Dockage			**Supplies**		**Services**					
VENICE AREA														
1. MarineMax of Venice 55.1	941-485-3388	68	16/72	12/9	call/60	–	GD	IMS	HEP	L	30/50	LS	P	GMR
2. Fisherman's Wharf Marina of Venice ▯ WiFi	941-486-0500	120	16/71	8/7	call/57	F	GD	IMS	E	–	30/100	S	P	GR
3. Venice Yacht Club 57.5	941-483-3625	100	16	10/10	3/67	–	GD	I	–	–	30/50	LPS	P	GMR
4. Crow's Nest Marina & Restaurant ▯ WiFi 58	**941-484-7661**	**140**	**16**	**12/12**	**24/34**	–	**GD**	**IS**	–	–	**30/50**	**LS**	**P**	**GMR**
CASEY KEY														
5. Gulf Harbor Marina 59	941-488-7734	45	16	10/6	–	–	GD	IMS	HEP	L	30/30	–	–	GMR
6. Escape at Casey Key Resort & Marina	941-882-4654	50	–	10/	call/15	–	–	–	–	–	30/30	LPS	–	GMR

▯ Internet Access WiFi Wireless Internet Access WG Waterway Guide Cruising Club Partner ⬭onSpot dockside WiFi facility

See WaterwayGuide.com for current rates, fuel prices, web site addresses, and other up-to-the-minute information. *(Information in the table is provided by the facilities.)*

VENICE AREA, NOAA CHART 11425

VENICE AREA, CASEY KEY, NOAA CHART 11425

Crow's Nest Marina & Restaurant / GIWW / Venice / Casey Key / Gulf of Mexico

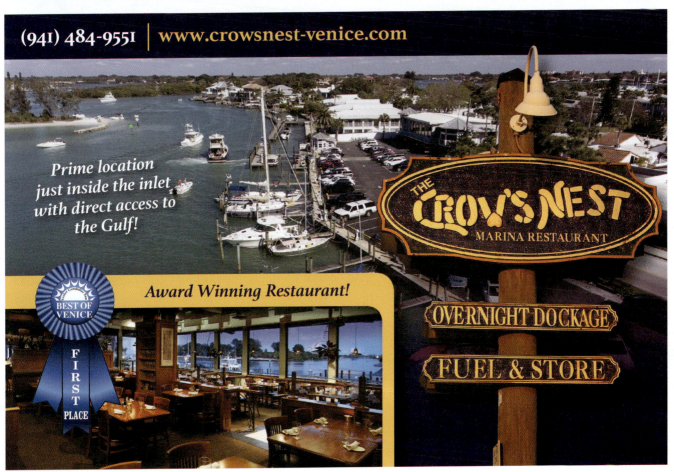

Little Sarasota Bay, FL

SIESTA KEY	Dockage						Supplies		Services					
	Largest Vessel Accommodated	VHF Channel Monitored	Transient Berths / Total Berths	Approach / Dockside Depth (reported)	Floating Docks	Gas / Diesel	Groceries, Ice, Marine Supplies, Snacks	Repairs: Hull, Engine, Propeller	Lift (tonnage), Crane, Rail	Laundry, Pool, Showers, Courtesy Car	Min/Max Amps	Pump-Out Station	Nearby: Grocery Store, Motel, Restaurant	
1. Bayfront Yacht Works 🖥 📶 66 **941-349-9449**	50	–	call/25	5/5	–	GD	IMS	HEP	L70	S	30/50	P	R	
2. Hidden Harbor Marina Boat Storage Sales & Service 941-927-4800	40	–	call/16	6/6	F	G	IMS	HEP	L	S	30/30	–	R	

🖥 Internet Access   📶 Wireless Internet Access   **WG** Waterway Guide Cruising Club Partner   ◉ onSpot dockside WiFi facility

See WaterwayGuide.com for current rates, fuel prices, web site addresses, and other up-to-the-minute information. *(Information in the table is provided by the facilities.)*

SIESTA KEY, NOAA CHART 11425

Fossilized sharks' teeth–either gray or black and with a triangular shape–are abundant here.

NAVIGATION: Use NOAA Chart 11425. Entering Venice waters, the first bridge is the **KMI (Hatchett Creek) Bascule Bridge** at GIWW Mile 56.9 has 30-foot closed vertical clearance and restricted openings year-round. It opens on signal, except from 7:00 a.m. to 4:20 p.m., Monday through Friday (except federal holiday), when the draw need only open on the hour and at 20 and 40 minutes past the hour (except between 4:25 p.m. and 5:25 p.m. when it is closed). On weekends and holidays, it opens from 7:30 a.m. to 6:00 p.m. on the hour and at 15, 30 and 45 minutes past the hour. Call ahead on VHF Channel 09.

After leaving the land cut, the GIWW runs through Roberts Bay. Lightly powered vessels should be cautious of the strong currents flowing in and out of Venice Inlet, which cross the route and create some navigational challenges. Shoaling is a recurrent condition, although the Army Corps of Engineers advises that 9-foot MLW depths are maintained in Venice Inlet. The inlet is jettied

and easily navigable, except when strong westerly winds oppose an ebbing tide.

The flashing red "2" was reported destroyed in fall 2017, so take care when locating the jetty from the Gulf side. Refer to the Waterway Explorer and NOAA online charts for the most up-to-date information.

North of Venice, the GIWW continues its sheltered path behind Casey Key through the **Albee Road (Casey Key) Bascule Bridge** (14-foot closed vertical clearance) at Mile 59.3 to the **Blackburn Point Swing Bridge** (9-foot closed vertical clearance) at Mile 63 in Osprey. Both bridges open on signal. Boaters who require an opening at the Albee Road Bridge should radio ahead on VHF Channel 09 before entering the channel. Passage through both bridges is on an angle in tight quarters (51-foot horizontal clearance), and little maneuvering room is available on either side of the bridge, so use caution.

Blackburn Bay, outside the GIWW at Mile 60, is very shallow and has only limited tie-ups. Proceed with caution and definitely do not attempt transiting this area at night. The course crosses Little Sarasota Bay, the approach to Sarasota.

Always a prime source of waterway shoaling, Midnight Pass, at Mile 65, which separates Casey Key from Siesta Key, has been closed for years by the action of nature. Despite continuing attention, the GIWW channel both north and south of the inlet tends to silt in at some point. Keep an eye on your depth sounder throughout this area. Overall, the channel is well marked and maintained and, if you keep to the middle of the channel, you should encounter no problems.

Dockage: Marine supplies are available at Mile 55.1 at MarineMax of Venice, with a well-stocked ship store, fuel and repairs. They may have space for you; call ahead.

Fisherman's Wharf Marina at GIWW Mile 57 has been serving the boating community in Venice since 1949. They offer all amenities and floating docks for monthly and yearly rentals as well as overnight stays. The on-site Dockside Waterfront Grill (941-218-6418) is accessible by land or sea. Fisherman's Wharf is just a short walk from historic downtown Venice.

At Mile 58, between quick-flashing green "13" and red daybeacon "14," a privately marked channel leads west toward the private Venice Yacht Club (with reciprocal privileges for members of the Florida Yacht Council only). Located just opposite the Venice Yacht Club docks is a small city dock at Higel Marine Park that five or six boats could tie up to for the day, but you must vacate the dock between midnight and 6:00 a.m.

Conveniently situated inside the inlet, the Crow's Nest Marina & Restaurant can accommodate deep-draft boats with slips up to 140 feet and offers the usual cruiser

Venice Inlet

amenities plus fuel, a laundry and the very popular on-site restaurant (941-484-9551). The restaurant serves a full range of moderately priced entrées, with fine foods upstairs and a tavern atmosphere downstairs. Courtesy bikes are available for the 1.5-mile ride to town (well worth the ride).

Gulf Harbor Marina at Mile 59, past Lyons Bay and red daybeacon "10," sells fuel but has no transient dockage. It is a storage facility. On the north side of the Albee Road Bridge is Escape at Casey Key Resort & Marina. Slips are reserved for guests staying at the resort.

Anchorage: You can drop the hook in Venice at Mile 58 at green daybeacon "15" with good holding in 6 feet at MLW with a sand bottom. This is somewhat exposed to the north and east and to GIWW wakes. This anchorage is small, but quiet until morning.

Siesta Key–GIWW Mile 65 to Mile 72

Writers and artists congregate on the slender, heavily wooded Siesta Key, which boasts large private estates and deluxe condos with their own docks. A favorite among people from all over the world, Siesta Beach's sand is soft and cool. The beach facilities include picnic areas, restrooms, concession stands, a playground, trails and tennis and volleyball courts.

Behind Siesta Key, the narrow, dredged GIWW runs up the center of Little Sarasota Bay until the bay narrows to the north. At the **Stickney Point (SR 72) Bascule Bridge** at GIWW Mile 68.6 (18-foot closed vertical clearance) the route moves over to the western shore, then swings out into the middle again at Roberts Bay. The bridge opens on signal daily, except from 6:00 a.m. to 7:00 p.m., when the draw opens need only open on the hour and half hour.

At the northern end of Siesta Key at GIWW Mile 71.6 is the **Siesta Drive Bridge** (25-foot closed vertical clearance). The bridge follows the same schedule as the Stickney Point Bridge.

Dockage: Bayfront Yacht Works at Mile 66 is a Suntex Marina offering an array of services, including engine repair, repower and restoration; hull cleaning and painting; electrical service and repair; and custom carpentry. They can haul vessels up to 70 feet. Call for details.

Across Little Sarasota Bay is the protected channel of Hidden Harbor Marina Boat Storage, which is primarily a storage and launching site that also offers repairs. They also sell gas. There are several small marinas along this stretch of the GIWW that cater to "day boats" such as center consoles and pontoon boats. Marinas with facilities and slips to handle transient cruisers are largely located in Venice and in Sarasota Bay.

Anchorage: You can anchor at White Beach at Mile 67.4 west of green daybeacon "55" in 5 to 6 feet at MLW with good holding. This is somewhat exposed to wakes from passing boats. There is another anchorage west of green daybeacon "79" at Mile 71. Here you will find good holding in 5 to 6 feet at MLW.

■ SARASOTA AREA– GIWW MILE 74

At Siesta Key, off to port heading north after clearing Little Sarasota Bay, the Sarasota area officially begins and then continues for about 15 miles. The passage starts with a well-marked stretch through the shoals of Roberts Bay and ends with the exit through Longboat Key Pass to the north of Sarasota Bay. This section of the GIWW traverses a sophisticated, fast-growing region and is a popular layover spot for cruising boats.

As such, facilities are plentiful, ranging from fishing camps to marina resorts, and all manner of boating needs and repairs can be handled here. As the mainland's focal point for a cluster of offshore island resorts (linked to it by causeways), Sarasota acts as the hub of an important agricultural and cattle-ranching district but is most proud of its cultural image.

NAVIGATION: Use NOAA Chart 11425. Use the St. Petersburg Tide Tables. For high tide, subtract 1 hour 38 minutes; for low tide, subtract 58 minutes.

After traversing Roberts Bay, the GIWW widens amidst a variety of marine facilities and then passes under the **Ringling Causeway (SR 684) Bridge** at Mile 73.6, with a fixed vertical clearance of 65 feet. Ringling Causeway crosses three Sarasota Bay keys (Bird, Coon and St. Armands) to link Lido Key to the mainland. The bridge span between Bird and Coon keys is fixed, with only a 10-foot vertical clearance. From flashing green "13" north of the causeway and opposite **New Pass Bascule Bridge** (23-foot vertical clearance). The draw opens on the hour, 20 minutes past the hour and 40 minutes past the hour from 7:00 a.m. to 6:00 p.m. From 6:00 p.m. to 7:00 a.m., the draw will open on signal if at least a 3-hour notice is given. Sarasota Bay opens up, both in width and–in certain areas–in depth.

Farther north from the Ringling Causeway, Longboat Key shields Sarasota Bay from the Gulf of Mexico and opens wide with central controlling depths of 7 to 12 feet at MLW. The low purple building on the east side of Sarasota Bay, just north of the causeway, is the Van Wezel (pronounced Vann WAY-zull) Theatre of Performing Arts. At about Mile 77, also on the east side, you can see the coral-colored mansion of John Ringling (of circus fame).

In this area, the GIWW runs a straight line down the middle of Sarasota Bay, with markers along this stretch spaced about 2 miles apart. At flashing green "17" (near the midpoint of Longboat Key, at Mile 80), the route turns sharply west, Sarasota Bay narrows, and you must observe all aids to navigation very carefully. Along this stretch, the GIWW follows a dredged path through shoal water (1- and 2-foot MLW outside the channel).

⚠ Near the northern end of Longboat Key, where the GIWW passes between it and Sister Keys, green daybeacon "35" was reported destroyed in April 2018.

Watch out for strong crosscurrents to and from Longboat Pass. The **Longboat Pass Bascule Bridge** (17-foot vertical clearance) opens on signal.

Dockage/Moorings: Many of Sarasota's marine facilities are on the mainland near the Ringling Causeway, in Whittaker Bayou and clustered around New Pass. Repairs and service are readily available.

Field Club is located on the east shore just to the south of the Siesta Drive Bridge with fuel. They only accommodate members of the Florida Council of Yacht Clubs (FCYC) for dockage.

Tucked in behind Island Park, Marina Jack (a Suntex Marina) is at the doorstep to downtown Sarasota. Full amenities include laundry facilities, and a concierge, shuttle and well-stocked ship store. There is a dining room, piano bar and patio bar and grill on site and live bands (on the patio) on weekends.

South of the Ringling Causeway before Lido Key are Bird Key Yacht Club and Sarasota Yacht Club, both of which may have transient space for reciprocating yacht club members only. Be sure to call ahead. Gas and diesel fuel are available from the two facilities.

Hyatt Regency Sarasota is north of the Ringling Causeway Bridge and to the east (Sarasota side) with resort amenities and facilities for hotel guests only. To the north, on Lido Key, are Sarasota Sailing

Squadron and MarineMax Sarasota. Both have fuel but no transient slips.

To get farther away from the crowd, take a mooring at the 287-slip Resort at Longboat Key Club Moorings. To reach its channel, steer 255 degrees true from flashing green "15." On this course, point toward the one farthest south of the three high-rise condominiums, where you will encounter the privately maintained entrance channel to the facility. Located adjacent to the marina are a supermarket and a pharmacy. The 20-slip Dock on the Bay is also on Longboat Key in the Buttonwood Harbor area and may have transient space for you.

At red daybeacon "16" in Sarasota Bay, steering a course of 038 degrees magnetic for 1.5 nm will bring you to the entrance markers to the Ramada Sarasota, which has a long seawall for tie ups and an on-site restaurant. Head towards the house with a white roof and chimney, take a hard left and hug the right shoreline. This facility shares an entrance with Sara Bay Marina, which offers ample amenities, including lodging and a restaurant. Be aware that there is only 4 feet at MLW on the approach near low tide.

At Longboat Pass, Cannons Marina (Mile 83.5) is a sales/service facility and offers no transient dockage.

Anchorage: Many transient and local boats anchor in Sarasota Bay. What used to be the main anchorage (south and west of Marina Jack on the outside of Island Park) is now the mooring field. You can still anchor here, but you must be at least 150 feet outside and away from any of the moorings. You will be exposed to weather coming out of the north and west.

There is a dinghy beach on the eastern side of Island Park near O'Leary's Sailing School, but that part of the beach is primarily for the sailing school and your dinghy might be removed by the city. O'Leary's charges a nominal fee for dinghy dockage. At the newspaper boxes near O'Leary's, pick up a Sarasota Visitors Guide, which includes a map of Sarasota's attractions and shopping centers. They also sell block ice here.

Privately owned Bickell's Bayou is offered for transient cruiser use and is located on the north (mainland) side of the Ringling Causeway Bridge. Be sure to anchor only in the area exposed to the west and not in the rest of the basin. The access channel has a controlling depth of about 6 feet at MLW. Approach from the GIWW directly eastward towards the basin where you will find 9-foot MLW. Please leave enough space in the central channel for other boats to access the rest of the basin.

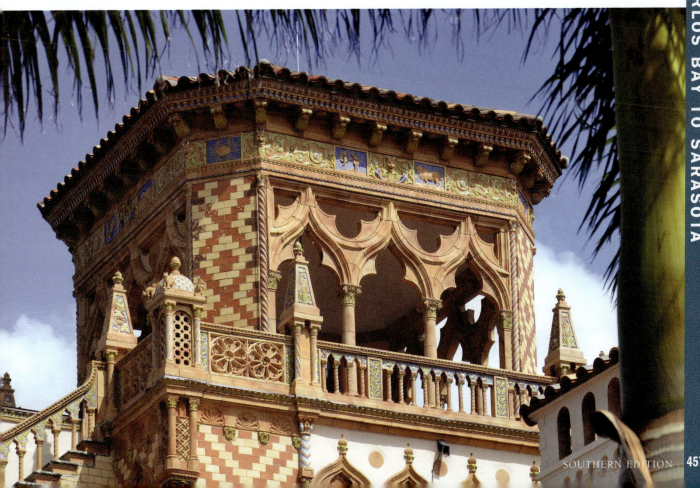

Sarasota Bay, FL

SARASOTA		Largest Vessel Accommodated	VHF Channel Monitored	Transient Berths / Total Berths	Approach / Dockside Depth (reported)	Floating Docks	Gas / Diesel	Groceries, Ice, Marine Supplies, Snacks	Repairs: Hull, Engine, Propeller	Lift (tonnage), Crane, Rail	Min/Max Amps	Laundry, Pool, Showers, Courtesy Car	Pump-Out Station	Nearby: Grocery Store, Motel, Restaurant
			Dockage				**Supplies**		**Services**				
1. Field Club	941-924-1201	-	16/68	-	5/5	-	GD	S	-	-	30/30	PS	-	GR
2. Marina Jack ▢ 🌐 onSpot 73.5	**941-955-9488 x1**	228	16/71	25/316	8/8	F	GD	IMS	HEP	-	30/100	LS	P	GMR
3. Bird Key Yacht Club ▢ WiFi	941-953-4455	50	16	call/42	12/8	-	GD	IMS	-	-	30/50	PS	P	R
4. Sarasota Yacht Club ▢ WiFi	941-365-4191	120	16/68	3/113	16/10	-	GD	IS	-	-	30/50	LPS	P	MR
5. Hyatt Regency Sarasota ▢ WiFi	941-812-4063	60	-	32/32	8/8	F	-	IS	-	-	30/50	LPS	P	GMR
6. Sarasota Sailing Squadron	941-388-2355	-	-	-	10/9	-	-	-	-	-	30/30	LS	-	MR
7. MarineMax Sarasota	941-388-4411	-	-	-	10/6	-	GD	IMS	-	L	-	-	-	R
8. Longboat Key Club Moorings onSpot WG 2.5 NW of 76	941-383-8383	145	16/08	30/287	8/20	-	GD	IMS	EP	-	30/100	LPS	P	GMR
9. The Dock on the Bay ▢ WiFi 2 SW of 80.5	941-383-3716	45	-	6/20	7/5	-	-	-	-	-	30/30	LPS	P	GMR
10. Ramada Sarasota ▢ WiFi 1.5 N of 78.5	941-358-1000	70	16	78/78	4/6	F	GD	IS	EP	-	30/50	LPS	P	GMR
11. Sara Bay Marina WiFi 1.5 N of 78.5	941-359-0390	50	16/74	20/60	4/4	F	-	IM	EP	L8	30/50	LPS	P	GMR
LONGBOAT PASS														
12. Cannons Marina 83.5	941-383-1311	-	-	-	5/5	-	G	IMS	HEP	-	-	-	-	-

▢ Internet Access WiFi Wireless Internet Access WG Waterway Guide Cruising Club Partner onSpot dockside WiFi facility

See WaterwayGuide.com for current rates, fuel prices, web site addresses, and other up-to-the-minute information. (*Information in the table is provided by the facilities.*)

LONGBOAT PASS, NOAA CHART 11425

SARASOTA, NOAA CHART 11425

GOIN' ASHORE: SARASOTA, FL

SERVICES		
1	Visitor Information	
ATTRACTIONS		
2	Florida Studio Theatre	
3	Sarasota Opera House	

4	Surrender Statue	
SHOPPING		
5	Publix	
6	Whole Foods	

DINING		
7	Marina Jack	
8	O'Leary's Tiki Bar & Grill	
MARINAS		
7	Marina Jack	

In 1929, John Ringling chose Sarasota as winter headquarters for his "Greatest Show on Earth" circus, and even though the circus has moved on, the Ringling legacy is very much alive here.

Attractions: The Ringling, formally named the John & Mable Ringling Museum of Art (5401 Bay Shore Rd., 941-359-5700), is a Renaissance-style palace that the circus king built to house his art collection. In addition to the 31 galleries of art, the Ringling includes a 66-acre bayfront garden, the Ringling's 56-room mansion (off site) and a circus museum where a large collection of circus memorabilia, from ancient Roman relics to contemporary carnival props, is on display. Next to his museum, Ringling reconstructed an 18th-century Italian theater with stones brought piece by piece from Asolo, Italy. Throughout the year, visitors can see plays and operas in the playhouse built for Queen Catherine. For additional musical/theatrical entertainment, the Florida Studio Theater (1241 N. Palm Ave., 941-366-9000)

and the Sarasota Opera House (61 N. Pineapple Ave., 941-328-1300) are to the south of Ringling and just a block apart.

Music lovers will especially enjoy Sarasota during the Sarasota Music Festival in the spring. On par with Tanglewood in the Berkshires, the festival is held annually in June and runs for two weeks. Concerts, lectures and seminars are open to the public. For program information, visit sarasotaorchestra.org/festival. Other musical events are held every weekend, as well as a jazz festival at City Island Park.

And speaking of City Island Park...Mote Marine Science Aquarium (1600 Ken Thompson Pkwy., 941-388-4441) and Save Our Seabirds, Inc. (1708 Ken Thompson Pkwy., 941-388-3010) are interesting stops there. Sarasota's efficient bus system can get you there and around town at bargain prices. On the way to City Island, you will pass Unconditional Surrender, one in a series of sculptures replicating an iconic photo taken of a sailor and nurse kissing in Times Square at the end of World War II.

For more ideas of things to see and do, visit the Sarasota County Visitor Information Center (1945 Main St., 941-706-1253).

Shopping: There is a Whole Foods (1451 1st St., 941-316-4700) not far from the marinas and a Publix (2031 Bay St., 941-366-4089) a bit farther away. There is also shopping on Main Street within just a couple of blocks of the waterfront.

Dining: Many excellent restaurants are within walking distance of the dinghy beach. Give them a try. You won't be disappointed. If you're in the mooring field, dinghy down the channel and tie up at The Old Salty Dog (1601 Ken Thompson Pkwy., 941-388-4311), a pleasant beer and burger place directly across from Mote Marine.

If you are staying in Marina Jack, you can take in their seafood spot (2 Marina Plaza, 941-365-4232) with an outdoor raw bar patio, upstairs dining room, piano bar and expansive water views. Or, take a nice stroll and visit Oleary's Tiki Bar & Grill (5 Bayfront Dr., 941-953-7505), with casual food and drinks in an open-air, tropical-themed joint on the beach.

Shallow-draft vessels should leave the deeper areas for those with deeper keels. There is no shore access here; please do not trespass on private land.

Dinghy access is available at the Ringling Bridge Causeway Park or the public boat ramp at 10th St. to the north of the anchorage. There is a free pump-out facility at Marina Jack's fuel dock. Do not trespass on the adjacent condominium properties. Anchor light regulations will be enforced after dark.

Other anchorages are between Otter and Lido Key (at least 6 feet at MLW with good holding in sand and mud with all-around protection), and also in the cove to port coming into New Pass from the Gulf, before the New Pass Bridge. Anchor by green daybeacon "9" here in 6 to 9 feet at MLW with excellent holding in sand and mud.

Closer to the north end of Longboat Key at Mile 78.4 there is an anchorage west of green daybeacon "15" where you will find 7 to 11 feet at MLW with good holding in sand and mud. Just before red daybeacon "40" to the north, a good anchorage in 13-foot MLW depths lies behind the tip of Longboat Key just off Longbeach.

The Mar Vista Dockside Restaurant (941-383-2391) is within dinghy range of this anchorage with good food and patio seating. You can also take your dinghy across the Longboat Pass Inlet, secure it to the dock next to the city boat ramp and catch a free trolley into Bradenton Beach. Here, you will find the laid-back old Florida feel, with shopping, shoreside restaurants and beaches. You can reach the Whitney Beach Plaza by taking the dinghy almost all the way down Bishop Bayou and tying up to the cement wall on the left side. The plaza offers a grocery, liquor store, Post Office and the Bayou Tavern (941-312-4975) with pizza, pasta and typical Italian entrées, plus views of the canal.

■ NEXT STOP

Continuing north, cruisers next encounter Anna Maria Island and the popular Tampa-St. Petersburg area. Beyond that Clearwater and its famous resort beaches beckon.

Marinas **Services** **Anchorages** **Bridges & Locks** **Nav Alerts** **Fuel**

6 Waterway Explorer provides different icons that overlay on the maps as modes

Modes

Info Pane with details

Plan your time on the water with Explorer

www.waterwayguide.com

Tampa Bay Area to Tarpon Springs

GIWW Mile 88–Mile 150   **VHF** FL Bridges: Channel 09

CHARTS NOAA 11411, 11415, 11416, 11425

One of the great natural harbors of the world, Tampa Bay extends about 25 miles north to south and about 10 miles east to west. It has two important cities (Tampa and St. Petersburg) and several large rivers that meander in from the east and north. Fringing the west side of the coast and extending northward is a pencil-thin chain of barrier islands with resort communities famous for their Gulf beaches.

The GIWW then runs from Tampa Bay to Anclote Key, via Boca Ciega Bay, at the mouth of the Anclote River leading to Tarpon Springs. Tarpon Springs on the Anclote River marks the end of the Florida GIWW at Mile 150. (The GIWW picks back up in Carrabelle, FL, where mileages are measured east and west of Harvey Lock, LA, notated as EHL or WHL.)

■ TAMPA BAY AREA

Tampa Bay comprises three vast bodies of water– Tampa Bay proper, Old Tampa Bay to the northeast and Hillsborough Bay to the northwest–providing excellent cruising. Lower Tampa Bay opens to the Gulf of Mexico, but enjoys the protection of barrier islands. Old Tampa Bay reaches northwest from Tampa Bay to the shoal water around Safety Harbor and Mobbly Bay. Hillsborough Bay branches off to the northeast between Interbay Peninsula and the mainland, to serve the city of Tampa, Ybor City and Davis Islands, with their extensive shipping and industrial areas.

From the open mouth of Tampa Bay, St. Petersburg lies due north, with metropolitan Tampa to the northeast. Each dominates one of the two big peninsulas that pierce the bay.

Pinellas, to the west, extends about 45 miles from the southern edge of St. Petersburg almost to Tarpon Springs. MacDill Air Force Base occupies the southern tip of Interbay, the second peninsula (about 3 miles wide and 10 miles long).

For the cruising skipper, Tampa Bay is a welcome change from the confines of the GIWW. Here, there are

If you are entering Tampa Bay from outside the U.S., the St. Pete/Clearwater International Airport (727-536-7311) is a **Port of Entry.** There is also one in nearby Tampa. Additionally, you can also use the U.S. Customs Local Boater Option and clear with a phone call (cbp. gov). For more information on Customs procedures, consult the Skipper's Handbook at the front of this guide.

Anna Maria Sound, FL

	Dockage					Supplies		Services				
Largest Vessel Accommodated	VHF Channel Monitored	Approach / Dockside Depth (reported)	Transient Berths / Total Berths	Floating Docks	Gas / Diesel	Groceries, Ice, Marine Supplies, Snacks	Repairs: Hull, Engine, Propeller	Lift (tonnage), Crane, Rail	Min/Max Amps	Laundry, Pool, Showers, Courtesy Car	Pump-Out Station	Nearby: Grocery Store, Motel, Restaurant

BRADENTON BEACH AREA

				Dockage				Supplies		Services						
1. Yacht Solutions @ Cortez Cove Marina WiFi	941-761-4554	70	–	call/35	7/7	–	–	M	HEP	L65	30/50	S	–	GMR
2. Bradenton Beach Marina 🖳 WiFi 87.2	941-778-2288	65	16/07	15/40	6/4	–	GD	GIM	HEP	L77	30/50	LS	P	GMR
3. Seafood Shack Marina, Bar & Grill 🖳 WiFi 87.4	941-807-1801	120	16/68	62/68	14/12	–	–	I	–	–	30/50	S	–	R
4. Cove Sound Moorings onSpot	941-795-4852	50	09	call/57	–	–	–	–	–	–	30/30	S	–	R

ANNA MARIA ISLAND

				Dockage				Supplies		Services						
5. Waterline Marina Resort & Beach Club, Autograph Collection 🖳 WiFi	888-849-2642	30	16/69	19/50	5/4	–	–	IS	–	–	30/50	LP	–	GMR
6. Galati Yacht Basin WiFi 1 W of 91.8	941-778-0755	105	16/68	12/60	7/7	F	GD	IMS	HEP	L75	50/50	LS	P	GMR

🖳 Internet Access WiFi Wireless Internet Access WG Waterway Guide Cruising Club Partner onSpot dockside WiFi facility

See WaterwayGuide.com for current rates, fuel prices, web site addresses, and other up-to-the-minute information. *(Information in the table is provided by the facilities.)*

BRADENTON BEACH AREA, ANNA MARIA ISLAND, NOAA CHART 11425

some 300 square miles of cruising waters, Gulf fishing, interesting ports, pleasant anchorages, good yacht facilities and superb sailing.

NAVIGATION: Use NOAA Charts 11425 and 11415. Traveling north from Sarasota Bay, there is no "quick" route north by going out into the Gulf of Mexico at Longboat Pass. Just stay on the inside. Even with a couple of bascule bridges that will have to open, you will save time and fuel. The inside route will bring you out in Tampa Bay at red daybeacon "68." Anna Maria Island is the barrier island that has been to the west since Longboat Pass.

Two bascule bridges cross the GIWW on this stretch before reaching Tampa Bay: the **Cortez (SR 684) Bridge** (Mile 87.4, 22-foot closed vertical clearance) and the **Anna Maria Island (Manatee Ave. West) Bridge** (Mile 89.2, 24-foot closed vertical clearance). Both open on signal, except from 6:00 a.m. to 7:00 p.m. daily, when the draw need only open on the quarter hour and three quarter hour.

After crossing The Bulkhead at red daybeacon "68, the mariner faces about 4.5 miles of open water across lower Tampa Bay to the continuation of the GIWW on the north side of the bay after crossing the main shipping channel. Commercial shipping traffic has the right-of-way, so be careful. Accidents (big ones) can and have happened here. With its long fetch, this stretch can kick up an uncomfortable chop. Flashing red buoy "70," near Mile 95, is a useful checkpoint on this open-water run.

On clear days, the high-level **Sunshine Skyway Bridge**, the span of which forms a 15-mile-long highway across lower Tampa Bay, is clearly visible from The Bulkhead. The span is 425 feet high at the top of the two cable towers. At a charted fixed vertical clearance of 175 feet at the center, it has 25 more feet of vertical clearance than the old bridge and is located 1,000 feet farther east. Small manmade islands (called dolphins) flank the 12 columns that support the Sunshine Skyway Bridge nearest the shipping channel. Their function is to deflect ships that might wander out of the channel. Half of the old southbound span, damaged when struck in 1980, remains on both sides as fishing piers.

Anna Maria Island–GIWW Mile 88

Lovely Anna Maria Island is noted for its white sandy beaches, good tarpon fishing and premium restaurants. Just north of Longboat Key, which is separated by **Longboat Pass (SR 789) Bascule Bridge**, the island lies between Sarasota Bay on the south, Anna Maria Sound (separating the island from the mainland at the towns of Cortez and Bradenton) and Tampa Bay on the north. Cruisers can reach Tampa Bay and points north either directly from the Gulf of Mexico or via the inside GIWW route from Sarasota Bay.

NAVIGATION: Use NOAA Chart 11425. The GIWW channel cuts through shoals in much of Anna Maria Sound and at red daybeacon "52," starts swinging toward Perico Island just south of the Anna Maria Bridge. A back range at Mile 90 helps you stay in the center of the channel until you reach the sand bar charted as "The Bulkhead," which is marked by flashing red "64" at Mile 92. After leaving red daybeacon "68," the water is deep, and you can head into Tampa Bay, go up the Manatee River to the east, or turn due west for about one-half mile to pick up green daybeacon "1." Head into the channel through Key Royale Bar to Bimini Bay on Anna Maria Island.

Dockage: South of the Cortez Bridge, on the mainland side of the west coast ICW at Mile 87 is Yacht Solutions @ Cortez Cove Marina, which has a lift and offer repairs. (Call ahead for slip availability.) To the west of the ICW on the south side of the Cortez Bridge is the Bradenton Beach Marina, which offers repairs (77-ton lift)and permits do-it-yourself work, sells fuel and has transient slips.

Shortly after flashing red "48" and the Cortez Bridge, on the eastern shore is the Seafood Shack Marina, Bar & Grill, a popular waterfront restaurant and marina with transient slips (for short-term stays of one to two nights). The helpful dockmaster answers on VHF Channel 16. A supermarket (941-795-4638) is several miles to the east at 75th St.

Also on the mainland side is Cove Sound Moorings, a facility geared more towards longer-term (one month or more) stays. Cortez Market, within walking distance, is just up the road, along with a Post Office and laundry. Several fish markets are located near the Cortez Coast Guard Station.

Waterline Marina Resort & Beach Club on Anna Maria Island is a modern resort with "old Florida authenticity." Boaters can enjoy resort amenities including laundry facilities, a resort-style pool and restrooms for a daily fee. Eliza Ann's Coastal Kitchen (941-238-6264) is on site serving breakfast, luch and dinner plus brunch on Saturday and Sunday and a daily happy hour.

To the northwest on Anna Maria Island, Galati Yacht Basin, located in Bimini Bay, offers slips and services, including fuel (both gas and diesel) and a ship store with an excellent parts department.

If you are coming in for the first time, it is easy to get confused by the marina markers. To enter the basin, go out of Anna Maria Sound northbound past quick flashing green "67," hang a sharp left heading west for a little more than a one-half mile to flashing green "1," and on your left you will see the markers to Bimini Bay, which are privately maintained. The Beachhouse Restaurant (941-779-2222) is at the southern end of Anna Maria Island and offers Gulf-front dining.

Anchorage: It is possible to anchor on the west side of the Cortez Bridge in 4 to 8 feet at MLW. Stay out of the channel.

Side Trip: Egmont Key–GIWW Mile 95

Square in the middle of the entrance to Tampa Bay at Mile 95 lies Egmont Key, 3 miles off the tip of Anna Maria Island. The island is a bird sanctuary, and you will also see a lot of gopher tortoises, which are on the endangered species list. Unfettered wandering is discouraged.

Anchorage: Egmont Key is a popular daytime anchorage that gets crowded on the weekends in the summer. You can anchor close to shore on the southeast end of the island and dinghy in. As an overnight anchorage, the waters on the east side off Egmont may be uncomfortable when an evening breeze kicks in and creates a lee shore. The bottom is hard sand with good holding.

City of Bradenton

The Manatee River's main city, Bradenton, is a popular layover port for those who want to explore the river and other waters. The protected marina basin has good depths and includes slips for liveaboards and weekenders alike.

NAVIGATION: Use NOAA Charts 11415 and 11425. Use the St. Petersburg Tide Tables. For high tide, subtract 1 hour 24 minutes; for low tide, subtract 55 minutes. From the exit at The Bulkhead in Anna Maria Sound, a sharp turn to the east, around red daybeacon "68," leads to the mouth of the lovely Manatee River, one of Tampa Bay's finest cruising and gunkholing areas. The almost-tropical Manatee River has a well-marked, deep channel (8-foot MLW depths), interesting side streams to explore by dinghy and friendly towns to visit. The entrance channel threads through shoals, but a series of ranges are strategically placed to keep the mariner from finding those shoals.

If you plan to enter the Manatee River, head for flashing red "2" northeast of The Bulkhead. When traveling in from the north, be aware of the shoal that is north of quick-flashing red "4," stay close to the buoy but inside the channel. Follow the markers closely until you are past DeSoto Point, marked by flashing red "12," where there is ample water. Continuing up the river, be aware of flashing red "14" and green daybeacon "15," as there are shoals growing in and around the markers. Give them a wide berth.

At Bradenton, three bridges cross the Manatee River within 1 mile of each other. The first (**Hwy. 41 Bridge**) has 41-foot fixed vertical clearance (known locally as the **Green Bridge**; the second (CSX Railroad Bridge) is untended and usually open (5-foot closed vertical clearance); and the third (**Hernando DeSoto Bridge**) has 40-foot fixed vertical clearance. The upper Manatee River, east of these three bridges, offers some cruising options and holds depths of 10 feet at MLW or better to the **I-75 Bridge** at Ellenton (40-foot fixed vertical clearance). After that, depths shallow considerably and venturing farther is not recommended. Two nautical miles beyond the last of the bridges, the Braden River opens to the south. A lush and scenic stream with plenty of wildlife, it is unmarked and full of shoals, but nonetheless offers some fine gunkholing by dinghy. Slim water and a fixed bridge with 10-foot vertical clearance limit exploration on bigger boats.

Dockage: Snead Island Boat Works Inc., located on the north bank of the river, opposite red flashing "14," is locally renowned for their repair service. At the Bradenton Yacht Club, east of McKay Point (northeast of red daybeacon "14") membership in a reciprocal yacht club is required.

Between Snead Island and Palmetto, a land cut beside the Bradenton Yacht Club leads into Terra Ceia Bay. This channel has depths of about 5 feet at MLW and a fixed bridge with a 13-foot vertical clearance. It leads to Marlow Marine Sales, Inc., Cut's Edge Harbor Marina and Tropic Isles Marina. Repairs and gas (no diesel) are available, however, they cater to small boats only due to the depth and height restrictions.

Conveniently located on the Manatee River, west of the Hwy. 41 Bridge, is the well-equipped and well-appointed Regatta Pointe Marina, which accommodates transient guests and sells all fuels.

Directly across the river, Twin Dolphin Marina is close to downtown Bradenton attractions and offers transient dockage at floating docks. The marina is at green daybeacon "21" and red daybeacon "22." Twin Dolphin Marina has a single-opening entrance configuration through its breakwaters; sound your horn going in or coming out. From red daybeacon "22" to daybeacon "41," there is an Idle-Speed/No-Wake Zone between the channel and the south shoreline. If you are staying at the marina, a must-stop is at the Pier 22 restaurant (1200 1st St., 941-748-8087), which features jumbo lobster tails along with many other menu choices. The upscale menu is balanced by the Florida-casual atmosphere.

Farther east, after the three bridges, on the south side of the Manatee River, is Tarpon Pointe Marina, which may have slips, sells gas and diesel and offers repairs.

On the opposite (north) shore is the full-service and lively Riviera Dunes Marina offering resort amenities, including two heated pools, on-site laundry facilities, pump-out service at slip or at fuel dock and individual bathrooms with showers. The on-site Blu Mangrove Grill (941-479-7827) is popular for its wide selection of seafood and smoked American BBQ menu choices. Riverfront dining with outdoor seating and live music make this a worthwhile stop. On 7th St., you will find a supermarket and pharmacy and a bank with an ATM.

Anchorage: Follow the channel past flashing red "12," then turn west into the cove behind DeSoto Point, being mindful of the charted shoal in the center of the cove (called "holy hole" due to the three crosses on shore). You can land your dinghy to visit the DeSoto National Memorial (nps.gov/deso.) DeSoto Point offers a good anchorage, regardless of the shoal. There is still plenty of room for several boats to anchor. It is protected except from the east and carries 9 to 10 feet at MLW. There is a second anchorage across the river at McKay Point, which is located east of Snead Island Boat Works. Depths range from 6 to 9 feet at MLW, but protection is good only from north winds.

Farther upriver, boats anchor just west of the bridge on either the Bradenton (near red daybeacon "22") or Palmetto (east of red daybeacon "18") side with good holding in mud in a least 7 feet at MLW.

Little Manatee River/Apollo Beach

NAVIGATION: Use NOAA Chart 11416.

Dockage: Located on the eastern side of Tampa Bay (north of the Little Manatee River) the Village Marina at Little Harbor offers dockage with full amenities and multiple restaurants. Antigua Cove at Little Harbor Marina has transient slips, sells all fuels and offers repairs, and to the south, near the mouth of the Manatee River, Shell Point Marina may have space and sells gas; call ahead.

DeSoto National Park

Manatee River, FL

WG

PALMETTO AREA		Largest Vessel Accommodated	VHF Channel Monitored	Dockage				Supplies				Services			
				Transient Berths / Total Berths	Approach / Dockside Depth (reported)	Floating Docks	Gas / Diesel	Groceries, Ice, Marine Supplies, Snacks	Repairs: Hull, Engine, Propeller	Lift (tonnage), Crane, Rail	Min/Max Amps	Laundry, Pool, Showers, Courtesy Car	Pump-Out Station	Nearby: Grocery Store, Motel, Restaurant
1. Snead Island Boat Works Inc.	941-722-2400	65	–	8/75	8/8	–	–	M	HEP	L70	30/50	S	–	–
2. Bradenton Yacht Club (WiFi)	941-722-5936	185	16/68	8/52	–	–	GD	IS	–	–	30/50	PS	P	R
3. Marlow Marine Sales, Inc.	941-729-3370	97	–	–	5/5	–	–	M	HEP	L	–	–	–	R
4. Cut's Edge Harbor Marina	941-729-4878	60	–	call/36	–	–	–	M	HEP	L40	30/30	–	–	–
5. Tropic Isles Marina	941-729-8128	40	–	call/15	10/9	F	G	IMS	–	–	30/30	–	–	GR
6. Regatta Pointe Marina 💻 WiFi WG	941-729-6021	120	16/71	75/350	10/10	–	GD	IMS	–	–	30/100	LPS	P	GMR
7. Twin Dolphin Marina 💻 WiFi WG	941-747-8300	80	16/72	25/225	12/9	F	GD	GI	–	–	30/50	LPS	P	GMR
8. Tarpon Pointe Marina	941-745-1199	38	–	–	13/5	–	GD	M	HEP	L9	–	–	–	–
9. Riviera Dunes Marina 💻 onSpot WG	**941-981-5330**	120	16/68	10/218	9/18	F	GD	I	–	–	30/100	LPS	P	GMR

💻 Internet Access WiFi Wireless Internet Access WG Waterway Guide Cruising Club Partner onSpot dockside WiFi facility

See WaterwayGuide.com for current rates, fuel prices, web site addresses, and other up-to-the-minute information. *(Information in the table is provided by the facilities.)*

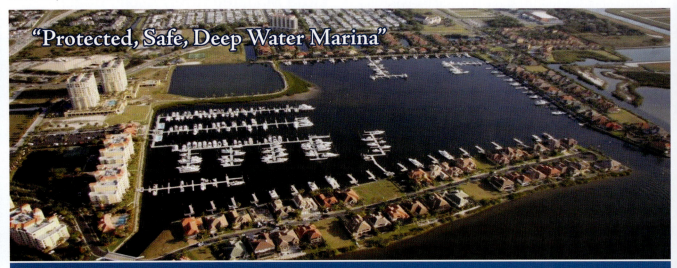

"Protected, Safe, Deep Water Marina"

Downtown Tampa

PALMETTO AREA, NOAA CHART 11415

MANATEE RIVER EXTENSION
SCALE 1:40,000

MANATEE RIVER
The controlling depths through dredged channels were:
8 feet from entrance to McNeil Point (MID 50 FT)
4 feet to Rocky Bluff (MID 50 FT)
½ foot to Rye (Centerline)   Dec 1994

PALMETTO AREA, NOAA CHART 11415

Hillsboro Bay, Tampa Bay, FL

		Largest Vessel Accommodated	VHF Channel Monitored	Transient Berths / Total Berths	Approach / Dockside Depth (reported)	Floating Docks	Gas / Diesel	Groceries, Ice, Marine Supplies, Snacks	Repairs: Hull, Engine, Propeller	Lift (tonnage), Crane, Rail	Min/Max Amps	Pump-Out Station	Laundry, Pool, Showers, Courtesy Car	Nearby: Grocery Store, Motel, Restaurant
LITTLE MANATEE RIVER				**Dockage**			**Supplies**		**Services**					
1. Village Marina at Little Harbor 🖳	813-645-2288	65	16/72	10/112	6/10	–	–	IMS	–	–	30/50	LPS	–	MR
2. Antiqua Cove at Little Harbor 🖳 WiFi	813-645-2288	75	16/72	5/105	8/10	F	GD	IMS	–	–	30/50	PS	–	MR
3. Shell Point Marina 🖳 WiFi	813-645-1313	60	–	2/40	6/9	–	G	–	HEP	L35	30/30	S	P	–
APOLLO BEACH														
4. Lands End Marina WiFi	813-645-5594	100	–	call/105	10/10	–	GD	IM	HEP	L5	30/50	LS	P	R
5. Appollo Beach Marina	813-645-0720	–	–	call/12	8/5	–	–	–	–	L	30/30	S	–	R
TAMPA AREA														
6. Tampa Yacht & Country Club – PRIVATE	813-831-1611	65	68	5/81	10/4	F	GD	GIMS	–	–	30/50	PS	–	GMR
7. Davis Island Yacht Club – PRIVATE	813-251-1158	55	–	call/114	10/8	F	–	IMS	–	R	30/30	PS	–	R
8. Marjorie Park Yacht Basin	813-259-1604	90	16	19/51	21/9	F	GD	GIMS	–	–	50/50	LPS	P	GR
9. The Westin Tampa Harbour Island 🖳 WiFi	813-229-5000	60	–	2/2	/6	–	–	IS	–	–	30/50	LPS	–	MR
10. Tampa Convention Center Transient Docks 🖳 WiFi	813-402-9352	160	16/68	27/27	19/19	F	–	IS	–	–	30/50	–	–	GMR
11. Marriott Tampa Waterside Hotel & Marina 🖳 WiFi	813-314-1006	60	16/72	12/32	19/19	F	–	IS	–	–	30/50	LPS	–	GMR

🖳 Internet Access   WiFi Wireless Internet Access   WG Waterway Guide Cruising Club Partner   onSpot dockside WiFi facility

See WaterwayGuide.com for current rates, fuel prices, web site addresses, and other up-to-the-minute information. *(Information in the table is provided by the facilities.)*

RUSKIN AREA, NOAA CHART 11416

APOLLO BEACH, NOAA CHART 11416

TAMPA AREA, NOAA CHART 11416

Lands End Marina at Apollo Beach is approached on a southeasterly course from the Cut "C" Channel range light. They have gas and diesel, some transient slips and a restaurant on site. Apollo Beach Marina is approached from the north via the Big Bend Channel. This facility is usually full with long-term rentals so be sure to call first for transient availability.

Anchorage: There is no room for anchoring in these tight harbors; its best to take a slip here or continue north to Boca Ciega Bay if you must anchor out.

City of Tampa

NAVIGATION: Use NOAA Chart 11415 and 11416. Use the St. Petersburg Tide Tables. For high tide at Davis Island, add 3 minutes; for low tide, add 32 minutes. To get to Tampa from The Bulkhead, at the exit of Anna Maria Sound, set a course of 022 degrees magnetic for flashing red buoy "70" well out in Tampa Bay at GIWW Mile 95. Continue on the same heading until you pick up quick-flashing red buoy "26" at Mullet Key Channel, the big-ship route up Tampa Bay. Go under the center spans of the Sunshine Skyway Bridge, and you may follow the big-ship channel the 20 to 25 miles all the way northeast to the City of Tampa.

Dockage: At the end of Davis Islands in Hillsborough Bay to the north is a park that offers a small beach area, off-leash area for dogs, picnic area, canoe launch and boat ramps. Davis Islands Park is adjacent to the Davis Island Yacht Club (private, no transients) and Davis Island Seaplane Basin. Tampa Yacht & Country Club across Hillsboro Bay at Ballast Point is also private.

Old Tampa Bay, FL

PORT TAMPA AREA		Largest Vessel Accommodated	VHF Channel Monitored	Transient Berths / Total Berths	Approach / Dockside Depth (reported)	Floating Docks	Dockage		Supplies		Services			
							Gas / Diesel	Groceries, Ice, Marine Supplies, Snacks	Repairs: Hull, Engine, Propeller	Lift (tonnage), Crane, Rail	Min/Max Amps	Nearby: Grocery Store, Motel, Restaurant	Pump-Out Station	Laundry, Pool, Showers, Courtesy Car
1. Florida Marina Clubs – Tampa Harbour (WiFi)	813-831-1200	80	16	call/48	25/12	F	GD	IMS	HEP	L15	30/50	L	P	GMR
2. Westshore Yacht Club (☐)	813-805-6871	150	16/71	call/149	25/8	F	–	IS	–	–	30/100	PS	P	GMR

☐ Internet Access (WiFi) Wireless Internet Access WG Waterway Guide Cruising Club Partner ☁onSpot dockside WiFi facility
See WaterwayGuide.com for current rates, fuel prices, web site addresses, and other up-to-the-minute information. *(Information in the table is provided by the facilities.)*

PORT TAMPA AREA, NOAA CHART 11416

Nearly all of the dockage at Harbour Island, which is in downtown Tampa, is private. A few restaurants are located in the Harbor Island complex and at the hotel. Marjorie Park Yacht Basin, on the channel between Harbor and Davis Islands is a full-service facility, with slips, all fuels and easy access to mass transit. The Westin Tampa Harbour Island has limited transient space, while the Tampa Convention Center Transient Docks has 27 reserved transient slips but no shore power or water. This facility is very convenient to the sights, sounds and activities of Downtown Tampa and Ybor City. Tampa Marriott Waterside Hotel & Marina may have transient slips on their floating docks, but call well in advance to check availability.

Old Tampa Bay

NAVIGATION: Use NOAA Chart 11416. On the opposite side of Interbay Peninsula from the City of Tampa is Old Tampa Bay, which is crossed by three bridges.

Dockage: Just south of the fixed **Gandy Twin Bridges** (43-foot vertical clearance) is Florida Marina Clubs–Tampa Harbor with slips and some repairs. To the south, on the same side (east), is Westshore Yacht Club, part of a condominium complex that has transient slips on floating docks for vessels up to 150 feet. Guests have access to the waterfront Bay Club with a spa, fitness center, tropical pool deck, tiki bar and ship store.

City of St. Petersburg

Facilities of one kind or another line all sides of the peninsula in St. Petersburg (often called St. Pete by locals). Boaters heading up Tampa Bay reach those at the south end first, but there are also facilities downtown on the east side of the peninsula and in Boca Ciega Bay on the west side.

NAVIGATION: Use NOAA Charts 11411, 11415 and 11416. Use St. Petersburg Tide Tables. Two routes, both clearly marked on Chart 11416, lead from Anna Maria Sound to St. Petersburg. Starting from The Bulkhead, as you would if going to Tampa, set a course of 022 degrees magnetic for flashing red "70" well out in Tampa Bay at Mile 95. Continue on the same heading until you pick up quick-flashing red buoy "26" at Mullet Key Channel, the big-ship route up Tampa Bay.

The Coast Guard is proposing to change the location of the Mullet Key Range Front Light. Refer to the Waterway Explorer and NOAA online charts for the most up-to-date information on where that light is located.

St. Petersburg is located on a peninsula, so water is everywhere, but unfortunately for boaters, much of it isn't very deep. Watching your charts is critical to avoid the shoals, which are often difficult to see. Unless you know the waters, stay in the well-marked channels to avoid bumping the sandy bottom. Also, keep an eye out for large ships heading to the ports of Manatee and Tampa.

The western approach to St. Petersburg begins with flashing green "1," north of quick-flashing green gong buoy "25" for Mullet Key Channel and before the enormous bridge. Channel depths were 6 feet at MLW nearly 10 years ago, but 5-foot MLW depths have been seen more recently.

The deeper route follows Mullet Key Channel eastward through the **Sunshine Skyway Bridge** (180-foot vertical clearance). The proper channel north takes off at flashing green buoy "3B," with a bearing of about 5 degrees magnetic. After leaving a 27-foot-high quick-flashing red to the east, you should pick up the twin, 16-foot-high flashing green "1" and flashing green "2." At quick-flashing green "3," turn west to flashing green "1" and take the channel under the 65-foot fixed vertical clearance bridge, known locally as the **Meisner Bridge**, and until it converges with the northbound channel to St. Petersburg at red daybeacon "14." In case you haven't guessed, this is a great place

for a good set of binoculars for sorting out the different channels' markers.

Be advised that if you are trying to avoid easterly winds out in Tampa Bay, you will have them right on your nose from green daybeacon "13A." It is several miles to the northbound channel.

If you are coming up the channel to St. Pete from Tampa Bay, you can get into Bayboro Harbor at flashing green "S." Coast Guard ships and cruise ships come in here, so the water is deep.

Dockage: The Renaissance Vinoy Resort Marina, near the big pink historic Vinoy Hotel, is a Marriott property offering resort amenities and deep water slips. The large (650-slip) St. Petersburg Municipal Marina in downtown St. Petersburg offers transient facilities with all amenities, including gas and diesel. Nearby is the St. Petersburg Yacht Club, where membership in a reciprocal yacht club is required.

The 340-slip Harborage Marina at Bayboro is around the bend from downtown but close to a trolley stop so you can get around if needed. The marina offers all fuels and slips. To the south, at the end of the entrance channel, are Sailor's Wharf Yacht Yard and Embree Marine. Both of these are strictly repair facilities (no transient slips). There might be limited space available at nearby Salt Creek Marina, but call in advance.

Moorings: Anchoring in the north basin, which is known as Vinoy Basin, has been eliminated. There are 13 moorings, which are managed by the St. Petersburg Municipal Marina (727-893-7927), in 14 to 16 feet at MLW. You should call ahead of your arrival to make sure that a mooring will be available. There is a handy dinghy dock nearby and great access to the city.

■ BOCA CIEGA BAY

NAVIGATION: Use NOAA Chart 11411. The GIWW runs from Tampa Bay to Anclote Key, at the mouth of the Anclote River leading to Tarpon Springs, through well-marked Boca Ciega Bay.

There are six bridges in the Pinellas Bayway Span Bridge system with only two of them coming into play with the GIWW. **Pinellas Bayway "C" Span** is a 65-foot fixed bridge, but **Pinellas Bayway "E" Bascule Bridge** has a 25-foot vertical clearance and a restricted schedule. There are plans for a new 65-foot vertical clearance fixed bridge to be completed

GOIN' ASHORE: ST. PETERSBURG, FL

SERVICES		
SERVICES		
1	Visitor Information	
ATTRACTIONS		
2	American Stage Theatre Company	
3	Mahaffey Theater	
4	Museum of Fine Arts	
5	Palladium Theater	
6	Salvador Dali Museum	

7	Saint Petersburg Museum of History
SHOPPING	
8	Al Lang Stadium (farmers market)
9	Publix
DINING	
10	400 Beach Seafood & Tap House
11	Fresco's Waterfront Bistro

12	The Mill Restaurant
MARINAS	
13	Renaissance Vinoy Resort Marina
14	St. Petersburg Municipal Marina
15	St. Petersburg Yacht Club

Dubbed the "Sunshine City" because of its climate and great weather, St. Petersburg also boasts an exciting arts and food scene, professional sporting events and a serious nightlife for those who aren't boating to run away from such things. Not only does St. Pete have the largest public waterfront park system of any U.S. city, it's also an easy city to negotiate by foot or public transportation.

Attractions: The downtown "Looper" trolley (727-821-5166) stops at many of the tourist spots and downtown locations, every 15 minutes, and carries only a nominal charge. The public bus service, PSTA (727-540-1800), can get you around the rest of the city and most lines run downtown near Williams Park.

Hopefully, you will be ready to get off the boat and enjoy some of the area's entertainment venues. You won't be at a loss for things to do. There are year-round plays at American Stage Theater Company (3rd St. N., 727-823-7529) and performing arts concerts by the symphony and traveling Broadway plays at the Mahaffey Theater (400 1st St. S., 727-892-5767). The Museum of Fine Arts (255 Beach Dr. N.E., 727-896-2667) exhibits antiquities and modern art and the Saint Petersburg Museum of History (335 2nd Ave. N.E., 727-894-1052) is nearby. The grand Palladium Theater (253 5th Ave. N., 727-822-3590) in a circa-1925 former church. This performing arts center hosts plays and films.

Perhaps the most well-known museum in the area is the Salvador Dali Museum (1 Dali Blvd., 727-823-3767), where a large collection of the artist's works can be seen, comprising paintings, sculpture, holograms and art glass. The collection spans Salvador Dali's entire career (1904-1989) and is the largest collection of the artist's works outside of Europe. The hulking modern concrete building itself is a work of art, as are the fantastical gardens around back, compete with a hedge maze and melting clock benches. There is also a museum shop and a café .

Another well-known and respected modern artist has his permanent collection in St. Pete. The Morean Arts Center is home to the Chihuly Collection (720 Central Ave., 727-896-4527) and has glass works commissioned specifically for this location as well as pieces collected from elsewhere.

The famous St. Petersburg Pier has been completely rebuilt and the ribbon-cutting was planned for early 2019. To find out whether it opened on schedule, check newstpetepier.com.

Shopping: Great boat provisioning can be had at a weekly Saturday farmers market in the Al Lang Stadium parking lot (100 1st Ave. S.) from October through May from 9:00 a.m. to 2:00 p.m. The Trolley stops 1.5 blocks north.

A Publix grocery store (250 3rd St. S., 727-822-1125) is about one-half mile from the Municipal Marina. Transportation will be necessary to reach the closest West Marine (2010 Tyrone Blvd. N., 727-342-8001).

Dining: The Mill Restaurant (200 Central Ave. #100, 727-317-3930) offers an innovative menu with a Southern spin. The popular 400 Beach Seafood & Tap House (400 Beach Dr. N.E., 727-896-2400) offers indoor or outdoor dining, lunch and dinner daily, plus an early bird special (3:00 p.m. to 6:00 p.m.), a Sunday brunch buffet and extensive liquor, beer and wine options.

Fresco's Waterfront Bistro (300 2nd Ave. N.E., 727-894-4429) is a laid-back spot at the foot of the pier with pastas, burgers, seafood entrées, and bay views.

As in all larger cities, there are many dining options–many more than we could list here–both indoors or at sidewalk cafés . See visitstpeteclearwater.com for suggestions.

Tampa Bay, FL

ST. PETERSBURG AREA		Largest Vessel Accommodated	VHF Channel Monitored	Transient Berths / Total Berths	Approach / Dockside Depth (reported)	Floating Docks	Gas / Diesel	Groceries, Ice, Marine Supplies, Snacks	Repairs: Hull, Engine, Propeller	Lift (tonnage), Crane, Rail	Min/Max Amps	Laundry, Pool, Showers, Courtesy Car	Pump-Out Station	Nearby: Grocery Store, Motel, Restaurant
				Dockage				Supplies		Services				
1. Renaissance Vinoy Resort Marina 🖥 📶	727-824-8022	130	16/68	22/74	12/12	–	–	IS	–	–	30/100	LPS	P	GMR
2. St. Petersburg Municipal Marina 🖥	727-893-7329	125	16/68	call/650	12/12	–	GD	IMS	–	–	30/100	LS	P	GR
3. St. Petersburg Yacht Club 📶	727-822-3227	150	16/69	13/80	10/14	–	GD	I	–	–	30/100	LPS	P	MR
4. Harborage Marina at Bayboro 🖥 📶	727-821-6347	200	16/68	15/340	24/12	F	GD	IS	–	–	30/200+	LPS	P	GMR
5. Sailor's Wharf Yacht Yard 🖥 WG	727-823-1155	80	–	1/23	10/9	F	–	M	HEP	L75,C2	30/50	S	–	GMR
6. Embree Marine	727-896-0671	70	–	–	7/7	–	–	M	HEP	L55	30/50	S	–	GMR
7. Salt Creek Marina 🖥 📶	727-895-4481	72	–	call/12	10/9	–	–	M	HEP	L50	30/50	S	–	GMR

🖥 Internet Access 📶 Wireless Internet Access WG Waterway Guide Cruising Club Partner ⬤ onSpot dockside WiFi facility

See WaterwayGuide.com for current rates, fuel prices, web site addresses, and other up-to-the-minute information. *(Information in the table is provided by the facilities.)*

ST. PETERSBURG, CHART 11416

in 2021. Be aware that there could be some activity in the area related to this construction. Check the *Local Notice to Mariners*.

The Pinellas Bayway "E" span opens on signal, except from 9:00 a.m. to 7:00 p.m., when it need only open on the hour and half-hour. Call ahead on your VHF radio to get the latest information. (Call "Structure Echo," so there will be no confusion about which one you are calling.) For more information, see the Bridges & Locks section at the front of this guide.

Two routes reach boating facilities on the west side of the Pinellas Peninsula. Those who can clear **Pinellas Bayway "A" Span** (with 18-foot fixed vertical clearance) can use the shortcut past Cats Point off the straight-line extension of the Sunshine Skyway Channel. Otherwise, follow the GIWW channel through the Pinellas Bayway Spans "E" and "C." At the northern end of the GIWW, approaching Clearwater, the waterway tends to narrow and bridges and shoaling become more frequent. Boats with significant draft should be very cautious.

Passes to the Gulf

From Tampa Bay to Clearwater, any one of three inlets affords easy access from the GIWW to and from the Gulf of Mexico (in good weather and daylight):

- **North Channel** (just north of Tampa Bay): Well marked and leads from the Gulf to Pass-a-Grille Channel.
- **Johns Pass**: Located about 6.5 nm north of North Channel. Connects with the GIWW between Mitchell and Sunshine beaches and is crossed by the twin **Johns Pass Bascule Bridges.** The closed vertical clearance is 27 feet at the center of the channel and the horizontal width has been expanded from 60 to 100 feet. The bridges open on request. All vessels operating with more than a 3-foot draft are advised to use extreme caution when transiting inbound and outbound of Johns Pass due to an encroaching shoal to the north in the vicinity of Johns Pass Buoy "3." This inlet tends to shoal rapidly. Calling for local knowledge from one of the tow services would be wise. Even though it is marked, it is shallow and a shoal is encroaching on the north part of the channel in the vicinity of green can buoy "3."

- **Clearwater Pass:** Located about 13 nm north of Johns Pass. Leads right into the heart of Clearwater proper. The 74-foot fixed vertical clearance **Clearwater Pass (SR 183) Bridge** spans the pass. This is the preferred channel unless you have solid local knowledge for the others. (Note that flashing green "1" may be missing.) Dredging last took place in May of 2018.

Pass-a-Grille Channel

At the start, the GIWW is a well-marked, dredged channel winding through shallows inside the barrier islands. From Pass-a-Grille Channel, it meanders northward inside the barrier islands referred to as the Holiday Isles: St. Petersburg Beach, Treasure Island and Sand Key. It threads around a maze of manmade islets pierced by canals.

⚠ Just north of the Pinellas Bayway Bridges is a shoal spot that sometimes catches the unwary. It is well marked, but do not be confused by the markers for the beginning of a side channel to Gulfport on the mainland. Red daybeacon "2," flashing red "26" and red "26A" lead past the shoal.

The route begins where the main GIWW channel intersects Pass-a-Grille Channel near Mile 114. If you explore Pass-a-Grille Channel, watch for shoaling and keep clear of the north side. The **Corey Causeway (SR 693) Bascule Bridge** (23-foot vertical clearance), **Treasure Island Causeway Bascule Bridge** (21-foot vertical clearance) and the **Welch Causeway (SR 699) Bridge** (at Madeira Beach, 25-foot vertical clearance) cross the GIWW. They have (varying) restricted schedules.

The Corey Causeway Bridge opens on signal, except from 8:00 a.m. to 7:00 p.m., Monday through Friday, and 10:00 a.m. to 7:00 p.m. Saturdays, Sundays and federal holidays, when the draw need only open on the hour, 20 minutes after the hour and 40 minutes after the hour.

The draw of the Treasure Island Bridge opens on signal, except from 7:00 a.m. to 7:00 p.m., when the draw need open on the hour, 20 minutes after the hour and 40 minutes after the hour (Monday through Friday) and on the quarter hour and three-quarter hour on Saturday, Sunday and federal holidays.

The Welch Causeway Bridge opens on signal, except from 9:30 a.m. to 6:00 p.m. on Saturdays, Sundays, and federal holidays, when the draw need open

Boca Ciega Bay, FL

WG

BOCA CIEGA BAY AREA		Largest Vessel Accommodated	VHF Channel Monitored	Transient Berths / Total Berths	Approach / Dockside Depth (reported)	Floating Docks	Gas / Diesel	Groceries, Ice, Marine Supplies, Snacks	Repairs: Hull, Engine, Propeller	Lift (tonnage), Crane, Rail	Min/Max Amps	Laundry, Pool, Showers, Courtesy Car	Pump-Out Station	Nearby: Grocery Store, Motel, Restaurant
		Dockage						**Supplies**			**Services**			
1. Magnuson Hotel Marina Cove [WiFi] 110.3	727-867-1151	55	16	32/32	5/8	–	–	IS	–	–	50/50	LPS	–	GMR
2. Suntex Marina at St. Petersburg [computer][onSpot]	**727-867-2600**	60	16	143/143	5/5	F	GD	GIMS	HEP	L	30/50	LPS	P	GMR
3. Maximo Marina (IGY) 1.5 NE of 115	727-867-1102	110	6/16	call/220	8/8	F	GD	IMS	HEP	L50,C	30/50	LS	P	GMR
4. Gulfport Municipal Marina [computer][WiFi] 1.5 NE of 115	**727-893-1071**	45	16/68	10/250	7/6	F	GD	IMS	P	–	30/50	S	P	GR
5. Pasadena Yacht & Country Club [computer][WiFi] 116.5	727-381-7922	70	16/69	6/82	10/6	–	–	IS	–	–	30/100	PS	P	GMR
6. MarineMax St. Petersburg	727-343-6520	75	16/72	call/130	8/6	F	–	IM	HEP	L80	30/100	S	P	GMR
7. Pasadena Marina [WiFi] 116	727-343-4500	56	–	1/125	6/6	–	–	I	–	–	30/50	LPS	P	GMR
8. Tierra Verde Marina Resort [computer][onSpot] 113	727-867-0400	120	16/71	20/107	12/12	F	GD	GIMS	HEP	L12	30/50	LPS	P	GMR
9. Tierra Verde Marina 113	727-866-0255	60	16	10/64	20/15	F	GD	GIMS	HEP	L10	30/50	–	P	GR
10. The Pass-A-Grille Marina [computer][WiFi] 113.8	727-360-0100	50	16	5/20	20/15	F	GD	IMS	HEP	L	30/100	–	–	GMR
11. Isla Del Sol Yacht Club Marina [computer][WiFi] 114.5	727-867-3625	65	16/68	3/74	20/6	–	–	I	–	L	30/50	LPS	P	R
12. Blind Pass Marina [computer] 118.5	727-360-4281	55	16/69	4/110	–	F	–	IS	–	L10	30/50	LS	P	GR
13. John's Pass Marina [WiFi] 1 S of 121.4	727-367-3835	75	16	15/34	10/5	F	GD	IMS	–	–	30/50	S	–	MR
14. Madeira Bay Docks, Inc. [computer][WiFi] 1 S of 121.4	727-639-2862	80	–	3/44	8/10	F	–	GIS	HEP	L77	30/50	LPS	P	GMR
15. Snug Harbor Inn 1 S of 121.4	727-395-9256	50	–	6/6	6/5	–	–	–	HEP	L35	–	PS	P	GMR
16. Madeira Beach Municipal Marina [computer] 122.2	727-399-2631	100	16/68	6/80	6/11	F	GD	IMS	HEP	–	30/50	LS	P	GMR
17. Bay Pines Marina [WiFi] 1.5 NE of 120.5	727-392-4922	50	16	call/60	5/7	F	G	IMS	E	L	30/50	–	P	R

[computer] Internet Access [WiFi] Wireless Internet Access [WG] Waterway Guide Cruising Club Partner [onSpot] dockside WiFi facility
See WaterwayGuide.com for current rates, fuel prices, web site addresses, and other up-to-the-minute information. *(Information in the table is provided by the facilities.)*

only on the hour, 20 minutes after the hour, and 40 minutes after the hour.

While openings are usually prompt, delays can occur. When approaching bridges in this section, bide your time and leave ample room for maneuvering while waiting. Call ahead on VHF Channel 09 if you are in doubt of the opening schedule and check the Waterway Explorer at waterwayguide.com for updates.

Dockage: Marine services run the gamut from small fishing camps and motel and restaurant docks to large, elegant marina complexes. You should contact these facilities ahead of time in to be sure they can accommodate you.

On the back side of Maximo Point is Magnuson Hotel Marina Cove, north of the Sunshine Skyway Bridge. Turn north at green daybeacon "13" to reach the marina. The marina welcomes transients up to 55 feet.

Suntex Marina at St. Petersburg is located in Frenchman Creek at Maximo Pt. They can accommodate vessels up to 60 feet and provide Category 4 hurricane-rated dry storage. Additionally, they have a captain's lounge, ship store, all fuels plus easy access to restaurants, shopping and activities.

Just North of Cats Point is Maximo Marina (IGY), which has slips, sells fuel and offers repairs (50-ton lift).

Two blocks from Maximo Marina is a shopping center with a large, well-stocked West Marine, a grocery store, a Post Office and a few restaurants.

To reach Gulfport and its boating facilities, turn to the northeast at GIWW Mile 114.5, just before flashing red "26." Slow down and take care as you round red daybeacon "2" and head carefully for green daybeacon "3." The red flashing light marks a shoal. Gulfport Municipal Marina is located here with a full complement of transient facilities in its well-protected basin. It offers pump-out service, fuel (gas and diesel), marine supplies, bait and tackle, and there is a restaurant nearby. This facility was renovated in 2017.

Other marinas in this area include Pasadena Yacht & Country Club, MarineMax St. Petersburg, Pasadena Marina, Tierra Verde Marina Resort, Tierra Verde Marina, The Pass-A-Grille Marina, Isla Del Sol Yacht Club Marina and Blind Pass Marina. All fuels and repairs are available here. Call ahead for transient dockage availability. See the "Boca Ciega Bay, FL" marina table in this chapter for details.

From Johns Pass at Mile 121 north to Sand Key are full-service municipal marinas and facilities on both shores, including John's Pass Marina, Madeira Bay Docks, Snug Harbor Inn and Madeira Beach Municipal

BOCA CIEGA AREA, NOAA CHART 11411

Boca Ciega Bay

GULFPORT MUNICIPAL MARINA

Gulfport

Marina. Refer to the marina table in this chapter for details. There are also motels and on-the-water restaurants with dockage.

To the northeast of Turtlecrawl Point, between two fixed bridges (32-foot vertical clearance on first bridge) is Bay Pines Marina with slips, gas and fuel.

Anchorage: When traveling the GIWW along its western leg beginning at Mile 104, you can anchor at the northeast corner of Boca Ciega Bay at Maximo Point West just east of the Sunshine Skyway Causeway. The area is exposed to winds from the southeast and the wakes of passing vessels, but can serve in a pinch. Depths are 9 to 12 feet at MLW. You can also anchor on the east side of the bridge in 7 to 9 feet at MLW outside Magnuson Hotel Marina Cove.

A number of anchorages can be found in Boca Ciega Bay just north of GIWW Mile 115. Proceed west between green daybeacon "31" and red daybeacon "30" from flashing red "32," then anchor where the chart shows 7- to 8-foot MLW depths. Proceed between the last two No-Wake markers to find the best depths. Or, proceed east at red daybeacon "32" in Cats Point Channel and anchor anywhere you can find sufficient depth and wind protection between Cats Point and Gulfport. One popular spot near the municipal marina has 5 to 7 feet at MLW and the other to the northwest has 6 to 10 feet at MLW. These offer protection from all but southern blows.

Just north of the Treasure Island Bridge at green daybeacon "17," turn west, and stay north of the charted spoil area for a well-protected anchorage. Mean low water depths around the spoil are roughly 4 to 6 feet, and the bottom is sand. Highly visible west of the GIWW on St. Pete Beach is the renovated Don CeSar Hotel, a longtime landmark for mariners. Finally, you can anchor north of the Welch Causeway Bascule Bridge (Mile 122.1) in 7 feet at MLW with good holding. Dinghy back to the first channel by the bridge (past the American Legion building) to the day dock to access restaurants and shopping.

The Narrows–GIWW Mile 126

NAVIGATION: Use NOAA Chart 11411. Nine nautical miles south of Clearwater, the GIWW enters the well-named Narrows, a deep, but narrow channel, connecting Boca Ciega Bay to Clearwater Harbor, which is comparatively broad and open. **Park Blvd. (SR 248) Bridge** at Mile 126.0 has a 20-foot closed vertical clearance and opens on request. Caddy's is just south

of green daybeacon "27A" and has docks available only while dining; no overnight dockage is permitted. The **Indian Rocks Beach (CR 694) Bascule Bridge** at Mile 129.3 has a 25-foot closed vertical clearance and opens on request.

Dockage: Indian Springs Marina at GIWW Mile 29 has a 30-ton lift and sells gas; call for slip availability.

Near the Indian Rocks Bridge is the Holiday Inn Harbourside Marina, offering transient slips, plus a pool, tiki bar and restaurant. On the beach side of the waterway just at red daybeacon "32" are the Indian Beach public docks at Keegan Clair Park. Call 727-595-2517 for information regarding these docks. These are free day-use docks only with no overnight stays allowed. Be careful when approaching these docks. It is very shallow, and we would advise only small shallow-draft boats attempt docking here. The 381-slip Largo Intercoastal Marina is at Mile 129.6 with gas and a few reserved transient slips.

■ CLEARWATER HARBOR

Although divided by the GIWW channel, Clearwater and Clearwater Beach constitute one very boat-minded community. The seat of Pinellas County and one of Florida's fastest-growing resort cities, Clearwater extends across the upper end of the Pinellas Peninsula.

Boaters are finding it an increasingly important port of call, both as a base of operations from which to enjoy the nearby resort attractions and also as a layover stop. The yacht services and elegant marinas here are mostly deepwater and capable of handling the largest boats that travel the GIWW. Marinas and repair installations are busy, but transient berths are generally available.

NAVIGATION: Use NOAA Chart 11411. The best access to Clearwater from the Gulf of Mexico is through Clearwater Pass, just south of Clearwater. This is one of the west coast's better daytime passes, and it is easy to use in good weather. North of the causeway, the channel has shoaled; proceed with caution.

From Clearwater Pass, 16-foot-high, flashing red "8" is followed by the 74-foot fixed vertical clearance **Clearwater Memorial Causeway (SR 60) Bridge**. At flashing red "14," turn north and into the channel marked by red daybeacon "2" and green daybeacon "3." A well-marked channel will take you to green daybeacon

The Narrows/ Clearwater Harbor, FL

		Largest Vessel Accommodated	VHF Channel Monitored	Transient Berths / Total Berths	Approach / Dockside Depth (reported)	Floating Docks	Gas / Diesel	Groceries, Ice, Marine Supplies, Snacks	Repairs: Hull, Engine, Propeller	Lift (tonnage), Crane, Rail	Min/Max Amps	Laundry, Pool, Showers, Courtesy Car	Pump-Out Station	Nearby: Grocery Store, Motel, Restaurant
INDIAN SHORES				Dockage				Supplies		Services				
1. Indian Springs Marina 129	727-595-2956	40	–	call/48	4.5/4.5	F	G	IM	HP	L30	30/30	–	–	GMR
2. Holiday Inn Harbourside Marina 💻 WiFi 129.4	727-517-3652	70	16	50/50	8/6	F	–	IMS	HEP	–	30/50	LPS	–	GMR
3. Largo Intercoastal Marina 129.6	727-595-3592	35	–	3/381	4/4	F	G	IMS	HEP	L	50/50	S	P	GMR
CLEARWATER BEACH AREA														
4. **Clearwater Municipal Marinas** (Clearwater Harbor Marina) WiFi **727-562-4981**		125	16/68	12/126	7/7	F	–	I	–	–	30/50	LS	P	GR
5. Chart House Marina WiFi 136	727-449-8007	–	–	26/26	7/7	–	–	–	–	–	30/30	LPS	–	GMR
6. Clearwater Yacht Club 💻 WiFi 136	727-447-6000	70	16/71	6/42	7/7	–	–	IS	–	–	30/50	PS	–	MR
7. **Clearwater Municipal Marinas** (Clearwater Beach Marina) WiFi **727-562-4955**		125	16/68	23/207	7/12	F	GD	GIS	–	–	30/100	LS	P	GMR

💻 Internet Access   WiFi Wireless Internet Access   WG Waterway Guide Cruising Club Partner   onSpot dockside WiFi facility
See WaterwayGuide.com for current rates, fuel prices, web site addresses, and other up-to-the-minute information. *(Information in the table is provided by the facilities.)*

Key West, FL	(305) 295-1316	24 Hours Daily	
Tampa Bay, FL	*(813) 645-2506	8:00 AM-4:00 PM (Mon-Fri)	
Tallahassee, FL	(850) 942-8833	8:00 AM-5:00 PM (Mon-Fri)	

*Recorded

NOAA VHF-FM WEATHER BROADCASTS

CITY	STATION	FREQ. (MHz)	BROADCAST TIMES
Tampa, FL	KHB-32	162.55	24 Hours daily
Sarasota, FL	WWG-59	162.40	24 Hours daily
Largo Marine, FL	KEC-38	162.450	24 Hours daily

POLLUTION REPORTS
Report all spills of oil and hazardous substances to the National Response Center via 1-800-424-8802 (toll free), or to the nearest U.S. Coast Guard facility if telephone communication is impossible (33 CFR 153).

broadcasting stations are subject to should be used with caution.
Station positions are shown thus:
⊙ (Accurate location)   o (Approximate

INDIAN SHORES, NOAA CHART 11411

CLEARWATER BEACH AREA, NOAA CHART 11411

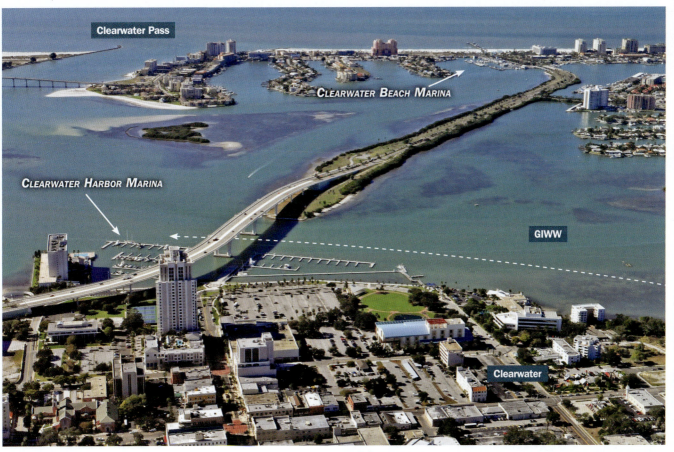

Clearwater Pass

CLEARWATER BEACH MARINA

CLEARWATER HARBOR MARINA

GIWW

Clearwater

Clearwater Harbor, FL

WG

DUNEDIN AREA		Largest Vessel Accommodated	VHF Channel Monitored	Transient Berths / Total Berths	Approach / Dockside Depth (reported)	Floating Docks	Gas / Diesel	Groceries, Ice, Marine Supplies, Snacks	Repairs: Hull, Engine, Propeller	Lift (tonnage), Crane, Rail	Min/Max Amps	Laundry, Pool, Showers, Courtesy Car	Pump-Out Station	Nearby: Grocery Store, Motel, Restaurant
		Dockage					**Supplies**		**Services**					
1. Dunedin Municipal Marina 139	727-298-3030	70	16	9/194	5/4.5	–	–	–	–	–	30/50	S	P	GMR
2. Marker 1 Marina 🖥 📶 .5 E of 141.5	727-733-9324	78	16/14	10/150	6/6	–	GD	IS	–	–	30/50	LPS	P	GMR
3. Caladesi Island State Park Marina	727-469-5918	–	–	call/108	4/4	F	–	IS	–	–	30/30	S	–	–

🖥 Internet Access 📶 Wireless Internet Access **WG** Waterway Guide Cruising Club Partner ⊙onSpot dockside WiFi facility

See WaterwayGuide.com for current rates, fuel prices, web site addresses, and other up-to-the-minute information. *(Information in the table is provided by the facilities.)*

DUNEDIN AREA, NOAA CHART 11411

"9," where you will turn west into the channel leading in from the GIWW to the Clearwater Municipal Marina.

If passing through, after passing under the bridge, you can follow the reds through a northward turn at quick-flashing red "10," and then an eastward turn at flashing red "14" before red daybeacons "16" and "20" bring you slightly south to the next 90-degree turn toward the north before the 16-foot-high, flashing red "12" and head under the Clearwater Causeway.

If heading south and looking to stop, find green daybeacon "1" just after the Clearwater Causeway. Turn west, and then follow the well-marked channel parallel to the causeway to green daybeacon "9," where that channel merges with the one coming in from Clearwater Pass. At this point, you can continue on to the marina of your choice.

Dockage: Approaching from the GIWW channel, the Clearwater Municipal Marinas (Clearwater Harbor Marina on the mainland side) is at green daybeacon "11." A sizable charter boat fleet is berthed here, as well as tour and fishing boats of all sizes. The marina takes reservations and the helpful marina staff can usually accommodate transients. The "Jolly Trolley" (clearwaterjolleytrolley.com) stops in front of the marina complex and provides a convenient ride to the grocery store. "Sunsets at Pier 60," a daily celebration similar to Key West's Mallory Square, includes music, entertainment, food and crafts for sale.

Clearwater's largest concentration of marinas is on the beach side between the Clearwater Pass and Clearwater Causeway. They can be approached either via a clearly marked and easy-to-navigate channel off the Clearwater

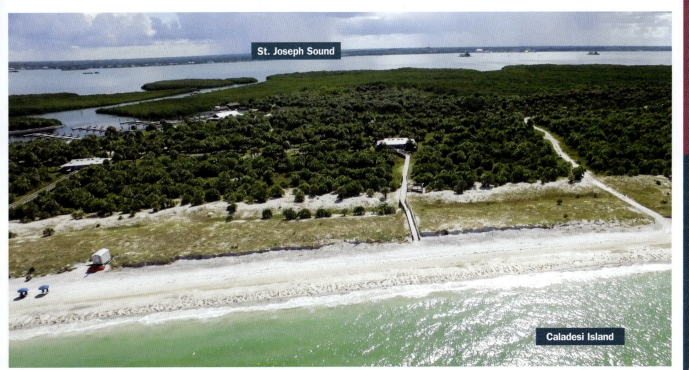

St. Joseph Sound

Caladesi Island

Pass entrance channel, if you are coming from the Gulf of Mexico, or by a channel from the GIWW, if you are traveling by the inside route. Facilities located between Clearwater Pass and the Causeway include Chart House Marina, Clearwater Yacht Club and the municipal Clearwater Beach Marina (on the beach end of the bridge). All have some transient space and the municipal marina sells fuel, both gas and diesel, plus some groceries. Adjacent to the municipal marina is The Bait House Tackle and Tavern (727-446-8134), featuring fresh bait and outstanding tackle, plus fresh local seafood, beer and wine. At the other end of the parking lot is Crabby's Dockside (727-210-1313) with a noteworthy happy hour from 3:00 p.m. to 6:00 p.m.

Anchorage: There are more anchoring choices in Clearwater Harbor than in Boca Ciega Bay, beginning with Belleair at GIWW Mile 131.9. On the northern side of the **Belleair Causeway Bridge** (75-foot fixed vertical clearance) you will find 7 to 8 feet at MLW with good holding in sand.

At Clearwater Beach, Clearwater Yacht Club has an anchorage with 6 to 9 feet at MLW. You can also anchor on either side of the west side of the **Causeway Blvd. (SR 60) Bridge** (14-foot fixed vertical clearance).

Dunedin Pass Area—GIWW Mile 139

Dunedin is home to several beaches, including Dunedin Causeway, Honeymoon Island, and Caladesi Island State Park (accessible only by boat), which is consistently rated among the best beaches in the world. The island has trails and quiet beaches and is definitely worth the effort to get there.

Dunedin is one of the few open waterfront communities from Sarasota to Cedar Key where buildings do not completely obscure the view of the waterway and the Gulf of Mexico beyond from the highway. There is also a lack of large commercial signage to obscure the view and no franchise restaurants or chain retail stores.

The Pinellas Trail, a 39-mile-long (63 km) bicycle and pedestrian trail that traverses all of Pinellas County, bisects downtown Dunedin. A large portion of the trail lies on the former roadbed of the Orange Belt Railway, the first railroad in Pinellas County, which arrived in 1888.

NAVIGATION: Use NOAA Chart 11411. The **Dunedin-Honeymoon Island Bascule Bridge** (opens on signal) crosses the GIWW at Mile 141.9. The bridge has an observed closed vertical clearance of 18 feet, even though it is charted as 24-foot vertical clearance.

⚠ There were several changes to the aids to navigation in this area in February 2018. Anclote Anchorage South flashing green "3" was relocated; green daybeacon "5" and red "6" were permanently discontinued; and flashing green "7" was renamed St. Joseph Sound Light "43." These changes may not be reflected on older NOAA charts.

St. Joseph Sound, FL

PALM HARBOR AREA		Dockage					Supplies		Services					
		Largest Vessel Accommodated	VHF Channel Monitored	Transient Berths / Total Berths	Approach / Dockside Depth (reported)	Floating Docks	Gas / Diesel	Groceries, Ice, Marine Supplies, Snacks	Repairs: Hull, Engine, Propeller	Lift (tonnage), Crane, Rail	Min/Max Amps	Laundry, Pool, Showers, Courtesy Car	Pump-Out Station	Nearby: Grocery Store, Motel, Restaurant
1. Island Harbor Marina	727-784-3014	30	–	call/43	5/5	F	–	–	EP	L	–	S	–	GMR
2. Home Port Marina onSpot	727-784-1443	42	–	call/187	5/5	–	GD	IMS	HEP	L	30/30	LPS	P	GMR
3. George's Marina	727-784-3798	40	–	call/11	/5	–	–	IS	HEP	L10	–	–	–	GMR
4. Ozona Fish Camp ⌨ WiFi	727-784-0143	37	68	–	6/4	–	G	IMS	–	–	30/30	–	P	GMR

⌨ Internet Access WiFi Wireless Internet Access WG Waterway Guide Cruising Club Partner onSpot dockside WiFi facility
See WaterwayGuide.com for current rates, fuel prices, web site addresses, and other up-to-the-minute information. *(Information in the table is provided by the facilities.)*

PALM HARBOR AREA, NOAA CHART 11411

Dockage: The Dunedin Municipal Marina has transient docks and is within walking distance to Dunedin's restaurants and shopping. The Bon Appetit Restaurant and Bar (727-733-2151) is next to the municipal marina and has docks for mariners who want to dine ashore. Immediately south of the Dunedin-Honeymoon Island Bascule Bridge, Marker 1 Marina offers transient dockage and gas and diesel fuel.

There are 90 slips in the wonderfully isolated Caldesi Island State Park Marina. To get to Caldesi Island, turn west just south of the Dunedin Bridge (green daybeacon "17") and then follow the Honeymoon Island Channel to a separate buoyed channel into Seven Mouth Creek. Only three slips here are wider than 11 feet; however, there are three "T" docks for larger boats. Average depths on the approach and dockside are reported at 4 feet at MLW, so you may need to travel at high tide, go slowly and obtain up-to-date local knowledge. Call ahead for reservations.

■ ST. JOSEPH SOUND

NAVIGATION: Use NOAA Chart 11411. About 3 miles north of Clearwater, the barrier islands fall away and the GIWW enters unprotected St. Joseph Sound and the approach to Anclote Key. After this final stretch on the GIWW, boaters continuing north beyond Anclote Key and the Anclote River have two choices. They may cross the open Gulf of Mexico for about 140 nm to Carrabelle, or they can follow a series of several markers relatively close in-shore around the Big Bend section of Florida for about 160 or 165 miles to Carrabelle.

 Stay well south of the green daybeacon "5" to avoid the marked shoal.

Anchorage: A popular anchorage in St. Joseph Sound is Three Rooker Bar, a narrow C-shaped island located between Honeymoon Island and Anclote Key, about 2.5 miles offshore from Tarpon Springs. Three Rooker's white sand beaches line the north and seaward sides of the island and offer some of the best shelling and beachcombing. The bay side of the island's shallow water teems with fish and birds. It is a well-protected anchorage from all but east winds. Enter around the north end of the bar, dropping anchor in the crescent near the beach in 4- to 8-foot MLW depths over a soft mud bottom. Use the depth sounder and line-of-sight navigation, avoiding the white sand bars that run out from the beach. On holiday weekends, this normally placid anchorage becomes a maelstrom of activity, with jet skis, small outboards and a floating hamburger stand all vying for space.

It is also possible to anchor at Anclote Key (Mile 151) in 8 to 10 feet at MLW with excellent holding and protection from the west. Anclote Key Preserve State Park has no provisions but the 403-acre park is home to at least 43 species of birds, including the American oystercatcher, bald eagle and piping plover. A picturesque 1887 lighthouse stands as a sentinel on the southern end of the island. Visitors can swim, grill and enjoy a picnic.

Palm Harbor Area–GIWW Mile 142

NAVIGATION: Use Chart 11411. North of the Dunedin-Honeymoon Island Bridge (24-foot vertical clearance, opens on demand), turn east at green daybeacon "17"

and follow the privately marked channel into Palm Harbor, which is shown on the chart as Smith Bayou.

Dockage: Note that the largest vessel accommodated here is 42 feet and 5-foot MLW approach depths are reported. To reach Island Harbor Marina and Home Port Marina, head up the channel toward the large dry stack buildings. Call ahead for slip availability. Home Port sells all fuels and is the site of waterfront Ozona Blue Grilling Co. (727-789-4540) serving grilled seafood, sandwiches and flatbreads. George's Marina is on the northeast side of the harbor and may have transient space; call ahead. Ozona Fish Camp has a marked channel to the north and they sell gas and may have transient space. There is no anchoring room here.

Side Trip: Anclote River (Tarpon Springs)– GIWW Mile 150

Tarpon Springs is the "Sponge Capital of the World" and has managed to diversify without losing its old-time flavor. While a large shrimp fleet and a lively boat-building industry make their homes in Tarpon Springs, colorful spongers still ply the waters as well.

NAVIGATION: Use NOAA Chart 11411. A range helps you through the big offshore shoal around the entrance to the Anclote River. (If you cannot see the onshore light, locate quick-flashing green "1.") Channel markers are no more than three-quarters of a mile apart. For help in orienting, you will see a tall, strobe-lighted power plant chimney on the north side of the Anclote River entrance, visible from 22 nm at sea on a clear day. The chimney, illuminated by flashing lights at night, is plotted on Chart 11411 ("STACK") and mentioned in the *U.S. Coast Pilot.*

Respect the shoal south of Anclote Key. When entering the GIWW south of Anclote Key, or entering the Anclote River, give flashing green "7" near Mile 150 its due respect. Older charts may not show the extension of the shoal southward. When traveling in this area, it is important to keep your charts current and your depthsounder on. Refer to the Waterway Explorer and NOAA online charts for the most up-to-date information.

⚠ Severe shoaling has been observed in the Anclote River in the vicinity of Anclote River turning basin daybeacons "51" and "53" at Tarpon Springs. Mariners are advised to use extreme caution while transiting the area.

Anclote River, FL

TARPON SPRINGS AREA		Largest Vessel Accommodated	VHF Channel Monitored	Approach / Dockside Depth (reported)	Transient Berths / Total Berths	Floating Docks	Gas / Diesel	Groceries, Ice, Marine Supplies, Snacks	Repairs: Hull, Engine, Propeller	Lift (tonnage), Crane, Rail	Min/Max Amps	Laundry, Pool, Showers, Courtesy Car	Pump-Out Station	Nearby: Grocery Store, Motel, Restaurant
		Dockage					**Supplies**			**Services**				
1. Anclote Village Marina 📶 WG	727-937-9737	55	–	2/20	5/7	F	GD	IMS	E	–	30/50	–	–	R
2. Port Tarpon Marina 🖥 📶	727-937-2200	75	16	10/58	9/9	F	GD	IMS	HEP	L50	50/100	S	–	R
3. Anclote Harbors Marina 📶	727-934-7616	45	16	4/30	9/6	F	G	I	HEP	L	50/50	LS	–	GMR
4. Anclote Isles Marina 🖥 📶 WG	727-939-0100	65	16	10/70	8/6	–	–	GIMS	–	–	30/100	S	P	GMR
5. Belle Harbour Marina 🖥 📶 WG	727-943-8489	50	16/68	3/18	6/5	F	G	IM	HEP	L7	30/50	LS	P	GMR
6. Tarpon Landing Marina	727-937-1100	65	–	5/50	5/6	–	GD	IM	HEP	–	30/50	–	P	GR
7. Tarpon Springs Yacht Club	727-934-2136	60	–	call/18	–	–	–	–	–	–	–	S	–	R
8. City of Tarpon Springs Municipal Marina 📶	727-946-5658	50	16	6/21	11/10	–	–	IS	–	–	30/50	S	–	GMR
9. River Energy–The New F & Y Inc.	727-937-4351	200	01	–	12/12	–	D	M	–	–	50/50	–	–	GMR
10. Gulf Marine Ways	727-937-4401	85	–	–	10/10	–	–	IM	HEP	R	50/50	–	–	GR
11. Turtle Cove Marina 📶	727-934-2202	50	16/72	10/56	5/6	F	GD	IMS	HEP	L12	30/50	LPS	P	GMR

🖥 Internet Access 📶 Wireless Internet Access WG Waterway Guide Cruising Club Partner onSpot dockside WiFi facility
See WaterwayGuide.com for current rates, fuel prices, web site addresses, and other up-to-the-minute information. *(Information in the table is provided by the facilities.)*

TARPON SPRINGS, CHART 11411

Take it easy going upriver the 3 miles to Tarpon Springs and observe the posted Idle-Speed/No-Wake Zone. There are many boats at slips in the river, and your wake can cause serious damage. Also, commercial fishing and sponging boats use the channel. The Cut C range's eastern mark is partially obscured by trees. Favor the southern side of the channel to avoid the shoal.

Dockage: You will pass several dry-stack marinas that may have space for transients. Just as you enter the river, on the northeast side is Anclote Village Marina. With some transient slips available, and "high and dry" storage for small boats, the marina offers a convenient stopping place if you do not have the time to go upriver.

Opposite green daybeacon "39" on the northeast side, Port Tarpon Marina has a convenient fuel dock with gas and diesel just off the river channel, transient slips and an on-site restaurant, Davidsons Dockside (727-487-0100), open 7 days a week. Next door, Anclote Harbors Marina welcomes cruising boats up to 45 feet. To the east, Anclote Isles Marina and Belle Harbour Marina have dockage and Belle Harbour sells gas.

Staying at any of the marinas on the north side of the river means you will need to arrange for transportation if you wish to get to the sponge docks and restaurants, most of which are on the south side of the river. The exception is Tarpon Landing Marina, from which sponge docks and Greek restaurants are a short walk across the fixed **SR 19 Alternate Hwy. Bridge** to the south side of the river. As evening approaches, the sounds of live music and laughter can be heard from Capt'n Jack's (727-944-3346) restaurant and bar at the head of the slips.

At the end of the navigable portion of the river, the City of Tarpon Springs Municipal Marina sits right next to the sponge docks and the Sponge Museum. It retains an old-time flavor and offers transient slips; reservations are a must. Its location at the east end of the sponge docks is ideal for exploring Tarpon Springs, with its sponge-diving trips, aquarium and many excellent Greek restaurants. The nearby Tarpon Springs Yacht Club welcomes members of reciprocating yacht clubs.

On the south side of the river are River Energy–the New F&Y Inc. and Gulf Marine Ways; both are repair and service facilities. River Energy sells diesel. Turtle Cove Marina is a full-service facility with all fuels and other amenities.

Anchorage: An anchorage with 6-foot MLW depths is located by the river's entrance east of green daybeacon "17" and just beyond the stack. There is a nearby park with a boat ramp and restrooms.

Up the river in Tarpon Springs, some boats anchor in front of the city marina, but shoaling and traffic may be a problem, and it is not recommended.

■ NEXT STOP

Tarpon Springs on the Anclote River marks the end of the Florida GIWW at Mile 150. (The GIWW picks back up in Carrabelle, FL, where mileages are measured east and west of Harvey Lock, LA, notated as EHL or WHL.) Beyond, from Anclote Key at the mouth of the Anclote River, lie the intriguing Big Bend (or Nature Coast) and the Florida Panhandle.

GOIN' ASHORE: TARPON SPRINGS, FL

SERVICES	
1	Library
2	Visitor Information
ATTRACTIONS	
3	Historic Tarpon Springs
4	Splash Museum
5	Sponge Docks
6	Sponge Factory

7	Tarpon Springs Heritage Museum
SHOPPING	
8	Save-A-Lot
DINING	
9	Captain Jack's Waterfront Bar & Grille
10	Rusty Bellies Waterfront Grill
11	ShrimpWrecked Restaurant & Dockside Bar

MARINAS	
2	City of Tarpon Springs Municipal Marina
10	Gulf Marine Ways
12	Anclote Isles Marina
13	Belle Harbour Marina
14	Tarpon Landing Marina
15	Tarpon Springs Yacht Club
16	Turtle Cove Marina

In reality, there are two Tarpon Springs. Both are intimately interrelated and well worth a visit. The sponge docks, the unbroken string of Greek restaurants and charming shops along Dodecanese Boulevard and the marinas are one aspect, while the other (historic downtown Tarpon Springs) is a charming complement to the docks. Be sure to stop at the Visitors Center at the City Marina (100 Dodecanese Blvd., 727-934-2952) to pick up a map of the area.

Attractions: A casual walk along the Dodecanese Boulevard waterfront brings Europe to mind more strongly than Florida. Many of the boutiques and restaurants are housed in former sponge warehouses. Your tour should include the Spongeorama's Sponge Factory (510 Dodecanese Blvd., 727-943-2164), where a brief movie tells the story of the original Greek sponge divers who made Tarpon Springs the "Sponge Capital of the World" and left an indelible mark on the city. Included in the theater is a museum, featuring sponge-diving exhibitions and exhibits of authentic sponging ships of bygone years; a 90-foot "mother" ship and a 38-foot diving boat. You can also buy from a broad range of sponges of all sizes, shapes and types. You can then take an hour-long trip on an authentic sponge boat and watch a diver go through his paces.

The second Tarpon Springs, Historic Tarpon Springs, is a 10-minute cab ride from the sponge docks or you can catch a ride on the city trolley or municipal bus; both have stops close by the city marina. This is an unusual and charming area, well worth the cruiser's attention.

For cruisers with dogs on board, a 10-minute walk from either marina leads to a dog park, with two separate fenced-in play areas where dogs can romp without leashes. Adjacent to the dog park is a Children's Splash Park with restrooms and a picnic pavilion, a children's play area, a fitness park with 10 pieces of outdoor equipment (under sail shades) and a lawn for yoga, etc.

From November to early spring, you will find manatees that make their home in the shallow Spring Bayou close to downtown. Craig Park offers a great vantage point for observing these gentle giants. It only takes a short dinghy ride to get to the Bayou, but it becomes a non-motorized area so you will need to row in and around the bayou to view the manatees.

While at Craig Park, why not stop in the Tarpon Springs Heritage Museum (727-937-0686)? The facility has two separate wings: The History Wing contains an exhibit about the Greek community of Tarpon Springs, as well as a collection of Native American archaeological artifacts from local excavations, while the ecology wing features large-scale murals of Tarpon Springs by artist Christopher Still. Visitors also can view a 16-minute documentary about the local sponge industry (727-937-0686).

Shopping: There is a Save-A-Lot downtown (780 S. Pinellas Ave., 727-934-0446), and to the east (near Rt. 19) is a Publix and Walmart plus other shopping. Dodecanese Blvd. and Athens St. on the Sponge Docks have hundreds of gift shops offering clothing, jewelry, sponges, souvenirs, and more. You will also find bakeries and a small convenience store on Athens St.

Dining: No visit is complete without sampling the Greek food on Dodecanese Boulevard. When you have worked up an appetite from a hard day of sightseeing, stop in at one of the many authentic restaurants lining the main street. If you do not go for the flaming saganaki (cheese appetizer) or the broiled octopus, their generous-sized Greek salads and hearty lamb dishes are particularly noteworthy (and available at too many restaurants to name here). After dinner or at snack time, sample some of the pastries sold at the bakeries inside each of the restaurants, especially the baklava.

For outdoor deck dining and entertainment, visit Captain Jack's Waterfront Bar & Grille (21 Oscar Hill Rd., 727-944-3346) at Tarpon Landing Marina. Rusty Bellies Waterfront Grill (937 Dodecanese Blvd., 727-934-4047) is a restaurant and seafood market that serves seafood fresh off the boats. ShrimpWrecked Restaurant & Dockside Bar (210 Dodecanese Blvd., 727-943-9879, next to the City Marina) offers expansive outdoor dining and a tiki bar. There are also Italian, Cuban, and Asian restaurants nearby. After dinner, you can catch a show, listen to live music or take in some belly dancing!

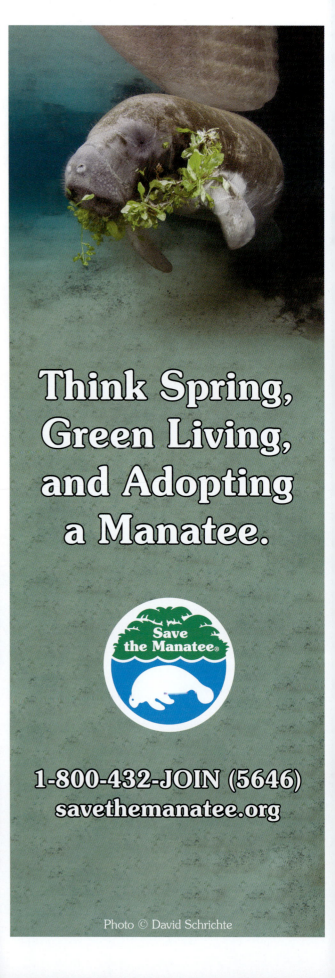

Upper Gulf Coast

■ THE BIG BEND: ANCLOTE KEY TO CARRABELLE ■ THE PANHANDLE: APALACHICOLA TO PENSACOLA
■ PERIDO KEY TO BAY ST. LOUIS, MS

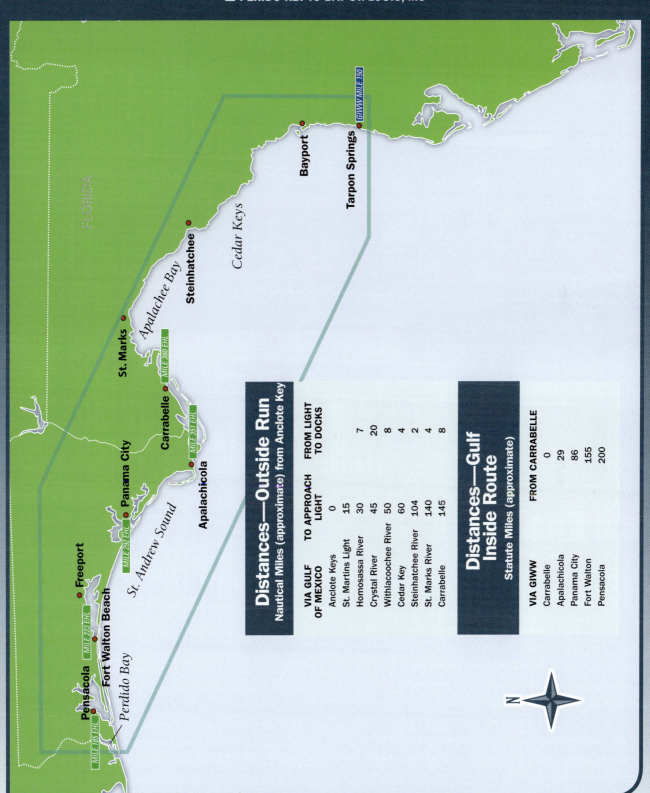

Distances—Outside Run
Nautical Miles (approximate) from Anclote Key

VIA GULF OF MEXICO	TO APPROACH LIGHT	FROM LIGHT TO DOCKS
Anclote Keys	0	
St. Martins Light	15	
Homosassa River	30	7
Crystal River	45	20
Withlacoochee River	50	8
Cedar Key	60	4
Steinhatchee River	104	2
St. Marks River	140	4
Carrabelle	145	8

Distances—Gulf Inside Route
Statute Miles (approximate)

VIA GIWW	FROM CARRABELLE
Carrabelle	0
Apalachicola	29
Panama City	86
Fort Walton	155
Pensacola	200

Visit Waterway Explorer at waterwayguide.com

Upper Gulf Coast

From the fascinating swampy marshland and wilderness of the Big Bend/Nature Coast to the stretches of blazing white sand beaches, spiked by high-rise condominiums, of the dazzling coastline that is Florida's Panhandle, Florida's Upper Gulf Coast provides definite variety for the skipper who has been on the ICW and/or GIWW for a while. The two distinct cruising regions range from the Anclote Keys on the eastern end to Pensacola and Perdido Bay on the west.

The 350-nm stretch from the Anclote Keys to Carrabelle across the Big Bend has no protected inside route. To transit the Big Bend area (officially called Florida's Nature Coast), mariners must make the trip across open waters in the Gulf of Mexico. For the second half, from Carrabelle on to Florida's Panhandle, you can travel the Gulf Intracoastal Waterway (GIWW) or continue outside in the Gulf.

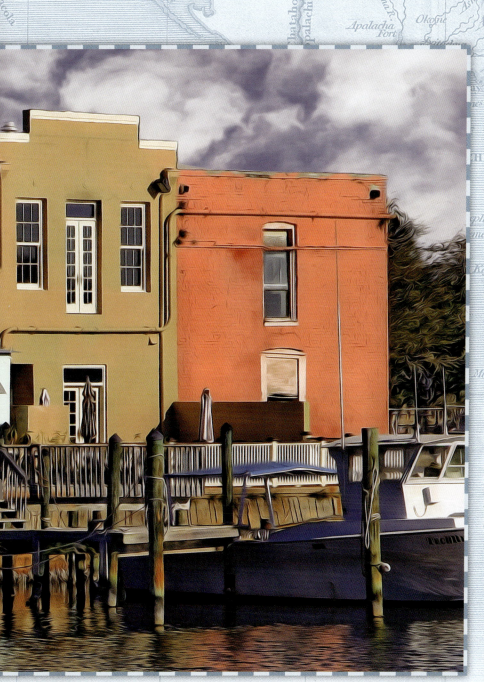

Pensacola, a seaport on Pensacola Bay, is protected by the barrier island of Santa Rosa and connects to the Gulf of Mexico.

Weather

A small change in latitude creates a perceptible difference in the weather of this region compared to southern Florida. The upper Gulf Coast of Florida is the only coastal section of the state that experiences a noticeable winter. For example, whereas "The Season" in South Florida runs generally from November to April, "The Season" in the Upper Gulf Coast, depending on the marine facility and location, may run from Memorial Day to Labor Day. It gets chilly in the winter, but it is still possible to enjoy these un-crowded, clear waters, award-winning beaches and boating-oriented communities.

Tides

Along the panhandle of Florida, a rather unique change occurs to tides. West of St. George Sound/Apalachicola Bay, there are only 2 tides per 24 hours (one high and one low, called diurnal tides), while east of this demarcation, the tides are the normal 4 per 24 hours (2 highs and 2 lows). Very few places on the planet can claim this distinction – the Java Sea, the Gulf of Tonkin, and a few others.

The Coastal Cruiser

Along the west coast shore of the Big Bend/Nature Coast, from Anclote Key almost to Carrabelle, the Gulf of Mexico is relatively shallow and the coastline low and indistinct. If you are running along the shore, keep a close eye on the depth sounder and tide charts and the little buoys for crab pots and lob-ster traps. This is a fine sailing area, but boats with deep drafts should be wary of the shoals.

Skippers with shallow-draft boats have the option of exploring the rivers of the "Lonesome Leg." They require time to spare, but provide strong satisfaction for those with a taste for exploring an area not yet swarming with cruising tourists. The long rivers offer splendid gunkholing and excellent fishing, but go in carefully and follow the approach and channel markers. Since many of these streams are loaded with weeds, check the strainers on all seawater intakes frequently. Brown pelicans are tricky neighbors up here: they have a tendency to deface buoy numbers, and a pelican perched on a green can buoy will, from a distance, change the outline to that of a red nun buoy. Get in the habit of checking floating marks carefully.

Offshore Crossing: To St. George Island

If you don't plan to cruise the Big Bend area, running the 130- to 140-nm rhumb line directly from Tarpon Springs or Clearwater to the St. George Island East Pass entrance buoy for Carrabelle can save a lot of time, but only an able boat enjoying good weather should attempt this passage. Many cruisers prefer to follow a route closer to the coastline. There used to be markers, called the Big Bend markers, which pro-vided an inshore route closer to the coastline. These were discontinued, but there are channel entrance markers that can be used to run a course closer to shore.

Before setting out, make sure your boat is seaworthy and your engine sound. Know your compass error. Refer to the Waterway Explorer and NOAA online charts for the most up-to-date information. There have been numerous changes to the navigation aids in recent years. Along the route, plot your courses carefully and stick to them. The land is low lying and it can be a long stretch between the navigation aids as you traverse this coastline. Always track your position, by dead reckoning and GPS. There are some remote sections of this coast and even though you are not far offshore, you may be far from help. A registered Emergency Position Indicating Radio Beacon (EPIRB) is an excellent addition to your safety equipment.

Those choosing the direct route, particularly in the Big Bend area, should leave a float plan with a friend or relative. If trouble occurs, rescue units will arrive much faster if they know your route. Unless you are very experienced, run only in daylight. It is particularly important to have daylight while you are within 20 nm or so of the Florida coast, as the crab pots can be very thick. Keep an eye to the sky and watch for changes in the weather. NOAA weather radio or local commercial AM or FM radio stations and satellite weather services, such as XM Weather, should be monitored regularly for the latest information.

Inside Route: Carrabelle to Pensacola

You can travel outside in the Gulf of Mexico by following the coastline all the way to Pensacola. The more interesting GIWW route connects big bays and sounds that are protected by narrow, wooded barrier islands. From Carrabelle to Pensacola, there are 200 statute miles of inside cruising with occasional passes to the Gulf of Mexico. Fixed bridge heights of 50 feet will prevent most sailboats from using some of the inside route.

On the east, the Florida Panhandle extends north beyond Carrabelle and inland to Tallahassee, the state capital. To the west, the Panhandle extends to Pensacola, once an outpost of the Spanish colony of New Orleans, and later the capital of British West Florida during the American Revolution. Midway along the route is Panama City, a well-equipped sportfishing and boating center surrounded by pure white beaches. Other worthwhile stops include Apalachicola, Port St. Joe, Destin and Fort Walton Beach. A fixed 49-foot bridge at Destin to the Gulf will dictate whether or not you can access the inner route to Fort Walton.

The Big Bend: Anclote Key to Carrabelle

 GIWW Mile 150–Mile 350 EHL

 VHF FL Bridges: Channel 09

CHARTS NOAA 11401, 11404, 11405, 11407, 11408, 11409

Floridians call it "The Big Bend." The State government and local Chambers of Commerce call it "The Nature Coast." For boaters, it is the longest open water unprotected passage for the 3,000 miles between Newport, RI, and Port Isabel, TX. It is a common topic of conversation between boaters in and near this region. For cruisers with the time, the right boat and the ability this is the area for those interested in lovely, and often isolated, wilderness grounds. Most cruising is done in the rivers entering the Gulf of Mexico, and there is no inside waterway or protected route to take. Fishing and hunting are the name of the game here. But sharpen up your navigation skills and cruise carefully. You may be a long and expensive distance from commercial assistance if you make a mistake.

North of Anclote Key and Tarpon Springs, as far as Carrabelle to the west, the coastline presents cruising skippers with a very different kind of Florida cruising. Shoaling normally extends so far out that cruisers are basically in open, although shallow, Gulf of Mexico waters. These are fishering waters, both fresh and saltwater. The entrance channels can be shallow and tricky but they are loaded with fish of all types.

Most of the coast is low and marshy. The countryside is still undeveloped, even primitive in spots, and any place you put in will offer fascinating and unique side trips with their own navigational challenges.

The Coast Guard station on the Withlacoochee River at Yankeetown, about 17 miles southeast of Cedar Key, covers this area and monitors VHF Channel 16. This station also operates and maintains three vessels for emergency search and rescue. In addition to VHF, the station can be reached by telephone at 352-447-6900.

■ EXPLORING THE BIG BEND

This section is uniquely different and purposefully prepared and included in this chapter to underline the care and caution warranted for navigating the Big Bend waters of Florida. You don't have to be apprehensive about sailing these waters; however, you must be attentive and responsible in all of your preparations.

Electronic charts are updated regularly, but not after every storm. Refer to the Waterway Explorer (waterwayguide.com) and NOAA online charts for the most up-to-date information, but remember that the only true, up-to-date indicator of depth comes from your depth sounder.

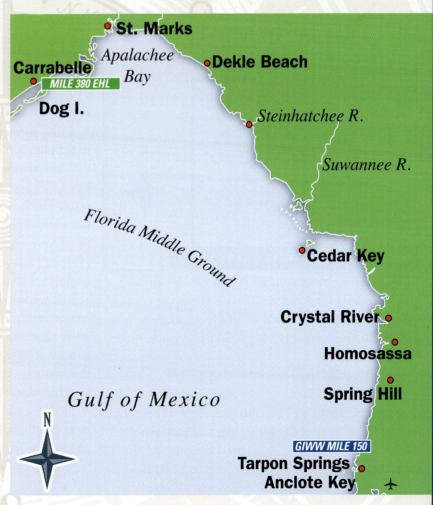

Little Pine Island Bay, FL

HERNANDO BEACH		Largest Vessel Accommodated	VHF Channel Monitored	Approach / Dockside Depth (reported)	Transient Berths / Total Berths	Floating Docks	Gas / Diesel	Groceries, Ice, Marine Supplies, Snacks	Repairs: Hull, Engine, Propeller	Lift (tonnage), Crane, Rail	Min/Max Amps	Laundry, Pool, Showers, Courtesy Car	Pump-Out Station	Nearby: Grocery Store, Motel, Restaurant
				Dockage				**Supplies**		**Services**				
1. Hernando Beach Marina	352-596-2952	40	-	call/31	4/4	F	GD	IMS	HEP	L30	30/30	S	-	GMR
2. Blue Pelican Marina	352-610-9999	30	-	4/4	4/4	F	G	IMS	HEP	L10	-	S	-	GMR

⌨ Internet Access 📶 Wireless Internet Access **WG** Waterway Guide Cruising Club Partner 💿**onSpot** dockside WiFi facility
See WaterwayGuide.com for current rates, fuel prices, web site addresses, and other up-to-the-minute information. *(Information in the table is provided by the facilities.)*

HERNANDO BEACH, NOAA CHART 11409

When sailing in difficult waters for which you have little knowledge and past experience, it may be safer to be farther out than nearer to land. Nevertheless, it is possible to safely make the Big Bend Passage and never lose sight of land.

The navigation sections in this chapter will provide information and options to help along each route as cruising boat crews and captains pick their way through the shallow depths of the Gulf of Mexico and into the unpredictable depths of the narrow channels and rivers. Considering the nature of these waters, it is not possible to guarantee total accuracy. Navigational information about shoals, location of river channels, aids to navigation and water depths are ever changing. On the land, marinas, facilities, restaurants, etc. come and go. Check the Waterway Explorer (waterwayguide.com) for the most up-to-date information.

Note: A **rhumb line** follows the shortest distance between two points on the globe, which isn't always the same thing as the shortest distance across a stretched-flat Mercator chart. The more area a chart covers, the less like it is that a straight line produces the shortest route. Electronic charting has made rhumb lines easy to create, but it is more complicated for those going long distances using small scale paper charts. To plot a rhumb line by hand, cut all the meridians at the same angle.

A Choice of Routes

Your trip through the Big Bend starts with making choices regarding your route:

1. Travel an outside route in deeper water from Anclote Key or Clearwater Beach for whatever time it takes to reach your western destination. Without extensive local knowledge, plan your arrival for daylight. Weather will be a serious consideration. You need a boat capable of the offshore passage, a captain and crew with the ability and confidence to make the voyage.

2. Travel an inside route closer to shore and find safe harbor before dark. Chart a careful course and do not travel after sunset. These are shallow waters. Know where you are going to go, how you are going to get there, and the condition of the water all along the route...before you leave the dock! There are reefs in the Big Bend. Many are oyster bars, and some are littered with rocks. Channel and river depths can be difficult. It is advisable to call ahead and ask for local knowledge if you can.

NAVIGATION: Use Chart 1114A. Let's start by drawing course lines. Most of your cruising will be in Gulf waters, so all distances are measured in nautical miles (nm). All routes will start from Anclote Key's 16-foot high, flashing red buoy "2" at N 28° 15.089'/ W 82° 52.896'. Its location is 2.6 nm at 290 degrees from the north end of Anclote Key, or 2.6 nm at 277 degrees from 15-foot high, flashing red "4."

Along both direct offshore routes you will be as much as 45 nm from land. Channel entrances to find shelter from weather are probably too far away and, in inclement weather, too dangerous to navigate. Waiting for an agreeable weather window will make a big difference in the comfort and safety of your trip along this course. The average cruising boat may want to wait for winds that are less than 10 knots with sea conditions less than 4 feet. Westerly winds are the least desirable. If winds are blowing greater than 15 knots wait 24 hours after they fall below 10 knots before you depart.

1. **Outside route from Anclote Key to Carrabelle:**
   From Anclote Key's 16-foot high, flashing red "2," draw a rhumb line all the way to East Pass's Carrabelle Channel flashing red buoy "2" at N 29° 44.541'/W 84° 39'199'. The distance is 130 nm at a course of 313 degrees magnetic.

2. **Outside route from Clearwater Beach to Carrabelle:** From the west end of Clearwater Pass's 20-foot flashing green "1" at N 27° 58.27'/ W 82° 50.84', draw a rhumb line to Carrabelle Channel flashing red buoy "2." This course will take you 142.5 nm on a course of 323 degrees magnetic.

3. **Inside route:** You will need to establish a series of courses for an inside route.
   A. Anclote Key's 16-foot high, flashing red "2" to St Martins Outer Shoal 16-foot high, lighted buoy flashing red "10" at N 28° 25.864'/W 82° 55.076'. The distance is 11 nm on a course of 354 degrees magnetic.
   B. St. Martins Outer Shoal 16-foot high, flashing red "10" to Crystal River flashing red buoy "2" at N 28°.47.542'/W 82°.58.571' (13 nm west of Homosasssa). The distance is 21.4 nm on a course of 350 degrees magnetic.

Planning Your Stops

For vessels traveling by day, along an inside route, consider the following as possible ports for shelter before the sun goes down. Do not attempt to enter these channels after the sun goes down. All distances are total daily nautical miles from point of departure to an anchorage or marina at the end of each day.

Daily distance of approximately 50 nm:
   1. Anclote Key to Hernando Beach—25 nm
   2. Hernando Beach to Crystal River—50 nm
   3. Crystal River to Yankeetown—30 nm
   4. Yankeetown to Suwannee River—50 nm
   5. Suwannee to Steinhatchee—40 nm
   6. Steinhatchee to St. Marks—60 nm
   7. St. Marks to East Pass—40 nm
(Note: It is possible to go directly from Hernando Beach to Yankeetown, a distance of 50 nm. The channel is shallow and it can take more time to find deep water and work your way in to the Withlacoochee River.)

Daily distance of approximately 60 nm:
   1. Anclote Key to Crystal River—55 nm
   2. Crystal River to Suwannee River—55 nm
   3. Suwannee River to Steinhatchee—40 nm
   4. Steinhatchee to St. Marks—60 nm
   5. St. Marks to East Pass—45 nm

(Alternate Route)
Daily distance of approximately 60 nm:
   1. Anclote Key to Yankeetown—55 nm
   2. Yankeetown to Suwannee—50 nm
   3. Suwannee River to Steinhatchee—40 nm
   4. Steinhatchee to East Pass—70 nm

Daily distance of approximately 80 nm:
   1. Anclote to Suwannee River—75 nm
   2. Suwannee River to Steinhatchee—40 nm
   3. Steinhatchee to East Pass—70 nm
(Note that it is possible to go directly from Suwannee to East Pass, a distance of 90 nm.)

Crystal River, Homosassa River, FL

HOMOSASSA		Largest Vessel Accommodated	VHF Channel Monitored	Transient Berths / Total Berths	Approach / Dockside Depth (reported)	Floating Docks	Gas / Diesel	Groceries, Ice, Marine Supplies, Snacks	Repairs: Hull, Engine, Propeller	Lift (tonnage), Crane, Rail	Min/Max Amps	Laundry, Pool, Showers, Courtesy Car	Pump-Out Station	Nearby: Grocery Store, Motel, Restaurant
			Dockage				**Supplies**		**Services**					
1. MacRae's of Homosassa **WiFi**	352-628-2602	35	16/68	call/10	6/3	F	G	IMS	P	–	30/30	LS	–	GMR
CRYSTAL RIVER														
2. Twin Rivers Marina 🖥 **WiFi**	352-795-3552	60	16	6/53	5/8	F	GD	IMS	HEP	L35	30/50	–	–	GR
3. Pete's Pier Inc. 🖥	352-795-3302	80	68	call/92	8/8	–	GD	IS	–	L	30/50	S	P	MR

🖥 Internet Access   **WiFi** Wireless Internet Access   **WG** Waterway Guide Cruising Club Partner   **onSpot** dockside WiFi facility
See WaterwayGuide.com for current rates, fuel prices, web site addresses, and other up-to-the-minute information. (*Information in the table is provided by the facilities.*)

HOMOSASSA, CRYSTAL RIVER, NOAA CHART 11409

C. Crystal River flashing red "2" to Seahorse Reef's 31-foot high, flashing white at N 28° 58.518'/ W 83° 09.182'. Do not get too close to this light, as it marks a shoal. The distance is 14.38 nm on a course of 319 degrees magnetic.

D. Seahorse Reef's 31-foot high, flashing white to Ochlockonee Shoal's flashing red buoy "24" at N 29° 51.485'/W 84° 10.318'. The distance is 75 nm at a course of 314 degrees magnetic.

E. Ochlockonee Shoal's flashing red buoy "24" to Carrabelle Channel flashing red buoy "2" at N 29° 44.541'/W 84° 39.199'. The distance is 26 nm on a course of 254 degrees magnetic.

Chart your course as you navigate. It is unlikely that your compass course will be exactly as those above. Keep a constant eye on your depth. Watch your time. These are difficult waters to navigate at night.

You can plot a course closer to shore by using entrance buoys to the various river channels. The caveat here is to make sure when plotting the course that your bearing does not carry you over shoals your vessel cannot negotiate. If weather is fair and winds are no more than 10 to 15 knots from the east, northeast or southeast, seas should be less than 4 feet.

◼ ANCLOTE KEY TO HOMOSASSA RIVER

....

NAVIGATION: Use NOAA Chart 11409. St. Martins Reef runs along the coast north from Anclote Key for some 40 nm. The shoals of this reef extend over 10 nm offshore. St. Martins Outer Shoal 16-foot high, flashing red "10" marks the outer limit of the shallow water. Many of the rocks and shoals are identified by private markers. Cruisers without local knowledge should approach the coast with care, and deep draft vessels should stand out in deeper waters. Smaller boats with drafts of 3 to 4 feet can usually follow the coast and find smooth water by keeping about 7 nm offshore.

Hernando Beach

Hernando Beach is a reachable stop between Anclote and Crystal River and is an easy daylight passage with a good weather window. It is a small community, but restaurants are within walking distance and Hernando Beach Marina has a small ship store.

NAVIGATION: Use NOAA Chart 11409. Travel the distance from Anclote Key's 16-foot high, flashing red "2" to St Martins Outer Shoal 16-foot high, flashing red "10," 11 nm at 350 degrees magnetic. From St. Martins Outer Shoal 16-foot high, flashing red "10" set a course of 60 degrees magnetic for 8.5 nm to the private Oc flashing 14-foot marker. Then, go 3.5 nm at 58 degrees magnetic to a point where you can turn toward the Hernando Beach Channel. The channel entrance is 1 nm at 142 degrees magnetic. Controlling channel depth is reported as 4 feet at MLW; however, mariners with local knowledge say it is common for boats with drafts of 5 feet to use the channel.

 Red daybeacon "4" was reported destroyed in July 2017; use caution.

Dockage: Hernando Beach Marina is the only marina here with transient slips; however, be aware that their widest slip is 14 feet. Blue Pelican Marina is primarily a dry stack facility and may not have transient space; call ahead for slip availability and to verify that shoaling is not a problem in this well-marked channel.

Homosassa River

The Homosassa River is a comparatively narrow and shallow waterway with winding channels and unforgiving oyster bars and rock beds, but it supplies some great fishing for both salt and freshwater species. The Homosassa River is another of the spring-fed rivers within the Springs Coast Watershed. The headwater springs of the Homosassa River are home to both freshwater and saltwater fish. This phenomenon is possible because the mineral content in the spring water resembles minerals found in salt water. The village of Homosassa is an attractive fishing center that grows more popular each year; more than 20 fishing guides operate year-round. Fishers should remember that the river qualifies as freshwater, so a fishing license is required.

NAVIGATION: Use NOAA Chart 11409. The channel into the Homosassa River is narrow and shallow. The route twists and turns its way to the fishing village of Homosassa, about 4 miles upriver. It may be best described as treacherous for mariners without local knowledge piloting boats with drafts greater than 4 feet. Boats with drafts greater than 4 feet should not

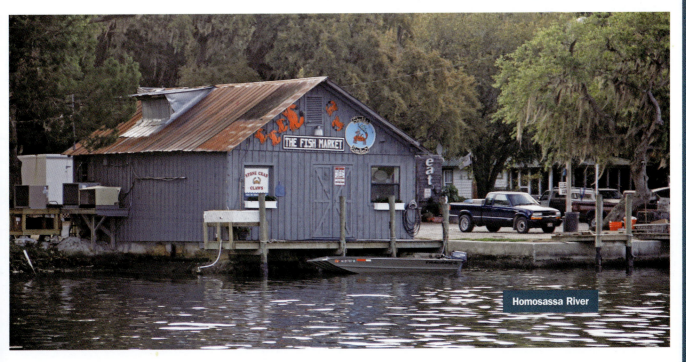
Homosassa River

Withlacoochee River, FL

YANKEETOWN		Largest Vessel Accommodated	VHF Channel Monitored	Transient Berths / Total Berths	Approach / Dockside Depth (reported)	Floating Docks	Gas / Diesel	Groceries, Ice, Marine Supplies, Snacks	Repairs: Hull, Engine, Propeller	Lift (tonnage), Crane, Rail	Min/Max Amps	Laundry, Pool, Showers, Courtesy Car	Pump-Out Station	Nearby: Grocery Store, Motel, Restaurant
			Dockage					**Supplies**		**Services**				
1. Yankeetown Marina	352-447-2529	50	16	1/50	6/6	–	–	GIMS	–	–	50/50	–	–	GMR
2. B's Marina & Campground 🖥 📶	352-447-5888	60	–	3/12	12/12	–	GD	I	–	–	30/30	LS	–	GMR
3. Riverside Marina & Cottages 📶	352-447-2980	60	–	3/15	25/6	–	–	–	–	–	30/30	LS	–	GMR

🖥 Internet Access 📶 Wireless Internet Access **WG** Waterway Guide Cruising Club Partner 🔵 onSpot dockside WiFi facility
See WaterwayGuide.com for current rates, fuel prices, web site addresses, and other up-to-the-minute information. *(Information in the table is provided by the facilities.)*

YANKEETOWN, NOAA CHART 11408

attempt this channel at low tide. Be aware that you may encounter many fast moving small fishing boats.

Travel the distance from Anclote Key's 16-foot high, flashing red "2" to St. Martins Outer Shoal 16-foot high, flashing red "10," 11 nm at 350 degrees magnetic. From St. Martins Outer Shoal 16-foot high, flashing red "10" set a course of 18 degrees magnetic for 16.5 nm to Homosassa Bay entrance 16-foot high, flashing red buoy "2" at N 28° 41.435'/W 82° 48.641'. Keep a close eye on your depth. Avoid the shoals to the southeast between that and red daybeacon "2A." Steer a careful, direct course between the first three reds, as there are shallows to both sides.

⚠️ From this point through the river entrance, depths are reported from 3.5 to 7 feet at MLW. Local mariners report depths of 3 feet at MLW at what they call "Hells Gate," a very narrow passage close the entrance of the marked channel. Proceed with great care. The channel and the river twist and turn and are very narrow. Currents can be strong. The slightest deviation could result in an encounter with rocks in the shoals.

Dockage: MacRae's of Homosassa has slips, sells gas and has a hotel, bait house (for anglers) and a riverfront tiki bar. They report 3-foot MLW dockside depths, so call ahead if that is a concern.

CRYSTAL RIVER TO CEDAR KEY

Crystal River

Crystal River and Crystal Bay are located 45 nm north of Anclote River and 23 nm southeast of Cedar Key. A marked channel leads from the Gulf through Crystal Bay and the Crystal River 6 nm to Kings Bay and the Town of Crystal River. When the water temperature drops in the Gulf of Mexico, manatees move to the warmer waters of the Crystal River, followed closely by nature-loving tourists and other visitors. Located along Central Florida's "Nature Coast," Crystal River is one of the few places where you can swim with manatees. (See sidebar.)

NAVIGATION: Use NOAA Chart 11409. Travel the distance from Anclote Key's 16-foot high, flashing red "2" to St Martins Outer Shoal 16-foot high, flashing red "10," 11 nm at 350 degrees magnetic. From there, continue on a course of 353 degrees magnetic for 21.4 nm to Crystal River flashing red buoy "2" at N 28° 47.542'/W 82° 58.571' (13 nm west of Homosasssa). As local channels and rivers go, Crystal River is navigable, and King's Bay is worth the trip. From flashing red buoy "2" through the channel and the river, depths are posted from 5 to 8 feet at MLW. Local mariners say the depth is 6 to 9 feet at MLW. During periods of north winds, depths can drop dramatically.

There is a posted 25 mph speed limit. King's Bay, at the head of Crystal River, is a designated Slow- and Idle-Speed Zone all along the river because of the manatee population.

Dockage: Transient slips, gas and diesel can be found at two marinas. At the junction of the Salt and Crystal Rivers, you will find the full-service Twin Rivers Marina. Use caution approaching the marina on the Salt River, and check your height; the charted overhead power cables have a 47-foot vertical clearance. This is the only complete full-service boatyard in Crystal River. Water depth to the marina and dockside is 5 feet at MLW.

Pete's Pier Inc. is located in the City of Crystal River at Kings Bay. They have some transient slips reserved and sell all fuels. This is the only transient marina near downtown Crystal River. A grocery store, fish market, liquor store and a laundry are all about 1 mile from the waterfront. You can get a bite to eat at Crackers Bar and Grill (352-795-3999), which has a fun tiki hut with live entertainment on the weekends. Transportation required

Swim with the Manatees

Crystal River is Florida's second largest system of natural springs, with a daily flow of about 3 million cubic yards of water, at a constant temperature of 72 degrees. When the water temperature drops in the Gulf of Mexico, manatees move to the warmer waters of the Crystal River. This area may host Florida's largest population of manatees.

Do not leave this area without checking out the spectacular caverns nearby. You can look down from King's Bay and see springs 60 feet under the surface. This is the only place where you can legally swim with manatees in the wild in the U.S. (during designated times). Be respectful of the manatees and remember that _you_ are in _their_ waters.

We recommend going with a local guide who can take you to the manatee "hot spots" and who will also educate you about them, giving you a more full experience and a greater understanding of these gentle creatures.

Another option is to board a free bus tour to Three Sisters Spring during the Florida Manatee Festival, held the third weekend in January in downtown Crystal River. Tours run continuously during the Festival. Manatee boat tours are also available for a nominal charge to take you out into Kings Bay and other favorite hangouts of the manatees.

Cedar Key, FL

CEDAR KEY		Largest Vessel Accommodated	VHF Channel Monitored	Transient Berths / Total Berths	Approach / Dockside Depth (reported)	Floating Docks	Gas / Diesel	Groceries, Ice, Marine Supplies, Snacks	Repairs: Hull, Engine, Propeller	Lift (tonnage), Crane, Rail	Min/Max Amps	Laundry, Pool, Showers, Courtesy Car	Pump-Out Station	Nearby: Grocery Store, Motel, Restaurant
		Dockage						**Supplies**		**Services**				
1. Cedar Key Marina II	352-543-6148	–	11	–	6/6	–	G	IMS	HEP	–	L6	–	–	–	GMR

⌨ Internet Access 📶 Wireless Internet Access WG Waterway Guide Cruising Club Partner onSpot dockside WiFi facility
See WaterwayGuide.com for current rates, fuel prices, web site addresses, and other up-to-the-minute information. *(Information in the table is provided by the facilities.)*

CEDAR KEY, NOAA CHART 11408 *(use inset)*

or you could dinghy over from Pete's Pier. There is a dock for small boats at the restaurant.

Anchorage: You can anchor anywhere in the wide part of Kings Bay before Pete's Pier. Kings Bay has very good holding and protection with plenty of room to swing. There is a full 3-foot tidal range, with 3 feet at MLW. From here you can kayak or dinghy to the springs or to town.

Withlacoochee River

There are two Withlacoochee Rivers in Florida. The other river flows from Georgia and empties into the Suwannee River. Big Bend's Withlacoochee River empties into the Gulf of Mexico 17 nm southeast of Cedar Keys. Yankeetown is the primary boating community on the river. It is a very small fishing and winter resort 3 nm above the mouth. The river is navigable for 8 miles upstream where it intersects with a bridge with a fixed vertical clearance of 10 feet. This is a navigable channel and river. The river itself is worth the trip to Yankeetown.

NAVIGATION: Use NOAA Charts 11408 and 11409. You need to work your way through the well-marked confusion of the Cross Florida Barge Canal into the channel for the Withlacoochee River. Back on your inside course through the Big Bend, leave Crystal River flashing red buoy "2" at N 28° 47.542'/W 82 °58.571' on a course of 3 degrees magnetic. Travel with a watchful eye on the depth sounder for 8 miles to the flashing red "4" at N 28° 55.512'/W 82° 58.004'. The Cross Florida Barge Canal runs in an easterly direction. Follow the canal to flashing green "17" where a channel will branch off to the right and a channel will go slightly left or straight. Take the channel straight ahead using flashing red "20" to set yourself up in the new channel.

At flashing green "23," take a course of 36 degrees magnetic and make for the 16-foot high, quick-flashing green "1" to take the Withlacoochee River Entrance channel. Green daybeacon "25" will be south, as will red daybeacon "26." The channel winds, with rocks on both sides. From green daybeacon "3" it is about 8 miles to Yankeetown. Depths for the channel, canal

Manatee Springs

and river are reported to be 5 feet or more at MLW. The Withlacoochee definitely fits the bill for those wanting to take the path less traveled.

Dockage: This is a great place to visit, but do not expect high end docks or amenities. It is a remote location. Yankeetown Marina (6-foot MLW approach depths) gets great reviews from boaters. B's Cypress Marina and Campground is farther upriver and has some transient space and sells gas. They can make arrangements for delivery of diesel. Riverside Marina and Cottages is a camping and RV resort with covered and open transient slips. They also rent pontoon boats and kayaks for further exploration.

Anchorage: Sailboats have been seen anchoring near the **Hwy. 19 Bridge** (40-foot fixed vertical clearance) on the Cross Florida Greenway.

Cedar Key

The Cedar Keys are a group of low sandy islets covered with mangrove trees. The outermost islet is Seahorse Key, where the white tower of an abandoned lighthouse stands on its south side. The lighthouse is visible from offshore.

Cedar Key is a small town on Way Key, located roughly one-third of the way between Anclote Key and Carrabelle. Named for the stand of cedar trees that once grew here, today the island is all logged out, and the town subsists on fishing, both commercial and sport, with tourism playing an increasingly important role. Cedar Key is the top U.S. producer of farm-raised clams.

NAVIGATION: Use NOAA Chart 11408. Resume your course for this route at Crystal River flashing red buoy "2" at N 28° 47.542'/W 82° 58.571'. Leave flashing red buoy "2" on a course of 341 degrees magnetic, and travel for 17 nm to Cedar Key's 16-foot high, flashing green "1" at N 29° 04.000'/W 083° 04.500'. Depths in the channel are at least 7 feet at MLW, but you must follow the well-marked channel carefully. Study an up-to-date chart in detail before you enter, and you should have no difficulty. Refer to the Waterway Explorer and NOAA online charts for the most up-to-date information.

Southwest from Seahorse Key, Seahorse Reef extends for 11 nm. This is a dangerous shoal with little depth. The outer end of the reef is marked by a 31-foot high, flashing white (N 28° 58.310'/W 83° 09.130'). The shoal between red daybeacons "10" and "12" is building out into the channel. When transiting this area, give red daybeacon "12" a wide berth, favoring the western, Seahorse Key side of the channel.

Be careful: Legions of unwary visitors seeking a shortcut have been grounded by the S-curve in the winding channel. Also, pay close attention at the junction of Ship and Northwest Channels, just past Grassy Key. Sorting out the maze of shoals and lights demands serious concentration. Go slowly, attempt no shortcuts and be aware of the currents.

When leaving northbound, take Northwest Channel, which leaves the main channel at quick-flashing red "30" about 1 nm from the town dock, off Grassy Key. Do not attempt Northwest Channel on a low tide if

Suwannee River, FL

SUWANNEE				**Dockage**				**Supplies**		**Services**				
		Largest Vessel Accommodated	VHF Channel Monitored	Approach / Dockside Depth (reported)	Transient Berths / Total Berths	Floating Docks	Gas / Diesel	Groceries, Ice, Marine Supplies, Snacks	Repairs: Hull, Engine, Propeller	Lift (tonnage), Crane, Rail	Min/Max Amps	Laundry, Pool, Showers, Courtesy Car	Pump-Out Station	Nearby: Grocery Store, Motel, Restaurant
1. Gateway Marina (formerly Miller's Marina of Suwannee, Inc.) 📟 WIFI 352-542-7349		70	16/17	10/200	10/6	F	GD	GIMS	HEP	L5,C40	30/30	L	P	GMR
2. Suwannee Marina Inc. 352-542-9159		38	16	call/47	7/7	F	G	GIMS	EP	–	–	–	–	GR

📟 Internet Access   WIFI Wireless Internet Access   WG Waterway Guide Cruising Club Partner   🌐 onSpot dockside WiFi facility
See WaterwayGuide.com for current rates, fuel prices, web site addresses, and other up-to-the-minute information. (*Information in the table is provided by the facilities.*)

SUWANNEE, NOAA CHART 11408

your draft exceeds 4 feet or during darkness or rough water conditions. Shoaling is particularly acute between green daybeacon "17A" and flashing red "18," and also between flashing green "19" and red daybeacon "20." Prominent marks in the Town of Cedar Key are a radio tower and 140-foot municipal water tank.

Dockage: There are no marinas with transient slips at Cedar Key. Cedar Key Marina II provides small boat dockage and dry storage as well as engine repair. They also sell boats and motors.

Anchorage: It is possible to anchor in depths around 8 feet at MLW on the north side of Atsena Otie Key. Feel your way in cautiously. The island is part of the Cedar Keys National Wildlife Refuge. The "cut" between the two halves of the island provides a great place to paddle a kayak. If you decide to go ashore,

don't miss the 19th-century cemetery and ruins of the once-thriving village.

Another alternative is to anchor just southwest of the fishing pier (out of the channel) in 8 to 14 feet at MLW, and then dinghy in under the bridge to the small-boat docking area in the basin. Because of the strong tidal current in the anchorage, you may want to use a two-anchor Bahamian moor. You can also find anchorage just north of the small boat basin and the restaurants on Dock St.

These are exposed anchorages with little protection. You should only anchor here in fair weather. This is not cruising boat territory.

SUWANNEE AND STEINHATCHEE RIVERS

The salt waters of the Gulf of Mexico intertwine with the spring-fed waters of the rivers in this area. As a result, you'll find plenty of water-related recreation: boating, fishing, paddling and "house-boating."

It is just over 100 statute miles from Cedar Keys to the town of St. Marks. Anchoring near the mouth of the St. Marks River cuts about 10 statute miles off this leg. Another good stopover is Steinhatchee about 45 nm from Cedar Keys.

Suwannee River

The river actually originates in Georgia's Okefenokee Swamp and meanders about 280 miles before reaching the Gulf of Mexico. The tannin-stained water here was the inspiration for Stephen Foster's Suwannee River from "Old Folks at Home," Florida's official state song. This is indeed Old Florida and you won't find much here but the beauty of the river and the 70 plus springs that feed millions of gallons of water into it every day .

On approach from the Gulf of Mexico there are three passes/channels into the Suwannee that can be confusing. Approaching from the south you will pass Derrick Key Gap at the south end of Suwannee Reef and Suwannee Sound. This is where you will find East Pass, the first of the three channels. Depths in East Pass are about 2 feet at MLW. You may see small fishing boats using the Pass, but it is doubtful you will be tempted to enter.

The second is West Pass, sometimes referred to as Alligator Pass by locals. It is the first marked channel and you may see small boats coming and going in West Pass. At high tide it should carry depths of 4 feet or more, but it is not recommended for a cruising boat.

The third channel you will encounter is the Main Pass, often referred to as Wadley Pass. It is the northernmost of the three channels. Depths are posted at a controlling depth of 3 feet at MLW; however, reports from March 2017 claim depths of at least 5 feet at MLW. If a north wind is blowing and a winter front is coming through depths can drop considerably.

NAVIGATION: Use NOAA Chart 11407. Starting at daybeacon green "1" at the entrance of the Crystal River Channel, travel 2 nm on a course of 269 degrees magnetic. Then, on a course of 281 degrees magnetic for 20 nm to the 31-foot tower, flashing "7M" at Sea Horse Reef. Make sure you leave this tower/marker to the east.

Leaping Sturgeons!

The Suwannee River appears to support the largest viable population of Gulf sturgeon, according to the Florida Fish and Wildlife Conservation Commission (FWC). Biologists estimate the annual population at 10,000 to 14,000 fish, averaging approximately 40 pounds each. Adult fish spend 8 to 9 months each year in the river spawning and three to four of the coolest months in Gulf waters.

The sturgeon can be hazardous to boaters, as they tend to leap unexpectedly straight up and out of the water, turning sideways and landing with a loud noise. Much like deer hit by cars, jumping sturgeon are sometimes struck by boats. A large sturgeon can weigh more than 100 pounds, so impact with a fast-moving boat can cause serious injury to both boat passengers and the sturgeon alike. Numerous people have been injured in accidental collisions with the jumping sturgeon on the Suwannee River.

Sturgeon are generally observed jumping during the summer and fall months (May-October). Jumping occurs most frequently in mid-summer (May-early August) when sturgeon are fasting. Researchers have determined that the sturgeon jump to communicate with other fish and to gulp air to fill their swim bladders. This allows the sturgeon to maintain neutral buoyancy. Sturgeon can leap more than 7 feet out of the water.

FWC officials have initiated a public awareness campaign to alert boaters to the risks of jumping sturgeon and recommended that boaters slow down to reduce the risk of impact and to have more reaction time if a jumping sturgeon is encountered. And boaters are always encouraged to wear their life jackets at all times while on the water. To report sturgeon collisions, call 888-404-FWCC (3922).

Steinhatchee River, FL

STEINHATCHEE		Largest Vessel Accommodated	VHF Channel Monitored	Approach / Dockside Depth (reported)	Transient Berths / Total Berths	Floating Docks	Gas / Diesel	Groceries, Ice, Marine Supplies, Snacks	Repairs: Hull, Engine, Propeller	Lift (tonnage), Crane, Rail	Min/Max Amps	Laundry, Pool, Showers, Courtesy Car	Pump-Out Station	Nearby: Grocery Store, Motel, Restaurant
				Dockage				**Supplies**		**Services**				
1. Sea Hag Marina ☐ 📶	352-498-3008	45	09	6/20	5/8	F	GD	IMS	HEP	L7	30/50	LPS	–	GMR
2. Good Times Motel & Marina ☐ 📶 WG	352-498-8088	45	09	3/50	9/9	F	GD	GIMS	–	–	30/30	S	–	GMR
3. River Haven Marina & Motel ☐ 📶	352-498-0709	70	10	4/51	3.5/10	F	GD	GIS	HEP	L15,C	30/50	LS	P	GMR
4. Steinhatchee Landing Resort	352-498-3513	28	–	12/12	8/5	F	–	S	–	–	30/30	LPS	–	GM

☐ Internet Access 📶 Wireless Internet Access WG Waterway Guide Cruising Club Partner 💬 onSpot dockside WiFi facility
See WaterwayGuide.com for current rates, fuel prices, web site addresses, and other up-to-the-minute information. *(Information in the table is provided by the facilities.)*

STEINHATCHEE, NOAA CHART 11407

Soon after you leave Crystal River and travel on a course of 281 degrees you will cross the Florida Barge Canal. Be mindful to avoid the markers as you cross the canal. From Sea Horse Reef, travel on a course of 352 degrees magnetic for 20 nm. Then, 68 degrees magnetic for 0.5 nm to the entrance channel for the Main/Wadley Pass to the Suwannee River. Along the route from Sea Horse Reef, in 16 nm, you will pass daybeacon flashing red "2" marking the entrance to West Pass. Do not enter West Pass, even though there are markers for the channel. This is not recommended for cruising vessels. The total distance from the Crystal River Channel entrance to the Main/Wadley channel entrance is 42 nm.

Follow the channel markers in to the Suwanee River. The average cruising boat should be able to enter the river and travel the 34 miles or so upriver to Fanning, where you will encounter the 34-foot Hwy. 19 Bridge. Depths in the river average 15 feet at MLW. Be wary and mindful of the unmarked shoal, Jack's Reef, about 13 miles above the river entrance, 3.7 miles north of Fowlers Bluff. The reef occupies about two thirds of the east bank with depths as shallow as 1 foot at MLW. Stay close to the west bank where you will find depths of more than 10 feet at MLW. The location of Jack's Reef is identified on some charts.

A trip to **Manatee Springs** and the State Park dock is well worth the 25-mile trip up river. You can anchor in the river and enjoy all the park has to offer.

Dockage: The full-service Gateway Marina (formerly Miller's Marine) has 200 slips (10 reserved for transients, sells gas and diesel and offers repairs (40-ton crane and 5-ton lift). Offerings include rental kayaks and bait, but their big draw is rental houseboats. Suwannee Marina Inc. sells gas and may have space for you. Call ahead.

You can tie up at Salt Creek Restaurant at the town of Suwannee (north of Barbree Island) if you plan to dine there. Choose from the large deck with water views, cozy indoor bar or cool outdoor tiki bar.

Anchorage: You can anchor in many places along the Suwannee River. North of Hog Island carries at least 5 feet at MLW and excellent holding in mud. Salt Creek, adjacent to the town of Suwannee, has 5 feet at MLW with good holding in mud. These both provide all-around protection.

Steinhatchee River

The interesting fishing village of Steinhatchee (pronounced "STEEN-hatchee") supports several seafood plants. Found about 4 nm from flashing green "1," which marks the entrance to the Steinhatchee River, Steinhatchee's dock space is limited, but locals try their best to make room for everyone.

NAVIGATION: Use NOAA Chart 11407. From the inside route penciled through the Big Bend leave the Cross Florida Barge Canal red buoy "2" on a course of 335 degrees magnetic. Stay on this course for 40 nm, until you are standing out from Bull Cove. At Bull Cove keep a distance from shore of about 6 nm. Keep a close eye on the depth to make sure you avoid shoals that extend as far as 4 nm from the coast. From Bull Cove change course to 17 degrees magnetic and run 7.5 nm to Steinhatchee River light green "1" at N 29° 39.357'/ W 83° 27.347'. Flashing green "1" marks the entrance to the channel for Steinhatchee River. Controlling depth is 5 feet at MLW. The channel is narrow in places, but depths of 6 plus feet at MLW are common. This is one of the more accessible ports of call along Florida's Big Bend.

Dockage: There is one marina with transient slips before the bridge. Sea Hag Marina is the most prominent marina in Steinhatchee and should be able to handle boats with a draft of 6 feet or more dockside, although they report 5-foot approach depths; call ahead. They sell gas and diesel and offer repairs. Good Times Motel & Marina has limited transient space (three slips) and sells fuel. River Haven Marina & Motel has transient slips for vessels to 70 feet. They are located past a 25-foot fixed vertical clearance bridge. They report 3.5-foot approach depths at MLW. Call for availability, directions and updated knowledge about water depths. Steinhatchee Landing Resort has transient space on floating docks and 5-foot dockside depths for vessels to 25 feet..

Anchorage: An anchorage is located on the outside of the bend, several hundred feet beyond red daybeacon "36," in 6- to 7-foot MLW depths. The holding is soupy, but protection from all directions is excellent. Anchorage is also available just above Sea Hag Marina after daybeacon red "48" before the **10th St. Bridge** (25-foot closed vertical clearance).

■ ST. MARKS

Four rivers flow into the eastern Apalachee Bay: St. Marks, Aucilla, Econfina and Fenholloway. Residential and commercial development is minimal along this part of the coast. This is truly a part of "old Florida." From Cedar Key it is 83 miles to the St. Marks River. Cape St. George is 54 miles to the northeast. The town of St. Marks is 5.5 miles above the river entrance. Barge traffic is prevalent in the river.

Wakulla Springs is less than 10 miles away. This immense freshwater spring reaches a maximum depth of 185 feet, and more than 600,000 gallons flow from the spring every minute, literally creating the Wakulla River.

NAVIGATION: Use NOAA Charts 11406, 11407, 11408 and 11405. A good reference for a route to St. Marks is to begin at the Cross Florida Barge Canal Approach lighted red "2" located 4 nm southwest of the Seahorse Reef's 31-foot high, flashing white. From Barge Canal red "2" set a course of 322 degrees magnetic for 76 nm to Ochlockonee Shoal's flashing red buoy "24." From there, it is 9.5 nm on a course of 3 degrees magnetic to the red and white "SM" buoy at the entrance of the St. Marks Channel.

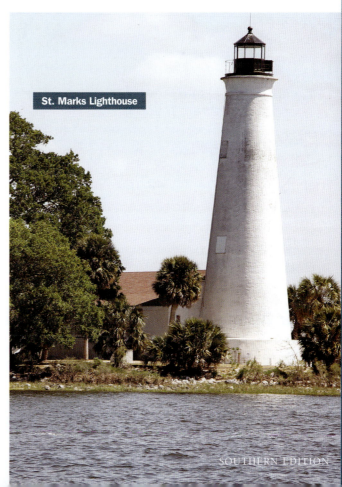

St. Marks Lighthouse

St. Marks River to Carrabelle River, FL

		Dockage						Supplies	Services					
	Phone	Largest Vessel Accommodated	VHF Channel Monitored	Transient Berths / Total Berths	Approach / Dockside Depth (reported)	Floating Docks	Gas / Diesel	Groceries, Ice, Marine Supplies, Snacks	Repairs: Hull, Engine, Propeller	Lift (tonnage), Crane, Rail	Min/Max Amps	Laundry, Pool, Showers, Courtesy Car	Pump-Out Station	Nearby: Grocery Store, Motel, Restaurant
ST. MARKS														
1. St. Marks Yacht Club	850-925-6606	50	–	1/25	7/7	F	–	–	–	–	50/50	LPS	–	GMR
2. Shields Marina	850-925-6158	60	16	2/100	12/10	–	GD	GIMS	EP	L	50/50	LS	P	GMR
3. Riverside Marina	850-925-6157	60	06	1/55	12/8	F	G	GIM	H	C	30/50	S	P	GMR
ALLIGATOR HARBOR														
4. Alligator Point Marina	850-349-2511	45	16	3/45	4/5	F	GD	IMS	–	–	30/50	S	–	R
CARRABELLE														
5. Carrabelle Boat Club	850-697-5500	–	–	call/18	–	–	–	IS	–	L	–	S	–	MR
6. The Moorings of Carrabelle 🖥 WiFi 380 EHL	850-697-2800	150	16/68	15/150	15/9	–	GD	IMS	–	–	30/50	LPS	P	GMR
7. C-Quarters Marina 🖥 WiFi 380 EHL	850-697-8400	100	16/68	30/67	12/9	–	GD	IMS	EP	–	30/50	LS	P	GMR
8. MS Dockside Marina	850-697-3337	65	16	call/22	16/19	F	–	IM	HEP	L60	30/50	–	–	R

🖥 Internet Access WiFi Wireless Internet Access **WG** Waterway Guide Cruising Club Partner onSpot dockside WiFi facility

See WaterwayGuide.com for current rates, fuel prices, web site addresses, and other up-to-the-minute information. *(Information in the table is provided by the facilities.)*

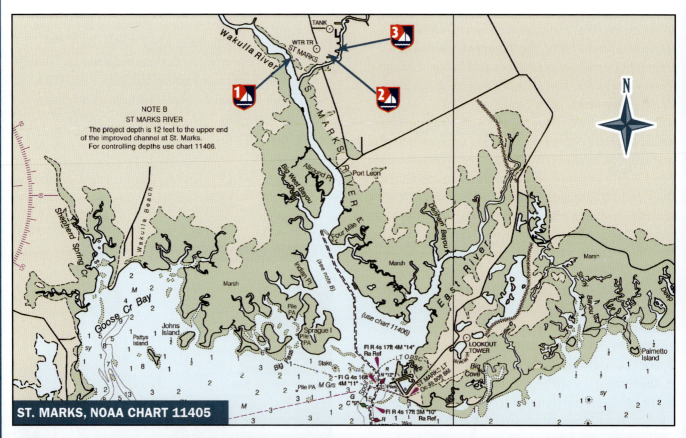

ST. MARKS, NOAA CHART 11405

NOTE B
ST MARKS RIVER
The project depth is 12 feet to the upper end of the improved channel at St. Marks. For controlling depths use chart 11406.

see our interactive charts

MARINAS ANCHORAGES FREE DOCK BRIDGES LOCKS NAV ALERTS FUEL

waterwayguide.com

ALLIGATOR HARBOR, NOAA CHART 11405

CARRABELLE, NOAA CHART 11404

GOIN' ASHORE: CARRABELLE, FL

SERVICES	
1	Post Office
2	Library
3	Visitor Information
ATTRACTIONS	
4	Camp Gordon Johnston WWII Museum
5	Carabelle History Museum
6	World's Smallest Police Station

SHOPPING	
7	Carabelle Medical Pharmacy
8	Ganders Gulf Supply Hardware
9	Gulfside IGA Plus
10	Millender & Son Seafood
DINING	
11	Fathon's Steam Room & Raw Bar

12	Harry's Bar & Package/Marine Street Grill
13	Marine Street Grill
14	The Fisherman's Wife
MARINAS	
15	C-Quarters Marina
16	MS Dockside Marina
17	The Moorings of Carabelle

Carrabelle is a small, quiet town known for relaxing, boating, fishing, hunting, friendly people and white sand beaches. The eastern panhandle area of Florida is largely undeveloped and unspoiled. Ecotourism has become the most popular aspect of the area; experienced "green guides" conduct tours (usually requiring advance reservations). This is a good way to explore the area's rich and diverse mixture of plants, flowers, wildlife, butterflies and birds. Land and water adventure tours are also available for hiking, kayaking, off-road trails, fishing and sightseeing.

Attractions: Carrabelle claims to be home to the World's Smallest Police Station. Located on US 98 at the corner of CR 67, the phone booth-sized police station has an interesting history. In the early 1960s policemen made phone calls from a pay phone located on the outside of the station to get around a regulation regarding making unauthorized long distance calls from a police phone. When the telephone company decided to replace its worn out phone booth in front of

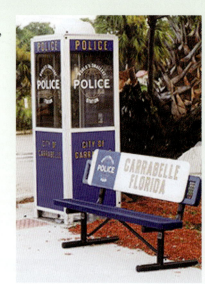

Burda's Pharmacy with a new one, they placed the police phone in the old booth. A replica of the booth is on display across the street from the Visitor Center at 105 St. James Ave. The tiny police station has been featured in multiple television shows and one movie (about nearby Tate's Hell State Forest, which is more fun than it sounds).

Other colorful history can be uncovered at the Carrabelle History Museum (106 SE Ave. B, 850-697-2141) and at the Camp Gordon Johnston WWII Museum, the largest WWII museum in Florida (1001 Gray Ave., 850-697-8575).

Most attractions are within walking/cycling distance or you can pre-arrange a shuttle for your visit. You will need transportation, for example, to visit the Crooked River Lighthouse & Keeper's House Museum (1975 Hwy .98 W., 850-697-2732).

Shopping: Grocery and convenience stores, hardware and marine supplies, a Post Office, a package store, a public library and a bank with 24-hour ATM are conveniently located within 1 mile of the marinas. The Carrabelle Medical Pharmacy also contains a gift shop. There are several other gift and antiques shops with a unique beachside flavor, to browse and shop.

For provisioning, a Gulfside IGA Plus is convenient to the marinas at 812 Ave. A N. (850-697-2710). If you want to prepare fresh seafood on the boat, the go to is Millender & Sons Seafood (607 Ave. B S., 850-697-3301).

Dining: Harry's Bar & Package (306 Marine St., 850-697-9982) is a true "locals" spot with a ton of character and has been in continuous operation in a historic waterfront building since 1942. At Marine Street Grill (304 Marine St., 850-646-3088), you can have a burger and a beer or wings and wine in a New Orleans-style courtyard.

Fathom's Steam Room and Raw Bar (201 St. James Ave., 850-697-9712) is not fancy but has good seafood and entertainment (open March through November). The Fisherman's Wife (201 8th St. W., 850-697-4533) offers seafood and burger baskets. You will find variety in menu choices in Carrabelle, and local seafood is generally available. It's a good idea to call ahead for hours and days of operation for the restaurants. Also, keep in mind that the pace is slower here than in some areas. Your patience will pay off when your seafood is fresh from the Gulf and made to order.

See carrabelle.org or call 850-697-2585 for more information on the area.

St. Marks is easily accessible from Steinhatchee. From 30-foot flashing green "1," marking the entrance to the Steinhatchee River Channel, set a course of 273 degrees magnetic for 9 nm to the yellow special purpose buoy at Steinhatchee Reef at N 29° 39.893'/ W 83° 37.823'. Depths at the reef are charted at 15 feet at MLW. From Steinhatchee Reef your course is 306 degrees magnetic for 36 nm to the red and white Morse (A) buoy "SM" marking the entrance to the St. Marks River.

Well before arriving at Morse (A) buoy "SM," you will see the 82-foot-high St. Marks Lighthouse (no longer lighted) on shore but do not shortcut this leg. The well-marked entry channel twists and turns through a maze of shoals. Daylight passage should present no problems but avoid going in at night. The single orange range marker is used in conjunction with the St. Marks Lighthouse; lining both up will keep you in mid-channel from flashing green "1" to the first dogleg at green can buoy "3A." (Note that green can "3" may be missing.)

St. Marks has a straightforward channel and river. Both are wide, well-marked and carry enough depth (6 feet plus at MLW) to accommodate most cruising boats that have made it this far.

Dockage: Up the St. Marks River, you will find St. Marks Yacht Club, Shields Marina and Riverside Marina. They all have limited (one to two) transient slips on their floating dock. Two restaurants and a small grocery store are within easy walking distance of Shields Marina. Riverside Marina sells gas. A call ahead is essential here, based on the minimal number of reserved transient slips.

Anchorage: About 1 mile above the marinas, around the first bend, the St. Marks River offers an anchorage completely different from the usual Gulf Coast beaches. Tropical plants line both riverbanks, wildlife abounds and you can anchor in complete solitude. Be sure to install your screens and apply plenty of insect repellent. You should have minimum 6-foot MLW depths.

Alligator Point

NAVIGATION: Use NOAA Chart 11405. To reach Alligator Point, take your departure from flashing red bell buoy "26" south of South Shoal. From there, take a course of 312 degrees magnetic to flashing green "1" at the northeast end of Dog Island Reef. At this point, you can alter course to 350 degrees magnetic. After just more than 3 nm, you will pick up red flashing "2," marking the entrance to Alligator Harbor. Follow the daybeacons all the way to the marina.

Dockage: Watch your depth. Charted shoals at the entrance to Alligator Point Marina are marked at 3 to 5 feet at MLW. The marina is primarily for small fishing boats, but transient slips are available. They also have a ship store with beer, fishing tackle, snacks and all fuels plus some boating accessories. End of the World Oasis–a seasonal on-site tiki hut–will cook your catch on site or you can choose from their (mostly grilled) menu (850-349-9792).

Anchorage: A protected anchorage can be found inside Bay Mouth Bar near red daybeacon "22" in at least 7 feet at MLW or off Wilson Beach (8 to 10 feet at MLW).

Carrabelle

East Pass into St. George Sound marks the end of the trek across Florida's Big Bend. Once again cruising boats, with a vertical clearance of less than 50 feet, can choose to travel the GIWW or go offshore in the Gulf of Mexico. To the west is the port city of Apalachicola, and to the east is the port city of Carrabelle. Carrabelle is the closest to East Pass. It is an excellent stop for boats looking for a place to rest after crossing The Big Bend.

NAVIGATION: Use NOAA Charts 11401, 11404 and 11405. If you are traveling west, this is the last leg of your trip along an inside passage for Florida's Big Bend. The inside route penciled on your chart runs from Ochlockonee Shoal's flashing red buoy "24" to the East Pass entrance to St. George Sound and on to Carrabelle.

For the cruising boaters coming from St. Marks, your transit begins at the red and white "SM" entrance buoy for the St. Marks River. From the "SM" buoy, travel on a course of 183 degrees magnetic for 9.5 nm to Ochlockonee Shoal's flashing red buoy "24" at N 29° 51.50'/W 84° 10.30'. From there, travel a course of 250 degrees magnetic for 9.3 nm to flashing red "26" at N 29° 47.50'/W 84° 20.00'. From red "26" change course to 265 degrees magnetic for 17 nm to flashing red "2" at N 29° 44.50'/W 84° 39.20', marking the entrance to East Pass and St. George Sound.

East Pass, one of the better Florida west coast passes, leads 5 nm through St. George Sound to the Carrabelle River. Follow the marked channel through East Pass and note the northeastern jog at flashing red can "12," which was reported to be sinking in January 2018. Stay in the channel to Carrabelle.

Dockage: One mile north of the GIWW on the Carrabelle River, three marinas offer transient dockage (Carrabelle Boat Club is private). The full-service Moorings of Carrabelle has slips and fuel plus provides complimentary bicycles. C-Quarters Marina also has slips and fuel and bicycles can be rented just across the street. MS Dockside Marina has slips and amenities and offers repairs (with a 60-ton lift). C-Quarters is closest to what the city has to offer, but bicycles allow you to access everything in the small downtown area of Carrabelle from the other local marinas.

Anchorage: You can anchor in the main river in 5-foot MLW depths south of green marker "17." Be sure not to block the channel.

Side Trip: Dog Island Anchorage

Due south of the Carrabelle River is Dog Island with numerous anchoring possibilities. Just inside the hook of the west end of Dog Island, you can anchor at Shipping Cove, an excellent spot in deep water (charted at 17 to 20 feet at MLW). A small embayment at the northeast end of Dog Island can provide limited shelter. Tyson Harbor, also at the northeast end of Dog Island, offers protection from all but northwest winds. The 6-foot plus channel leading to the small ferry dock is narrow, but well-marked. Stay in the center, and watch for the abruptly shoaling edges.

The island's hospitable owners allow cruising mariners to explore the beaches but please stay off private docks and property. A portion of the island is a bird breeding and nesting area, posted with "Keep Out" signs. Please honor them. (The posted section does not include the beach.)

■ NEXT STOP

At this point, we will leave the Big Bend area and enter the Florida Panhandle area. You will need to decide if you want to travel outside in the Gulf of Mexico by following the coastline all the way to Pensacola or take the GIWW route (200 statute miles). Fixed bridge heights of 50 feet will prevent most sailboats from using some of the inside route.

The Panhandle: Apalachicola to Pensacola

 GIWW Mile 375 EHL-Mile 170 EHL   **VHF** FL Bridges: Channel 09

CHARTS NOAA 11378, 11385, 11389, 11390, 11391, 11393, 11401, 11402, 11404

The Panhandle is a strip of land in northwest Florida that runs some 200 miles from Apalachicola to Pensacola and is 50 to 100 miles wide. Sometimes this region is referred to as the Emerald Coast, describing the beaches and resorts spanning the western section from Port St. Joe to Pensacola.

Cruisers from parts west, such as Texas and southbound Loopers exiting the Tombigbee River into Mobile Bay will reach The Panhandle from the west. Boaters who skirt the shores of Florida's Big Bend or make the 140- to 170-nm run offshore from Anclote Key or Clearwater will approach from the southeast.

Bridges with vertical clearances as low as 50 feet limit the inside route along this coast, but those who can manage that have many options. If you have the time and boat for it, this part of the GIWW is much more intriguing and enjoyable than many segments of the ICW. It meanders along for a couple of hundred miles, sometimes along the barrier island beaches and sometimes inland through the woods and marshlands. Real estate development is not as dense. You can enjoy the cypress- and hardwood-lined banks of the waterway, state parks, national seashore, secluded anchorages or a good marina at the end of each day.

The region is rich with cypress and hardwood trees, sugar white beaches, clear natural springs, clear blue waters and abundant seafood. Fish the ageless Steinhatchee, explore the wilderness of St. Vincent Island, enjoy the history of Apalachicola, the beach and nightlife of Panama City Beach and the rich history and culture of Pensacola. The pace of life here is slow. Embrace the laid-back southern style that is all mixed in a magnificent blueprint that makes the Florida Panhandle a great place to hang out for a while.

> As mentioned in the introduction to this section, along the panhandle of Florida, a rather unique change occurs to **tides.** West of St. George's Sound/Apalachicola Bay, there are only 2 tides per 24 hours—one high and one low—while east of this demarcation, the tides are the normal 4 per 24 hours—2 highs, and 2 lows.

OFFSHORE TO PENSACOLA

For the cruising boat that reaches St. George Sound (and has a vertical clearance of less than 50 feet), it is difficult to recommend an offshore passage to Pensacola. The GIWW distance from Mile 375 EHL to Mile 180 in Pensacola Bay is 195 statute miles through an enjoyable, low-stress section of the GIWW.

The GIWW has three bridges, spaced conveniently between offshore inlets, with fixed vertical clearances of 50 feet. The offshore passage from East Pass must go around the shoals that extend from Cape St. George and Cape San Blas. The offshore distance from Mile 375 EHL to the entrance at Pensacola Bay is 158 nm (182 statute miles).

From the flashing red "2" at the end of East Pass, set a course of about 230 degrees magnetic for 25 nm to avoid the shoals at Cape St. George and Cape San Blas. Then, for Pensacola, set a course of about 295 degrees magnetic for 130 nm (for a total distance of 155 nm).

There are two inlets that will allow you to break the trip into two days to enjoy this part of the Emerald Coast. The well-marked inlet at St. Andrews Bay will be a total distance of 80 nm from East Pass. There are two sets of red and green nuns and cans marking shoals inside the inlet that may not be shown on your charts. Refer to the Waterway Explorer (waterwayguide.com) and NOAA online charts for the most up-to-date information and check electronic charts at different zooms.

The channel at Destin is passable but not as well marked. It has a controlling depth of 6 feet at MLW and a width of 50 feet and is a total distance of 120 nm from East Pass. From this channel, you can reach marinas before the 49-foot bridge that blocks the pass to the GIWW.

An alternate, recommended offshore route is to enter St. George Sound at East Pass and proceed along the GIWW to Port St. Joe. To reach Port St. Joe, turn to the southwest at Mile 328 EHL at the Gulf County Canal. (There are signs at this intersection.). The distance to Port St. Joe from Mile 375 EHL is 52 statute miles. The offshore run from Port St. Joe to the entrance at Pensacola Bay is 100 nm) on a course of 283 degrees.

⚠️ This area of the Gulf is used extensively by the U.S. Air Force. Along the entire route you will be passing by and over areas marked as missile testing, unexploded ordnance and fish havens. Check the *Local Notice to Mariners* and the Waterway Guide Explorer at waterwayguide.com for updates.

CARRABELLE TO APALACHICOLA

The segment of the GIWW from East Pass to Pensacola covers 195 statute miles of relatively pleasant inside cruising. There is very little white-knuckle cruising here. The GIWW passage along the Florida Panhandle ranges in ambiance from lovely and lonesome, narrow channels winding through swamp and bayou areas to more northern settings of deciduous trees and modern housing, connecting big, clear bays, bayous and sounds. Narrow barrier islands protect the entire passage.

Depths range from 10 to 12 feet at MLW but shoaling is possible, so be sure to keep an eye on your depth sounder. There are three bridges with a fixed vertical clearance of 50 feet: DuPont Bridge in East Bay (Mile 295.4 EHL), Brooks Memorial Bridge at Fort Walton Beach (Mile 223 EHL) and Navarre Beach Bridge (Mile 206.6 EHL).

Apalachicola–GIWW Mile 351 EHL

A worthwhile layover along this stretch of the GIWW is Apalachicola, with its village-like atmosphere, excellent local oysters and unique shopping opportunities within walking distance of the marinas.

NAVIGATION: Use NOAA Chart 11404. It is a pleasant trip through the Sound and Apalachicola Bay to the unique and beautiful City of Apalachicola. If you go into Carrabelle, you will have to come back out the same way. After exiting the Carrabelle River and retracing your course into St. George Sound, pick up flashing red "2" (Mile 374 EHL) just inside East Pass. From there, flashing red "6" becomes visible, about 2.5 statute miles to the southwest. From flashing red "6," the GIWW is clearly marked as it jogs south by southwest at quick flashing red "20" for about two statute miles to quick-flashing red "28" (Mile 365 EHL), where it resumes its southwest direction. From that point, it is a straight shot southwest for about 9.3 statute miles under the fixed

Apalachicola–St. George Island Bridge at Mile 361.4 EHL (65-foot vertical clearance) over Apalachicola Bay at Bulkhead Shoal (red nun buoy "48"). Watch your depths carefully in the area of Bulkhead Shoal where the oyster beds come right to the edge of the channel. The channel is especially narrow on the east side of the bridge, so keep an eye on the markers ahead and behind to keep from crabbing into the shallows. The bridge is the boundary of demarcation between St. George Sound and Apalachicola Bay.

After traversing much of Apalachicola Bay, at quick-flashing red "76," make a 90-degree turn north and follow the GIWW about 3.5 statute miles to red nun buoy "24," marking the entrance to the Apalachicola River and the town of Apalachicola.

Dockage: After passing red nun buoy "24," and just south of the fixed **John Gorrie Memorial (U.S. 98/319) Bridge** at Mile 351.4 EHL (65-foot vertical clearance), is the easily sighted Apalachicola municipal marina (Battery Park Marina). Transient slips are available and the marina sells gas. This facility is open to wakes left by passing boaters transiting the GIWW, so be sure to use ample spring lines and fenders.

Transients are welcome north of the bridge at Apalachicola Marina, Inc., which has 12-foot MLW dockside depths and full amenities, including gas and diesel and some marine supplies. A supermarket, drug store and restaurants are within easy walking distance. Close by is the Apalachicola River Inn (850-653-8139) with slips, guest rooms and dining options.

Most of the other transient facilities are located farther north, along with various fuel docks and a waterfront hotel (Water Street Hotel and Marina) with ample dock space. J.V. Gander Distributors, Inc. sells gas and diesel fuel but has no transient space. Take care while fueling and docking, as the Apalachicola River can have a strong current depending on tidal flow.

If you want to get away from GIWW traffic, Scipio (the "c" is silent) Creek Marina is a popular stopover for cruisers. It has less tidal current than facilities located directly on the Apalachicola River. The marina is located to the northwest of the river at green-red can "A." Motels, restaurants and provisions are within a 3-block walk.

Anchorage: It is possible to anchor in Apalachicola, just north of the John Gorrie Memorial Bridge. Here you will find 9 to 12 feet at MLW with good holding. You will be exposed to wakes; be sure to anchor well out of the channel. There are also anchorages at Shell Point on St. George Island in 7 to 10 feet at MLW.

Apalachicola

GOIN' ASHORE: **APALACHICOLA, FL**

SERVICES	
1	Post Office
2	Library
3	Visitor Information
ATTRACTIONS	
4	Apalachicola Maritime Museum
5	Battery Park
6	John Gorrie State Museum
7	Veterans Memorial Park
SHOPPING	
8	Bowery Art Gallery
9	Down Town Books and Purl
10	Forgotten Coast Books
11	On the Waterfront
12	Tin Shed
DINING	
13	Caroline's River Dining/Boss Oyster
14	Gibson Inn
15	Papa Joe's Oyster Bar & Grlll
MARINAS	
13	Apalachicola River Inn
16	Apalachicola Marina, Inc.
17	Battery Park Marina
18	J.V. Gander Distributors, Inc.
19	Scipio Creek Marina
20	Water Street Hotel & Marina

While taking a rest from the rigors of the sea, stretch your legs as the shadows fall and the heat subsides. The golden sunset light flatters the preserved historic buildings, Victorian homes, and the restored antebellum houses, a number of which have been turned into bed and breakfasts. As an interesting side note, several of the larger houses in Apalachicola were originally built in Port St. Joe (40 miles to the west) but were moved after a yellow fever outbreak in the 1800s.

Attractions: A visit to the John Gorrie State Museum (42 6th St., two blocks from the municipal pier) might be in order. He doesn't get much recognition for his discovery today, but in the 1830s Dr. John Gorrie invented a machine that made ice. While Dr. Gorrie's

invention was originally designed to help yellow fever patients, it changed the world by making southern climes more habitable. The museum displays a replica of the mechanical refrigerator for which he was granted the first U.S. patent in 1851.

The Apalachicola Maritime Museum (103 Water St., 850-653-2500) sponsors many local events, including educational tours, kayaking, a wooden boat school, a maritime library and exhibits. The Veterans Memorial Park (18 Seventh St.) features a bronze sculpture cast from the same molds used to craft the Three Servicemen Statue at the Vietnam Veteran's Memorial in Washington, DC.

Annual features include the Seafood Festival, held during the first week of November at Battery Park, and the Antique Boat Show held on the waterfront in April.

Shopping: The Tin Shed near the marinas boasts "the most comprehensive maritime collection east of the Mississippi." Several art galleries have opened in recent years, thanks to the influx of artists and tourists to this riverside town. Bowery Art Gallery (149 Commerce St., 850-653-2425) and On the Waterfront (117 Market St., 850-653-9699) are particularly noteworthy.

Down Town Books and Purl (67 Commerce St., 850-653-1290) offers a very wide selection of books that should pique the interest of everyone. They also sell exquisite yarns, games and diversions. Forgotten Coast Books (236A Water St., 850 653-2080) is a gem for browsing. They feature regional literature from old and new Florida and the south, with special editions of classic and modern authors as well as travel, hiking and water guides.

Dining: The fully-restored and expanded Gibson Inn (51 Ave. C, 850-653-2191), just a block from the municipal pier, is an early 1900s "cracker" style structure. Florida cracker homes are characterized by metal roofs, raised floors, large porch areas (often wrapping around the entire home) and straight central hallways from the front to the back of the home (sometimes called "dog trot" or "shotgun" hallways). The Inn offers lodging, a bar and one of the many area restaurants that specialize in seafood, especially the renowned local Apalachicola oysters brought fresh from the bay's shell beds. Papa Joe's Oyster Bar & Grill (301-B Market St., 850-653-1189) has some of these oysters and also great seafood.

Happy hour at the various bistros draws an interesting hodgepodge of oystermen, artists and, naturally, cruisers. Locals and transients keep an eye on the weather fronts via the Weather Channel, which is usually on at the Apalachicola River Inn (123 Water St., 850-653-8139). Caroline's River Dining and Boss Oyster are both located at the Inn. Boss Oyster has a more casual atmosphere with charm and character, serving oysters prepared a whopping 17 different ways.

Apalachicola River, FL

APALACHICOLA		Dockage					Supplies		Services					
		Largest Vessel Accommodated	VHF Channel Monitored	Approach / Dockside Depth	Transient Berths / Total Berths	Floating Docks	Gas / Diesel	Groceries, Ice, Marine Supplies, Snacks	Repairs: Hull, Engine, Propeller	Lift (tonnage), Crane, Rail	Min / Max Amps	Laundry, Pool, Showers, Courtesy Car	Pump-Out Station	Nearby: Grocery Store, Motel, Restaurant
1. Battery Park Marina 351 EHL	850-653-9319	50	–	15/	6/5	–	–	G	–	–	50/50	–	P	GR
2. Apalachicola Marina, Inc. **WIFI** 351 EHL	**850-653-9521**	100	16/09	3/6	15/12	–	GD	IM	–	–	30/50	S	–	GMR
3. Apalachicola River Inn 351 EHL	850-653-8139	90	16	17/17	6/6	–	–	I	–	–	50/50	S	–	GMR
4. Water Street Hotel and Marina ☐ WIFI WG 351 EHL	850-653-3700	55	16	20/20	12/8	F	–	GIMS	–	–	50/50	PS	–	GMR
5. J.V. Gander Distributors, Inc. 351 EHL	850-653-8889	150	–	–	9/9	–	GD	GIMS	–	–	–	–	–	GMR
6. Scipio Creek Marina **WIFI** 351 EHL	850-653-8030	100	16	6/14	12/10	–	GD	IMS	HEP	L	30/50	LS	P	GMR

☐ Internet Access **WIFI** Wireless Internet Access **WG** Waterway Guide Cruising Club Partner **onSpot** dockside WiFi facility
See WaterwayGuide.com for current rates, fuel prices, web site addresses, and other up-to-the-minute information. *(Information in the table is provided by the facilities.)*

APALACHICOLA, NOAA CHART 11401

Side Trip: St. Marks Island

Boaters seeking a side trip can follow the Apalachicola River upstream through a few miles of heavily wooded swampland to the St. Marks, East and Brothers Rivers, after exiting the GIWW at red daybeacon "30." There is ample depth of water here for smaller vessels. (Controlling depths of 9 and 10 feet MLW are available to St. Marks Island on the St. Marks River.) The really adventurous can navigate the river up to the Jim Woodruff Dam at Chattahoochee, but be advised to obtain local knowledge. A grounding requiring commercial assistance will take a large amount of money, especially if you don't have unlimited towing.

APALACHICOLA TO PANAMA CITY

Apalachicola to White City–GIWW Mile 351 to Mile 329 EHL

The GIWW leaves Apalachicola Bay and the Gulf of Mexico at Mile 350 EHL, and then winds along on the scenic Apalachicola River, undulating generally northwest to the **Apalachicola Railroad Swing Bridge** at Mile 347.0 EHL (11-foot closed vertical clearance, usually open). Keep a sharp eye out for tree limbs and other floating debris. Night passages are not recommended.

NAVIGATION: Use NOAA Charts 11393, 11401 and 11402. From the mouth of the Apalachicola River, the GIWW is well marked. Past red daybeacon "30," the Apalachicola River turns north, and the GIWW continues along the Jackson River (named for Stonewall Jackson who was governor of the territory) to Lake Wimico at Mile 340 EHL.

You will soon take a hairpin turn to the south past flashing green "9," just west of Mile 345 EHL, and about 1 mile later, take a sharp curve to the west and proceed to Lake Wimico at Mile 340 EHL and green daybeacon "3" and red daybeacon "4." The course for the straight shot across the lake is about 310 degrees magnetic. Follow the daybeacons carefully as the spoil areas are close to the narrow channel.

At flashing green "15," enter Searcy Creek at the end of Lake Wimico (Mile 335 EHL). Follow the well-marked channel from here about 6 miles to the **White City (SR 71) Bridge** (65-foot fixed vertical clearance) at Mile 329.3 EHL. The waterway is relatively wide, relatively deep and there is little to intrude on an enjoyable view from all sides as you traverse swamp country (described on the charts as "impenetrable," "cypress" and "low swampy area").

Dockage: There is a free dock at White City with restrooms in the adjacent park. Tie up to either the seawall or floating dock. There is a convenience store with minimal supplies 1 mile north on the highway. The bulkhead is subject to wakes from GIWW traffic.

Anchorage: Just after the Jackson River splits off from the Apalachicola, head to Saul Creek (northeast at Mile 345 EHL between green "7" and red "8"). There is an excellent protected anchorage in 8 feet at MLW at the junction of Saul Creek and the Saul Creek Cutoff. Depths exceed 30 feet in much of this lovely creek; for optimum holding, use your depth sounder to find an appropriate depth to set the hook. Alligators and birds are abundant.

After exiting Lake Wimico into Searcy Creek, the oxbow around the island at Mile 334 EHL normally carries 10 feet at MLW or better and provides an excellent secluded anchorage.

Port St. Joe, which is southwest of White City, is on **Eastern Time**. You will have to switch your watch back and forth a bit if you don't continue on in the GIWW and, instead, come out into St. Joseph Bay.

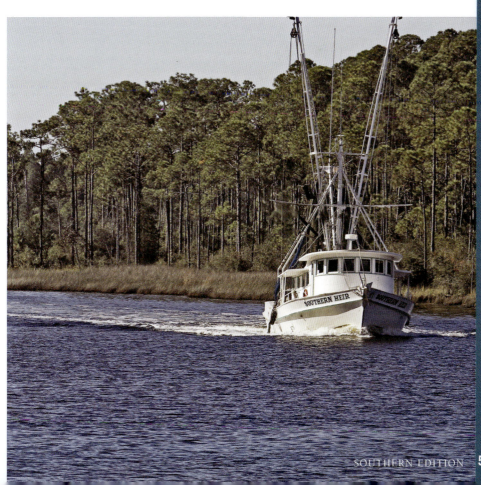

St. Joseph Bay, FL

PORT ST. JOE			Dockage				Supplies		Services					
		Largest Vessel Accommodated	VHF Channel Monitored	Approach / Dockside Depth (reported)	Transient Berths / Total Berths	Floating Docks	Gas / Diesel	Groceries, Ice, Marine Supplies, Snacks	Repairs: Hull, Engine, Propeller	Lift (tonnage), Crane, Rail	Min/Max Amps	Laundry, Pool, Showers, Courtesy Car	Pump-Out Station	Nearby: Grocery Store, Motel, Restaurant
1. Port St. Joe Marina 🖥 📶	850-227-9393	120	16/10	25/114	15/7	–	GD	IMS	–	–	30/50	LS	P	GMR
MEXICO BEACH														
2. Mexico Beach Marina 🖥 📶	850-648-8900	–	16/11	10/34	/6	–	G	IMS	HEP	L7	30/30	–	–	GMR

🖥 Internet Access 📶 Wireless Internet Access **WG** Waterway Guide Cruising Club Partner ☺ onSpot dockside WiFi facility
See WaterwayGuide.com for current rates, fuel prices, web site addresses, and other up-to-the-minute information. *(Information in the table is provided by the facilities.)*

PORT ST. JOE, MEXICO BEACH, NOAA CHART 11389

White City to Panama City via Gulf County Canal and Gulf Route

NAVIGATION: Use NOAA Charts 11389, 11393 and 11401. About 1.5 statute miles from White City on the GIWW, at about Mile 328 EHL, the Gulf County Canal cuts off 90 degrees south and extends 5 miles southwest from the waterway to Port St. Joe on St. Joseph Bay. The controlling depth is 12 feet at MLW, and there is a 75-foot fixed **Port St. Joe (U.S. 98) Bridge** near the exit to St. Joseph Bay. Exiting into St. Joseph Bay, if you are heading for the pass to the Gulf of Mexico, the channel from Port St. Joe to the Gulf is clearly marked. You will have been coming southwestward on the canal. When you intersect the ship channel, you will turn to the northwest and later, north to get around St. Joseph Point at the tip of St. Joseph Peninsula and out of St. Joseph Bay. You will be doing this incrementally, with the last straight run to the southwest until you get into the Gulf of Mexico and 30-plus feet of water.

To get to the entrance buoy (RW "SA") off Panama City, steer northwest. The distance is 21 miles. The "SA" stands for either St. Andrew or St. Andrews, depending on whether you are looking at a chart or listening to the locals; it is best to be flexible. Dead ahead, to the northeast across the bay, you will spot the Panama City Municipal Marina.

Dockage: Port St. Joe can be a convenient stopover point, regardless of the direction you are traveling.

To reach Port St. Joe Marina, follow the deep, well-marked channel into the harbor. The marina welcomes transients, has a well-stocked ship store, sells gas and diesel and is home to the popular open-air Dockside Seafood and Raw Bar (850-229-5200). Have a tropical drink at the tiki bar on the deck or order off the ample menu. The large Bluewater Outriggers is close by, selling clothing and equipment for anglers and other outdoor enthusiasts (850-229-1100). There is a supermarket next door to Bluewater with an ATM and a pharmacy and several fast food establishments are just a short walk from the marina.

Mexico Beach Marina to the north has slips and sells gas. There's not much to do in Mexico Beach, and there isn't even a stoplight. This is a place to slow down and enjoy the white sandy beach.

White City to Panama City–GIWW Mile 329 to Mile 290 EHL

NAVIGATION: Use NOAA Charts 11390, 11391 and 11393. From White City, the GIWW continues to run clean, relatively wide and deep, with no need for navigational aids. At about Mile 318 EHL, it becomes the South Prong of Wetappo Creek and continues beneath **Overstreet (SR 386) Bridge** at Mile 315.4 EHL (65-foot fixed vertical clearance) to about Mile 314 EHL, where it joins the North Prong and becomes Wetappo Creek.

At that point, aids to navigation appear again, starting with green daybeacon "1" at about Mile 313 EHL and continuing down the Wetappo Creek and into Big Cove. At that same green daybeacon "1," eastbound vessels need to stay alert, as the channel bends southeast here and the small bay to the south can be confused with the GIWW.

During strong southerlies, the narrow channel leading west to the sharp turn at Mile 310 EHL (quick-flashing red "28") can pose serious difficulties to barge traffic. If meeting a tow along this stretch, be sure to coordinate on VHF Channel 13 to clarify your intentions. As a matter of practical concern, if you have your VHF radio cycling between Channel 16 and Channel 13 on this section of the GIWW, you will be in great shape.

The GIWW channel runs southwest from Raffield Island, and turns west at red "44" to Murray Point. Near Mile 306 EHL, favor the southwestern side of the channel to avoid oyster reefs on the northeast side (generally marked with "Danger" signs).

On this part of your journey, you will be passing a bay that leads to Sandy Creek just past Mile 310 EHL. You will pass Raffield Island to the south (at 3 feet mean sea level). From there, the GIWW into East Bay winds through well-marked, but relatively narrow channels. Watch your markers carefully in this area, as some very shoal water can be found out of the channel. For example, at red daybeacon "38" off Piney Point (Mile 300.75), there is a 4-foot-deep shoal charted just northeast of the channel. Refer to the Waterway Explorer and NOAA online charts for the most up-to-date information.

Just past Long Point is the **Dupont (U.S. 98) Bridge** at Mile 295.4 (50-foot fixed vertical clearance). From here to Panama City, the GIWW runs through relatively deep water (25 to 35 and even 40 feet).

⚠️ Study the chart carefully for the run up East Bay to Panama City. Flashing green "29" (Mile 294.2 EHL) off Parker Bayou should be left to starboard here, as the GIWW buoy system gives way to the Panama City buoy system (red-right-returning from the Gulf). This can be confusing, as red buoys are now on your port side as you travel west, switching back to red on the right with flashing red "6" off Buena Vista Point west of Panama City.

Anchorage: Between White City and Panama City on the GIWW, a pleasant, protected overnight anchorage is located at Wetappo Creek (Mile 314.5). Just around the first bend of the creek (North Prong), you can safely anchor over a soft mud bottom in about 10 feet of water. Because of the current, a Bahamian moor might be appropriate here, preferably on the side of the river by the marshlands.

In East bay, Walker Bayou (Mile 307.5 EHL), Murray Bayou (Mile 305.7 EHL) and California Bayou (Mile 302

EHL) are options. For boats with shallow draft, Laird Bayou (Mile 299.5 EHL) provides ample protection from north winds in 6 to 8 feet of water with plenty of room to swing. This anchorage is northeast of the GIWW, across from Cedar Point in East Bay. One cove over is Callaway Bayou with good holding in 8 feet of water and all-around protection.

Panama City–GIWW Mile 290 EHL

Panama City boasts a large year-round charter fishing fleet, party boats, fishing piers, diving and surf fishing. Gulf fishing has greatly improved in the area, thanks to conservation efforts, and inshore light-tackle catch-and-release fishing on the bay has become very popular. Snapper, grouper and scamp are plentiful, and offshore fishing is considered magnificent. Boaters can also enjoy the area's sparkling white sugar sand beaches, rated as some of the finest in the country.

NAVIGATION: Use NOAA Chart 11389 and 11390. Shell Island, the barrier island forming the southern side of the main pass from the Gulf of Mexico into St. Andrew Bay, provides shelter for Panama City, which is a major harbor for transient yachts. The cut itself is considered one of the best deep-water channels on the Gulf Coast.

St. Andrew Bay, one of Florida's finest bays and home to Panama City, is deep and almost landlocked. It is a good hurricane hole for larger vessels, but cruising boats should, if possible, seek shelter in a more protected bayou. The Bay's exit to the Gulf of Mexico is a land cut through St. Andrews Park that has a rock jetty and is well marked. The Navy operates a lab on the west end of the bay and south of the **Hathaway (U.S. 98) Bridge** at Mile 284.6 EHL (65-foot fixed vertical clearance); you will frequently see helicopters, hovercraft and some esoteric "special ops" equipment here.

⚠️ Under no circumstances should cruisers attempt to navigate the entrance to St. Andrew Bay at the eastern tip of Shell Island, labeled "Lands End" on the chart. It is unmarked and, with the bottom continually shifting, is considered unsafe. Rest assured that the boats fishing or anchored in this area arrived from St. Andrew Bay, not the Gulf.

Dockage: Panama City is probably the best-equipped harbor north of Tampa and St. Petersburg, and berths are usually available except on holiday weekends. It is a good idea, particularly during the season, to call ahead and reserve a berth. There are facilities throughout the area, beginning from the east at Watson Bayou (north

Waterway Guide Preferred Destination

WG

DESTINATION PANAMA CITY

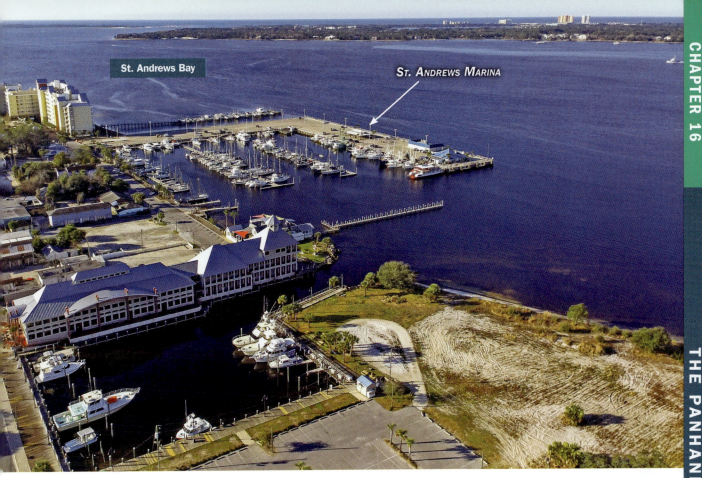

St. Andrews Bay

St. Andrews Marina

The City of Panama City Florida Welcomes You to Their Two Marinas

marinas@pcgov.org

ST. ANDREWS · Marina ·

St. Andrews Marina is newly renovated with floating docks and conveniently located in Historic St. Andrews where a short walk will lead you to coffee shops, famous seafood restaurants, raw bars, live music, and Oaks by the Bay. St. Andrews Marina is a recreational marina that embraces it's working waterfront heritage.

St. Andrews Marina
3151 West 10th Street • 850-872-7240
Buoy Marker Red 6 • MM 287

PANAMA CITY Marina

Panama City Marina is a 240-slip marina designed for vessels up to 120 feet with drafts to 10 feet. Open 7AM to 5PM, 7 days a week • Competitive fuel prices, Ethanol Free Fuel • Fully stocked Ship's store • Clean showers and laundry facilities • FAX and copier service • Nighttime security • Easy Walk to restaurants, coffee shops, Marina Civic Center, and art galleries.

Panama City Marina
1 Harrison Avenue • 850-872-7272
Buoy Marker Green • Flashing 17 • MM 290

GOIN' ASHORE: PANAMA CITY, FL

	SERVICES
1	Visitor Information
	ATTRACTIONS
1	Oyster Trail
2	Oaks by the Bay Park
3	Panama City Publishing Co.
	SHOPPING
4	Floriopolis
5	Little Village
	DINING
6	Hunt's Oyster Bar
7	Just the Cook
8	St. Andrews Coffee House & Bistro
9	Uncle Ernie's Bayfront Grill
	MARINA
7	St. Andrews Marina

It's no surprise that a city with the slogan "Where life sets sail" is a popular boater destination. Panama City welcomes cruisers year-round. Check in with the friendly staff at Destination Panama City Visitors Center at 1000 Beck Ave. (850-215-1700) when you arrive. They can point you to the unique art galleries and specialty shops, a thriving music scene and dining opportunities that range from casual dockside cafés to upscale eateries, with local Gulf oysters as the fare of choice.

Attractions: It's easy to find oysters here…just follow the Panama City Oyster Trail to more than a dozen raw bars and restaurants where you can have oysters any way you desire–raw, baked, char-grilled or fried. The Oyster Trail opened on August 5, 2017 (National Oyster Day) to support and celebrate the watermen who harvest the local oysters. Go to destinationpanamacity.com/oyster-trail for more on the importance of the trail to the oyster industry.

Panama City is unique in that it has not only preserved many of its original downtown buildings, but some of its original downtown businesses as well. The Panama City Publishing Company building at

1134 Beck Ave. in historic St. Andrews, for example, was constructed around 1920 and housed the local newspaper. The building contains more than 70 major historical items, including original printing presses and office furnishings, and is open for tours. Call 850-872-7208 for details.

The Panama City web site (destinationpanamacity. com) provides suggested itineraries based on visitor interest–Fit for Foodies, On the Waterfront and Ecotourism are among the offerings. Whatever you choose, try to end your day on the boardwalk at Oaks by the Bay Park (2715 W. 10th St.), a perfect location to watch the sun set over St. Andrews Bay.

Shopping: Bring a good pair of walking shoes because there are a number of shops you'll want to explore. Antiques, boutiques and art galleries flourish here. Floriopolis, at 1125 Beck Ave. (850-249-9295), features a gallery showcasing the work of more than 100 local artists. Here you will find pottery, jewelry, sculpture, paintings, photography and more. Little Village (2808 W. 12th St.) is a waterfront shopping and entertainment venue. Discover handmade, eco-friendly, fair trade,

PANAMA CITY
Oyster
TRAIL

23rd Street

15th Street (US Hwy 98)

Sun Harbor Rd

PANAMA·CITY
FLORIDA
Where Life Sets Sail

Brought to you by Destination Panama City
For more information visit
DestinationPanamaCity.com

Beck

Bayview

Harrison

Laverne

12th Street

11th Street

10th Street

6th Street

4th Street

E. 3rd Court

E. 3rd Street

1. Gene's Oyster Bar
2. Sue's
3. Bayou Joe's Marina & Grill
4. Millie's Cafe
5. Black & White Tavern
6. Destination Panama City Visitors Center
7. Alice's on Bayview
8. Uncle Ernie's Bayfront Grill & Brewhouse
9. Barefoot on the Bay
10. The Shrimp Boat
11. Hunt's Oyster Bar
12. Captain's Table Fish House
13. g. Foley's
14. Shipyard Grill

Graphic courtesy of Destination Panama City

recycled and re-purposed items from around the globe, as well as a special selection of local artists' work.

You will need transportation to reach groceries or other such shopping. While not a full-service grocery store, Grocery Outlet on Hwy. 98 carries some brand-name groceries (and possibly beer and wine). Call ahead at 850-785-4841 for hours.

Dining: Start your day with a leisurely breakfast at St. Andrews Coffee House & Bistro (1006 Beck Ave.), where they brew a perfect cup of coffee, along with their constantly changing breakfast specials and deli sandwiches. For lunch (or dinner), go see Chef Ernie Hall, who was named by Food Network as one of the Top 16 Cooks in America. Chef Ernie's floating restaurant, Just the Cook, is located in Slip 80 at the St. Andrews Marina. Stop in for his award-winning Dan-D-Donut Burger, a rosemary-seasoned all-beef burger topped with Canadian bacon, Swiss and bleu cheeses, and a grilled red pepper, sandwiched between two locally-made grilled doughnuts. Just the Cook also serves up some killer Latin Caribbean-inspired fare, such as Shrimp Tortuga.

Other dining choices are varied and unique. Gene's Oyster Bar, for example, is a quintessential oyster bar that is so well known, it earned its own historical marker. You can find it at 302 Sherman Ave. (850-785-1232). The sophisticated g. Foley's at 3212 W. 23rd St. (850-481-0354) serves an eclectic menu made up of locally sourced ingredients. And don't miss Hunt's Oyster Bar (1150 Beck Ave., 850-763-9645), where you can witness firsthand the skills of Honor Allen, who won both the 2016 and 2017 U.S. National Oyster Shucking Championship and placed 13th worldwide in the International Oyster Shucking Competition held in Galway, Ireland, in 2017. Also convenient to St. Andrews Marina and part of the Oyster Trail is Uncle Ernie's Bayfront Grill, located in a waterfront historic house at 1151 Bayview Ave. (850-763-8427). They specialize in seafood and house-brewed beers.

St. Andrew Bay, FL

		Largest Vessel Accommodated	VHF Channel Monitored	Approach / Dockside Depth (reported)	Transient Berths / Total Berths	Floating Docks	Gas / Diesel	Groceries, Ice, Marine Supplies, Snacks	Repairs: Hull, Engine, Propeller	Lift (tonnage), Crane, Rail	Min/Max Amps	Laundry, Pool, Showers, Courtesy Car	Pump-Out Station	Nearby: Grocery Store, Motel, Restaurant
PANAMA CITY				**Dockage**				**Supplies**			**Services**			
1. Pier 98 Marina (WiFi)	850-874-8723	66	–	call/10	12/12	–	GD	GIM	–	–	30/50	S	P	GMR
2. Panama City Marina 🖥 (WiFi) [WG] 290 EHL	**850-872-7272**	110	16/12	20/240	10/10	–	GD	GIMS	–	–	30/100	LS	P	GMR
BUENA VISTA POINT														
3. St. Andrews Marina (WiFi) 287 EHL	**850-872-7240**	200	16/10	15/102	15/8	F	GD	IMS	–	–	30/50	LS	P	GR
4. Sun Harbor Marina 🖥 (WiFi) 285 EHL	**850-785-0551**	55	16	6/96	12/12	–	GD	IMS	–	–	30/50	LS	P	GMR
GRAND LAGOON														
5. Bay Point Marina 🖥 (WiFi) 280 EHL	**850-235-6911**	120	16/78	20/180	6/7	–	GD	I	EP	–	30/200+	LPS	P	GMR
6. Lighthouse Marina (WiFi) 280 EHL	850-625-2728	70	16/68	20/50	8/8	–	GD	IMS	HEP	L55	30/50	LSC	–	GMR
7. Treasure Island Marina 280 EHL	850-234-6533	70	16	6/85	8/6	–	GD	GIMS	HEP	L35	30/50	S	–	GMR
8. Pirates Cove Marina (WiFi) 280 EHL	850-234-3939	60	16/68	25/400	6/8	–	GD	I	HEP	L12	30/50	LPSC	–	GMR
NORTH BAY														
9. Miller Marine 🖥 (WiFi)	850-265-6768	–	–	–	–	–	–	M	HEP	L88	–	C	–	GR

🖥 Internet Access (WiFi) Wireless Internet Access [WG] Waterway Guide Cruising Club Partner 📶 onSpot dockside WiFi facility
See WaterwayGuide.com for current rates, fuel prices, web site addresses, and other up-to-the-minute information. *(Information in the table is provided by the facilities.)*

PANAMA CITY, BUENTA VISTA POINT, GRAND LAGOON, NOAA CHART 11390

NORTH BAY, NOAA CHART 11390

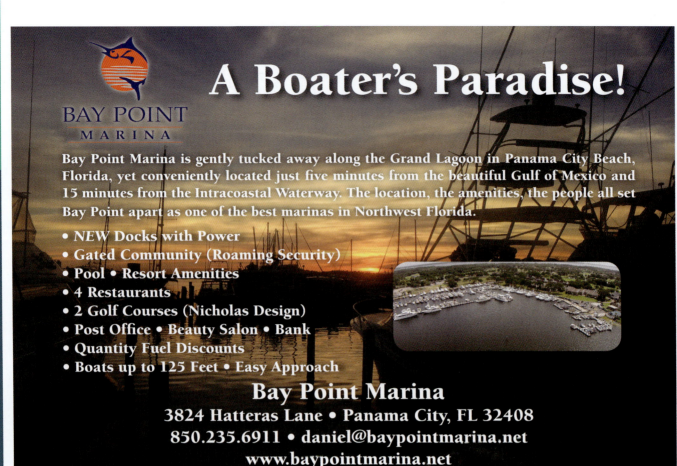
of flashing green "25") and extending west to flashing red "14" off Dyers Poin, including Pier 98 Marina at Pitts Bayou, which sells fuel and may have space for you; call ahead.

Directly northeast of the pass from the Gulf, and due north of Redfish Point and quick-flashing green "17" (Mile 290.5 EHL) are the office, ship store and fuel dock of the Panama City Marina. The marina's transient docks are to the east of the fuel dock. Other amenities at the municipal marina include a pump-out station, clean showers and laundry facilities, a ship store and gift shop and WiFi. The marina is one block from downtown Panama City, with several fine restaurants, a Post Office and a variety of amenities and services. Unique local and traveling exhibits are on display at the nearby Visual Arts Center. Banks, delis, bookstores, the public library, theaters and performing arts centers all lie within a perimeter of about 10 blocks from the marina. Marine parts are available here as well, but you will need transportation to get to the local West Marine. Consult local boaters for the best places to get repairs. Virtually all of the boatyards and several of the marinas have fallen prey to condominium development.

Moving westward up the GIWW, Buena Vista Point is 0.5 mile north of flashing red "6." The newly renovated St. Andrews Marina welcomes transients on their floating docks (102 slips with 16 reserved for transients) and fuel service is available 24 hours a day, 7 days a week. This is a recreational marina that embraces its working waterfront heritage

Continuing west on the GIWW, just south of the Hathaway Bridge is the deep-water Sun Harbor Marina, where deep-water transient berths for vessels up to 55 feet are available. They sell all fuels, have a well-stocked ship store and there is popular on-site restaurant, Shipyard Grill (850-640-0900). Sun Harbor Marina is home to the *Columbia*, a 141-foot replica of a 1923 Gloucester fishing schooner.

Anchorage: Along this stretch of the GIWW, from the Dupont Bridge to Panama City, virtually any cove well away from the channel offers good anchorage. Pitts and Parker Bayous are viable anchorages. Pearl Bayou used to be a nice anchorage, but it is said to be full of crab pots. It could, however, be considered as a hurricane hole.

Watson Bayou before a 9-foot fixed bridge offers 360-degree protection and good holding in 8 to 10 feet. It is a short walk to the store from a landing near the bridge. Farther west of Watson Bayou, on the southern side of the GIWW (near flashing red "20"), Redfish Point and Smack Bayou offer protection from southerly winds. There is one mooring ball in Smack Bayou but we cannot vouch for its safety. You can get in pretty close to shore at Redfish Point for great protection. Expect to hear jets flying over in the mornings. Bunkers Cove is across the water if you need northerly protection.

West of Watson Bayou, and just east of Panama City Marina, you will find some anchoring room and restaurants ashore in Massalina Bayou. The drawbridge at the entrance (7-foot closed vertical clearance) opens on demand 24 hours a day. If you are hungry, tie up at Bayou Joe's (112 E. 3rd Ct., 850-763-6442). They serve breakfast, lunch and dinner daily, featuring southern-style breakfast and fried seafood platters.

Shell Island has some excellent anchorages off the beach, over a hard sand-and-shell bottom. If boat wakes from the channel bother you, head farther east on the island. Be wary of the charted sandbars between Davis Point and Shell Island. If your depth sounder shows less than 7-foot depths, you are in the wrong place! (You are either too close to the island or too far north over the Camel Humps.)

Side Trip: Grand Lagoon

NAVIGATION: Use NOAA Charts 11390 and 11391. Grand Lagoon, immediately inside and west of St. Andrews Inlet, off St. Andrew Bay, offers an interesting side trip and some superior hospitality. Follow the marked channel and this trip should not provide too many challenges.

Dockage: At flashing green "5," a well-marked channel leads to Bay Point Marina off to the northeast. The resort-style marina is a very impressive facility in the sheltered Marriott Hotel complex. Marina guests can explore the resort on complimentary bicycles and take advantage of waterfront dining, the only Nicklaus-designed golf course in Northwest Florida, a spa, clay tennis courts and more. The tradition of flying weather flags is still honored there, and cruisers are definitely welcome on their newly renovated docks.

Lighthouse Marina, Treasure Island Marina and Pirates Cove Marina are about 1 mile farther into Grand Lagoon. All have some transient space reserved, sell all fuels and offer repairs. Past the Hathaway Bridge, on North Bay is Miller Marine, which is a repair facility with an 88-ton lift (no transient slips).

Anchorage: The anchorage at Grand Lagoon has 10 to 13 feet of water with good holding in sand. It is open and exposed, however, to the southeast and wakes. Note that jets flying overhead (often early in the morning) is pretty typical of the entire area.

■ PANAMA CITY TO FORT WALTON BEACH

From Panama City, westbound cruisers will find about 12 miles of relatively trouble-free transit through West Bay, then about 16.5 miles of transit through a land cut known to some as the "Grand Canyon," ending up in Choctawhatchee Bay, about 30 miles long and 3 to 5 miles wide.

NAVIGATION: Use NOAA Charts 11385 and 11390. When westbound from Panama City and approaching the Hathaway Bridge at Mile 284.6 EHL (65-foot fixed vertical clearance), don't hug the 17-foot high, flashing red "14" off Dyers Point (Audubon Island), as shoaling off the small island reaches into the marked channel. Beyond Hathaway Bridge, the GIWW opens up. Heading north, give the 17' flashing green "5" at Shell Point a wide berth. From there, the GIWW curves northwest through West Bay, cuts under the **West Bay Creek (SR 79) Bridge** at Mile 271.8 EHL (65-foot fixed vertical clearance) and then enters the relatively narrow channel of West Bay Creek, the start of the land cut known as the "Grand Canyon." For purposes of careful navigation, however, you may assume that you are in narrow circumstances at quick-flashing green "15."

⚠ Shoaling was reported in June 2017 in West Bay Channel in the vicinity of the bridge between red nun "32" and "34" and is encroaching approximately 30 feet into the channel along the north edge. Mariners are urged to exercise caution when transiting the area.

While in the "Grand Canyon," watch aids to navigation and your course carefully, as shoal water with depths of 2 to 4 feet at MLW runs very close to either side of the channel. The narrow channel persists past green daybeacon "39," and then aids to navigation cease, as they are not needed. The channel here runs relatively wide and deep. This situation continues for about 16.5 statute miles to Mile 254.5 EHL, entering Choctawhatchee Bay.

In the event of strong crosswinds, make it a point to check with any tows (VHF Channel 13) in the channel east of the **Clyde B. Wells (Choctawhatchee Bay) Bridge** at Mile 250.4 EHL (65-foot fixed vertical clearance), as the narrow channel may require coordinated meeting or passing. Barges, especially empties, are exceptionally difficult to handle for towboat operators in heavy wind and current.

While the cut is frequently dredged to 10.5-foot MLW depths, shoaling is chronic, so hold to the center except when passing and realize that hugging the shore while passing will likely run you aground in soft mud. Also, use particular caution when transiting after strong winds or heavy rain, as large pine trees frequently break away from the nearly vertical banks. From time to time, when high winds are expected on Choctawhatchee Bay, be prepared to find westbound barges waiting inside the "Grand Canyon" at about Mile 254 EHL for better conditions. Cautious mariners might follow suit. Tying up to a commercial barge here is entirely possible, if you make a proper approach to the towboat's skipper.

Anchorage: Burnt Mill Creek at Mile 277. 7 EHL in West Bay has 7 to 9 feet at MLW. If you need it, you can find anchorage in 7 feet at MLW over good holding ground in the lee of the causeway on either side of the Choctawhatchee Bay Bridge at Mile 250.3 EHL.

Choctawhatchee Bay– GIWW Mile 253.5 EHL

NAVIGATION: Use NOAA Chart 11385. As you travel into Choctawhatchee Bay from the east, the water deepens from about 9 feet (MLW) to 38 feet but is generally shallow along its southern shore. Be cautious passing Tucker Bayou (Mile 254 EHL), as it sometimes shoals to 3-foot depths or less at its mouth.

The route is closely pegged with markers for the first 5 to 6 nm, but as the bay broadens and deepens, buoys thin out. Markers are used mainly to indicate shallows to the south, and these should be given a wide berth due to the possibility of shoaling. There is room to roam on this big open bay, but be aware that it can get rough in hard easterly or westerly blows because of the 20-mile east–west fetch. The approach to the 64-foot fixed vertical clearance **Mid-Bay Bridge** (Mile 234.2 EHL) is well marked from both east and west.

Dockage: In La Grange Bayou, off the north side of the Choctawhatchee Bay, are two marinas with limited services: Fisherman's Boatyard (repairs only) and Freeport Marina and Yacht Club (slips and gas).

Near the center of the long Choctawhatchee Bay, south of Mile 239 EHL in Horseshoe Bayou, is the full-service Sandestin's Baytowne Marina, part of a large resort community that stretches from the bay to the beach. The gated community offers marina guests all resort amenities. A small ferry runs between the marina and the Village of Baytowne Wharf, or you can take a walk on the boardwalk built over the marshland. The Village of Baytowne Wharf has many charming shops and boutiques, restaurants, nightclubs, art galleries and other facilities.

To approach Baytowne Marina, head south once you are clear of Four Mile Point and line up for flashing green "1" and flashing red "2" at the beginning of the entrance to the facility. Be careful to avoid the shoal depths when approaching shore to the east.

Located at the southeastern foot of the Mid-Bay Bridge is Legendary Marina, which offers dockage with amenities and sells fuel; call ahead for details.

After passing under the Mid-Bay Bridge and passing flashing red "58," head northwest a little more than 3 miles along the northern shore to flashing green "1," and turn north for Rocky Bayou. Ward Cove is to the east as you approach Rocky Bayou on the north side of Choctawhatchee Bay. Green daybeacon "1" and flashing red "2" mark the entrance to Ward Cove and Bluewater Bay Marina. Bluewater Bay is a full resort complex with an outstanding ship store and an excellent restaurant and oyster bar. Nearby Boggy Bayou is home to North Light Yacht Club, which may have transient space. Both facilities sell fuel.

Anchorage: Rocky Bayou on the north shore provides a scenic anchorage. To enter Rocky Bayou, follow the directions above for Bluewater Bay Marina but pass Ward Cove. Before the 20-foot fixed vertical clearance bridge, anchorage can be found in 12 to 14 feet at MLW with protection from the south and only a small amount of fetch from the north. A tighter but even more protected (except from the south) option is in the Northwest Fork in 7 to 10 feet at MLW.

You can also anchor in Boggy Bayou to the west, either at Toms Bayou with 13-foot MLW depths or Niceville, by North Light Yacht Club, in 11 to 12 feet at MLW.

For an anchorage on the south side of the bay, a turn to the south at Mile 230 EHL will bring you to a marked entry to Joes Bayou, a 360-degree protected anchorage, with a soft mud bottom and depths of 10 feet or more at MLW.

Destin–GIWW Mile 227 EHL

A major sportfishing and recreational center on northwest Florida's "Miracle Strip," Destin is renowned for its sparkling beaches, crystal-clear waters and seaside resort activities, which attract thousands of tourists and boaters year-round. This is possible because the Gulf Coast's temperatures are relatively moderate from October through March. The average air temperature is 67.3 degrees maximum, with a minimum average of 52.2 degrees. Winter visitors throng from the north by both boat and car for respite from the chill and snow. Destin lies just north and east of the Choctawhatchee Bay entrance on the barrier peninsula sheltering Choctawhatchee Bay on the south. Full-service marinas, waterfront hotels and restaurants abound.

Destin sponsors a bill-fishing tournament each year, while the month of October is mainly devoted to the more than 50-year-old Deep Sea Fishing Rodeo. Big game fish that ply the Loop Current that circulates clockwise in the Gulf of Mexico are the reason, and the current comes relatively close to shore near Destin. The rodeo draws thousands of expectant anglers who search the offshore waters, inshore bays and bayous for prize-winning fish, worth thousands of dollars. Scuba divers get their chance for fun and games at the annual Destin Underwater Easter Egg Hunt in April. Great food and friendly people add to the attraction of these events.

NAVIGATION: Use NOAA Chart 11385. The main docking area in Destin is immediately south and east of the twin fixed bridges over the Choctawhatchee Bay entrance from the Gulf (south of the GIWW). The charted vertical bridge clearance at the **Destin Twin Bridges** is 49 feet, but there have been reports that 48 feet is closer to reality, so sailors should use caution if their vessel's mast height is more than 48 feet.

⚠️ If entering East Pass from the Gulf, care should be taken when crossing the bar if there is a swell running. Also note that buoys are not charted in the Choctawhatchee Bay entrance channel, as constant shoaling necessitates frequent relocation. This is a pass that needs to be negotiated with local knowledge, in flat water, with good visibility and during reasonable tides. (Refer to Tide Tables in front of this guide.)

To enter the main Destin Harbor, commonly known as Old Pass Lagoon, from Choctawhatchee Bay to the north, turn sharply to east after passing under the bridges. The channel into the large harbor is narrow, but well-marked with daybeacons. It runs between the mainland to the north and the protective sandbar to the south.

Many facilities line the northern shore of the harbor. The pristine beaches and dunes of Santa Rosa Island are located across the peninsula on the Gulf side. Because of the substantial development along the beach, you will have to search for a spot with public access.

Dockage: Along the north shore of the harbor are Destin Marina, Harborwalk Marina and Destin Fishermen's Co-op. Many locally popular eating establishments also offer dockage along with everything from snacks to gourmet meals. Destin Marina (northeast side of the twin Destin Bridges) has only 8 slips and no amenities; however, the marina is within walking distance of downtown.

Fuel and transient dockage is available at HarborWalk Marina, located southeast of the bridge and on the north side of Destin Harbor. This facility gets high marks from cruisers for the friendly and helpful staff. They have a ship store and gift shop on site. Their Destin Harborwalk web cams are pretty fun too; check them out on the marina's web site. Restaurants and provisions are within walking distance of the marina.

Destin Fisherman's Co-op is located on the north side of the harbor and can accommodate vessels to 100 feet and sells fuel. Farther in Destin Harbor is Dockside Watersports, which does not offer transient space.

Many restaurants lacking dockage welcome customers coming ashore in their dinghies. You can have a great time just dinghy-hopping from one bistro to the next. For a first-class meal, tie up at the Marina Café Yacht Club or dinghy to the beach. Others to explore include the Boathouse Oyster Bar (288 Harbor Blvd. East, 850-837-3645) with outdoor music; Harry T's (46 Harbor Blvd., 850-654-4800) with excellent cuisine and bands; and McGuire's Irish Pub and Brewery (33 Harbor Blvd., 850-433-6789), the legendary Pensacola bistro, which now has a Destin counterpart just across the road near the bridge. Florida law requires that a dinghy carry a life jacket (with whistle attached) for every passenger. If you don't want a flashing blue light from a law enforcement boat from the Florida Fish and Wildlife Conservation Commission (FWC) approaching you, make certain you pay attention to this decree. It is actively enforced and not negotiable.

Anchorage: Destin Harbor provides excellent anchorage with no surge, and wakes are strictly

East Pass

HarborWalk Marina

Destin

controlled. The entrance is a little tricky. Turn directly after passing under bridge and follow the (unlit) channel and stay closer to the north side of harbor. You can anchor on the southwest side of the harbor or just off Harbor Docks Restaurant to the east. There are restaurants all around with dinghy docks. A municipal water taxi service is available during the summer months. Note that the harbor is a No-Discharge Zone.

Fort Walton Beach–GIWW Mile 224 EHL

Fort Walton Beach combines the many charms of a major seaside resort and is well worth a cruising layover. Besides the swimming and snorkeling in crystal-clear water (locals swear you can see a quarter on the bottom at 30 feet), the area is an angler's delight.

Fort Walton Beach continues to be an Air Force town. The linchpin is Eglin Air Force Base, a military facility that's larger than the entire state of Rhode Island.

This captivating town is a shopper's bonanza with its many antiques stores, novelty shops, boutiques, upscale dress shops and bookstores. Golf and tennis

Did You Know? You can thank the Apalachicola River, 130 miles east of Ft. Walton Beach, for the fine, white of sand found here. The quartz–sand combination, delivered to the Gulf from the Appalachian mountains via the river, was deposited along the shores when Santa Rosa Island began to extend from Destin. This extension continues today as these small, white grains of quartz sand move to the west before reaching their final destination at the Pensacola Pass. The sand here is so fine that it actually "squeaks" underfoot.

facilities abound, and there is an eclectic variety of restaurants and nightclubs.

NAVIGATION: Use NOAA Chart 11385. The channel at Fort Walton Beach is well marked on the approach from the east. Flashing green "1" and red nun "2" are almost 2 miles west of the entrance to North Channel.

Dockage: Transient space may be found on the eastern shore of the entrance to Garnier Bayou, approximately 2 miles northwest of Mile 225 EHL on the GIWW. A well-marked channel entrance with a tall cylindrical water tower serves as a beacon to the Shalimar Yacht Basin, a full-service repair facility with slips and fuel. This area has comprehensive cruiser amenities and services. While Cinco and Garnier Bayous offer a number of marine facilities, the 19-foot fixed vertical clearance **Elgin Parkway Bridge** limits access to both.

At Mile 225 EHL, the GIWW narrows down considerably, and you will come across a series of floating marks that will get that point across to you quite well. On the west side of the **Brooks Memorial Bridge** (50-feet fixed vertical clearance), Brooks Bridge Bait & Tackle Inc. offers pump-out service at their dock or they can also come to you. They also sell fuel but do not have transient slips.

Fort Walton Beach offers a free pump-out station at a city park about one block west of Brooks Bridge, on the north side, where you can also stay overnight after obtaining approval by calling the city manager's office at 850-833-9500. Depth at the dock's T-Head is 6 feet at MLW, but it is considerably shallower near the shore. From the GIWW make your turn toward the Ft. Walton Beach Landing Dock, on the north shore, between red "6" and red "8."

On the southern shore, Legendary Marine's Fort Walton Beach may have transient space and they offer repairs. Nearby Emerald Coast Boatyard has a 75-ton lift and offers repairs but no transient slips. Fort Walton Beach Yacht Basin sells gas and has some transient space reserved. Call ahead for slip availability in this area and refer to the marina table in this chapter for more details.

■ FORT WALTON BEACH TO PERDIDO BAY

The Narrows and Santa Rosa Sound— GIWW Mile 223 to Mile 189 EHL

From the southwestern terminus of Choctawhatchee Bay, west of Fort Walton Beach, the GIWW enters a section known as The Narrows. This waterway, which is actually the eastern end of Santa Rosa Sound, is appropriately named. Although well-marked, the channel twists back and forth through shallows for about 6 statute miles before it widens somewhat as it approaches Santa Rosa Sound proper.

As the GIWW winds through Santa Rosa Sound to Pensacola Bay, you will see an abundance of attractive homes along the mainland side, with beach communities dotting the barrier side. Santa Rosa Sound, which is almost as narrow as The Narrows has numerous coves and good anchorages along its shores. However, check your depths, and remember the effect of the wind on tides, as the anchorages could be somewhat more shallow than charted.

Pensacola Bay, west of Deer and Fair Points, has always been considered one of Florida's largest and safest harbors. It has served as a heavy weather refuge for commercial and naval ships, as well as for smaller craft.

NAVIGATION: Use NOAA Charts 11378 and 11385. At Mile 206.7 EHL, the **Navarre Beach Causeway (CR 399) Bridge** has a charted fixed vertical clearance of 50 feet but may have only a 48-foot fixed vertical clearance due to tide conditions. East of the bridge, between flashing green "87" and quick-flashing red "88," is a shoal into the channel, so favor the green (south) side.

While transiting The Narrows, monitor VHF Channel 16 and Channel 13 for barge traffic to avoid a "squeeze"

Destin to Fort Walton Beach, FL

		Dockage					Supplies		Services					
	Phone	Largest Vessel Accommodated	VHF Channel Monitored	Transient Berths / Total Berths	Approach / Dockside Depth (reported)	Floating Docks	Gas / Diesel	Groceries, Ice, Marine Supplies, Snacks	Repairs: Hull, Engine, Propeller	Lift (tonnage), Crane, Rail	Min/Max Amps	Laundry, Pool, Showers, Courtesy Car	Pump-Out Station	Nearby: Grocery Store, Motel, Restaurant
LA GRANGE BAYOU														
1. Fisherman's Boatyard	850-835-4848	–	–	–	–	–	–	–	HP	L88	–	–	–	GR
2. Freeport Marina and Yacht Club [WiFi]	850-835-2035	55	09/16	8/38	15/10	–	G	IMS	–	–	30/30	S	P	GR
HORSESHOE BAY														
3. Sandestin's Baytowne Marina ⌨ [WiFi] 240 EHL	850-267-7773	130	16/10	20/113	8/7	–	GD	GIS	HEP	–	30/100	LPS	P	GMR
MORENO POINT														
4. Legendary Marine 234 EHL	850-337-8200	50	16	call/350	8/	F	GD	GIMS	HEP	L	30/50	S	P	GMR
WARDS COVE														
5. Bluewater Bay Marina ⌨ [WiFi] 232 EHL	850-897-2821	110	16	10/120	8/8	–	GD	GIMS	HE	–	30/50	LPSC	P	GMR
6. North Light Yacht Club [WiFi] 232 EHL	850-678-2350	65	16	10/55	15/8	–	GD	IMS	HEP	L	50/50	LPS	P	GMR
DESTIN														
7. Destin Marina	850-837-2470	30	–	8/10	6/6	–	GD	GIMS	–	–	–	–	–	GMR
8. HarborWalk Marina ⌨ [WiFi] 230 EHL	**850-650-2400**	**85**	**16**	**2/52**	**10/6**	**F**	**GD**	**GIMS**	**–**	**–**	**30/50**	**–**	**P**	**GMR**
9. Destin Fisherman's Co-op 230 EHL	850-654-4999	100	–	call/40	8/8	–	GD	IM	HEP	L88	30/30	–	–	MR
10. Dockside Watersports	850-428-3313	–	–	–	10/8	–	–	IS	–	–	–	–	–	GMR
FORT WALTON BEACH														
11. Two George's Marina at Shalimar Yacht Basin [WiFi]	850-651-0510	125	16	6/134	32/8	–	GD	IMS	HEP	L35	30/50	S	P	GMR
12. Brooks Bridge Bait & Tackle Inc. 223 EHL	850-243-5721	130	16	–	8/8	–	GD	IS	–	–	–	–	P	GMR
13. Ft. Walton Beach Landing Dock 223 EHL	850-833-9504	50	–	6/6	6/	–	–	–	–	–	30/30	–	P	GMR
14. Legendary Marine's Fort Walton Beach	850-244-1099	40	–	10/15	30/5	–	–	M	HEP	–	30/50	–	–	GMR
15. Emerald Coast Boatyard	850-244-2722	–	–	–	9/7	–	–	–	HEP	L75	–	–	–	GMR
16. Fort Walton Beach Yacht Basin 222 EHL	850-244-5725	50	16	4/94	9/7	–	G	I	–	–	30/50	S	P	GMR

⌨ Internet Access [WiFi] Wireless Internet Access [WG] Waterway Guide Cruising Club Partner ⦿ onSpot dockside WiFi facility

See WaterwayGuide.com for current rates, fuel prices, web site addresses, and other up-to-the-minute information. *(Information in the table is provided by the facilities.)*

LA GRANGE BAYOU, NOAA CHART 11385

HORSESHOE BAY, NOAA CHART 11385

MORENO POINT, NOAA CHART 11385

WARDS COVE, NOAA CHART 11385

DESTIN, NOAA CHART 11385

FORT WALTON BEACH, NOAA CHART 11385

when meeting with an oncoming barge. "Passing one whistle" means that you both agree to alter course to starboard and pass port to port. "Two whistles" means that you are altering course to port and will pass starboard-to-starboard. If you are clever enough to ask the skipper of the tow what is best for him, you will get extreme cooperation. Remember, barges are not maneuverable like your pleasure craft, so give the barge traffic the benefit of the doubt.

At Mile 205 EHL, the GIWW emerges from shoal territory into Santa Rosa Sound. Though the GIWW does move through some shoal areas in Santa Rosa Sound (5- and 6-foot MLW depths), for the most part it carries respectable depths of 13 to 17 feet at MLW.

⚠️ On your westward journey near Mile 200 EHL, note that red daybeacon "124" (between flashing green "123" and "125") marks a shoal encroaching into the channel. Some charts do not show this marker. At this point, you should switch to Chart 11378 for your approach to the Pensacola Beach Twin Bridges.

Anchorage: Anchorages abound in The Narrows. Mary Esther at Mile 219.7 EHL has at least 4 feet at MLW and good holding. On Santa Rosa Island, there are viable anchorages at Mile 217.4 EHL (green daybeacon "51"); Mile 215 EHL (green daybeacon "69"); and Mile 213.9 EHL at Manatee Point (red daybeacon "74A").

On the north shore at Mile 208.6, you can drop the hook at Lower Pritchard Long Point in 9-foot MLW depths. You can also anchor on either side of the Navarre Bridge (Mile 206.7 EHL) at green daybeacon "89" (Navarre Park) or at "93" on the south shore or on the north shore, just east of the bridge.

Pensacola Bay–GIWW Mile 189 to Mile 179 EHL

NAVIGATION: Use NOAA Charts 11378. Keep within all channel markers if you are entering the bay from the Gulf of Mexico. This good all-weather passage is subject to shoaling, which is almost always well marked. A principal mark for the entrance is the 171-foot conical brick Pensacola Light. Currents can be significant in this channel, especially at the 90-degree turn into the Bay. The Pensacola Coast Guard Station is 1 mile east of Pensacola Light.

Pensacola Bay is relatively narrow (3 statute miles) and stretches in an east–west direction for about 22 statute miles. On its west side, Escambia Bay and East Bay extend some 10 statute miles north. Pensacola Bay carries depths of 20 to 50 feet, but the bays to the north run 9 to 12 feet (MLW) with more extensive shoals as you go north.

⚠️ For westbound skippers, as you enter Pensacola Bay, note that after passing flashing green "145" (at about Mile 184.2 EHL) the buoys shift to that of the Pensacola Ship Channel (red-right-returning for vessels inbound from the Gulf to Pensacola). Thus, traveling the GIWW from this point, all the way across Pensacola Bay to the Pensacola Landcut and re-entering the GIWW at about Mile 179.5 EHL, you should leave red markers to port and green to starboard. (These markers carry the appropriate small yellow triangles and squares indicating their dual role as GIWW route markers.)

The City of Pensacola lies about 5 statute miles north of the GIWW. The **Pensacola Beach Twin Bridges** (65-foot fixed vertical clearance) span the GIWW at Mile 189.1 EHL.

Dockage: Immediately east of the Pensacola Beach Twin Bridges at Mile 190 EHL, on the north side of Santa Rosa Sound is the Santa Rosa Yacht & Boat Club, offering transient dockage and fuel. Just past the bridges, if you turn south and parallel the bridges, you will see channel markers for Little Sabine Bay. Pensacola Beach Marina is the first marina on the port side after entering Little Sabine Bay. It provides dockage, fuel, restaurants and a grocery store. Just to the south in Little Sabine Bay is Sabine Marina, which may also have transient space. Call ahead as these facilities only have four to five reserved transient slips.

The Palafox Pier Yacht Harbor facility is 6 miles northeast of the GIWW, on the west side of the Commercial Port of Pensacola. The slips are on floating piers with deep water. The marina is home to Jaco's Bayfront Bar and Grille (850-432-5226) and is within walking distance of downtown. Nearby Baylen Slips Marina may also have transient space on their floating docks. Call first. There are literally hundreds of "best" spots to eat within the city, but just a few blocks up Palafox Street from Palafox Pier you can find any number of restaurant choices.

One nautical mile southwest of the Port of Pensacola is a channel running northwest to Bayou Chico (Mile 185 EHL), which has a yacht club, full-service boatyards with facilities to handle most repairs and a number of full-service marinas. The 65-foot fixed vertical

Pensacola

clearance **Bayou Chico (Barrancus Ave.) Bridge** crosses Bayou Chico. Before the bridge to the north are Pensacola Yacht Club and MarineMax Pensacola at Bahia Mar. Both sell all fuels. There are restaurants nearby plus a bed-and-breakfast. To the south-southwest before the bridge are Yacht Harbor Marina and Palm Harbor Marina. Both have slips on floating docks.

Beyond the Bayou Chico high-rise bridge on the south side, full-service repairs and transient dockage is available at Pelican's Perch Marina & Boatyard. Past Pelican's Perch are Bell Marine Service and Island Cove Marina, which has a barbecue area and a community kitchen. Call ahead for slip availability.

A little farther up Bayou Chico is the Pensacola Shipyard Marina & Boatyard, a full-service facility with a 110-ton lift and a 14-ton crane, plus mechanical, fiberglass, carpentry, electrical systems and painting services.

Anchorage: At Pensacola Beach, to the east of the bridge, Quiet Water Beach Pier is a free dock. If the dock is full, you can anchor nearby in 7 to 11 feet at MLW. It is also possible to anchor in Little Sabine Bay in 5 to 11 feet at MLW. On the north shore of Santa Rosa Sound, English Navy Cove carries 11 to 15 feet at MLW.

In Bayou Chico to the north, you can anchor north of the marinas in 9 to 11 feet at MLW with good holding in mud and all-around protection. The public boat ramp before the Barrancus Ave. Bridge allows access to the main road. Shopping is a two-mile walk west or take the bus.

Bayou Grande at Jones Point (Mile 183 EHL) has 9-foot depths and offers good protection from wind and wakes in the basin before the **Murray Rd. Bridge** (13.8-foot fixed vertical clearance).

Big Lagoon to Perdido Bay– GIWW Mile 179 to Mile 172 EHL

Continue west from Pensacola Bay into the GIWW. The intersection is about 1 statute mile from the exit into the Gulf of Mexico. It is a run of about 8 to 10 miles from Fort McRee at Pensacola's Gulf entrance to the Alabama line at about Mile 170 EHL. Ahead on the GIWW are some fabulous anchorages, great waterfront restaurants and fine repair facilities.

NAVIGATION: Use NOAA Chart 11378. Traffic here can get confusing, because the markers change to red-right-returning for vessels inbound from the Gulf to Pensacola, to GIWW red on the north or land side, green on the south or Gulf side. Refer to the Waterway Explorer and NOAA online charts for the most up-to-date information.

After flashing green "15," in the middle of the Caucus Channel between Forts Pickens and Barrancus, head west-southwest to green can "1" and flashing red "2" to transit the short and narrow, but well-marked passage known locally as the Pensacola Land Cut (about Mile 178 to Mile 179 EHL) leading to Big Lagoon.

Be careful not to confuse green can buoy "1" with green can buoy "13" just to its south, which is a marker for the Caucus Channel. You can also line up the range markers to get to the land cut, which leads into Big Lagoon. As you enter, keep an eye out for shoaling caused by strong tidal currents through the Caucus Channel. The shallows are easily seen on sunny days, but if it is overcast, they will be harder to make out, so stay to the center except to pass. If you see a barge entering the pass, wait. There is not much room in there.

Anchorage: There is a great anchorage in 10 to 13 feet at MLW in Big Lagoon at GIWW Mile 178.4 EHL. This

Pensacola Bay, FL

WG

	Largest Vessel Accommodated	VHF Channel Monitored	Transient Berths / Total Berths	Approach / Dockside Depth (reported)	Floating Docks	Groceries, Ice, Marine Supplies, Snacks	Gas / Diesel	Repairs: Hull, Engine, Propeller	Lift (tonnage), Crane, Rail	Min/Max Amps	Laundry, Pool, Showers, Courtesy Car	Pump-Out Station	Nearby: Grocery Store, Motel, Restaurant
PENSACOLA BEACH			**Dockage**			**Supplies**					**Services**		
1. Santa Rosa Yacht & Boat Club ▢ WiFi 189 EHL 850-934-1005	70	16	5/40	8/8	-	GD	I	-	-	30/100	LS	P	GMR
2. Pensacola Beach Marina ▢ WiFi 189 EHL 850-931-2030 x4	100	16	4/30	-	-	GD	GIS	-	-	30/50	S	P	GMR
3. Sabine Marina ▢ WiFi 189 EHL 850-932-1904	57	16	5/64	9/8	-	-	IS	-	-	30/50	LS	P	GMR
SAYVILLE HARBOR													
4. Palafox Pier Yacht Harbor WiFi 186 EHL 850-432-9620	175	16/09	10/88	20/13	F	GD	I	-	-	30/50	LS	P	R
5. Baylen Slips Marina WiFi 850-432-9620	55	16/09	call/24	20/13	F	GD	I	-	-	30/50	LS	P	R
PENSACOLA AREA													
6. Pensacola Yacht Club ▢ 185 EHL 850-433-8804	100	16	call/58	8/8	-	GD	I	-	-	30/50	LPS	P	MR
7. MarineMax Pensacola at Bahia Mar WiFi 185 EHL 850-477-1112	50	16/09	6/60	6/4	F	GD	IMS	HEP	L50	30/30	LS	P	GR
8. Yacht Harbor Marina ▢ WiFi 185 EHL 850-455-4552	65	16	8/52	9/6.5	F	-	-	-	-	30/50	S	P	GMR
9. Palm Harbor Marina ▢ WiFi 850-455-4552	70	-	10/64	9/6.5	F	-	I	-	-	30/50	S	P	GMR
10. Pelican's Perch Marina & Boatyard WiFi 185 EHL 850-453-3471	50	-	call/55	15/6	F	-	MS	HEP	L50,C	30/30	S	-	-
11. Bell Marine Service 185 EHL 850-455-7639	48	-	call/20	5/6	-	-	M	E	-	30/30	-	-	G
12. Island Cove Marina ▢ WiFi 185 EHL 850-455-4552	75	-	6/94	7/6	F	-	IMS	-	-	30/50	S	P	GMR
13. Pensacola Shipyard Marina & Boatyard WiFi 185 EHL 850-439-1451	150	-	4/52	18/7	F	-	MS	HE	L110,C14	30/100	LS	P	-

▢ Internet Access WiFi Wireless Internet Access WG Waterway Guide Cruising Club Partner onSpot dockside WiFi facility

See WaterwayGuide.com for current rates, fuel prices, web site addresses, and other up-to-the-minute information. *(Information in the table is provided by the facilities.)*

PENSACOLA BEACH, NOAA CHART 11378

SAYVILLE HARBOR, PENSACOLA AREA, NOAA CHART 11378

Perdido Key, FL

PERDIDO KEY			Dockage					Supplies		Services					
		Largest Vessel Accommodated	VHF Channel Monitored	Transient Berths / Total Berths	Approach / Dockside Depth (reported)	Floating Docks	Gas / Diesel	Groceries, Ice, Marine Supplies, Snacks	Repairs: Hull, Engine, Propeller	Lift (tonnage), Crane, Rail	Min/Max Amps	Laundry, Pool, Showers, Courtesy Car	Pump-Out Station	Nearby: Grocery Store, Motel, Restaurant
1. Perdido Key Oyster Bar Restaurant & Marina, LLC 🖥	850-492-5600	150	16	20/50	10/12	–	GD	IS	–	–	30/50	–	–	R
2. A & M Perdido Resort & Marina WiFi	850-492-7304	–	–	call/24	–	–	–	–	–	–	–	LPS	P	M
3. Holiday Harbor Marina and Grill 🖥 WiFi WG	172 EHL 850-492-0555	125	16/14	2/48	7/7	–	GD	GIMS	EP	L10	30/50	LS	P	GR

🖥 Internet Access   WiFi Wireless Internet Access   WG Waterway Guide Cruising Club Partner   ⬮onSpot dockside WiFi facility
See WaterwayGuide.com for current rates, fuel prices, web site addresses, and other up-to-the-minute information. *(Information in the table is provided by the facilities.)*

PERDIDO KEY, NOAA CHART 11378

is adjacent to Fort McRee, so expect to see planes flying overhead. Dinghy to the beaches on the Bay or Gulf side. This anchorage is somewhat exposed to the west.

Redfish Point is a good anchorage south of the GIWW that is well protected in most weather. Turn south before flashing red "10," which marks a very shallow shoal; you can anchor as close to shore as your draft permits in hard sand. You can also turn north at red "10" to access Trout Point with 11 feet at MLW and good holding.

If you continue to flashing green "15" and double back toward the beach on Perdido Key, you will find 12-foot MLW depths. For a bit of shore side recreation, you can swim or dinghy to the beach. The Gulf beach is a short walk across the dunes, which are part of the Gulf Coast Island National Seashore Park. This is a favorite weekend getaway for locals, but there is a bothersome chop during a northerly.

You can anchor before the bridge at Siguenza Cove (Mile 172 EHL) in 5 to 7 feet at MLW. This is somewhat exposed to the east and wakes.

Perdido Bay–GIWW Mile 172 to Mile 170 EHL

From Big Lagoon, it is a short trip to Perdido Bay, down the middle of which runs the state line separating Florida from Alabama. Perdido Bay offers a variety of enticements for the cruising yachtsman.

NAVIGATION: Use NOAA Chart 11378. Leaving either the anchorage or the marinas, as you approach the left turn at the west end of Big Lagoon, be careful not to shortcut the channel, as flashing red "12" is well up in the cove and hard to see. The area southeast of green can buoy "11" is shallow (you will realize this when you see pelicans walking on the bar) so favor the center of the channel to avoid joining the many who have run aground here. Follow the markers because this entire area is surrounded by shoal water. After a turn at flashing red "16" and green daybeacon "15," you will see the Gulf Beach Bridge at Mile 171.8 EHL with a 73-foot fixed vertical clearance.

Marinas   **Services**   **Anchorages**   **Bridges & Locks**   **Nav Alerts**   **Fuel**

6 Waterway Explorer provides different icons that overlay on the maps as modes

Modes

Info Pane with details

Plan your time on the water with Explorer

www.waterwayguide.com

After flashing green "35," enter the open but shoaled area between Perdido Key (FL) and Ono Island (AL, Mile 170 EHL). The GIWW is well marked as it extends along the northern side of Ono Island and Innerarity Peninsula. From there at flashing green "57," the GIWW swings north into Perdido Bay. At this stage, the last of Florida, Innerarity Point, is now north of you, and the first part of Alabama, Ono Island, is now to the south. (Contrary to popular belief, not all of Alabama is west of Florida.)

Dockage: Immediately before the bridge on your left is the Perdido Key Oyster Bar Restaurant & Marina. The marina has transient slips and fuel. The Oyster Bar Restaurant & Marina offers slips and a face dock for larger vessels (to 150 feet) They also sell fuel. The restaurant serves lunch and dinner, has an outdoor bar and frequently host live music. Call ahead for reservations.

Just after the bridge is A&M Perdido Resort, an RV resort with condos and a marina. Call ahead for slip availability.

If you are in need of repairs or a break, just 0.5 mile west of the bridge and immediately past flashing green "35," you can turn south and follow the private markers a short distance to Holiday Harbor Marina and Grill. The marina offers transient dockage, gas and diesel and boat work/repairs. They are either the last marina in Florida heading west, or the first marina in Florida heading east, depending on your perspective.

Anchorage: On the western side of Perdido Bay there are anchorages at Soldier and Palmetto Creeks, which offer protection from the north and good holding in mud. Tarkiln Bay (Mile 166.3 EHL) to the east offers 7- to 9-foot MLW depths and protection from all but southwest winds.

■ NEXT STOP

From here you will be entering the waters of Alabama's Gulf Coast and the vast delta of Mobile Bay. Those traveling the Great Loop will exit the inland river system here.

Perdido Key to Bay St. Louis, MS

 GIWW Mile 170 EHL–Mile 40 EHL

 VHF FL Bridges: Channel 9/AL Bridges: Channel 13

CHARTS NOAA 11376, 11378

West of the Pensacola Inlet you will enter the GIWW, pass Sherman Cove to the north, and enter Big Lagoon. You will begin to notice that the waters are not as clear and as you continue west, they become cloudy to murky. As you approach Mobile Bay you are entering a vast delta basin fed by many rivers. These rivers feed into the Bay and spread across the area to comprise the second largest drainage basin in the United States, with the largest being the Mississippi River Delta. The hundreds of GIWW miles west are an adventure with a rich history, scenic beauty, and endless opportunities to entice the cruising boater.

Along this stretch of the GIWW, you cross into Alabama waters. The waterway route from the Alabama border, Mile 170 EHL to Mile 160 EHL is a wonderland of excellent protected anchorages, including Perdido Bay, Terry Cove, Cotton Bayou, Soldier Creek, Roberts Bayou, Ingram Bayou and Wolf Bay. Check your charts, and pick any one of these places for a pleasant, protected overnight stop.

There are also plenty of marinas in the area, along with repair facilities, restaurants and other amenities. Until you get to Mobile Bay, the only water-accessible town is Orange Beach, AL, named for the orange groves that once were plentiful there.

■ ORANGE BEACH

At Mile 170 EHL, heading west on the GIWW, the tip of private Ono Island appears to the south as you cruise the straight westward line of the GIWW to the entrance to Perdido Bay. At flashing green "57," turn north to explore Perdido Bay or southwest to explore Bayou St. John.

NAVIGATION: Use NOAA Chart 11378. From flashing green "57" on the GIWW, there is a marked channel extending from the GIWW through Bayou St. John to Perdido Pass to the Gulf of Mexico. The pass has a 9-foot MLW controlling depth and the **Perdido Pass**

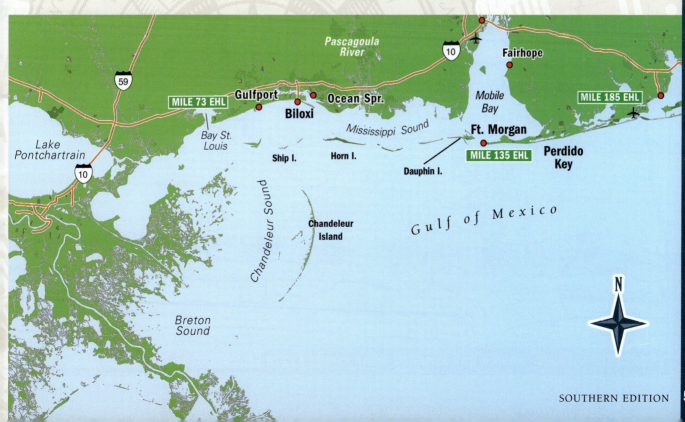

Perdido Key, FL to Bon Secour Bay, AL

		Largest Vessel Accommodated	VHF Channel Monitored	Transient Berths / Total Berths	Approach / Dockside Depth (reported)	Floating Docks	Gas / Diesel	Groceries, Ice, Marine Supplies, Snacks	Repairs: Hull, Engine, Propeller	Lift (tonnage), Crane, Rail	Min/Max Amps	Laundry, Pool, Showers, Courtesy Car	Pump-Out Station	Nearby: Grocery Store, Motel, Restaurant
				Dockage			**Supplies**			**Services**				
ORANGE BEACH AREA														
1. SanRoc Cay Marina [wifi] 167 EHL	251-981-5423	150	16	75/75	5/5	–	GD	GIMS	–	–	50/50	S	P	GMR
2. Zeke's Landing Marina 163 EHL	251-981-4044	100	69	4/50	7/7	–	GD	GIMS	–	L	50/50	LS	P	GMR
3. Saunders Marine Center – Orange Beach 💻 [wifi]	**251-981-3700**	**75**	**–**	**0/1**	**6/6**	**–**	**–**	**IMS**	**HEP**	**L60,C6**	**30/50**	**LS**	**P**	**GMR**
4. Orange Beach Marina 💻 [wifi] 163 EHL	**251-981-4207**	**130**	**16/69**	**30/161**	**9/8**	**–**	**GD**	**IMS**	**HEP**	**L60**	**30/100**	**LSC**	**P**	**MR**
5. Sportsman Marina 💻 [wifi] 163 EHL	251-981-6247	140	19	25/100	12/8	–	GD	GIMS	HEP	L15	30/100	LS	P	GR
ARNICA BAY														
6. Bear Point Harbor [wifi] 165 EHL	251-981-2327	47	16	5/83	12/6	–	GD	IS	–	–	30/50	LS	P	R
ELBERTA														
7. Barber Marina 💻 [wifi] 163 EHL	251-987-2628	125	16	30/155	12/12	F	GD	GIMS	HEP	L110	30/200+	LSC	P	G
8. Pirates Cove Marina & Restaurant 165 EHL	251-987-1224	65	–	16/16	10/10	–	–	I	–	–	30/30	LS	P	R

💻 Internet Access [wifi] Wireless Internet Access **WG** Waterway Guide Cruising Club Partner onSpot dockside WiFi facility

See WaterwayGuide.com for current rates, fuel prices, web site addresses, and other up-to-the-minute information. (*Information in the table is provided by the facilities.*)

ORANGE BEACH AREA, ARNICA BAY, ELBERTA, NOAA CHART 11378

Experience
ORANGE BEACH MARINA

Home of the **MOBILE BIG GAME FISHING CLUB** *Est. 1966*

Haven or Heaven
Enjoy the experience.

Relax. Every need is met at our beautifully secluded, secure location with covered and open slips available. Enjoy on site waterfront dining and shopping as your yacht gets all the attention it needs with on site service and repair. Located just minutes from the Gulf of Mexico at Perdido Pass and the Intercoastal Waterway.

marinalife **Best Marina 2016**

marinalife **Best Large Marina 2017**

Voted **Top 25 US Marina**

HOW TO Navigate Through Thick Fog Safely
POWER & MOTORYACHT
25 Best Marinas

Orange Beach Marina
ORANGE BEACH, ALABAMA

TENANT AMENITIES
Outstanding Marina Staff
2 Restaurants On Site
24 Hr Security
6 Bay Fuel Dock
Free Wi-Fi & Cable TV
Upscale Dock Store
Courtesy Cars & Ample Parking
Dockage to 130'
Covered Grilling & Picnic Areas
Laundry Center
Private Showers & Restrooms

ON SITE SERVICES
Fisher's at Orange Beach Marina
    Upstairs & Dockside
Saunders Yachtworks
Bluewater Yacht Sales
Coldwell Banker Seaside Realty
Orange Beach Marina Water Sports
Mobile Big Game Fishing Club
Boat Washing & Detailing Service
Inshore & Offshore Charters

NEARBY
White Sand Beaches
Commercial & Private Airports
Walking, Biking & Nature Trails
Shopping & Outlet Centers
Grocery & Drug Stores
Golf Courses - 6 within 20 Minutes

27075 Marina Road • Orange Beach, AL • 251.981.4207 • OrangeBeachMarina.com

GOIN' ASHORE: ORANGE BEACH, AL

Spanish explorer Carlos Sequenza was looking for a permanent base when he stumbled upon Perdido Bay, which means "lost" in Spanish. Presumably Perdido Bay was named "lost" because of its narrow entrance. Pirates reportedly once favored the bay and the many coves and bayous in the area because they made good hiding places. Citizens using picks and shovels opened the Perdido Pass Inlet from the Gulf in Orange Beach proper in 1906.

Attractions: The 222-acre Wharf Resort contains a full-service marina on the GIWW, condominiums, several restaurants, a variety of specialty and retail shops, a 10,000-seat amphitheater, a movie theater and a record-height (112-foot) Ferris wheel. Coastal Alabama Business Chamber coordinates the annual Shrimp Festival on the second weekend in October, drawing more than 200,000 people to Pleasure Island at the Gulf Shores Beach Boardwalk for four days of entertainment, savory foods and numerous booths featuring arts and crafts of all kinds.

Shopping: The beachside communities of Gulf Shores and Orange Beach have numerous restaurants, nightclubs and shopping. For provisioning, there is a Publix (25771 Perdido Beach Blvd.), convenient to Cotton Bayou. There is a Winn-Dixie and Walmart nearby as well. A West Marine is located at 24369 Canal Rd. (251-981-1329, requires transportation). Close by at 25472 Canal Rd. is Orange Beach Auto Marine with boating supplies and needs. OBA Canvas at 4161 Orange Beach Blvd. can handle all your canvas needs.

Dining: Orange Beach, long known as the "Fishing Capital of Alabama," has a large charter fleet and boasts a variety of restaurants offering everything from Cajun cuisine to seafood specialties. Fisher's Dockside (27075 Marina Rd. #300, 251-891-7308) at the Orange Beach Marina offers casual dockside dining downstairs or more upscale fare upstairs. Tacky Jack's (27206 Safe Harbor Dr., 251-981-4144) is nearby.

SanRoc Cay Marina, on the south shore, offers easy access to the upscale Louisiana Lagniappe (9990 Perkins Rd., 251-981-2258). Also not to be missed is the cheeseburger at Pirates Cove (6664 County Rd. 95, 251-987-1224), north of Bear Point Marina at the end of Orange Beach, just across Amica Bay. It is rumored to be the home of the original "cheeseburger in paradise." Anchor just off the restaurant and dinghy in for a carnivore's extravaganza. Call ahead for dockside depths before bringing a cruising vessel to the docks.

Channel Bridge has a 54-foot fixed vertical clearance. This pass is a popular well-marked gateway to and from the Gulf of Mexico.

A number of restaurants and marinas are located in the bays and bayous on the way to Perdido Pass. To visit here, turn southwest off the GIWW at flashing green "57," then head for green daybeacon "17," which is the last buoy of the Perdido Pass Inlet channel. Pass between green daybeacon "17" (which will be to the west) and quick flashing red "18" (to the east), and then continue that orientation toward the Perdido Pass Inlet as you come around to the west. Note that at the beginning of this channel, there are several private markers to a small cut into Ono Island to the south, which you should not follow.

If you want to explore marinas and facilities in Cotton Bayou, Terry Cove or Johnson Cove, make a soft turn further west at green can buoy "1," without cutting the shallows between that and red nun buoy "8" for the Perdido Pass Channel. Parallel the bridge running west, on the bridge's north side. At the western end of the bridge there are two channels: one that goes farther west into Cotton Bayou, and the other going north from red nun buoy "8" and green can buoy "9." This will take you into the body of water holding both Terry Cove and Johnson Cove.

If you choose to enter Cotton Bayou, be careful of shoal water. Downtown Orange Beach amenities can be reached from the bayou. There is a moderate current here as you pass the inlet, so be careful. Boaters with deep-draft vessels should use caution in Cotton Bayou; keep an eye on your depth sounder. Experience shows 6-foot MLW depths here, even though the chart shows differently.

Dockage: On the south side of Cotton Bayou, SanRoc Cay Marina can accommodate transient vessels to 150 feet and sells gas and diesel. Zeke's Landing Marina primarily handles charter fishing boats; however, gas and diesel fuel are available here, along with marine supplies and groceries.

Either from Cotton Bayou or Perdido Pass, if you are heading up to Terry Cove for Saunders Marine Center– Orange Beach or Orange Beach Marina, you will pass a boat ramp on the west headland. Just past this boat ramp is flashing red "12."

For Orange Beach Marina, look due west (about 150 to 200 yards) to see green daybeacon "1" and red daybeacon "2." This privately marked channel curves southward and then westward along private docks and residences. Follow it, keeping red to starboard and at the very end you will see Orange Beach Marina's private channel, running due south. The full-service Orange Beach Marina has plenty of transient dockage in a secluded and fully protected harbor. They offer all the usual amenities, plus two restaurants (the upscale Fisher's Upstairs and the more casual Fisher's Dockside) and a full-service boatyard, Saunders Marine Center. Saunders is equipped with a 60-ton lift and handles repairs from minor to extensive.

Located on the north shore of Johnson Cove or eastern end of Terry Cove, Sportsman Marina is easy to reach. At flashing red "12" in Johnson Cove, carefully proceed north by northeast, but give flashing red "12" a wide berth to avoid shoals lying east of the marker.

Anchorage: There is an anchorage at Bayou St. John at Mile 167 EHL with 7 to 8 feet at MLW and excellent holding in sand. (Somewhat exposed to the west.)

■ BEAR POINT TO BON SECOUR BAY

There are even more "must-see" spots off the GIWW, particularly for gunkholers. Many cruisers have a problem when they visit this bountiful area; they do not want to leave. Some who plan to stay for a week or so can only tear themselves away after several weeks. Some stay permanently.

NAVIGATION: Use NOAA Chart 11378. Reversing course toward the GIWW, as you leave Bayou St. John, you can safely cut across from green daybeacon "17" (which will be to the west) to GIWW flashing red "58" (leave to the east, as you are back on the GIWW westbound) at Mile 166 EHL.

The channel around Mill Point is well marked, but it is narrow and shallow on the edges; a sharp watch is required. Once in Arnica Bay, the channel opens up– particularly to the north–before it closes down again off Hatchett Point at flashing red "68." From flashing red "68" to red daybeacon "90," the GIWW is relatively open through Bay La Launch, past Sapling Point and through the straight shot across Wolf Bay to red daybeacon "90" at the entrance to Portage Creek.

From here (Mile 160 EHL) the GIWW is bordered by land to Oyster Bay at Mile 152.5 EHL. Along this route you will pass under **Foley Beach Expressway Bridge** at Mile 158.7 EHL, which has a fixed vertical clearance of 73 feet. The next and last bridges along this route are the **Gulf Shores Parkway (Portage Creek) Twin Bridges** at Mile 154.9 EHL with fixed vertical clearances of 73 feet.

A tugboat crew-change station and supply store is east of the Gulf Shores Parkway Twin Bridges. There is an Idle-Speed/No-Wake Zone along this stretch. Shrimp boats and barges sometimes tie up to both banks east of the bridge to wait out inclement weather.

Dockage: Most of the marinas in the Orange Beach/Bear Point area welcome transients (and there are several small ones not listed here). These and the facilities at Gulf Shores, AL, are the last recreational boat marinas located on or near the GIWW east of New Orleans. Full-service marinas at Mobile and Fairhope, AL; Biloxi and Gulfport, MS; and Slidell, LA, all require side trips of up to 20 miles from the GIWW proper.

Curving around the green buoys off Bear Point into Arnica Bay, you will soon find the 83-slip Bear Point Harbor south of green daybeacon "65" at Mile 165 EHL. This has traditionally been a favorite stopover for cruising boats. Both gas and diesel are available.

Barber Marina is located north off the GIWW (Mile 163 EHL) at red daybeacon "74." This marina can accommodate boats on floating docks and sells fuel. Nearby (at Mile 165 EHL) Pirates Cove Marina & Restaurant may have transient space. You will see the entrance to the marina docks and boatyard off to the west as you approach the narrow cut into Roberts Bayou.

At this point, activity increases on the GIWW. Heading west, just past the Foley Beach Bridge, is The Wharf Marina at Mile 158.8 EHL. In addition to slips on floating docks and all fuels, a variety of restaurants, shopping centers and condominiums are here.

The full-service Saunders Yachtworks–Gulf Shores is located at GIWW Mile 155.5 EHL. They have a 165-ton lift and 6-ton crane and can handle most any repair.

The protected Homeport Marina is located at Mile 155.0 EHL just under the Gulf Shores Parkway Twin Bridges with plenty of room for transients at its concrete floating docks, along with gas and diesel fuel. They offer all the usual amenities plus the on-site LuLu's restaurant, operated by Lucy Buffett (Jimmy's sister). There is a 120-foot-long dock in front of the restaurant where you can tie up if you are stopping to eat. The daily "countdown to sunset" is not to be missed. Call 251-967-5858 to check availability.

Anchorage: You can anchor just to the west of Bear Point Marina and dinghy in. This is open and exposed to the north and west as well as wakes. Almost due north from Bear Point Marina, on the other side of Arnica Bay, is Roberts Bayou, commonly known both to cruisers and locals as "Pirates Cove." There is a narrow entrance with private markers leading to the bayou. While the narrow entrance may seem intimidating, a local sailing charter boat, the 50-foot former world cruiser *Daedelus* often transits the channel under sail. There is a spot at the mouth of Roberts Bayou and the end of the entrance channel that narrows to one boat width, so plan ahead. Roberts Bayou is a popular anchorage for cruisers and locals, with about 8 feet at MLW and good holding ground. As in any anchorage that is or might be crowded, it is a good idea to buoy your anchor with a trip line, not only so someone will not drop their hook over your rode, but to prevent snarling and tangling in tight quarters.

An idyllic location for cruisers and locals alike is Ingram Bayou (Mile 164 EHL, due north of red daybeacon "72") about 1.5 miles west on the GIWW from Roberts Bayou. Turn right at red daybeacon "72," and then go straight into Ingram Bayou, right down the center. There is shoaling on either side of this excellent, all-weather anchorage, but 9-foot MLW depths hold most of the way in. Larger boats can find 8-foot MLW depths just past the sharp bend to the left at the head of Ingram Bayou. This is a favorite spot. Once inside, you will be surrounded by total greenery and quiet (except on a busy weekend), and there is usually a breeze to keep most of the bugs away.

There are also plenty of places to anchor in 5- to 8-foot MLW depths at Wolf Bay, including in Graham Bayou and at Wolf Bay Lodge. This is a busy thoroughfare, so expect wakes and anchor appropriately.

Bon Secour Bay–GIWW Mile 151 EHL

Bon Secour lies at the southeasterly reaches of Mobile Bay. Moving west on the GIWW, enter Bon Secour Bay at the 17 foot flashing green "103" and red nun buoy "104." The next marker will be the 17-foot flashing red "2" marking the beginning of a well-marked channel north into the Bon Secour River.

The GIWW tracks west across lower Mobile Bay and crosses the Main Ship Channel at flashing red "26" on the channel (Mile 133.75 EHL). This is where the cruising sailor with plenty of time might be tempted to change course, head north and sample some of the breezy bay's delights.

Dockage: Gulf Shores Marina, located near Fort Morgan at the southeastern end of Mobile Bay (Mile 135 EHL), offers transient dockage, dry storage, a fuel dock and an on-site restaurant, Tacky Jacks 2 (251-968-8341).

Anchorage: You can anchor up the Bon Secour River by red daybeacon "38" in 4 to 7 feet at MLW with good holding in mud. Note that local boats may buzz by you here, throwing wakes. A better anchorage is located south of flashing green "135" in Bon Secour Bay. There is a cut through the spoil area at flashing green "123" to reach the Edith Hammock anchorage. Watch your chart and take care to avoid the fish haven and submerged pilings as you head toward the water tower. Anchor in sand in 7 to 9 feet at MLW. You are protected from the southwest through southeast, and exposed to northerly winds. Holding is good.

Dauphin Island–GIWW Mile 130 EHL

On the west side of the entrance to Mobile Bay, Dauphin Island, with its long sandy spit to the west, is the first of the barrier islands running from Mobile Bay to New Orleans. Of the many recreational and boating centers in the Mobile area, Dauphin Island is the closest to the GIWW. The island is a pleasant and interesting stopover, with a sizable marina, anchorages along the entire length of the island and excellent beaches.

Dauphin Island is home to Fort Gaines, once a Confederate stronghold used to defend the east entrance to Mobile Bay. Now a historic site and museum, it can be explored daily (except Thanksgiving and Christmas). Every year, Fort Gaines hosts a variety of theme weekends, such as Civil War reenactments. For details visit dauphinisland.org or call 251-861-3607.

The island is also home to Dauphin Island Sea Lab, Alabama's marine education and research center. The lab operates the Estuarium, an extensive public aquarium, displaying features of coastal Alabama's ecosystems: the Delta, Mobile Bay and the Gulf of Mexico. For more information, call 251-861-2141 or visit disl.org.

NAVIGATION: Use NOAA Chart 11378. It is possible to enter Dauphin Island Bay via two channels. The first channel, for boats heading west across Mobile Bay, Middle Ground, is on the east side of the island by Fort Gains at Pelican Point. This entrance is referred to locally as "Billy Goat Hole." Move west through the channel in the spoil areas at flashing green "25" and flashing red "26." Local knowledge suggests that

Oyster Bay Area, AL

GULF SHORES			Dockage				Supplies		Services				
	Largest Vessel Accommodated	VHF Channel Monitored	Approach / Dockside Depth (reported) Transient Berths / Total Berths	Floating Docks	Gas / Diesel	Groceries, Ice, Marine Supplies, Snacks	Repairs: Hull, Engine, Propeller	Lift (tonnage), Crane, Rail	Laundry, Pool, Showers Courtesy Car Min/Max Amps	Pump-Out Station	Nearby: Grocery Store, Motel, Restaurant		
1. The Wharf Marina ▭ WIFI WG 158.8 EHL 251-224-1900	150	16/68	30/210	10/10	F	GD	GIMS	EP	–	30/200+	LPS	P	GMR
2. Saunders Yachtworks – Gulf Shores ▭ WIFI 155.5 EHL 251-981-3700	130	–	call/14	10/8	–	–	IM	HEP	L165, C6	30/200+	–	P	GMR
3. Homeport Marina ▭ WIFI WG 155 EHL 251-968-4528	115	16	10/77	10/8	F	GD	GIS	–	–	30/100	LS	P	GMR

▭ Internet Access WIFI Wireless Internet Access WG Waterway Guide Cruising Club Partner ⊙onSpot dockside WiFi facility
See WaterwayGuide.com for current rates, fuel prices, web site addresses, and other up-to-the-minute information. *(Information in the table is provided by the facilities.)*

GULF SHORES, NOAA CHART 11378

depth over the spoils is about 10 feet at MLW. Turn south to the well-marked channel through Billy Goat Hole. You will pass a Coast Guard Station and ferry dock just inside the entry. Depths are charted at 4.5 feet at MLW. Refer to the Waterway Explorer (waterwayguide.com) and NOAA online charts for the most up-to-date information.

The second channel is Aux Heron's Channel, 1.6 miles west of the **Dauphin Island Causeway Bridge** (fixed 83-foot vertical clearance) at Mile 127.8 EHL. Entrance via this second channel is limited by a fixed bridge (**Dauphin Island Bridge**) with a 25-foot vertical clearance. At red "22" in the Aux Heron's Channel, leave the GIWW on a southeast course and pick up flashing green "1" marking the entrance to a channel to Bayou Aloe. Proceed on a southeast course past the 17-foot flashing red "2" and green "3." The next marker should be flashing green "1," leading into a privately marked channel to Chugae Point and the clearly visible Dauphin Island Bridge. Depths are charted at 4.5 feet at MLW.

⚠️ Dauphin Island Channel daybeacons "5" and "7" were reported destroyed in April 2018.

Dockage: The only marina here, Dauphin Island Marina, is a full-service facility welcoming transients. It would be prudent to call ahead for reservations and the latest information on markers and water depths. Motels and restaurants are a short walk from the marina. This marina also has good access to a Post Office, bank and groceries.

Anchorage: Dauphin Island has many fine anchorages protected from southerly winds but not from the north. Hurricane Rita broke through the middle of Dauphin Island, leaving a breach in the island. Keep this in mind when deciding where to anchor.

If you need someplace close to the channel entrance on the east side of the island, you can anchor in Billy Goat Hole. With a draft less than 5 feet you can travel 400 to 500 feet then go east to the beach at Billy Goat Hole. To make sure you stay away from service boats and the ferry, put you bow on the beach and carry an anchor to shore. A deeper anchorage (6 to 9 feet at MLW) is Confederate Pass on the eastern end. This is well protected and marked and is within dinghy distance of a restaurant; however, it is usually occupied by commercial boats.

Other options are Bayou Aloe with good holding in sand (very shallow), and near green daybeacon "27" at the west end of the island in 7 to 9 feet at MLW. On the south side of the island you can find a quiet anchorage in Pelican Bay. Leave the main ship channel at green "15" and navigate past the shoals at Pelican Island, which has become more of a peninsula, then into the smaller bay/lagoon where you should find depths of 10 to 12 feet at MLW with good holding.

GOIN' ASHORE: **DAUPHIN ISLAND, AL**

On Dauphin Island, less is more. The little island in the southwest tip of Alabama is well known and much loved for being less congested than other Gulf Coast resorts. It's also noted for its breathtaking sunsets, pristine beaches, walking and biking trails, bird sanctuaries, charter fishing boats, ferry across Mobile Bay, outdoor recreation and historic sites. Truth is, Dauphin Island is awash in history.

Long before modern-day folks were opening oysters on the island, the Pensacola people of the Mississippian period (1100 to 1550) were steaming and roasting them and then discarding the shells at a site now called Indian Shell Mound Park, which is on the National Register of Historic Places. The arrival of Europeans first brought new displaced Choctaw, Creek and Seminole people to replace or absorb the Pensacola, but the Spanish and French eras were a time of shared use of the island as a trading port. The early 19th century saw waves of settlers from Georgia, the Carolinas, and Virginia, which created the pressure for the forced relocation of all those tribes to Oklahoma.

Attractions: When you visit Dauphin Island, you can golf; rent bicycles, kayaks, canoes and stand-up paddle boards; take a nature tour, a dolphin watch boat ride, a lighthouse cruise or a sunset cruise; and visit the Island Heritage and Art Gallery, which features high-quality paintings, pottery, woodworking, jewelry and other items produced by local artists.

In addition, visitors won't want to miss historic Fort Gaines, built in the early 19th century and a key coastal fortification in the Civil War's Battle of Mobile Bay. Besides cannons, artifacts and regular blacksmithing demonstrations, the fort annually hosts re-enactors from throughout the Southeast who fire weapons and re-create living conditions at the fort during that August 1864

conflict. Just off the beach, U.S. Admiral David Farragut uttered his (probably paraphrased) order: "Damn the torpedoes; full speed ahead!" This fort is one of the eleven most endangered historical sites in the U.S., due to shoreline erosion, so make your visit now.

Birds and birders love the island, too. Dauphin Island is home to a 137-acre Audubon Bird Sanctuary, which draws bird-watchers from all over the country, especially during the annual fall and spring migrations. The National Audubon Society calls the island "globally important" for birds, and it has been voted the "Birdiest Small Coastal City in America" several years in a row.

Dauphin Island holds a special place in the hearts of fishermen and boaters, who love the fact that it is surrounded by water: The Mississippi Sound is on the north side, the Gulf of Mexico is on the south, and there are small bays, inlets and bayous all over the 14-mile-long island. Boaters will find easy access to marinas as well as to public and private boat launches.

Fishermen converge on the island each July for the three-day Alabama Deep Sea Fishing Rodeo, which is nearing its 85th anniversary. Sailors come for the annual Dauphin Island Sailboat Regatta, held in April and billed as the largest one-day point-to-point regatta in the United States.

Shopping/Dining: The marina or Bayou Aloe anchorage put you right in the shopping and eating area, though farther from Fort Gaines and the bird sanctuary. The Lighthouse Bakery (919 Chaumont Ave, 251-861-2253) gets good marks for its light breakfasts and cozy atmosphere. Miquel's Beach'n Baja (916 Bienville Blvd., 251-861-5683) has a simple but flavorful menu. JT's Sunset Grill (1102 De Soto Ave., 251-861-2829) is the waterfront seafood option with a deck, but it's down-home, not dinner-jacket.

Locally owned boutiques, restaurants and gift shops dot the island, adding to its old-fashioned, charming atmosphere. As the day draws to an end, folks across the island can look to the west, knowing that as the "Sunset Capital of Alabama," Dauphin Island is the perfect place to watch Mother Nature paint the sky in spectacular shades of scarlet, orange, yellow and copper.

Want to learn more about this unique beach community? Go to.dauphinislandchamber.com and. townofdauphinisland.org, and follow the Town of Dauphin and Friends of Dauphin Island Facebook pages.

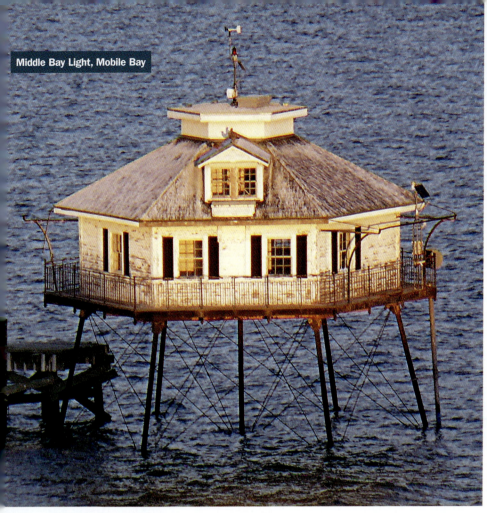
Middle Bay Light, Mobile Bay

Mobile Bay is shallow and with its long fetch running south to north it can build substantial waves. In 15-knot winds it will be rough. Winds at greater speeds will and have made the bay dangerous.

The best way to cover cruising in Mobile Bay is through a literary "tale of two shores."

City of Fairhope

The allure of the east is its attractive, character-filled communities. There are fewer facilities and they are more widely spaced. Marinas are mostly self-contained, resort-type facilities.

NAVIGATION: Use NOAA Chart 11376, 11378. Westbound on the GIWW you will enter the Mobile Bay area via Bon Secour Bay. You can cruise north into Mobile Bay by leaving the GIWW and navigating through the open waters of the bay, or continue east and turn north when you enter the Main Ship Channel.

The Ship Channel provides a well-defined, well-marked route to follow north. You can leave the channel almost anywhere. It is bordered by spoils, but local boaters say the depth over the spoils is usually about 10 feet at MLW. You may choose to leave the GIWW for a shorter route, but be aware that this requires navigating the more open shallower waters of the Bay. Eastbound cruisers will almost surely choose the Main Ship Channel, which is a shorter route to the north and east.

For the north route in the bay, leave the GIWW at Mile 145 EHL, at green "129," on a course of 337 degrees magnetic. Continue for 10 statute miles to the 30-foot red "2" at Mullet Point. Continue on a course of 337 degrees magnetic for another 7.25 statute miles to the 37-foot "4" at Great Point Clear. Leave the charted shoals to the east. From this point, head northwest if you are going to the marina at the Grand Hotel Marriott Resort.

If you are continuing on a northerly route, turn to starboard on a course of 142 degrees magnetic. The

MOBILE BAY

Mobile Bay sits on the northern Gulf Coast, 40 miles west of Pensacola and 90 miles northeast of South Pass at the Mississippi River. It is the approach to the City of Mobile and to the Alabama and Tombigbee Rivers. The Bay has depths of 7 to 12 feet at MLW outside the dredged channels. The Gulf approach to the Bay is 3 miles wide and is bordered by Mobile Point on the east and Pelican Point on the west. Stay in the dredged channel to avoid shoals that extend 4 miles south (into the Gulf) on both sides. The Port of Mobile is 25 miles to the north. Expect heavy traffic.

High rise condominiums are prominent along the shoreline and can be seen on approach. West of the entrance is a chain of low wooded islands for 50 nm. The black conical tower that is Sand Island Light is the most prominent landmark near the entrance at 131 feet. On the east side of the entrance, the pentagon-shaped walls of Fort Morgan at Mobile Point are clearly visible. To the west of the entrance, a spherical, elevated tank two miles west of Fort Gains on the east end of Dauphin Island at Pelican Point is clearly visible.

Bon Secour Bay to Mobile Bay, AL

	Largest Vessel Accommodated	VHF Channel Monitored	Transient Berths / Total Berths	Approach / Dockside Depth (reported)	Floating Docks	Gas / Diesel	Groceries, Ice, Marine Supplies, Snacks	Repairs: Hull, Engine, Propeller	Lift (tonnage), Crane, Rail	Min/Max Amps	Laundry, Pool, Showers, Courtesy Car	Pump-Out Station	Nearby: Grocery Store, Motel, Restaurant
GULF SHORES AREA				**Dockage**			**Supplies**			**Services**			
1. Gulf Shores Marina 135 EHL 251-540-2628	70	16	6/70	4/4	–	GD	GIMS	–	L10	30/30	S	P	GR
DAUPHIN ISLAND													
2. Dauphin Island Marina 📶 127.8 EHL 251-861-2201	60	16	5/90	6/6	–	GD	IMS	–	L5	30/50	LPS	P	GMR

🖥 Internet Access 📶 Wireless Internet Access **WG** Waterway Guide Cruising Club Partner ⬤ onSpot dockside WiFi facility
See WaterwayGuide.com for current rates, fuel prices, web site addresses, and other up-to-the-minute information. *(Information in the table is provided by the facilities.)*

GULF SHORES AREA, DAUPHIN ISLAND, NOAA CHART 11378

Town of Fairhope is 4 miles farther on this course, then 1 mile to the east. To reach the marinas at Fly Creek, continue a course of 142 degrees magnetic for 1 mile, then turn east for 1 mile. If you want to continue a northerly trek in the Bay, it is best to go west to the Ship Channel. Refer to the Waterway Explorer (waterwayguide.com) and NOAA online charts for the most up-to-date information.

Dockage: The Fairhope Municipal Pier is in Fairhope Park at the end of Fairhope Ave., and is a short walk into town. It is the only place where a boat can tie up within walking distance of the historic town. Shux on the Pier may have dockage for diners. Call ahead at 251-421-4554.

To get to the Grand Hotel Marriott Resort & Spa, use the charted Point Clear approach and follow the daybeacons that line the entrance channel. The depth in the channel and in the harbor is at least 7 feet at MLW.

Gas and diesel fuel are available here as well as dockage for vessels to 115 feet.

Stay to the south side of channel as you enter Fly Creek. Fairhope Docks is on the north side of the channel. The facility was undertaking a major renovation at press time in summer 2018 and will remain open during the process. The marina has covered and open slips, as well as plans for a new fuel dock and pump-out facility. A full-service repair facility is expected by 2019.

Fly Creek Marina is located further up Fly Creek, at the town of Seacliff. Follow the Fly Creek Channel from Mobile Bay, holding to the south side until you are inside the breakwater; it is the second facility just past the private Fairhope Yacht Club's docks. This marina, similar to other eastern shore marinas, is heavily populated by sailboats. It is a tidy, clean marina in a lovely wooded area.

Fairhope

Mobile Bay: Western Shore

On the western shore of Mobile Bay, boaters will find facilities that are work-a-day marinas with good basic services but fewer frills. Other facilities, however, are within convenient reach to downtown Mobile, either by rental car or marina courtesy car.

The City of Mobile is a metropolis with an recently expanded and updated commercial waterfront, and since the completion of the Tennessee-Tombigbee Waterway in 1985, heavy barge traffic has greatly increased in the area, especially on the northern end near the mouth of the Mobile River. There is also a cruise ship terminal, which increases waterfront traffic.

NAVIGATION: Use NOAA Chart 11376. All cruising boats visiting the west shore will want to move north in the large ship channel. Boats heading west across Bon Secour Bay can leave the GIWW at the 17-foot green "147." Set a course of 298 degrees magnetic for 6.5 miles to a cut through the spoil into the ship channel. Follow the same course through the cut for 1.5 miles and enter the ship channel at the 17-foot flashing red "34." Boats coming from the east through Pass Aux Heron can leave the GIWW at red nun "10" and green can "9" after passing under the Dauphin Island Causeway Bridge. Set a course of 61 degrees magnetic for 5 miles to the cut entering the ship channel. Follow the same course for 1.5 miles and enter the ship channel at the 17-foot flashing green "33."

Moving north in the ship channel for 8 miles, you will come to a cut in the spoil just before 17-foot green "49." To access the facilities on the western shore at Fowl River, exit the ship channel before green "49" on a course of 275 degrees magnetic for 4.3 miles to the channel entry at green "1" and red "2."

Further north (2.7 miles) in the ship channel you will pass the Hollinger Island and Theodore Ship Channel, opposite the 17-foot red "54." The channel leads to an industrial complex with no facilities for cruising boats.

Continuing north past the 17-foot green "63" and red "64" for 5 miles where you will intersect the channel to Dog River to the west. Enter the channel between green daybeacon "1" and red daybeacon "2." Stay in the channel on a heading of about 305 degrees magnetic for 2.5 miles to green "5." Channel depths are charted at 6.5 feet at MLW. Turn west at green daybeacon "5" and follow the channel for 2 miles to the **Dauphin Island Parkway (Dog River) Bridge**. The bridge has a

GOIN' ASHORE: **FAIRHOPE, AL**

SERVICES		
1	Library	
2	Post Office	
3	Visitor Information	
ATTRACTIONS		
4	Fairhope Municipal Pier	

5	Fairhope Museum of History	
6	Marietta Johnson Museum	
SHOPPING		
7	Greer's Market	
DINING		
4	Shucks on the Pier	

8	Panini Pete's Café & Bakeshoppe
9	Pinzone's Italian

In 1894 a group of 28 Populist reformers led by E.B. Gaston landed on the eastern shore of Mobile Bay to establish a Single Tax Colony, as prescribed by noted economist Henry George (1839-1897). Their mission was to: "establish and conduct a model community or colony, free from all forms of private monopoly, and to secure to its members therein equality of opportunity, the full reward of individual efforts, and the benefits of co-operation in matters of general concern."

Incorporated as the Fairhope Industrial Association, the group purchased a large tract of land and then leased it back to individuals, charging an annual rent (the Single Tax) in return for municipal services. They retained the bluff and the best waterfront property for the use and enjoyment of the community. As new people moved in, services expanded and the model community thrived. The Fairhope Single Tax Corporation, a non-profit entity, owns 4,200 acres. Homeowners and merchants still lease parcels of land from the Corporation. The Corporation pays all state and local taxes from the rent and manages a fund to make community improvements.

There is much to intrigue and delight visiting cruisers to Mobile Bay's eastern shore. The people who began the initial experimental community were a freethinking,

intellectual group. Fairhope continues to attract artists, philosophers, musicians, and writers. The town boasts independent bookstores and hardware stores in the thriving downtown district. Unique art galleries, shops and restaurants abound.

Attractions: The Fairhope Municipal Pier is a gathering place where townspeople and visitors meet, picnic, fish, stroll the pier, and enjoy the sunsets. There are benches for watching Mobile Bay, and walking paths for walking and running. The Fairhope Welcome Center (20 N. Section St., 251-928-5095) is your resource for maps, brochures and restaurant and lodging guides for the Fairhope area.

The Marietta Johnson Museum (10 S. School St., 251-990-8601) is housed in the Bell Building. Marietta Johnson, a leader in the Progressive Education Movement, founded Fairhope's first school, the School for Organic Education in 1907. The fascinating story of this visionary educator and author and her school that boasted "no tests, no grades, no shoes" is told at this delightful museum. For more information call 251-990-8601.

The Fairhope Museum of History (24 North Section St., 251-929-1471) features permanent displays highlighting the unique history of Fairhope. The museum is located in a Spanish Mission Revival structure originally built in 1928 as the city's first municipal building and rehabilitated in 2007 for the museum (with the help of the Single Tax Corporation).

There is a Dog Park at 701 Volanta Ave. near Fly Creek Marina that caters to free spirits of your canine pals. Watering stations are provided, as are waste bag and collection stations.

For cruisers interested in touring by bicycle, there is a designated bike route from the *USS Alabama Battleship* Memorial Park south through Daphne and Fairhope and ends at Point Clear. For detailed information, visit thetrailblazers.org.

Special Events: Each February Fairhope celebrates Mardi Gras with colorful parades and related festival events. In mid-March cruisers can enjoy the three-day Annual Arts & Crafts Festival featuring several hundred artists from across the nation. There is live entertainment and unique cuisine throughout the show. This prestigious juried art exhibition draws over 200,000 visitors each year.

An Art Walk featuring art exhibits and musical entertainment is held the first Friday of every month in downtown Fairhope. Between 20 and 30 venues are open between 6:00 p.m. and 8:00 p.m. for the Art Walk.

Shopping: It is easy to provision in Fairhope. A Publix Supermarket is within 1 mile of Fly Creek Marina and Eastern Shore Marina, both located on Fly Creek. Greer's Market (75 S. Section St., 251-928-8029) sells quality meat and produce and has a deli counter. The summer and fall Farmers' Markets are held on Thursday afternoons on Bancroft St., behind the Fairhope Public Library. The downtown shopping area features a hardware store, art galleries, gift shops, boutiques, a locally owned bookstore, antiques and collectibles shops and a bicycle shop.

Dining: There is a smörgåsbord of options for dining in Fairhope. These are well worth the trip ashore, but a vehicle or the desire to pedal long distances and possibly uphill is recommended. Check your marina for a courtesy car.

On the municipal pier you can tie up and enjoy seafood served over the water at Shucks on the Pier (251-421-8021). For those seeking Italian food, try Pinzone's Italian (18 Laurel Ave., 251-990-5535). Panini Pete's Café & Bakeshoppe at 42 1/2 S. Section St. (251-929-0122) comes highly recommended, as does Sunset Pointe at Fly Creek Marina, which has the same owner. Sunset Pointe offers vivid sunsets along with your meal.

Mobile Bay to Dauphin Island, AL

		Largest Vessel Accommodated	VHF Channel Monitored	Transient Berths / Total Berths	Approach / Dockside Depth (reported)	Floating Docks	Gas / Diesel	Groceries, Ice, Marine Supplies, Snacks	Repairs: Hull, Engine, Propeller	Lift (tonnage), Crane, Rail	Min/Max Amps	Laundry, Pool, Showers, Courtesy Car	Pump-Out Station	Nearby: Grocery Store, Motel, Restaurant
FAIRHOPE AREA														
1. Grand Hotel Marriott Resort & Spa 🖥 WiFi	251-928-9201	115	16	34/34	6/5	-	GD	GIMS	-	-	30/50	PS	P	GMR
2. Fairhope Docks Marina (formerly Eastern Shore Marine) 🖥 WiFi	251-929-0365	80	16/79	12/70	6/6	-	GD	IM	-	-	30/50	LS	P	GR
3. Fly Creek Marina 🖥 WiFi	251-928-4868	36	16	10/50	9/6	-	GD	I	-	-	30/50	LS	P	MR
DOG RIVER AREA														
4. Fowl River Marina	251-973-2670	50	16	3/60	5/5	F	GD	GIMS	-	-	50/50	S	P	GR
5. Beachcomber Marina	251-443-8000	65	-	15/96	9/16	-	-	-	HEP	L40	30/30	-	-	R
6. Grand Mariner Marina & Mariner Restaurant 🖥 WiFi	251-525-8395	200	16/68	20/100	15/12	-	GD	IMS	-	L35	30/50	LS	-	R
7. Turner Marine Supply Inc. 🖥 WiFi WG	251-476-1444	100	16	40/150	8/7	-	-	M	HEP	L55,C2	30/50	LSC	-	R
8. Dog River Marina and Boat Works Inc. 🖥 WiFi	251-471-5449	200	16	50/100	8/10	-	GD	IM	HEP	L70	30/100	LSC	P	-
9. Dockside Marina	251-479-2772	-	-	-	-	-	-	-	-	-	30/50	S	P	R
10. River Yacht Basin Marina WiFi	251-776-4435	70	-	10/72	6/6	-	-	-	-	-	30/50	LS	-	GR

🖥 Internet Access　WiFi Wireless Internet Access　WG Waterway Guide Cruising Club Partner　onSpot dockside WiFi facility

See WaterwayGuide.com for current rates, fuel prices, web site addresses, and other up-to-the-minute information. *(Information in the table is provided by the facilities.)*

73-foot fixed vertical clearance. Several marinas can be found just under the bridge.

Dockage: Working clockwise around Mobile Bay from the southwest corner, Fowl River Marina appears first. The channel into Fowl River is well marked. The marina is located 0.5 miles upriver on the north side at red daybeacon "16," before the 45-foot fixed vertical clearance **East Fowl River Bridge**. The on-site Pelican Reef Restaurant (251-973-2670) is open daily and serves fresh seafood straight from its own boats.

There is a cluster of marinas on Dog River to the north on the western shore of Mobile Bay, roughly two-thirds of the way up the Ship Channel from the pass entering Mobile Bay. Marinas are on each side of the river within 100 yards of the Dauphin Island (Dog River) Parkway Bridge.

Beachcomber Marina is the first marina on the south side of the bridge. They have slips and a 40-ton lift for repairs. The large Grand Mariner Marina & Mariner Restaurant is the second marina south of the bridge, heading upriver. This full-service marina has ample dockage and a fantastic restaurant.

Turner Marine Supply Inc. is about 150 yards past the bridge on the north shore with slips and repairs (55-ton lift). The full-service Dog River Marina and Boat Works Inc. is on the same side, a little farther north around the curve. They have a very complete West Marine store on the premises as well as a 70-ton lift. To the north is the new (in 2018) Dockside Marina in a quiet, protected harbor. There is a sandy beach in a family friendly environment.

Farther upriver is River Yacht Basin Marina, which may have space for you. If you plan to transit north up the Tennessee-Tombigbee Waterway, see *Waterway Guide's* Great Lakes edition.

Anchorage: There is room to anchor up the East Fowl River in 6 to 8 feet at MLW if you can fit under the 45-foot fixed East Fowl River Bridge. Dog River offers a good anchorage near River Yacht Basin Marina. Anchor according to wind direction.

◼ PORT OF MOBILE

Mobile is a busy deep-water port. It moves around 54 million tons of cargo per year, ranking it within the top dozen or so ports in the nation. It is also home to the GulfQuest National Maritime Museum of the Gulf of Mexico, which is dedicated to the rich traditions, history and culture of the Gulf. The museum has 90 interactive exhibits, simulators and theaters covering an array of maritime topics including early settlements and trade routes, marine archeology and shipwrecks, marine life, weather and hurricanes, marine and coastal environments, maritime commerce and shipbuilding, ship navigation and communication, offshore oil/gas platforms and much more (gulfquest.org).

Mobile is also a cultural center with numerous festivals, museums and historical sites. See details at mobile.org.

FAIRHOPE AREA, NOAA CHART 11376

DOG RIVER AREA, NOAA CHART 11376

Dockage: There is a free dock at the Mobile Convention Center. This is a fixed dock with 25-foot dockside depths at MLW and no amenities. It is a short walk to town. Call 251-208-2165 for details.

Anchorage: There are several anchorages north of Mobile on the Mobile River. The south side of Twelve-Mile Island offers at least 10 feet at MLW and all-around protection. Note that commercial traffic uses this area, so display good anchor light.

Big Bayou Canot offers two anchorages. The south anchorage is just south of the 7-foot fixed vertical clearance bridge, while the north anchorage can be accessed via the Mobile River, north of the CSX Railroad (14-Mile) Lift Bridge (opens on signal). Both have 15 feet at MLW with good holding in mud and all-around protection.

Big Briar Creek is located 1 mile east of the Mobile River on a canal that runs between the Mobile River and the (unmarked) Tensaw River. Turn north into Big Briar Creek for a wide anchorage with enough current to keep you straight. Here you will find at least 10 feet at MLW and good holding. You can take your dinghy east to the island used by locals to walk the dog.

> Note: It would be best if you and your pet don't swim here. There seem to be more and more **alligators** every year, and there's no need to feed the wildlife!

■ MISSISSIPPI SOUND

West of Mobile Bay, the GIWW opens up to the Mississippi Sound, a bay-like expanse of water between the mainland and a string of barrier islands known as the Gulf Islands National Seashore. This open stretch of waterway extends from east to west for 85 statute miles. The width of the sound is 10 to 12 miles. This long stretch and significant width, when combined with a 15-knot wind, will result in considerable chop. When the winds blow over 15 knots, consider staying in a safe harbor or looking for shelter if you find yourself underway in these conditions. Wait for fair weather and the Sound can be a very enjoyable and rewarding cruising area worth exploring in detail. Sunrise over the beaches of Horn Island has been heralded as truly spectacular.

Shoreside facilities in this area are limited. The number and quality of destinations is growing, however, due to both the popularity of the area as well as the ongoing rebuilding effort from past hurricanes.

Anchorage is often available in the lee of the Gulf Islands during warm weather months when a south wind prevails. Pleasure boaters should keep in mind that traveling west from this point will increase the frequency of encounters with commercial vessels, most often towboats. Give these vessels a wide berth, particularly in shallower waters and narrow channels. As suggested earlier, it is advisable to monitor both VHF Channels 13 and 16. Additionally, AIS is used extensively on the GIWW.

Gulf inlets (usually referred to in these waters as "passes") are not all trustworthy. Only the three inlets at Pascagoula, Biloxi and Gulfport provide reliable access to the Gulf of Mexico.

Pass Aux Heron to Pascagoula– GIWW Mile 125 EHL to 104 EHL

Pascagoula is primarily a commercial shipping port. The harbor, located about 9 miles north of Horn Island Pass is one of the important deep water ports on the Gulf Coast. The city, which is located at the mouth of the Pascagoula River, is home to many large industries, which will contribute to commercial ship traffic.

Steeped in a past with French Louisiana influence, the area was settled in the 1700s by French and French Canadians. After the Louisiana Purchase, a militia group took control of the city and raised the American flag. In 1870 a railroad route that ran directly through the city was completed. The railroad–combined with the deep water port–ensured the economic success of the city.

NAVIGATION: Use Charts 11367, 11372, 11373, 11374, 11375. From Mobile Bay, the GIWW passes through Pass Aux Herons Channel and then enters Mississippi Sound. When leaving the channel at Mile 124 EHL, most markers are lighted and elevated, although some are as many as 4 miles apart. Pay close attention to compass headings and position fixes on the long run between markers. The next 70 or more miles are a long and only partially protected passageway. Natural depths of 12 to 18 feet are found throughout the Sound, and a channel from Mobile Bay to New Orleans is regularly dredged.

Stay in the channel to GIWW Mile 118.5 EHL at 17-foot flashing red "40" and green "41." The next channel marker is 17-foot green "5" at GIWW Mile 114 EHL at a distance of 4.5 statute miles on a course of about 255 degrees magnetic. Chart your course to stay in or close to the GIWW channel through the rest of the sound.

It is 10.5 miles from the large ship channel at Horn Island Pass to Pascagoula. North in the Pascagoula Channel you will encounter a Y at red buoy"36." To port is the route to Pascagoula; to starboard is Bayou Casotte.

Dockage: Pascagoula Inner Harbor Marina is at Lake Yazoo and has limited space. They report 3-foot MLW dockside depths, so call ahead. Also off of the Pascagoula River to the north and west is the Mary Walker Marina, catering mostly to sportfishermen (reporting 5-foot dockside depths), but welcoming to transients of all kinds.

Anchorage: It is possible to anchor in Lake Yazoo in 5 feet of water with all-around protection. Another option is north of the **CSX Railroad (Pascalouga-Singing River) Swing Bridge** (8-foot vertical clearance, opens on request) and the **US 90 (Pascagoula-Singing River) Bridge** (80-foot fixed vertical clearance), where you will find 8 to 15 feet of depth on the Pascagoula River.

Pascagoula to Biloxi—GIWW Mile 104 EHL to Mile 87.5 EHL

Biloxi is a city on a peninsula jutting east into Mississippi Sound. The port is accessible from the Gulf through Dog Keys Pass and Little Dog Keys Pass and from the GIWW, which passes through Mississippi Sound about 6 miles south of the city. It is an important sportfishing and resort area with a large commercial seafood industry. Keesler Air Force Base and a large veteran's hospital are at the west end of the city. The waterfront on the sound is protected by Deer Island, and the harbor in Back Bay of Biloxi is landlocked.

NAVIGATION: Use Charts 11372, 11373 and 11374. Cross the Pascagoula Channel at green buoy "29" and red "30." Continue west in the Mississippi Sound and the next GIWW mark will be flashing green "1" in 4.4 miles. From here continue for 2 miles to 17-foot red "2" and 17-foot green "3." Turn to starboard (north) on a course of about 320 degrees magnetic for 2.5 miles to 17-foot flashing green "5." The GIWW makes this turn to the north to avoid the shoals at Middle Ground, and will shoal slightly (8 to 12 feet) until you reach green "5." Continue west for 9 miles to Biloxi Bay Channel.

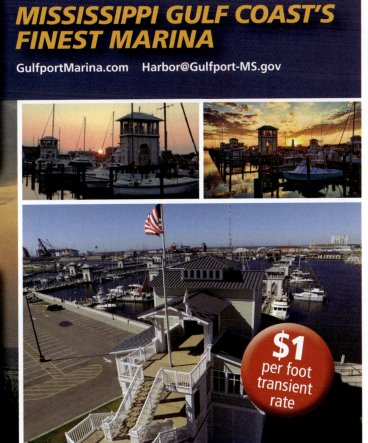

Biloxi Bay, MS to St. Louis Bay, MS

		Largest Vessel Accommodated	VHF Channel Monitored	Transient Berths / Total Berths	Approach / Dockside Depth (reported)	Floating Docks	Gas / Diesel	Groceries, Ice, Marine Supplies, Snacks	Repairs: Hull, Engine, Propeller	Lift (tonnage), Crane, Rail	Min/Max Amps	Laundry, Pool, Showers, Courtesy Car	Pump-Out Station	Nearby: Grocery Store, Motel, Restaurant
PASCAGOULA AREA				Dockage			Supplies				Services			
1. Pascagoula Inner Harbor Marina	228-938-6627	40	–	1/60	7/3	–	–	–	–	–	30/50	–	P	–
2. Mary Walker Marina WIFI	228-497-3141	50	–	6/150	6/5	–	GD	GIMS	–	–	30/50	LS	P	GMR
BILOXI AREA														
3. Biloxi Small Craft Harbor	228-436-4062	50	16	call/124	–	–	GD	IMS	–	–	30/50	S	P	GMR
4. Biloxi Schooner Pier Complex 🖥 WIFI 88 EHL	228-435-6320	–	–	6/27	10/	F	–	I	–	–	30/50	–	P	GMR
5. Point Cadet Marina 88 EHL	228-436-9312	100	16	20/246	12/10	F	GD	IMS	–	–	30/50	LS	P	MR
6. Biloxi Boardwalk Marina WIFI WG	228-432-2628	60	16/11	25/72	6/5.5	–	GD	GIMS	HEP	L19	30/50	S	P	GMR
GULFPORT														
7. Gulfport Municipal Marina-MS WIFI	228-867-8721	140	16/68	50/327	12/11	–	GD	IMS	–	–	30/100	LS	P	GMR
8. Long Beach Harbor WIFI	228-863-4795	65	16/08	20/213	8/8	–	GD	GIMS	–	–	30/100	LS	P	GMR
BAY ST. LOUIS														
9. Pass Christian East Harbor Expansion	228-452-5128	70	16	21/164	10/10	–	GD	I	–	–	30/50	LS	P	R
10. Pass Christian Harbor	228-452-5128	100	–	20/370	10/10	–	GD	IMS	–	–	30/50	–	P	R
11. Bay St. Louis Municipal Harbor WIFI 55 EHL	228-467-4226	110	16	13/160	8/8	–	GD	I	E	–	30/100	S	P	GMR
12. Bay Marina & R.V. Park WIFI 55 EHL	228-466-4970	50	16	10/75	5/5	–	GD	IMS	–	–	30/50	LS	P	GMR

🖥 Internet Access WIFI Wireless Internet Access WG Waterway Guide Cruising Club Partner 🌐 onSpot dockside WiFi facility

See WaterwayGuide.com for current rates, fuel prices, web site addresses, and other up-to-the-minute information. *(Information in the table is provided by the facilities.)*

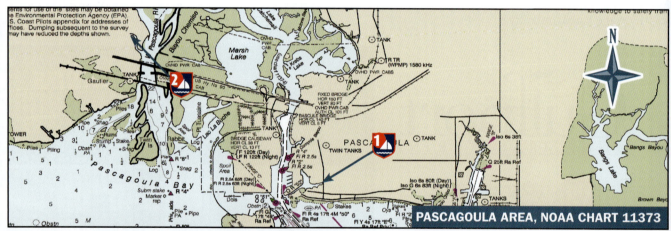

PASCAGOULA AREA, NOAA CHART 11373

BILOXI AREA, NOAA CHART 11372

GULFPORT, NOAA CHART 11372

BAY SAINT LOUIS, NOAA CHART 11372

At Mile 87.5 EHL, follow the Biloxi Ship Channel into Biloxi Bay, and turn to port at green daybeacon "35" and quick-flashing red "26." Do not drift outside the channel, as the water depth is as low as 2 to 4 feet on the edges with an oyster shell bottom. Deer Island is south of the channel. Heading west-southwest, the channel opens up to the Biloxi waterfront and many marine facilities at red daybeacon "26."

Eastbound cruisers can return to the GIWW along the Biloxi Ship Channel as described above. Westbound cruisers can save some time by continuing along the Biloxi Channel extending east to west along the city and then changing direction to the south toward the GIWW. From the Biloxi waterfront, travel west to flashing red "12," and then turn south to green daybeacon "5" and flashing red "6." This section of the channel is 150 feet wide and 6 feet deep with a soft mud bottom.

Dockage: Biloxi Small Craft Harbor has slips and sells fuel. The Biloxi Schooner Pier Complex, 0.5 mile west of Point Cadet, includes some transient slips as part of the Maritime & Seafood Industry Museum facility. This complex is walking distance to several casinos. It is also the home base of the two historic Biloxi Schooners, replicas of turn-of-the-century oyster ships that make daily sails around Mississippi Sound.

The 246-slip Point Cadet Marina, at the eastern tip of Biloxi, offers transient berths and sells fuel. After passing under the railroad bridge you will see smaller (72-slip) Biloxi Boardwalk Marina, which has slips and fuel and offers repairs too.

Back Bay of Biloxi

NAVIGATION: Use Chart 11372. The Biloxi Ship Channel continues north into Back Bay of Biloxi. Three bridges cross the channel. The first is the **Biloxi Bay (U.S. 90) Bridge** with a fixed 95-foot vertical clearance; the second is an abandoned bridge (now used as a fishing pier) with channel sections removed, and the third is the **Biloxi Bay (CSX Railroad) Swing Bridge** with a 14-foot closed vertical clearance (opens on signal).

Anchorage: You can drop the hook anywhere in Back Bay. For northeast protection, anchor at Big Lake in deep water (at least 14 feet).

Biloxi to Gulfport–GIWW Mile 87.5 EHL to Mile 72.5 EHL

NAVIGATION: Chart 11372. Cross the Biloxi Bay Channel south of channel markers green "1" and red "2." Set a course to the west for 15 miles to Gulfport Sound Channel. The first GIWW channel marker you will see is 17-foot red "2" in 5.5 statute miles. Continue west 5.5 miles to 17-foot red "4" then 4 miles to the Gulfport Sound Channel.

City of Gulfport

Gulfport, the seat of Harrison County, is a seaport and tourist center. It is one of Mississippi's most successful commercial ports. For the cruising boater Gulfport features casinos, restaurants, museums and the ferry to Ship Island, all near marinas. Take a bus or taxis to the mall and outlet stores on I-49, about 3.5 miles north of the harbor.

NAVIGATION: Use Chart 11372. At Mile 73 EHL, travel northwest for 6 miles until you reach Gulfport. Pass between flashing green "43" and flashing red "44," and then travel along Gulfport Shipping Channel to flashing red "62." From here, follow the channel markers into the Gulfport Small Craft Harbor, just east of the Mississippi State Port.

Dockage: The friendly Gulfport Municipal Marina is deep-water marina that can accommodate vessels up to 140 feet. This modern facility offers easy access (no bridges to negotiate) and all amenities, including showers, laundry, security, wide fairways and full-length finger piers. They offer a 24-hour fuel dock and a beautiful white sand beach right on the gulf. There is only one tidal cycle per day here with a very small tidal range of just over 1 foot. Casinos and downtown restaurants are within walking distance.

Long Beach Harbor is about 3 statute miles to the west of Gulfport. The marina here may have transient space for you and sells all fuels.

Anchorage: Drop the hook north of Long Beach Harbor in 8 to 9 feet of water with excellent holding in soft mud. Keep in mind that this is exposed to the south.

■ GULFPORT TO BAY ST. LOUIS

Side Trip: To Lake Ponchartrain–GIWW Mile 72.5 EHL to Mile 40 EHL

NAVIGATION: Use Charts 11367, 11371 and 11372. From the Gulfport Channel the GIWW follows a route west for 7.5 miles to GIWW Mile 65 EHL, at flashing green "1." Here it makes a southerly turn to about 225 degrees magnetic and passes through 17-foot "WR2" and 17-foot green "3." Channel markers begin to get closer together, but are still at distances of 1 mile or more. In 7.5 miles, at GIWW Mile 58 EHL you enter the well-marked Marianne Channel at 17-foot red "14." At 17-foot "1," GIWW Mile 54 EHL, turn west into Grand Island Channel. Grand Island Channel ends at GIWW Mile 48 EHL at 17-foot "15."

Turn south to a course of about 255 degrees magnetic and make way through St. Joe Pass. The channel through St. Joe Pass is wide and has good depths along the GIWW. The next GIWW marker you will see is daybeacon red "2" at Mile 45 EHL. St. Joe Pass leads to Lake Borgne and the Louisiana State Line. The state line is marked by the entrance to the Pearl River and then GIWW Mile 40 EHL. Avoid the charted obstruction north of the GIWW at the Pearl River.

Bay St. Louis–North of GIWW Mile 55 EHL

At the western entrance to St. Louis Bay, the town of Bay St. Louis is the last of the Mississippi coastal resorts. In Bay St. Louis, visiting shallow-draft vessels will find many suitable anchorages and fine fishing.

The John C. Stennis Space Center (where NASA does research work) offers free tours, but you will need ground transportation to get there. It is well worth the trip for those who are interested in the technical side of space travel. Visit nasa.gov/centers/stennis for more information.

NAVIGATION: Use Chart 11372. From GIWW Mile 54 EHL, at the junction of Marianne Channel and the Grand Island Channel, travel 5 miles north to flashing red "2" (west side of Square Handkerchief Shoal) and then 2.5 miles to the **Bay St. Louis Railway Swing Bridge** (13-foot closed vertical clearance), which opens on signal. This is followed by the **Bay St. Louis (US 90) Highway Bridge** (85-foot vertical clearance).

Bayou Caddy, located along the shoreline just a few miles west of Bay St. Louis, is mostly a commercial fishing port. Carefully follow the 50-foot-wide channel (5.5-foot depths) into the bayou, which itself has 6-foot depths. The atmosphere is very friendly toward visiting pleasure boaters. Many interesting hours can be spent watching the commercial and private fishermen as they come and go.

Heron Bay, just northwest of Lighthouse Point and north of flashing green "3," may look like a good anchorage or fishing hole, but note its shallow depths. The many fishing boats you see are of the Lafitte skiff type, which draw less than 2 feet.

Dockage: There are two marked channels leading to the Pass Christian Harbor, located about 4 miles east of Bay St. Louis. The eastern channel reportedly has better depths. Pass Christian Harbor & the East Harbor Expansion both have slips and sell all fuels. Water and pump-out service are available at each slip. The fun, open-air Shaggy's (228-452-9939) restaurant is located near the marina. This is the original Shaggy's; there are now four Gulf Coast locations. Also close by is a gas station with a well-stocked convenience store.

Bay St. Louis Municipal Harbor is conveniently located between the bridges and offers transient slips for vessels up to 110 feet with full amenities (including free WiFi). They also sell gas and diesel fuel. Groceries and restaurants are nearby. Courtesy transportation to nearby casinos is also available. Bay Marina & R.V. Park is located just west of the casino on the Jourdan River. They have transient slips and fuel.

■ NEXT STOP

The northern entrance into Mobile Bay marks the end of the inland river system portion of the Great Loop. The Great Loop trail turns east from here and follows the Florida Panhandle, but do not overlook the intrigue of going west, as westward lies New Orleans, the Louisiana low country and the windswept Texas coast all the way to Mexico. This area is detailed in our Skipper Bob publication, Cruising the Gulf Coast. Due to several hurricanes that have visited the area in the past several years, cruisers are advised to carefully research available facilities and waterway conditions before proceeding west.

Waterway Guide Cruising Club Partners

Simply show your Cruising Club membership card at these participating businesses to start saving money on fuel, dockage, supplies and more.

Also receive discounts on Waterway Guide and Skipper Bob products online at www.waterwayguide.com

To sign up for your **FREE** membership call **800-233-3359** or go to **www.waterwayguide.com**

List current as of 8/2018

Alabama

Homeport Marina
251-458-7135
www.homeportmarina.net

The Wharf Marina
251-224-1900
www.thewharfmarina.com

Turner Marine
www.turnermarine.com

Bahamas

Abaco Inn
800-468-8799
www.abacoinn.com

Bimini Big Game Club Resort & Marina
800-867-4764
www.biggameclubbimini.com

Blue Marlin Cove Resort & Marina
242-349-4101
www.bluemarlincove.com

Brendals Dive Center
242-365-4411
www.brendal.com

Davis Harbour Marina At Cotton Bay Club
242-334-6303

Green Turtle Cay Club
242-365-4271
www.greenturtleclub.com

Leeward Yacht Club & Marina
242-365-4191
www.leewardyachtclub.com

Marina at Emerald Bay
242-336-6102
www.marinaatemeraldbay.com

Master Harbour Marina
242-345-5116
www.turnquestinvestments.com

Port Lucaya Marina
242-373-9090
www.portlucaya.com

Sail and Dive
242-577-0867
www.sailanddive.net

Spanish Cay Marina
242-365-0083
www.spanishcay.com

Sunrise Resort and Marina
800-932-4959
www.sunriseresortandmarina.com

Connecticut

Cedar Island Marina
860-669-8681
cedarislandmarina.com

Landfall Navigation
203-487-0775
www.landfallnavigation.com

Mystic River Marina
800-344-8840
www.MysticRiverMarina.com

North Cove Yacht Club
860-388-9132
www.northcoveyc.com

Norwalk Cove Marina
203-838-5899
norwalkcove.com

Saybrook Point Marina
860-395-3080
www.saybrookpointmarina.com

Seaview House Marina
203-219-4693
www.seaviewhousemarina.com

Delaware

Indian River Marina
302-227-3071
www.destateparks.com/marinas

Florida

Adventure Yacht Harbor
386-756-2180
www.adventureyachtharbor.com

All American Covered Boat Storage
941-697-9900
www.aaboatstorage.com

Always for Sail
904-625-7936
www.alwaysforsail.com

Amelia Island Yacht Basin
904-277-4615
www.aiyb.net

Anclote Isles Marina
727-939-0100
www.ancloteisles-marina.com

Anclote Village Marina
727-937-9737
www.anclotevillagemarina.com

Anglers Avenue Marine Center
954-962-8702
www.aamcmarina.com

Aquamarina Daytona
386-252-6421
www.ilovemymarina.com

Austral International Marina
305-325-0177
www.australinternational.net

Belle Harbour Marina
727-943-8489
www.belleharbourmarina.com

Bimini Bar & Grill
941-451-8634
biminibarandgrill.com

Boater's Edge
321-383-4173
www.boatersedge.us

Burnt Store Marina
941-637-0083
www.burntstoremarina.com

Camachee Cove Yacht Harbor
904-829-5676
www.camacheeisland.com

Cape Haze Marina
941-698-1110

Captains License Class
888-937-2458
www.captainslicensclass.com

City of Fort Myers Yacht Basin
239-321-7080
www.cityftmyers.com

Delray Harbor Club Marina
561-276-0376
www.delrayharborclub.com

Dolphin Marina and Cottages
305-797-0878
www.dolphinmarina.net

Everglades National Park Boat Tours

Fernandina Harbor Marina
904-491-2089
www.fhmarina.com

Fishermens Village Yacht Basin
941-575-3000
www.fishville.com

Florida Marina's Clubs
239-489-2969

Fort Pierce City Marina
772-464-1245
www.fortpiercecitymarina.com

Glades Boat Storage, Inc.
863-983-3040
www.gladesboatstorage.com

Good Times Motel And Marina
352-498-8088
www.goodtimesmotelandmarina.com

Gulf Harbour Marina
239-437-0881
www.gulfharbormarina.net

Halifax Harbor Marina
386-671-3603
www.halifaxharbormarina.com

Harbour Isle Marina
772-461-9049
www.harbourisleflorida.com

Hawks Cay Resort & Marina
305-743-9000 x2
www.hawkscay.com

Holiday Harbor Marina
850-492-0555
myholidayharbor.com

Holly Bluff Marina
386-822-9992
www.hollybluff.com

Hopkins-Carter Marine Supply
305-635-7377
www.hopkins-carter.com

Huckins Yacht
904-389-1125
www.huckinsyacht.com

Kennedy Point Yacht Club & Marina
321-383-0280
www.kennedypointyachtclub.com

Laishley Park Municipal Marina
941-575-0142
www.laishleymarina.com

Lake Park Harbor Marina
561-881-3353
www.lakeparkmarina.com

Lambs Yacht Center, Inc.
904-384-5577
www.lambsyachtcenter.com

Loblolly Marina
772-546-3136
www.loblollymarinainfo.com

Loggerhead Club and Marina
561-625-9443
www.loggerheadjupiter.com

Longboat Key Club Moorings
941-383-8383
www.longboatkeymarina.com

LukFuel, LLC
305-432-3487
LukFuel.com

Marathon Marina & Boat Yard
305-743-6575
www.marathonmarinaandresort.com

Marina at Naples Bay Resort
239-530-5134
naplesbayresort.com

Marina Bay Marina Resort
954-791-7600
www.marinabay-fl.com

Mariner Cay Marina
772-287-2900
www.marincaymarina.org

Marker 1 Marina
727-487-3903
www.marker1marina.com

METROPOLITAN PARK MARINA
904-630-0839
www.coj.net

Naples Boat Club Marina
239 263 2774
www.naplesboatclub.com

Nettles Island Marina
772-229-2811
www.nettlesislandmarina.com

New Port Cove Marine Center
561-844-2504
www.opch.com

Night Swan Intracostal B&B
386-423-4940
www.nightswan.com

North Palm Beach Marina
561-626-4919
www.opch.com

Old Port Cove Marina
561-626-1760
www.opch.com

Palm Coast Marina
386-446-6370
www.palmcoastmarina.net

Palm Cove Marina
904-223-4757
www.palmcovemarina.com

Panama City Marina
850 872 7272
www.pcmarina.com

Pirates Cove Resort & Marina
772-223-9216
www.piratescoveresort.com

Port Canaveral Yacht Club
321-297-3441
pcyc-fl.org

Prosperity Pointe Marina
239-995-2155
www.prosperitypointemarina.com

Regatta Pointe Marina
941-729-6021
www.regattapointemarina.com

Rivers Edge Marina
904-827-0520
29riveredgemarina.com

Riviera Dunes Marina
941-981-5330
www.rdmarina.com

RMK Merrill-Stevens
305-324-5211
www.rmkmerrill-stevens.com

Sailfish Marina of Stuart
772-283-1122
www.sailfishmarinastuart.com

Sailor\'s Wharf Yacht Yard
727-823-1155
sailorswharf.com

Sandy Beach Catamaran Sailing Charters
954-218-0042
www.catamaransailcharter.com

Sea Tech & Fun USA / Spade Anchor
321-409-5714
www.spadeanchorusa.com

Seaside Sailing
800-569-7245
www.seasidesailing.com

Sombrero Marina Condo. Assc.
305-743-0000
www.sombreromarina.com

Stock Island Marina Village
305-294-2288
www.stockislandmarina.com

Telemar Bay Marina
321-773-2468
telemarbay.com

The Jacksonville Landing
904-353-1188
www.jacksonvillelanding.com

The Marina at Ortega Landing
904-387-5538
www.ortegalanding.com

Thunderboat Marine Service Center
954-964-8859
www.thunderboatmarinecenter.com

Titusville Municipal Marina
321-383-5600
www.titusville.com/marina

Turnberry Isle Marina Yacht Club
305-933-6934
www.turnberryislemarina.com

Twin Dolphin Marina
941-747-8300
www.twindolphinmarina.com

Water Street Hotel and Marina
850-653-8801
www.waterstreethotel.com

Yacht Haven Park & Marina
954-583-2322
yachthavenpark.com

Yacht Management Marina
954-993-9368
www.YMISF.com

Georgia

Fort McAllister Marina
912-727-2632
fortmcallistermarinaga.com

Hidden Harbor Yacht Club
912-261-1049
www.hiddenharboryachtclub.com

Hinckley Yacht Services
912-629-2400
www.hinckleyyachts.com

Hyatt Regency Savannah
912-721-4654
www.hyattdockssavannah.com

Isle of Hope Marina
912-354-8187
www.iohmarina.com

Morning Star Marinas at Golden Isles
912-634-1128
www.morningstarmarinas.com

River Supply Inc.
912-354-7777
www.riversupply.com

Sunbury Crab Co. Restaurant & Marina
912-884-8640
www.sunburycrabco.com

Thunderbolt Marina
912-210-0363
www.thunderboltmarine.us

Tybee Island Marina
912-786-5554
tybeeislandmarina.com

Illinois

31st Street Harbor (A Westrec Marina)
312-742-8515
www.chicagoharbors.info

Louisiana

Lake Pontchartrain Harbor Marina
985-626-1517

Retif Oil and Fuel
504-349-9113
www.retif.com

Ship To Shore Co.
337-474-0730
www.shiptoshoreco.com

Maine

Edwards Harborside Inn
207-363-2222
www.EdwardsHarborside.com

Landings Restaurant & Marina
207-594-4899

Maryland

Annapolis Harbor Boatyard
410-268-0092
www.annapolisharbor.net

Back Creek Inn B&B
410-326-2022
www.backcreekinnbnb.com

Calvert Marina LLC
410-326-4251
calvertmarina.com

Campbell's Bachelor Pt. Yacht Co.
410-226-5592
www.campbellsboatyards.com

Campbell's Boatyard @ Jack's Pt.
410-226-5105
www.campbellsboatyards.com

Campbell's Town Creek Boatyard
410-226-0213
www.campbellsboatyards.com

Fawcett Boat Supplies
410-267-8681
fawcettboat.com

Galloway Creek Marina
410-335-3575
www.dredgeanddock.com

MarinaLife
410-752-0505
www.marinalife.com

Maritime Solutions Inc.
410-263-1496
MSI-1.com

Paradise Marina
301-832-6578
www.Paradise-Marina.com

Point Lookout Marina
301-872-5000
www.pointlookoutmarina.com

Quality Inn Beacon Marina
410-326-6303
www.beaconsolomons.com

Rock Hall Landing Marina
410-639-2224
www.rockhalllanding.com

Rockhold Creek Marina & Yacht Repair
410-867-7919
www.rockholdcreekmarina.com

Somers Cove Marina
410-968-0925
www.somerscovemarina.com

Sunset Harbor Marina
410-687-7290
www.sunsetharbor.com

Massachusetts

Constitution Marina
617-241-9640
www.constitutionmarina.com

Fireside Insurance Agency,Inc.
508-487-0754
fireside Insurance.com

Newburyport Harbor Marina
978-462-3990
www.newburyportmarinas.com

Pickering Wharf Marina
978-740-6990
www.pickeringwharf.com

Seaport Inn and Marina
508-997-1281
www.seaportinnandmarina.com

Vineyard Haven Marina
508-693-0720
www.mvhm.com

Michigan

Belle Maer Harbor
586-465-4534
www.bellemaer.com

Crosswinds Marine Service
231-894-4549
www.crosswindsmarineservice.com

Detroit Yacht Club
313-824-1200
www.dyc.com

Harbour Towne Marina
231-755-2218
htownemarina.com

Jacobson Marina Resort, Inc.
231-620-0474
www.jacobsonmarinaresort.com

Onekama Marine Inc.
231-889-5000
www.onekamamarine.com

Port Austin Harbor
989-738-8712
www.michigan.gov/
portaustinharbor.com

Terry's Marina
586-709-9559
www.terrysmarina.com

Toledo Beach Marina
734-243-3800
www.toledobeachmarina.com

Woodland Harbor Marina
269-743-3624
www.woodlandharbormarina.com

Mississippi

Biloxi Boardwalk Marina
228-432-2628

Isle Casino Biloxi
916-834-4112
www.biloxi.isleofcapricasinos.com

New Jersey

Beach Haven Yacht Club Marina
609-492-9101
beachhavenyachtclubmarina.com

Captains License Class
888-937-2458
www.captainslicensclass.com

Green Cove Marina
732-840-9090
www.greencovemarina.com

Hinkley Yacht Services
732-477-6700
www.hinckleyyachts.com

Hoffman's Marina
732-528-6200
www.hoffmansmarina.com

Kammerman's Marina
609-348-8418
www.kammermansmarina.com

Lincoln Harbor Yacht Club
201-319-5100
www.lincolnharbormarina.com

Marina At Southwinds
609-693-6288
www.marinaatsouthwinds.com

Miss Chris Marina
609-884-3351
www.misschrismarina.com

Riverside Marina & Yacht Sales
856-461-1077
www.riversideys.com

Seaboard Marine Inc.
732 264 8910
www.seaboardmarineinc.com

Seaside Sailing
800-569-7245
www.seasidesailing.com

New York

Brewerton Boat Yard Inc.
315-676-3762
www.brewertonboatyard.com

Essex Shipyard
518-963 4024
essexshipyard.net

Ess-Kay Yards
315-676-7064
www.ess-kayyards.com

Glen Cove Marina
516-759-3129
www.glencovemarina.com

Half Moon Bay Marina
914-271-5400
www.halfmoonbaymarina.com

Halsey's Marina
631-324-5666
www.seaincorp.com

Harbor's End Marina
315-938-5425
www.harborsendmarina.com

Hudson River Maritime Museum
845-338-0071 x12
www.hrmm.org

Hutchinson's Boat Works, Inc.
315-482-9931
www.hbwboats.com

Hyde Park Marina
845-473-8283
www.hydeparkmarina.com

Minneford Marina
718-885-2000
www.minnefordmarina.com

New Rochelle Municipal Marina
914-235-6930
NewRochelleNY.com

New Whitehall Marina
518-499-9700

Patsy's Bay Marine
845-786-5270
www.patsysbaymarina.com

Pier 225 Marina LLC
315-569-6153
pier225marina.com

Riverside Marine Services Inc.
518 943-5311
www.riverviewmarineservices.com

Rondout Yacht Basin
845-331-7061
www.rondoutyachtbasin.com

Sell My Boat For Me LLC
888-511-5441
www.sellmyboatforme.com

Smith Boys Marine Sales
716-695-3472
smithboys.com

Star Island Yacht Club & Marina
631-668-5052
www.starislanddyc.com

Sunset Harbour Marina
631-289-3800
ILoveMyMarina.com

Tappan Zee Marina
845-359-5522
tappanzeemarina.com

Three Mile Harbor Marina
631-324-1320
www.seaincorp.com

Treasure Cove Resort Marina
631-727-8386
www.treasurecoveresortmarina.com

Triangle Sea Sales
631-477-1773
www.triangleseasales.com

North Carolina

Albemarle Plantation
252-426-4037

Anchors Away Boatyard
910-270-4741
www.anchorsawayboatyard.com

Bald Head Island Marina
910-457-7380
www.baldheadislandmarina.com

Bennett Brothers Yachts
910-772-9277
www.bbyachts.com

Cape Fear Marina
910-772-9277
www.bbyachts.com

Cypress Cove Marina
252-796-0435
www.cypresscovenc.com

Dawson Creek Boatworks
252-617-2630
www.dawsoncreekboatworks.webs.
com

Deep Point Marina
910-269-2380
www.deeppointmarina.com

Dismal Swamp Welcome Center
252-771-8333
www.DismalSwampWelcomeCenter.
com

Dowry Creek Marina
252-943-2728
dowrycreekmarina.com

Joyner Marina
910-458-5053
www.JOYNERMARINA.com

Morehead City Yacht Basin
252-726-6862
www.mcyachtbasin.com

Ocean Isle Marina & Yacht Club
910-579-6440

Page After Page Bookstore
252-335-7243
www.pageafterpagebook.com

Portside Marina
252-726-7678
www.portsidemarina.com

River Forest Manor And Marina
252-943-0030
www.riverforestmarina.com

River Forest Shipyard & Marina
252-943-2151
www.riverforestmarina.com

Sailcraft Service
252-249-0522
www.waterwayguide.com/marina_
close-ups/sailcraft-service-inc

South Harbour Village Marina
910-799-3111
www.southharboursales.com/
marina.html

**St. James Plantation / St. James
Marina**
910-253-3001
www.stjamesplantation.com

T/A Poor Man's Hole
910-326-1953

**The BoatHouse At Front Street
Village**
252-838-1524

Town Creek Marina
252-728-6111
towncreekmarina.com

**Uncorked By The Sea Wine Shop
& Gallery**
910-454-0633
uncorkedbythesea.com

Washington Waterfront Docks
252-975-9367 ext 221
www.washingtonncmarina.com

Whittaker Pointe Marina
252-249-1750
www.whittakerpointe.com

Wilmington Marine Center
910-395-5055
www.wilmingtonmarine.com

Ontario, Canada

Boblo Island Marina
519-736-1111
www.boblomarina.com

Cobourg Marina
905-372-2397
www.cobourg.ca/municipal-departments/marina.html

General Wolfe Marina
613-385-2611
www.generalwolfehotel.com

Rawley Resort And Marina
705 538 2272
www.rawleyresort.com

White Sea Resort
705-283-1483
www.whitesearesort.ca

Quebec, Canada

Yacht Club Montreal
514-789-9264
www.ycmi.com

Rhode Island

Apponaug Harbor Marina
401-739-5005
www.apponaugmarina.com

Newport Yachting Center Marina
800-653-3625
www.newportyachtingcenter.com

South Carolina

Bucksport Marina & RV Resort
843-397-5566
www.bucksportplantation.com

Cooper River Marina
843-554-0790

Coquina Yacht Club
843-249-9333
coquinayachtclub.com

Harborwalk Books
843-546-8212
www.harborwalkbooks.com

Harbour Town Yacht Basin
843-363-8335

Harbourgate Marina
843-249-8888
www.Harbourgatemarina.com

Heritage Plantation Marina
843-237-3650
www.heritageplantation.com

Lady's Island Marina
843-522-0430

Osprey Marina
843-215-5353
www.ospreymarina.com

Pierside Boatworks
843-554-7775
www.piersideboatworks.com

Port Royal Landing Marina, Inc.
843-525-6664
www.portroyallandingmarina.net

Skull Creek Marina
843-681-8436
www.theskullcreekmarina.com

St. Johns Yacht Harbor
843-557-1027
www.sjyh.com

UK-Halsey Charleston
Sailmakers
843-722-0823
www.ukhalseycharleston.com

Texas

Freeport Municipal Marina
979-236-1221
www.myfreeportmarina.com

Kemah Boardwalk Marina
281-334-2284

Vermont

Champlain Marina
802-658-4034
www.champlainmarina.com

Virginia

Bay Point Marina
757-362-3600
www.littlecreekmarina.com

Carter's Cove Marina
804-438-5273
www.carterscovemarina.com

Chesapeake Boat Works
804-776-8833
www.chesapeakeboatworks.com

Cobb's Marina
757-588-5401
cobbsmarina.com

Deltaville Marina
804-776-9812
deltavillemarina.com

Deltaville Yachting Center
804-776-9898
www.dycboat.com

Downtown Hampton Public Piers
757-727-1276
www.downtownhampton.com

Dozier's Port Urbanna Marine Center
804-758-0000
www.doziermarine.com

Dozier's Regatta Point Yachting Center
804-776-6711
www.doziermarine.com

Little Creek Marina
757-971-8411
www.littlecreekmarina.com

Mobjack Bay Marina, Inc.
804-725-7245
www.mobjackbaymarina.com

Norton Yachts
804-776-9211
www.nortonyachts.com

Ocean Marine Yacht Center
757-321-7432
www.oceanmarinellc.com

Regent Point Marina
804-758-4457
www.regent-point.com

River's Rest Marina and Resort
804-829-2753
www.riversrest.com

Scott's Creek Marina
757-399-BOAT

Signature CanvasMakers
757-788-8890
www.SignatureCanvasMakers.com

Smithfield Station
757-357-7700
www.smithfieldstation.com

Stingray Point Boat Works
804-776-7500
www.stingraypointboatworks.com

The Boathouse Marina
804-224-7614
theboathousemarina-va.com

The Tides Inn & Marina
804-438-4465
www.tidesinn.com

Top Rack Marina
757-227-3041
www.toprackmarina.com

Urbanna Town Marina at Upton's Point
804-758-5440

Vinings Landing Marine Center
757-587-8000
www.viningslanding.com

White Point Marina
804-472-2977
www.whitepointmarina.com

Whitehouse Cove Marina
757-508-2602
www.whitehousecovemarina.com

Willoughby Harbor Marina
757-583-4150
www.viningsmarine.com/marinas/willoughby-harbor-marina.htm

Yankee Point Marina
804-462-7018
www.yankeepointmarina.com

Washington, DC

Capital Yacht Club
202-488-8110
www.capitalyachtclub.com

Wisconsin

Harborside Yacht Center
414-273-0711
www.harborsideyachtcenter.com

Marina/Sponsor Index

Sponsors are listed in **BOLD**.

O

Oasis Boatyard & Marina, 158, 161

Ocean Club Marina at Port Canaveral, 190-191

Ocean Divers, 356, 374

Oceans Edge Key West Resort Hotel & Marina, 388, 390, 392

Old Naples Seaport Marina, 418, 420

Old Port Cove Marina, 276-278

Olde Fish House Marina, 434, 437

Olsen Marine Service Inc., 422, 426

One Island Park - Miami Beach (IGY), 330, 334

Orange Beach Marina, 546-549

Ortega River Marina, 128-129

Outta the Blue Marina, 368, 377

Owl Creek Boat Works, 254-255

Oyster Bay Harbour Marina, 109, 112

Ozona Fish Camp, 486-487

P

Pahokee Marina and Campground, 246, 248

Palafox Pier Yacht Harbor, 538, 540

Palatka City Dock, 135-136

Palm Bay Marina, 200-201

Palm Beach Town Docks, 282, 285

Palm Beach Yacht Center, 286

Palm Beach Yacht Club & Marina, 282, 284

Palm Coast Marina, 164-165

Palm Cove Marina, 150-152

Palm Harbor Marina, West Palm Beach, 282, 284

Palm Harbor Marina, Pensacola, 539-540

Palmeiras Beach Club at Grove Isle, 344

Panama City Marina, 525, 528, 530-531

Pancho's Marina and Fuel Dock, 368, 380, 382

Pasadena Marina, 478, 481

Pasadena Yacht & Country Club, 478, 481

Pascagoula Inner Harbor Marina, 562, 564

Pass Christian East Harbor Expansion, 564, 567

Pass Christian Harbor, 564, 567

Pass-A-Grille Marina, The, 478, 481

Pelican Bend Restaurant & Marina, 414, 416

Pelican Harbor Marina, 330, 332

Pelican Isle Yacht Club, 420, 425

Pelican Yacht Club, 214, 216

Pelican's Perch Marina & Boatyard, 539-540

Pensacola Beach Marina, 538, 540

Pensacola Shipyard Marina & Boatyard, 539-540

Pensacola Yacht Club, 539-540

Perdido Key Oyster Bar Restaurant & Marina, LLC, 542, 544

Pete's Pier Inc., 500, 503

PGA Marina, 276, 278

Pier 98 Marina, 528, 530

Pilot House Marina, 356, 358, 371, 374

Pineda Point Marina, 197-198

Pineland Marina, 434, 437

Pink Shell Beach Resort and Marina, 422, 424, 426

Pirate's Cove Resort & Marina, 224-226, 228

Pirates Cove Marina, FL, 528, 531

Pirates Cove Marina & Restaurant, AL, 546, 550

Plantation Yacht Harbor Marina, 356, 360-361, 363

Playboy Marine Center, 318-319

Point Cadet Marina, 564, 566

Port Canaveral Marine, 190-191

Port Canaveral Yacht Club, 190-191

Port Consolidated, 108, 112

Port LaBelle Marina, 250, 252

Port of the Islands Marina, 410, 412

Port Salerno Marine, 224, 226, 228

Port Sanibel Marina, 428, 430

Port St. Joe Marina, 522-523

Port Tarpon Marina, 488-489

Prime Marina Miami, 342-344

Prosperity Pointe Marina, 256, 258

Punta Gorda Marina, 439-440

Q

Quality Inn & Suites Riverfront, 135-136

R

Ramada Sarasota, 457-458

Ranger Tugs, 5

Regatta Pointe Marina, 467-468

Renaissance Vinoy Resort Marina, 474, 476-477

Reynolds Park Yacht Center, 133, 136

Rickenbacker Marina Inc., 339, 340

River City Brewing Co. & Marina, 126-127

River Cove Marina, 336, 338

River Deck Marina, 178-179

River Energy- The New F & Y Inc., 488, 492

River Forest Yachting Center - LaBelle, 236, 250-251

River Forest Yachting Center - Stuart, 236, 241-242

River Haven Marina & Motel, 508-509

River House Marina, 250-251

River Palms MHP, 190, 192

River Yacht Basin Marina, 560

Riverbend at LMC, 308, 313

Riverfront Marina, 308, 310, 312

Rivers Edge Marina, 158, 161

Riverside Marina, St. Marks, 510, 513

Riverside Marina & Cottages, Yankeetown, 502, 505

Riverside Marina Fort Pierce, 213-216

Riverwatch Marina and Boatyard, 232, 234

Riviera Beach City Marina, 278, 280-281

Riviera Dunes Marina, 468, 471

RMK Merrill-Stevens, 336, 338

Robbie's of Key West LLC, 390, 392

Roland and Mary Ann Martins Marina & Resort, 248-249

Rolly Marine Service, Inc., 308, 313

Roscioli Yachting Center, 308, 313

Rose Marina, 414, 416

Royal Palm Marina, 450-451

Royale Palm Yacht Basin, 318-319

Rybovich Marina, 282, 284

Rybovich Marine Center, 278, 280

S

Sabine Marina, 538, 540

Sadler Point Marine Center, 128-129

Safe Cove Boat Storage, 438, 440

Sag Harbor Yacht Club, 19

Sailfish Marina of Stuart, 226-228

Sailfish Marina Resort, 278, 282

Sailor's Wharf Yacht Yard, 474, 476-477

Subject Index

Most relevant pages are listed in **BOLD**.

SUBJECT INDEX

Goin' Ashore Index

Inlets Index

Skipper's Notes

Skipper's Notes